INTERMEDIATE PRICE THEORY

INTERMEDIATE PRICE THEORY

ANALYSIS, ISSUES, AND APPLICATIONS

Micha Gisser
University of New Mexico

McGraw-Hill Book Company

New York   St. Louis   San Francisco   Auckland   Bogotá   Hamburg   Johannesburg   London
Madrid   Mexico   Montreal   New Delhi   Panama   Paris   São Paulo   Singapore
Sydney   Tokyo   Toronto

This book was set in Times Roman by Better Graphics.
The editors were Bonnie E. Lieberman, Ellen R. Friedman,
and James B. Armstrong;
the designer was Jo Jones;
the production supervisor was Charles Hess.
The drawings were done by J & R Services, Inc.
R. R. Donnelley & Sons Company was printer and binder.

INTERMEDIATE PRICE THEORY:
Analysis, Issues, and Applications

1234567890DODO8987654321

Library of Congress Cataloging in Publication Data

Gisser, Micha.
 Intermediate price theory.

 Includes index.
 1. Microeconomics. 2. Prices. I. Title.
HB172.G57   338.5   80-22505
ISBN 0-07-023312-8

To Rivka

CONTENTS

PREFACE

This textbook takes the traditional approach to the theory of price, or microeconomics. But it brings the theory to life by emphasizing its connections to contemporary economic, social, and political problems. Throughout the text there are real-life examples and applications. In addition, there are optional sections and chapters which allow the student and the instructor to explore new topics in price theory, such as *economic regulation*, *intertemporal pricing of exhaustible natural resources*, and *externalities*. There are also numerous diagrams, accompanied by descriptive captions, which graphically illustrate the theoretical concepts. At the end of each chapter are a glossary, a summary, and a series of problems, which are designed to ensure the student's thorough understanding of elementary microeconomics.

WHO CAN USE THE BOOK

This text is appropriate for intermediate-level microeconomics courses offered by economics departments and for similar courses offered by business schools. It is also ideal for MBA programs and BBA programs.

ORGANIZATION OF THE BOOK

This text can be used in either a one-term course or a two-term course. For a one-term course, the instructor may opt to teach Chapters 1–3, 5–9, 11, and 14. These are the traditional chapters covering the theory of the consumer, the producer, perfect competition, monopoly, and input markets. If the book is to be used in a two-term (one-year) course, the instructor may teach the optional chapters—4, 10, 12, 13, and 15–18—in the second term. These chapters cover topics such as index numbers, unit taxes, markets for futures, oligopoly and monopolistic competition, labor markets, the theory of interest and capital, and welfare economics, with emphasis on externalities and Coase's theorem.

There are problems at the end of each chapter. Hints and answers to the *numerical* problems can be found following Chapter 18. All the problems can be discussed in a lab if a lab time and an assistant are provided. Otherwise, students may work out the problems on their own with the aid of the hints and answers to the numerical problems. The Instructor's Manual provides answers to all text problems and contains additional problems that the instructor may want to incorporate in tests.

CHAPTER ORGANIZATION

While traditional in organization, this book has particular features that are worth mentioning, because they can assist the students in grasping the theory of price.

1. The theory is developed step by step in a logical order.
2. Each major theoretical development is accompanied by an example or an application or both. These examples and applications upgrade microeconomics from a cut-and-dry theory to a lively social science that sheds light on the real world.
3. Diagrams are explained by detailed captions, which are helpful to students for reviewing the theory and for preparing for tests.
4. A short, convenient summary follows each chapter.
5. A glossary of terms is provided at the end of each chapter, again to assit students in reviewing the theory and in preparing for tests.
6. There are 10 to 20 problems at the end of each chapter. (The more advanced problems are marked by an asterisk.) Hints to the solution of most problems and all *numerical* answers are provided at the end of the book. These are given because some students need a bit of help in order to crack a problem, while all students would like to verify answers to the numerical problems. For the benefit of the professor, solutions to *all* problems are included in the Instructor's Manual.
7. There are mathematical appendixes at the end of many chapters for those students interested in tasting the mathematical flavor of rigorous economic analysis.

UNIQUE FEATURES

All chapters include unique features and topics which enliven the presentation by showing the student why price theory is relevant to real life. Some of the features of those chapters that can be used for a one-term or one-semester course are as follows:

Chapter 1, "Consumer Preferences and Choice": Allotment in the kibbutz; the food-stamp program; commodity rationing; negative income taxes.

Chapter 2, "Consumer, Consumption, and the Theory of Demand": Income elasticities for selected countries; a strange PCC in developing countries; the demand for sugar.

Chapter 3, "Aggregate (Market) Demand and Demand Shifts": Price elasticity and fluctuations in farm income; the demand for electricity in the United States; the demand for automobiles.

Chapter 5, "The Production Function": Statistical values of elasticities of substitution in some manufacturing industries; the semantics of relating inputs to each other; education as an input in the production function.

Chapter 6, "The Theory of Cost and Production": Empirical cost curves; refuse collection, economies of scale in electric-power generation, the survival technique (petroleum refining), and cotton farms in Texas High Plains.

Chapter 7, "The Competitive Firm": The challenge to the classical tradition; the "smart" farmer and the "not-so-smart" farmer; accounting versus economic costs.

Chapter 8, "Production and the Theory of Supply": Long-run supply elasticity of natural gas; empirical supply curves of agricultural commodities; technological progress; farm supply response in the Punjab.

Chapter 9, "The Competitive Market": Farm price support; price control of natural gas; frost in Brazil and coffee supply; the bituminous coal industry; hybrid corn and technological innovations; rent and old oil; crime and punishment.

Chapter 11, "Monopoly": Welfare loss due to monopolistic pricing; why regulate the utilities; the market for physicians' services; a cartel that failed—the electrical conspiracy of the early 1960s; a cartel that succeeded—OPEC.

Chapter 14, "Demand and Supply of Inputs": Who is afraid of the energy crisis?; the energy crisis and United States manufacturing; the market for water rights in the Southwest United States; the problem of common property resource.

The optional chapters cover a wide variety of unique and interesting topics:

Chapter 4, "Special Issues in Consumer Theory": Index numbers; escalation clauses in wage agreements; the theory of utility under uncertainty; workmen's compensation.

Chapter 10, "Special Issues in the Competitive Market": Excise taxes; imports and exports; the economics of regulation; the futures market.

Chapter 12, "Monopolistic Competition": Price dispersion and the market for gasoline.

Chapter 13, "Oligopoly": Concentration ratios versus the Herfindahl index; the extended Lerner formula; empirical evidence of trends in concentration ratios over time; the rate of return and barriers to entry; three examples—the steel industry, the airlines (1938–1978), and the car industry.

Chapter 15, "The Labor Market": Population doctrines; the demand for children, an empirical study; black enslavement in the South; barbers in

Illinois; discrimination in labor markets; welfare loss due to unions; is the minimum wage rate a political puzzle?

Chapter 16, "The Theory of Interest, Capital, and Exhaustible Resources": capital budgeting; capital recovery factor; the problem of the internal rate of return; the Trans-Alaskan pipeline; the price of exhaustible natural resources over time; forecasting OPEC prices in the future; the economics of semiexhaustible natural resources: water and trees.

Chapter 17, "Welfare Economics": Coase's theorem; the fable of the bees; the proposed Proxmire tax on sulfur dioxide; farmers under stress in arid environments; public goods in theory and practice.

Chapter 18, "Quantitative Tools": Testing economic theories; econometrics in the service of economists; linear programming; nonlinear programming; dynamic programming and water pollution along a river; queueing theory; inventories; simulation.

ACKNOWLEDGMENTS

I am indebted to my colleagues Peter Gregory and Ronald N. Johnson for their stimulating conversations, especially during jogging hour. I am also indebted to the following educators who reviewed the manuscript: Michael Behr, University of Wisconsin, Superior; Michael Metzger, George Washington University; Hugh O. Nourse, University of Georgia; and Victor Tabbush, UCLA.

I am indebted to Bonnie E. Lieberman and Ellen R. Friedman of McGraw-Hill, who participated in this project during various stages of its development, and to Gail Hughes for her assistance in securing permissions to quote from books and journals.

Micha Gisser

INTRODUCTION

WHY IS PRICE THEORY IMPORTANT?

Price theory (microeconomics) is important basically because it can provide solutions to problems that cannot be solved by common sense. On many occasions common sense fails because it ignores what is known as the *fallacy of composition*. The fallacy of composition can be explained by the following example: A person who is watching a movie in a theater that is full to capacity estimates that it will take 2 seconds to reach the exit in case of fire. After a fire does break out, it actually takes that person 40 minutes to get to the exit. Why did the person miscalculate so grossly? The answer lies in the fallacy of composition: Because everybody in the theater rushed to the door simultaneously, individual calculations of the exit time no longer held.

A few more examples might be useful.

After the so-called energy crisis of 1974, some famous writers fell into the trap of the fallacy of composition. Barry Commoner, an advocate of solar energy, told us how the petrochemical industry, by clever salesmanship that lasted from the turn of the century to 1973, entrapped farmers by selling them cheap chemical fertilizers and fuels. Then came the energy crisis. Prices of fuels and chemical fertilizers started to rise significantly. Commoner wrote that "the process has left U.S. agriculture in a vulnerable economic position; if the selling price of farm commodities should fall, farmers will be hard pressed to meet the elevated prices of agricultural chemicals, and of fuel, that have been imposed on them by the energy and petrochemical corporations."[1] Common sense would go along with this conclusion, but not microeconomics: It is true that a single farmer who was hit by the energy crisis would be hard pressed to meet the elevated prices of fuels and fertilizers. But contrary to common sense, when all farmers are hit at the same time, the energy crisis turns into a blessing. Microeconomics explains why (Chapter 14).

The energy crisis provided another illustration along these lines. If crude oil were unlimited but there was only one individual who owned an exhaustible field of oil, given that the oil in the field was distributed uniformly, the owner would continue to mine oil at a price which would remain stable over time, and the oil field would be exhausted sooner or later. If we commit the fallacy of composition, we conclude that if all oil fields were exhaustible, the price of oil would not change over time, but one day ("doomsday") all oil fields would be depleted and there would be no oil substitutes. Price theory provides a different scenario: Over time the price of an exhaustible resource (like crude oil) must rise until, at the time of exhaustion, a new resource replaces the old one; moreover, the transition in price is as smooth as the transition from the old to the new resource (Chapter 16).

Reducing the rate of a tax will deprive the government of important revenue, says common sense. Not always, says microeconomics. Sometimes

---

[1] Barry Commoner, *The Poverty of Power: Energy and the Economic Crisis,* Alfred A. Knopf, New York, 1976, p. 172.

reducing the rate of a tax will increase both output (of the taxed good) and the revenue for the government (Chapter 10).

Some politicians tell us that physicians would charge their patients higher fees if the supply of physicians increased. This is based on the *target income* doctrine, a derivative of common sense. Price theory disagrees. Studies have shown price theory to be correct (Chapter 11).

Common sense tells us that labor unions will hurt the consumer by causing prices to rise. Microeconomics shows that in the United States, where only about a third of the labor force is unionized, the damage to the consumer is minimal. The main impact of unions is on the nonunion employees rather than on consumers (Chapter 15).

If light bulbs were produced by a monopoly, would it suppress an innovation that could increase the illumination hours per bulb? Regardless of what common sense tells us, price theory says that under some conditions a monopoly will introduce the innovation, and under other conditions it will suppress the innovation.

ECONOMICS IS A SCIENCE

Is there any doubt that economics is a science? Everybody knows that physics is a science. What makes it a science? One afternoon in 1665, when Sir Isaac Newton was sitting under a tree, the famous apple fell on the ground; the theory of gravity was born. This new theory explained why the moon moves around the earth. But the fact that Newton's theory made a lot of sense was not sufficient to make it a science. *Confirmation* was needed in order to upgrade logic into science. The planet Uranus provided astronomers with the opportunity to confirm the gravity theory: Since they could not figure out Uranus's orbit around the sun, they knew there must be another planet far off in space which pulled Uranus. J. C. Adams, a Cambridge student, applied the theory of gravity and figured out the whereabouts of that planet. In 1846, an astronomer aimed his telescope in the direction suggested by the calculations based on Newton's theory and discovered the planet Neptune, which had never been seen before. Newton's theory was *confirmed*. Modern Einsteinian physics did not escape the need to test a theory. For example, the general theory of relativity predicted that light rays would bend in gravitational fields. Albert Einstein predicted that the image of a star relatively near the sun would be displaced compared with the image of a star relatively remote from the sun. These minute deflections could be photographed only during a solar eclipse and then only from a particular position on earth. A famous scientist, Sir Arthur Eddington, traveled to the Gulf of Guinea and photographed the sun during the eclipse of 1919. He *confirmed* Einstein's theory.

Economics was upgraded from a branch of logic to a science a bit after the turn of the century, when economists started to test theories by using real data and statistical procedures. The pioneers were those who showed for the first time that consumers behaved in the marketplace as predicted by the theory. A perusal of contemporary economic journals reveals page after page of mathematical notations. The student should not think that economics is scientific because economists frequently apply mathematics. Rather, the fact that economists can test their theories to either confirm or refute them makes economics a science. Economics uses statistical procedures to confirm or refute economic theories having to do with the behavior of consumers and producers in the marketplace (Chapter 18).

Those who measure precision in terms of achievements of the physical sciences will say that economics is not a precise science. The lay person tends to separate subjects into "hard" sciences (like physics) on the one hand and "soft" sciences (like economics) on the other. If hardness is measured by the ability to predict, however, it is not clear what is hard and what is soft. For example, before the July 16, 1945, atomic test, the physicists of Los Alamos had a betting pool on the size of the explosion. Most estimates were far too low. A few were too high. According to Robert Jungk, only one guess came close to the target, and it was made by a scientist who was absent from Los Alamos for some time.[2]

If physical scientists could predict precisely how physical systems would work under different conditions, certainly the 1965 blackout which hit the Northeast could never occur again. Yet in July of 1977, during a hot, wet night in New York, it happened again; lights went out, and subways and air conditioners stopped. For the better part of a day there was no electricity in many parts of the city.

And what about the physical and chemical science of the atmosphere known as meteorology? Does it predict the precipitation for next year better than econometric models predict the rate of inflation for next year?

We can summarize that economics is a science that, like the physical sciences, generates theories that must be either refuted or confirmed by real data. But because economics investigates human beings, testing in economics is different from testing in the physical sciences. In particular, it is difficult if not impossible to create laboratory conditions to test economic theories. Economists therefore apply mathematical and statistical procedures which are known as *econometrics* (Chapter 18).

ECONOMICS IS A SOCIAL SCIENCE

As noted in the previous section, economics is a science that bears many similarities to the physical sciences, particularly in the form of research which involves postulating, developing a theory, and then either confirming or refuting the theory. Moreover, the power of the theory in both physical sciences and economics lies in the ability to predict. But as the subject matter of economics is human beings, it has a lot in common with other social sciences. Economics investigates the interaction of people in the mar-

---

[2]Robert Jungk, *Brighter than a Thousand Suns*, Harcourt, Brace, New York, 1958.

ketplace. *Anthropology*, another social science, studies cultural variations and how they involve family and larger group relationships. Anthropology is indirectly related to economics. For example, in Israel, farmers raise carp in artificial ponds for profit. The demand for carp stems from the cultural Jewish tradition of eating gefilte fish on holidays. In 1967, prices of fish declined when the Catholic church in the United States abolished the prohibition against eating meat on Friday.

Sociology, one of the major social sciences, is involved in studying classes. For example, sociology may study the evolvement of the women's liberation movement. There is no doubt that this movement affected the attitudes of employers toward female employees in the United States. Economists who study the labor markets confirmed that this movement had a positive impact on the salaries of female secretaries. Demographers, social scientists who study population trends, found, however, that this movement had a negative impact on the fertility rate in the United States. Finally, economists concluded that in the long run, the decline in the fertility rate will shrink the rate of growth of the labor force until it will reach a steady state. Economists accept cultural norms (Jews eating gefilte fish), cultural variations (Catholics beginning to eat meat on Fridays), and group movements (women's liberation) as data. These data enter their studies of markets (carp in Israel, fish in the United States, and the labor market for women in the short run and for women and men in the long run).

MICROECONOMICS (PRICE THEORY) AS A FIELD IN ECONOMICS

As noted, the main concern of economics as a social science is interaction of human beings in the marketplace. When they study markets, economists sometimes apply the microscope in order to study problems of specific markets such as the market for gasoline during the so-called energy crisis or the change in the market for female employees as a result of the women's liberation movement. Whenever the "microscope" is applied to study a problem of a specific market, we enter the field of *microeconomics, or price theory.* At other times, economists apply the "macroscope" in order to investigate the entire economy and its well-being. For example, the issue of inflation, which is signified by a rise in all prices in all markets, or of unemployment, which is insufficient demand for labor in all labor markets, is studied by applying the macroscope to the entire economy, glossing over the micro-components of the economy. Such macrostudies are in a field known as *macroeconomics.*

Microeconomics (price theory) and macroeconomics are the two major components in economics. Accordingly, they are the prerequisites for all other studies in economics. There are also subjects that are taught in management schools that draw heavily on these two major fields in economics: finance, money and banking, marketing, and cost accounting. Figure I-1 illustrates the relationships of some of the fields in economics and how they are related to macroeconomics and microeconomics (price theory).

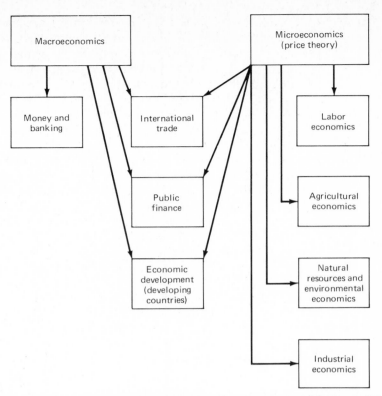

FIGURE I-1   THE VARIOUS FIELDS IN ECONOMICS AND HOW THEY ARE RELATED TO
MICROECONOMICS (PRICE THEORY) AND MACROECONOMICS.

Figure I-1 does not enumerate all the fields in economics, however. Fields are born out of need. For example, urban problems in the 1960s gave rise to a field known as *urban economics*. Welfare economics and general equilibrium, taught at the graduate level, are not mentioned as separate fields because they are viewed as advanced topics in price theory. *Econometrics*, a major field in economics derived neither from macroeconomics nor from microeconomics (price theory), is a statistical-mathematical apparatus applied by economists either to confirm or to refute their theories.

ARE ECONOMISTS IN DISAGREEMENT?

It is said that if you get two economists together, you will get from them three opinions about a single issue. Though amusing, this saying is not a good summary. The state of the art of microeconomics is such that most general theories have been tested and confirmed many times over. If economists disagree on anything, it is the selection of the policy tool rather than the theory, and this happens because they have different goals. As an example, consider the hot issue of American reliance on foreign oil. Economists agree that the demand for gasoline is negatively sloped, implying that less gasoline will be purchased at higher prices and, conversely, more gasoline will be purchased at lower prices. (This is in spite of suggestions at the outset of the 1974 energy crisis that Americans love their big cars so much, they would pay any price for gasoline and would never adjust to rising prices by switching to compacts.) Many economists supported deregulation with a bonanza tax on oil companies, others supported an excise tax on gasoline, and still others thought that the deregulation should not be accompanied by any tax. What happened? All economists agreed that deregulation would raise the price to the consumers and thus induce them to consume less gasoline. However, some economists had an additional goal, that is, to punish the oil companies. For others, the only goal was to reduce American reliance on foreign oil. Those who advocated an excise tax on gasoline were determined to expedite the process of extricating the United States from the grip of foreign oil producers.

In macroeconomics, some major issues have not been resolved. These issues gave rise to the "big debates" that centered mainly around the role of money and monetary policy versus fiscal policy in stabilizing the economy. The controversies in macroeconomics resulted from the lack of a clear-cut empirical test that would confirm the theory of one group and refute the theory of another.

POSITIVE VERSUS NORMATIVE ECONOMICS

Positive economics is interested in *what is,* while *normative economics* is interested in *what should be.* For example, as a result of industrial development, rivers became polluted, particularly after World War II. Positive economics, among other things, provides analysis known as *externalities* which analyzes, for example, why fishermen, water skiers, and others who enjoy clean water fail to bargain with municipalities and factories that dispose of their effluents in the streams. This positive theory is sometimes known as *Coase's theorem.* Normative economics says, however, that the public ought to clean rivers. In order to preserve the fishing industry, the government may therefore decide that the dissolved oxygen (DO) in rivers should not be less than a certain level. Economic theory would then be called upon to determine the least-cost pollution-abating policy subject to the DO constraint imposed by the government. Thus economic analysis contributes to normative economics.

FREE MARKETS ARE EFFICIENT

Adam Smith was the father of the dictum that each individual in a free market economy, by pursuing his or her own selfish economic goals, is led, as if by an invisible hand, to attain bliss for society as a whole. This bliss has many faces, one of which is an efficient system that allocates limited resources among many consumer goals. In a free enterprise system we rarely observe a shortage of a good or a waiting line for the good that is in short supply. Yet, in the summer of 1979 in California long waiting lines for gasoline became part of the daily scene: One could mistake it for a normal situation in a socialist economy. What went wrong? The Department of Energy did not trust the market mechanism and decided to embark on a system of administrative allocation of gasoline in the United States. Ignoring the rapid rate of growth of the California economy relative to the rest of the economy, the Department of Energy did not allocate sufficient amounts of gasoline to California.

By contrast, look at the coffee situation in 1975–1977: In the summer of 1975, frost reduced the 1976 Brazilian coffee harvest significantly. The 1976–1977 exportable production of coffee dropped 18 percent below the 1975–1976 level. There were no coffee shortages and no lines for coffee. How come? The market was left alone; so the price of coffee rose, leading consumers to adjust to buying less. An important role of price theory (microeconomics) is to demonstrate how free markets function efficiently and why, if tampered with, they malfunction. In socialist economies, the market plays a limited role. The government decides what and how much of each good to produce. Although it is impossible to compare the two systems from a moralistic viewpoint, it is evident that Western Europe, with its free markets, enjoys higher standards of living than does Eastern Europe; and Taiwan is developing much faster than the People's Republic of China.

Why can a central government not replace the invisible hand of the free market? Instead of a formal answer, consider the following nightmare of a socialist economy, where the government assigns production quotas to factory managers. If they fulfill only their quota, they get a salary; if they exceed their quota, they receive a bonus as well. Consequently, when the manager of a nail factory was assigned a quota measured in the number of nails produced per annum, for a while there was a glut of small nails in the shops. To correct it, the government assigned quotas in terms of weight: Quotas were measured in pounds of nails produced in a year. Small nails vanished from the market; now there was a glut of large nails in the shops. There has never been a shortage of small or large nails or nails of any size in a free enterprise system: Free markets foster the smooth functioning of markets. And it is price theory (microeconomics) that explains how free markets work.

THE CIRCULAR FLOW OF AN ECONOMIC SYSTEM

Price theory (microeconomics) concerns itself with three basic problems that confront every society:

1. What goods can be produced and in what quantity?

2. How can the different goods be produced?
3. For whom are the different goods being produced?

Even Robinson Crusoe on his island confronted the first two problems. Crusoe had limited resources on his island, only himself, some tools, and land. First, he had to determine how to allocate his limited resources among the different goods (fish, meat, and grains) that could be produced on the island. We note that leisure was one of many goods that Crusoe could produce by simply performing less work every day. He then faced the second basic problem. He could sacrifice leisure or hunting time by devoting more time to preparing additional fields so that in the future he would have more corn and vegetables. This would enable him to combine more capital with his labor and increase his production capacity. The third problem arose only after Friday joined Crusoe on the island. As an example, they could have distributed production by agreeing that Friday would specialize in hunting and Crusoe in producing grains, and they would exchange grains for meat by bargaining with each other.

A modern society differs from Crusoe's lonely island mainly because money is used as a unit of measurement. Assume for this discussion that Crusoe and Friday had $50 each. Would this fact make any difference to them? The answer is that it would make it easier for them to trade with each other, but it would not change the basic nature of the problems that they had to solve. For example, they might agree that Friday would sell Crusoe 10 pounds of meat for 2 bushels of corn. Assume that meat is the *numeraire* commodity, that is, everything is measured in terms of meat. In our illustration the price of corn is 5 pounds of meat. Imagine now hundreds of individuals producing and selling hundreds of different goods. Using meat as a medium of exchange would not be very convenient to accommodate such a complex market operation. Introducing money can solve the problem if everyone simply agrees to measure everything in terms of money. In our example we may start by assuming that the price of meat is $1 per pound. Accordingly, the price of corn is $5 per bushel. The monetary transaction would go as follows: Friday sells Crusoe 10 pounds of meat: Crusoe pays Friday $10 (10 pounds times $1). Crusoe sells Friday 2 bushels of corn; Friday pays Crusoe $10 (2 bushels times $5). Notice that if each week Crusoe and Friday trade with each other $10 worth of corn and $10 worth of meat and they have a stock of money for $100, then $1 out of $10 makes a complete round (Crusoe-Friday-Crusoe) during each week. If we gave each of the island residents an additional $50, the stock of money would double (from $100 to $200). Crusoe and Friday would have the illusion of possessing more wealth and would begin to spend more money on corn and meat. But since their productivity has not changed, more money would be chasing a fixed flow of goods, and prices would rise. Finally prices will double: A pound of meat will sell for $2 and a bushel of corn will sell for $10. What we have described is the process of *inflation,* which is a subject of macroeconomics. The relevant point for microeconomics is that although *nominal prices* doubled, real prices are the same: One bushel of corn still buys 5 pounds of the numeraire good, namely, meat: $10/$2 = 5. Notice also that the relationship between the stock of money and money in circulation is the same: $20 now makes a round during each week, but the stock of money is $200; again $1 out of $10 makes the round.

In Figure I-2 we illustrate the circular flow diagram for a more complex economy. We assume that a certain stock of money is available to this economy. We are not going to worry about the size of this stock because, as shown above, its size will determine the nominal level of prices of goods but not their prices *relative* to some numeraire commodity. In microeconomics we are interested only in *relative prices,* such as the price of corn in terms of meat. In macroeconomics we are interested in *nominal prices,* such as doubling the price of both corn and meat in terms of money.

In Figure I-2 the outer circle with an arrow pointing in the counterclockwise direction is the monetary flow. The inner circle with the arrow pointing clockwise is the physical flow of goods, including such goods as labor and capital services. Let us start with households. (In a circular flow the starting point is arbitrary.) Households receive an income in form of salaries, wages, interest, and so on. Their income is spent on goods represented by the physical flow of finished goods. Chapters 1 through 4 deal with the households box, and particularly with the flow of finished goods and the opposite flow of expenditures on finished goods. In these chapters the flow of income (wages, salaries, rentals interest, and profit) is assumed to be

FIGURE I-2   THE CIRCULAR FLOW DIAGRAM.

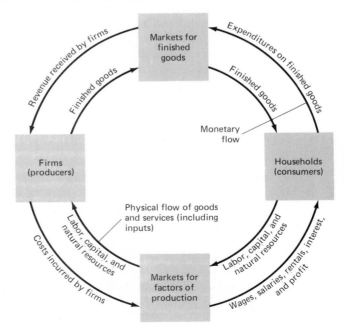

given, as are the prices confronting consumers. This part of the book is known as the *theory of the consumer*. The theory of the consumer gives rise to the theory of demand.

Firms are considered next. First, in order to be able to produce the flow of finished goods, firms must buy inputs from households. Inputs are represented by the inward flow in the direction of the firms box; these inputs are labor, capital, and land services, and natural resources such as minerals and water. The cost flow, which is payment for these factors of production, is in the form of salaries, wages, rentals, profit, and so on. The physical flow of finished goods produced by firms is sold in exchange for revenue received by firms. Chapters 5 through 8 deal with firms and the flows that go into and out of firms; this part of the book is known as the *theory of producer and supply*.

How are prices of finished goods determined? The upper box in the circular flow diagram represents the marketplace for finished goods. Firms bring the physical supply of finished goods to the marketplace. This is represented by the inward flow of finished goods from the firms box to the market of finished goods box. From the other direction, households receive the inward flow of finished goods in exchange for a monetary flow of expenditures on finished goods. Prices are determined in the marketplace by a simple principle that requires that the entire output flow of finished goods will be taken off the shelves, namely, be converted into a flow of consumption, and also that the entire flow of expenditures on finished goods, which is the budgets of households, will be converted into the flow of revenue received by firms. Chapters 9 and 10 deal with *perfect competition*. In perfectly competitive markets there are many small producers, none of whom has any appreciable influence over the market, and they produce a homogeneous product, say, wheat.

Chapters 11, 12, and 13 deal with *monopoly and imperfect competition;* in such markets firms are not numerous, and hence single firms have some influence over the price in the marketplace. Firms in imperfect markets cover a wide spectrum. Economists classify such markets into *monopoly* (a single firm dominates the market; for example, telephone services are produced by a monopoly), *oligopoly* (a small number of firms dominate a significant share of the market; for example, the automobile industry is dominated by four corporations), and *monopolistic competition* (many small firms produce a good which is slightly differentiated; for example, furniture is produced by a relatively large number of firms and the product is differentiated).

How are the prices of *inputs* (factors of production) determined? The lower box on the circular flow diagram helps us answer this. First consider the physical flow representing the supply of labor, capital, and land services as well as the supply of minerals and other natural resources. This inward flow originates at the households box, passes through the markets for factors box, and ends up in the firms box. We can picture it as households bringing these services to the marketplace of factors of production to be sold to firms. The monetary flow from firms to the markets for factors is the amount of money firms are willing to pay for the various inputs. Prices of labor (salaries and wage rates), price of capital services (interest and dividends), and prices of natural resources (such as crude oil) are determined in the marketplace. The cost of production is a flow which originates in the firms box; it flows into the markets for factors box, where it becomes a flow of wages, salaries, rentals interest, and profit going into the households box. The rule of the market for factors of production is familiar: Prices will vary until whatever households bring into the marketplace is cleared by firms, namely, until firms use as much labor, capital services, and other resources as are offered by the owners of these resources; simultaneously, in the marketplace the cost of production is converted into income received by households. Chapters 14, 15, and 16 deal with the markets for factors of production. These chapters analyze how the market forces determine wages and salaries, returns to capital, payments to exhaustible resources, and so on.

In Figure I-2 everything depends on everything else. For example, if, say, households want to consume more pianos and fewer cucumbers, prices of pianos will rise while prices of cucumbers will fall in the marketplace for finished goods. This is a signal for firms producing pianos to hire more labor and use more capital services, and a signal for the firms producing cucumbers to release (employ less) labor and capital. If the process of producing pianos is capital-intensive relative to the production of cucumbers (which is labor-intensive relative to pianos), the price of labor in the marketplace for inputs (factors of production) will fall slightly and the price of capital will rise slightly. *General-equilibrium analysis* considers what occurs in one market in conjunction with what results in other markets, even if they are remote from the market under focus. Since in most cases what occurs in a single market has only imperceptible impacts on other remote markets, we ignore these secondary impacts and focus on the market under consideration, or at most, we may also focus on a closely related market. This type of analysis, known as *partial-equilibrium analysis,* is our main concern in this book. Partial-equilibrium analysis is very simple and efficient; yet occasionally general-equilibrium analysis is called for to keep partial-equilibrium analysis "honest."

PART ONE

THE THEORY OF THE CONSUMER AND DEMAND

A *consumer,* the decision maker in a household or any other organization engaged in consumption (e.g., a hospital), is confronted daily with the problem of allocating a budget among the various goods which can be purchased in the marketplace. This part of the book will develop the *theory of the consumer and demand.* Chapter 1 discusses the theory of *utility* and *indifference curve analysis,* which deals with how a consumer spends a budget in order to maximize his or her utility (satisfaction). Chapter 2 considers a consumer's response to variations in income and the price of a good. This is known as the *theory of demand.* Chapter 3 expands the theory of demand by considering the change in a consumer's consumption of one good when the price of another good varies. The individual demand curves are aggregated in order to obtain the *market demand curve,* and the impact of population growth on market demand is also examined. Chapter 4 covers optional topics such as *index numbers* and *consumer behavior in situations involving risk,* which, while relevant, are not essential for a basic course in price theory.

At this point students might want to review the circular flow diagram in Figure I-2. In particular, they should observe the role of the households box in that model.

C H A P T E R

CONSUMER PREFERENCES AND CHOICE

Our study of price theory begins with the individual consumer, whose preferences and consumption and demand patterns determine all economic activity. The economic problem can be stated as follows: *How to satisfy alternative ends with limited resources.* If resources were unlimited, there would not be an economic problem; all ends would be completely satisfied. If resources were limited and only one end were to be satisfied, again there would be no economic problem. For instance, a Robinson Crusoe, stranded on an island with limited resources, faces a purely technological problem if he wants to grow wheat, namely, how to produce maximum wheat with the given limited resources. If leisure is also an end for Robinson Crusoe, however, he must decide how to allocate his limited time between wheat production and leisure. This is an economic problem. In the modern economy, limitation of resources is reflected in the size of individual spendable income, which is never infinitely large. With their limited income individuals satisfy alternative ends such as food, shelter, and leisure. The individual who allocates limited income among alternative ends is called a *consumer*, and the process of satisfying the alternative ends is called *consumption*. The ends are denoted simply as *goods*. The consumer has limited income which he or she wants to allocate among alternative goods available for a price in the marketplace. The goal is to maximize satisfaction. The consumer will therefore be considered as a decision-maker faced with a variety of choices. The objectives in Chapter 1 are, first, to understand the nature of the consumer satisfaction (utility); second, to develop a theory of rational consumer behavior aimed at achieving maximum satisfaction; and third, to develop the indifference curve apparatus which will allow us to summarize the theory of consumer behavior conveniently by applying simple geometric devices.

1.1 CONSUMER BEHAVIOR AND WANT SATISFACTION

There is little to be added to the doctrine of Jeremy Bentham, a nineteenth century English philosopher, who postulated that utility is power in goods which creates satisfaction, and that the happiness of the individual is the sum total of his or her satisfactions. From observing consumers, ourselves included, we know that consumption is far from being a stagnant process. Consumers substitute goods whose price falls for other goods. This implies that all goods have something in common: As income increases, consumers attempt to increase the consumption of preferred goods over the consumption of less preferred goods. According to Bentham, what guides people's behavior is the principle of "greatest happiness," which modern economists call *maximizing utility*. The modern theory of consumer's behavior, which is based on the postulate of utility maximization, will be considered next.

1.1a Cardinal versus Ordinal Utility

To illustrate further what utility means, let us imagine a consumer with two shopping carts, each containing a different combination of goods. We tell that person to choose only one cart. The consumer is likely to examine the two carts and choose the one that provides more satisfaction; in other words, to maximize the utility. In choosing between the shopping carts, the consumer has clearly compared the two, measured their respective utility, and chosen the one that gives more utility. But how do we measure utility for the purpose of comparison?

Early economists led by Leon Walras and Alfred Marshall believed that *cardinal* measurement of utility was possible. Cardinal measurement means that a basic unit of measurement exists, such as a pound for weight, a yard for distance, and a dollar for money, and that utility can be measured in terms of such a basic unit. Cardinal numbers are quantitatively related to each other, and the units of measurement of utility under the cardinal system are sometimes called *utils*. In our example, if we denote the two carts A and B, respectively, under a cardinal system our consumer may tell us that B yields 40 utils while A yields only 20 utils. Since B yields twice as much utils as A, B is preferred.

Late in the nineteenth century, the English economist Francis Edgeworth (a contemporary of Walras and Marshall) introduced the concept of *ordinal* measurement of utility. Ordinal measurement accepts only qualitative comparison and thus denies the existence of a basic unit of measurement for utility. Under an ordinal utility system the consumer in our example will tell us that B ranks over A, but not by how much B ranks over A. Since in reality we rank goods qualitatively rather than quantitatively, modern economics has accepted ordinal measurement of utility as a basis for the theory of consumer behavior.

1.2 CARDINAL UTILITY

If ordinal utility is realistic and cardinal utility impractical, why bother with cardinal utility? The answer is multifold. First, cardinal utility is easier to grasp on a more intuitive basis. Second, theories should not be tested directly. Rather, theories are tested indirectly, and then they are either confirmed or refuted. It so happens that cardinal and ordinal utility measurement lead to the same theoretical structure. Accordingly, they are equally relevant if economics is a true science. Third, in some economic studies cardinal utility is chosen as the standard for analysis, and it might therefore prove a useful tool for the student of economics.

1.2a The Concepts of Total and Marginal Utility

If cardinal measurement of utility were possible, we could design experiments in which utility could be quantitatively associated with consumption. Imagine that your friend Ben has designed an experiment to determine the amount of satisfaction he derives from drinking beer after his daily 4-mile jog in July. The conditions of the experiment are set as follows: He must run 4 miles at noon. He must drink beer during the first hour immediately following his jogging. We assume that the temperature, his health, and all other relevant conditions do not vary from day to day. On the first day he drinks 1 cup of beer; on the second day he drinks 2 cups; the amount of beer he drinks per hour increases by 1 cup each day. Each day Ben records the amount of utility derived from drinking the ice-cold beer after jogging. He notes that his thirst is quenched after drinking 5 cups. The sixth cup detracts from his satisfaction. Denoting utility by U and quantity by X, we can record the results of the experiment graphically, as shown in Figure 1-1. The *total utility* Ben derives from drinking beer is depicted by the curve labeled U. Notice that this utility curve rises up to a level of 5 cups, where it attains its maximum level. Beyond that point utility begins to fall. From the diagram we learn that 1 cup of beer yielded 2.5 utils, 2 cups yielded 4 utils, and so on. Total utility increased to 5 utils from 3 cups, 5.5 utils from 4 cups, and 5.9 utils from 5 cups. The fact that the maximum satisfaction was reached at some level of consumption implies that as the quantity of the good consumed per unit of time increases, the additional utility gained diminishes. This is the topic of Section 1.2b.

Marginal utility is defined as the extra utility obtained from a small (unit) change in the consumption of a given good when taste and the consumption of all other goods remained unchanged. Marginal utility (MU) is calculated by applying the following formula:

$$MU = \frac{\Delta U}{\Delta X} = \frac{U_1 - U_0}{X_1 - X_0} \qquad (1\text{-}1)$$

where ΔX is the small change in quantity from X_0 to X_1 and ΔU is the resulting change in utility from U_0 to U_1. The subscripts 0 and 1 denote two consecutive quantities (of beer and utility, etc.). In the example, if we select

FIGURE 1-1 TOTAL UTILITY CURVE
The total utility curve relates total utility to the consumption of a certain good per unit of time. Here, the consumption of beer (after jogging) varies while all other things are kept constant. Total utility rises up to a certain point (5 cups of beer per hour) and then it begins to fall.

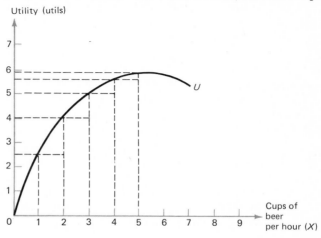

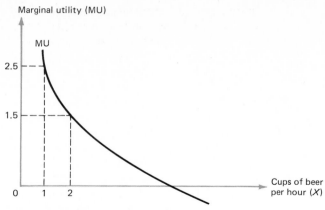

FIGURE 1-2   MARGINAL UTILITY CURVE
The horizontal axis is the same as in Figure 1-1. Along the vertical axis we measure the marginal utility, namely, the changes in utility derived from varying consumption by small changes. For example, a marginal utility of 1.5 utils for the second cup of beer is obtained from Figure 1-1 by noting that adding a second cup of beer increases the total utility of the jogger from 2.5 to 4 utils. The marginal utility curve is negatively sloped.

$X_0 = 1$ (cup) and $X_1 = 2$ (cups), then, as indicated by the utility curve U, the corresponding U_0 is 2.5 utils and the corresponding U_1 is 4 utils. Accordingly, the marginal utility of the second cup of beer is

$$\text{MU (second cup)} = \frac{4 - 2.5}{2 - 1} = \frac{1.5}{1} \text{ utils}$$

Having defined marginal utility, we now draw the *marginal utility curve*. In Figure 1-2 beer is measured along the horizontal axis and marginal utility along the vertical axis. We notice that the marginal utility of the first cup is 2.5 utils. We have already calculated that the marginal utility of the second cup is 1.5 utils. The marginal utility of the third cup is 1 util, and so on. This information, which is read off Figure 1-1, is plotted in Figure 1-2. The resulting marginal utility curve is denoted by MU. We note finally that the smaller the change in X, the closer we get to the definition of marginal utility at a given point.

1.2b The Law of Diminishing Marginal Utility

The law of diminishing marginal utility states that, *ceteris paribus*, the marginal utility derived from consuming a certain good diminishes when the quantity of that good consumed per unit of time increases. Notice that *ceteris paribus* means that tastes and the consumption of all other goods remain unchanged. The law of diminishing marginal utility summarizes our experience that the more we consume of one commodity per unit of time the less important to us is one additional unit of it. In Figure 1-1 the law of diminishing marginal utility is illustrated by the fact that as consumption of beer increases, utility increases at a decreasing rate. For example, while the marginal utility of the second cup is 1.5 utils, the marginal utility of the third cup is only 1 util, and so on. After the fifth cup marginal utility becomes negative. Note, by comparing Figures 1-1 and 1-2, that marginal utility is zero at the quantity where total utility is maximum.

1.2c Maximization of Utility

In the example that follows we shall assume that consumption is a smooth process, namely, that commodities are divisible. Moreover, we shall assume that utility is a smooth function of consumption, as implied in Figure 1-1, where a smooth curve passes through points $X = 1, U = 2.5, X = 2, U = 4$, and so on.

Suppose as a consumer you are confronted in the marketplace with only two goods, X and Y and fixed prices of X, P_x and Y, P_y. To compare utilities (derived from two different goods), X and Y must be subject to the same measure. We must therefore redefine the unit of X and Y to be equal to "$1's worth." For example, if the price of X is \$2, then \$1's worth of the new unit of X is half of the normal unit. If the price of Y is 25 cents, then \$1's worth of each new unit of Y is equal to four normal units. Now we can restate the marginal utils of X and Y in comparable terms. The new marginal utility of X is denoted by MU_x/P_x. That is, the marginal utility of each \$1's worth is equal to the marginal utility of X divided by the price of X. To illustrate, assume that the marginal utility of X is 5 utils for the third unit consumed. Since the price of X is \$2, the third normal unit represents six new units, i.e., \$6's worth. Thus the marginal utility of the sixth \$1's worth of good X is 5/\$2 = 2.5 utils. Having determined the marginal utility of \$1's worth of X and Y, let us now define your available budget. We first assume that your budget is fixed and that savings have been subtracted. The budget of any consumer is then expressed as follows:

$$I = P_x \cdot X + P_y \cdot Y \qquad (1\text{-}2)$$

where I stands for the budget available to the consumer, and the budget must be exhausted on the goods X and Y. For example, if your budget is \$100, P_x is \$2, and P_y is \$0.25, your budget equation is

$$\$100 = \$2X + \$0.25Y$$

You could exhaust your budget on buying 50 (normal) units of X or, alternatively, 400 (normal) units of Y, or any intermediate combination such as 25 units of X and 200 units of Y. However, only one combination of X and Y would yield maximum utility. Maximizing utility to obtain the optimal combination of X and Y subject to the budget constraint is illustrated in Figure 1-3.

The space in Figure 1-3 is used for simultaneously depicting the marginal utility of \$1's worth of X (MU_x/P_x) and the marginal utility of \$1's worth of Y (MU_y/P_y). O_y denotes the origin of the Y diagram. The quantity of Y increases as we move from left to right. O_x is the origin of the X diagram. The quantity of X increases as we move (unconventionally) from right to left. If

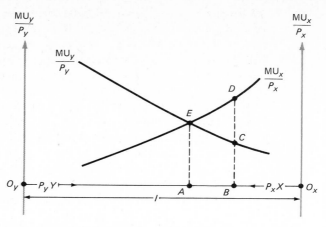

FIGURE 1-3   MAXIMUM UTILITY COMBINATION OF TWO GOODS
Units of goods such as apples or loaves of bread are transformed into $1's worth. The marginal utility for such units are MU/P, that is, additional utility obtained from spending one additional dollar on the good under consideration. Money spent on Y is measured from left to right, and money spend on X from right to left. Equilibrium occurs where the two marginal utility curves (adjusted for the new scales) intersect. At the point of intersection MU_x/P_x = MU_y/P_y.

the consumer is at O_y, he is exhausting his entire budget on X. If he is at O_x, he is exhausting his entire budget on Y. Assume he is at O_x. He begins to move to the left. Moving one unit to the left means forgoing the consumption of $1's worth of Y and increasing the consumption of $1's worth of X. If he stops at point B, spending $\overline{O_xB}$ dollars on X and $\overline{O_yB}$ dollars on Y, he has not yet maximized utility: As indicated by the MU_x/P_x curve, the marginal utility per the last dollar spent on X is $\overline{BD}$, while as indicated by the MU_y/P_y curve, the marginal utility per the last dollar spent on Y is only $\overline{BC}$. Accordingly, moving to the left one additional dollar, or what is the same, shifting one more dollar from Y to X would roughly increase the utility of the consumer by $\overline{CD}$ utils. ($\overline{CD}$ is a rough approximation of the gain in utility because a movement to the left continuously raises MU_y/P_y and depresses MU_x/P_x.) Assume that finally the consumer reaches point A: The two curves intersect at point E, where $\overline{O_xA}$ dollars are spent on X and $\overline{O_yA}$ dollars are spent on Y. At the point of intersection the additional utility from spending the last dollar on X is the same as the additional utility from spending the last dollar on Y. This situation can be expressed as follows:

$$\frac{MU_x}{P_x} = \frac{MU_y}{P_y} \tag{1-3}$$

It states that consumers have maximized utility when there is no incentive to shift money from spending on X to spending on Y, and vice versa. As a numerical example, assume that when you allocate your budget of $100, $60 to X and $40 to Y, the marginal utility of (normal) X is 16 utils and of (normal) Y is 2 utils. The prices of X and Y are, respectively, $2 and $0.25. The marginal utility of $1's worth of X is 16/$2 = 8 utils, and the marginal utility of $1's worth of Y is 2/$0.25 = 8 utils. This means that you have maximized your utility: $\overline{O_xA}$ = 60 $1's worth of X, $\overline{O_yA}$ = 40 $1's worth of Y, and $\overline{AE}$ = 8 utils. If you move $1 to the right, say, by shifting the last dollar from X to Y (spend $59 on X and $41 on Y), your gain from consuming more Y (ΔY = 4 normal units) would be less than 8 utils; your loss from consuming less X (ΔX = minus a half of a normal unit) would be more than 8 utils. Thus, you will suffer a net loss of utility. It is left for the student to show that a movement of $1 to the left of point A would also result in a net loss of utility.

We can summarize and say that at point E the consumer maximizes his utility. There he is indifferent between spending his last dollar on X or alternatively on Y; the consumer has reached *equilibrium*.

1.2d Cardinal Utility and Indifference Curves

Consider now a consumer with only two goods in her budget, X and Y. Looking at Figure 1-4, we know that each point in the X, Y space represents a basket of some combinations of units of X and Y consumed per unit of time. While in Figure 1-3 the consumer was restricted to combinations of X and Y that are exactly covered by her budget, in Figure 1-4 she is free to consider any combinations of X and Y whatsoever. Consider any arbitrary pair of X and Y, say, point K. Now, suppose we took away one unit of Y ($\overline{KQ}$) from the consumer and asked her the following question: "What is the

FIGURE 1-4 DERIVING INDIFFERENCE CURVES: CARDINAL UTILITY

The indifference curve U_0 is derived by selecting a starting point at random in the X, Y space. This point is K. Equal amounts of Y (such as $\overline{KQ}$, $\overline{LR}$, etc.) are taken away from the consumer. He or she is compensated by positive changes in X (such as $\overline{QL}$, $\overline{RM}$, etc.) such that he or she remains indifferent between points such as K, L, and M. A new indifference curve such as U_1 reflecting a higher level of utility can be constructed by selecting a starting point, say, Z, which represents either more Y or more X or both, relative to a point such as M on the old indifference curve. Z could be the starting point for the new indifference curve.

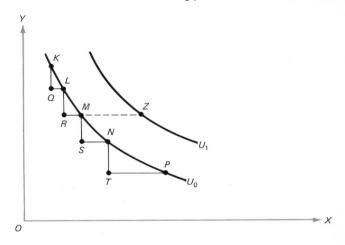

additional amount of X which will compensate you for the loss of one unit of Y?'' Assume the answer is ''$\overline{QL}$ units of X will compensate me for that loss.'' The consumer is indifferent between the pair of X and Y depicted by K or the pair depicted by L. We proceed with the experiment by asking the consumer to forgo the consumption of a second unit of Y $(\overline{LR})$, and she tells us that this time an additional amount of $\overline{RM}$ of X will compensate her. The loss of the third unit of Y$(\overline{MS})$ requires a compensation of $\overline{SN}$ units of X, and the loss of the fourth unit of Y $(\overline{NT})$ is compensated by adding $\overline{TP}$ units of X. Thus the consumer is indifferent between the pairs of X and Y depicted by the points K, L, M, N, and P. In other words, the consumer derives the same amount of utility from combinations K, L, M, N, and P, respectively. Assuming smoothness, we can connect these points and obtain the indifference curve denoted by U_0.

Any point in the space of X and Y in Figure 1-4 which does not lie on U_0 represents more utility if it lies to the right of U_0 and less utility if it lies to the left of U_0. Consider, for example, point Z, which relative to point M represents the same amount of Y but more X. Later the formality of the statement that *consumers prefer more to less* will be discussed. For the time being we accept this as a natural phenomenon and hence agree that point Z yields more utility than point M. We than construct another indifference curve which passes through point Z and denote it by U_1. In a like manner we can fill the entire space in Figure 1-4 with an infinitely large number of indifference curves. The space containing many indifference curves is known as the *indifference map*.

Finally, we notice two interesting results obtained tacitly by drawing U_0: First, since the consumer must be compensated by a certain amount of X if she loses a small amount of Y, the indifference curve must have a *negative slope*. Second, as we slide down an indifference curve in the southeasterly direction, the marginal utility of X diminishes and the marginal utility of Y rises. This must lead to a *convex* indifference curve because, if we were to reduce the amount of Y by equal small changes, the changes in X would have to increase in order for the consumer to achieve the same amount of satisfaction. These two important points will be expanded later.

1.2e Can Utility Be Measured Cardinally?

Utility cannot be measured cardinally. At least no method has been invented to date. We are stating the known fact that consumers, if given the choice of consuming only one of two baskets of goods, would be able to rank one basket over the other on the basis of preference. But consumers are not able to assert meaningfully that one basket contains so many more utils than the other basket.

As stated earlier, ordinal utility measures relative utility. That is, it measures what is preferred to what, but not by how much. Fortunately, we do not really need to know the degree to which a consumer prefers A to B, only that A is preferred to B. In the following sections we shall turn our attention to the process of derivation of the indifference map under the realistic assumption that consumers rank goods ordinally.

1.3 ORDINAL UTILITY

1.3a The Three Axioms of Rational Behavior

The derivation of indifference curves under the (realistic) assumption that utility can be measured only ordinally is based on the following three axioms:

1. *Comparison*. A rational consumer comparing two alternative baskets of goods denoted by A and B must reach one and only one of the following conclusions: A is preferred to B; B is preferred to A; A and B are indifferent.
2. *Transitivity*. If a rational consumer prefers basket B to basket C, and basket A to basket B, then A must be preferred to C. In the same vein, if the consumer is indifferent between B and C and between A and B, then he or she must be indifferent between A and C.
3. *More is preferred to less*. Consider two baskets containing goods that have positive marginal (ordinal) utility. A rational consumer would always prefer basket A to basket B if the two baskets contain identical goods but the quantity of one good is larger in A than in B. This axiom is also known as the *axiom of greediness*.

It is important to note that not all consumers are necessarily rational. The young and old will sometimes violate the three axioms above. However, the theory of the consumer's choice is based on the assumption that the majority of consumers behave rationally. As we shall see, these axioms coupled with the postulate that consumers maximize their utilities will lead to theories that must be either confirmed or refuted.

1.3b The Negative Slope of the Indifference Curve

We now utilize the axioms of rational behavior to derive the indifference curve. As before, there are only two goods in the budget of the consumer, X and Y. In Figure 1-5 point K represents some original basket, arbitrarily chosen. Through point K we pass two straight lines parallel to the X and Y axes, respectively. The (positive), X, Y space is accordingly divided into four quadrants, namely, I, II, III, and IV. According to the third axiom, which states that more is preferred to less, any basket in quadrant III, such as point F, is preferred to basket K. The same holds true with regard to "borderline" baskets such as F' and F''. Also by the third axiom, K is preferred to any basket in quadrant I, such as G. It is also preferred to "borderline" baskets such as G' and G''. Thus we conclude that baskets that are indifferent to K can be found only in quadrants IV and II. Geometrically this leads to the conclusion that the indifference curve must be negatively sloped. The construction of the indifference curve is carried out by applying

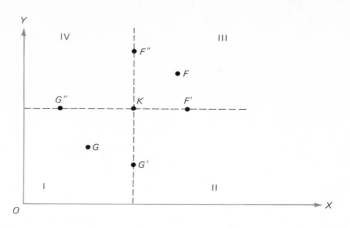

FIGURE 1-5 PROVING THAT INDIFFERENCE CURVES ARE NEGATIVELY SLOPED
In the X, Y space, point K, representing a certain basket, is selected at random. Then, the third axiom (greediness) is invoked in order to demonstrate that K is preferred to baskets in quadrant I, but baskets in quadrant III are preferred to K. The conclusion is then drawn that an indifference curve passing through K must go from quadrant IV to quadrant II; i.e., the indifference curve must be negatively sloped.

a procedure similar to that illustrated by Figure 1-4: In both cases point K depicts the original basket. In both cases the consumer is asked by how many units of X he must be compensated for the loss of one unit of Y. The only difference is that in the experiment conducted under the assumption that cardinal utility is possible the consumer equates the number of utils gained from adding units of X with the number of utils lost from forgoing one unit of Y. In the experiment conducted under the assumption that only ordinal utility is possible, the consumer does not count utils. He simply tells how many additional units of X would compensate him for the loss of one unit of Y. We can summarize finally and say that the property that the indifference curve is negatively sloped has been proved by utilizing the third axiom.

1.3c The Indifference Map

By selecting arbitrary points like K in Figure 1-5 and by applying the procedure of constructing indifference curves as mentioned above, we can fill the X, Y space with as many indifference curves as we desire. In fact, between any two indifference curves one can pass as many additional indifference curves as one pleases. To prove the property that two indifference curves cannot intersect, we use Figure 1-6. The second and third axioms are invoked in the proof as follows: Assume that two indifference curves U_1 and U_0 intersect at point E. Thus the two are ranked equally by the consumer. Baskets G and E on U_1 are indifferent. Baskets F and E on U_0 are indifferent. Thus, by transitivity (the second axiom), baskets G and F are indifferent.

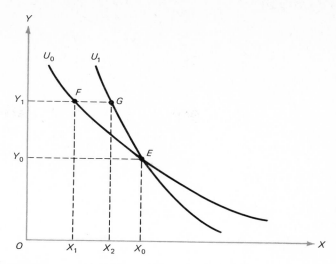

FIGURE 1-6 TWO INDIFFERENCE CURVES CANNOT INTERSECT
Indifference curves cannot intersect. We assume the contrary—that U_0 and U_1 do intersect. E is the point of intersection. On U_0, F and E are indifferent; on U_1, G and E are indifferent; by the second axiom (transitivity) F and G are indifferent; but by the third axiom (greediness) G represents more Y as compared with F; hence G is preferred to F. This contradiction leads to the rejection of the possibility of intersection.

But by the third axiom (more is preferred to less), G is preferred to F, hence the contradiction leading to the nonintersection.

The indifference map is illustrated in Figure 1-7. Note that an indifference curve lying to the right of another indifference curve must be preferred by the consumer. The reason is that moving on the map either north or east means having more of either Y or X; by the third axiom, which states that more is preferred to less, the consumer thus moves to a preferred position. The indifference curves in Figure 1-7 are ordinally labeled 1, 2, 3, 4, etc. Any other consecutive ordering such as a, b, c, d, etc., or 1, 1,000,000, 1,000,000.5, 3,000,000, etc., which conveys the message that moving outward gets the consumer to preferred positions is acceptable.

1.3d The Slope of the Indifference Curve

The *slope of the indifference curve* is known as the *marginal rate of commodity substitution* (RCS). It is simply defined as a small change in Y over a small change in X, namely, $\Delta Y/\Delta X$. Consider Figure 1-8 and assume that we are back in the world of cardinal utility. The two baskets on U_0 depicted by points K and L are very close to each other. Following the indifference curve from point K to point L means giving up $\overline{KQ}$ units of Y, which is ΔY, and being compensated by $\overline{QL}$ units of X, which is ΔX. Since points K and L are in proximity, we can assume that when we move from basket K to basket L

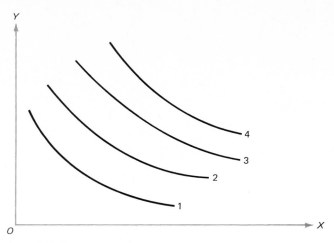

FIGURE 1-7   A MAP OF INDIFFERENCE CURVES
The indifference curves 1, 2, 3, and 4 represent just a few of the infinitely large number of such curves that can be drawn in the *X, Y* space. The numbers 1, 2, 3, and 4 are ordinal. We know that any point on indifference curve 2 is preferred to any point on 1, and so on. We can replace the numbers 1, 2, 3, and 4 by a, b, c, and d or any other set of values that will convey the message that as we move outward the consumer is better off.

the marginal utility of Y does not rise appreciably and the marginal utility of X does not fall appreciably. Thus the loss of utility due to moving south from K to Q is roughly $\Delta Y \cdot MU_y$ and the gain in utility due to moving from Q to L is roughly $\Delta X \cdot MU_x$. Since the movement along the indifference curve implies that the net gain must be zero, we can write

$$\Delta Y \cdot MU_y + \Delta X \cdot MU_x = 0 \qquad (1\text{-}4)$$

Adding $-\Delta X \cdot MU_x$ to both sides of Equation 1-4, we obtain an expression $\Delta Y \cdot MU_y = -\Delta X \cdot MU_x$. If we divide this equality first by MU_y and then by ΔX, we obtain the following expression for RCS:

$$RCS = \frac{\Delta Y}{\Delta X} = -\frac{MU_x}{MU_y} \qquad (1\text{-}5)$$

This expression for RCS will prove useful in the discussion of welfare economics in Chapter 17. It is important to note that RCS was derived under the assumption that cardinal utility is possible. This is nothing more than a procedural convenience. In Mathematical Appendix 1 we show that the transformation from cardinal to ordinal utility leaves the result as given in Equation 1-5 unaltered.

Finally, the student should be able to show that if $\Delta Y = -2$, $MU_y = 3$, and $MU_x = 4$, then $\Delta X = 1.5$ and $RCS = -1.333$.

In summary, the three axioms of rational consumer behavior given in Section 1.3a led us to conclude that indifference curves (1) are *negatively sloped* and (2) *cannot intersect with each other*. We named the collection of

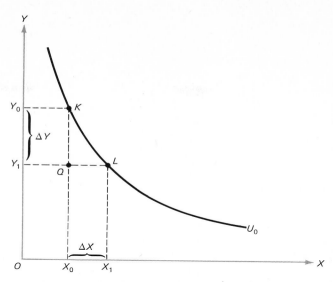

FIGURE 1-8 THE SLOPE OF THE INDIFFERENCE CURVE
The segment $\overline{KQ}$ is ΔY. The segment $\overline{QL}$ is ΔX. The slope of the indifference curve (RCS) is $\Delta Y/\Delta X$. Since the level of utility enjoyed by the consumer when moving from K to L does not change, it can be shown that RCS $= \Delta Y/\Delta X = -MP_x/MP_y$. (RCS is the marginal rate of commodity substitution.)

all the indifference curves in the X, Y space the *indifference map*. The slope of the indifference curve is defined as being equal to $-MU_x/MU_y$ by using terms taken from the world of cardinal utility. But this result is valid in the world of ordinal utility.

The student must have noticed that indifference curves are drawn convex (bulging) toward the origin. In the world of ordinal utility this property can be verified empirically. How this can be done will be demonstrated when the theory is developed further (Section 1.4c).

1.4 EQUILIBRIUM OF THE CONSUMER

1.4a The Budget Line

The *budget line* has already been defined by Equation 1-2 as $I = P \cdot X + P_y \cdot Y$. Recall that I is the income of the consumer minus her savings. The geometric properties of the budget line are illustrated in Figure 1-9. If the consumer spends her entire budget on X, she buys I/P_x units of X, and if she spends her entire budget on Y, she buys I/P_y units of Y. Thus, as illustrated by Figure 1-9, the budget line cuts the X axis at I/P_x and the Y axis at I/P_y. For example, if the budget is $100 per unit of time, the price of X is $4 and the price of Y is $2, the X intercept is 25 units (25 = 100/4) and the Y intercept is 50 units (50 = 100/2). The slope of the budget line is constant because of

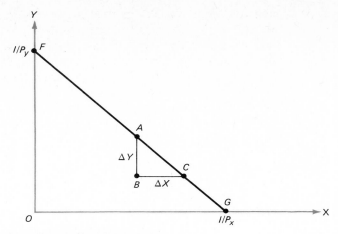

FIGURE 1-9 THE SLOPE OF THE BUDGET LINE

FG is a budget line. The formula of the budget line is $P_x \cdot X + P_y \cdot Y = I$. The intercepts of the budget lines are I/P_y and I/P_x, and the slope of the budget line is the ratio of the intercepts, namely, $-P_x/P_y$. Another way to derive the slope is to note that $\overline{AB}$ is ΔY and $\overline{BC}$ is ΔX. Since the budget constraint implies that the same amount of money is spent on basket C as on A, the slope of the budget line, namely, $\Delta Y/\Delta X$, is $-P_x/P_y$.

linearity.[1] It can be obtained by considering the small triangle denoted by ABC. Assume that you are the consumer and you are moving down on your budget line, meaning you sell Y and use the proceeds to buy X. Alternatively we can view it as a situation in which you are forgoing the opportunity to purchase $\overline{AB}$ units of Y and enabling yourself to buy additional $\overline{BC}$ units of X. Moving from point A to point B would provide you with a cash flow of $\Delta Y \cdot P_y$ dollars. But spending it for the movement from B to C would deplete your cash by $\Delta X \cdot P_x$. Since your budget is exhausted when you are moving along the budget line, the inflow of cash from forgoing the consumption of ΔY must be equal to the outflow of cash for buying ΔX. That is, the two flows must add up to zero, which we express as follows:

$$\Delta Y \cdot P_y + \Delta X \cdot P_x = 0 \qquad (1\text{-}6)$$

If we subtract $\Delta X \cdot P_x$ from both sides of the equality sign and then divide both sides first by P_y and then by ΔX, we obtain the expression for the slope of the budget line:

$$\text{Slope} = \frac{\Delta Y}{\Delta X} = -\frac{P_x}{P_y} \qquad (1\text{-}7)$$

In other words, the slope of the budget line is the price ratio P_x/P_y with a

---

[1]Linearity stems from the following simple derivation: Divide Equation 1-2 by P_y and subtract $X \cdot (P_x/P_y)$ from both sides of the equality. The result is a linear form, namely, $Y = I/P_y - (P_x/P_y) \cdot X$. The general form of a linear function is $Y = a + bX$. In our case $a = I/P_y$ and $b = -(P_x/P_y)$. In other words, the intercept with the Y axis is equal to I/P_y, and the slope of the budget line is a price ratio with minus sign.

negative sign. We can check this result by recalling that in Figure 1-9 the small triangle ABC was congruent with the large triangle FOG. Thus $\Delta Y/\Delta X$ is equal to $\overline{FO}/\overline{OG}$, which is the Y intercept with a negative sign divided by the X intercept. The result is $(-I/P_y)/(I/P_x) = -P_x/P_y$. In our example the slope is $-(\$4)/(\$2) = -2$. We can verify this result by dividing the X intercept into the negative Y intercept: $-50/25 = -2$. Thus the ratio $-P_x/P_y$ determines the slope of the budget line.

The budget I and the two prices simultaneously determine the position of the budget line. A change in one price would lead to a budget line rotation. In Figure 1-10, I_0 depicts our original example ($I = \$100$, $P_x = \$4$, and $P_y = \$2$). I_1 depicts the new budget line after the price of X has fallen to \$2.5. I_2 depicts the new budget line after income has doubled from \$100 to \$200. As expected, I_2 is parallel to I_0. I_2 could have alternatively resulted from a 50 percent cut in P_x and P_y, respectively. Consider a situation in which the consumer receives his income in kind, say, basket A containing 10 units of X and 30 units of Y. The consumer receives no pecuniary income. How would the budget line change if both prices rise by 10 percent? If both prices fall by 10 percent? If the price of X rises and the price of Y falls?

1.4b Determining Equilibrium

In order to obtain the equilibrium combination of X and Y, leading to the highest level of satisfaction, we impose the budget line on the indifference

FIGURE 1-10   SHIFTING BUDGET LINES
I_0 represents the budget line $\$4 \cdot X + \$2 \cdot Y = \$100$. In I_1, P_x declined from \$4 to \$2.5. In I_2 (relative to I_0) either prices are cut by half or the budget is doubled.

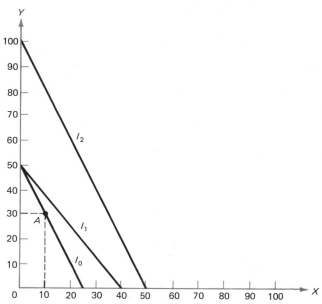

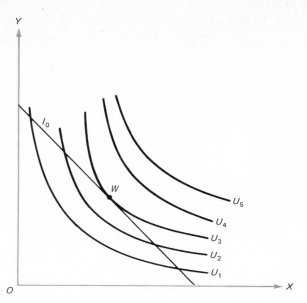

FIGURE 1-11 DETERMINING EQUILIBRIUM

The budget line I_0 is imposed on an indifference map. At point W the budget line is tangent to an indifference curve (U_3). Accordingly at W the consumer reaches equilibrium: His or her utility is maximized. Going away from W, either in the southeasterly direction or in the north-westerly direction, will carry the consumer to lower indifference curves such as U_2 and U_1. At W the following is satisfied: $MU_x/P_x = MU_y/P_y$. W is also known as an *interior solution*.

map as shown in Figure 1-11. We assume that the consumer moves along the budget line until reaching the point of maximum satisfaction on the line. Points to the right of the budget line are unattainable because of the budget constraint. However, points to the left of the budget line are attainable. Since we assume that the entire budget is exhausted on X and Y, the consumer's movements are restricted to the budget line. Logically, the best point on the budget line is the one coinciding with the highest indifference curve. This point is W, at which budget line I_0 just touches indifference curve U_3. In other words, I_0 is tangent to U_3 at W. From geometry we know that at the point of tangency the slope of indifference curve U_3 (RCS) must be equal to the slope of budget line I_0. Recall that RCS is the ratio of the two marginal utilities with a negative sign (Equation 1-5). The equality of the slopes, respectively, can be expressed as follows:

$$\text{Slope of budget line} = -\frac{P_x}{P_y} = -\frac{MU_x}{MU_y} = \text{RCS} \qquad (1\text{-}8)$$

We can rearrange Equation 1-8 to yield the familiar Equation 1-3, which states what is intuitively very appealing, namely, that in equilibrium, spending the last dollar on X or, alternatively, on Y would yield the same additional amount of utility. Geometrically, the consumer is restricted to moving along a straight line on the indifference map, and W is the point representing the highest level of utility that can be attained.

1.4c The Convexity of Indifference Curves

We are now ready to demonstrate that an indifference curve will be convex toward the origin. First, recall that under the assumption of cardinal utility convexity was intuitively derived from the law of diminishing marginal utility. Diminishing marginal utility was a property derived from empirical observation rather than a logical result of the theory. Under the assumption of ordinal utility the convexity is a property that has to be verified empirically. (Empirically does not necessarily imply statistical studies. It may simply mean casual observation of consumer behavior in reality.) Let us hypothesize the opposite of convexity toward the origin, namely, concavity. In Figure 1-12 a concave indifference curve is depicted by U_1 with the consumer at point K on the curve and taking quantities X_1 and Y_1 of the two goods.

The indifference curve, by definition, indicates the consumer would be just as satisfied at point L with X_2 and Y_2. That is, the consumer is agreeable to trading ΔY for ΔX. Similarly, from point L to point M the consumer will trade $\Delta Y'$ for $\Delta X'$. But if (in absolute value) $\Delta Y = \Delta Y'$, $\Delta X > \Delta X'$, we are forced to the conclusion that the consumer will trade away Y for ever smaller amounts of X. If we contemplate some given money prices for X and Y, we find that buying less Y and more X is increasingly attractive because \$1 transferred from Y to X results in a constant *ability* to trade Y for X; but the consumer is *willing* to take ever *less* X in exchange for Y; thus the more X he

FIGURE 1-12   A CONCAVE INDIFFERENCE CURVE

The consumer moves along the concave indifference curve. It will pay him or her to move either to the X axis or to the Y axis.

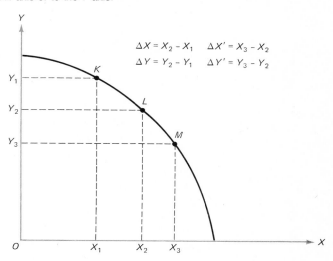

has, the better the buy it is and the greater the rush to trade away still more (all) Y for still more (all) X. We have thereby shown that the consumer can be expected to purchase one good to the exclusion of all others; we have a theory that denies the preference for variety! On these empirical grounds the concave indifference curve is rejected.

This result is known, in the economic jargon, as a *corner solution*. The result obtained in Figure 1-11 is known as an *interior solution*. A corner can occur on either the X axis or the Y axis. How can we determine on which axis the corner solution will occur? Consider Figure 1-13 in which a map of concave indifference curves is drawn. Tangency between budget line I_0 and indifference curve U_2 occurs at point W. Notice, however, that W is the basket yielding the lowest level of satisfaction along the budget line. The highest indifference curve that has at least one point common with the budget line is U_4. This common point, denoted by E, must lie on the X axis in our illustration. It is left for the reader to show that had the price of Y started to fall, at a certain low level of the price of Y the consumer would switch from spending his or her budget entirely on X to spending his or her budget entirely on Y. It is evident from examining Figure 1-13 that given concave indifference curves the point of tangency leads to a minimum satisfaction and that in order to attain the highest level of satisfaction the consumer must move either to the X axis or to the Y axis. In Figure 1-13 the corner solution occurs at point E, where I_0 and U_4 intersect on the X axis. The other corner solution is not optimal: Point D lies on an indifference curve which is lower than U_4. Corner solutions would indicate that consumers specialize in consumption. In such a world of concavity some consumers would specialize in

FIGURE 1-13   CONCAVE INDIFFERENCE MAP AND A CORNER SOLUTION
A budget line (I_0) is imposed on a concave indifference map. The interior solution (W) is a point yielding minimum utility. Either corner solution (D and E) will yield more utility than W. In this case E is preferred to D.

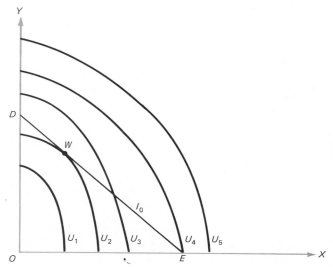

eating cucumbers only. Others would gorge only on noodles. If we extend the two-commodity world into an n-commodity world, some consumers would gorge on noodles and others would starve but would listen to music day in and day out. In reality we observe that consumers do not specialize in consumption. Rather, they diversify by spending money on a variety of goods. Moreover, they normally react to price changes in the marketplace by varying the mix of their baskets rather than by switching abruptly from one good to another. This is another way to show why concavity is rejected.

Lest the reader conclude that a corner solution is impossible if the indifference map is convex, we hasten to mention the possibility of a corner solution in spite of the convexity of indifference curves. Geometrically this is possible by rotating a budget line clockwise about a point on the Y axis. At a certain sharp angle (with the Y axis) the budget line will not have even one point of tangency with any indifference curve. In reality such a case may represent a poor consumer for whom Y is all other goods and X is a mink coat. The student should illustrate this case as an exercise.

The following section is optional, yet the student is urged to study at least one or two applications. Indifference curve analysis can be a powerful tool in analyzing the impact of governmental programs on social welfare.

1.5 APPLICATIONS (Optional)

This section is not essential for understanding the following chapter, in which we derive the demand curve from the indifference map and the budget line. However, one can become familiar with the process of applying indifference curve analysis to real world problems by considering one or two of the following examples.

1.5a Allotment in the Kibbutz

In the kibbutzim (plural for kibbutz) in Israel members work and consume collectively. Until recently they were on an allotment system whereby each member was allotted food, clothing, and other goods in equal amounts. That this type of allotment leads to a *welfare loss* can be shown by applying indifference curve analysis. Welfare loss is interpreted here as a movement from a certain indifference curve to a lower one. Assume that there are only two goods in the kibbutz, say, clothing (X) and food (Y). The kibbutz allots to each member X_0 units of X and Y_0 units of Y; as Figure 1-14 shows, this combination is denoted by point T on budget line I_0. Consider two kibbutz members who, by definition, both have an identical budget line. If they were allowed to spend their budget in a free market, one consumer would purchase point R, namely, a smaller amount of X and a larger amount of Y, and the other would purchase a combination denoted by point S, namely, more X and less Y. For the first consumer, the indifference curve passing through T and denoted by U_0' occupies a lower position than the indifference curve denoted by U_1', which is tangent to the budget line at the equilibrium point R. His or her loss of utility is $U_1' - U_0'$, and although we cannot measure it cardinally, it is a certain loss. Likewise, for the second consumer who in a free market would select combination S, the loss of utility would be $U_1 - U_0$. Only the "lucky" kibbutz member who happened to be at point T (tangency) would not suffer any welfare loss. It is not surprising, therefore, that many kibbutzim are switching from the allotment system to the system of allocating equal budgets to their members.

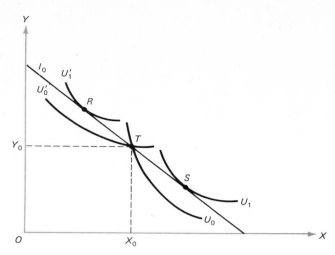

FIGURE 1-14 ALLOTMENT IN THE KIBBUTZ
All kibbutz members are allotted basket T. This leads to a loss of welfare: If instead of income-inkind (T) they were allotted a pecuniary budget I_0 (which can buy basket T), the consumer with a strong preference for Y would move to point R and upgrade his or her utility from U_0' to U_1'. The consumer with a strong preference for X will move to point S and upgrade his or her utility from U_0 to U_1.

1.5b The Food Stamp Program in the United States

Sometimes we find it convenient to focus on one good, say, food, and view all other goods as being a unified commodity (nonfood). The advantage of such an approach is that the analysis becomes two-dimensional. Had we opted for an n-dimensional analysis, the simplicity of applying geometry would have been lost. Moreover, the complexity of the analysis would have increased manyfold.

Under the provisions of the Food Stamp Act of 1964, as amended, poor households are entitled to purchase food stamps which enable them to obtain food for less than its market price. Consider Figure 1-15. Originally the poor consumer is at point R, where indifference curve U_0 is tangent to budget line EF. This budget line reflects the ability of the consumer to purchase combinations of food and nonfood. For convenience we can define units of nonfood as "dollars worth," such that each unit is a dollar. At the start of the month the poor consumer receives an income of $\overline{OE}$ dollars. If he qualifies as a poor person, he can forgo a portion of his income depicted by the segment $\overline{EK}$ for food stamps that would entitle him to $\overline{KM}$ units of food. In the marketplace $\overline{EK}$ dollars could have purchased only $\overline{KL}$ units of food. Assume that

the consumer is at point M. If his tastes are reflected by the indifference map containing U_0, U_1, and U_2, he would move to point T, where U_2 is just tangent to budget line HG passing through M and reflecting the market price ratio (of food to nonfood). This would be exactly equivalent to giving the poor person a pecuniary subsidy of $\overline{EG}$ dollars and allowing him the freedom of choosing his best basket along the new higher budget line. (If the administrative cost of a food stamp program is the same as that of a pecuniary subsidy, the cost to the government of subsidizing the consumer in the amount of $\overline{EG}$ dollars is the same as the cost of food stamps.) But since it is illegal and perhaps embarrassing for him to sell food on the market, the poor person is more likely to stay at point M, through which indifference curve U_1 passes. The difference between U_1 and U_2 reflects the loss of utility of a food stamp program relative to a pecuniary subsidy. Only a consumer with a very high preference for food would not suffer a loss of satisfaction relative to a pecuniary subsidy. Having purchased the food stamps, this consumer would end up at some point between M and H, say, point S.

Kenneth W. Clarkson estimated that in 1973, $1 (in

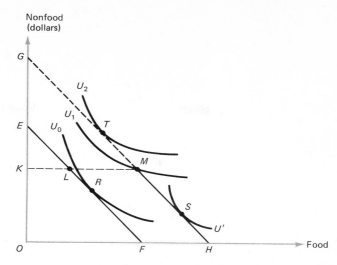

FIGURE 1-15 WELFARE LOSS DUE TO THE FOOD STAMP PROGRAM IN THE UNITED STATES

Prior to the introduction of the Food Stamp Program the budget line of the poor person is EF. The person is allowed to pay $\overline{EK}$ dollars for food stamps that entitle him or her to purchase $\overline{KM}$ units of food. Had the poor person been allowed to sell food in the market, his new budget line would have been GH. But since he is not allowed to sell food, he is restricted to MH. Assuming that he does not have a strong preference to food, he will end up at point M. Had he been allowed to sell food, or what is equivalent, had the government given him $\overline{EG}$ dollars (the pecuniary value of $\overline{LM}$ units of food) he would have settled at point T. Thus the welfare loss of food stamps as compared with a pecuniary subsidy to the poor is $U_2 - U_1$. A consumer with a strong preference for food will end up at point S either under a Food Stamp Program or under a pecuniary subsidy.

the market) worth of food is valued by the recipient at only 83 cents.[2] In other words, the welfare loss to the poor is roughly estimated at 17 percent compared with a monetary subsidy. Clarkson estimated that in 1973 the federal government spent $1.09 for each $1.00 in the form of food stamps. We do not know, however, what the administrative cost of running the alternative program of a direct pecuniary subsidy would be.

1.5c Commodity Rationing

Governments may resort to commodity rationing during or after wars. Assume that because of the war commodity X is in short supply. The government decides to guarantee each citizen a certain amount X_0 units of X at a price lower than the prevailing price of X in the market prior to rationing. There is a strict law forbidding the trade in commodity X. The consumer who would consume the combination indicated by point F in Figure 1-16 is not affected by the law: He or she normally consumes less than the rationed amount. But a consumer who would consume the basket depicted by point G is adversely affected: He or she is forced to move to point H, which belongs to a lower indifference curve.

[2]Kenneth W. Clarkson, "Welfare Benefits of the Food Stamp Program," *Southern Economic Journal*, vol. 34, July 1976, pp. 864–878.

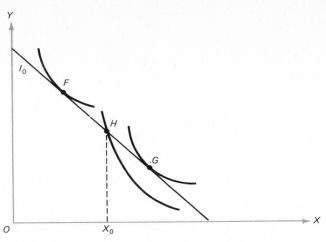

FIGURE 1-16   COMMODITY RATIONING
After a war the government decides to ration good X. Each family is limited to buying a maximum amount of X_0 units of X. A consumer with a strong preference for X will have to move from G to H, i.e., a movement to a lower indifference curve. A consumer with a strong preference for Y will remain at point F and will not suffer any loss in utility.

Next consider the case where citizens are allowed to trade in their rations. Let us adopt the realistic assumption that scarcity would lead to a situation in which the market price of X denoted by P_m is higher than the rationing price denoted by P_r. Figure 1-17 illustrates the benefits to consumers from the relaxation of the restrictive law; the citizen who would previously consume basket F would now buy the rationed X_0 units of X at a low price of P_r and sell them at a higher price of P_m. This would increase the citizen's budget by $X_0(P_m - P_r)$. Originally, this budget amount to I_0 and it cut the Y axis at $Y_1 = I_0/P_y$ and the X axis at $X_1 = I_0/P_r$. After trade is allowed, the new budget amounts to $I_1 = I_0 + X_0(P_m - P_r)$, and the new budget line cuts the Y axis at $Y_2 = [I_0 + X_0(P_m - P_r)]/P_y$ and the X axis at $X_2 = [I_0 + X_0(P_m - P_r)]/P_m$. The new budget line I_1 intersects with I_0 at point H. (Can you show why?) Clearly the result of allowing trade is a gain in utility: Jane, who indicated a low preference for the rationed commodity, now moves from point F to a superior point L on a higher indifference curve. Linda, who indicated a high preference for the rationed commodity, is no longer restricted to basket H. If there is a higher indifference curve touching I_1, she can move to point K. Note that the indifference curve that passes through H may lie above I_1 throughout. In that case the shift from H to a point like K is impossible.

1.6 LEISURE VERSUS ALL OTHER GOODS

So far in our discussion we have generously provided our consumers with a fixed income (budget) to spend on the combination of goods that puts them in equilibrium. In real life, of course, most consumers earn their incomes in exchange for the work they perform. This suggests that we can view work as *leisure sold in the labor market in exchange for all other goods*. And further, by applying indifference curve analysis, we can derive the optimal amount of work that consumers are prepared to perform. In other words, if we view as a "commodity" the amount of leisure available to consumers in a year (24

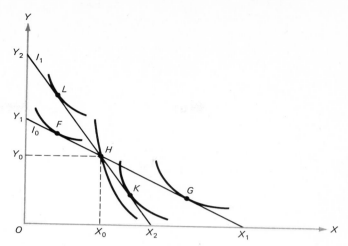

FIGURE 1-17   COMMODITY RATIONING WITH A BLACK MARKET
The diagram depicts a situation similar to Figure 1-16. We relax the assumption that there is
no black market. In fact we assume that there is a black market and that the government
looks the other way. In the black market the price is P_m, which is higher than the regulated
price of P_r. The consumer who was at point F can advance along the old budget line to point
H, and then go back in the northwesterly direction along a new budget line with a new slope
of $-P_m/P_y$. His new equilibrium will be at point L, representing a higher level of utility as
compared with the previous point F. The consumer with a strong preference for X *might* be
able to move from H to a better point such as K.

hours $\times$ 365 days), we can say that a consumer exchanges some amount of
leisure for some amount of all other goods (income) until an optimum point is
reached. Consumers can control the amount of work performed by varying
the number of days worked per year, the number of hours worked per day,
or some combination of both, until maximum satisfaction is attained. To
know that leisure is a source of satisfaction, we need only know that workers
in the United States "purchased" more leisure as their earnings increased.
For example, the *Handbook of Labor Statistics*[3] reports that the average
weekly hours performed by manufacturing workers was 51 in 1909, 44.5 in
1925, and 42.1 in 1930. In other words, manufacturing workers in the United
States on average purchased close to 10 hours of leisure per week between
1909 and 1930. Although the average weekly hours of manufacturing workers was stable at a level of slightly over 40 hours from the beginning of the
1950s, workers continued to purchase leisure in various other forms such as
longer vacations and more holidays.

By applying the theory of indifference curves to leisure and all other
goods, we can shed light on the supply of labor. Moreover, this theory seems
a useful tool for analyzing the impact of taxes on the behavior of workers in
the labor market. For example, income taxes lower the rate of exchange of
leisure in the market: One hour of leisure can be exchanged for less of all

[3]Published by the Bureau of Labor Statistics.

other goods, the higher the income tax. If the hourly wage rate for a typical worker is $5, the worker can exchange 1 hour of leisure for $5 worth of all other goods. If an income tax of 20 percent is imposed, the rate of exchange falls to $4. The basic analysis of indifference curves as applied to leisure and all other goods is discussed below. The analysis concludes by examining the interesting case of negative income taxes.

1.6a The Optimum Amount of Work Performed

Brenda, a consumer, has available a maximum amount of leisure in hours, say, 24 hours. For this example leisure is measured in hours, although any other relevant measure, such as days, would be acceptable. Each unit of all other goods will be measured in terms of $1's worth, as in Figure 1-15. Figure 1-18 illustrates Brenda's situation: The horizontal axis denotes leisure L; the vertical axis denotes all other goods $Y;$ the slope of the budget line is simply the hourly wage if leisure is measure by hours and all other goods are measured by $1's worth. This is true because if all other goods are measured by $1's worth, the price of all other goods is $1, and the slope of the budget line (according to Equation 1-7) is expressed as follows:

$$\text{Slope} = \frac{\Delta Y}{\Delta L} - \frac{W}{1} = -W \tag{1-9}$$

where W is the wage rate, L is leisure, and Y is all other goods. Brenda achieves maximum satisfaction at the point of tangency E, at which she consumes L_1 units of leisure. She sells $L_0 - L_1$ hours of leisure for $\overline{L_1 E}$ dollars worth of all other goods. This is equivalent to saying that she works $L_0 - L_1$ hours in exchange for $\overline{L_1 E}$ dollars.

FIGURE 1-18 DETERMINING THE OPTIMAL AMOUNT OF LEISURE SOLD
L represents leisure and Y represents all other goods. If one day represents the unit of time, then L_0 is the maximum amount of leisure a consumer has, namely, 24 hours. Going along the budget line in the northwesterly direction means selling leisure, or what is equivalent, performing work. In this diagram the consumer decided to sell $L_0 - L_1$ leisure hours, which is also the number of hours that he worked per day. The slope of the budget line is simply $-W$, where W is the wage rate.

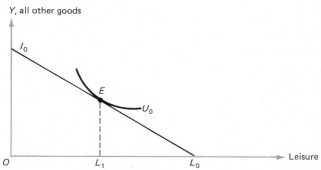

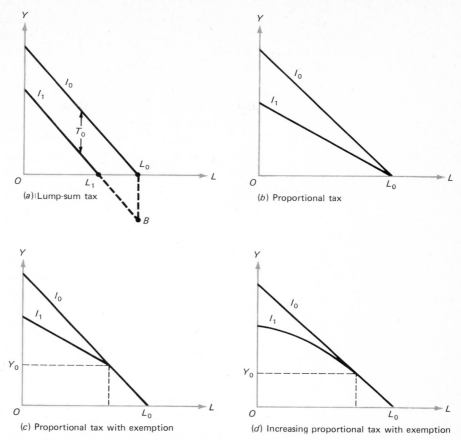

FIGURE 1-19 THE IMPACT OF THE VARIOUS FORMS OF INCOME TAX ON THE OPPORTUNITY SET OF THE INDIVIDUAL

I_0 in the panels a, b, c, and d is the same as I_0 in Figure 1-18. Panel (a): A lump-sum tax of T_0 dollars is imposed. The consumer must pay the same tax of T_0 dollars regardless of the work effort. I_1 is the budget line net of the lump-sum tax. Panel (b): A proportional tax is imposed ($t = 0.1$ means that the consumer pays 10 percent of earned income) I_1 is the budget line net of the tax. Panel (c): The same as in panel (b), except that Y_0 is exempted from the tax. Between the origin and Y_0 the budget line does not change. For income above Y_0 the budget line net of the tax is I_1. Panel (d): As in panel (c), Y_0 is exempted from the tax. But the rate of the tax is not fixed; rather, it increases with earned income.

1.6b The Effect of Income Taxes

Income taxes can be imposed in a variety of forms. Some of these forms are illustrated in Figure 1-19. Panel (a) illustrates a *lump-sum tax* of T_0 dollars. A lump-sum tax is a fixed tax imposed per unit of time; its size is not related to the amount of income earned by the worker. For example, consider Figure 1-18 again. Brenda sells $\overline{L_0 L_1}$ hours of leisure in exchange for $\overline{L_1 E}$ dollars. That is, she moves from L_0 to L_1 and then vertically to E. But if a lump-sum tax is imposed she must move down from E by T_0 dollars, the amount that she pays the government. Since wherever she ends up on I_0 she must move T_0 downward, the new budget line, net of the tax, which is denoted by I_1 in panel (a) of Figure 1-19, is parallel to I_0. Notice that after the lump-sum tax is imposed, the new budget line, which is also known as an opportunity set, begins at point B directly beneath L_0 at a vertical distance equal to the amount of the tax. This indicates that Brenda starts the day in debt. She must perform $\overline{L_0 L_1}$ hours of work in order to pay her debt to the government.

Panel (b) illustrates a *proportional tax,* which is simply a certain proportion of total income earned. Consider Figure 1-18 again. If Brenda performs $\overline{L_0 L_1}$ hours of labor she earns $\overline{L_1 E}$ dollars. If $t = 0.1$, it means that she must pay the government 10 percent of this $\overline{L_1 E}$ dollars. At L_0 no income is earned and the tax is zero ($t \cdot 0 = 0$). The new opportunity set, which is denoted by I_1 in panel (b) of Figure 1-19 is thus obtained by rotating the budget line counterclockwise from I_0 to I_1, where L_0 is the pivot. The student should be able to show that if the budget line of the individual I_0 was $\$5 \cdot L + \$1 \cdot Y = \$120$ before the tax, the new budget line I_1 is $\$4 \cdot L + \$1 \cdot Y = \$96$ after a 20 percent tax is imposed ($t = 0.2$).

In panel (c), Y_0 dollars are exempted from the tax. For any level of income Y in excess of Y_0 the taxable income is defined as $Y - Y_0$. In panel (c) for income in excess of Y_0 the tax is proportional to the taxable income; namely, it is $t(Y - Y_0)$. For levels of income lower than Y_0 the tax is zero. Let us define the rate of the tax as the amount of the tax paid divided by income earned. Do you expect the rate of the tax to increase, decrease, or remain unchanged as earned income rises?

In panel (d) the exemption is the same as in the previous case. However, for taxable income $(Y - Y_0)$ the rate of the tax increases with income. Consider Table 1-1, where before the imposition of the tax I_0 is expressed as $\$5 \cdot L + \$1 \cdot Y = \$120$ and $Y_0 = \$20$. If the results of Table 1-1 are drawn such that earned income denotes I_0 and net income denotes I_1, the linear I_0 and the concave I_1 are obtained as in panel (d) of Figure 1-19. Given a map of parallel indifference curves, it is likely that the imposition of such a tax will result in a decline in the work effort.

TABLE 1-1   An Illustration of Panel (d) in Figure 1-19

Amount of labor performed, hours per day	Earned income, $	Rate of the tax (t) on taxable income, percent	Tax paid $t(Y - \$20)$, $	Net income, $	Rate of the tax $\dfrac{t(Y - Y_0)}{Y}$, percent
2	10	0	0	10	0
4	20	0	0	20	0
6	30	10	1	29	3.3
8	40	20	4	36	10.0
10	50	30	9	41	18.0

1.6c An Example: Negative Income Taxes (Optional)[4]

The idea of *negative income taxes,* whereby the government pays money to the poor, became popular in the 1960s. The example of negative income taxes is selected for two reasons: First, microeconomic analysis can be applied to analyze the impact of such taxes on consumer behavior. Second, since the theory cannot resolve the issue of whether negative income taxes strengthen or weaken the incentive to work, limited experiments were conducted in the United States. The results of these experiments are reported later; they are relevant for the student in that they show that price theory must be either confirmed or refuted by empirical testing.

Negative income taxes are the reverse of regular income taxes: The government pays money to individuals in some proportion to their income. More specifically, the idea is that an individual whose income is below a certain level receives money from the government. This view of the negative income tax was motivated by pragmatism rather than ideology: If the poor are to be supported, it should be done in as simple and effective a way as possible. The prevailing consensus is that the existing welfare system is complex and not particularly effective.

Indifference curves analysis can shed light on the issue of negative income taxation. Before geometrical analysis is applied, the following terms are needed: The *support level S* is the guaranteed amount of money a family (or a household in general) will receive if it has no income at all, while t is the rate at which the payment from the government to the poor is reduced for every additional dollar the poor family earns. Let Y denote the income the family earns. Let Y_b denote the break-even income at which the tax switches from a negative to a positive tax. Then, for Y less than Y_b the formula of the negative income tax becomes

$$\text{Negative income tax} = S - tY \qquad (1\text{-}10)$$

As mentioned before, when income reaches the break-even level Y_b, the negative income tax is zero. Accordingly, we obtain the following formula for the break-even level of income:

$$Y_b = S/t \qquad (1\text{-}11)$$

For example, if the support level S is \$1,000 and t is 0.4, Y_b is \$2500. In Figure 1-20 the horizontal axis measures leisure and the vertical axis measures income (all other goods and services). In the absence of any welfare programs the budget line of the individual is negatively sloped line GL_0. At L_0 the individual does not work. He enjoys 24 hours of leisure a day. Moving to the left and upward along the budget line means selling leisure in the labor market, namely, working. The slope of the budget line reflects the price of the (labor) services the individual can sell in the market.

With the introduction of the negative income tax program the individual receives a support income of S dollars (which is also equal to $\overline{L_0E}$). His budget line is now L_0EFG. Segment $\overline{EF}$ is flatter than Segment $\overline{L_0F}$ because between L_0 and L_b each additional dollar he earns is reduced by a rate of t. For example, assume leisure is measured in hours. If the hourly wage rate is \$3, the slope of GL_0 is (negative) \$3. However, reducing the additional income in the range L_0 to L_b by a rate of t which is, say, 0.4 yields a slope of \$1.8. In the example in Figure 1-20 the indifference curve of the individual is tangent to his budget line at point A. His leisure is L_1 and his income is $\overline{L_1A}$. He works $L_0 - L_1$ hours. For this he earns $\overline{L_1B}$ dollars. The negative income tax he receives from the government is $\overline{BA}$ dollars, which is $S - t(\overline{L_1B})$. (Recall that S is the support level, which is equal to $\overline{L_0E}$.)

The negative income tax scheme gave rise to a dilemma: Assume that the support level is \$4000 for a family without any income. If t is 0.4, the break-even level of income Y_b is \$10,000. This means that families with incomes less than \$10,000 do not pay taxes and become the recipients of government assistance. This may mean a revolution in the entire tax system. The solution might be to raise the rate t. Suppose t is raised from 0.4 to 0.8. In that case the break-even income is lowered to \$5000, which is more feasible from the fiscal viewpoint but is likely to create work disincentives. This is illustrated in Figure 1-21. The support level is the same for the two alternative schemes: $\overline{L_0E}$. For a relatively low t the budget line is L_0EF_2G. Equilibrium occurs at point A_2. The head of the family works $L_0 - L_2$ hours. If t is in-

---

[4]The discussion in this section is based on M. Kurz, "Negative Income Taxation," printed in *Federal Tax Reform: Myths and Realities,* Institute for Contemporary Studies, San Francisco, 1978.

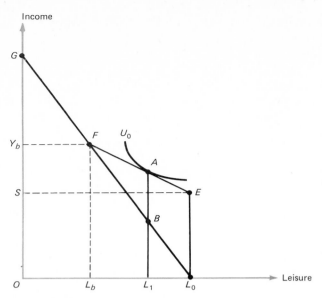

FIGURE 1-20 NEGATIVE INCOME TAXES
The original budget line of the consumer is the same as in Figure 1-18. L_0 represents a starting point at which no work is performed. A support income of S dollars $(= \overline{L_0 E})$ is given to the poor person who earns no income at all. The person moves to E. If he or she earns money, out of each additional dollar the government "confiscates" a certain fraction in order to reduce the support level given initially. The person has to work $L_0 - L_b$ hours in order to switch from being a recipient of money from the government to a taxpayer. Y_b is the break-even level of income at which the negative income tax reduces to zero.

creased (say, from 0.4 to 0.8) the budget line becomes $L_0 E F_1 G$ and the point of equilibrium is A_1. The head of the family reduces her work to $L_0 - L_1$. (Note that if the budget line becomes flatter and if the slope of the indifference curves does not change appreciably in the move from one indifference curve to the next, the point of tangency between the new budget line and the new indifference curve is likely to move to the right.)

The above analysis indicates that for a fixed rate t there is a tradeoff between t and the break-even level Y_b: The smaller t is the higher Y_b will be.

Since the issue of disincentive to work because of negative income taxation could not be resolved theoretically, Congress decided to fund a unique social experiment in selected areas in New Jersey and

Pennsylvania. A sample of families with low incomes was placed under a negative income tax regime. The support level was set at the poverty line and the rate t was set at 0.5. The experiment lasted for 3 years. The results were as follows: On average, males revealed a tendency to neither increase nor decrease their work effort. But while white males slightly decreased their effort, black males slightly increased their effort. Married women decreased their effort by 20 percent. A second experiment based on a larger sample was conducted in Seattle and Denver. This experiment confirmed the New Jersey and Pennsylvania results for working wives. In this experiment, however, working husbands decreased their work effort by slightly over 5 percent.

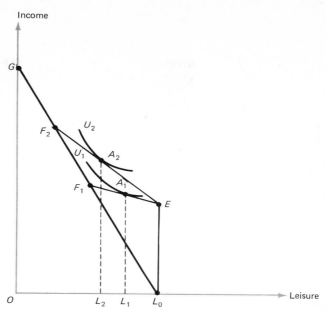

FIGURE 1-21 NEGATIVE INCOME TAX: TWO RATES AND THE SAME SUPPORT LEVEL
The same as Figure 1-20, except that two rates of paying back are shown. The support level S is the same amount of $\overline{L_0E}$ dollars. If the rate t is relatively high, the poor person will advance along the segment $\overline{EF_1}$. There will be a smaller incentive to work, but fiscally the cost of the program will be relatively small. If the rate t is relatively low, the poor person will advance along $\overline{EF_2}$. The incentive to perform work will be stronger, but the cost of the program to the government will be relatively higher. Under the assumption that the indifference curves are vertically parallel, the tangency point rises from A_1 to A_2 as the rate t falls.

1.7 THE UTILITY HILL: GOODS AND BADS

A contour line on a map is a representation of an imaginary line on the surface of a hill that has a constant elevation above sea level. The indifference map can be imagined as the map of a "utility hill." If John has only two goods in his budget, X and Y, we can ask him what is the most desirable combination of X and Y for him. His answer would provide us with the coordinates of the top of the utility hill. Going away from this point must lead to a reduction in utility and hence is equivalent to going down the utility hill. Moreover, going along a contour, namely, keeping the amount of utility unchanged, boils down to following an indifference curve. Clearly, if John follows an indifference curve (such as in Figure 1-8) in the southeasterly direction, at a certain point he has too much of X and thus X begins to be a nuisance, or a source of disutility. From that point and on, in order to keep John on the same indifference curve, we must allow him to consume more of Y to compensate him for agreeing to consume more of X. We say that initially both X and Y were "goods." Now since X becomes a source of disutility, X becomes "bad."

Imagine now that John's utility hill for X and Y can be mapped as illustrated in Figure 1-22. The top of the hill is depicted by point A. The indifference curves denoted by U_1, U_2, etc., are projections of contours of constant elevation which completely encircle the hill. Next, we divide the map into four regions as follows: region I: Indifference curves are negatively sloped and convex; region II: Indifference curves are positively sloped and convex; region III: Indifference curves are negatively sloped and concave; region IV: Indifference curves are positively sloped and concave. As an exercise, the student should show that in regions I, II, III, and IV commodities X and Y are "good" and "good," "bad" and "good," "bad" and "bad," and "good" and "bad," respectively.

SUMMARY   Consumer preference is a major factor in economic activity. Economists want to be able to measure and analyze consumer behavior in the marketplace in order to be able to make predictions about responses of consumers to changes in market conditions. The theory of consumer behavior rests on the postulate of utility maximization. Early economists believed that *cardinal measurement of utility* was possible. And they developed the *util* as the unit of measure for ranking combinations (baskets) of goods for compari-

FIGURE 1-22   A MAP OF THE UTILITY HILL
In this map of the utility hill, U_1, U_2, U_3, and U_4 are samples of the infinitely large number of "round" indifference curves, representing contours of the utility hill. Point A is the top of the hill. The map is divided into four regions as follows: I: X and Y are "goods." II: X is "bad" and Y is "good." III: X and Y are "bads." IV: X is "good" and Y is "bad." The rule to find out whether a good is "good" or "bad" is to keep the other good unchanged and increase the amount of the good under investigation; if we go down hill, the good is "bad"; if we go up hill, the good is "good."

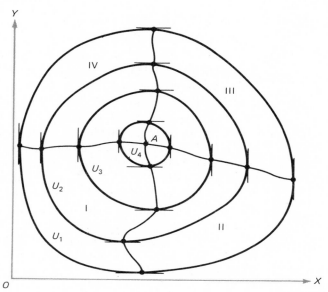

son. Although experience has shown that cardinal measurement is not possible, cardinal utility is an effective approach to understanding how consumers act to maximize their utility (satisfaction). The concepts of *marginal utility* and *diminishing marginal utility* were derived from cardinal utility.

Consumer behavior was then viewed under the more realistic assumption of *ordinal utility*. Ordinal utility measures what is preferred to what—but it does not say by how many degrees. Using the concepts we derived from cardinal utility, plus the axioms of *comparison, transitivity,* and *greediness,* we derived the *indifference curve*. We established that indifference curves (1) are *negatively sloped,* (2) are *convex to the origin,* and (3) *cannot intersect.* It was then demonstrated that the slope of the budget line is also negatively sloped. In other words, we derived the apparatus for *indifference curve analysis*, which enables us to demonstrate how the consumer maximizes utility, that is, reaches equilibrium, given the *budget constraints* and the prices of goods in the marketplace.

That idea was then extended and the consumer's leisure was viewed as a resource that can be exchanged for all other goods (income). Using indifference curve analysis it was demonstrated that the same principle of maximizing satisfaction applies: Individuals will sell some leisure (perform work) in exchange for some amount of all other goods (income) until an optimal amount of work and income is reached.

The following chapter will investigate the response of the consumer to changes in incomes and prices, which is the core of the consumer's theory.

GLOSSARY   **Utility** The common denominator of all goods. Satisfaction derived from the process of consumption.

Cardinal utility Utility that can be measured cardinally. Implying that the utility derived from different baskets of goods can be compared quantitatively.

Ceteris paribus All other things being constant.

Ordinal utility Utility that can be measured only ordinally. Implying that a basket of goods is preferred to another basket, or the other basket is preferred to it, or the two baskets are equally desired.

Marginal utility Extra utility obtained from a small change (unit) in the consumption of a given good, when the consumption of all other goods is kept constant. Formally it is written as $\Delta U/\Delta X$.

The law of diminishing marginal utility *Ceteris paribus,* the marginal utility derived from consuming a good diminishes when the quantity of that good consumed per unit of time increases.

Budget line The budget is the limited amount of money that is available for the consumer to spend on goods per unit of time. If there are only two goods in the budget of the consumer, the budget must be exhausted on the two goods. Formally this is written as $I = P_x \cdot X + P_y \cdot Y$. This is the formula of the budget line, which is linear and negatively sloped.

Indifference curve The locus of points representing pairs of goods (X and Y)

with the same level of utility. If utility is measured ordinally, all the pairs along the indifference curve are ranked as equally desirable.

Indifference map An X, Y space containing all the possible indifference curves.

The Marginal Rate of Commodity Substitution The slope of an indifference curve, denoted by $\Delta Y/\Delta X$. This slope is equal to $-MU_x/MU_y$ and is known as the RCS.

Consumer's equilibrium The combination of goods leading to maximum utility. Geometrically equilibrium occurs at a point of tangency between the budget line and an indifference curve. This is known as an interior solution. At this point $MU_x/P_x = MU_y/P_y$. Sometimes equilibrium occurs on either the X axis or the Y axis. This is known as a corner solution.

PROBLEMS An asterisk indicates an advanced problem.

1-1. $MU_x = 30$ utils and $P_x = \$10$. $MU_y = 9$ utils and $P_y = \$3$. This (cardinal) equilibrium is destroyed by a 40 percent decline in the price of X. (a) How much utility would the consumer gain by transferring the first dollar from Y to X? (b) Will the consumer gain the same amount of utility by transferring the second dollar from Y to X?

1-2. The same as problem 1-1, except that the consumer is not subject to the law of diminishing marginal utility, nor does the MU of one good depend on the consumption of other goods. What would the consumer do after realizing that P_x has declined 40 percent? Does it matter by how much P_x falls?

1-3. What would be the shape of the indifference curves in the following cases:
(a) X is bread in one supermarket and Y is bread in another supermarket across the street.
(b) X is left and Y is right shoes.

1-4 The consumer receives his income in kind: 10 units of X and 30 units of Y (point A in Figure 1-10). How would his budget line change if both prices rise by 10 percent? If both prices decline by 10 percent? If the price of X rises and the price of Y falls?

1-5 A consumer receives her income in kind, 8 units of Y and 7 units of X. Given the market prices, she reaches equilibrium when she sells 4 units of Y in exchange for 3 units of X.
(a) Show the behavior of the consumer on a diagram.
(b) The price of X rises relative to the price of Y. The consumer decides to consume 5 units of X. Can you determine whether her welfare increased or decreased relative to a?
(c) Would your answer change if the consumer had decided to consume 8 units of X in b?
(d) Assume that, relative to a, both prices decrease 15 percent. Analyze.

1-6. Can a corner solution be obtained even if indifference curves are convex?

1-7. John receives a present of three units of X (food stamps) from his uncle (Sam) on Monday each week. He cannot sell the present because his uncle would be offended and would stop giving him the present. If his uncle were to allow him to sell the present on the market, would he be better off?

1-8. Before imposition of a tax the budget line in the L, Y space is $5 \cdot L + \$1 \cdot Y = \$120$. Show that after a proportional tax of 20 percent ($t = 0.2$) is imposed the new (net) budget line is $4 \cdot L + \$1 \cdot Y = \$96$.

1-9. Show that if a tax is proportional with respect to taxable income, and taxable income is defined as income earned minus income exempted [Y_0 in panel (c) of Figure 1-19], the rate of the tax (relative to earned income) diminishes with income earned.

1-10. If X is work performed and Y represents all other goods, which of the four regions in Figure 1-22 would you select to depict this case? What would be the shape and the meaning of the budget line?

1-11.* Currently a lump-sum tax (T_0 dollars per year without regard to income) is imposed on Mrs. Smith. The government changes the tax to a proportional tax. (She now pays a certain percentage t of her income.) If the new tax brings in the same revenue to the government, does Mrs. Smith perform more or less work under the proportional tax as compared with the fixed tax?

MATHEMATICAL APPENDIX 1

In what follows we shall derive the necessary and sufficient conditions for the equilibrium of the consumer. First, the assumption will be made that utility can be measured cardinally. This assumption will be relaxed later by transformation from cardinal to ordinal utility.

M1.1 NECESSARY CONDITIONS FOR EQUILIBRIUM

Consider a consumer whose budget per unit of time amounts to I dollars. The entire budget is spent on goods $X_1, X_2, \ldots, X_n$. By agreement, X_i will denote both the ith good and the quantity consumed of that good. The prices of these goods confronting the consumer are P_1 (for X_1), P_2, etc. The (cardinal) utility function of the consumer is

$$U = u(X_1, X_2, \ldots, X_n) \tag{m1-1}$$

In equilibrium, Equation m1-1 is maximized subject to the budget constraint

$$\sum_{i=1}^{n} P_i \cdot X_i = I \qquad \text{(m1-2)}$$

Let λ be the Lagrange multiplier; then we have to maximize

$$L = U + \lambda(I - \sum_{i=1}^{n} P_i \cdot X_i) \qquad \text{(m1-3)}$$

Let $u_i = \partial U/\partial X_i$, $i = 1, 2, \ldots, n$. Differentiating Equation m1-3 with respect to λ and X_i gives

$$\sum_{i=1}^{n} P_i \cdot X_i = I$$
$$-\lambda P_1 + u_1 = 0$$
$$-\lambda P_2 + u_2 = 0 \qquad \text{(m1-4)}$$
$$\vdots$$
$$-\lambda P_n + u_n = 0$$

We note that u_i stands for MU_i, and so on.

It is easy to derive the following set of equations from Equation m1-4:

$$\frac{u_1}{P_1} = \frac{u_2}{P_2} = \cdots = \frac{u_n}{P_n} = \lambda \qquad \text{(m1-5)}$$

Since the marginal utility derived from spending the last dollar on X_i is u_i/P_i, the above set of equations shows that λ is the marginal utility of the last dollar spent when the consumer is in a state of equilibrium. This is sometimes known as the marginal utility of money.

Note finally that Equation m1-4 is a set of $n + 1$ equations. These equations determine the value of $n + 1$ unknowns; these are $X_1, X_2, \ldots, X_n$, and λ.

M1.2 SUFFICIENT CONDITIONS FOR EQUILIBRIUM

Equations m1-4 do not tell us whether consumers have really reached a point of maximum utility (tangency between a convex indifference curve and a budget line). In fact, they may have minimized their utility (tangency between a concave indifference curve and a budget line). If L denotes the Lagrange (Equation m1-3) and h denotes the constraint

$$(h = I - \sum_{i=1}^{n} P_i \cdot X_i),$$

then $L_{ij} = \partial L^2/(\partial X_i \partial X_j)$ and $h_i = \partial h/\partial X_i$.

Next we form the following determinants:

$$\begin{vmatrix} L_{11} & h_1 \\ h_1 & 0 \end{vmatrix} \quad \begin{vmatrix} L_{11} & L_{12} & h_1 \\ L_{21} & L_{22} & h_2 \\ h_1 & h_2 & 0 \end{vmatrix} \quad \cdots \quad \begin{vmatrix} L_{11} & L_{12} \ldots L_{1n} & h_1 \\ L_{21} & L_{22} \ldots L_{2n} & h_2 \\ \vdots & & \\ L_{n1} & L_{n2} \ldots L_{nn} & h_n \\ h_1 & h_2 \ldots h_n & 0 \end{vmatrix} \qquad \text{(m1-6)}$$

The last determinant in m1-6 is known as the bordered Hessian, and the rest of the determinants are known as bordered principal minors of the Hessian. The above determinants should be alternatively negative and positive for L in Equation m1-3 to be maximized.

M1.3 THE TRANSFORMATION FROM CARDINAL TO ORDINAL UTILITY

The transformation from cardinal to ordinal utility is achieved by replacing U in Equation m1-1 by an arbitrary function of itself; call it $f(U)$. The only restriction imposed on $f(U)$ is that it should rank combinations of goods as U does. This restriction is imposed by requiring that $f'(U) > 0$. For example, if $U = X \cdot Y$ and $f(U) = U^2$, the same ranking would be performed by the two functions because for $U > 0, f'(U) = 2U > 0$. [You can try ranking various baskets alternatively under U and $f(U) = U^2$ to verify that indeed the two functions rank various baskets alike.]

Fortunately, the transformation from cardinal to ordinal utility does not invalidate the conclusions derived in Sections M1.1 and M1.2. For the first-order conditions the proof is easy. Differentiating $f(U)$ instead of U with respect to X_i gives

$$\frac{\partial}{\partial X_i} f(U) = f'(U) \cdot u_i$$

Since $f(U)$ is arbitrary, $f'(U)$ is arbitrary too, and marginal utility cannot be measured. But the first-order equilibrium conditions in Equation m1-5 are unchanged, since the ratios are all multiplied by a common factor $f'(U)$ that cancels out. The proof for the second-order conditions is more difficult. It involves performing column operations on the Hessians obtained when U is replaced by $f(U)$.

C H A P T E R

2

CONSUMER, CONSUMPTION, AND THE THEORY OF DEMAND

The indifference curve apparatus we developed in Chapter 1 enabled us to show how the consumer maximizes satisfaction (utility) in the marketplace. We made two assumptions: First, the budget was fixed, and second, the prices of goods were fixed. Realistically this is not the case. Budgets can and do change because of a rise in the wage rate paid for work performed, an increase in stock dividends, and other such variables. Consumers also face commodity price changes daily; some are seasonal (for example, vegetables and fruits) and some are for the long run (for example, energy). Therefore, to describe and rationalize consumer behavior in the marketplace more accurately, we must look at how consumers respond to changes in budget (income) and prices. We will, in other words, develop the *theory of demand*. Demand theory enables us to make predictions about the response of consumers to changes in income, changes in prices, and changes in tastes. For example, the so-called energy crisis is manifested by rising prices of energy resources. We want to know in what manner consumers (of gasoline) would respond to rising prices of gasoline. We also want to know what the impact of rising levels of income and growing populations would be on the consumption of energy. To go even further, we want to know what the impact of imposing duties on imported oil from abroad would be on the behavior of consumers in the United States. The theory of demand will help us to organize our thinking on important issues such as energy, taxation, imports and exports, and government regulation.

To develop the theory of demand, we will first look at the consumer's patterns of consumption related to changes in income. Then we will examine patterns of consumption as related to commodity price changes. First, we assume that consumers are in equilibrium; that is, given a certain budget and certain prices, they have achieved an optimal allocation of that budget among the various goods consumed. We then assume that a change occurs either in that budget or in a price of a good, causing consumers to change their consumption patterns in order to regain equilibrium.

We remind the student that a consumer is any unit such as a family or household, school, individual, or branch of government that has a budget and spends it on goods. The bulk of consumers is made up of millions of families and individuals who continuously earn money and spend it in the marketplace.

2.1 A NOTE ON THE UNIT OF TIME, FLOWS, AND STOCKS

Although we mentioned in Chapter 1 that consumption is usually a flow, it is appropriate at this junction to dwell a bit more on *time units*, *flows*, and *stocks*. In most cases, when we discuss consumption we have in mind a *flow*. For example, if at a certain price a family consumes a loaf of bread a day, this is equivalent to a daily flow of one loaf of bread. It would also be equivalent to a weekly flow of seven loaves of bread and an annual flow of 365 loaves of bread. In that sense, consumption is a *rate* associated with a unit of time. Normally the unit of time associated with consumption flows is

1 year, but other units of time used are quarters (of years), months, and days. As an example, the consumption of crude oil in the United States would sometimes be quoted in daily rates and at other times in annual rates.

A *stock* is a quantity of a good which exists at a moment of time. Consider light bulbs. Suppose you count 32 light bulbs in your home, your stock of light bulbs is 32. You are interested in possessing that stock because it provides a flow of service, namely, illumination. If each light bulb burns on the average 1 hour a day, the daily flow of the service rendered by the stock of light bulbs is 32 hours of illumination per day. A similar example would be a family that owns a fleet of three cars. This fleet is a stock that provides a service which is defined as miles traveled per unit of time. If the total miles traveled by the fleet amounted to 25,000 in 1981, the service rendered by the stock (fleet of three cars) was 25,000 miles per annum.

Most of our analysis will be related to flows. Throughout this book, we shall refer to "quantities of goods and services consumed per unit of time" as simply "quantities." Thus, if X denotes a certain good measured along the horizontal axis, the student should read it as "X per unit of time."

2.2 THE CONCEPT OF ELASTICITY

Elasticity is a concept used to describe responsiveness. It measures the responsiveness of consumers to changes in incomes and prices. It also measures the responsiveness of producers to prices, and accordingly, its importance cannot be exaggerated. We now attempt to develop this concept, both intuitively and formally.

Picture a spring attached to the ceiling with a basket tied to the bottom end of the spring. Initially a piece of lead weighing 10 pounds is placed in the basket; the resulting distance between the ceiling and the basket is 5 feet. We now add an additional piece of lead weighing a ½ pound and observe that as a result the distance from the ceiling to the basket increases from 5 to 6 feet. We can summarize this experiment by saying that the spring "responded" to an additional ½ pound of weight by stretching 1 additional foot. Is 1 foot of stretch relative to ½ pound a "generous" or a "stingy" response? In order to answer this question meaningfully, we have to come up with a measure which is independent of units of measurement. Elasticity is such a measure. Let us agree to denote the variable that causes the change as the *independent variable,* and the responding variable as the *dependent variable*. In the above example, the weight in the basket is the independent variable and the length of the spring is the dependent variable. Elasticity is then defined as the *relative change in the dependent variable divided by the relative change in the independent variable.* Since the relative change may also be expressed as a percentage change, elasticity may similarly be defined as a *percentage change in the dependent variable over the percentage change in the independent variable.* Upon carrying out the division, we determine that elasticity is the percentage change in the dependent variable per 1 percent change in the independent variable. (For example, 10 percent over 5 percent is equivalent to 2 percent over 1 percent). If the independent variable is denoted by X (X is the weight placed in the basket) and the dependent variable is denoted by Y (Y is the length of the spring), we can express elasticity as follows:

$$\text{Elasticity} = \frac{\dfrac{\Delta Y}{Y}}{\dfrac{\Delta X}{X}} = \frac{\text{percentage change in } Y}{\text{percentage change in } X} \qquad (2\text{-}1)$$

We note that elasticity is measured in pure numbers, rather than in units such as pounds or feet.

Consider Figure 2-1. The curve $Y = f(X)$ represents the relationship between Y, the length of the spring, and X, the weight of the lead in the basket. As the weight increases from X_0 to X_1 (namely, from 10 to 10.5 pounds), the length of the spring increases from Y_0 to Y_1 (namely, from 5 to 6 feet). In Figure 2-1 this is equivalent to a movement from point A to point B. *Arc elasticity* is the elasticity calculated between the two distinct points A and B. Put differently, ΔX and ΔY are calculated as $\Delta X = X_1 - X_0$, and $\Delta Y = Y_1 - Y_0$. We have three options for calculating the arc elasticity: divide the ΔX by $X_0, \overline{X}$, or X_1; and similarly, divide the ΔY by $Y_0, \overline{Y}$, or Y_1. Notice that $\overline{X}$ and $\overline{Y}$ represent midpoints: $\overline{X} = (X_1 + X_0)/2$ and $\overline{Y} = (Y_1 + Y_0)/2$.

The results are as follows:

$$\eta_0 = \frac{\dfrac{1}{5}}{\dfrac{0.5}{10}} = \frac{20 \text{ percent}}{5 \text{ percent}} = 4$$

FIGURE 2-1   AN ILLUSTRATION OF ARC ELASTICITY

Y is the dependent variable (length of spring), and X is the independent variable (weight). The effect of increasing X by ΔX is to cause a change in Y by ΔY. The *arc elasticity* is defined as $(\Delta Y/Y)/(\Delta X/X)$. If ΔX becomes smaller and smaller, $\Delta Y/\Delta X$ becomes the slope of the curve (at point A). We then estimate *point elasticity*.

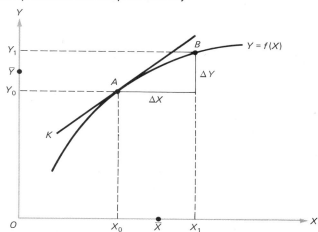

$$\bar{\eta} = \frac{\dfrac{1}{5.5}}{\dfrac{0.5}{10.25}} = \frac{18 \text{ percent}}{4.9 \text{ percent}} = 3.7$$

$$\eta_1 = \frac{\dfrac{1}{6}}{\dfrac{0.5}{10.5}} = \frac{16.7 \text{ percent}}{4.8 \text{ percent}} = 3.5$$

where η (eta) is the symbol for elasticity. The most appropriate of the three estimates is the "middle" η, which we denoted $\bar{\eta}$. The closer we move point B to point A, the closer the three estimates of the arc elasticity will be to each other.

Assume that we do not change the position of point A but that we move point B toward point A. As point B moves closer to point A, ΔX and ΔY become progressively smaller and the value of the arc elasticity approaches a limit. This limit is known as the *point elasticity*. Elasticity as defined in Figure 2-1 can be rearranged and written as follows:

$$\eta = \frac{\dfrac{\Delta Y}{Y}}{\dfrac{\Delta X}{X}} = \frac{\Delta Y}{\Delta X} \cdot \frac{X}{Y} = (\text{slope of curve}) \cdot \frac{X}{Y}$$

where $\Delta Y / \Delta X$ is the slope of the curve at point A when B is moving ever closer to A. In the limit, the slope of the curve at point A is the slope of the tangent line denoted by k which just touches the curve $Y = f(X)$ at point A. The point elasticity calculated at A would have the expression

$$\eta = (\text{slope of line } k) \cdot \frac{X_0}{Y_0}$$

The student may wonder why we do not rush to calculate the point elasticity of our curve at point A. The answer is simply that we do not have a specific mathematical form for the length of the spring as a function of the weight in the attached basket.

To illustrate the fact that arc elasticity is a reasonable proxy for the point elasticity, consider a function expressed as $Y = 20 + 5\sqrt{X}$. In this function Y is the dependent variable and X is the independent variable. We consider an arc (like the segment of the curve going from A to B in Figure 2-1). Equivalently, we can say that we consider the function in the *domain* stretching from X_0 to Y_0. The data generated by this function for points at the ends of the arc are given in Table 2-1. The arc elasticity is calculated as follows:

$$\text{Arc elasticity} = \frac{\dfrac{\Delta Y}{Y}}{\dfrac{\Delta X}{X}} = \frac{\dfrac{5}{37.5}}{\dfrac{7}{12.5}} = \frac{0.133}{0.56} = 0.237$$

TABLE 2-1   Calculating Arc Elasticities

	X	Y
Original quantity	9	35
Second quantity	16	40
Δ quantity	7	5
Average quantity	12.5	37.5

The two point elasticities are 0.214 for point A and 0.250 for point B.[1] We notice that the value of the arc elasticity is close to the average of the two point elasticities.

The following points should be stressed:

1. In most cases elasticity is not constant along a curve such as $Y = f(X)$ in Figure 2-1. There are, however, some special functions that will yield constant elasticity along a curve which describes the function. An example is $Y = aX^b$, in which the elasticity of Y with respect to X is equal to b throughout.

2. Elasticity (either *point* or *arc*) can assume a value of less than 1, exactly 1, or more than 1. Correspondingly, the curve [representing a function $Y = f(X)$] between two points, or at a point, is said to be *inelastic*, of *unitary elasticity*, or *elastic*. For example, the curve representing our experiment with the weight and the spring is elastic between points A and B: a 1 percent increase in the weight will cause the spring to respond by stretching by 3.7 percent.

2.3 THE SENSITIVITY OF THE CONSUMER TO CHANGES IN INCOME

2.3a Real Income versus Nominal Income

To understand the consumer's sensitivity to changes in income, we must first understand the relationship between *nominal* income and *real* income. Recall from Section 1.4a that the opportunities set of the consumer will increase—namely, the budget line will shift to the right—if either the budget increases and prices remain unchanged, or alternatively if the budget remains unchanged and the prices of goods confronting the consumer in the marketplace fall. We can utilize the case illustrated in Figure 1-10 to explain further the meaning of nominal and real budgets. Assume that you are the consumer in that example. Let X and Y denote apples and oranges, the only goods you consume. Initially your budget (I_0) is \$100, the price of apples is \$4, and the price of oranges is \$2. The slope of the budget line is $-P_X/P_Y$

---

[1]Since the slope of the curve at a point is the derivative of Y with respect to X, denoted by dY/dX, elasticity can be written as $\eta = (dY/dX) \cdot (X/Y)$. In our example $Y = 20 + 5\sqrt{X}$. We first calculate dY/dX as being equal to $2.5/\sqrt{X}$ and then multiple it by the ratio X/Y in order to obtain a point elasticity.

namely, $-(\$4)/(\$2) = -2$. The two intercepts are determined by noting that you can exhaust your entire budget on 25 apples, or alternatively, on 50 oranges. In this example, the *nominal* budget is initially equal to $100. Now note that if your nominal budget increases from $100 to $200 and the prices of apples and oranges are unchanged in the marketplace, your opportunities set increases: You can exhaust the budget on 50 apples, or alternatively on 100 oranges, or on any mixed basket lying on the new opportunities set, which we call I_2. We can summarize this by saying that if your nominal budget increases and prices of goods remain unchanged, your real income increases. In fact, if prices are kept unchanged, real income changes in direct proportion to nominal income. In our example, the movement from I_0 to I_2 doubled both your nominal and your real income. Recall from the same example that your real income could also increase without any change in nominal income. If the prices of apples and oranges were each cut by a half, your opportunity set would have shifted from I_0 to the more desirable I_2. In this example, your real income also doubled.

We note finally that when we discuss a change in real income due to a change in prices, we insist on a *proportional* change in all prices. In our example, the prices of apples and oranges were cut by a half. Why is that? For convenience of analysis, we separate changes in income from changes in *relative* prices. A change in *relative* prices may be defined as a change leading to a change in the slope of the budget line of the consumer. On a more intuitive basis, a change in relative prices will result in making some goods more expensive than other goods. To illustrate this point, assume that currently your budget is I_2 (still Figure 1-10), which is equal to $200. The prices of apples and oranges are, respectively, $4 and $2. The slope of I_2 is -2. Now suppose there is a rise in prices: the price of apples rises to $5 and the price of oranges rises to $4. Your new budget line is I_1. The new slope is $-P_X/P_Y = -\$5/\$4 = -1.25$. Oranges became more expensive relative to apples. In fact, the price of apples rose by 25 percent; the price of oranges rose by 100 percent. The result of this is the budget line I_1, which reflects both a decrease in opportunites and a change in relative prices. We can separate the two effects by first assuming that both prices doubled, leading you to shift from I_2 to I_0, which is parallel to I_2; next, only the price of apples declined from $8 to $5, leading to a rotation of the budget line from I_0 to I_1.

2.3b The Income Consumption Curve (ICC)

We are now ready to investigate the way in which consumers respond to changes in income (budget). The analysis will be carried out in two stages. First, we shall focus on the X, Y space and see what happens when the budget increases or decreases. In the next section we shall translate our findings to a more practical presentation where the response of the consumer is presented in the I, X space.

Assume, as before, that apples and oranges are the only goods in your budget. Refer to Figure 2-2, where oranges are measured along the Y axis and apples are measured along the X axis. Your initial equilibrium occurs at

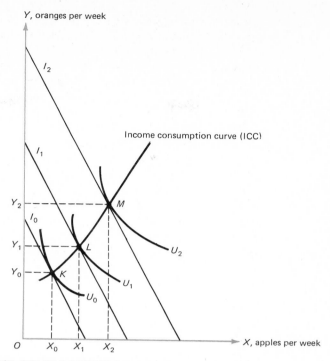

Y, oranges per week

Income consumption curve (ICC)

I_2

I_1

Y_2 --------------- M

I_0

Y_1 ---------- L

Y_0 ----- K

U_0

U_1

U_2

O X_0 X_1 X_2 X, apples per week

FIGURE 2-2   THE INCOME CONSUMPTION CURVE (ICC)
Income of the consumer increases while prices are kept unchanged. As a result the budget
line shifts in a parallel manner from I_0 to I_1 and then to I_2. The respective equilibrium points
are K, L, and M. The ICC is traced out by passing a curve through points like K, L, and M.

point K on budget line I_0. At that point indifference curve U_0 just touches
budget line I_0. Let us assume that $X_0 = 10$ apples and $Y_0 = 30$ oranges. The
budget is exhausted, that is, $100 = \$4 \cdot 10 + \$2 \cdot 30$. Next, assume that your
income rises from $100 to $160. Your budget line shifts to I_1 and you regain
equilibrium at point L where a new indifference curve, U_1, just touches the
new budget line. Let us assume that at point L your weekly consumption is
$X_1 = 20$ apples and $Y_1 = 40$ oranges. And this new budget is exhausted: $160
$= \$4 \cdot 20 + \$2 \cdot 40$. Finally, your income increases to $240, and you regain
your equilibrium at point M, where you consume 32 apples and 56 oranges.
Your budget is exhausted, as $240 = \$4 \cdot 32 + \$2 \cdot 56$. By connecting points
K, L, and M, we trace out the *income consumption curve* (ICC). In Figure
2-2, we show only three points of tangency. In principle the ICC should be
drawn by continuously varying the income of consumers from zero to the
highest income that they are likely to earn, keeping prices of goods unchanged. A continuous increase in income would lead to a continuous shift
in the budget line, thus tracing out all the points of tangency in the X, Y
space. We conclude by defining the ICC as the *locus of all points of
tangency between all possible budget lines and indifference curves where
prices (nominal and relative) are unchanged.* The ICC is an important

theoretical tool, but it is not particularly convenient for practical studies of consumers' sensitivity to variations in income. Accordingly, in the next section we develop a more convenient framework for handling this type of analysis.

2.3c The Engel Curve

The *Engel curve*, named after the German statistician Ernst Engel (1821–1896), is obtained by mapping the ICC from the X, Y space into the I, X space. Mapping in our example simply means utilizing the information in Figure 2-2 in order to draw a curve in the I, X space in Figure 2-3, which shows your consumption of apples as related to income. One Engel curve is shown, but we note that since the consumption of two goods is involved, two Engel curves can be derived—one for X and one for Y. Going back to the example, your Engel curve is obtained by mapping K, L, and M in Figure 2-2 into K', L', and M', where the coordinates of the new points are: $I_0 = \$100$, $X_0 = 10$ apples; $I_1 = \$160$, $X_1 = 20$ apples; $I_2 = \$240$, $X_2 = 32$ apples.

2.3d Normal and Inferior Goods

A good is called *normal* if its consumption increases in response to an increase in income and conversely decreases in response to a decrease in income. Normal goods are also called *superior* goods. In our example, both X and Y (apples and oranges) were normal; as your income increased, you increased the consumption of both goods. Since in the case of a normal good, a positive relationship exists between income and consumption, it follows that the Engel curve must have a positive slope.

A good is called *inferior* if its consumption decreases in response to an increase in income, and vice versa, if it increases in response to a decrease in income. To illustrate the case of an inferior good, consider your sister Ellen, who consumes fewer oranges and more apples in response to a rise in her

FIGURE 2-3   THE ENGEL CURVE
Points K', L', and M' were mapped from Figure 2-2 (K, L, and M). As the income of the consumer rises from I_0 to I_1 and then to I_2, his or her consumption of good X increases from X_0 to X_1 and then to X_2.

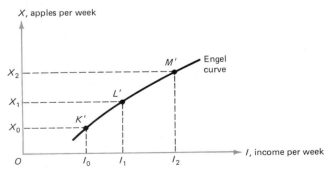

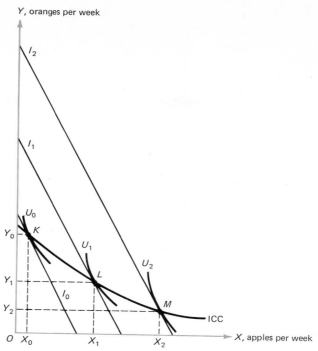

FIGURE 2-4 DERIVING THE ICC FOR AN *INFERIOR GOOD* (Y)
As income rises from I_0 to I_1, and then to I_2, the point of tangency moves in the southeasterly direction. Hence consumption of Y falls from Y_0 to Y_1 and then to Y_2.

income. Assume that she started in equilibrium with an income of $100 spent on 5 apples and 40 oranges. (Recall that in the marketplace prices are $P_x = 4 and $P_y = 2.) As her income rose to $160, she regained her equilibrium by consuming 30 apples and only 20 oranges. As her income rose to $240, Ellen responded by consuming 55 apples and 10 oranges. Ellen's ICC is displayed in Figure 2-4. Notice that the curve is falling as income rises because for Ellen oranges are inferior. The ICC in Figure 2-4 is mapped into an Engel curve in Figure 2-5. The negative relationship between Ellen's income and her consumption of oranges renders the Engel curve negatively sloped.

We note that only a few commodities are confirmed to be inferior by statistical studies. Most commodities are normal (superior). In fact, if we talk about aggregates of goods such as food, clothing, and transportation, we find that these aggregates are normal in the sense that consumers always increase consumption of these aggregate goods in response to a rise in their incomes. We shall return to this issue in the next and later sections.

2.3e Income Elasticity

Income elasticity of demand measures how a consumer responds in the consumption of a good, given a change in the income of that consumer.

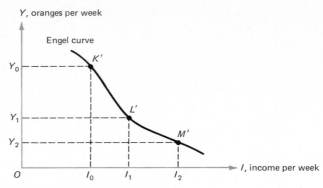

Y, oranges per week

Engel curve

FIGURE 2-5 ENGEL CURVE FOR AN INFERIOR GOOD Y
As income rises from I_0 to I_1 and then to I_2, consumption of good Y falls from Y_0 to Y_1, and
then to Y_2. The points K', L', and M' were mapped from Figure 2-4 (K, L, and M). The *Engel
curve* for an inferior good is negatively sloped.

Following the discussion in Section 2.2, we define income elasticity as the
relative change in the consumption of the good over the relative change in
income, namely,

$$\alpha = \frac{\dfrac{\Delta X}{X}}{\dfrac{\Delta I}{I}} = \frac{\text{percentage change in the consumption of } X}{\text{percentage change in the income of the consumer}} \quad (2\text{-}2)$$

where α (alpha) is used to denote income elasticity.

Let us use the previous example to demonstrate how income elasticities
are calculated. First, refer to Figure 2-3. Recall that moving from point K'
to point L' reflected a change in your income from $100 to $160 per week, to
which you responded by increasing your consumption of apples from 10 to
20. Accordingly, the income elasticity for the arc K'L' is calculated as follows:

$$\alpha = \frac{\dfrac{\Delta X}{X}}{\dfrac{\Delta I}{I}} = \frac{\dfrac{20 - 10}{15}}{\dfrac{160 - 100}{130}} = \frac{66.7 \text{ percent}}{46.1 \text{ percent}} = 1.45$$

How should we interpret this finding? Intuitively, we note that you responded to an increase in income of 46.1 percent by increasing your consumption of apples by 66.7 percent. More conclusively, we interpret the
value of 1.45 as indicating that between K' and L' a 1 percent increase in
your income led you to *increase* consumption of apples by 1.45 percent.

Let us now calculate the income elasticity for an inferior good. Consider
Ellen's Engel curve (Figure 2-5) for oranges in the arc L'M'. Going from L'
to M', her income rose from $160 to $240. She responded by decreasing her
consumption of oranges from 20 to 10. Her income elasticity is calculated as
follows:

$$\alpha = \frac{\frac{\Delta Y}{Y}}{\frac{\Delta I}{I}} = \frac{\frac{10 - 20}{15}}{\frac{240 - 160}{200}} = \frac{-66.7 \text{ percent}}{40.0 \text{ percent}} = -1.67$$

First, we note that income elasticity is negative. We interpret the result as indicating that between points L' and M', Ellen responded to a 1 percent increase in her income by *decreasing* her consumption of oranges by 1.67 percent.

We can now generalize our findings to the following result:

Since Engel curves of normal goods are positively sloped and Engel curves of inferior goods are negatively sloped, it follows that income elasticities of normal goods are positive and income elasticities of inferior goods are negative.

Economists divide normal goods into two subgroups: just *normal* and *ultrasuperior* (also known as luxuries). Goods whose income elasticity is between 0 and 1 are just normal, and goods whose income elasticity is greater than 1 are normal, but they are also known as ultrasuperior.

In summary, we can state:

1. If the commodity is inferior, income elasticity is negative.
2. If the commodity is just normal, income elasticity is between zero and 1.
3. If the commodity is normal, but also ultrasuperior, income elasticity is greater than 1.

We now turn around to look at income elasticities in reality.

2.3f Income Elasticities in Reality

Income elasticities are relevant to producers of goods and services. In Chapter 3 we shall see that two factors, *income per capita* and *population,* are critical in determining how much of the growing purchasing power of consumers (their budgets or incomes) will be spent on one good or another. The first factor is considered here. The reader can already intuitively feel that if Ellen in our example were a typical consumer, producers of apples should expect a feast and producers of oranges should expect a famine. It should be evident from this example that knowledge of the value of income elasticities of apples and oranges is valuable to owners of orchards. It is not surprising, therefore, that economists devote great effort to estimating income elasticities. A pioneer economist, Herman Wold, estimated income elasticities for foodstuffs based on three family budget surveys conducted in Sweden in 1913, 1923, and 1933.[2] He found few goods were inferior. For workers and low-grade employees, the only inferior commodities in 1933 were skim milk, margarine, and flour, with income elasticities of -1.17, -0.37, and -0.50. Wold estimated the income elasticity of butter, which is

---

[2]Herman Wold and L. Jureén, *Demand Analysis, A study in Econometrics,* Wiley, New York, 1953.

closely related to margarine, at 0.64, and eating out in restaurants at 2.14. In other words, according to his study skim milk, butter, and eating out in restaurants are inferior, normal, and ultrasuperior goods.

In the United States as well, inferior goods are not often encountered. Recent studies of consumers' responses to changes in income indicate that commodities are either normal or ultrasuperior. Goods such as furniture, cars, and whiskey are ultrasuperior. Most foods and fuels are normal goods.

2.3g Replacing the Physical Quality of the Good by Expenditures on the Good

When we observe the response of consumers to changes in income, should we consider goods such as rye bread separately from whole wheat bread, or should we consider aggregates of commodities such as bread? Should we study consumer behavior toward sofas separately from that toward armchairs, or should we consider the aggregate of all furniture as a more useful objective of our analytical efforts? The answer is that it depends on the purpose of the study. Bakers and farmers are more likely to be interested in *aggregate bread* than in a specific kind of bread such as rye. Producers of furniture who sell a wide spectrum of items are interested in the consumption of aggregate furniture. But producers of soft drinks might be interested in studying the income elasticity for the aggregate of all soft drinks as well as the income elasticity of their own brands.

If it is clear that we are sometimes interested in studying aggregates of goods, how can we lump together closely related but still different commodities such as rye bread and whole wheat bread? We may do it by simply considering the expenditures on goods rather than the physical quantities of goods. To begin with, we can measure along the respective axes of Figures 2-3 and 2-5 expenditures on apples and oranges instead of the number of apples and oranges. Consider Figure 2-3. Instead of measuring X along the vertical axis, we could replace the X by $P_x \cdot X$ (in our example, $P_x = \$4$) and redraw a new curve known as the *Engel expenditure curve*. We leave it for the student to show that if consumers have more than one good in their budgets, the Engel expenditure curve (for any aggregate not covering all goods) must lie below the *cross diagonal*. The cross diagonal is a ray starting at the origin and forming a 45° angle with both axes. Let us extend this to a case in which there are closely related goods such as apples, peaches, and plums. We may denote them as X_1, X_2, and X_3 and aggregate these three closely related fruits by adding together the amount of money that a consumer spends on them as follows:

Money spent on apples, peaches, and plums $= P_{x1} \cdot X_1 + P_{x2} \cdot X_2 + P_{x3} \cdot X_3$

We can express this aggregate symbolically as $\Sigma P_{xi} \cdot X_i$. An Engel expenditure curve showing how consumers would vary consumption of apples, peaches, and plums in response to changes in income will be drawn in a diagram in which income I is measured along the horizontal axis and $\Sigma P_{xi} \cdot X_i$ is measured along the vertical axis.

We are now equipped to consider one of the most important studies of income elasticities of Engel expenditure curves.

2.3h An Example: Empirical Estimates of Income Elasticities for Engel Expenditure Curves

As noted before, estimates of income elasticities are relevant for producers of various goods and services. For such purposes, we can now add governments, and in particular governments of developing countries. For example, the government of a developing country considers a huge irrigation project for reasons relating to food production. Since the project, if undertaken, will be on line in only 20 years, the government should have an estimate of expenditures for food 20 years hence. Knowledge of the income elasticity of food in that country is critical for forecasting future expenditures for food.

Engel studied patterns of consumption in the kingdom of Saxony. *Engel's law,* based on accumulated statistics, states that the proportion of income spent on food declines as income rises. In other words, the income elasticity of (aggregate) food is less than unity. Engel's law can be written as follows:

$$\frac{\Delta(\text{expenditures on food})}{(\text{expenditures on food})} < \frac{\Delta I}{I}$$

If we divide both sides of the inequality by $\Delta I/I$, we obtain the result that

$$\alpha = \frac{\dfrac{\Delta(\text{expenditures on food})}{\text{expenditures on food}}}{\dfrac{\Delta I}{I}} < 1$$

Or, to put it differently, food is just a normal good rather than an ultrasuperior good. For example, if income elasticity of food is 0.5 and you currently spend 20 percent of your income on food, a 10 percent increase in your income will induce you to increase your expenditures on food by 5 percent. You should be able to verify that after the change in income takes place, you will devote only 19 percent of your income to food.

Hendrik Houthakker estimated income elasticities in a variety of countries by applying statistical methods. His studies are important because they not only bear out Engel's law but also provide both producers and governments with useful estimates of income elasticities for aggregate groups of goods and services. He studied the specific aggregates of food, clothing, and housing, as well as miscellaneous items such as transportation, entertainment, and furniture.

Table 2-2 shows some of Houthakker's results for three countries.

Houthakker found that income elasticities for food were less than unity in all countries studied, again confirming Engel's law. The elasticities for clothing were higher than unity but in most cases were less than 1.5. Thus we conclude that clothing is ultrasuperior. In the case of housing, income elasticities were likewise found to be less than unity in most countries. In the United States, these elasticities were higher in suburbs compared with cities—an indication that families with preferences for large homes tend to move to the suburbs. The elasticities for miscellaneous items were higher than unity; except for the United States and a few other countries, they were higher than 1.4.

TABLE 2-2   Income Elasticities for Selected Countries

Country	Food	Clothing	Housing	Miscellaneous
United States, 1950, all cities	0.692	1.280	0.895	1.248
France	0.483	1.158	1.098	1.656
Poland	0.731	1.784	0.662	1.774

Source: H. S. Houthakker, "An International Comparison of Household Expenditure Patterns, Commemorating the Century of Engel's Law," *Econometrica,* vol. 25, October 1957, pp. 532–551.

2.3i The Interdependency of Income Elasticities

If a consumer has n goods in his or her budget, there are n income elasticities associated with these goods. The n income elasticities do not exist independently of each other. To explain it intuitively, if the consumer has only two goods in his or her budget, a decision to increase the rate of spending on X in response to a change in his or her income is necessarily at the expense of the other good Y. Or to give a more convincing example, if Y is inferior, X must be ultrasuperior. This is true because if both X and Y were inferior, as income rose the consumer would have decreased the consumption of both goods, leading to a situation in which the amount of money actually spent on X and Y was smaller than the budget. This, however, would have violated our basic assumption that the budget was exhausted; hence we conclude that at least one good in the budget of the consumer must be normal. This intuitive notion that there is some interdependency among the income elasticities of the various goods in the budget of the consumer can be formulated as follows: Assume that the budget of the consumer is exhausted on only two goods X and Y, namely, $P_x \cdot X + P_y \cdot Y = I$. If such is true, it must also be true that a change in the budget must be exhausted on the change in the consumption of the two goods, namely,

$$P_x \cdot \Delta X + P_y \cdot \Delta Y = \Delta I$$

If we divide through by ΔI, we obtain an expression

$$\frac{P_x \cdot \Delta X}{\Delta I} + \frac{P_y \cdot \Delta Y}{\Delta I} = 1$$

Consider the expression $(P_x \cdot \Delta X)/\Delta I$. If we multiply both the numerator and the denominator of this expression by $I \cdot X$, we obtain

$$\frac{P_x \cdot \Delta X}{\Delta I} \cdot \frac{I \cdot X}{I \cdot X} = \frac{P_x \cdot X}{I} \cdot \frac{\Delta X \cdot I}{\Delta I \cdot X} = K_x \cdot \alpha_x$$

where K_x is the fraction of income which is spent on X, namely, $(P_x \cdot X)/I$. Manipulating the expression for Y in the same way yields the following formula, which relates the income elasticity of $X(\alpha_x)$ to the income elasticity of $Y(\alpha_y)$.

$$K_x \cdot \alpha_x + K_y \cdot \alpha_y = 1 \qquad (2\text{-}3)$$

Note: Since $P_x \cdot X + P_y \cdot Y = I$, it follows that $K_x + K_y = 1$.

To understand this further, recall that in Section 2.3d Ellen's income increased from \$160 to \$240. Her consumption of apples increased from 30 to 55, and her consumption of oranges fell from 20 to 10. In Section 2.3e, we calculated α_y to be equal to -1.67. By applying the formula for income elasticity, we calculate Ellen's α_x for that range to be 1.47. Now, at a midpoint between L and M in Figure 2-4, Ellen spends \$170 on apples and \$30 on oranges. Accordingly, $K_x = \$170/\$200$ and $K_y = \$30/\$200$. Substituting these values in Equation 2-3, we obtain

$$0.85 \cdot 1.47 + 0.15 \cdot (-1.67) = 1$$

We conclude this section by noting that the weighted average of all income elasticities is equal to unity. That is to say, a 1 percent change in income will lead to a 1 percent change in spending on all goods in the budget, which is another way of saying that the budget is exhausted.

2.3j A Note on Semantics

In the section that follows, we shall attempt to derive a new concept, the *demand curve*. It is important for the student to realize, however, that this chapter so far is not merely an introduction to the theory of demand. To set matters straight, we stress that "consumption" is synonymous with "demand" and that indeed the Engel curve indicates the consumer's adjustment of his or her *demand* for a certain good to a change in his or her income. Why the curve which relates consumption, or demand for a good, to income is called an *Engel curve* and not a *demand curve* is an interesting question that we leave for economic historians to answer. This semantic confusion would perhaps be resolved if the student would consider the following: the opportunities set of the consumer can change either if income varies or if prices change. Changes in income lead to parallel shifts in budget lines and are conveniently summarized by demand curves known as "Engel curves." Changes in prices lead to nonparallel shifts in budget lines and are conveniently summarized by demand curves known as "demand curves."

2.4 THE SENSITIVITY OF THE CONSUMER TO CHANGES IN PRICE

2.4a The Response of Consumers to Price Changes

The evidence that consumers are sensitive to price changes is abundant. Department stores hold sales after Christmas in order to clear leftovers from December. In the fall of 1979, Chrysler offered $500 rebates on cars that were priced at $8000 and cleared a stock of some 80,000 cars. Vegetables are sold at relatively low prices during the season in order to clear the market. As a result of the energy crisis, the annual rate of growth of the consumption of electric power in the United States fell from 8 to 3 percent. Moreover, importers of compact cars enjoyed a boom while domestic producers in the United States who could not adjust quickly to the new market conditions suffered losses. In this section, we organize and formalize our thinking about this type of consumer sensitivity to price variations. In later chapters, it will become evident to the student that this analysis is essential for the understanding of complex economic systems. An example of such a complex system is the regulation of the crude oil market that was implemented after the energy crisis of 1974. According to this scheme, refineries in the United States were forced in 1977 to purchase oil in three price tiers: old oil at $5.25

per barrel, new oil at $11.28 per barrel, and imported and stripper oil at the OPEC price. The issue was "to regulate or not to regulate." The point made by most economists was that deregulation would reduce the United States reliance on imported oil. In this type of analysis, among other things, economists must take into account the sensitivity of consumers to rising prices of gasoline.

2.4b The Price Consumption Curve (PCC)

The format of this and the following section is similar to that of our earlier derivations of the ICC and the Engel curve. We shall assume that the consumer is in equilibrium. Then, we shall assume that the relative price of one good changes, leading to a rotation in the consumer's budget line. The consumer regains equilibrium on the new budget line, which allows us to record the response to the change in price. In the next section we shall translate our findings into a more convenient tool, exactly in the same way that the ICC curve was translated into an Engel curve.

Let us assume again that your income is $100 per week, and apples and oranges are denoted by X and Y. The prices are, to begin with, $4 for apples and $2 for oranges. Since we are interested in the relative price of one good, we shall assume that the price of oranges remains unchanged throughout the analysis of this and the next section. More formally, $P_{y0} = \$2$. During the initial week, $P_{x0} = \$4$. Now consider Figure 2-6, panel (a). Your initial budget line is I_0 and an initial indifference curve U_0 is tangent to I_0 at point K. Assume that at K you consume 10 apples and 30 oranges. During the second week the price of apples declines to $2. Accordingly the intercept of the budget line with the X axis increases from 25 ($100/$4) to 50 ($100/$2). The intercept of the budget line with the Y axis remains unchanged at point $T(50 = \$100/\$2)$.

Equilibrium is regained at L where U_1 just touches I_1, the new budget line. At point L, you consume $X_1 = 30$ apples and $Y_1 = 20$ oranges. Finally, during the third week, the price of apples falls to $1. While T remains the intercept of the new budget line with the Y axis, the intercept of the new budget line I_2 with the X axis is 100 ($100/$1). Your third point of equilibrium is M, where you consume $X_2 = 54$ apples and $Y_2 = 23$ oranges. Passing a curve through points like K, L, and M traces out the *price consumption curve* (PCC). In other words, the PCC is the *locus of all points of tangency between all budget lines that have a common intercept with the Y axis and indifference curves in the X, Y space.*

Like the ICC, the PCC is not a particularly convenient tool of analysis. Recall that the ICC was transformed into the Engel curve, which was easy to relate to the real world. For the same reason, in the next section we shall transform the PCC into a more convenient tool, the demand curve.

Finally, note the similarity between a rise in income and a fall in the price of one good: Both lead to an increase in the set of opportunities that are open to the consumer. The only difference is that a rise in income results in a

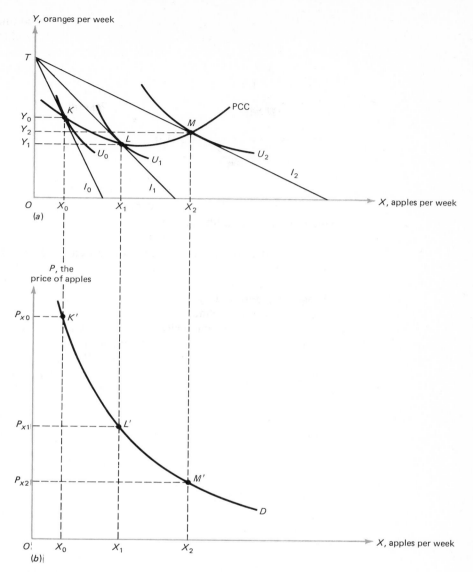

FIGURE 2-6 DERIVING THE PCC

Panel (a): The budget line rotates about the pivot T from I_0 to I_1 and then to I_2. The rotation takes place as a result of a fall in the price of X from P_{x0} to P_{x1} and then to P_{x2}. As the budget line rotates due to the fact that X becomes cheaper relative to Y, tangency point changes from K to L, and then to M. The PCC is traced out by passing a curve through points like K, L, and M. Panel (b): Points K', L', and M' are mapped from panel (a) (K, L, and M). The *demand curve* is obtained by passing a curve through points like K', L', and M'.

parallel shift in the budget line as in Figure 2-2, while a fall in the price of a good (a decline in its relative price) results in a rotation of the budget line.

2.4c The Demand Curve

The *demand curve* is obtained by mapping the PCC in the X, Y space into the P, X space as shown in Figure 2-6, panel (b). P denotes the price of good X. Since economic tradition dictates that the price should be measured along the vertical axis, we can place the price and quantity-of-X diagram right below the Y, X diagram and line the two up with exactly the same horizontal scale. The mapping thus becomes very simple: First, we extend vertical lines from the X axis in panel (a) to the X axis in panel (b) at levels of X_0, X_1, and X_2 (10, 30, and 54 apples). We next mark on the price axis of panel (b) the prices P_{x0}, P_{x1}, and P_{x2} ($4, $2, and $1). The pairs X_0, P_{x0}; X_1, P_{x1}; and X_2, P_{x2} are denoted by the points K', L', and M'. In other words, the points K, L, and M were mapped from the X, Y space into the points K', L', and M' in the P,X space. Passing a curve through points like K', L', and M' traces out the demand curve, which is denoted by D. We can say that the demand curve is the locus of all points in the P,X space telling us how many units of X per unit of time will be consumed by the individual at various prices. The following two properties of the demand curve are important:

1. Under normal conditions, the demand curve is negatively sloped. In a later section in this chapter, we shall show that this is always true for normal (including ultrasuperior) goods, and in most cases it is true for inferior goods. This property of the demand curve has been borne out by numerous statistical tests.

2. Moving down on the demand curve (in a southeasterly direction) enhances the satisfaction of the consumer. This is true because a downward movement along the demand curve, from K' to L' and then to M' in panel (b), reflects a movement from U_0 to U_1 and then to U_2 in panel (a).

2.4d The Sensitivity of the Consumer to Changes in Prices of Other Goods

Let us reconsider Figure 2-6, panel (a). While the price of apples was falling from one week to the next and the price of oranges remained unchanged at $P_{y0} = \$2$, your consumption of oranges did not remain unchanged. Rather, it changed from $Y_0 = 30$ to $Y_1 = 20$ and finally to $Y_2 = 23$. Likewise, if the price of oranges were to vary and the price of apples remained unchanged, we would expect you to respond by changing the quantity of apples you consumed per week. The reason for this is intuitively clear: first, as the relative price of one good falls, the opportunities set of consumers increases and they can now afford to consume more of all goods, not only the good whose price falls. Second, as the price of one good falls, consumers find it beneficial to shift some money from the other good to this good and thus increase the utility. (See Equation 1-3. $MU_x/P_x = MU_y/P_y$. If P_x falls, the marginal utility obtained from spending the last dollar on X exceeds the marginal utility obtained from spending the last dollar on Y. Hence, by transferring a small amount of money ordinarily spent on Y to X, the consumer gains utility.) This topic will be discussed in greater detail in Chapter 3.

2.4e An Example: A Strange PCC in Developing Countries

It is sometimes asserted that the masses in developing countries respond to rising incomes by working less. It is alleged that these poor people have "fixed wants": when their income rises, they work less. Recall from Section 1.6 that earning money is equivalent to selling leisure in the marketplace. Consider Figure 2-7. Along the horizontal axis we measure leisure, and along the vertical axis we measure the aggregate of all other goods, denoted by Y. As earnings per unit of time rise, the budget line rotates from l_0 to l_1. L_0 serves as the pivot point because the individual is endowed with a fixed amount of leisure, for example, 24 hours per day. A rotation, rather than a parallel shift, occurs because a rise in earnings indicates a change in the relative price of leisure versus all other goods. Now, if it is true that people in developing countries have fixed wants, say, equal to Y_0 units of all goods and services, their PCC must be flat as shown in Figure 2-7. As earnings rise, leading to a rotation of the budget line from l_0 to l_1, workers move along the flat PCC from point A to point B. They increase the amount of leisure enjoyed from L_1 to L_2. The amount of labor performed by the poor worker is reduced from $L_0 - L_1$ to $L_0 - L_2$.

The anthropologist Erenstine Friedl disagrees with the idea of a flat PCC in developing countries. According to Friedl, the villagers of Vasilika, an "underdeveloped" village in modern Greece, try to emulate the living standards and tastes which they perceive as existing in the modern city—a point important to the economics of developing countries. When Friedl was writing her book, the majority of villagers used wooden outbuildings as their latrines. Some villagers with higher incomes bought modern latrines. Friedl wrote, "From the villagers' point of view, the newer latrines are not valued because they constitute better sanitation, but because the villagers' urban relatives have been ridiculing them for not having some kind of toilet." With rising income the villagers would often buy new goods because of the sophistication they represented. Friedl goes on to tell the story about one of Vasilika's less prosperous inhabitants whose house nevertheless was electrified in 1959. This man "had one naked bulb hanging in the center of his small upstairs room. This man described for us his feelings about a recent visit he made to the *paniyiri*[3] of a mountain village which had no electricity. 'I couldn't stay there more than a day,' he said. 'They had no electric light, and I cannot live like that any more. I have become a European,' he concluded, with a smile, using the terms that Greeks use for the inhabitants of Europe west of the Adriatic."[4]

2.4f Price Elasticity of Demand

Price elasticity measures how consumers respond in consumption of a good, given a change in the price of that good in the marketplace. We define price elasticity as

$$\eta = \frac{\dfrac{\Delta X}{X}}{\dfrac{\Delta P_x}{P_x}} = \frac{\text{percentage change in the quantity of } X \text{ consumed}}{\text{percentage change in the price of } X} \quad (2\text{-}4)$$

where η is the symbol used to denote price elasticity of demand. Following

---

[3] Festival.

[4] Erenstine Friedl, *Vasilika, A Village in Modern Greece,* Holt, Rinehart and Winston, New York, 1965.

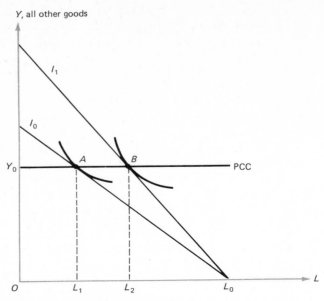

FIGURE 2-7 AN ALLEGED PCC IN DEVELOPING COUNTRIES
The flat PCC reflects the (erroneous) philosophy that poor consumers in developing countries have "fixed wants": They need only a fixed amount of Y_0 units of all other goods. Thus, as their earnings rise, leading to a rotation of the budget line from I_0 clockwise to I_1, they increase the amount of leisure they "buy" from L_1 to L_2, which is equivalent to decreasing their work effort from $L_1 - L_0$ to $L_2 - L_0$.

Section 2.2, let us illustrate how we calculate the price elasticity of your demand curve for the arc $L'M'$, as presented in panel (*b*) of Figure 2-6.

$$\eta = \frac{\frac{\Delta X}{X}}{\frac{\Delta P_x}{P_x}} = \frac{\frac{54 - 30}{42}}{\frac{1 - 2}{1.5}} = \frac{57 \text{ percent}}{-67 \text{ percent}} = -0.85$$

Following Section 2.2, the demand curve is *inelastic* in the arc $L'M'$. In fact, a 1 percent drop in the price of apples induced you to increase consumption of apples by less than 1 percent. Because the relationship between price and quantity consumed is negative, price elasticity is negative. The definitions of an *elastic demand,* a demand of *unitary elasticity,* and an *inelastic demand* are slightly modified. First, recall that the *absolute value of a number* is defined as the number multiplied by -1 if the number is negative. (The absolute value of a positive number is the number itself.) The absolute value of η is written as $|\eta|$. For example, if $\eta = -2$, then $|\eta| = 2$. We accordingly accept the following definitions of the degree of price elasticity:

If $|\eta| < 1$, the demand curve is *inelastic.*
If $|\eta| = 1$, the demand curve has *unitary elasticity.*
If $|\eta| > 1$, the demand curve is *elastic.*

The student is reminded that, except for special cases, the elasticity applies only for the arc for which it has been calculated. In your example, you are allowed to claim that in the arc $L'M'$ your demand curve is inelastic and is equal to -0.85.

Price elasticity is important not only as a measure of the responsiveness of consumers to changes in prices but also as an indicator of how *total revenue*—defined as price times quantity demanded—will change given a movement along the demand curve. The concept of total revenue will be covered again in Chapter 3.

Let us return to Figure 2-6. Applying the formula as given in Equation 2-4, we calculate price elasticity for arc $K'L'$ as being equal to -1.49. We also note that, moving from K' to L', your expenditures on apples increased from $40 to $60, and, moving from L' to M', your expenditures on apples fell from $60 to $54. This is not a coincidence. It is a finding that can be generalized into a rule which is illustrated in Figure 2-8: When PCC is falling, up to X_0,

FIGURE 2-8 THE RELATIONSHIP BETWEEN THE SLOPE OF THE PCC AND η
In panel (a) the PCC decreases from the origin to X_0, and thereafter it rises. Correspondingly, in panel (b) the associated demand curve is elastic between the origin and X_0 and inelastic beyond X_0. At a level of output of X_0 the demand curve has unitary elasticity.

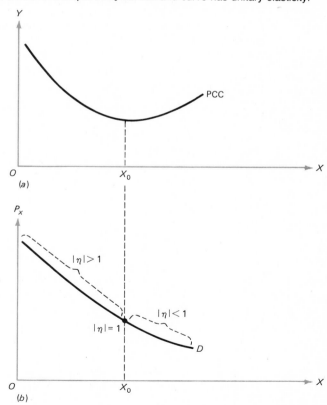

total revenue increases and the demand curve is elastic. When PCC is rising, beyond X_0, total revenue decreases and the demand curve is inelastic. What is the logic behind this relationship? Total revenue is $P_x \cdot X$. Since the budget is exhausted, we can write $P_x \cdot X = I - P_y \cdot Y$. (Subtract $P_y \cdot Y$ from both sides of the budget equation.) Recall that P_y and I are held constant along the PCC. When PCC is falling, $P_y \cdot Y$ shrinks and the expression $I - P_y \cdot Y$ must increase. This explains why total revenue ($P_x \cdot X$) must rise. The reverse holds true when PCC is rising. Next consider the portion of the demand curve in Figure 2-8, panel (b), between the origin and X_0. If the demand curve there were of unitary elasticity, a 1 percent fall in the price would have led to a 1 percent rise in the consumption of X, the two opposite changes would have offset each other, and total revenue would have remained unchanged. But since we showed that total revenue must rise between the origin and X_0, we conclude that the percentage increase in the consumption of X must exceed 1 percent, implying an elastic demand curve. The same argument in reverse applies to the rising portion of the PCC.[5]

2.4g Substitution Effects and Income Effects

In the conclusion of Section 2.4c, we stated that under normal conditions the demand curve is expected to have a negative slope. This was in doubt only where the demand for inferior goods was concerned. The doubt arises because when the price of X falls, the opportunities set of consumers increases. Since we feel intuitively that this, in a way, is equivalent to giving the consumer additional income, might he or she not decrease the consumption of good X if X is inferior? In order to handle this problem less intuitively, we may disjoint the effect of the increased opportunities set from the effect of the change in relative price. The effect of the increased opportunities set is known as the *income effect,* and the effect of the change in relative price is known as the *substitution effect.* To illustrate how we may separate the income effect from the substitution effect, consider Figure 2-9. The original equilibrium occurs at point K, where indifference curve U_0 is tangent to the budget line I_0. After the price of X falls from P_{x0} to P_{x1}, the budget line rotates from I_0 counterclockwise to I_1. The new equilibrium is achieved at L, where U_1 is tangent to I_1. As a result the consumer increases his or her consumption of X from X_0 to X_1, and the *total effect* of the change in price is

---

[5]For the reader who fails to follow the intuitive argument, note that $R = P_x \cdot X$, where R denotes total revenue. Take the log of the above function to obtain $\log R = \log P_x + \log X$. Taking the whole differential and replacing d by Δ, we get

$$\frac{\Delta R}{R} \doteq \frac{\Delta P_x}{P_x} + \frac{\Delta X}{X}$$

which can be written as

Percentage change in R = percentage change in P_x + percentage change in X

This formula, which is good for relatively small changes, says that given a 1 percent fall in the price of X, the quantity of X consumed will have to increase by more than 1 percent in order to yield a positive change in total revenue, etc.

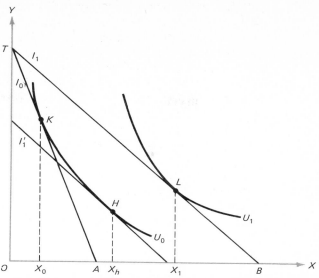

FIGURE 2-9 SEPARATING THE INCOME EFFECT FROM THE SUBSTITUTION EFFECT
As the price of X falls the budget line rotates from I_0 to I_1, and equilibrium changes from K to L. We then confiscate income from the consumer so as to shift his or her new budget line back to position I_1' such that it is tangent to the initial indifference curve at point H. Correspondingly, the movement from X_0 to X_h is the *(Hicksian) substitution effect*. The movement from X_h to X_1 is the *(Hicksian) income effect*.

$X_1 - X_0$. If we forced the consumer to stay on the original indifference curve U_0, after the price of X fell, the consumer would move to point H on U_0. Forcing the consumer to move to point H can be achieved by confiscating some of his or her income, thus shifting his or her budget line inward from I_1 to I_1'. In fact, the amount of money confiscated must be sufficient to shift I_1 inward until it is just touching the original indifference curve U_0. I_1' is parallel to I_1 because the two lines reflect different incomes but the same prices for X and Y. The movement from K to L has been broken into two parts: first, the movement along the original indifference curve from K to H, and then the movement from H to L. These movements are projected on the X axis as a movement from X_0 to X_h which is known as the *Hicksian substitution effect*[6] and a movement from X_h to X_1 which is known as the *income effect*. The amount of money that was confiscated from consumers in order to shift I_1 to I_1' could be thought of as the increase in his or her opportunities set due to the decline of the price of X. Geometrically, the opportunities set shifted from I_1' outward to I_1.

Good X in Figure 2-9 is normal. A parallel shift in the budget line from I_1' to I_1 leads to an increase in the consumption of X (from X_h to X_1). We can summarize this finding as follows: The demand curve for a normal good must

---

[6]Named after Sir John Hicks, an English economist, the author of *Value and Capital*, Oxford University Press, London, 1946, pp. 29–33.

have a negative slope. First, as the price of the good falls, the consumer will consume more of this good because of the substitution effect. This results from the negative slope and convexity of the original indifference curve. Second, since the good is normal, a parallel shift of the budget line from I_1' to I_1 must lead to a further increase in the consumption of the good. We note, however, that in reality the income effect is relatively small.

2.4h Inferior Goods and the Giffen Paradox

Let good X be inferior and let its price fall, thus leading to a rotation from I_0 to I_1 as pictured in Figure 2-10 (both panels). Consider panel (a). The movement from point K to point H is the (Hicksian) substitution effect. However, since by assumption X is an inferior good, the parallel displacement of the budget line from I_1' to I_1 results in a decline in the consumption of X from X_h to X_1. The income effect and the substitution effect work at cross purposes. The substitution effect is to increase the quantity demanded of X by $X_h - X_0$; the income effect is to decrease the quantity demanded of X by $X_1 - X_h$. Since the substitution effect dominates, the net effect is still a positive change of $X_1 - X_0$. Notice that in panel (a) the PCC curve still moves outward. The decline in the price of X stills leads to an increase in the quantity of X demanded.

Let us now shift our attention to panel (b). The situation is identical to that in panel (a) except that as the budget line shifts from I_1' to I_1, the consumer moves from the temporary point H to the new point of tangency L which lies to the left of point K; the income effect of lowering the consumption of X from X_h to X_1 (associated with the movement from H to L) is stronger than the substitution effect of moving from X_0 to X_h. As a result, the PCC is backward-bending (the direction of the arrowhead). A good with a backward-bending PCC curve is known as a *Giffen good*, after the economist Robert Giffen. A falling price of X leads to a fall in its quantity demanded. Hence the associated demand curve is positively sloped. We can summarize our analysis as illustrated in panel (b) as follows:

1. Inferiority is a *necessary condition* for a good to be a Giffen good.
2. The dominance of the income effect (the distance from X_0 to X_h is smaller than the distance from X_h to X_1) is sufficient for a good to be a Giffen good.

The Giffen paradox was formally introduced by Alfred Marshall in his *Principles* (1895). Marshall said that Giffen pointed out that a rise in the price of bread is a drain on the resources of the poor consumer who curtails the consumption of meat and other fancy foods and consumes more bread, which is still the cheapest food available. Stigler studied the history of the Giffen paradox out of curiosity "which was and is far from satisfied."[7] Stigler brings data on per capita consumption and price of wheat in the United Kingdom for the period 1889–1890 to 1903–1904. The data do not

---

[7]George J. Stigler, "Notes on the History of the Giffen Paradox," *The Journal of Political Economy*, vol. 55, April 1947, pp. 152–156.

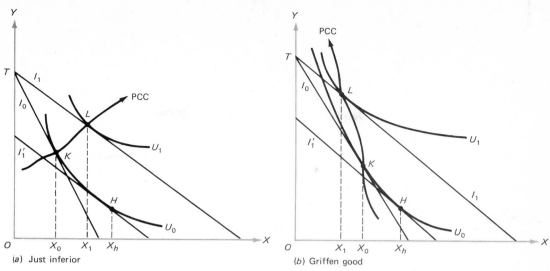

FIGURE 2-10 THE SUBSTITUTION EFFECT AND THE INCOME EFFECT WHEN THE GOOD IS INFERIOR

Panel (*a*): The price of *X* falls, leading to a rotation of the budget line from I_0 to I_1. Income is confiscated sufficiently to shift the new budget line back to I_1'. I_1' is tangent to the initial indifference curve at point *H*. The movement from X_0 to X_h is the substitution effect. However, since *X* is inferior, the movement from *H* to the final point *L* is in the northwesterly direction. Correspondingly, the movement from X_h to X_1, which constitutes the income effect, is negative. Since the substitution effect $(X_h - X_0)$ dominates the income effect $(X_1 - X_h)$, the net result is a net increase in consumption by $X_1 - X_0$. Panel (*b*): The same as in panel (*a*), except that the income effect $(X_1 - X_h)$ dominates the substitution effect $(X_h - X_0)$, and hence the net effect $(X_1 - X_0)$ is negative. *X* is a *Giffen good*.

reveal a positive relationship between quantity and price. Stigler cites another study of workmen's budgets by the Board of Trade in 1904. The conclusion of the study was that except in the highest income class, income was uncorrelated with consumption of bread. Thus, although theoretically the Giffen paradox is possible, Stigler could not verify that a positively sloped demand curve for wheat actually reflected the behavior of English consumers at the turn of the century.

2.4i Slutsky Substitution Effect (Optional)

The exact shape of indifference curve U_0 in Figure 2-10 is unknown. Accordingly, we cannot estimate the change in income that will shift the consumer's budget line from I_1 back to I_1' such that I_1' is tangent to the original indifference curve U_0. In order to get around this difficulty, the Russian economist Eugene Slutsky suggested that after the price of *X* declines we should confiscate an amount of money from the consumer so that his or her new budget line, I_1', will pass through the initial basket *K*. In other words, instead of confiscating an amount of money that will leave the consumer with the initial amount of utility (indicated by U_0), we confiscate an amount of money such that with the income left, the consumer can buy the initial basket K. The derivation of the *Slutsky substitution effect* is presented in Figure 2-11. To illustrate how we shift the budget line from I_1 back to I_1', let us consider the example in Section 2.4b. Recall that your initial budget was $I_0 = \$100$, and the prices were $P_{x0} = \$4$ and $P_{y0} = \$2$. Notice that (see Figure 2-11) $I_1 = I_0$. In our example, $I_1 = I_0 = \$100$. Thus the income which is confiscated may be written as $I_1 - I_1' = I_0 - I_1'$. The initial equilibrium K represented $X_0 = 10$ apples and $Y_0 = 30$ oranges. During the second week, the price of apples fell to $P_{x1} = \$2$. You regained your equilibrium by moving to $L(X_1 = 30$ apples and $Y_1 = 20$ oranges). How much of your income should we confiscate so as to move you to a budget line passing through the initial basket K? We calculate it as follows:

$$
\begin{aligned}
\text{Money confiscated} &= I_1 - I_1' \\
&= I_0 - I_1' \\
&= P_{x0} \cdot X_0 + P_{y0} \cdot Y_0 - (P_{x1} \cdot X_o + P_{y0} \cdot Y_0) \\
&= P_{x0} \cdot X_0 - P_{x1} \cdot X_0 \\
&= X_0(P_{x0} - P_{x1}) \\
&= -X_0(P_{x1} - P_{x0}) \\
&= -X_0 \cdot \Delta P_x
\end{aligned}
$$

The expression $-X_0 \cdot \Delta P_x$ is called the *change in apparent real income*. Given a change in the price of a good in the budget of the consumer, the change in apparent real income indicates the variation in income required to leave him or her an amount of money with which he or she can buy the initial basket K. In our example, the change in apparent real income was $-10(\$2 - \$4) = \$20$.

In Figure 2-11, after we shift the budget line from I_1 to I_1', a temporary equilibrium position is established at point S where an indifference curve, U_s, just touches I_1'. In analogy with the Hicksian substitution effect, the movement from X_0 to X_s is the *Slutsky substitution effect* and the movement from X_s to X_1 is the *Slutsky income effect*.

It is left as an exercise for the student to show that for a normal good the Slutsky substitution effect slightly exceeds the Hicksian substitution effect. However, it has been shown that if the change in price is not too large, the Slutsky substitution effect is a good proxy for the Hicksian substitution effect.

Sometimes the substitution portion of the change in quantity demanded $(X_s - X_0)$ is called the *compensated* change in quantity demanded. A demand curve derived by ignoring the income effect is sometimes called the *compensated demand*.

The main advantage of the Slutsky approach over the Hicksian approach is that it yields quantitative results. These aspects of the Slutsky approach are covered in Mathematical Appendix 2.[8]

---

[8] A very useful formula which we derive in Mathematical Appendix 2, disjoints the price elasticity of the demand curve into two components as follows:

$$\eta = \bar{\eta} - K_x \cdot \alpha$$

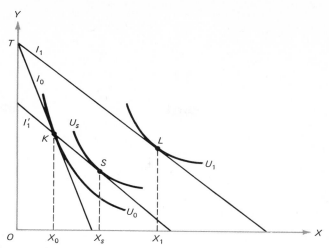

FIGURE 2-11 THE SLUTSKY SUBSTITUTION EFFECT
The price of X falls leading to a budget line rotation from I_0 to I_1. Income is confiscated, leading the new budget line to shift back until it passes through the initial equilibrium point K. An indifference curve U_s is tangent to I'_1 at point S. The corresponding movement from X_0 to X_s is the *Slutsky substitution effect*, and the movement from X_s to X_1 is the *Slutsky income effect*.

2.4j Short-Run and Long-Run Demand Curves

Short-run demand curves reflect the responsiveness of consumers to price changes in the short run. Although under normal conditions, the short-run demand curve is not different from the *long-run* (regular) demand curve, conditions may exist under which the consumer cannot respond in the short run as he or she intend to do in the long run. For example, in 1973 the price of gasoline rose dramatically; this is illustrated in Figure 2-12, where the price rises from P_0 to P_1. Assume that Carl had already bought a station wagon in 1972. It would not have been reasonable for him to replace it with a compact in 1973. So he responded to the price increase in the short run by economizing his driving habits and thus reducing his gasoline consumption from X_0 to X_s. Looking again at Figure 2-12, note that the pair P_1 and X_s is point S on his short-run demand curve D_s. In 1978, Carl bought a compact that further reduced his consumption of gasoline to X_e per unit of time. The pair P_1 and X_e is point L on his long-run demand curve D_e. Since Carl responded more drastically in the long run as compared with the short run, the long-run demand curve is more elastic than the short-run demand curve.

---

where η is the price elasticity of demand, $\bar{\eta}$ is the price elasticity of the compensated demand, K_x is the fraction of the budget the consumer spends on the good under consideration, and α is the income elasticity with respect to good X. By examining this formula, we can appreciate the fact that the income effect is small. As an example, if consumers devote only 3 percent of their budget to good X, then $K_x = 0.03$. If, in addition, $\bar{\eta} = -1$ and $\alpha = -2$, then $\eta = -1 - 0.03$ $(-2) = -0.94$. In other words, if K_x is relatively small, a good cannot be a Giffen good even if it is inferior.

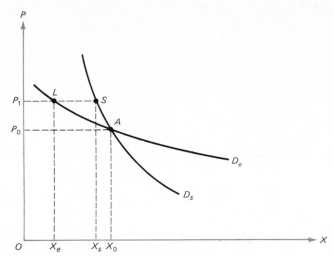

FIGURE 2-12   SHORT-RUN AND LONG-RUN DEMAND CURVES
The initial equilibrium of the consumer is depicted by A. The *regular demand curve*, which we also call the *long-run demand curve*, is denoted by D_e. If the price rises from P_0 to P_1, the consumer would like to lower his or her consumption from X_0 to X_e. But if there are difficulties in adjusting quickly, the consumer, in the short run, will lower his or her consumption to X_s units only. Connecting points like L (P_1, X_e) with A (P_0, X_0) traces out the regular (long-run) demand curve. Connecting points like S (P_1, X_s) with A traces out the short-run demand curve, D_s.

2.5 STATISTICAL DEMAND CURVES

Economics moves from logic to science only when its theories are confirmed by facts. Theoreticians do not have the obligation to confirm their own theories, but they have the responsibility to call the attention of others to the testable implications of their theories. For example, one economic theory asserts that indifference curves are negatively sloped and convex toward the origin. Chapter 1 pointed out that if this theory holds, consumers can be expected to spread their budgets on a variety of goods, rather than concentrate on a single commodity. This is a testable implication. Indeed, we observe that consumers do spread their budgets on a variety of goods, and thus the theory is confirmed. This chapter has developed an economic theory which claims that consumers respond to a decline in the price of a good by consuming more of that good. In other words, the demand curve is negatively sloped. In order to either confirm or refute the theory that demand curves are negatively sloped, we need to apply a special technique in mathematical statistics known as *econometrics*. In Chapter 18 the tools used by economists will be described in some detail. Here it is sufficient to mention that econometrics is an elaborate tool which is widely used by economists to estimate empirical economic functions such as demand functions. In addition to confirming theories, statistical demand curves are useful for private firms and governments. For example, sugar producers would like to know how much the demand for sugar will grow in the future. For this they need good estimates of income elasticities. Chapter 3 will illustrate how, given a

TABLE 2-3 Price Elasticity for Sugar, as Estimated by Schultz[10]

Period	Price elasticity
1875–1895	−0.38
1896–1914	−0.27
1915–1929	−0.31

statistical demand curve for electricity, a forecast about future demand is derived.

One of the earliest studies confirming the negative slopes of demand curves was conducted by Henry Schultz.[9] His book contained, for the first time, statistical estimates of the demand function for various agricultural goods. Since Schultz's pioneer work, economists have estimated a variety of demand functions for goods whenever the data were available.

Among other things, Schultz studied the demand for sugar for three periods. Table 2-3 presents some of his findings.

---

[9]Henry Schultz, *The Theory and Measurement of Demand,* University of Chicago Press, Chicago, 1938.

[10]Statistical demand curves are in most cases estimated in either linear form, logarithmic form, or (if time trend is present) semilogarithmic form. Linear demand curves could be of the form $X = a + bP + cI$ for cross-sectional data (data are for different groups of consumers at a point of time), or $X = a + bP + cI + dt$ for time-series data (data for the same group of consumers at different points in time). Note that elasticities are not constant for the linear demand curve. If the demand curve is linear, then at the X intercept price elasticity is zero, at the P intercept price elasticity is $-\infty$, and exactly at the midpoint between the two intercepts price elasticity is -1. [*Hint*: Use the form $\eta = (\Delta X / \Delta P) \cdot (P/X)$.] Nonlinear demand curves are usually of the form $X = aP^{\eta}I^{\alpha}$ for cross-sectional data and $X = aP^{\eta}I^{\alpha}e^{rt}$ for time-series data. Such nonlinear equations are estimated by transformation into natural logarithm forms such as $\ln(X) = \ln(a) + \eta \ln(P) + \alpha \ln(I) + rt$. The powers of P and I (η and α) are constant price and constant income elasticities, respectively. In other words, when such logarithmic forms are used (for mathematical convenience), we force upon the data the assumption of constant elasticities throughout. In time-series data the growth of demand over time is estimated by the rate r. Schultz estimated both linear and constant-elasticity forms of demand-for-sugar functions. The accompanying table provides a summary of his empirical demand functions. X stands for consumption of sugar per capita per year. P is price per pound in cents and t is time in years. The interpretation of the results of the linear equation in the second period, for example, is that an increase of 1 cent in the price of sugar would lead to a decline of 3.34 pounds of sugar consumed per capita. The time trend indicates a growth of 0.92 pound per year. The interpretation of the nonlinear form is that the price elasticity is -0.27 and that growth was occurring at an annual rate of 1.2 percent. Time does not appear in the third period because demand ceased to grow and reached its ceiling. Had Schultz estimated the demand curves for sugar today he might have introduced income per capita I as an explanatory variable.

Statistical Demand Curves for Sugar

Period	Linear form	Constant elasticity form
1875–1895	$X = 70.62 - 2.26P + 0.84t$	$X = 113.7P^{-0.38}e^{0.016t}$
1896–1914	$X = 92.90 - 3.34P + 0.92t$	$X = 117.5P^{-0.27}e^{0.012t}$
1915–1929	$X = 134.51 - 7.80P$	$X = 157.8P^{-0.31}$

Source: Henry Schultz, *The Theory and Measurement of Demand,* University of Chicago Press, Chicago, 1938.

The findings in Table 2-3, in addition to confirming that demand curves for sugar are negatively sloped, could be interpreted as saying that in the period 1875–1895 a 1 percent rise in the price of sugar would have induced consumers to reduce consumption of sugar by 0.38 percent, and so on.

2.6 THE EFFECT OF A CHANGE IN TASTES ON CONSUMERS' BEHAVIOR

So far the impact of changes in income, self-price, and the price of other goods on the consumption of a certain good has been discussed. In Section 2.3j, it was mentioned that *consumption* and *demand* are synonymous; hence we can summarize by saying that we investigated the impact of income and price changes on consumers' demand. So far we have assumed that *tastes* are unchanged throughout the analysis. We will relax the assumption that tastes are fixed.

Sometimes a change in tastes can be as important as changes in income and prices. As an example, consider cigarette smoking. In 1965, Congress enacted the Cigarette Labeling and Advertising Act, which required the printing of a health warning on cigarette packages. James Hamilton studied the impact of the "health scare" on smoking.[11] The results of this study are shown in Table 2-4. The effect of income and price was to increase consumption by 114 cigarettes: 124 (income) − 10 (price) = 114. The change in tastes led to a decline in consumption of 158 cigarettes: 95 (advertising) − 253 (scare effect) = −158. The effect of price and income was, by 44 cigarettes, *less* important than the change in tastes (114 − 158 = −44). The results of Table 2-4 are reproduced graphically in Figure 2-13. The original budget line is I_0, with equilibrium occurring at point E. A rise in the price of cigarettes rotates the budget line clockwise to position I_p. The new equilibrium is depicted by point P. The decline in consumption amounts to 10 cigarettes. Next, because of the rise in income (per capita), the budget line

TABLE 2-4 Cigarette Smoking
Change per capita per annum, 1964–1970

Change in		Quantity of cigarettes consumed
Income		124
Price		−10
Tastes		
Advertising effect	95	
"Health scare" effect	−253	
		−158
Net effect		−44

Source: James L. Hamilton, "The Demand for Cigarettes, Advertising, the Health Scare, and the Cigarette Advertising Ban," *The Review of Economics and Statistics,* vol. LIV, November 1972, pp. 401–411.

---

[11]James L. Hamilton, "The Demand for Cigarettes, Advertising, the Health Scare, and the Cigarette Advertising Ban," *The Review of Economics and Statistics,* vol. LIV, November 1972, pp. 401–411.

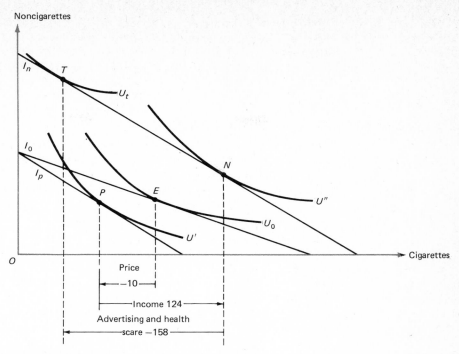

FIGURE 2-13   CHANGES IN PRICE, INCOME, AND TASTES

A rise in the price of cigarettes leads to a budget-line rotation from I_0 to I_p. Equilibrium changes from E to P and smoking per annum decreases by 10 cigarettes. Then income rises leading to a parallel shift of the budget line from I_p to I_n, accompanied by an equilibrium change from P to N. Since cigarettes are normal, smoking rises by 124 cigarettes per year. Finally, the net effect of advertising and the "health scare" (in favor of the latter) is to displace the entire indifference map (a change in tastes) leading to a tangency shift from N to T, which is the final point. This amounts to a reduction of smoking by 158 cigarettes.

shifts to I_n, which is parallel to I_p, and equilibrium shifts from point P to point N. Consumption increases by 124 cigarettes. Up to this point the indifference map has not changed. Curves U_0, U', and U'' reflect the initial tastes, and hence they belong to the same map. But the net impact of advertising and the "health scare" is a change in tastes leading to a new orientation of the entire indifference map. Such a shift in the map reflects an increasing distaste for smoking. Figure 2-13 does not show the entire new indifference map, but only a single new indifference curve, U_t, belonging to a new set. This single indifference curve is tangent to budget line I_n at point T. The shift from N to T reflects the change in tastes, leading to a decline in the consumption of cigarettes.

2.7 CONSUMER'S SURPLUS

To understand about the consumer's surplus, we must first consider what has become known as the *diamond-water paradox*. Water is essential for human survival; hence it is of utmost importance to people. Diamonds are not essential for survival; hence they are not very important to human beings. Yet the price of diamonds relative to water is very high. This paradox led the early classicists to reject utility as the apparatus for explaining value. The answer, of course, lies in the law of diminishing marginal utility: The more water we have available for use, the lower is the marginal utility of water. On the other hand, since diamonds are not abundant, the marginal utility of the last pound of diamonds is relatively very high. Recall that in equilibrium the marginal utility obtained from spending the last dollar on diamonds is the same as the marginal utility obtained from spending the last dollar on water. This relationship was summarized by Equation 1-3 as $MU_x/P_x = MU_y/P_y$. If X is diamonds and Y is water measured in pounds, we can rewrite Equation 1-3 as follows: $MU_x/MU_y = P_x/P_y$. Clearly the abundance of water and the relative rarity of diamonds makes MU_x very high relative to MU_y. Hence P_x must be very high relative to P_y in order to satisfy Equation 1-3. So what did the early classicists have in mind when they were misled by the usefulness of water relative to its price? They apparently had in mind the "all or nothing" proposition, which asks the consumer, "How much would you be willing to pay rather than go without water altogether?" Intuitively they felt that consumers would pay a lot rather than give up the consumption of water.

We can accordingly define the *consumer's surplus* as the amount of money a consumer would be willing to pay rather than go without a certain good altogether.

The intuitive process of estimating the monetary value of the consumer's surplus is illustrated in Figure 2-14. D_0 is the demand curve for water. For arithmetic simplicity, it is assumed to be a 45° line. When the price is $7, the consumer buys only one unit per unit of time. The utility which the consumer derives from the first unit is the same as the utility which he or she could obtain by spending the $7 alternatively on other goods. When the price falls to $6, the consumer could, if he or she wanted, continue to buy only one unit of water and thus get for $6 what was worth $7 to him or her. This is a surplus of utility, which is $7 minus $6, or $1. When the price falls to $5, he or she consumes three units of water per unit of time. The surplus of utility for the first unit is worth $7 − $5 = $2, and for the second unit it is worth $6 − $5 = $1. Altogether it is $3. When the price falls to $2, the surplus of utility is roughly estimated at $5 + $4 + $3 + $2 + $1 = $15, which is indicated by the shaded area. If we let units of water become smaller and smaller, the consumer's surplus becomes the area of the triangle indicated by points A, B, and C.

In Figure 2-15, D_w, the demand curve for water, occupies a position far to the right compared with D_d, the demand curve for diamonds. This shows that water is more important than diamonds. Since diamonds are rare (only X_d pounds are available), the price of diamonds is relatively high; it is $\overline{X_dC'}$. Since water is abundant (X_w pounds are available), its price is relatively very low; it is only $\overline{X_wC}$. However, the consumer's surplus on account of diamonds (the area of triangle $A'B'C'$) is small relative to the consumer's surplus on account of water (the area of triangle ABC.)

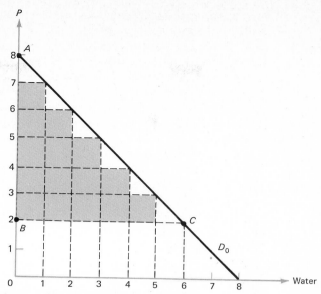

FIGURE 2-14 ESTIMATING THE CONSUMER'S SURPLUS

When the price is $7, the consumer buys 1 unit. After the price declines to $6, the consumer buys 2 units. Since the consumer indicates that for him or her the value of the first unit is $7, and actually he or she pays only $6, there is a gain of one dollar on the first unit ($7 − $6), which is called the consumer surplus. We continue to reduce the price dollar by dollar to $2. The *consumer's surplus* is the shaded area (for the first unit $7 − $2, for the second unit $6 − $2, and so on).

FIGURE 2-15 THE WATER-DIAMOND PARADOX

D_w denotes the demand for water. D_d denotes the demand for diamonds. Water is abundant (X_w) relative to diamonds (D_d); hence the price of water is lower ($\overline{X_w C}$) relative to the price of diamonds ($\overline{X_d C'}$). However, the consumer's surplus of water, the area of the triangle ABC, is larger than the consumer's surplus of diamonds, the area of the triangle $A'B'C'$. This is the solution to the water-diamond paradox.

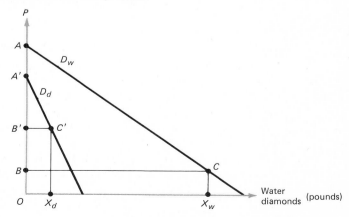

We note that the area of the triangle indicated by *ABC* in Figure 2-14 is the consumer's surplus for neutral (neither normal nor inferior) goods only. Otherwise the triangle is a close approximation of the true consumer's surplus. The advance approach to consumer's surplus involves a derivation using indifference curves and budget lines. We postpone this discussion until Chapter 4.

The concept of the consumer's surplus helped economists to get out of the water-diamond confusion. It will serve other purposes in succeeding chapters.

SUMMARY   In this chapter we investigated the response of consumers to changes in income and prices.

First, we considered the sensitivity of consumers to income changes. We have seen that when income increases, the consumer will consume more of most goods and less of some goods. This information was summarized by *Engel curves*. Goods were divided into two major groups: *normal goods*, of which the consumer consumes more when his or her income rises, and *inferior goods*, of which the consumer consumes less when his or her income rises and vice versa.

The *income elasticity* of Engel curves was defined as the relative change in consumption of a good over a small relative change in income. Income elasticity of an inferior good is negative and income elasticity of a normal good is positive. If income elasticity of a normal good is greater than 1, the good is classified as *ultrasuperior*.

Next, we examined the concept of *Engel expenditure curves*, in which quantities of commodities are replaced by expenditures on commodities. We noted that Engel expenditure curves allow us to consider *aggregates* of goods such as food and clothing.

Second, we considered the sensitivity of consumers to changes in prices of goods in the marketplace. We have seen that except in the rare case of a Giffen good, consumers will consume more of a good when its price falls and, conversely, consume less of it when its price rises. This information was summarized by *demand curves*.

We defined the *price elasticity* of demand curves as the relative change in consumption of a good over a small relative change in its price.

We then continued to disjoint the effect of a change in price on consumption into the *substitution effect* and the *income effect*. The substitution effect was derived by confiscating some of the consumers' income after the price of a good fell until he or she returned to an equilibrium point on his or her initial indifference curve. We stressed that in reality the income effect is negligible.

A *change in tastes* was defined as a displacement of the entire indifference map of the consumer. We stressed that a change in tastes may have a significant effect on the preferences of the consumer.

Finally, to explain how the *water-diamond* paradox was resolved, we discussed the *consumer's surplus*, which was defined as the amount of money a consumer would be willing to pay rather than go without a good altogether.

GLOSSARY **Elasticity** A concept used to describe responsiveness. If Y is functionally related to X, elasticity is the relative change in Y over a small relative change in X. Elasticity can be measured over an *arc* or at a *point*.

A change in real income A change in nominal income unaccompanied by a change in prices.

A change in relative price A change in the price of a good occurring when the prices of all other goods are kept unchanged.

The income consumption curve (ICC) The locus of all points of tangency between all possible budget lines and indifference curves in the X, Y space, where prices (nominal and relative) are kept unchanged.

The Engel curve A curve showing how the consumer responds in his or her consumption of a good to a change of his or her income. The Engel curve is obtained by mapping the ICC from the X, Y space to the X, I space.

Income elasticity The relative change in the consumption of a good over a small relative change in income. $\alpha = (\Delta X/X)/(\Delta I/I)$.

Inferior goods Goods with income elasticity less than zero.

Normal goods Goods with income elasticity between zero and 1.

Ultrasuperior goods Goods with income elasticity greater than 1. Ultrasuperior goods are also classified as normal goods with income elasticity greater than 1 (unity).

Engel expenditure curve The same as *Engel curve*, except that the physical amount of the good is replaced by the expenditures on the good. (X is replaced by $P_x \cdot X$.) Engel expenditure curves are particularly useful when *aggregates* of goods are studied.

The price consumption curve (PCC) The locus of all points of tangency between all budget lines that have a common intercept with the Y axis and indifference curves in the X, Y space. The family of all budget lines that have a common intercept with the Y axis is derived by varying the price of X and keeping unchanged nominal income and all prices of all other (non-X) goods.

The demand curve A curve showing how the consumer responds in his or her consumption of a good to a change in the price of the good. The demand curve is obtained by mapping the PCC from the X, Y space into the P, X space.

Price elasticity of demand The relative change in consumption of a good over a small relative change in the price of that good. $\eta = (\Delta X/X)/(\Delta P_x/P_x)$.

The degree of price elasticity of demand The demand curves are defined as being *price-inelastic* or *price-elastic* if their price elasticity (absolute value)—in an arc—is less than 1 or more than 1. The borderline case where the price elasticity is equal to 1 (absolute value) is known as a *demand curve of unitary elasticity*.

The substitution effect The change in consumption due to a change in price derived in principle by forcing the consumer to remain with his or her initial level of utility after the price of a good changes.

The income effect The total change in consumption minus the *substitution effect,* given a change in the price of a good.

A Giffen good An inferior good for which the *income effect* dominates the *substitution effect.* The slope of the demand curve of a Giffen good is positive.

Short-run demand curve A demand curve which is less elastic than the *regular* or the *long-run demand curve,* owing to difficulties in adjusting quickly to price changes.

Statistical demand curves Demand curves that are estimated empirically from data. Such demand curves are needed for confirming (or refuting) theories, and in order to enable policymakers (private and government) to forecast the demand for goods.

A change in tastes A displacement of the entire indifference map of a consumer.

The consumer's surplus The amount of money a consumer would be willing to pay rather than go without a good altogether. The *consumer's surplus* is approximated by measuring the area above the price line but below the demand curve.

PROBLEMS An asterisk indicates an advanced problem.

2-1.   A light bulb burns on average 10 hours a day. Its lifetime is 1000 hours of illumination. Define the *stock,* the *weekly flow,* and the frequency of changing the light bulb.

2-2.   Can two ICC (of the same consumer) intersect?

2-3.   Prove that a linear Engel curve for a normal good starting at the origin has unitary income elasticity.

2-4.   Which of the following four baskets belong to the same ICC?

Basket	X	Y	P_x	P_y	I
1	2	3	9	8	42
2	4	3	6	6	42
3	4	5.5	4.5	4	40
4	5	6	11	10	115

2-5.   Jane's income has increased from $24 to $26 a day. As a result she decreased her consumption of margarine by 2 percent. Calculate her (arc) income elasticity with respect to margarine.

2-6.   If your income elasticity with respect to potatoes is $-\frac{1}{2}$, by how much would you increase or decrease your demand for potatoes as a result of a 4 percent increase in your (real) income?

2-7. Show that if the consumer has more than one good in his budget, the *Engel expenditure curve* for any good X must lie below the *cross diagonal* (45° line) in the I, $(P_x \cdot X)$ space.

2-8. Income elasticity with respect to food is 0.50. Currently 20 percent of a consumer's income is spent on food. Show that after her income rises by 10 percent she devotes only 19 percent of her budget to food.

2-9. David has only three goods in his budget: they are bread, wine, and milk. The budget is allocated 20, 50, and 30 percent to bread, wine, and milk, respectively. What is the income elasticity of milk if the income elasticity of bread is 3 and of wine is −1?

2-10. Can two PCC (of the same consumer) intersect?

2-11. The price elasticity of demand for tomatoes is −¼. By what percentage will total revenue change as a result of a 16 percent decrease in the price of tomatoes?

2-12. Solve problem 2-11 again, with (a) price elasticity −1, and (b) price elasticity −4.

2-13. Your income is $100. The prices of goods A, B, C, and D are $10, $4, $3, and $1, respectively. Currently you consume 4, 5, 4, and 28 units of the above goods, respectively. As a result of a 20 percent decrease in the price of A, you increase your consumption of A by 50 percent, you consume 5.5 units of B, and you do not change your consumption of C. Will you change your consumption of D, and if so, by how much?

2-14. Explain (intuitively) why a Giffen good would be likely to occur only if the fraction of income which is spent on that good is very large.

2-15.* Show that if X is a normal good, then resulting from a decline in the price of X, the *Slutsky substitution* effect will exceed the *Hicksian substitution effect*.

2-16.* Prove that the price elasticity of a linear demand curve is equal to 0 at the quantity intercept, to $-\infty$ at the price intercept, and to −1 at the midpoint between the two intercepts.

2-17.* The price per drink at the faculty club is $1. The demand curve of Professor Smith is given by

$$X = 100 - 50 \cdot P$$

where X denotes the number of drinks per unit of time. What is the maximum lump-sum membership fee (per unit of time) that can be charged by the faculty club without losing the professor as a customer?

MATHEMATICAL APPENDIX 2

In Mathematical Appendix 1 necessary and sufficient conditions for utility maximization, subject to the budget constraint, were derived. In this Mathematical Appendix we devote our main effort to the derivation of the Slutsky equation, which separates the income from the substitution effect (Sections 2.4g, 2.4h, and 2.4i). In order to simplify the notations, the number of goods will be limited to three. The method applied to the case of three goods can be easily generalized to n goods.

M2.1 A CHANGE IN INCOME

In order to analyze the response of the consumer to a change in income, Equation m1-4 (for $n = 3$) is partially differentiated with respect to income I. We obtain

$$P_1 \frac{\partial X_1}{\partial I} + P_2 \frac{\partial X_2}{\partial I} + P_3 \frac{\partial X_3}{\partial I} = 1$$

$$-P_1 \frac{\partial \lambda}{\partial I} + u_{11} \frac{\partial X_1}{\partial I} + u_{12} \frac{\partial X_2}{\partial I} + u_{13} \frac{\partial X_3}{\partial I} = 0$$

$$-P_2 \frac{\partial \lambda}{\partial I} + u_{21} \frac{\partial X_1}{\partial I} + u_{22} \frac{\partial X_2}{\partial I} + u_{23} \frac{\partial X_3}{\partial I} = 0 \qquad \text{(m2-1)}$$

$$-P_3 \frac{\partial \lambda}{\partial I} + u_{31} \frac{\partial X_1}{\partial I} + u_{32} \frac{\partial X_2}{\partial I} + u_{33} \frac{\partial X_3}{\partial I} = 0$$

where $u_{ij} = \partial^2 u / (\partial X_i \partial X_j)$. From m1-5 we know that $P_i = u_i / \lambda$. Substituting u_i / λ for P_i, Equation m2-1 can be written as

$$\begin{vmatrix} 0 & u_1 & u_2 & u_3 \\ u_1 & u_{11} & u_{12} & u_{13} \\ u_2 & u_{21} & u_{22} & u_{23} \\ u_3 & u_{31} & u_{32} & u_{33} \end{vmatrix} \begin{vmatrix} -\dfrac{1}{\lambda} \cdot \dfrac{\partial \lambda}{\partial I} \\ \partial X_1 / \partial I \\ \partial X_2 / \partial I \\ \partial X_3 / \partial I \end{vmatrix} = \begin{vmatrix} \lambda \\ 0 \\ 0 \\ 0 \end{vmatrix} \qquad \text{(m2-2)}$$

Let the determinant of the 4×4 matrix of coefficients in Equation m2-2 be denoted by U. Let the cofactor of u_i be denoted by U_i and the cofactor of u_{ij} be denoted by U_{ij}. Solving for $\partial X_1 / \partial I$ by Cramer's rule gives

$$\frac{\partial X_1}{\partial I} = \frac{\lambda U_1}{U} \qquad \text{(m2-3)}$$

Since U_1 may be either positive or negative, $\partial X_1 / \partial I$ is also either positive or negative. Income elasticity is obtained by multiplying $\partial X_1 / \partial I$ by I/X_1, which is positive. By definition then, if $\partial X_1 / \partial I$ is positive, X_1 is a normal good. If $\partial X_1 / \partial I$ is negative, X_1 is an inferior good.

M2.2 A CHANGE IN PRICE

The response of the consumer to a change in the price of a good is obtained by partially differentiating Equation m1-4 ($n = 3$) with respect to the price of that good. Selecting X_1 to be the representative good, carrying out the differentiation, and then replacing P_i by u_i/λ give the following set of four equations in four unknowns:

$$
\begin{vmatrix}
0 & u_1 & u_2 & u_3 \\
u_1 & u_{11} & u_{12} & u_{13} \\
u_2 & u_{21} & u_{22} & u_{23} \\
u_3 & u_{31} & u_{32} & u_{33}
\end{vmatrix}
\begin{vmatrix}
-\dfrac{1}{\lambda}\dfrac{\partial \lambda}{\partial P_1} \\
\partial X_1/\partial P_1 \\
\partial X_2/\partial P_1 \\
\partial X_3/\partial P_1
\end{vmatrix}
=
\begin{vmatrix}
-\lambda X_1 \\
\lambda \\
0 \\
0
\end{vmatrix}
\qquad \text{(m2-4)}
$$

By Cramer's rule,

$$\frac{\partial X_1}{\partial P_1} = \lambda \frac{U_{11}}{U} - X_1 \frac{\lambda U_1}{U} \qquad \text{(m2-5)}$$

We identify in Equation m2-3, $\lambda \cdot U_1/U$ as $\partial X_1/\partial I$; hence Equation m2-5 can be written as a *Slutsky equation:*

$$\partial X_1 = \lambda \frac{U_{11}}{U} \partial P_1 - X_1 \cdot \partial P_1 \frac{\partial X_1}{\partial I} \qquad \text{(m2-6)}$$

Since $-X_1 \cdot \partial P_1$ is the change in apparent real income, the second term on the right side of Equation m2-6 is the change in apparent real income (Section 2.4i) times the marginal propensity to consume X_1. Thus this term is the Slutsky income effect. The first expression on the right side of Equation m2-6 must accordingly be the Slutsky substitution effect written as

$$\frac{\overline{\partial X_1}}{\partial P_1} = \lambda \frac{U_{11}}{U} \qquad \text{(m2-7)}$$

where $\overline{\partial X_1}/\partial P_1$ is the change in the quantity demanded for good X_1 per \$1 change in its own price, accounted for by the substitution effect only. Since the determinants in Equation m1-6 are alternatively positive and negative, U_{11}/U must be negative. (*Hint:* Rearrange the goods such that X_1 becomes X_3.) Saying that $\overline{\partial X_1}/\partial P_1$ is negative is equivalent to stating that the compensated demand curve must be negatively sloped.

Substituting Equation m2-7 into Equation m2-6, we obtain

$$\eta = \bar{\eta} - K_1 \alpha$$

where η is the self-price elasticity of X, $\bar{\eta}$ is the substitution portion of the price elasticity, K_1 is $(P_1 \cdot X_1)/I$, and α is income elasticity. Normally, K_1 is very small, and thus the income effect is negligible. The necessary condition for a Giffen good is that the good be inferior; i.e., $\alpha < 0$. The sufficient condition is that K_1 be so large that $|-K_1\alpha| > |\bar{\eta}|$. The chance that the sufficient condition and the necessary condition will be satisfied simultaneously is negligible.

C H A P T E R

AGGREGATE (MARKET) DEMAND AND DEMAND SHIFTS

In Chapter 2 we focused on the individual consumer's response first to changes in income and second to changes in prices in the marketplace. To sum up, the consumer changes the amount and mix of goods he or she consumes with any change in income, price, or taste. An increase in income will induce greater consumption of normal goods and less of inferior goods. On the other hand, a decrease in income will induce less consumption of normal goods and more of inferior goods. Moreover, a decrease in the relative price of a good will generally induce the consumer to consume more of that good; conversely, when the price of a good rises, the consumer will generally consume less of that good. Finally, we illustrated how a change in taste may lead a consumer to change his or her pattern of consumption. It must be evident that an individual demand for goods and services is not important per se, but it is important as a component of the demand of all individuals in the community, which is known as either the *aggregate demand* or the *market demand*.

Examples abound to convince the student that *aggregate demand* is an important tool of analysis. Succeeding chapters will include diverse illustrations, examples, and applications where aggregate demand is crucial. For instance: Adoption of medical insurance in the United States affected physician's incomes. To understand its impact on the welfare of physicians (and patients), we must study the impact of medical insurance on demand for physician services from the standpoint of the physicians. In discussing the "health scare effect" of the Cigarette Labeling and Advertising Act of 1965, we pointed to a significant change in consumer attitudes toward smoking. The study of the demand changes due to the "health scare effect" is of utmost importance to the cigarette industry. In 1966, the Roman Catholic church in the United States started allowing its followers to eat meat on Friday. Knowledge of the demand functions would have made it possible for both farmers and fishermen to assess their respective losses and gains. Chapter 10 will describe a sales tax that was increased by the City of New York during the 1950s and early 1960s. The city government was surprised to learn that a rise of one percentage point in the tax rate resulted in a $575 million loss of taxable sales. Had they taken time to study the elasticity of the demand curves of their constituents, keeping in mind that New York is surrounded by shopping areas in sales tax–free counties, they would have avoided the embarrassment of losing taxable sales. Most of the water (rights) in New Mexico is owned by farmers. They are interested in forecasting the future demand for water by the growing urban population. They want to know whether it is smart to sell some or all of their water now or to wait some time before selling. Demographers are currently studying the demand for children. They are interested in identifying the "price" of having children, the impact on children of having a higher level of income, and so on. Forecasting the populations of the future is of utmost importance to pension funds and to legislators concerned about social security taxes. In summary, it is hard to find a single economic issue in which market demand does not play a critical role.

The plan of this chapter is first to show how we aggregate all the individual demand curves in order to obtain the market demand curve, and second to analyze demand changes resulting from changes in prices, incomes of consumers, and populations.

3.1 THE PROCESS OF AGGREGATION

3.1a An Illustration of Aggregation

The aggregate demand curve is obtained by horizontally totaling all the demand curves of all consumers. Given that the price of X is P_{xo}, and given that at that price the first consumer would demand (consume) X_1 units of X, the second consumer would demand X_2 units of X, and so on up to the last consumer, who would demand X_n units of X, the aggregate demand is $X_1 + X_2 + \cdots + X_n$, or using the summation notation, it is simply

$$\sum_{i=1}^{n} X_i$$

Varying the price of X from zero to the highest likely price of X that might occur in the marketplace, and aggregating the consumption of X over all individuals for each price, yields the *aggregate*, or what we sometimes call the *market demand curve*.

To illustrate the process of aggregating individual demand curves, consider Sara and Jack, who want to get married. Figure 3-1, panel (*a*), shows Sara's demand curve for potatoes; Figure 3-1, panel (*b*), is Jack's demand for potatoes. Note that at prices of $3, $5, $7, and $10 per bushel, quantities consumed per week by Sara are 15, 9, 6, and 4 bushels, and by Jack 8, 6, 5,

FIGURE 3-1   AGGREGATING INDIVIDUAL DEMAND CURVES
The demand curves of Sara and Jack are presented in panels (*a*) and (*b*). The aggregate demand curve is derived in panel (*c*) by horizontally adding the two individual demand curves. For example, at a price of $5, 9 + 6 = 15.

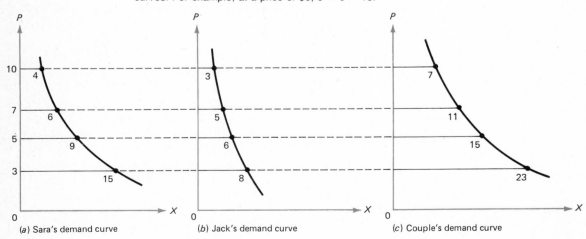

(*a*) Sara's demand curve   (*b*) Jack's demand curve   (*c*) Couple's demand curve

and 3 bushels, respectively. The process of horizontal aggregation yields the aggregate demand curve of the household, which is shown in panel (c): The household consumes 23, 15, 11, and 7 bushels per week at prices of $3, $5, $7, and $10 per bushel, respectively.

In principle, we can, in the same manner, derive the market demand curve for potatoes in the United States by horizontally totaling all the demand curves of potato consumers in the United States. A market demand curve for potatoes summarizes the functional relationship between the price of potatoes and the aggregate amount of potatoes bought per unit of time.

It should be clear from the way we derived the market demand curve that the individual demand curve possesses the same properties as the market demand curve. In reality, not all individuals follow the same pattern of behavior. Accordingly, we shall always refer to the *typical individual consumer* whenever we mention the *consumer*. As an example, if the short-run demand curve of the typical consumer is less elastic than his or her long-run demand curve, the short-run market demand curve is less elastic than the long-run market demand curve.

3.1b Price Elasticity of the Aggregate Demand Curve

If, as we stressed earlier, the market demand curve is of utmost importance to economists, its elasticity is crucial as a tool of analysis. The elasticity of the market demand curve is relevant not only as a measure of the sensitivity of all consumers to price changes but also where total revenue is an issue. As illustration, the so-called energy crisis was a blessing to the farm sector, since the demand for farm output is inelastic. That this is possible will become clear as we develop understanding of the relationship between price elasticity and total revenue yield along a market demand curve.

At this stage the student may want to review Sections 2.2 and 2.4f. The price elasticity of the aggregate demand curve is not basically different from the price elasticity of the individual demand curve as summarized in Equation 2-4. The only difference lies in what X represents: In the case of an individual demand curve, X stands for the consumption of an individual consumer. In the case of an aggregate demand curve, X stands for the summation of consumption over all the individuals in the market.

As mentioned before, the individual demand curve possesses the same properties as the aggregate demand curve. This implies that the price elasticity of the aggregate demand curve should somehow reflect the price elasticities of the individual demand curves. To illustrate how the individual elasticities influence the elasticity of the aggregate demand curve, let us denote Sara's and Jack's consumption of X by X_s and X_j, respectively. If the price of X changes by ΔP, the individual quantities demanded will change by ΔX_s and ΔX_j, respectively, leading to an aggregate change in the consumption of aggregate X which is equal to ΔX as follows:

$$\Delta X_s + \Delta X_j = \Delta X$$

If the above equation is multiplied by $P/(X \cdot \Delta P)$, we get

$$\frac{\Delta X_s \cdot P}{\Delta P \cdot X} + \frac{\Delta X_j \cdot P}{\Delta P \cdot X} = \frac{\Delta X \cdot P}{\Delta P \cdot X}$$

Following Section 2.2, the right-hand side of the above equation is the price elasticity of the aggregate demand; the two expressions on the left should be developed further. If we multiply Sara's expression by X_s/X_s and Jack's expression by X_j/X_j and rearrange, we get

$$\frac{X_s \cdot \Delta X_s \cdot P}{X \cdot \Delta P \cdot X_s} + \frac{X_j \cdot \Delta X_j \cdot P}{X \cdot \Delta P \cdot X_j} = \frac{\Delta X \cdot P}{\Delta P \cdot X}$$

since $X_s + X_j = X$, X_s/X is Sara's share and X_j/X is Jack's share in aggregate consumption. If we denote these shares by K_s and K_j, respectively, we can obtain the following important formula:

$$K_s \cdot \eta_s + K_j \cdot \eta_j = \eta \tag{3-1}$$

where η_s, η_j, and η are the price elasticities of Sara's demand, Jack's demand, and the aggregate demand. Equation 3-1 can be extended to n consumers. The interpretation of this equation is that the elasticity of the aggregate demand is the weighted average of the individual demand curves. The weights used in calculating the weighted average are the shares of the individual consumers (K_s, K_j, etc). As an illustration, consider Figure 3-1 again. Let us first calculate the arc elasticities for the range between a price of $5 and a price of $7:

Sara:

$$\eta_s = \frac{\dfrac{(6-9)}{7.5}}{\dfrac{(7-5)}{6}} = -1.2$$

Jack:

$$\eta_j = \frac{\dfrac{(5-6)}{5.5}}{\dfrac{(7-5)}{6}} = -0.545$$

Aggregate:

$$\eta = \frac{\dfrac{(11-15)}{13}}{\dfrac{(7-5)}{6}} = -0.923$$

If we consider the midpoints inside the arc, then $X_s = 7.5$, $X_j = 5.5$, and $X = 13$. Accordingly, we calculate K_s to be 0.577 (7.5/13) and K_j to be 0.423 (5.5/13). The weighted average of the two individual price elasticities is

$$0.577 \cdot (-1.2) + 0.423 \cdot (-0.545) = -0.923$$

This result confirms Equation 3-1.

3.2 PRICE ELASTICITY OF THE AGGREGATE DEMAND CURVE, TOTAL REVENUE, AND MARGINAL REVENUE

3.2a Total Revenue and Marginal Revenue

In Section 2.4f we defined total revenue as the price times the quantity demanded (consumed) by the individual consumer. Total revenue, which is related to the market demand curve, is the price times the aggregate quantity demanded (at that price) by all individual consumers. The term total revenue is somewhat misleading because what is total revenue to the producers of a product is total expenditures to the buyers of that product. But here we will use total revenue, which we denote by R. Formally total revenue is defined as

$$R = X \cdot P \tag{3-2}$$

The way in which total revenue varies when we move along a demand curve is related to another tool, known as *marginal revenue*. Marginal revenue is defined as the change in total revenue over a small change in the amount of the good consumed. If we denote marginal revenue by MR, the change in total revenue by ΔR, and the change in the quantity demanded (consumed) by ΔX, we obtain the following expression for marginal revenue:

$$\text{MR} = \frac{\Delta R}{\Delta X} \tag{3-3}$$

Consider Figure 3-2. As the price declines from P_0 to P_1, the quantity demanded increases from X_0 to X_1. This is a movement from point A to point B. We can divide the revenue change ΔR into two components: The first component is the rectangle covered with diagonal stripes. This area is a loss in revenue; it is the initial quantity demanded times the decline in the price, namely, $X_0 \cdot \Delta P$. The second component is the shaded rectangle. This area is a revenue gain; it is the additional quantity demanded times the new price, namely, $\Delta X \cdot P_1$. If the gain in revenue $\Delta X \cdot P_1$ exceeds the loss $X_0 \cdot \Delta P$, then ΔR is positive and so is MR. Conversely, if the gain falls short of the loss, ΔR is negative and so is MR. If we now imagine a movement along the demand curve in the opposite direction, from B to A, the analysis does not change, except that $\Delta X \cdot P_1$ becomes a loss and $X_0 \cdot \Delta P$ becomes a gain in revenue. Consider Figure 3-1 again. At a price of $7, Sara purchases 6 units. She spends $42. At a price of $5, she purchases 9 units, spending $45. When the price declines, Sara spends more money on the good under consideration. Now let us turn to Jack: At a price of $7, he purchases 5 units and spends $35. At a lower price of $5, he purchases 6 units and spends $30. When the price declines, Jack spends less money on the good under consideration. Recall from Section 3.1 that in the price range of $5 to $7, Sara's price elasticity was -1.2 and Jack's price elasticity was -0.545. We seem to have discovered the following relationship between price elasticity and total revenue: (1) *For an elastic demand curve:* Going down the demand curve (price falls, leading to a larger quantity demanded) results in a higher total revenue; going up the demand curve (price rises, leading to a smaller quan-

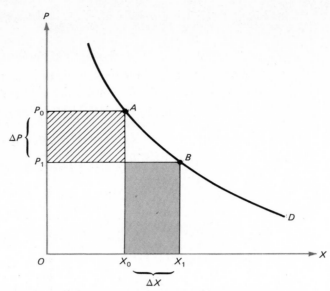

FIGURE 3-2 A GEOMETRIC ILLUSTRATION OF MARGINAL REVENUE
When we move from A to B, the price falls by ΔP and the quantity increases by ΔX. The loss in total revenue is the area with diagonal stripes, namely, $\Delta P \cdot X_0$. The gain in total revenue is the shaded area, namely, $\Delta X \cdot P_0$.

tity demanded) results in a lower total revenue. (2) *For an inelastic demand curve:* Going down the demand curve results in a lower total revenue: going up the demand curve results in a higher total revenue. It is left for the student to confirm this rule for the aggregate demand curve [Figure 3-1, panel (c)].

Let us now develop an important formula to help summarize the above relationship. Focus again on Figure 3-2. Let R_0, X_0, and P_0 denote original total revenue, original quantity demanded, and original price. Let R_1, X_1, and P_1 denote second total revenue, second quantity demanded, and second price.
Since

$$\Delta X = X_1 - X_0$$

and

$$\Delta P = P_1 - P_0$$

then

$$X_1 = X_0 + \Delta X$$

and

$$P_1 = P_0 + \Delta P$$

Now

$$R_0 = X_0 \cdot P_0$$

and

$$R_1 = X_1 \cdot P_1$$
$$= (X_0 + \Delta X)(P_0 + \Delta P)$$

Then
$$\Delta R = R_1 - R_0 = (X_0 + \Delta X) \cdot (P_0 + \Delta P) - X_0 \cdot P_0$$
$$= X_0 \cdot P_0 + X_0 \cdot \Delta P + \Delta X \cdot P_0 + \Delta X \cdot \Delta P - X_0 \cdot P_0$$
$$= X_0 \cdot \Delta P + \Delta X \cdot P_0 + \Delta X \cdot \Delta P$$

When the change in price is very small, the change in quantity demanded is also relatively small. Thus $\Delta X \cdot \Delta P$ is negligible and can be ignored. So

$$\Delta R = X_0 \cdot \Delta P + \Delta X \cdot P_0$$

Dividing through by ΔX, we obtain

$$\text{MR} = \frac{\Delta R}{\Delta X} = \frac{X_0 \cdot \Delta P + \Delta X \cdot P_0}{\Delta X}$$

$$= X_0 \frac{\Delta P}{\Delta X} + P_0$$

where MR stands for marginal revenue, as before. Factoring P_0 out and changing the order gives

$$\text{MR} = P_0 \left(1 + \frac{X_0 \cdot \Delta P}{P_0 \cdot \Delta X} \right) = P_0 \left(1 + \frac{1}{\eta} \right) \qquad (3\text{-}4)$$

We are now ready to prove the relationship between total revenue and price elasticity by utilizing Equation 3-4. For this, consider the three cases of price elasticity (recall from Section 2.4f that $|\eta|$ is the absolute value of η; namely, it is η without its negative sign).

1. *Elastic demand curves.* As $|\eta|$ is larger than unity, $1/|\eta|$ is smaller than unity. Since $1 + 1/\eta = 1 - 1/|\eta|$, and since one minus a number smaller than unity is positive, we conclude that the expression $1 + 1/\eta$ is positive. Marginal revenue, which is price times this expression, must be positive, too. A positive marginal revenue means that total revenue increases when quantity demanded increases and decreases when quantity demand decreases. *Example:* Let $P_0 = \$10$ and $\eta = -2$. MR $= \$10 \cdot [1 + 1/(-2)] = \$5$. Therefore, one additional unit sold in the market would increase total revenue by \$5, and conversely, one unit less sold in the market would reduce total revenue by \$5.

2. *Unitary elasticity.* As $|\eta|$ is equal to unity, $1 - 1/|\eta|$ is equal to zero. Thus marginal revenue is zero. *Example:* If $P_0 = \$10$ and $\eta = -1$, MR $= \$10 \cdot [1 + 1/(-1)] = \$0$. Moving along the demand curve would not induce any change in total revenue.

3. *Inelastic demand curve.* As $|\eta|$ is smaller than unity, $1/|\eta|$ is larger than unity, and the expression $1 - 1/|\eta|$ must be negative. We conclude that marginal revenue must be negative. A negative marginal revenue means that total revenue decreases when quantity demanded increases and increases when quantity demanded decreases. *Example:* $P_0 = \$10$ and $\eta = -1/2$. MR $= \$10 \cdot [1 + 1/(-1/2)] = -\$10$.

In Table 3-1 we summarize the above findings. A *rise, no change,* and a *fall* in total revenue are denoted by a $+$, 0, and $-$, respectively.

TABLE 3-1   Changes in Total Revenue along the Demand Curve

	Demand curve		
	Inelastic	Unitary elasticity	Elastic
Moving down along the demand curve	−	0	+
Moving up along the demand curve	+	0	−

In the following example we shall demonstrate the importance of the price elasticity of market demand.

3.2b Case Study: Price Elasticity and Fluctuations in Farm Income

A certain fixed quantity of output per unit of time is dumped in the marketplace. This fixed quantity is denoted by X_0 in Figure 3-3. If we trace a vertical line from X_0 to point A on the demand curve D, we find the magnitude of the price which will clear the market; this price is P_0. The reason for this is simple: At a higher price of, say, P_1, producers who bring to the marketplace X_0 units of X will find out that the market clears only X_1 units and hence that they are stuck with inventories of unsold merchandise accumulating at a rate of $X_0 - X_1$ per unit of time. Since inventories are costly to handle, sellers will reduce the price until inventories are no longer accumulating. Conversely, at a lower price of, say, P_2 producers will find out that their inventories vanish and some customers who cannot buy all they want at such a low price are offering to pay higher prices. Such pressures from customers will induce the sellers to raise the price to P_0. The price of P_0 is known as the *clearing price,* namely, the price at which whatever is brought into the marketplace by producers (sellers) is taken away by customers.

The demand for farm output is price-inelastic at the farm level. Farm output is the aggregate of all farm products, as discussed in Section 2.3g. The price of farm output is the average of prices of all commodities sold by farmers.[1] With this introduction we are ready to describe the dilemma of fluctuations in farm income.

During the period 1973–1974, farmers in the United States were content with the free market. This was true in spite of the so-called energy crisis. But in 1976–1978, those farmers took their tractors to the streets and protested low prices. They threatened that unless they got a huge price support from the government, they would not plant and thus would deprive the population of essential food.

---

[1]These averages are *index numbers.* The reader who is interested in more than the intuitive appeal is referred to Chapter 4.

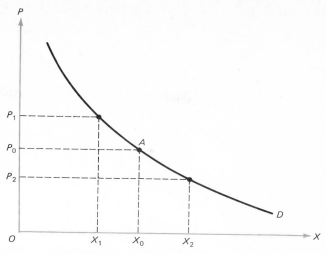

FIGURE 3-3   FIXED QUANTITIES DUMPED IN THE MARKETPLACE

An amount of X_0 units of output (per unit of time) is brought into the marketplace. At a price of P_1 only X_1 will be taken by consumers. Producers will get stuck with an inventory which will accumulate at a rate of $X_0 - X_1$ per unit of time. This will induce them to lower the price to a level of P_0. At a price of P_2 consumers would want to buy X_2 units. Since only X_0 units are available, inventories will dwindle, and producers will raise the price to P_0 in order to build up their inventories to the normal level.

Economists have recognized two main problems related to this farm issue. First, there are long-run adjustments having to do with the long-run adjustment of supply and demand for food. For example, population growth affects the long-run increase of the demand curve for food; technological changes affect the long-run growth of food supply. The issue of the long run will be discussed in Chapter 9. Second, there are short-run problems related to the market for farm produce.

Farm output is sensitive to weather conditions; favorable weather conditions result in good crops. But since the demand is price-inelastic, good crops lead to low farm revenue. To simplify our analysis, we assume that in the short run farmers dump on the market whatever they produce in a certain season (or year). Actually, this is only approximately correct. *Future markets* will be discussed in Chapter 10, where we will see that in the case of a nonperishable commodity the impact of a glut on the market in a certain year will, to some extent, spread into the future. For now, however, consider Figure 3-4. If farmers dump on the market a quantity X_n denoting a "normal" crop, the price they can command in the marketplace is P_n. If weather conditions are favorable, the quantity dumped in the market is X_h, and the price becomes P_h. Finally, if weather conditions are unfavorable, the quantity dumped on the market is X_l, and price becomes P_l. The total revenues of the three cases associated with points L, N, H on the demand curve are R_l ($= X_l P_l$) for unfavorable weather conditions, R_n ($= X_n P_n$) for normal weather conditions, and R_h ($= X_h P_h$) for favorable weather conditions.

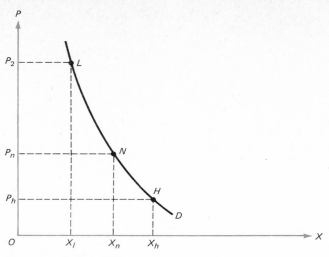

FIGURE 3-4 FLUCTUATIONS IN FARM OUTPUT

The demand curve D is inelastic. Bad, normal, and good weather conditions would result in farm outputs of X_l, X_n, and X_h, respectively. Total revenue resulting from bad weather conditions (L) will exceed total revenue resulting from normal weather conditions (N), and so on.

Clearly, since the demand curve for farm output is inelastic, R_l is higher than R_n, and R_n is higher than R_h. That is to say, farmers would benefit from unfavorable weather conditions as compared with favorable weather conditions.

An increase in exports means a rightward shift in the demand for farm output. To understand why this is true, go back to Figure 3-1. Assume that Sara's demand for potatoes represents the domestic demand and Jack's demand represents the foreign demand, which is exports. Producers of potatoes perceive the aggregate demand curve as drawn in panel (c). If Jack's demand for potatoes increases, that is, at each price he wants to consume more potatoes, his demand curve will shift to the right. In other words, exports will increase, leading also to a rightward shift in the aggregate demand in panel (c). Let us consider Figure 3-5. Because of, say, drought in India, the aggregate demand for American farm output increases, leading to a rightward shift from D_0 to D_1. We again simplify our analysis by assuming that farmers dump on the market a quantity denoted by X_0. If we trace a vertical line to point A on the demand curve, we conclude that the clearing price must be P_0. The increases in exports lead to a shift in the demand curve from D_0 to D_1. At a price of P_0 farmers face a deterioration of inventories: The quantity demanded is X_1 (movement from A to C), meaning that there is pressure to raise the price. The new clearing price is discovered by tracing a vertical line from X_0 to a new point B lying on the new demand curve D_1. The new price is P_1, and since the demand is price-inelastic, we know that the percentage rise in the price (from P_0 to P_1) will exceed the percentage increase in the demand (from X_0 to X_1). The change in the price resulting from the demand shift is calculated by applying the formula of price

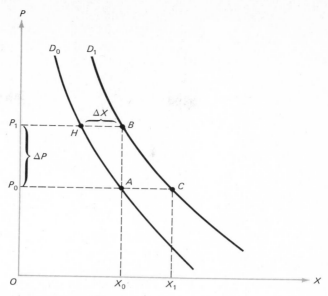

FIGURE 3-5 THE EFFECT OF FARM EXPORTS
Initially X_0 units of farm output are sold in the marketplace at a price of P_0. Due to the sale of exports the demand shifts from D_0 to D_1. As a result the price received by farmers rises to P_1, sufficient to shrink domestic consumption by $\Delta X (=\overline{BH})$, which is the amount exported. The change in the price is calculated as $\Delta P/P = (\Delta X/X)/\eta$.

elasticity, $\eta = (\Delta X/X)/(\Delta P/P)$; ΔX is interpreted as the movement from B to H, and ΔP is interpreted as the movement from A to B. We can write it as $\Delta P/P = (\Delta X/X)/\eta$. Recall from Section 2.4f (Equation 2-4) that $\Delta X/X$ is the percentage change in quantity demanded and $\Delta P/P$ is the percentage change in price. Then, for example, if increased exports shifted demand 10 percent to the right, given a price elasticity of $-1/2$, the change in price received by farmers in the marketplace is calculated as

Change in price received by farmers =

$$\frac{\text{percentage change in quantity demanded}}{\eta} = \frac{-10 \text{ percent}}{-1/2} = 20 \text{ percent}$$

We can read the result as follows: Since the demand is inelastic, the price of farm output has to increase 20 percent (from A to B) in order to shrink domestic consumption by 10 percent (from B to H); this fall of domestic consumption by 10 percent enables foreigners to purchase ΔX ($= \overline{HB}$) units of food from farmers.[2]

Now let us look at the situation of the farmers in the United States between 1968 and 1978. During the period 1968–1972 real realized annual

---

[2]This result is only approximately correct. If we assume constant elasticity of demand, namely, $X = k \cdot P^\eta$, then for $\eta = -0.5$ a 10 percent demand shift will lead to a 21 percent price rise.

farm income[3] averaged $12 billion. In 1973, realized net farm income rose to $22 billion and in 1974 to $19 billion. During the period 1968–1972 annual farm exports averaged slightly over $6 billion. In 1973, real farm exports rose to almost $10 billion, and in 1974 exports reached a peak of $14 billion. During 1973 and 1974 farmers reaffirmed their allegiance to the free market system. In 1975–1977, however, farm exports started to fall while output increased. Realized net real farm income fell from $19 billion in 1974 to $13 billion in 1975 and 1976. Thus in 1977, farmers took to the streets demanding that the government intervene in the market and provide a high price support.

3.3 AGGREGATE DEMAND SHIFTS

In Section 3.2 we introduced a demand shift which resulted from a rise in the level of exports. We are now ready to formalize the theory of demand shifts to help organize our thinking about problems involving changes in individual incomes, prices, and population. It is important to note the distinction between a *change in demand* and a *change in quantity demanded*. A change in aggregate demand for a good is caused by a change in either population or individual income or prices of other goods or tastes. Such changes in demand are described geometrically as demand shifts. A change in (aggregate) quantity demanded is caused by a change of the price of the good under consideration. Such a change is described geometrically as a movement along the demand curve. The distinction between *demand shifts* and *moving along demand curves* stems from organizational convenience.

3.3a The Process of Aggregation and the Effect of Population Change

In Western Europe there are countries in which populations are at a *steady state*; that is, they are neither growing nor falling over time. In such countries the impact of population changes on market demand is not an issue. In the United States the rate of population growth is currently around 1 percent per year. In many developing countries the rate of population growth is over 2 percent per year. In such countries the effect of population on aggregate demand cannot be ignored. In fact, in some developing countries lowering the rate of population growth is the key for economic progress.

Let us now return to Figure 3-1. Assume that the population consists of two members only, Sara and Jack. We use this trivial example to bring out some technical relationships between the individual demand curve and the aggregate demand curve.

At a price of $5 Sara demands 9 units and Jack demands 6 units. Together

---

[3]Real income, as defined in Section 2.3a, is distinct from nominal income. If, for example, *net income* increases by 50 percent, but during the relevant period the *general price level* rises by 20 percent, then *real farm* income rises by only 25 percent (150/120). The general price level is a *price index*. The theory of *price indices* is presented in Chapter 4.

they demand 15 units. If each demand increases by 20 percent, that is, Sara increases her demand by 1.8 units and Jack by 1.2 units, aggregate demand increases by 3 units, which is also 20 percent of 15 units. Moreover, assume that Sara increases her demand by 1 unit and Jack by 2 units, then on average the *typical consumer* increases consumption of the good by 20 percent (= 1.5/7.5); aggregate consumption also increases by 20 percent. To summarize:

> *Ceteris paribus,*[4] *the aggregate demand curve will shift by the same percentage as the typical individual demand curve.*

Next, let us examine the situation where the conditions affecting individual consumer behavior do not change, but population does change. Assume that Bonnie joins the community of Sara and Jack. Following our assumption that on the average those who join the existing population are not different in their tastes, we assume that Bonnie's demand curve is an average of Sara's and Jack's. In particular, at a price of $5 Bonnie consumes 7.5 units. We note that a population growth of 50 percent (½) led to a proportional change in demand of 50 percent (7.5/15). Because of the population change of 50 percent the aggregate demand shifts 50 percent. To summarize:

> *Ceteris paribus, the aggregate demand curve will shift by the same percentage as the percentage change in population.*

We are now ready to discuss the various changes in factors such as individual income and prices of other goods that give rise to changes in individual demand curves and hence to changes in the aggregate demand curve.

3.3b Demand Shifts due to Changes in Incomes

We derived the demand curve by mapping the PCC into a quantity-price relationship (Figure 2-6). Since a change in income would lead to a parallel shift in all budget lines, the PCC must be displaced too. Therefore, any change in income would lead to a corresponding shift in the demand curve. The association between the displacement of the PCC and the shift in the demand curve is pictured in Figure 3-6. We assume that good X is normal. The geometry of an inferior good is left for the student to determine. Income rises from a low level to a relatively high level. In panel (a), we first consider a low level of income I and two prices: A price of P_{x0} and a relatively lower price of P_{x1}. The price of Y is held constant at P_{y0}. The intercept with the Y axis does not change ($\overline{OT} = I/P_{y0}$). As the price of X falls from P_{x0} to P_{x1}, the budget line rotates from I_0 to I_1 (the X intercept moves from $\overline{OA} = I/P_{x0}$ to $\overline{OB} = I/P_{x1}$). The two points of equilibrium (tangency between budget lines and indifference curves) are K and L. The points K and L are mapped into

---

[4]*Ceteris paribus* means "all things are kept constant." In this instance it means population is constant.

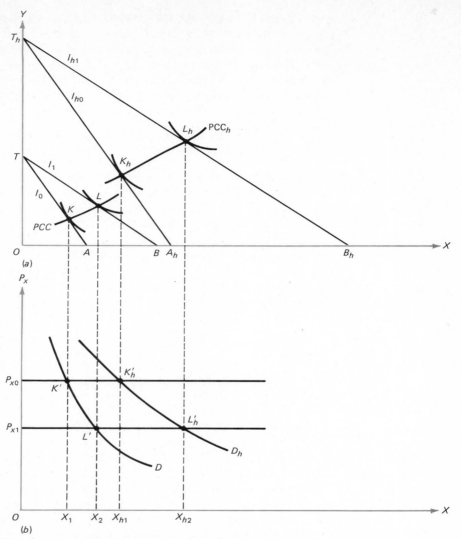

FIGURE 3-6 A DEMAND SHIFT DUE TO A CHANGE IN INDIVIDUAL INCOME
In panel (a) there are two PCC's: PCC which corresponds to a relatively low level of income and PCC$_h$ which corresponds to a relatively high level of income. ($\overline{OT} = I/P_{y0}$, and $\overline{OT}_h = I_h/P_{y0}$). The two PCC's are mapped into two demand curves in the P_x, X space in panel (b). Since X is assumed to be a normal good, D_h lies to the right of D.

K' and L' in panel (b). Demand curve D passing through K' and L' is the image of the PCC. Next we let income rise to a higher level of I_h. The intercept with the Y axis now shifts from T to T_h. ($\overline{OT}_h = I_h/P_{y0}$.) The new budget line, I_{h0} ($\overline{OA}_h = I_h/P_{x0}$), is parallel to the initial budget line, I_0. The new budget line, I_{h1} ($\overline{OB}_h = I_h/P_{x1}$), is parallel to the initial budget line, I_1. This time the points of equilibrium are K_h and L_h. The curve passing through K_h and L_h is denoted by PCC$_h$, and it is the PCC associated with a higher level of individual income. Points K_h and L_h are mapped into K_h' and L_h', and D_h is the image of PCC$_h$. It is a demand curve associated with a relatively higher level of income. Since by assumption X is normal, K_h must lie to the right of K and L_h must lie to the right of L. Correspondingly, K_h' must lie to the right of K' and L_h' must lie to the right of L'. Thus the new demand curve, D_h, occupies a position to the right of D. If income declines [panel (a)], the associated demand will shift leftward from D_h to D. We can summarize:

A rise in the income of the individual will lead to a rightward shift in his or her demand for a normal good. Conversely, a fall in the income of the individual will lead to a leftward shift in his or her demand for a normal good. If the individual is typical, the percentage shifts in the market (aggregate) demand curve will be identical with the percentage shift of his or her demand curve.

In the case of an inferior good the shifts are in the opposite direction: A rise in income leads to a leftward shift in demand, and conversely, a fall in income leads to a rightward shift in income.

Consider the following example: At a price of P_{x0} [panel (b) of Figure 3-6] Bonnie consumes 10 whatnots per week. By how much will her demand for whatnots change if her income rises from \$90 to \$110 per week and her income elasticity with respect to whatnots is known to be 0.5? The solution is as follows: Equation 2-2 states that $\alpha = (\Delta X/X)/(\Delta I/I)$, where α is income elasticity, X is consumption of whatnots, and I is Bonnie's income. We can rewrite Equation 2-2 as $\Delta X/X = \alpha(\Delta I/I)$. Since the change from \$90 to \$110 amounts to 20 percent, we can solve for the percentage change in demand as follows:

Percentage change in demand = $0.5 \cdot 20$ percent = 10 percent

In other words, a 20 percent change in Bonnie's income led to a 10 percent rightward shift in her demand for whatnots (which is equal to one whatnot).

If whatnots are inferior and $\alpha = -0.5$, the demand curve would shift 10 percent to the left [$(-0.5) \cdot 20$ percent]. (Bonnie would consume 9 whatnots.)

We stated that the demand curve shifted by 10 percent to the right at a price level of P_{x0}. Income elasticity does not have to be equal to 0.5 at a price level of P_{x1}. It may be different. Thus a 20 percent increase in Bonnie's income coupled to a price of P_{x1} might result in a different percentage shift. However, for reasonably small price ranges we normally assume that the same value of income elasticity exists. *Note:* If gross national product (GNP) increases at an annual rate of 6 percent, population increases at a rate of 2 percent, and income elasticity is 0.5, we first calculate the change in income per capita as being 6 percent $-$ 2 percent = 4 percent. (See Footnote 5 in Chapter 2.) Then the shift in demand is 2 percent because of population change and $0.5 \cdot 4$ percent = 2 percent because of the change in income per capita (Equation 2-2: $\Delta X/X = \alpha(\Delta I/I)$.

3.3c Demand Shifts due to Changes in Prices of Other Goods

In Section 2.4d we mentioned the sensitivity of the consumer to changes in prices of other goods. When the price of tomatoes rises, some consumers respond by consuming more cucumbers; when the price of beef falls, some consumers decrease their consumption of poultry; when the price of natural gas rises, some consumers buy equipment to collect solar energy; when the price of gasoline rises, some consumers buy smaller cars. The importance of this relationship between demand for goods and price variations of other goods cannot be exaggerated: A car manufacturer who failed to perceive the demand shift from full-sized cars to compact cars following the rise in gasoline prices suffered a famine; European manufacturers of compact cars had a feast.

From experience we know that margarine and butter and chicken and turkey are *pairs of substitutes*. On the other hand, coffee and cream, tea and sugar, and bread and butter are *pairs of complements*. The crude rule that we apply in order to test whether two goods are substitutes or complements with respect to each other is: *Ceteris paribus*, when the price of a good falls, a consumer buys more of the good itself, less of its *substitute*, and more of its *complement*.

We will first assume that X and Y are substitute goods. We will start with demand curve D, which is derived from the PCC in panel (a) of Figure 3-7. In panel (a) budget line I_0 reflects a price (of X) of P_{x0}, and I_1 reflects a relatively lower price (of X) of P_{x1}. The two equilibrium points between these budget lines and the relevant indifference curves are K and L, respectively. We then transform K and L into K' and L' in panel (b). Suppose the price of Y rises above the original price of P_{y0}. As a result the Y intercept shrinks from $\overline{OT}$ to $\overline{OT^*}$. (The superscript * will denote a higher price of good Y.) The new budget lines are I_0^* ($\overline{T^*A}$) and I_1^* ($\overline{T^*B}$). The new optimum baskets are K^* and L^*, respectively. Since X and Y are substitutes, K^* lies to the right of K and L^* lies to the right of L. PCC* is obtained by passing a curve through points like K^* and L^*. The demand curve associated with PCC* is D^*. In summary, we observe that a rise in the price of Y gave rise to a shift to the right in the demand curve for X, which is a substitute good.

Before we extend these results to the case of two complements, we should pause. We cannot use a two-dimensional diagram to analyze two complement goods, because if there are only two goods in the budget of the consumer, they must be related to each other as substitutes. The correct rule that must be applied is to ask if a fall in the price of one good leads to a *decrease* in the consumption of the other good when only the (Hicksian) substitution effect counts. Looking at Figure 2-9, we see that this is actually a movement from K to H (rather than from K to L). Clearly, since such a movement is nothing more than scalloping an indifference curve (U_0) which is negatively sloped and convex toward the origin, the consumption of one good must fall as the consumption of the other rises. Being aware that the substitution effect is by far more important than the income effect, we can conclude that since X and Y in Figure 3-7 are substitutes, the demand for X must increase because of a rise in the price of Y. Conversely, had we started the analysis with a relatively high price of Y and then let it drop to a lower level, the demand for X would have shifted in panel (b) leftward from D^* to D.

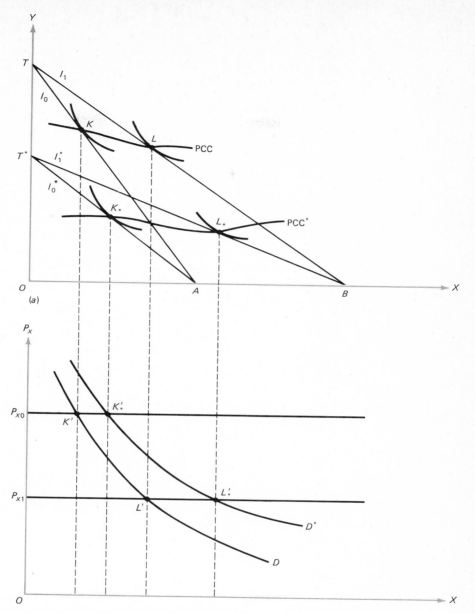

FIGURE 3-7 A SHIFT IN THE DEMAND FOR X DUE TO A CHANGE IN THE PRICE OF Y
Initially the price consumption curve is PCC in panel (a). After the price of Y rises we obtain a new PCC, namely PCC*. The two PCC's are mapped into two associated demand curves in the P_x, X- space in panel (b). The demand curve D^* associated with a higher price of Y lies to the right of D, because X and Y are substitutes.

We can extend the rules derived for demand shifts due to changes in the price of a substitute good to the case of complementarity. Dick has three goods in his budget, X (tea), Y (coffee), and Z (cream). Let us assume he adds cream to coffee but not to tea. Thus Y and X are a pair of substitutes and Y and Z a pair of complements. As the price of coffee (Y) rises, Dick consumes less coffee, more tea (X), and less cream (Z). Looking at Figure 3-8, we see that when the price of coffee increases from P_{y0} to P_{y1}, the quantity demanded for coffee decreases from Y_0 to Y_1; the demand for tea increases, shifting the demand curve for tea to the right, and as a result the consumption of tea increases from X_0 to X_1; the demand for cream decreases, shifting the demand curve for cream to the left, and as a result the consumption of cream decreases from Z_0 to Z_1.

In summary, given a rise in the price of a good, we would expect a rightward shift in demand curves of substitutes and a leftward shift in demand curves of complements. Conversely, given a fall in the price of a good, we would expect a leftward shift in demand curves of substitutes and a rightward shift in demand curves of complements.

3.3d Cross Price Elasticities

Cross price elasticity, which is sometimes called just *cross elasticity*, measures the responsiveness of the consumption of a good, given a change in the price of another good. To put it differently, it is the percentage change in the demand of one good, per 1 percent change in the price of another good. Following Section 2.2, we state the cross elasticity of X with respect to the price of Y as follows:

FIGURE 3-8 AN ILLUSTRATION OF SUBSTITUTES AND COMPLEMENTS
In panel (a) the price of coffee rises, leading to a movement in the northwesterly direction along D_{y0}. In panel (b) the result is a rightward shift in the demand for the substitute good, tea. In panel (c) the demand curve for a complement, cream, shifts to the left.

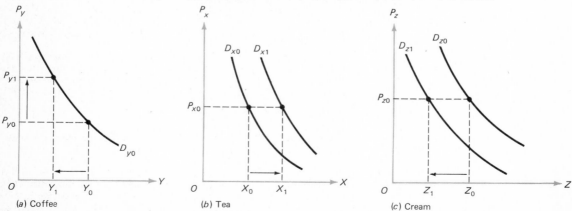

$$\eta_{xp_y} = \frac{\dfrac{\Delta X}{X}}{\dfrac{\Delta P_y}{P_y}} = \frac{\text{percentage change in the demand for } X}{\text{percentage change in the price of } Y} \qquad (3\text{-}5)$$

Cross elasticity is positive if the two goods are substitutes (Y and X in Figure 3-8) and negative if the two goods are complements (Y and Z in Figure 3-8). In Figure 3-8 a rise in the price of coffee induces a positive change in the consumption of tea, hence the positive sign of the cross elasticity when the two goods are substitutes; a rise in the price of coffee induces a negative change in the consumption of cream, hence the negative sign of cross elasticity when two goods are complements. As an example consider a situation in which the price of coffee rises from \$3 to \$5, and as a result consumption of tea increases from 6 to 7 units per unit of time, while the consumption of cream decreases from 11 to 9 units per unit of time. The cross elasticities are estimated as follows:

$$\eta_{xp_y} = \frac{\dfrac{\Delta X}{X}}{\dfrac{\Delta P_y}{P_y}} = \frac{\dfrac{7-6}{6.5}}{\dfrac{5-3}{4}} = \frac{15.38 \text{ percent}}{50 \text{ percent}} = 0.31$$

$$\eta_{zp_y} = \frac{\dfrac{\Delta Z}{Z}}{\dfrac{\Delta P_y}{P_y}} = \frac{\dfrac{9-11}{10}}{\dfrac{5-3}{4}} = \frac{-20 \text{ percent}}{50 \text{ percent}} = -0.4$$

Finally, a demand shift due to a change in the price of other goods may be disjointed into *income* and *substitution* effects exactly in the same manner as

---

[5]In Mathematical Appendix 3 a formula for cross elasticity is proved; it can be written as

$$\eta_{xp_y} = \bar{\eta}_{xp_y} - K_y \cdot \alpha_x$$

where $\bar{\eta}_{xp_y}$ is the cross price elasticity when only the substitution effect is counted. K_y is the fraction of the budget of the consumer devoted to good Y and α_x is income elasticity with respect to good X. If Y and X are substitutes, $\bar{\eta}_{xp_y}$ is positive. If X is inferior, α_x is negative and the expression $-K_y \cdot \alpha_x$ is also positive.

If X is normal, α_x is positive and $-K_y \cdot \alpha_x$ is negative. Hence the substitution effect (represented by $\bar{\eta}_{xp_y}$) and the income effect (represented by $-K_y \cdot \alpha_x$) might work at cross purposes. However, we can count on the smallness of K_y to ensure that the substitution effect will dominate. *Example*: $\bar{\eta}_{xp_y} = 2$. $K_y = 0.03$. $\alpha_x = 2$. The value of the cross elasticity is calculated as follows:

$$\eta_{xp_y} = 2 - 0.03 \cdot 2 = 1.94$$

If the two goods are complements, the formula is the same. Assume that Y and Z are the two complements, we then write

$$\eta_{zp_y} = \bar{\eta}_{zp_y} - K_y \cdot \alpha_z$$

where $\bar{\eta}_{zp}$ is the cross price elasticity for two complements when only the substitution effect counts. $\bar{\eta}_{zp}$ is negative. If Z is normal, α_z is positive and hence $-K_y \cdot \alpha_z$ is also negative. If Z is inferior, α_z is negative and hence $-K_y \cdot \alpha_z$ is positive, and the substitution effect and the income

the change in quantity demanded due to a change in self-price was disjointed into *income and substitution effects* (Section 2.4g).[5] The income effect is very small compared with the substitution effect; thus it can be ignored for all practical matters.

3.3e An Example: Substitution of Hospital Outpatient Care for Inpatient Care

Expenditures for medical care accounted for 4.8 percent of the income of urban wage earners and clerical workers in 1952. In 1977, this figure was 6.9 percent. Medical care professionals have maintained that economic factors do not influence medical decisions. Some studies, however, indicate that consumers are sensitive to prices of medical services. Karen Davis and Louise B. Russel studied the responsiveness of consumers to prices of outpatient and inpatient care.[6] A demand function for outpatient and inpatient visits was empirically estimated by employing cross-sectional data for 48 states for 1969.

The cross elasticity of outpatient visits to the price of 1-day in-hospital care was estimated at 0.85. This means that a 10 percent increase in the price of 1-day in-hospital care would induce an increase of 8.5 percent in outpatient visits. The cross elasticity of inpa-

tient services to the price of outpatient care was estimated at 0.25. It shows that a 10 percent decline in the price of outpatient care would lead to 2.5 percent decline in hospital admissions. The bottom line of this study is that if outpatient care can be provided at a reduced cost, the pressure on hospitals can be relieved to some extent. For example, if better organization of outpatient care lowered outpatient cost by 10 percent, in addition to saving money to outpatients, some inpatients will convert to outpatients (partially or totally).

Note that the cross elasticity of outpatient care with respect to the price of inpatient care was by far larger as compared with the cross elasticity of inpatient care with respect to the price of outpatient care. Intuitively this is so because expenditures on inpatient care by far exceed expenditures on outpatient care.[7]

3.4 AN EXAMPLE AND AN APPLICATION OF AN EMPIRICAL DEMAND FUNCTION

By now we know that quantity demanded of a good will change in response to changes in the price of that good. We also know that demand for a good will change as a result of either a change in population or a change in income per capita or a change in prices of other goods (close substitutes and close comple-

ments) or a combination of the above. This knowledge, which in sum is the theory of demand, is useful in shedding light on policy issues as well as in forecasting. The link between theory and policy in real life can be illustrated by an example of an empirical demand curve and an application.

---

effect might work at cross purposes. However, the smallness of K_y would ensure that the substitution effect will dominate. *Example:* $\bar{\eta}_{zp} = -2$. $K_y = 0.03$. $\alpha_x = -2$. The value of the cross elasticity is calculated as follows:

$$\eta_{zp_y} = -2 - 0.03\,(-2) = -1.94$$

[6]Karen Davis and Louise B. Russel, ''The Substitution of Hospital Outpatient Care for Inpatient Care,'' *The Review of Economics and Statistics,* vol. LIV, May 1972, pp. 109–120.

[7]More formally, if X and Y are two substitutes, then, as we shall prove in Mathematical Appendix 3, the following holds (assuming negligible income effects):

$$P_x \cdot X \cdot \eta_{xp_y} = P_y \cdot Y \cdot \eta_{yp_x}$$

where X denotes outpatient care and Y inpatient care. If $(Y \cdot P_y)/(X \cdot P_x)$ is roughly 4, the cross elasticity of outpatient care (X) with respect to the price of inpatient care (P_y) is expected to be four times the cross elasticity of inpatient care (Y) with respect to the price of outpatient care (P_x).

3.4a An Example: The Demand for Electricity in the United States

Whenever there is an economic crisis, doomsday prophets become popular. After the energy crisis of 1973, doomsday prophets began constructing input-output models, or simple extrapolation models, in order to tell us when we shall run out of fossil fuel, that is, when doomsday will arrive. Oil, they said, could be mined at a fixed cost per gallon to the very last drop. When the last drop is squeezed out of mother earth, doomsday is here. Natural resources, however, are not evenly distributed in nature.

An analogy to minerals in nature is the following: A fixed number of beads is thrown into a pile of hay. A person is responsible for finding the beads. The more beads the person finds, the more difficult it is to find new beads. If difficulty is measured by time, the marginal time of finding beads increases with discovery of new beads. The beads-in-the-hay theory applies to all minerals such as oil, gas, and coal. Thus, as the best mines are exhausted, marginal mines are discovered and the cost to consumers must rise.[8]

The theory of demand should tell how consumers react to changes in (self) prices, population, income, and prices of other goods. Statistical studies can be utilized to estimate the various elasticities of demand. The findings show that consumers are sensitive to changes in prices of energy resources. Most electricity in the United States is derived from petroleum, coal, and natural gas. Thus a rise in the price of these fossil fuels must lead to a rise in the price of electricity. Robert Halvorsen applied statistical methods to estimate the demand elasticities for electricity.[9] He used cross-sectional data for the 48 contiguous states for 1969. Some of the results obtained by Halvorsen are shown in Table 3-2.

Results for the commercial and industrial sectors are included in the table, although these sectors represent derived demand. The theory of derived demand for factors of production will be covered in Chapter 14. The reason why households and businesses use less electricity when its price rises is practically the same: They find substitutes for it.

If we examine closely the results for the residential sector, we find that, as expected, demand is proportional to the number of customers (population): A 10 percent increase in population will result in a 10 percent increase in the demand for electricity. The sign of the price elasticity is negative, as expected: a 10 percent rise in the price of electricity is expected to result in a 9.74 decline in the quantity demanded for electricity. Electricity is a normal good: A 10 percent

---

[8] In fact we do not need the "theory of beads" in order to show that the price of exhaustible resources must rise over time. In Chapter 16 we shall see that even if all deposits of a certain natural resource are finite and known, and even if their quality is uniform (in the sense that exploring and excavating are the same for all deposits), the price of such natural resources must rise over time.

[9] Robert Halvorsen, "Demand for Electric Energy in the United States," *Southern Economic Journal,* vol. 42, April 1976, pp. 610–625.

TABLE 3-2   **Selected Elasticities in the Demand Function for Electricity**

Residential		Commercial		Industrial	
Variable	Value	Variable	Value	Variable	Value
				Value of mineral production	0.669
Customers	1.000	Population	0.924	Value added in production	0.187
Price	−0.974	Price	−0.916	Price	−1.404
Per capita income	0.714	Per capita income	1.249		
Price of gas	0.159	Price of gas	−0.193	Price of gas	0.293

Source: Robert Halvorsen, "Demand for Electric Energy in the United States," *Southern Economic Journal*, vol. 42, April 1976, pp. 610–625.

increase in income per capita is expected to result in 7.14 percent increase in demand. Finally, gas and electricity are substitutes. The sign of the cross elasticity is positive (0.159). This result indicates that a 10 percent rise in the price of gas will induce consumers to increase their demand for electricity by 1.59 percent.

3.4b An Application

The Federal Power Commission (FPC) predicted for 1970–1990 an annual growth in demand for electricity of 7.14 percent. At the same time they predicted a price rise at a rate of 28 percent for the period 1970–1990. Halvorsen points out that, had they considered price elasticities properly, they would have concluded that the annual rate of growth of demand for electric energy should be 3.34 percent, less than half the rate adopted by the FPC. Halvorsen's demand forecasts under various price scenarios are presented in Table 3-3.

Table 3-3 clearly shows that one cannot ignore the rise in the price of a commodity when forecasting its future demand. While the increase in population, income per capita, and the price of gas will lead to a rise in the demand for electricity, the rise in the price of electricity will lead to a decline in the quantity of electricity demanded. How do economists calculate the net result of the impact of all the forces that influ-

ence the demand for a good? The theory covered in previous sections which relates the aggregate response of consumers to changes in various factors affecting the demand for a good is summarized in Table 3-4.

If we collect the impacts from changes in the various factors affecting the demand for a good, as summarized in Table 3-4, we obtain the following convenient equation:[10]

$$\frac{\Delta X}{X} = \eta \cdot \frac{\Delta P_x}{P_x} + \frac{\Delta \pi}{\pi} + \alpha \cdot \frac{\Delta I}{I} + \eta_{xp_y} \cdot \frac{\Delta P_y}{P_y} \quad (3\text{-}6)$$

where π stands for population and Y stands for a related good.

Assume that we expect the (relative) price of electric power, population, income per capita, and the (relative) price of gas to rise at annual rates of 3, 1, 2, and 10 percent, respectively. Using the values of elasticities for the residential demand for electricity as

---

[10]Equation 3-6 may be obtained by assuming a demand function of the form $X = P_x^\eta \cdot \pi \cdot I^\alpha \cdot P_y^{\eta_{xp_y}}$. Taking the natural logarithm of this demand function, we get $\ln X = \eta \cdot \ln P_x + \ln \pi + \alpha \cdot \ln I + \eta_{xp_y} \cdot \ln P_y$. Taking the whole differential of the logarithmic form gives the form

$$\frac{dX}{X} = \eta \cdot \frac{dP_x}{P_x} + \frac{d\pi}{\pi} + \alpha \cdot \frac{dI}{I} + \eta_{xp_y} \cdot \frac{dP_y}{P_y}$$

For reasonably small changes, the symbol d may be replaced by the symbol Δ. Note that tastes may be incorporated by adding a coefficient such as T, that is, $X = T \cdot P_x^\eta \cdot \pi \cdot I^\alpha \cdot P_y^{\eta_{xp_y}}$. The expression dT/T ($\Delta T/T$) will represent demand shifts due to changes in tastes.

TABLE 3-3   Total Demand for Electricity under Alternative Price Scenarios (Millions of kilowatthours)

	Real electricity and gas price assumed to:				
	Decrease at past rates	Decrease at one-half past rates	Remain constant	Increase 28%	Increase 50%
a. Demand in 1990	6,238,633	4,500,602	3,285,277	2,575,112	198,366
b. Ratio of 1990 to 1970	4.680	3.376	2.464	1.929	1.649
c. Compound growth rate, %	8.02	6.27	4.61	3.34	2.53

Source: Robert Halvorsen, "Demand for Electric Energy in the United States," *Southern Economic Journal*, vol. 42, April 1976, pp. 610–625.

TABLE 3-4   A Summary of Factors Influencing the Demand for a Good X

Section source	Influencing factor		Elasticity		Impact on demand	
	Description	Symbol	Description	Symbol	Description	Equation source
2.4f	(Self) price of good	P_x	Self-price	η	$\eta \cdot \dfrac{\Delta P_x}{P_x}$	2-4
3.3a	Population	π	Proportional change	Unity	$\dfrac{\Delta \pi}{\pi}$	
2.3e and 3.3b	Income per capita (budget)	I	Income elasticity	α	$\alpha \cdot \dfrac{\Delta I}{I}$	2-2
3.3c and 3.3d	Price of a related good	P_y	Cross elasticity	η_{xp_y}	$\eta_{xp_y} \cdot \dfrac{\Delta P_y}{P}$	3-5

given in Table 3-2, we obtain the following estimate of expected change in the residential demand:

Percentage change in demand for electricity
$$= -0.974 \cdot 3 \text{ percent} + 1 \text{ percent}$$
$$+ 0.714 \cdot 2 \text{ percent} + 0.159 \cdot 10 \text{ percent}$$
$$= 1.1 \text{ percent}$$

That is, we forecast a net annual increase in the demand for electricity by the residential sector at a rate of 1.1 percent. This result is illustrated in Figure 3-9. Initially the demand curve is marked by D_0. It shifts from D_0 to D_π (1 percent) because of population growth; it then shifts from D_π to D_I (1.43 percent) because of the rise in income per capita; it finally shifts from D_I to D_{P_y} because of the rise in the (relative) price of gas; all the above shifts are measured along the level of the initial price P_0. The rise in the (relative) price of electricity leads to a movement in the northwesterly direction along the demand curve D_{P_y}. This movement contributes to a reduction in the quantity demanded by 2.92 percent.

3.5 THE DEMAND FOR DURABLE GOODS: AUTOMOBILES (Optional)

In Section 2.1 we mentioned that some goods are purchased in the form of stocks. In this section we give an example of an empirical demand for stocks, namely, the demand for automobiles.

A consumer who purchases a car purchases a stock that renders a service, in this case transportation and prestige, for a relatively long period. Thus the demand for a car is really a demand for the related service. But since someone must own the car to enjoy the service, we must begin the analysis by estimating the demand for the stock. New car purchases are related to the demand for the stock of cars. The demand for purchases is equal to the demand for the stock in period t minus the demand for the stock in period $(t-1)$ plus the *depreciation* of the old stock.

Gregory C. Chow studied the demand for cars in the United States for the period 1920–1953.[11] He theorized that the demand for the stock of cars per capita is a function of price and income per capita. It is worthwhile to go into

---

[11]Gregory C. Chow, *Demand for Automobiles in the United States*, North Holland, Amsterdam, 1957.

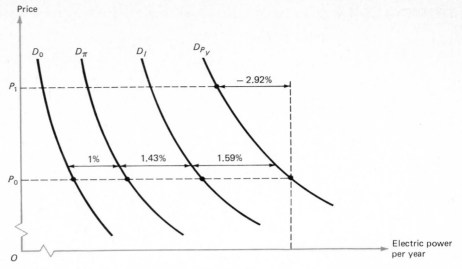

FIGURE 3-9 THE IMPACT OF CHANGES IN VARIOUS FACTORS ON THE DEMAND FOR ELECTRIC POWER

The 1 percent shift in the demand for electricity from D_0 to D_π is due to the growth of population. The 1.43 percent shift from D_π to D_I is due to the change in income per capita (0.74 · 2 percent). The shift from D_I to D_{P_y} is due to the rise in the price of gas (0.159 · 10 percent). The decrease in quantity demanded by 2.92 percent is due to the fact that the price of electricity goes up from a level of P_0 to a level of P_1, a 3 percent increase ($-$ 0.974 · 3 percent).

the data definitions of the study; 1937 was selected as the base year. Stocks of cars were estimated by multiplying the physical stocks of cars in different age groups by the average price ratios of the corresponding groups at the end of December 1937. For example, if on average in 1937 a 1-year-old car sold in the market for $644 and a 5-year-old car sold for $247, then a 5-year-old car is equivalent to 0.38 of a new car. The entire stock was divided by population in order to establish the stock of cars per capita. The price index for the stock for each year was derived by multiplying the retail prices of cars of different age groups by the corresponding stocks on December 31, 1937, and dividing this by the entire value of stocks which existed at the end of December 1937. (This price was deflated by a general price index[12] in order to express it in real terms.) Instead of regular income per capita, a concept of *expected* income per capita was applied in this study. Expected income per capita is obtained by taking the weighted average of current and past income, where the weights of preceding years are (exponentially) declining.

The results of the statistical estimates are as follows: Chow estimated the price elasticity at -0.95 and income elasticity at 2.03. Since Chow's study took place before the era of rising gasoline prices, the price of gasoline could not be included in order to estimate the cross elasticity of cars with respect to (complementary) gasoline.

---

[12]The concept of a price index will be discussed in Chapter 4. It is akin to an average price.

3.6 DEMAND SHIFTS DUE TO CHANGES IN TASTES

In Section 2.6 we mentioned the 1965 Cigarette Labeling and Advertising Act, which led to a change in tastes of consumers against smoking. On average consumers wanted to smoke less. Had we aggregated the demand of all smokers, it is clear that the aggregate demand for cigarettes would have decreased, leading to a leftward shift in the aggregate demand for cigarettes. We can summarize by saying that a change in taste against a good would lead to a leftward shift in its aggregate demand curve, and conversely, a change in taste in favor of a good would lead to a rightward shift in its aggregate demand curve.

SUMMARY This chapter introduced the concept of *market demand*, which was defined as the *aggregate* demand of all consumers in the economy. In principle the *aggregate demand curve* was obtained by adding horizontally the demand curves of all consumers for a certain good.

We have seen that the price elasticity of the aggregate demand curve is the weighted average of all price elasticities of all consumers. It was proved that *marginal revenue* is positive where the demand curve is *elastic* and negative where the demand curve is *inelastic*. (Marginal revenue is zero where the demand curve has unitary elasticity.) From the above relationship the relationship between *price elasticity* and *total revenue* along the demand curve was derived. Total revenue increases when we go down an elastic demand curve, and it decreases when we go down an inelastic demand curve. These relationships are reversed when we move up along a demand curve. Total revenue does not change when we move along a demand curve with unitary elasticity.

Next, *demand shifts* were discussed. It was concluded that market demand curves are proportional to population: Demand curves shift over time equiproportionately to changes in populations. We saw that demand for normal goods increases when income (per capita) increases, and conversely, it decreases when income (per capita) decreases. Demand for *inferior* goods decreases when income (per capita) increases, and conversely, it increases when income (per capita) decreases. Finally, demand shifts due to changes in prices of other goods were considered. If the price of a good falls, the demand for its substitute goods will decrease, while the demand for its complement goods will increase. Conversely, if the price of a good rises, the demand for its substitute goods will increase, while the demand for its complement goods will decrease. In conjunction with the theory of demand shifts due to changes in prices of other goods, the concept of *cross elasticity* was defined as the change in the demand of one good over the small change in the relative price of another good.

Given the (empirical) values of the elasticities with respect to self-price, income, and prices of other goods, we saw how we can forecast the change in demand for a given good if we have estimates of the projected change in the self-price, population, income per capita, and prices of related goods.

Such forecasts may be made by considering statistical estimates of the demand function for electricity.

GLOSSARY   **Aggregate demand curve** A demand curve which is obtained by horizontally totaling several individual demand curves for a certain good.

Market demand curve The aggregate demand curve of all individual consumers in the economy.

Typical consumer A consumer who, in his or her behavior, represents most consumers.

Price elasticity of the aggregate demand curve Measures the response of many (or all) consumers to a change in the price of a good. It is the relative change in the quantity demanded by many (or all) consumers over a small relative change in the price of the good under consideration. The price elasticity of the aggregate demand curve is equal to the weighted average of the individual price elasticities. The weights are the *shares* of individual consumers in the total consumption of a good.

Total revenue Each point on the (aggregate) demand curve represents a price and a quantity. Total revenue is the product of the price and the quantity. Total revenue *increases* when we move *down* an *elastic* portion of a demand curve and *decreases* when we move *down* an *inelastic* portion of a demand curve. Total revenue does not vary when we move along a demand curve that has unitary elasticity.

Marginal revenue A change in total revenue over a small change in the quantity demanded. Marginal revenue is related to the elasticity of the demand curve (from which it is derived) as follows: $MR = P(1 + 1/\eta)$. Accordingly marginal revenue is *negative* where the demand curve is *inelastic, positive* where the demand curve is *elastic,* and *zero* where the demand curve has *unitary elasticity.*

Demand shift due to population changes *Ceteris paribus,* the *market demand* is proportional to the population. Accordingly, the shift in the *market demand* is proportional to the population change.

Demand shifts due to changes in income per capita An increase in income per capita will lead to an increase in the demand for a *normal* good. A decrease in income per capita will lead to a decrease in the demand for a normal good. A rise in income per capita will lead to a decrease in the demand for an inferior good. A fall in income per capita will lead to an increase in the demand for an inferior good. An increase in demand is equivalent to a rightward shift, and a decrease in demand is equivalent to a leftward shift in the demand curve. *Ceteris paribus,* demand shifts due to changes in income per capita are forecast by multiplying *income elasticities* by the expected changes in income per capita.

Substitutes and complements If the price of a good falls, the demand for a *substitute* good decreases and the demand for a *complement* good increases. Conversely, if the price of a good rises, the demand for a *substitute* good increases and the demand for a *complement* good decreases. An increase in demand is equivalent to a rightward shift, and a decrease in demand is equivalent to a leftward shift in the demand curve.

Cross price elasticity The relative change in the demand for a good over a small relative change in the price of another (related) good. Cross price elasticity, which is sometimes called *cross elasticity*, measures the responsiveness of the consumption of a good, given the change in the price of another good. Cross elasticity is positive for a pair of substitutes and negative for a pair of complements. *Ceteris paribus*, demand shifts due to changes in prices of substitutes or complements are obtained by multiplying *cross elasticities* by expected changes in prices of other goods.

PROBLEMS An asterisk indicates an advanced problem.

3-1. The only source of water on an island is owned by a single person. Assume it costs the owner of the water nothing to distribute the water to customers. Consider the aggregate demand for water on the island: The higher part of this demand curve is elastic and its lower part is inelastic. How much water and at what price should the owner sell to the community?

3-2. GNP grows at a rate of 8 percent per annum. Population grows at an annual rate of 3 percent. By how much (percentage) does the demand for whatnots shift over a period of 1 year if income elasticity of whatnots is −0.4?

3-3. Cattle ranchers consume more meat when the price of meat rises. Assume that the ranchers' income rises with the rise in meat prices. Can you rationalize the ranchers' increased consumption of meat by assuming that for them (a) meat is superior, (b) meat is inferior (but not a Giffen good), (c) meat is a Giffen good?

3-4. The stock of cars may be defined as the number of cars times the average size of cars. By treating cars and gasoline as complementary goods, explain why consumers shifted from full-sized cars to compact cars after the so-called energy crisis.

3-5. Given the elasticities of residential demand for electricity in Table 3-2 and assuming that the annual rate of population growth, income per capita, and the price of gas are 1, 2, and 10 percent, respectively, what should be the annual rate of growth of the price of electric power in order to leave residential demand at a steady state?

3-6. Production of food at the farm level is *energy-intensive*. (The process of production takes relatively a lot of energy.) Some people say that when the price of energy rises farmers produce less and thus suffer the most from the energy crisis. Do you agree? Why or why not?

3-7. There are only two goods in the budget of a consumer. How would the demand curve for Y shift as a result of a fall in the price of X? The demand curve of X is price-inelastic.

3-8.* If the demand curve of one consumer can be described by the linear equation $P = 10 - 20X$, what would be the aggregate demand curve of 100 such consumers?

3-9.* Consider the demand curve of the 100 consumers in problem 3-8. Assume that all producers of the good X live 10 miles away from where consumers live. Assume that shipping costs 20 cents a mile. What would be the net demand curve facing producers? Net means the price producers can get in the market, net of shipping costs.

3-10.* Consider Footnote 5 and answer the following:
(a) If X and Y are substitutes, under what conditions would cross elasticity η_{xp_y} be negative?

(b) If Y and Z are complements, under what conditions would cross elasticity η_{zp_y} be positive?

MATHEMATICAL APPENDIX 3

This Appendix is a continuation of Mathematical Appendix 2. We recall that Equation m2-4 was obtained by differentiating Equation m1-4 (first-order conditions for consumer's equilibrium) with respect to the price of one good, say, P_1. In Mathematical Appendix 2 we focused on $\partial X_1/\partial P_1$. Here we want to focus on the cross relationships, for example, on $\partial X_2/\partial P_1$.

Solving Equation m2-4 by Cramer's rule gives

$$\frac{\partial X_2}{\partial P_1} = \lambda \cdot \frac{U_{12}}{U} - X_1 \cdot \frac{\lambda \cdot U_2}{U} \tag{m3-1}$$

In analogy with the derivation of Equation m2-8, we can change m3-1 to

$$\eta_{21} = \bar{\eta}_{21} - K_1 \cdot \alpha_2 \tag{m3-2}$$

If $\bar{\eta}_{21} > 0$, X_1 and X_2 are substitutes. If $\bar{\eta}_{21} < 0$, X_1 and X_2 are complements.

If we replace 2 and 1 by X and Y, we obtain

$$\eta_{xp_y} = \bar{\eta}_{xp_y} - K_y \cdot \alpha_x \tag{m3-3}$$

the notation used in Footnote 5.

Since U is symmetrical, $U_{12} = U_{21}$. By utilizing the result $\overline{\partial X_2/\partial P_1} = \lambda \cdot (U_{12}/U)$, we derive the result $\overline{\partial X_2/\partial P_1} = \overline{\partial X_1/\partial P_2}$. This result can be written as

$$X_1 \cdot P_1 \cdot \bar{\eta}_{12} = X_2 \cdot P_2 \cdot \bar{\eta}_{21} \tag{m3-4}$$

Again, 2 and 1 can be replaced by X and Y to obtain

$$P_x \cdot X \cdot \bar{\eta}_{xp_y} = P_y \cdot Y \cdot \bar{\eta}_{yp_x} \tag{m3-5}$$

which was used in Footnote 7.

Finally, consider U, which appears on the left side of Equation m2-2 (and m2-4). If the second row of this determinant is replaced by the first row, the value of the new determinant is zero. We may write it as

$$0 \cdot U_1 + u_1 \cdot U_{11} + u_2 \cdot U_{12} + u_3 \cdot U_{13} = 0$$

Substituting λP_i for u_i (Equation m1-5), dividing by U, and utilizing the fact that $\overline{\partial X_i / \partial P_j} = \lambda \cdot (U_{ji}/U)$, we obtain

$$P_1 \cdot \frac{\overline{\partial X_1}}{\partial P_1} + P_2 \cdot \frac{\overline{\partial X_2}}{\partial P_1} + P_3 \cdot \frac{\overline{\partial X_3}}{\partial P_1} = 0 \qquad \text{(m3-6)}$$

If there are only two goods in the consumer's budget (say, X_1 and X_2), then, since $\overline{\partial X_1 / \partial P_1}$ is always negative, $\overline{\partial X_2 / \partial P_1}$ must be positive. This is the proof of the theorem that if there are only two goods in the budget, these goods must be substitutes.

CHAPTER

4

SPECIAL ISSUES IN CONSUMER THEORY
(optional)

The modern theory of demand includes a wealth of concepts which have useful and interesting applications. Examples considered in this chapter are measurement by *index numbers*, decision making on the basis of *risk*, and determination of the *consumer's surplus* through indifference curves. Because these concepts are not essential for understanding most of the following chapters, study of this chapter is optional.

4.1 INDEX NUMBERS

Suppose we want to know when a consumer was better off than he is now. For example, did he have a larger buying capacity in 1977 compared with 1975? Or suppose we want to compare a worker's well-being in two countries. Consider, for example, an employee transferred from an office in the United States to an office in Brazil. How does the firm adjust her salary so she can buy the goods she normally consumes in the United States? To make such determinations, both *quantity index numbers* and *price index numbers* are helpful.

Index numbers are also useful in countries where inflation is a way of life. For example, if you lend Ann $1000 today for a period of 1 year at a 5 percent interest rate, you will end up with $1050 in 1 year. But if the annual rate of inflation is 10 percent, the purchasing power of your $1050 is only $954.54. How can you protect yourself from the inflation? You need some measure of the rate of inflation, which is a price index number. Another example is the period following 1973, which was disturbed by both inflation and rising energy prices. Economists who wanted to know how much energy prices rose *relative* to prices of other (nonenergy) goods needed two price indices. They needed first a general price index which measures the change in the prices of all goods, and second, the price index of energy items such as oil and gas. Consider this: If all prices, including the prices of energy items, rose by 10 percent in 1 year, we could not say that there was an energy crisis. But if all prices rise at an annual rate of 10 percent and the prices of energy items rise by 20 percent, we can say that the relative price of energy rose by 9 percent. To give another example relevant to the so-called energy crisis, some policy makers said that deregulation of the energy sector would lead to rising prices of energy resources. Such deregulation, they said, must be accompanied by properly compensating the poor. To compensate the poor properly, one must consider a certain price index which is based on the goods and services normally consumed by the average (typical) poor.

First *quantity index numbers* and how they are used to compare the well-being of consumers in different situations will be discussed. *Price index numbers* and how they relate to quantity index numbers will then be considered.

4.1a Quantity Index Numbers and Revealed Preference

Intuitively, *quantity index numbers* help us to examine the quantity of goods consumed by a person in one situation compared with another situation. The problem is to compare 10 concerts and 60 loaves of bread consumed in 1975 with 15 concerts and 45 loaves of bread consumed in 1977. As will become clear from the following analysis, if the basket contents (Figure 4-1) vary from situation to situation because of changes in income and prices but not because of changes in taste, we can conduct a meaningful comparison of the two baskets, and in most (but not all) cases we can determine which basket provided greater satisfaction to the consumer.

The concept of a quantity index number is illustrated by the data in Table 4-1 and Figure 4-1, which show the hypothetical consumption of two goods in two time periods. (The first period is sometimes referred to as the *base* period.)

In Figure 4-1 the consumption in time period 0 is depicted by point A and the consumption in time period 1 is depicted by point B. We distinguish between two kinds of quantity index numbers, *Laspeyre* and *Paasche*. Before the formulas for the two kinds of quantity indices are presented, let us see what they mean technically.

The Laspeyre quantity index denoted by Q_l is basket B in Figure 4-1 evaluated by prices of period *0*, divided by basket A, also evaluated by prices of period *0*. (To evaluate a basket means to convert the physical quantities into dollars.) In order to calculate the Laspeyre quantity index, we multiply the quantities in each basket by the prices that prevailed in the *base* period. Using data from Table 4-1, we write

$$Q_l = \frac{7 \cdot \$2 + 8 \cdot \$5}{3 \cdot \$2 + 4 \cdot \$5} = \frac{\$54}{\$26} = 2.08$$

The *Paasche quantity index* denoted by Q_p is calculated by following a similar procedure, except that we evaluate the baskets by using the prices of the second period as weights:

$$Q_p = \frac{7 \cdot \$4 + 8 \cdot \$6}{3 \cdot \$4 + 4 \cdot \$6} + \frac{\$76}{\$36} = 2.11$$

If instead of X, Y, P_x, and P_y we use more general notations, namely, X_1, X_2, P_1, and P_2, and in addition we adopt a second subscript for time, say, $0 =$ base time period and $1 =$ second time period, the numerator in the expression for Q_l will be

$$X_{11} \cdot P_{10} + X_{21} \cdot P_{20} = 7 \cdot \$2 + 8 \cdot \$5$$

In order to save space, we may use the summation notation Σ as follows:

$$\sum_{i=1}^{2} X_{i1} \cdot P_{i0} = X_{11} \cdot P_{10} + X_{21} \cdot P_{20}$$

TABLE 4-1 **Consumption Data**

Period	X	P_x	Y	P_y	I
0 (base)	3	$2	4	$5	$26
1	7	$4	8	$6	$76

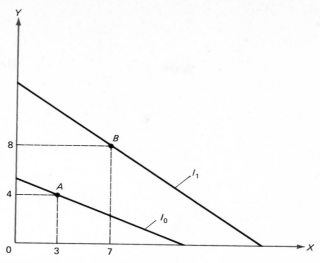

FIGURE 4-1 A GRAPHIC ILLUSTRATION OF TABLE 4-1

I_0 and I_1 are the budgets corresponding to the base and second periods, respectively. Point A represents the base-period basket, and point B represents the second-period basket.

For the case of n goods the summation extends from 1 to n; that is, the summation is written as

$$\sum_{i=1}^{n}$$

Since it is evident that the summation covers all goods, namely, from 1 to n, sometimes the subscript i is dropped and we may write

$$\sum_{i=1}^{n} X_{i1} \cdot P_{io} = \Sigma X_1 \cdot P_0$$

By the same token, the denominator in the expression for Q_l is written as $\Sigma X_0 \cdot P_0$. We are now ready to write the formulas for the quantity index numbers Q_l and Q_p as

$$Q_l = \frac{\Sigma X_1 \cdot P_0}{\Sigma X_0 \cdot P_0} \tag{4-1}$$

$$Q_p = \frac{\Sigma X_1 \cdot P_1}{\Sigma X_0 \cdot P_1} \tag{4-2}$$

Quantity indices are useful in welfare analysis for comparing the satisfaction of the same consumer in two different situations. As mentioned before, two distinct situations may be two different time periods, or alternatively two different countries. As we shall see in the subsequent analysis, our main concern is the size of the quantity index number relative to unity. For example, when both Laspeyre and Paasche quantity indices are greater than 1, an improvement of satisfaction from the *base* to the *second* time period is implied. Since each of Q_p and Q_l can be either less than, equal to, or greater than 1, we have nine possible outcomes of combinations of Q_p and Q_l. These outcomes are summarized in Table 4-2. In Table 4-2 a + denotes an improvement, a − denotes a deterioration, and 0 denotes no change in satisfaction. A c denotes a change in taste, and ct stands for "cannot tell." For example, in cell$_{12}$ (first row, second column), which corresponds to $Q_l > 1$ and $Q_p = 1$, we entered with a +, indicating an improvement in satisfaction.

Some of the more important cases of welfare comparison by applying geometric analysis will now be considered. At the end of each analysis the appropriate sign will be entered in the relevant cell in Table 4-2.

The initial equilibrium of the consumer in the base period is denoted by A, and the new equilibrium in the second period is denoted by B. In order not to crowd the diagrams, indifference curves are not generally shown. The reader should, however, imagine A as being a tangency point between budget line I_0 and indifference curve U_0, and B as being a tangency point between budget line I_1 and indifference curve U_1.

Case 1 Consider Figure 4-2. Panel (*a*) serves to explain the Laspeyre quantity index. Budget line I_0^* is parallel to I_0 and passes through point B. It must be equal to the cost of basket B at prices of the base period. We can express it as

$$I_0^* = \Sigma X_1 \cdot P_0 (= 7 \cdot \$2 + 8 \cdot \$5 \text{ in the example})$$

Budget line I_0 simply represents the amount of money actually spent on basket A in period *0* (base period). Hence it is written as

$$I_0 = \Sigma X_0 \cdot P_0 \ (= 3 \cdot \$2 + 4 \cdot \$5 \text{ in the example})$$

Thus the Laspeyre quantity index can be written as

$$Q_l = \frac{I_0^*}{I_0} = \frac{\Sigma X_1 \cdot P_0}{\Sigma X_0 \cdot P_0} \tag{4-3}$$

We now shift to panel (*b*). Budget line I_1 contains point B. It represents the sum of money actually spent on basket B in period 1. Hence it is written as

$$I_1 = \Sigma X_1 \cdot P_1 \ (= 7 \cdot \$4 + 8 \cdot \$6 \text{ in the example})$$

Budget line I_1^* is parallel to I_1 and passes through point A. Thus it represents the cost of basket A at the prices of the second time period. It is written as

$$I_1^* = \Sigma X_0 \cdot P_1 (= 3 \cdot \$4 + 4 \cdot \$6 \text{ in the example})$$

Accordingly, the Paasche quantity index can be expressed as

$$Q_p = \frac{I_1}{I_1^*} = \frac{\Sigma X_1 \cdot P_1}{\Sigma X_0 \cdot P_1} \tag{4-4}$$

Could the consumer buy basket A in period 1 at prices of the second time period? The answer is yes, because the budget in the second time period

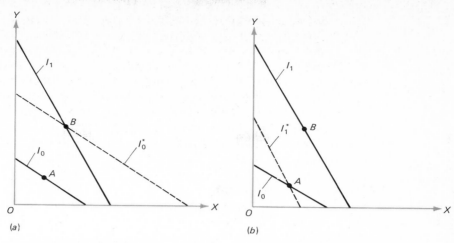

FIGURE 4-2   QUANTITY INDEX NUMBERS: CASE 1—B IS RANKED OVER A
(a) I_0 and I_1 represent the budget lines of the base and the second periods, respectively. I_0^* is parallel to I_0 and passes through B. It reflects the cost of B evaluated in prices of the base period.
   (b) I_1^* is parallel to I_1 and passes through A. It reflects the cost of A evaluated in prices of the second period.

exceeds the cost of basket A evaluated at prices of the second time period. This fact can be summarized as an inequality.

$$I_1 > I_1^* \tag{4-5}$$

The inequality states that I_1 is greater than I_1^*, and it means that if the consumer had wanted to, he or she could have bought basket A in period 1, but he or she preferred basket B. The consumer's preference has been revealed: He or she ranks B over A. *Note:* we do not need to have knowledge of the consumer's indifference map in order to deduce that B is preferred to A. An *axiom of revealed preference,* which is a summary of our intuition, states that given unchanging tastes, if B is revealed as preferable to A when evaluated at prices of period 1, then A cannot be revealed as preferable to B when evaluated at prices of the base period (or any other period). In other words, given Inequality 4-5, I_0 cannot exceed I_0^*, or

$$I_0 < I_0^* \tag{4-6}$$

The above presentation is only a crude version of the important axiom of revealed preference.[1]

   Geometrically, Inequality 4-5 is pictured by the fact that in Figure 4-2,

---

[1]We are referring here to the *weak axiom of revealed preference.* The axiom states that if basket B (X_1, Y_1) is revealed as preferable to basket A (X_0, Y_0), that is, if $X_1 \cdot P_{x1} + Y_1 \cdot P_{y1} \geq X_0 \cdot P_{x1} + Y_0 \cdot P_{y1}$, then basket A cannot be revealed as preferable to basket B. Basket A can be revealed as preferable to basket B only if there exists a price set $(P_{x0} \, P_{y0})$ such that $X_1 \cdot P_{x0} + Y_1 \cdot P_{y0} \leq X_0 \cdot P_{x0} + Y_0 \cdot P_{y0}$. But, since this cannot be, the following inequality must be satisfied: $X_1 \cdot P_{x0} + Y_1 \cdot P_{y0} > X_0 \cdot P_{x0} + Y_0 \cdot P_{y0}$.

panel (b), budget line I_1 occupies a position to the right of I_1^*. Inequality 4-6 is pictured by the fact that in Figure 4-2, panel (a), budget line I_0 occupies a position to the left of I_0^*. *Note:* The fact that one budget line is parallel to the other means that they reflect the same (relative) prices. Moreover, any point lying on the lower budget line represents a basket that can be bought with the budget represented by the higher budget line (with some money left over); not even one point lying on the higher budget line can be bought with the budget represented by the lower budget line.

Dividing both sides of Inequality 4-5 by I_1^* gives

$$Q_p = \frac{I_1}{I_1^*} > 1 \tag{4-7}$$

and dividing both sides of Inequality 4-6 by I_0 gives

$$Q_l = \frac{I_0^*}{I_0} > 1 \tag{4-8}$$

We are now ready to summarize case 1: Assuming no change in taste, if the Paasche and Laspeyre quantity indices are each greater than unity, the consumer is better off in the second period. We enter a + in cell$_{11}$ of Table 4-2.

If the positions of points A and B (as well as I_0 and I_1) are interchanged, the order of ranking the baskets would be reversed: Basket A would be ranked over basket B. As shown in Figure 4-3, panel (b), I_1 will be smaller than I_1^* and, as shown in Figure 4-3, panel (a), I_0 will be greater than I_0^*; the signs of Inequalities 4-5, 4-6, 4-7, and 4-8 will be reversed. Thus Q_l and Q_p are each smaller than unity. We conclude that if Q_l and Q_p are each smaller

FIGURE 4-3   QUANTITY INDEX NUMBERS: CASE 1—A IS RANKED OVER B
It is the same as Figure 4-2, except that the roles of I_0 and I_1 have been reversed. In Figure 4-2, I_1 was higher than (and to the right of) I_0; in Figure 4-3, I_0 is higher than (and to the right of) I_1.

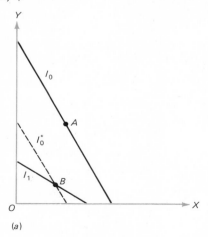

(a)

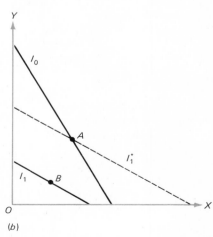

(b)

than unity, the well-being of the consumer has deteriorated from the base period to the second period. Accordingly we enter a $-$ in cell$_{33}$ in Table 4-2.

Case 2 So far we have considered the case in which one budget line lies entirely to the right of the other budget line. One budget line thus represents a set of market opportunities which is clearly superior to that of the other budget line. We now turn to the ambiguous situation where the two budget lines intersect. Consider Figure 4-4. In panel (a) the situation is similar to the previous case of nonintersection: In the second period, the consumer has sufficient income to buy basket A but selects basket B: $I_1 > I_1^*$. At the base period the consumer could not buy basket B: $I_0 < I_0^*$. Again, if we divide the first inequality by I_1^* and the second inequality by I_0, we obtain the result that the quantity indices are each greater than unity. In panel (b) optimum point A occurs at the intersection of budget line I_0 and I_1. Clearly, I_1 is identical with I_1^*, and Q_p ($= I_1/I_1^*$) is equal to unity. Note that at the second period, although the consumer has the opportunity to buy basket A, he or she selects basket B. However, at the base period, he or she did not have sufficient income to buy basket B: $I_0 < I_0^*$ and hence $Q_l > 1$. In other words, if tastes remain the same, and we observe that the Paasche quantity index is equal to unity but the Laspeyre is greater than unity, the consumer is better off in the second period. In cell$_{12}$ of Table 4-2 we enter a $+$.

If points A and B were to travel in the southeasterly direction along their respective budget lines until they occupy positions to the right of the intersection point [Figure 4-4, panel (a)], we would obtain a situation in

FIGURE 4-4   QUANTITY INDEX NUMBERS: CASE 2

(a) I_0 and I_1 intersect. However, since both A and B lie on the same side of the intersection point (here to its left), B is unambiguously preferred to A: I_1^*, which is parallel to I_1, and passes through A, lies to the left of I_1; the consumer can buy A in the second period. I_0^*, which is parallel to I_0 and passes through B, lies to the right of I_0; the consumer cannot buy B in the base period.

(b) Obtained by slowly moving I_1^* toward I_1, until they merge. The result is the same as in panel (a), except that $I_1^* = I_1$.

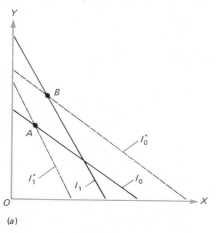

(a)

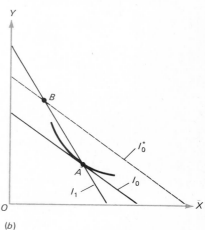

(b)

which A is revealed as preferable to B. The consumer would be better off in the base period, and the quantity indices would each be smaller than unity. This result is similar to the situation depicted by Figure 4-3. In Table 4-2 it fits into cell$_{33}$.

Case 3 Consider Figure 4-5, panel (a). Basket A lies to the right of the intersection point, and basket B lies to the left of the intersection point between the two budget lines. In the second period the consumer does not have sufficient income to buy basket A: $I_1 < I_1^*$. Also, in the base period, the consumer did not have an opportunity to buy basket B: $I_0 < I_0^*$. Thus we cannot tell which basket is preferred. The inequalities lead to the result that $Q_p < 1$ and $Q_l > 1$: In cell$_{13}$ of Table 4-2 we enter a ct. In Figure 4-6, panel (a), we illustrate this case further by drawing two alternative indifference curves. First, the solid indifference curve U' is tangent to both I_0 and I_1 at points A and B, respectively. The consumer is as well off in the two periods. But we can draw the dashed indifference curve U'' such that it is tangent to I_1 at B, but it is higher than point A. In other words B may yield more satisfaction than A. The third possibility would be to draw an indifference curve tangent to I_0 at A and passing above point B, indicating that A is preferred to B. This is left for the student to do.

FIGURE 4-5   QUANTITY INDEX NUMBERS: CASE 3

(a) I_0 and I_1 intersect. A lies to the right of the intersection point, and B lies to the left of the intersection point. I_0^*, which is parallel to I_0 and passes through B, lies above I_0; in the base period the consumer cannot buy B. I_1^*, which is parallel to I_1 and passes through A, lies above I_1; in the second period the consumer cannot buy A. Thus we cannot tell whether A is preferred to B or, conversely, B is preferred to A.

(b) This arrangement is obtained by moving A and B to the other side of the intersection between I_0 and I_1. Since now I_0^* lies below I_0, the consumer can buy in the base period basket B. This means that A is preferred to B. But I_1^* also lies below I_1, indicating that in the second period the consumer can buy A. That is, B is preferred to A. The result that A is preferred to B and B is preferred to A contradicts the axiom of revealed preference: A change in taste must have occurred.

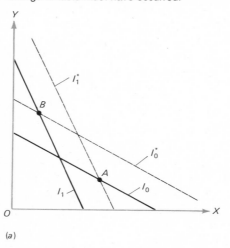

(a)

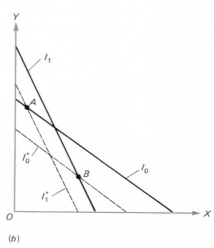

(b)

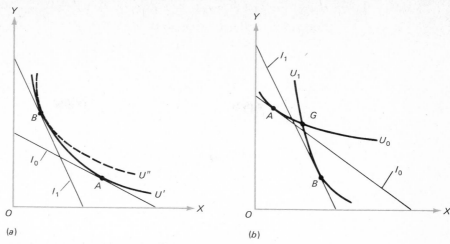

(a)

(b)

FIGURE 4-6 QUANTITY INDEX NUMBERS: CASE 3—SPECIAL SITUATIONS
(a) This sheds light on panel (a) of Figure 4-5. It is a replica of panel (a) of Figure 4-5, except
that two indifference curves are added—U' is tangent to I_0 and I_1 at A and B, respectively:
The consumer is indifferent between A and B. An alternative is U'', which is tangent to I_1 at B
but passes above A. Thus B may be preferred to A. (The case in which A is preferred to B is
left for the student to draw.)
(b) This sheds light on panel (b) of Figure 4-5. U_0, the indifference curve which is tangent
to I_0, must intersect with U_1, the indifference curve which is tangent to I_1. G is the point of
intersection between the two indifference curves. The intersection of two indifference curves
contradicts a theorem proven in Section 1.3c: A change in taste must have occurred.

Two additional situations should be explored in Figure 4-5, panel (*a*).
First, if point *A* traveled in the northwesterly direction along I_0 to the point
of intersection between the two budget lines (not shown), we would obtain
the same situation as depicted in Figure 4-4, panel (*b*). Second, if point *B*
traveled southeasterly along I_1 to the point of intersection between the two
budget lines (not shown), basket A would be ranked over basket B. Such a
displacement of point *B* would lead to a situation in which the consumer can
buy basket B at the base period: $I_0 = I_0^*$, but he or she revealed his or her
preference for basket A. In the second period the consumer could not buy
basket A: $I_1 < I_1^*$. Dividing both sides of the equality by I_0 and both sides of
the inequality by I_1^*, we obtain the result that $Q_l = 1$ and $Q_p < 1$. We
conclude that the consumer is better off in the base period. In other words
there was a deterioration of well-being in the second period compared with
the base period. We enter a $-$ sign in cell$_{23}$ of Table 4-2.

Consider Figure 4-5, panel (*b*). In the second period the consumer has an
opportunity to buy basket A: $I_1 > I_1^*$. Since the consumer opted to buy
basket B, we conclude that B is ranked over A. But in the base period there
was an opportunity to buy basket B: $I_0 > I_0^*$. The consumer opted for A; thus
we conclude that A is ranked over B. This result contradicts the axiom
stating that if B is revealed as preferable to A when evaluated by one set of
prices, then A cannot be revealed as preferable to B when evaluated by
another set of prices. A change in taste must therefore have occurred. Again

TABLE 4-2 A Summary: Quantity Index Numbers*

Q_I	Q_p > 1	= 1	< 1
> 1	+	+	ct
= 1	c	c or o	−
< 1	c	c	−

*Improvement, deterioration, and no change in utility are indicated by +, −, and 0, respectively. "Cannot tell' and a change in taste are indicated by ct and c, respectively.

we divide the first inequality by I_1^* and the second inequality by I_0 to obtain the result that $Q_p > 1$ and $Q_l < 1$. We enter a c in cell$_{31}$ of Table 4-2. In Figure 4-6, panel (b), we show that given the situation depicted by Figure 4-5, panel (b), the two indifference curves associated with equilibrium (U_0 touches I_0 at A, and U_1 touches I_1 at B) must intersect (point G). But in Section 1.3c it was proved that given a fixed indifference map, two indifference curves cannot intersect. The intersection of U_0 with U_1 in Figure 4-6, panel (b), implies that these two indifference curves belong to two different indifference maps.

We leave it for the student to show that if point B [Figure 4-5, panel (b)] is moved to the intersection of the two budget lines, a change in taste must have occurred and $Q_p > 1$ and $Q_l = 1$. Similarly, if point A is moved to the intersection, a change in taste must have occurred and $Q_p = 1$ and $Q_l < 1$. Given these results, the sign c should be entered in cell$_{21}$ and cell$_{32}$ of Table 4-2. The trivial case in which A and B coincide is left as an exercise for the reader.

4.1b Price Index Numbers

Recall that quantity indices were calculated by dividing the weighted average of quantities of a given period by the weighted average of quantities of the base period. The choice of weights determined whether the index would be Paasche or Laspeyre. In the case of *price indices* the role of quantities and prices is interchanged; We divide the weighted average of prices of a given period by the weighted average of prices of the base period. Quantities serve as weights, and the choice of which period quantities we select for weighting determines whether the price index number is a Paasche or Laspeyre type.

To illustrate the concept of a price index number consider again the example in Table 4-1 and Figure 4-1. (Recall that in Table 4-1 and Figure 4-1 we presented hypothetical data of hypothetical consumption of two goods in two periods.) We denote the *Laspeyre price index by* P_l and the Paasche price index by P_p. To evaluate the Laspeyre price index, we consider the *base basket* (point A in Figure 4-1), that is, 3 units of X and 4 units of Y. This basket is evaluated at \$36 by the prices of the second period and \$26 by the prices of the base period. Accordingly, we obtain the Laspeyre price index as follows:

$$P_l = \frac{\$4 \cdot 3 + \$6 \cdot 4}{\$2 \cdot 3 + \$5 \cdot 4} = \frac{\$36}{\$26} = 1.38$$

To evaluate the *Paasche price index*, we consider the second basket (point B in Figure 4-1), that is, 7 units of X and 8 units of Y. This basket is evaluated at $76 by the prices of the second period and at $54 by the prices of the base period. Accordingly, we obtain the Paasche price index as follows:

$$P_p = \frac{\$4 \cdot 7 + \$6 \cdot 8}{\$2 \cdot 7 + \$5 \cdot 8} = \frac{\$76}{\$54} = 1.40$$

Geometrically, the Laspeyre price index P_l is basket A evaluated by prices of period 1 divided by the same basket evaluated by prices of period 0. As the calculation shows, the cost of basket A rose 38 percent from period 0 to period 1. By the same token, the Paasche price index P_p is basket B evaluated by prices of period 1 divided by the same basket evaluated by prices of period 0. As the calculation shows, the cost of basket B rose 40 percent from period 0 to period 1.

Using the summation notations, defined previously, we can define the price indices as follows:

$$P_l = \frac{\Sigma P_1 \cdot X_0}{\Sigma P_0 \cdot X_0} \tag{4-9}$$

$$P_p = \frac{\Sigma P_1 \cdot X_1}{\Sigma P_0 \cdot X_1} \tag{4-10}$$

Let us now turn to the economic analysis of price index numbers. In Figure 4-7, I_0 is the budget of the consumer in the base period; given the prices of the base period, the consumer prefers basket A to all other opportunities on I_0. In period 1 the budget of the consumer amounts to I_1 dollars; given the prices of the second period, he or she prefers basket B to all other opportunites on I_1. The cost of basket B in the second period is I_1. The cost of the same basket B at prices of the base period is I_0^*. I_0^* is a budget line parallel to I_0 and passing through point B. The Paasche price index measures the cost of basket B at prices of the second period relative to the cost of the same basket B at the base period prices. This is written as

$$P_p = \frac{I_1}{I_0^*} = \frac{\Sigma P_1 \cdot X_1}{\Sigma P_0 \cdot X_1} \tag{4-11}$$

Notice in Figure 4-7 that I_0^{**} is another budget line parallel to I_0 and touching indifference curve U_1 at point G. Indifference curve U_1 contains point B. I_0^{**} tells what is the budget required for "buying" the same level of utility U_1 at prices of the base period. Recall that the cost of U_1 at the second period is I_1. If instead of a basket of goods such as B we focus on a fixed amount of utility such as U_1, then comparing the cost of U_1 in the second period (I_1) with its cost in the base period (I_0^{**}) yields an *ideal Paasche price index*. Let us de-

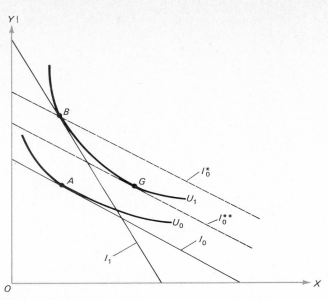

FIGURE 4-7 PAASCHE PRICE INDEX

I_0 represents the budget of the consumer in the base period; I_1 represents the budget of the consumer in the second period. I_0^*, which passes through B and is parallel to I_0, reflects the cost of basket B evaluated by prices of the base period. The Paasche price index is accordingly defined as I_1/I_0^*. I_0^{**} is parallel to I_0 and is tangent to U_1 at G; it tells the cost of U_1 satisfaction evaluated by prices of the base period. The *ideal* Paasche price index is I_1/I_0^{**}, and it is larger than the Paasche price index.

note the ideal Paasche price index by *ideal* P_p and we obtain

$$\text{Ideal } P_p = \frac{I_1}{I_0^{**}} > \frac{I_1}{I_0^*} = P_p \qquad (4\text{-}12)$$

That is, the Paasche price index is smaller than the *ideal* Paasche price index. Since the shape of the indifference map is not known, the ideal Paasche price index cannot be estimated. But Inequality 4-12 does indicate that the Paasche price index is biased downward. For example, if you consume basket B (7 units of X and 8 units of Y) in the second period, the Paasche price index for Table 4-1 is calculated as 1.40. But Inequality 4-12 tells you that since 1.40 is less than the ideal Paasche price index, the cost of U_1 rose by more than 40 percent from the base to the second period.

Figure 4-7 is partially reproduced in Figure 4-8. Instead of focusing on basket B of the second period, we now focus on basket A of the base period. The cost of basket A at prices of the base period is I_0. The cost of basket A at prices of the second period is I_1^*. Geometrically, I_1^* is a budget line parallel to I_1 and passing through A. The Laspeyre price index measures the cost of basket A at prices of the second period relative to the cost of the same basket A at prices of the base period. This is written as

$$P_l = \frac{I_1^*}{I_0} = \frac{\Sigma P_1 \cdot X_0}{\Sigma P_0 \cdot X_0} \qquad (4\text{-}13)$$

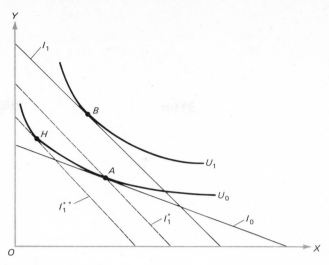

FIGURE 4-8 LASPEYRE PRICE INDEX

I_0 represents the budget of the consumer in the base period; I_1 represents the budget of the consumer in the second period. I_1^*, which passes through A and is parallel to the I_1, reflects the cost of basket A evaluated by prices of the second period. The Laspeyre price index is accordingly defined as I_1^*/I_0. I_1^{**} is parallel to I_1 and is tangent to U_0 at H. It tells the cost of U_0 satisfaction evaluated by prices of the second period. The *ideal* Laspeyre index is I_1^{**}/I_0 and is smaller than the Laspeyre price index.

We note that I_1^{**} is a budget line parallel to I_1 and touching indifference curve U_0 at point H. U_0 passes through A. I_1^{**} tells what is the budget required for "buying" the same level of utility U_0 at prices of the second period. Recall that the cost of U_0 in the base period is I_0. We define the *ideal Laspeyre price index* as the cost of U_0 in the second period relative to its cost in the base period. Thus we obtain the comparison of the *ideal* Laspeyre price index with the Laspeyre price index as follows:

$$\text{Ideal } P_l = \frac{I_1^{**}}{I_0} < \frac{I_1^*}{I_0} = P_l \qquad (4\text{-}14)$$

That is, the Laspeyre price index is greater than the *ideal* Laspeyre price index. This indicates that the Laspeyre price index is biased upward. As we shall see later, the upward bias of the Laspeyre price index is important in determining compensation. Let us go back to Table 4-1. Assume that in the base period you received an income of $26 and you purchased 3 units of X and 4 units of Y. From the base period to the second period the price of X rose from $2 to $4, and the price of Y rose from $5 to $6. As we have seen, P_l is 1.38; for you to consume basket A (3 units of X and 4 units of Y) in the second period your budget must increase by 38 percent from $26 to $36 (= 1.38 · $26). However, we note that in the base period you paid $26 for U_0. Inequality 4-14 tells us that the ideal Laspeyre price index in less than 1.38; in other words, for you to attain in the second period a satisfaction as indicated by U_0, your budget should increase by less than 38 percent.

4.1c Deflating Nominal Income

When we talk loosely about *price levels*, we have in mind a price index. As shown in Section 4.1b, a price index tells us what is the change in the *average* price of a certain basket of goods. We also noted that the change in the *average* price may be due to the passing of time, or alternatively, to a change in location. Consider Table 4-1 again. Suppose X represents energy and Y represents nonenergy resources. The price of energy increased by 100 percent; the Laspeyre price index increased by only 38 percent. If we talk in terms of price indices, the price index of energy in our example is 2.00 (= \$4/\$2). To *deflate* the price of energy means to divide the energy price index by the general price index. If we select the Laspeyre price index as the deflator, we obtain the deflated price of energy as follows: $2.00/1.38 = 1.45$. The interpretation is that the relative price of energy rose by 45 percent. We can also convert the *nominal* price of \$4 in the second period into a *real* price of \$2.9 (= \$4/1.38). Note that \$2.9 makes sense only if we refer to the base period. Thus if 1977 is the base year, we may say that the real price of energy in 1978 was \$2.9 in 1977 prices.

Consider Table 4-1 again. Consumer income rose from \$26 in the base period to \$76 in the second period. If we deflate \$76 by a Laspeyre price index of 1.38, we obtain \$55.07. Dividing this number by \$26, we get 2.11, which is the Paasche quantity index. If we deflate \$76 by the Paasche price index, we obtain \$54.28. Dividing this number by \$26 gives 2.08, the Laspeyre quantity index. Let us prove this result formally. Let $Y_1 = \Sigma X_1 \cdot P_1$ denote the nominal income of the consumer in the second period and $Y_0 = \Sigma X_0 \cdot P_0$ denote that income in the base period. The change in nominal income (Y_1 relative to Y_0) is

$$\frac{Y_1}{Y_0} = \frac{\Sigma X_1 \cdot P_1}{\Sigma X_0 \cdot P_0}$$

The change in real income may be calculated by dividing the change in nominal income by the change in price. If the Laspeyre price index is used, we obtain

$$\text{Change in real income} = \frac{\dfrac{Y_1}{Y_0}}{P_l} = \frac{\dfrac{\Sigma X_1 \cdot P_1}{\Sigma X_0 \cdot P_0}}{\dfrac{\Sigma P_1 \cdot X_0}{\Sigma P_0 \cdot X_0}} = \frac{\Sigma X_1 \cdot P_1}{\Sigma X_0 \cdot P_1} = Q_p$$

In other words, deflating the change in nominal income by a Laspeyre price index yields a Paasche quantity index. Since P_l has an upward bias, Q_p must have a downward bias. Alternatively, deflating the change in nominal income by a Paasche price index yields a Laspeyre quantity index as follows:

$$\text{Change in real income} = \frac{\dfrac{Y_1}{Y_0}}{P_p} = \frac{\dfrac{\Sigma X_1 \cdot P_1}{\Sigma X_0 \cdot P_0}}{\dfrac{\Sigma P_1 \cdot X_1}{\Sigma P_0 \cdot X_1}} = \frac{\Sigma X_1 \cdot P_0}{\Sigma X_0 \cdot P_0} = Q_l$$

Since P_p is biased downward, Q_l must be biased upward. In other words, since the Paasche price index is smaller than the ideal Paasche price index, had we divided the change in nominal income by the ideal Paasche price index instead of the Paasche price index, we would have received a smaller (ideal) Laspeyre quantity index.

The Laspeyre price index can be written as

$$P_l = \Sigma w_0 \cdot \frac{P_1}{P_0} \tag{4-15}$$

If, for convenience, commodities are denoted by X, Y, etc., then w is (base period) weight. For example, w for X is $(X_0 \cdot P_{x0})/(X_0 \cdot P_{x0} + Y_0 \cdot P_{y0})$. In Table 4-1 the Laspeyre price index would be calculated as follows:

$$P_l = \frac{6}{26} \cdot \frac{4}{2} + \frac{20}{26} \cdot \frac{6}{5} = 0.23 \cdot \frac{4}{2} + 0.77 \cdot \frac{6}{5} = 1.38$$

4.1d The Consumer Price Index

The consumer price index (CPI) is a statistical measure of changes in prices of goods and services which has been calculated by the Bureau of Labor Statistics since 1917–1919.

The CPI is used as a measure of changes in the purchasing power of the dollar for a variety of purposes, including welfare payments and pensions. Also, wage contracts between labor and management often contain escalation clauses based on changes in CPI.

The monthly index is calculated for the United States as a whole and for standard metropolitan areas. Prices are obtained by periodic visits to a representative sample of about 18,000 retail stores and other service establishments. Rental rates are obtained from close to 40,000 tenants. From time to time the Bureau of Labor Statistics revises the weights of the various commodities in the basket, as patterns of consumption change. For example, some items consumed in the early 1960s, such as bobby pins and garter belts, were hardly seen on the market in the late 1970s.

The *wholesale price index (WPI)* is another important index calculated by the Bureau of Labor Statistics. The WPI is a Laspeyre index that measures the price changes for goods sold in primary markets. The Department of Commerce calculates the gross national product (GNP) deflators, which are also known as the *implicit deflators. These price indices are used specifically to calculate GNP in real terms.*

4.1e An Application: Escalation Clauses in Wage Agreements

To illustrate how an escalation clause might work, consider a typical worker, one whose relative weights in the basket of goods are identical to the relative weights of the basket as calculated by the Bureau of Labor Statistics. As shown in Figure 4-9, originally the worker's budget line was I_0, and the optimum basket on it was depicted by point A. Because of inflation, prices rise and the budget line shifts inward to I_1. The new optimum point is B. To compensate the employee, the employer must increase the wage rate

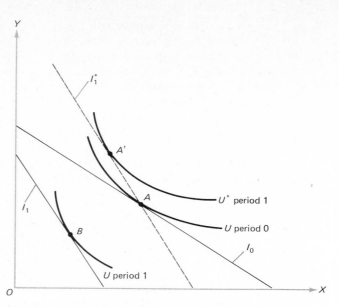

FIGURE 4-9 AN ESCALATION CLAUSE IN WAGES

The initial equilibrium of the consumer is A. At A the initial indifference curve is tangent to I_0. Due to inflation the budget line shifts down to a new position—I_1. B is the new equilibrium point. The compensation due to the escalation clause now takes place: The consumer's budget is now increased by a proportion equal to Laspeyre price index; this enables the consumer to shift the budget line to a new position denoted by I_1^*, which is parallel to I_1 and passes through A. The consumer climbs to a still higher indifference curve which is tangent to I_1^* at point A': The conclusion is that a compensation based on a Laspeyre price index will result in a higher level of satisfaction for the consumer.

from I_0 to I_1^*. The employer restores the employee's purchasing power so that the employee can again buy basket A. The amount of compensation is calculated by applying Equation 4-13, namely, $P_I = I_1^*/I_0$, which is the rate of inflation. For example, if the rate of inflation according to the CPI was 9 percent, the nominal wage rate of the consumer is raised 9 percent. But recall that the ideal Laspeyre price index is smaller than the Laspeyre price index. In other words, the escalation clause allows the typical consumer to "buy" more utility than he or she had in the first time period: He or she moves from A to A', which belongs to a higher indifference curve. This blessing may or may not accrue to the nontypical consumer. We leave this question as an exercise for the student.

4.2 THE THEORY OF UTILITY UNDER UNCERTAINTY

4.2a Introduction

Some people insure their homes against fire and their cars against accident and take a day off and go to Las Vegas to gamble. Are they irrational? M. Friedman and L. J. Savage proposed a special utility function of income which rationalizes the behavior of a person who insures and gambles simultaneously.[2] In this section the theory of utility under uncertainty and the special Friedman-Savage utility curve will be presented to illustrate how insurance and gambling can coexist. Then the claim of some policy makers that *workmen's compensation laws* force employers to introduce safety measures will be considered. This is another illustration of behavior affected by the possibility of risk.

First, let us briefly go over the concept of probability: If an urn contains 100 tags, say, 20 red and 80 white, the probability of blindly drawing a red tag is 20 out of 100, namely, 0.20, and the probability of drawing a white tag is 80 out of 100, namely, 0.80. If we denote the probability of drawing a red tag by p, then $p = 0.20$. Hence the probability of drawing a white tag is $(1 - p)$ and $1 - p = 0.80$.

In Chapter 1 the theory of utility of sure prospects was developed. Sure prospects could be baskets of commodities. In this section we introduce the notion of an uncertain prospect of having "basket A or basket B," where the probability of having A is p and the probability of having B is $(1 - p)$. For example, assume that if anyone who draws a red tag from the urn that contains 20 red tags and 80 white tags wins basket A and anyone who draws a white tag wins basket B, then $p = 0.20$ and $(1 - p) = 0.80$. If instead of baskets we consider incomes measured in dollars, the uncertain propect has an associated concept known as an *expected income*. If instead of the two baskets A and B, we introduce two levels of income, respectively, a lower level I_1 and a higher level I_2, and if the probability of having I_1 is p and that of having I_2 is $(1 - p)$, then the expected income denoted by $\overline{I}$ is expressed as

$$\overline{I} = p \cdot I_1 + (1 - p) \cdot I_2 \tag{4-16}$$

For example, if the uncertain prospect is a 20 percent chance of having \$10 and an 80 percent chance of having \$20, the expected income is $\overline{I} = 0.2 \cdot \$10 + 0.8 \cdot \$20 = \$18$. Now, since more income is preferred to less income, we can state that the utility derived from a level of income I_2 exceeds the utility derived from I_1. Let these utilities be denoted by $U(I_2)$ and $U(I_1)$, respectively. The *expected utility* of the uncertain prospect [the probability associated with I_1 is p and the probability associated with I_2 is $(1 - p)$] is expressed as

$$\overline{U} = p \cdot U(I_1) + (1 - p) \cdot U(I_2) \tag{4-17}$$

In our example, if the utility of having \$10 is 900 utils and the utility of having \$20 is 1600 utils, then the expected utility of the uncertain prospect is $\overline{U} = 0.2 \cdot 900 + 0.8 \cdot 1600 = 1460$ utils. There is a convenient geometric property associated with expected income and expected utility that should be illustrated here. Consider Figure 4-10. Let the points G and H depict the pairs I_1 and its associated $U(I_1)$ and I_2 and its associated $U(I_2)$, respectively, in the I

---

[2] Milton Friedman and Leonard J. Savage, "The Utility Analysis of Choices Involving Risk," *Journal of Political Economy*, vol. LVI, August 1948. Friedman and Savage avoided using cardinal utility. In order to simplify the presentation here, cardinal utility is used.

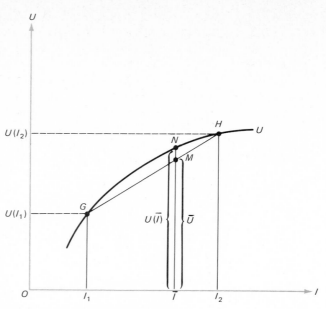

FIGURE 4-10   EXPECTED INCOME AND EXPECTED UTILITY
The curve U represents utility as a function of income. Points $G[I_1, U(I_1)]$ and $H[I_2, U(I_2)]$ represent the two components (certain prospects) which make up the uncertain prospect. The expected income of the uncertain prospect is $\bar{I}$. $\bar{U}$ is the expected utility of the uncertain prospect. $U(\bar{I})$ is the utility of a sure level of income, which is equal to $\bar{I}$. Given any pair of probabilities p and $(1 - p)$, we calculate $\bar{I}$ and then trace a vertical line from $\bar{I}$ all the way to the segment $\overline{GH}$ in order to find the value of $\bar{U}$.

and U space. First, if $p = 1$, uncertainty vanishes and there is certainty of having an income of I_1. As p is decreased, we trace out the expected income $\bar{I}$ by moving along the horizontal axis from I_1 to I_2. Finally, when p is reduced to zero, I coincides with I_2. The geometric convenience is rendered by the fact that the straight line $\overline{GH}$ is the locus of all points satisfying $\bar{U} = p \cdot U(I_1) + (1 - p) \cdot U(I_2)$ for $I = \bar{I}$. For example, in Figure 4-10 we mark $\bar{I}$ on the horizontal axis and then we trace a vertical line from $\bar{I}$ to point M on the $\overline{GH}$ segment in order to obtain $\bar{U}$.

The special theory of Friedman and Savage simply states that uncertain prospects (like the one illustrated by Figure 4-10) can be ranked by their associated expected utility. Put differently, if the expected utility of an uncertain prospect is higher than the expected utility of another uncertain prospect, the first should be preferred to the latter. Moreover, uncertain prospects can be compared with certain prospects: In Figure 4-10 the utility function of income assumes the normal shape of being concave from below, reflecting the law of diminishing marginal utility (Section 1.2b). Assume the consumer had to rank the uncertain prospect of having either I_1 with probability p or I_2 with probability $(1 - p)$ with the certain prospect of having sure income equals $\bar{I}$. Since the utility of the expected income is higher than the expected utility, the consumer would rank the certain prospect over the uncertain prospect. Let us extend our example ($I_1 = \$10$, $I_2 = \$20$, and $p = 0.20$) further by imagining that the utility function is $U = 100I - I^2$ (which would behave nicely between $I = 0$ and $I = 50$). The utility of the expected income is 1476 utils ($= 100 \cdot 18 - 18^2$). The expected utility is (as shown before) 1460 utils. A consumer behaving according to the special theory would rank the utility of the expected income over the expected utility. The theory just described is "good" or "bad" depending on whether it can rationalize behavior of consumers in situations involving risk. As we see in the next section, in order for the theory to be "good," the utility curve cannot be concave throughout.

4.2b Insurance and Gambling

First, let us examine insurance. In Figure 4-11 the utility function has a concave segment which is followed by a convex segment. The convex segment will be needed to explain the fact that people who insure themselves may simultaneously indulge in gambling. Earned income is equal to $\overline{OC}$ dollars. There is a very small probability that fire will occur, leading to a great loss of income. In that case income will be reduced to $\overline{OA}$. Expected

FIGURE 4-11   INSURANCE

U is the utility curve. $\overline{OC}$ is the income of the consumer. If fire were to damage his home, the income of the consumer would be reduced to $\overline{OA}$. The expected value of this uncertain prospect (probability of p to have $\overline{OA}$ and probability of $(1 - p)$ to have $\overline{OC}$) is $\overline{OH}$. The expected utility of this uncertain prospect is $\overline{HH'} = p \cdot \overline{(AA')} + (1 - p) \cdot \overline{(CC')}$. This is less than the utility from a sure income of $\overline{OH}$, which is $\overline{HH''}$. Thus it pays the consumer to convert his uncertain prospect to a sure income of $\overline{OH}$, so long as the cost of insurance is less than $\overline{BH}$.

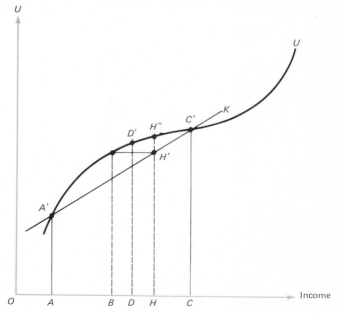

income is $\overline{OH}$ [$= p \cdot \overline{OA} + (1 - p) \cdot \overline{OC}$]; the corresponding expected utility is $\overline{HH'}$. Clearly, since the utility curve is concave, a sure income of $\overline{OH}$ with associated utility of $\overline{HH''}$ is better than the uncertain prospect yielding an expected utility of $\overline{HH'}$ only. It is impossible to convert an uncertain prospect with an expected income of $\overline{OH}$ dollars into the same amount of sure income. The reason for this is explained by the following example: A thousand homeowners each owning a home worth $100,000 decided to pool in order to insure their homes. The risk of a fire destroying a home (per year) is 1/1000. Thus the cost of pooling (converting uncertain to certain prospects) without administrative expenses amounts to $100 per homeowner. If the administrative cost is $10,000 per year, each person will have to pay $110 per year to insure a home. In Figure 4-11 if $10 is less than $\overline{BH}$, the homeowner will find it worth his or her money to pay the insurance premium of $110 because the utility of the new sure income will exceed the expected utility of the expected income. For example, suppose the segment $\overline{DH}$ is equal to $10. In that case the sure income of the homeowner will be $\overline{OD}$ and his or her utility will be $\overline{DD'}$, which is in excess of $\overline{HH'}$.

How can we explain the fact that a person who yesterday insured his or

FIGURE 4-12 GAMBLING

U is the utility function of the consumer. We now focus on its convex as well as concave portion. The consumer has an income of $\overline{OC}$. She can purchase a lottery of $\overline{LC}$ that entitles her to a small probability of winning $\overline{LN}$ dollars. The expected value of her income after she buys the lottery is $\overline{OM}$. The corresponding expected utility is $\overline{MM'} = p \cdot (\overline{LL'}) + (1 - p) \cdot (\overline{NN'})$. It exceeds the utility of the sure prospect marked by $\overline{CC'}$. The consumer should gamble.

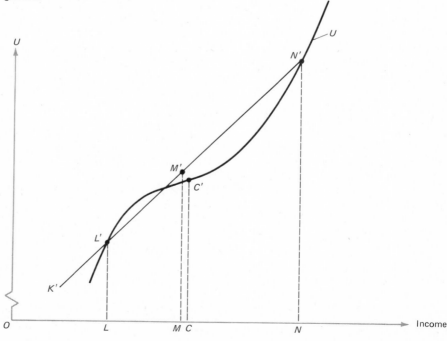

her home today indulges in gambling? Figure 4-12 is a replica of Figure 4-11 except that we now focus on both its concave and convex segments. Earned income is again $\overline{OC}$ dollars. The consumer can buy a lottery ticket at a price of $\overline{LC}$. There is a small probability of winning a relatively large sum of money $\overline{LN}$. If the person loses, his or her income will be $\overline{OL}$, if the person wins, his or her income will be $\overline{ON}$. The expected income is $\overline{OM}$ [$(= p \cdot \overline{OL} + (1 - p) \cdot \overline{ON})$]. Clearly, $\overline{OM}$ has to be less than $\overline{OC}$ for the house to be profitable. Yet the consumer buys the lottery because the expected utility of the uncertain prospect, namely, $\overline{MM'}$, exceeds the utility of the sure income, namely, $\overline{CC'}$. It is evident from the shape of the utility curve that the consumer has to be near the point of inflection (the point separating the concave from the convex zone) in order for him or her to insure his or her home and indulge in gambling simultaneously. Indeed, this is what Friedman and Savage suggested. Economists later raised the question about a person whose income grows to a level somewhere in the middle of the convex zone. Obviously, such a person might buy lottery tickets that will either make him or her very rich or leave him or her with nothing. But it is known that middle-class families do not engage in such unusual gambling. To settle this issue, Harry Markowitz suggested that the position of the utility curve changes with wealth: The inflection point roughly coincides with the *customary* level of wealth of the consumer. Should his or her wealth rise, the entire curve would shift to the right.[3]

4.2c An Application: Workmen's Compensation

The theory of utility in situations involving risk is remotely applicable to workmen's compensation. State workmen's compensation laws were enacted during the first 40 years of the twentieth century to provide compensation to injured workers. For the time being it can be stated intuitively that workers would like to insure against the risk of on-the-job injury to no lesser degree than they would like to insure against car accidents. In absence of workmen's compensation laws workers would insure themselves privately if they perceived the risk of injury on the job. Moreover, *ceteris paribus,* in a free market the wage rate in *risky* employment will exceed the wage rate in *less risky* employment by the cost to workers of a policy insuring against income loss, medical expenses, and associated nonpecuniary psychic losses resulting from on-the-job injuries. (If such a wage differential in favor of risky employment did not exist, workers

would prefer less risky jobs. The resulting shift in employment would thus raise the wage rate in risk-associated work and depress the rate in less risky work, until a differential which is equal to the cost of an insurance policy is created.)

The question then arises: Are not workmen's compensation laws superfluous? Students of workmen's compensation justified the enactment of the laws (at least in part) by assuming that such laws stimulated employers to invest in safety measures which significantly reduced the incidence of injuries. Gregory and Gisser furnished evidence supporting a different hypothesis, namely, that employers invested in safety measures where the firm required a relatively high degree of skill since the cost of replacing an injured worker would be high.[4] (When a worker with skills specific to the firm is injured on the job, the firm has to recruit a new employee and invest in job training. A

---

[3]Harry Markowitz, "The Utility of Wealth," *Journal of Political Economy,* vol. LX, April 1952, pp. 151–158.

[4]Peter Gregory and Micha Gisser, "Theoretical Aspects of Workmen's Compensation," in Monroe Berkowitz (ed.), *Supplemental Studies for the National Commission on State Workmen's Compensation Laws* (Director Peter S. Barth), vol. 1, Washington, 1973.

TABLE 4-3   Frequency Rates of Occupational Injury
(Frequency rate, injuries per million worker-hours)

Total manufacturing		Warehousing and storage (skills are general to the firm)		Steel (skills are specific to the firm)	
Period	Rate	Period	Rate	Period	Rate
1942–1944	19.4	1942–1944	35.9	1921–1925	31.3
1954–1956	12.0	1957–1959	29.6	1946–1948	9.6
1966–1968	13.8	1966–1968	26.9	1964–1967	5.4

Source: P. Gregory and M. Gisser, "Theoretical Aspects of Workmen's Compensation Laws," in Monroe Berkowitz (ed.), vol. I, *Supplemental Studies for the National Commission on State Workmen's Compensation Laws* (Director Peter S. Barth) Washington, 1973.

worker with general skills who is injured on the job can be replaced with minimal costs.) Gregory and Gisser used data furnished by the National Safety Council on frequency rates of occupational injury by selected occupations and years. Industries were divided into two groups, one in which skills are general to the firm and the other in which skills are specific to the firm. Table 4-3 gives results for *total manufacturing, warehousing and storage,* and *steel*.

Although the periods in Table 4-3 are not comparable, it is evident from examining the data presented that the frequency rate declined more rapidly in the steel industry than in the warehousing and storage industry. Why? It is possible that direct production costs, rather than the enactment of workmen's compensation laws, induced employers to increase investment in safety measures.

4.3 THE CONSUMER'S SURPLUS: A MORE ADVANCED APPROACH

In Section 2.7 the concept of the *consumer's surplus* was developed by applying an intuitive method. We saw that the operational meaning of the consumer's surplus is the maximum amount of money a consumer would be willing to pay for a good rather than go without that good. Geometrically, we saw that the consumer's surplus is approximately the area under the demand curve and above the price confronting the consumer in the marketplace (Figure 2-14). It was also mentioned that the concept of the consumer's surplus is useful in analyzing loss of social well-being due to monopolistic pricing and taxes. These topics will be covered in later chapters. This section gives the interested student a chance to study consumer's surplus at a more advanced level.

Why have we separated the "intuitive" approach from the "indifference curves" approach? The answer lies in a technical difficulty: It is relatively easy to show that the area under the demand curve and above the price line measures the consumer's surplus. It is also relatively easy to show that the consumer's surplus is a certain vertical distance between two indifference curves in an indifference map. However, relating the area under the demand curve to the vertical distance between two indifference curves is rather difficult, as the following section illustrates.

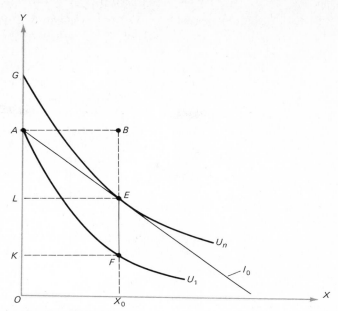

FIGURE 4-13 THE CONSUMER'S SURPLUS

X represents the good under consideration; Y represents all other goods. Given a certain price of X and assuming that $P_y = \$1$, we obtain the budget line I_0. Initially the budget of the consumer amounts to $\overline{OA}$ dollars. To get to the equilibrium point E, she gives up $\overline{BE}$ dollars in exchange for $\overline{AB}$ ($= X_0$) units of X. The consumer's surplus is $\overline{EF}$. Had the consumer been asked how much more income she would give up rather than go without X altogether, she would indicate a willingness to sacrifice up to $\overline{EF}$ dollars, because point F and point A lie on the same indifference curve; point A means to go without X altogether.

4.3a The Indifference Curves Approach[5]

Let Y in Figure 4-13 represent all goods but commodity X. If we agree to a scale such that $P_y = \$1$, the vertical axis measures money income in dollars. If consumers are confronted with a certain price of X on the market, say, P_{x0}, and given that their income is $\overline{OA}$ dollars per unit of time, the position and slope of their budget line are determined. Let this budget line be I_0. The consumers' equilibrium point is E, where the indifference curve U_n is just tangent to the budget line I_0. They now consume X_0 units of X and pay $\overline{BE}$ dollars (which is equal to $\overline{AL}$) for X_0 units of X. The first question we ask the consumer is: "How much would you pay rather than go without X altogether?" The answer must be $\overline{BF}$ dollars, because going without X would get the consumer to point A, which would yield the same satisfaction as point F: Both points are on the same indifference curve U_1. As a matter of logic if confronted with this "all or nothing" proposition, the consumer

---

[5] For a more rigorous treatment see Richard A. Bilas, *Microeconomic Theory*, McGraw-Hill, New York, 1971, 2d ed., pp. 97–107.

should be ready to pay $\overline{EF}$ minus a penny in addition to $\overline{BE}$ dollars which was already paid. $\overline{EF}$ dollars can be defined as the *consumer's surplus*. A second question we can ask the consumer is: "Given that you are at point A, how much would you pay for the opportunity to trade Y for X?" The answer must be $\overline{AG}$ dollars, because the trade would enable the consumer to climb to a higher indifference curve U_n, compared with U_1. Looking at it differently, $\overline{AG}$ indicates what is the maximum license fee that could be levied from the consumer for the right to trade.

The concept of the consumer's surplus was invented by Dupuit in 1844. Alfred Marshall later developed the concept technically and included it in his *Principles*. Marshall stated that if the marginal utility of money income is constant, the segment $\overline{EF}$ in Figure 4-13 is equal to the area of the triangle under the demand curve and above the price line (Figure 2-14). Moreover, $\overline{EF}$ (Figure 4-13) is equal to $\overline{AG}$: If to the assumption of constant marginal utility of money income we add the assumption of separability, which states that the marginal utility of X is not affected by the amount of Y (money income) consumed, then the indifference curves are vertically parallel. For example, the indifference curve U_1 at point F has the same slope as U_n at point E. Geometry also tells us that if indifference curves are vertically parallel they are also vertically equidistant. Thus $\overline{FE} = \overline{AG}$, etc. Vertical parallelism results from the fact that the slope of the indifference curve RCS is equal to $- MU_x/MU_y$ (Equation 1-5). Since the marginal utility of money income MU_y is constant and since tracing a vertical line such as X_0FE in Figure 4-13 also means keeping MU_x constant, the ratio MU_x/MU_y is kept constant along any vertical movement throughout the indifference map.

Figure 4-13 is duplicated in panel (a) of Figure 4-14. In panel (b) the associated demand curve is shown. As before, the consumer's income is $\overline{OA}$. The amount of X purchased is X_0, and the amount of money paid for it is $\overline{BE}$. Recall that consumers would be willing to pay $\overline{BF}$ dollars rather than go without X. Actually, he or she pays $\overline{BE}$ dollars; so his or her surplus is $\overline{EF}$. Now, $\overline{BF}$, the maximum amount of money the consumer would be willing to pay for X_0, is equal to the sum of the ΔY's obtained by "scalloping" U_1 from point A to point F: Consider a relatively high price of X, say, P_x^*, reflected in budget line I^* which touches indifference curve U^* at E'. Because indifference curves are assumed parallel, the slope of U^* at E' is the same as the slope of U_1 at F'. But by the tangency of I^* and U^* at E', budget line I^* has the same slope as U_1 at F'. Thus we can write the following (for small ΔX):

$$\frac{\Delta Y^*}{\Delta X} = \text{slope of } I^*$$

Multiplying by ΔX gives

$$\Delta Y^* = \Delta X \cdot (\text{slope of } I^*)$$

The slope of I^* is $-P_x^*/P_y$, and since by assumption (that Y is money income) $P_y = \$1$, and ignoring the negative sign, the slope of I^* becomes simply P_x^*. Substituting P_x^* for the slope to I^* in the above equation, we obtain

$$\Delta Y^* = \Delta X \cdot P_x^*$$

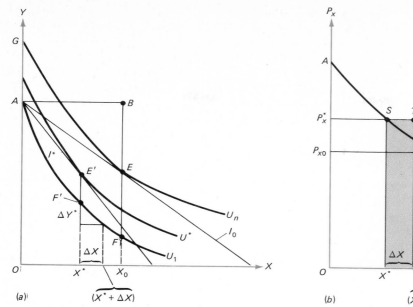

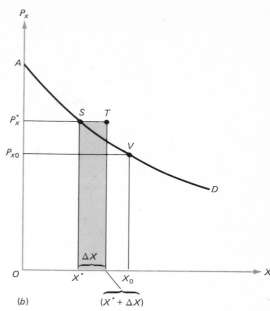

FIGURE 4-14   THE CONSUMER'S SURPLUS—AN ADVANCED APPROACH

(a) The indifference curve U_n is tangent to I_0 at E. The indifference curve U_1 has the same intercept as I_0 with the Y axis, namely, point A. As in Figure 4-13, $\overline{EF}$ is the consumer's surplus. I^* is a budget line representing a certain price of X. The equilibrium point on I^* is E'. The slope of I^* is $-p_x^*/P_y$. Since $P_y = \$1$, and ignoring the minus sign, the slope is equal to P_x^*. Separability (between MU_x and Y and between MU_y and X) and the assumption that the marginal utility of income (here Y) is constant renders U_n, U^* and U_1 vertically parallel. Hence the slope of I^* at E' is equal to the slope of U_1 at F'. Thus the slope of I^* equals $\Delta Y^*/\Delta X$, leading to the result that $\Delta Y^* = P_x^* \cdot \Delta X$.

(b) D is the demand curve derived from the indifference map in panel (a) of Figure 4-14. In particular, P_x^* is associated with I^* in panel (a) of Figure 4-14. The shaded rectangle is $P_x^* \cdot \Delta X$, and it is equal to ΔY^* in panel (a) of Figure 4-14.

which in panel (b) is the shaded rectangle denoted by $X^*(X^* + \Delta X)TS$. The entire length of $\overline{BF}$ can be built by a series of increments like ΔY^*, starting with a very high price of X near point A and slowly reducing the price of X to P_{x0}. If the increments are very small, adding their associated rectangles in panel (b) will yield the area under the demand curve denoted by $OAVX_0$. Subtracting $OP_{x0}VX_0$ in panel (b) [associated with $\overline{BE}$ in panel (a)] yields the triangular area $P_{x0}AV$, namely, the consumer's surplus.

If the assumption of constant marginal utility of money income is relaxed, the Marshallian triangular area $P_{x0}AV$ [panel (b)] is only approximately equal to $\overline{EF}$ [panel (a)]

SUMMARY   Three topics have been covered in this optional chapter: *index numbers, the theory of utility under uncertainty*, and a *more advanced approach to the consumer's surplus.*

Index numbers We discussed both *quantity index numbers* and *price index numbers*. Quantity index numbers were divided into *Laspeyre* and *Paasche* indices and were used to determine whether the well-being of the consumer increases or decreases over time or from location to location. The key to making the determination about a change in well-being was to compare the quantity index number with unity. *Price index numbers* measure the variations of price levels of groups of goods. Price index numbers are also divided into *Laspeyre* and *Paasche* indices. The Laspeyre price index has practical application because the base period basket can be used to weight the prices of the various goods in the consumer's budget. The *consumer price index (CPI)* in the United States is a Laspeyre price index which is used in introducing wage escalation clauses into labor contracts and in other situations where consumers seek protection against inflation. We saw that the Laspeyre price index is biased upward and the Paasche price index is biased downward. We therefore concluded that escalation clauses based on Laspeyre price index numbers compensate consumers by more than is necessary to leave them with the intitial level of satisfaction. Finally the concept of *deflation* was discussed; we found that a relative price of a good may be derived by deflating that (nominal) price by a price index such as the CPI. Nominal income can also be deflated by a price index. Deflating nominal income by a Paasche price index would yield real income series in which the numbers relate to each other as quantity Laspeyre index numbers, and conversely, deflating nominal income by a Laspeyre price index would yield real income series in which the numbers relate to each other as quantity Paasche index numbers.

The theory of utility under uncertainty In Section 4.2 the concept of *uncertain prospects* was introduced. A special utility theory was discussed which enables the consumer to compare uncertain prospects with both certain and uncertain prospects. In this connection the concept of *expected income* and *expected utility* was also introduced. We saw how insurance can be explained by a concave utility function, which implies that the utility of sure income (which is equal to the expected income) exceeds the expected utility. We also saw that the behavior of people who simultaneously insure their homes and gamble can be rationalized by assuming a utility curve which is first concave and then convex.

An advanced approach to the consumer's surplus In Chapter 2 the consumer's surplus was defined as the amount of money a consumer would pay for a good rather than go without the good altogether. We saw that the consumer's surplus is equal to the area under the demand curve and above the price. In Section 4.3 we saw that the consumer's surplus is a vertical distance between two specific indifference curves: One has a common intercept with the budget line on the Y (all-other-goods) axis, and the other is tangent to the budget line. The vertical distance between the two indifference curves was proved to be equal to the area under the demand curve and above the price.

Quantity index number The weighted average of quantities consumed in one situation relative to the weighted average of quantities consumed in another situation. A situation may be a period or alternatively a location. The quantity index is *Laspeyre* if the prices in the base period are used as weights. The quantity index is *Paasche* if the prices of the second period are used as weights. Symbolically, the Laspeyre quantity index is $Q_l = (\Sigma X_1 \cdot P_0)/(\Sigma X_0 \cdot P_0)$ and the Paasche quantity index is $Q_p = (\Sigma X_1 \cdot P_1)/(\Sigma X_0 \cdot P_1)$.

Revealed preference An axiom stating that if B (basket) is revealed as preferable to A when evaluated by one set of prices, then A cannot be revealed as preferable to B when evaluated by another set of prices.

Price index number The weighted average of prices in one period (or location) relative to the weighted average of prices in another period (or location). The price index is *Laspeyre* if the basket of the base period serves for weighting the prices. The price index is *Paasche* if the basket of the second period serves for weighting the prices. Price index numbers are useful in converting *nominal* prices into *relative* (real) prices and *nominal* incomes into *real* flows in income. Symbolically the Laspeyre price index is $P_l = (\Sigma P_1 \cdot X_0)/(\Sigma P_0 \cdot X_0)$. The Paasche price index is $P_p = (\Sigma P_1 \cdot X_1)/(\Sigma P_0 \cdot X_1)$.

The consumer price index (CPI) A statistical measure of changes in prices of goods and services. It is a *Laspeyre* price index. The Bureau of Labor Statistics has been calculating the CPI since 1917–1919.

An uncertain prospect Given two certain prospects, such as A and B, the *uncertain prospect* is having *either A or B*, where a probability p is associated with A and a probability $(1 - p)$ is associated with B. A prospect could represent a basket, a level of income, or a level of utility.

Expected value The expected value of an uncertain prospect is the sum of all the components (certain prospects) of the uncertain prospect, each multiplied by its associated probability. If the components of an uncertain prospect are the certain prospects I_1 and I_2 with associated probabilities of p and $(1 - p)$, the expected value of the uncertain event is $\overline{I} = p \cdot I_1 + (1 - p) \cdot I_2$, where $\overline{I}$ stands for *expected value*.

Insurance Converting an uncertain prospect of two levels of income into a certain prospect of income.

Gambling Converting a certain income prospect into an uncertain prospect involving two levels of income.

Consumer's surplus The maximum amount of money a consumer would be willing to pay for a good rather than go without a certain good altogether.

An asterisk indicates an advanced problem.

4–1. Prove that if points A and B in Figure 4–5 coincide, unless I_0 and I_1 are identical, tastes must have changed.

4–2. The Paasche quantity index of a consumer increased from 1974 to 1975. Is he better off in 1975? Assume that his tastes have not changed, and 1974 is the base year.

4-3. The Paasche quantity index of a consumer (base year is 1974) is given as follows:

Time	Q_p
1974	100
1975	110
1976	120

Is she better off in 1976 compared with 1975?

4-4. The United Nations sent an economist from the United States to Brazil. His income in Brazil was increased by 20 percent over his income in the United States. His consumption of X and Y (the only two goods in his budget) is summarized as follows:

Country	X	P_x	Y	P_y	I
United States	8	$2	1	$4	$20
Brazil	2	$3	6	$3	$24

(a) Is the economist better off in Brazil than in the United States?
(b) By how much should his income be increased in Brazil to ensure that he is at least as well off as he was in the United States?
(c) If the economist is compensated according to (b), can you predict the magnitudes of the new quantity indices Q_l and Q_p comparing Brazil with the United States (< 1, $= 1$, or > 1)?

4-5. In country A, a Laspeyre price index was calculated as follows for the period 1974–1975:

Time	P_x	P_y	Laspeyre price index
1974	100	100	100
1975	105	110	108.5

The average weights (for 1974) applied in calculating the index were 30 percent for X and 70 percent for Y. Assume that X and Y are the only two goods in the budgets of consumers. The salaries of three employees were accordingly raised by 8.5 percent, respectively. In

1974 the first, second, and third employees spent 20, 30, and 50 percent of their respective budgets on X. Whose satisfaction increased and whose satisfaction declined from 1974 to 1975?

4-6. Following the deregulation of natural gas some economists suggested compensating poor families (below the poverty line) by an amount equal to the average consumption of natural gas at the base year times the change in the price of natural gas. Would the typical poor consumer benefit from the compensation? How about the nontypical consumer? You should compare the satisfaction of the consumer before the rise in the price of natural gas with his or her satisfaction after the rise in the price of natural gas was compensated.

4-7. A person who earns $600 a month is persuaded to accept an 80-20 chance of winning or losing $100. What is the marginal utility of the seventh $100 if the marginal utility of the sixth $100 is set at 10 utils. What would you conclude about a person who under the same circumstances was persuaded to accept a 20-80 chance?

4-8. A person insures her home but does not insure her car. Can you rationalize it?

4-9.* A faculty club has been established. The price per drink was fixed at $1. When the annual membership fee was set at $25, Professor Smith refused to join. When the fee was reduced to $20, he decided to join the club. He bought 100 drinks during the entire year. What is the shape (equation) of his demand curve if it is linear?

PART TWO

THE THEORY OF
THE PRODUCER
AND SUPPLY

Now that the theory of demand has been covered in some detail, we can turn our attention from the consumer to the *producer*. The analysis of producers will be separated from that of consumers because the two groups in reality are separate. The growers of coffee, for example, make up but a small minority of coffee consumers. (This point will be considered again in Chapter 9.)

The *theory of the producer and supply* will be developed as follows: Chapter 5 will cover the technical aspects of the theory of production. Prices will not be mentioned at this early stage of analysis. Chapter 6 will analyze the least-cost combination of factors of production, leading to the derivation of cost curves. In order to figure out its least-cost combination of inputs, a firm has to take into consideration its process of production, known as the *production function*, and prices of *inputs* such as *labor, capital,* and *land.* Chapter 7 will introduce into the analysis the price of final output, enabling the *competitive firm* to select the optimum level of output. (The theory dealing with optimum output of noncompetitive firms will be covered in Chapters 11, 12, and 13.) Finally, Chapter 8 will discuss the response of competitive firms to variations in the price of output, which boils down to the *theory of supply.*

At this point students will benefit from reviewing the circular flow model as illustrated in Figure I–2. In particular they should observe the role of the firms' box in that model.

C H A P T E R

THE PRODUCTION FUNCTION

This chapter will focus on the *process of production*. Any process of production obeys some important rules that stem from the scarcity of resources. If resources such as labor, knowledge, machinery, and energy were available in unlimited amounts, goods could be produced at zero cost in any desired quantity. This is not true for the world we live in; even if we had at our disposal unlimited resources of energy, machinery, raw materials, land, and all that was needed to combine these resources, we would have scarcity because of the simple fact that performing work means sacrificing leisure. Leisure is an important good in the budget of every consumer; after all, without leisure a consumer cannot enjoy most other goods that are available in the marketplace. Now, scarcity of resources implies that producers must pay a price for such things as labor, machinery, and natural resources. And to maximize profit, producers must combine these resources in the most efficient and economical way, namely, in the least-cost way. Before the least-cost combination of scarce resources is discussed, however, the physical rules that govern any process of production will be analyzed.

5.1 THE PROCESS OF PRODUCTION

Resources, inputs, and *factors of production* are synonyms; they are commodities and services transformed into *output*. The process of transformation of resources is known as the process of production. We make note of the fact that output, which is the end of one process of production, may become an input used in another process of production. For example, coal, capital, labor, and water are inputs in the production of electricity. Electricity is an input in the production of bread. Bread is *final output*. Final outputs are goods.

Section 2.1 differentiated between *stocks* and *flows*. It is worthwhile to explain the difference between stocks and flows in inputs. A worker is a stock; at a point in time so many workers are employed in a certain factory; the amount of labor that a worker performs per unit of time is a flow. For example, the stock of one worker performing work during 2 hours or, alternatively, the stock of two workers performing work during 1 hour results in the same flow: 2 hours of labor. Land is another stock; the stock of land can be converted into a flow by using it for the production of wheat, say, for an entire winter. In what follows, flows of labor, land, capital, and the like will be referred to as either *inputs* or *factors of production*.

5.1a The Firm

In the early stages of human history man and woman used only two kinds of inputs in the process of production, *labor power* and *natural resources*. In that respect people did no better than animals. Lions, for example, use lion power and natural resources (water and zebras) to provide a meal. Once man and woman started to form capital, say, in the form of bows and arrows, their capacity to produce increased, but so did their dependence on other men and women. With capital accumulation came *specialization* and *division of labor*.

Adam Smith, in the *Wealth of Nations*, illustrated this principle by describing the production of straight pins: Without specialization and division of labor each worker could produce 20 pins a day. But if the process of transforming iron into pins was divided into 18 separate operations, output per worker could rise to 4800 pins a day. Production of cars on the assembly line is an extension of the same principle to a higher level of specialization. Specialization and division of labor required an elaborate form of organization. For example, in Smith's example it would be impossible to organize production of straight pins if one worker decided to show up for work 2 hours on Friday while fellow workers opted to work only on Monday morning from 10:00 A.M. to 12:00 noon. In other words, since modern production requires fine tuning and coordination among many workers and owners of capital and natural resources, some kind of commitment must be made by the participants in the process of production. This commitment has two aspects: One is physical-organizational; the other is legal. Physically and organizationally, there must be a place where owners of capital install their machinery and owners of labor are committed to perform their labor daily during specified hours. This place, or physical entity, sometimes known as a *plant*, can be a factory, a shop, a farm, an office, a studio. It is owned by a *firm*, which is a *legal entity*.

If individuals who are the owners of labor, capital, and natural resources signed contracts with one another in order to commit their resources simultaneously to a certain process of production, the transaction costs arising from the signing and enforcing of the contracts would be enormous. To minimize such transaction costs, people invented three forms of legal entities: *single proprietorships, partnerships,* and *corporations*. Usually only a fraction of the physical entity is owned by a single firm, and ownership is in the hands of more than one person. Moreover, the owners usually borrow money to supplement their own capital. This borrowed money is known as the *liability* of the firm. The owners of capital, not the lenders, are the owners of the firm. They enter into contracts with labor and owners of natural resources who commit themselves to participate in the process of production.

Most small firms in the United States are single proprietorships or partnerships. Typically these firms have unlimited liabilities of the owners and nonseparability between ownership and management. On the other hand, corporations, which are normally large firms, are legally *fictitious persons*. Ownership in corporations is achieved by purchase of stocks issued by the corporation. Liabilities of stock owners are limited.

In all three major forms of business organization (firms) the owners are claimants of the *profit*, which is left over after costs are subtracted from revenue. Costs are contractual payments to factors of production (or their owners). Revenue is simply the flow of output times the price received in the market. No wonder the major economic force moving the free enterprise system is the never-ending endeavor to maximize profit.

In what follows the concept of the firm will be separated from its legal and organizational complexities. Here, the firm is an agent involved in transforming factors of production into goods for the purpose of maximizing profit. This chapter will be limited to some basic and simple laws that govern every process of production.

5.1b The Production Function

Consider farmers who own land and machinery such as tractors and tools. They can combine their land and capital with many applications of water, seeds, and fertilizers per season. From experience farmers know what level of output to expect from each combination of inputs. This information, which assigns a level of output to each combination of inputs, is the *production function*. Farmers could write their production functions in the form of a huge table enumerating all the possible relationships between inputs and outputs. If a farmer uses only two inputs in the process of production, the production function could be formally stated as

$$X = f(A, B) \tag{5-1}$$

In Equation 5-1, X represents output and A and B represent any combination of two inputs, say, labor and capital. This form of a production function could be extended to any number of inputs which are transformed into output X. Equation 5-1 should be interpreted with care: For each pair of A and B there corresponds a number X, which is the *maximum* level of output that can be produced by using the indicated amounts of the inputs A and B per unit of time. The relevance of Equation 5-1 to reality will be discussed in the following section.

5.1c Production Functions in Reality

In reality, especially in the short run, the firm may be aware of a finite number of processes of production. For example, a hypothetical firm may be aware of only three processes of production, as shown in Table 5-1.

In the long run, when enough time is allowed for adjustment, many additional processes of production may be introduced. This knowledge, accumulated by the management of the firm, may be summarized conveniently by a production function as follows:

TABLE 5-1 Three Hypothetical Processes of Production

Process	Maximum output X	Inputs A	B
1	10	4	25
2	10	5	20
3	10	6	$16\frac{2}{3}$

$$X = \sqrt{A \cdot B} \qquad\qquad (5\text{-}2)$$

When first exposed to the idea of the production function, the student may find it difficult to accept the notion of variable proportions between factors of production. For example, the particular production function described by Equation 5-2 allows a wide variety of proportions between the different factors. While it may be true that in the short run proportions between factors of production such as labor and capital tend to be fixed or nearly so, in the long run substitutability between the various factors is almost endless.

Section 3.4a mentioned that the price elasticity of the demand for electricity by the industrial sector is greater than unity (in absolute value). This relatively high degree of responsiveness of manufacturing industries to the change in the price of electricity is large due to the ease with which electricity can be replaced by other inputs. In the 1940s most elevators were still operated manually. In the 1970s elevators were automatic. In the coal industry a major union drive to increase wages started in the 1940s. The real cost of labor was rising rapidly while the cost of mining machinery was falling. While production of coal between 1940 and the mid-1950s remained roughly the same, employment declined sharply and use of machinery increased sharply. (This example is considered further in Chapter 9.) In underdeveloped countries bookkeeping is entirely manual. In the United States it is largely computerized. In farming, land and fertilizers are known to be good substitutes for each other in the process of production. We would expect the application of fertilizers to rise as land becomes scarcer. This expectation is tested by comparing the average application of fertilizer per hectare in four developed countries as illustrated in Table 5-2.

As land grows scarcer, farmers increase the application of fertilizers relative to land. In Japan the proportion of fertilizers to land is 18, 4, and 2.5 times larger than in Australia, the United States, and Israel, respectively. It is well known that land scarcity increases when we move down the list from Australia to Japan.

We conclude that a production function which allows a wide variety of proportions between factors of production is realistic.

TABLE 5-2 **Consumption of Fertilizers per Hectare of Agricultural Area (Arable Land and Permanent Crops) Data for 1976**

Country	Land scarcity	Fertilizers, in 100 grams of N, P_2O_5, and K_2O
Australia	Very low	235
United States	Low	1065
Israel	High	1719
Japan	Very high	4305

Source: 1977 Annual Fertilizer Review, Food and Agriculture Organization of the United Nations, Rome 1978, Table 12.

5.2 THE BASIC CONCEPTS

5.2a The Production Hill

We begin our discussion of the laws that govern the production function by considering an agronomic production function. Earl O. Heady and John Dillon studied agricultural production functions extensively.[1] Only corn will be discussed here. Corn production experiments were conducted in western Iowa in 1952. In those experiments land, labor, and machinery were kept constant while two types of fertilizer were varied from one experiment to the next. Nitrogen (N) and phosphate (P_2O_5) were varied from zero to 320 pounds per acre. The increment from experiment to experiment was 40 pounds. Thus, altogether there were 81 different plots of land, each yielding a different amount of corn per acre. To obtain the empirical production function, the resultant yields per acre were regressed (estimated statistically) against the independent variables nitrogen and phosphate. Heady and Dillon tried a variety of forms for their production functions. The results for one version are summarized in Table 5-3. Let the input phosphate be denoted by P and the input nitrogen by N. Table 5-3 then is a production function as stated by Equation 5-1. For example, if we plug in $X = f(P,N)$, $P = 120$ (pounds of phosphate), and $N = 80$ (pounds of nitrogen), we obtain $90.7 = f(120,80)$.[2]

Table 5-3 can be transformed into a three-dimensional diagram as illustrated in Figure 5-1. The two horizontal dimensions measure the amounts of phosphate and nitrogen (in pounds per season). These are the two variable inputs

---

[1]Reprinted by permission from Earl O. Heady and John Dillon, Agricultural Production Functions, (c) 1961 by the Iowa State University Press, Ames, Iowa 50010.

[2]The production function that Heady and Dillon used to generate the results in Table 5-3 is

$$X = -7.51 + 0.584 \cdot N + 0.664 \cdot P - 0.0016 \cdot N^2 - 0.0018 \cdot P^2 + 0.00081 \cdot N \cdot P$$

It will not be discussed at this level.

TABLE 5-3 An Empirical Production Function of Corn
Corn = f(phosphate, nitrogen)

Pounds of phosphate per acre	Pounds of nitrogen per acre								
	0	40	80	120	160	200	240	280	320
0		13.3	29.2	39.8	45.5	46.1	41.7	32.2	17.6
40	16.2	38.3	55.4	67.4	74.4	76.3	73.1	64.9	51.6
80	34.1	57.5	75.9	89.2	97.5	100.7	98.8	91.9	79.9
120	46.3	71.0	90.7	105.3	114.9	119.4	118.8	113.2	102.5
160	53.0	78.7	99.8	115.6	126.6	132.3	133.0	128.7	119.3
200	53.4	80.7	103.0	120.2	132.3	139.4	141.5	138.4	130.4
240	48.3	76.9	100.5	119.0	132.5	140.8	144.1	142.4	135.7
280	37.5	67.4	92.3	112.0	126.8	136.5	141.1	140.7	135.2
320	20.9	52.1	78.3	99.4	115.4	126.4	132.3	133.2	129.0

Reprinted by permission from Earl O. Heady and John Dillon, *Agricultural Production Functions*, (c) 1961 by The Iowa State University Press, Ames, Iowa 50010.

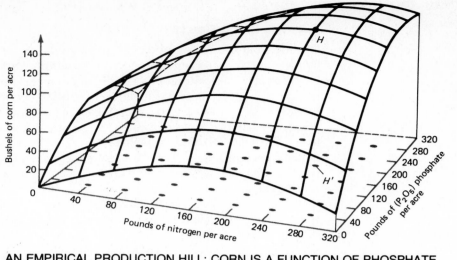

FIGURE 5-1 AN EMPIRICAL PRODUCTION HILL: CORN IS A FUNCTION OF PHOSPHATE AND NITROGEN

On the horizontal plane two inputs, phosphate and nitrogen, are measured. The vertical axis along which output of corn is measured is perpendicular to the horizontal plane. For each combination of phosphate and nitrogen such as H' on the horizontal plane (200 pounds of phosphate and 240 pounds of nitrogen) there corresponds an output point on the surface of the production hill such as H. $\overline{H'H}$ = 141.5 bushels of corn. [*Source:* Reprinted by permission from Earl O. Heady and John Dillon, *Agricultural Production Functions*, © 1961 by the Iowa State University Press, Ames, Iowa 50010.]

applied (per acre) in the production of corn. The vertical dimension measures the amount of the output corn generated by pairs of inputs. The result is a *production hill*. For example, the pair of 200 pounds of phosphate and 240 pounds of nitrogen is denoted by H' on the horizontal plane. In Table 5-3 the associated level of output is 141.5 bushels of corn. Tracing up from point H', 141.5 (bushels of corn), point H is obtained. In other words, $\overline{H'H}$ is equal to 141.5 bushels of corn. In principle, this is how the production hill is drawn, point by point.

Figure 5-2 is a general production hill, where inputs A and B represent nitrogen and phosphate or any other inputs such as labor and capital or energy and labor.

Note: For convenience of presentation the direction of measurement of input B is changed from Figure 5-1 to Figure 5-2. It is measured from left to right in Figure 5-1 and from right to left in Figure 5-2. The production hill in Figure 5-2 is drawn in the exact same manner as in Figure 5-1: Point H' represents a pair of A_0 units of A and B_0 units of B, lying on the horizontal plane; point H on the production surface is obtained by tracing up an amount of output X_0 which is $X_0 = f(A_0, B_0)$.

5.2b Slicing the Production Hill

The production hill may be viewed as half an orange that can be sliced in many different ways. For a particular slice, the shell of the orange at the

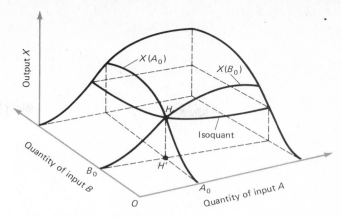

FIGURE 5-2 A THREE-DIMENSIONAL DIAGRAM

Inputs *A* and *B* are measured along the two axes that form the horizontal plane. The output axis is perpendicular to the horizontal plane. In principle the production hill is drawn by plotting a point like *H'* representing pair A_0 and B_0, and then tracing a vertical line from *H'* to *H* such that $\overline{H'H} = f(A_0, B_0)$. Segment $\overline{H'H}$ is perpendicular to the *A*, *B* plane.

edge of the slice represents production patterns. Two special slices will be considered in what follows: the *vertical slice* and the *horizontal slice*.

5.2c The Vertical Slice: The Total Output Curve

Consider the production hill in Figure 5-1. This hill can be sliced vertically for fixed amounts of phosphate in order to obtain output curves as functions of nitrogen, or alternatively, it can be sliced for fixed amounts of nitrogen in order to obtain output curves as functions of phosphate. Following Heady and Dillon, Figure 5-3 shows the total output curves of corn as related to nitrogen. The "slices" selected are for an amount of phosphate equaling 0 and an amount of phosphate equaling 320 pounds. Notice that in Figure 5-3 the total output curves are concave downward; that is, they increase at a decreasing rate throughout the entire relevant range of nitrogen application. In theoretical arguments, such as those to be presented in Figure 5-4, total output curves display first increasing output at increasing rates up to a point, and thereafter increasing output at decreasing rates. The Heady-Dillon study may have excluded the first stage simply because the statistical tools applied to estimate the production function were too crude for estimation. Note, by the way, that the slice for phosphate = 320 pounds is not the highest one. A glance at Table 5-3 should convince the student that a vertical slice for phosphate = 240 pounds would trace a curve which occupies a higher position than phosphate = 320 pounds. Note also that the vertical slices could be drawn directly off Table 5-3 by transforming the first row and the last row into curves in the corn, nitrogen space. In economic jargon, vertical slices like those shown in Figure 5-3 are *total output curves*. Such curves indicate how output responds to variations in one input when all other inputs are held unchanged.

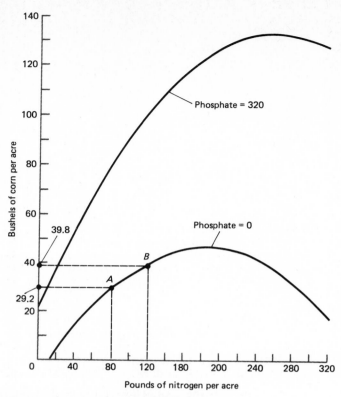

FIGURE 5-3 TWO SLICES OF THE CORN PRODUCTION HILL
The lower curve is a vertical cut for a zero level of phosphate; the higher curve is a vertical cut for a level of phosphate of 320 pounds per acre. (*Source:* Reprinted by permission from Earl O. Heady and John Dillon, *Agricultural Production Functions*, © 1961 by the Iowa State University Press, Ames, Iowa 50010.)

We now turn back to Figure 5-2. We can take a vertical slice that is parallel to the X,B plane; this slice yields a total output curve for a fixed input $A(= A_0)$ and a variable input B. Such a curve is denoted by $X(A_0)$. The vertical slice that is parallel to the X,A plane yields a total output curve for a fixed input $B(=B_0)$ and a variable input A. This curve is denoted by $X(B_0)$. Imagine now that we take three slices of the production hill in Figure 5-2. These three slices, which are parallel to the X,A plane, are cut at $B = B_0, B = B_1$, and $B = B_2$, as shown in Figure 5-4. Notice that B_2 is larger than B_1 and B_1 is larger than B_0. Since the vertical cuts were taken at the slope of the hill facing us, the total output curves in Figure 5-4 occupy higher and higher positions as B increases (from B_0 to B_1 and from B_1 to B_2). Had we continued to take more vertical slices until we passed the peak of the hill, total output curves would have begun to occupy lower and lower positions. It should be stressed again that the total output curves in Figure 5-4 display the same properties as the curves in Figure 5-3, except that having been cut from a theoretical production hill they are first convex downward and then concave

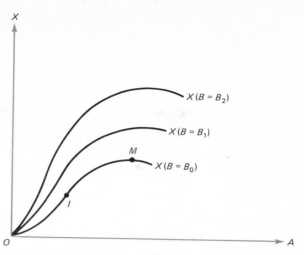

FIGURE 5-4 THREE VERTICAL SLICES OF THE PRODUCTION HILL OF FIGURE 5-2
The cutting knife is parallel to the X, A plane. Each curve obtained in this manner is known as a total output curve. The point of inflection is denoted by I and the maximum point (of the lowest curve) is denoted by M.

downward. For example, the curve $X(B = B_0)$ is convex downward up to point I; this means that up to point I output increases at an increasing rate. From point I on, the curve is concave downward; this means that output increases at a decreasing rate. Note that beyond point M, $X(B = B_0)$ is falling. Still, the concavity of the curve in the proximity of M implies that for equal ΔAs, the values of the changes in output ΔX continue to decline.[3] Point I is a transition point: At I the curve ceases to be convex and begins to be concave. Point I is known as the *inflection point*.

We are now ready to consider new concepts that will prove useful in the coming chapters.

5.2d Marginal Physical Product and Average Physical Product

The *marginal physical product* of a factor of production is the change in total output (production) over a small change in the factor used (per unit of time) when all other factors are kept constant. The marginal physical product of factor A is denoted by MP_a, etc. Formally it is written as

$$MP_a = \frac{\Delta X}{\Delta A} \tag{5-3}$$

where ΔX is the change in output and ΔA is the small change in factor A, all per unit of time.

---

[3]For curves that are convex downward the second-order derivative is positive: $\partial^2 X/\partial A^2 > 0$. For curves that are concave downward the second-order derivative is negative: $\partial^2 X/\partial A^2 < 0$. Geometrically, if the curve bulges toward the horizontal axis, it is convex downward and if it bulges upward it is concave upward.

The *average physical product* of an input is simply total output over the amount of the input used. The average physical product of A is denoted by AP_a, and is written as

$$AP_a = \frac{X}{A} \tag{5-4}$$

Consider Figure 5-3. Assume that you are a farmer in Iowa and you want to figure out the marginal physical product and the average physical product of nitrogen in producing corn. In particular, you move along the total output curve for phosphate = 0 from point A to point B by increasing the application of nitrogen from 80 to 120 pounds per acre; you want to calculate the marginal physical product and the average physical product for that domain. Given that the resulting outputs associated with these points will be 29.2 and 39.8 bushels of corn, you calculate the following:

$$\text{Marginal physical product of nitrogen} = \frac{39.8 - 29.2}{120 - 80} = \frac{10.6}{40} = 0.265$$

That is, in the domain of the total output curve between points A and B, 1 additional pound of nitrogen would yield 0.265 additional bushel of corn.

The average physical product of nitrogen can be calculated either for a level of 80 pounds or for a level of 120 pounds. You calculate it for the first level as follows:

$$\text{Average physical product of nitrogen} = \frac{29.2}{80} = 0.365$$

The fact that average physical product is higher than marginal physical product is not accidental. This will be discussed later as a law of logic.

5.2e Further Geometric Properties of the Marginal and Average Physical Products

Some additional geometric properties of the marginal physical product and the average physical product will now be clarified. Figure 5-5 is a total output curve denoted by $X(A)$ for the hypothetical production function $X = \sqrt{A \cdot B}$. Factor B is held constant at 10 units. Factor A is increased from 4 to 5 units per unit of time, and the associated levels of output are calculated as 6.32 ($=\sqrt{10 \cdot 4}$) and 7.07 ($=\sqrt{10 \cdot 5}$). Accordingly, the marginal physical product of A for the domain extending from 4 to 5 units of A is calculated as

$$MP_a = \frac{\Delta X}{\Delta A} = \frac{7.07 - 6.32}{5 - 4} = 0.75$$

Section 2.2 discussed the difference between *arc elasticity* and *point elasticity*. Point elasticity was defined as the arc elasticity for a change in the independent variable, which is becoming smaller and smaller. By the same token ΔA can become smaller and smaller. For example, if we increased A by ½ unit, from 4 to 4.5 units, the output associated with $A = 4.5$ would be 6.71 ($=\sqrt{10 \cdot 4.5}$). The marginal physical product would be

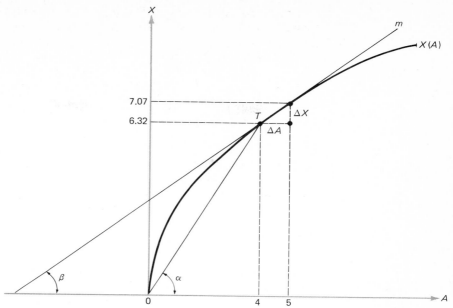

FIGURE 5-5 SOME GEOMETRIC PROPERTIES OF MP_a AND AP_a

$X(A)$ is an output curve associated with the production function $X = \sqrt{A \cdot B}$, where $B_0 = 10$. The slope of the line connecting the origin and point T (tangent of angle α) is the AP_a. The slope of the line m, which is tangent to the total output curve at T (tangent of angle β), is the MP_a. When A increases from 4 to 5 units, output increases from 6.32 to 7.07 units. Hence, in that domain we can calculate ΔA as being $5 - 4$ and ΔX as being $7.07 - 6.32$, etc.

$$MP_a = \frac{\Delta X}{\Delta A} = \frac{6.71 - 6.32}{4.5 - 4} = 0.78$$

The student will benefit from illustrating that, as ΔA decreases, MP_a for $A = 4$ (and $B_0 = 10$) approaches 0.79.[4] Let point T denote the level of output associated with $A = 4$ and $X = 6.32$. Consider the line denoted by m which is tangent to $X(A)$ at T. The slope of this line is equal to 0.79. More generally, given any total output curve, the slope of the line which is tangent to the curve at a certain point is equal to the marginal physical product at that point. We also recall from geometry that since the line m forms an angle β with the horizontal axis, it follows that the slope of the line is the tangent of the angle β.

The average physical product at point T in Figure 5-5 is calculated by dividing output by the variable input, which is

$$AP_a = \frac{X}{A} = \frac{6.32}{4} = 1.58$$

---

[4]Given a production function $X = f(A, B)$, $MP_a = \partial X / \partial A$. In our example

$$\frac{\partial X}{\partial A} = 0.5 \cdot A^{-0.5} \cdot B^{0.5} = 0.5 \cdot 4^{-0.5} \cdot 10^{0.5} = 0.79$$

It is evident from Figure 5-5 that if we connect the origin with point T, we obtain a line whose slope is equal to AP_a. Moreover, since this line forms an angle α with the horizontal axis, it follows from geometry that the tangent of α is equal to the average physical product.

The student may wonder why we need this geometric apparatus at all. The answer is that by comparing angles α and β we can tell which of the two, the AP_a or the MP_a, is greater.

5.2f The Horizontal Slice: Isoquants

First consider Figure 5-1. If we take a horizontal slice of the production hill, we obtain as a result a *production indifference curve* known as an *isoquant*. Recall from Section 1.7 that in a map of certain landscape a contour line is a representation of an imaginary line on the surface of a hill having a constant elevation above sea level. The indifference map was defined as a map of the *utility hill*. Contour lines can in principle be derived by cutting the hill horizontally, starting with a low elevation and gradually raising the elevation of the cutting knife until the entire map is produced. Figure 1-22 showed the indifference map obtained from cutting a utility hill horizontally. The utility hill can be viewed as a process of production in which two inputs, X and Y, are involved in the production of utility. If in Figure 1-22 we replace X, Y, and utility by phosphate, nitrogen, and corn, the indifference curves in Figure 1-22 can be considered isoquants of corn. To follow an isoquant means to remain at the same production elevation or, to put it differently, to produce the same amount of corn with various combinations of phosphate and nitrogen. Let us now turn to the general case. If we cut the production hill in Figure 5-2, we can obtain isoquants as presented in Figure 5-6. We show only three isoquants, X_0, X_1, and X_2, out of an infinitely large number of isoquants. X_2 represents a higher level of output than X_1, X_1 represents a higher level of output than X_0, and so on. Point M denotes the peak of the production hill. Following Section 1.7 and Figure 1-22, the isoquant map is divided into four regions. Similar notations can be used by agreeing to call an input "good" if using more of it in the process of production (per unit of time) would increase output, that is, would lead us to climb the production hill. We can call an input "bad" if using more of it in the process of production would decrease output, that is, would lead us to descend the production hill. Let us now examine the regions one by one.

Region I Both inputs are "good." Increasing the amount of either A or B used leads to a higher point on the production hill.

Region II Input A is "bad." Applying more of A to the process of production would drag us downhill. B is "good." Producers should avoid region II by retreating in the westerly direction. In fact, so long as producers are in region II, retreating in the westerly direction will get them to a still higher production elevation, which is a double blessing: they produce more, and

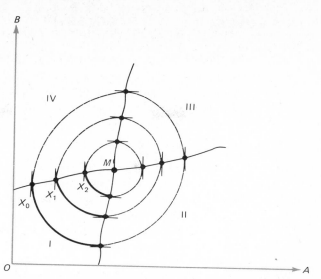

FIGURE 5-6   THE HORIZONTAL SLICES OF A PRODUCTION HILL
Curves X_0, X_1, and X_2 represent horizontal cuts at different production elevations, where the elevation rises from X_0 to X_1 and from X_1 to X_2. Each cut generates a round isoquant. The producer would avoid regions II, III, and IV and produce only in region I, where both inputs are "good."

they have to use less of factor A. *Note*: Factor A is costly. In summary, producers should avoid region II.

Region III   Both inputs are "bad." Producers should retreat to region I in the westerly direction or in the southerly direction or both. In summary, they should avoid region III.

Region IV   Input B is "bad." Input A is "good." Producers should retreat in the southerly direction. They should avoid region IV.

These findings are summarized as follows: Producers should avoid regions II, III, and IV. This leaves region I, in which both A and B are "good." If you are tempted to think that the peak of the production hill (point M) is of any significance to producers, you are wrong. In coming chapters, we shall see why maximum output is of little significance to producers: They are after another point.

When drawing isoquants, we shall now ignore regions II, III, and IV and focus on region I. In other words, we shall draw isoquants that are negatively sloped and convex toward the origin.

Having investigated the basic concepts in the theory of production in some detail, we are now ready to begin the discussion of some important laws that govern the theory of production.

5.3 THE LAWS GOVERNING THE PROCESS OF PRODUCTION: ONE INPUT IS FIXED AND THE OTHER IS VARIABLE

5.3a The Relationship between Marginal and Average Magnitudes

Before proceeding with the theory of production, we must pause to consider a *law of logic* that governs the relationship between *marginal* and *average* magnitudes.

In Chapter 3 a formula (Equation 3-4) was developed that relates the marginal revenue to the price. The formula, written as $MR = P(1 + 1/\eta)$, implied that since normally price elasticity of demand is negative, marginal revenue (MR) must be smaller than the price. Since the price may be viewed as average revenue (revenue divided by the quantity purchased), it must be true that when average revenue is falling, marginal revenue is smaller than average revenue.[5] Is this relationship accidental or a reflection of a general law? It so happens that marginal and average magnitudes are confined in their relationship to each other.

If Y is a function of X, then when the average Y (Y/X) is falling, marginal Y (ΔY/ΔX) is smaller than the average; when the average Y is level, marginal Y is equal to the average Y; and when average Y is rising, marginal Y is greater than the average Y.

These three basic relationships are depicted by Figure 5-7: When the average magnitude (solid) is rising, the marginal magnitude (dashed) is above it. When the average magnitude reaches its maximum (level), the marginal magnitude cuts the average magnitude from above. When the average magnitude is falling, the marginal magnitude is below it. As the average magnitude reaches its minimum, the marginal magnitude cuts it from below, and so on. The proof proceeds as follows:

If the average magnitude is declining, we have

$$\frac{Y + \Delta Y}{X + \Delta X} < \frac{Y}{X}$$

which, after proper rearrangements, gives

$$X(Y + \Delta Y) < Y(X + \Delta X)$$

and, carrying out the multiplications, gives

$$X \cdot Y + X \cdot \Delta Y < Y \cdot X + Y \cdot \Delta X$$

Subtracting $X \cdot Y$ from both sides of the inequality gives

$$X \cdot \Delta Y < Y \cdot \Delta X$$

---

[5]In general, let M, A, and E stand for *marginal magnitude, average magnitude,* and *elasticity of the average magnitude. M* is then related to A as follows:

$$M = A\left(1 + \frac{1}{E}\right)$$

If A is positively sloped, $E > 0$ and M is greater than A. If A is negatively sloped, $E < 0$ and M is smaller than A.

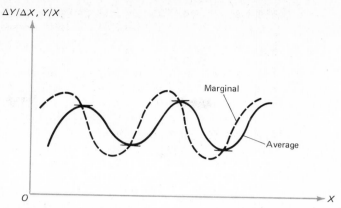

FIGURE 5-7 THE RELATIONSHIPS BETWEEN AVERAGE AND MARGINAL MAGNITUDES
It is assumed that Y is functionally related to X: $Y = f(X)$. The average magnitude is Y/X and the marginal magnitude is $\Delta Y/\Delta X$. The graph shows that the marginal is greater than the average when the average is rising, and conversely, it is smaller than the average when the average is falling. The marginal cuts the average at the maximum and minimum points of the average curve.

Dividing through by $X \cdot \Delta X$ gives

$$\frac{\Delta Y}{\Delta X} < \frac{Y}{X}$$

The proof for the second and third relationships proceeds along similar lines, except that the $<$ sign is replaced by an $=$ sign and a $>$ sign, respectively.

5.3b The Relationships between Total Output and Average and Marginal Physical Products

Recall that if we slice the production hill vertically we obtain total output curves. The projections of such vertical slices were illustrated by Figure 5-4. This section will focus on the properties of total output curves, mainly vis-à-vis the two curves that are derived from it, i.e., the AP_a curve and the MP_a curve. If we pick any vertical slice in Figure 5-4, say, $X(B = B_o)$, we obtain a relationship between output and a variable input. Let us now focus on a single total output curve, say, for $B = B_0$. This curve is redrawn in panel (*a*) of Figure 5-8. The associated MP_a and AP_a curves are drawn in panel (*b*) of Figure 5-8. Sometimes the theory of production, when one input is held constant while the other varies, is called the *law of variable proportions,* because as we move rightward on the A axis the proportion of A to B increases. When we move leftward on the A axis, the proportion of B to A increases. Thus, instead of considering a fixed and a variable factor, respectively, we may consider variable proportions between the two factors.

Factors may be increased equiproportionately. For example, if in Figure 5-2 we send a ray from the origin to point H' on the A,B plane, points on such a ray would represent combinations of inputs A and B which are kept in fixed proportions. Increasing output by advancing along such a ray is known as a change in *scale*. In reality it is hard to find a case in which a change in scale is pure in the sense that all factors, without exception, vary in fixed proportion; there is one factor, namely, the *entrepreneurial capacity*,[6] which is fixed even in the very long run. Thus, in reality, when n inputs are involved in the process of production, one could think of two extreme cases: At one extreme is the case where all inputs but one are fixed. At the other extreme, all inputs but one, the entrepreneurial capacity, are variable.

In panel (a) of Figure 5-8 the domain[7] of feasible production extends from the origin, denoted by O, to A_4. Beyond the point A_4 output is zero. We proceed to analyze the properties of the total output curve and the two associated curves MP_a and AP_a.

Domain $\overline{OA}_1$: Total output curve is convex downward, or in other words, output increases at an increasing rate: The greater the amount of A employed, the greater the ΔX associated with ΔA. Hence, in panel (b) Figure 5-8, MP_a, which is the ratio of ΔX *to* ΔA, is rising. We can summarize it geometrically as follows: In domain $\overline{OA}_1$, to the convex-downward total output curve OR [panel (a) of Figure 5-8] there corresponds an increasing MP_a curve OF [panel (b) of Figure 5-8]. The technical reason for this relationship is that the firm is stuck with a fixed factor of production, and when small amounts of the variable input are used, the fixed factor is too abundant relative to the variable input. Thus, as more of the variable input is added to the process of production, the fixed factor is utilized more intensively. As an example consider a process of production involving painting, bending bars, and drilling holes. If there is only one employee, the manager must tell that

---

[6]In small firms, mainly *partnerships* and single *proprietorships*, the *entrepreneur* is the owner of the firm. Thus a farmer is the entrepreneur of the farm, the owner of a small shop is the entrepreneur of the shop, and so on. In large firms it is difficult to identify a single person as the entrepreneur. Rather, the top management and the majority stockholder, together, constitute the entrepreneurial capacity that makes the important decisions concerning the actions taken by the firm.

[7]If Y is functionally related to X such that X is the independent variable and Y is the dependent variable, we may limit our interest to a segment of X starting at X_0 and ending at X_1 and call it a *domain*. The collection of all the values of Y corresponding to X in the domain is called *range*. Geometrically, the *domain* and the *range of* $Y = f(X)$ are illustrated as follows:

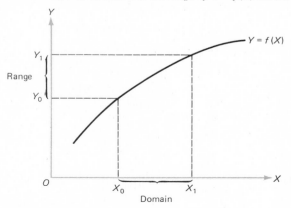

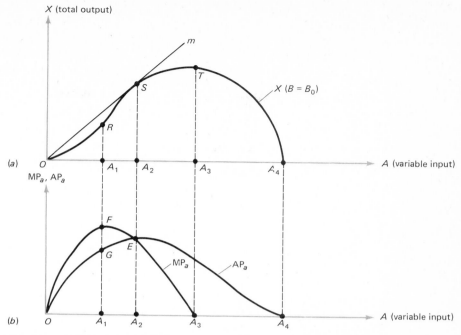

FIGURE 5-8 THE RELATIONSHIPS BETWEEN TOTAL OUTPUT MP_a AND AP_a

(*a*): The variable input A is measured along the horizontal axis; output X is measured along the vertical axis. X is an output curve at the $B = B_0$ level. X becomes negative at A_4. R is a point of inflection, S is the point where the tangent line m also passes through the origin, and T is a point of maximum.

(*b*): The variable input A is measured along the horizontal axis; MP_a and AP_a are measured along the vertical axis. Point F, where the curve MP_a attains its maximum, corresponds to point R in panel (*a*). Point E, where MP_a and AP_a curves intersect, corresponds to point S in panel (*a*). At the level of A_3, MP_a vanishes. In panel (*a*) total output reaches its maximum level at this level of employment. Zone I extends from the origin to A_2. Zone II, known as the *zone of production,* extends from A_2 to A_3. Zone III extends from A_3 to A_4.

employee to perform the three operations. After a second employee is hired, the manager evaluates their talents and assigns painting to the more cautious worker and bending bars to the stronger of the two. As a result, output more than doubles. When a third employee joins, reevaluation takes place: The most cautious worker paints, the strongest of the three bends bars, and the one with the steadiest hand drills holes. The additional output as a result of adding the third worker exceeded the additional output that resulted from adding the <u>second</u> worker, and so on.

Domain $\overline{A_1 A_3}$: Total output curve is concave downward, or in other words output increases at a decreasing rate. This means that the greater the amount of A employed the smaller is ΔX associated with ΔA. Hence, in panel (*b*) of Figure 5-8, MP_a is falling. Notice that point R separates the convex from the concave portion of the total output curve. It is called a *point of inflection*. In panel (*b*) of Figure 5-8 the associated point is denoted by F, which marks the maximum of the MP_a curve. Point T on the total output curve occurs where output is maximized. Since output at that point is level, the associated MP_a in panel (b) of Figure 5-8 is zero. Moreover, thereafter total output diminishes and MP_a becomes negative. We can summarize it geometrically as follows: In domain $\overline{A_1A_3}$, to the concave-downward total output curve RT [panel (a) of Figure 5-8] there corresponds a diminishing MP_a curve FA_3 [panel (b) of Figure 5-8]. The technical reason for the diminishing MP_a curve is evident: As more and more of the variable factor is added to the process of production, the variable input becomes too abundant relative to the fixed factor. In the long run, the manager cannot cope efficiently with the multiplicity of problems as the scale of production increases. In the short run the reason might be technological or agronomic. As more fertilizer is added, a certain level of output is reached beyond which output increases at a decreasing rate. The empirical observation that in domain $\overline{A_1A_3}$, MP_a falls is summarized as the law of *diminishing marginal physical product* as follows:

> *If the use of one factor of production is increased while all other factors are kept constant, a level of output is reached beyond which the marginal physical product of that factor declines.*

Domain $\overline{A_3A_4}$: Total output curve TA_4 declines. Correspondingly, MP_a is negative. The firm would avoid this domain because the more of the variable input the firm uses there, the less output will be generated. In the example of the agronomic production function (Table 5-3) it was shown that (for phosphate specified at 160 pounds per acre) when nitrogen per acre is increased beyond 240 pounds, marginal physical product of nitrogen is negative.

The AP_a curve: The relationship between the average magnitude and the marginal magnitude was discussed in the previous section. Accordingly, we know that the AP_a must have the shape of an inverted U and that the MP_a must cut it at the maximum of the AP_a (point E), as shown in panel (b) of Figure 5-8. To see how to determine level A_2 at which the intersection between AP_a and MP_a occurs, we focus again on panel (a) of Figure 5-8. Recall that if we send a ray from the origin to any specific point on the total output curve, the slope of this ray is equal to AP_a. (The slope of the ray connecting T with the origin in Figure 5-5 was the tangent of angle α, and it was equal to AP_a associated with point T.) In panel (a) of Figure 5-8 the slope of such a ray, denoted by m, is the greatest when it just touches the total output curve at point S. Correspondingly, at that level of output, AP_a attains its maximum. This is the only level of output at which the slope of the ray is also the slope of the tangent line (denoted by m). Hence this must be the point of intersection between AP_a and MP_a. The results of the previous section are confirmed.

We sometimes find it convenient to divide the domain of the positive output [$\overline{OA_4}$ in panel (a) of Figure 5-8] into three zones: zone I, $\overline{OA_2}$; zone II, $\overline{A_2A_3}$; zone III, $\overline{A_3A_4}$. The firm would always avoid zone III; marginal physical product of the variable input is negative there, meaning that hiring more of factor A would lead to output reduction. The firm would be producing primarily in zone II, known as the *zone of production*, where MP_a is positive. For reasons that will become clear in Chapter 7, the firm would also avoid zone I.[8]

While this section may seem irrelevant now, the material will prove useful in the coming three chapters.

5.3c The Elasticity of Production

Once again we find the concept of elasticity very useful. (The student may want to review Section 2.2.) We want to measure the responsiveness of output to a change in one input. In order to do this, we define the *elasticity of production* with respect to factor A (or any other factor) as the relative change in output over the relative change in the amount of the variable factor used in the process of production. (If there is more than one variable input, the elasticity of production can be calculated for one factor at a time.) If we denote the elasticity of production by E_a, we obtain the following formula:

$$E_a = \frac{\Delta X / X}{\Delta A / A} = \frac{\Delta X \cdot A}{\Delta A \cdot X} = \frac{\Delta X / \Delta A}{X / A} = \frac{MP_a}{AP_a} \qquad (5\text{-}5)$$

For example, in the case of the production function $X = \sqrt{A \cdot B}$, as illustrated by Figure 5-5, the elasticity of production in the domain extending from 4 to 5 units of A is calculated as

$$E_a = \frac{MP_a}{AP_a} = \frac{0.75}{1.49} = 0.50$$

---

[8]The horizontal axis of Figure 5-8 assumes that A varies and B is kept constant. In the following sections of this chapter some additional assumptions are made concerning the production function (constant returns to scale) which allow us to conclude that AP_a and MP_a are determined by the ratio A/B rather than by the amounts of A and B used. We can accordingly express the horizontal axis in panel (*b*) of Figure 5-8 as A/B, and consider either A or B as fixed. We can then read the scale either left to right (B is fixed and A/B increases), or right to left (A is fixed and B/A increases). The result is the following diagram:

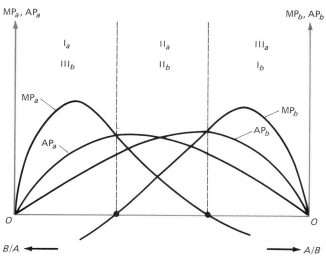

This finding is interpreted as follows: A 1 percent change in input A would lead to 0.50 percent change in output (in the domain $A = 4$ to $A = 5$). It is left for the student to show that from O to A_2 output with respect to the variable input is elastic.

5.4 THE LAWS GOVERNING THE PROCESS OF PRODUCTION: THE TWO INPUTS ARE VARIABLE

A situation in which the firm can vary only one input is typical of the short run. For example, a firm producing electric power by burning oil would achieve variations of output in the short run by varying the amount of oil (factor A) while the number of generators is fixed (the B factor). In the long run, however, the firm can vary both the amount of oil burned and the number of generators. The analysis carried out in Section 5.3 is suitable for the short run. The analysis to be developed here is suitable to the long run, when all, or almost all, inputs can be varied. Since for simplicity the analysis is limited to two factors of production, symbolically the short run will be represented by a case in which input B is fixed and input A is variable (Section 5.3); the long run will be represented by a case in which both input A and input B are variable.

The long-run analysis, in which both A and B are variable, draws heavily on the horizontal slices of the production hill as presented in Figure 5-6. In the long run producers are no longer limited to climbing (or descending) the production hill along a horizontal line that moves only in the easterly or the westerly direction. They can choose any direction they please. The following chapter will discuss an optimal route for a producer in the long run. Let us now discuss some technical properties of isoquants.

5.4a Substitution and the Isoquant

Focus on a single isoquant (both A and B are "good") for which the level of output is held constant at X_0. Such an isoquant is reproduced in Figure 5-9. Movement along the isoquant in the southeasterly direction means producing the same amount of X_0 with less B and more A. The analysis that follows is formally identical with the theory of the consumer developed in Section 1.3d. First consider points K and L, which are very close to each other. A movement from K to L implies a reduction in the employment of B by ΔB_0 and, to produce the same level of X_0, adding ΔA_0 units of A (per unit of time) to the process of production. Since points K and L are near each other, we can assume that the marginal physical product of B does not rise appreciably and the marginal physical product of A does not fall appreciably. Thus the loss of output due to the diversion of ΔB_0 away from production is roughly $\Delta B_o \cdot \mathrm{MP}_b$, and the gain in output due to adding ΔA_0 is roughly $\Delta A_0 \cdot \mathrm{MP}_a$. Since, when we move from K to L, the net gain in ouput is zero, we can write

$$\Delta B \cdot \mathrm{MP}_b + \Delta A \cdot \mathrm{MP}_a = 0 \qquad (5\text{-}6)$$

TABLE 5-4   An Isoquant:
$$10 = \sqrt{A \cdot B}$$

A	B	$X = \sqrt{A \cdot B}$
1	100	10
2	50	10
3	$33\frac{1}{3}$	10
4	25	10
5	20	10
6	$16\frac{2}{3}$	10
7	$14\frac{2}{7}$	10
8	$12\frac{1}{2}$	10
9	$11\frac{1}{9}$	10
10	10	10

(The subscripts 0 are deleted because the property as stated in Equation 5-6 is valid for any pair of points like K and L on the isoquant.) Substracting $\Delta A \cdot \mathrm{MP}_a$ from both sides of Equation 5-6 gives $\Delta B \cdot \mathrm{MP}_b = -\Delta A \cdot \mathrm{MP}_a$. Dividing first by MP_b and then by ΔA yields

$$\mathrm{RTS} = \frac{\Delta B}{\Delta A} = -\frac{\mathrm{MP}_a}{\mathrm{MP}_b} \tag{5-7}$$

where RTS stands for (marginal) *rate of technical substitution* between B and A, which is sometimes denoted by RTS_{ab}. In Table 5-4 a numerical isoquant is calculated for the production function $X = \sqrt{A \cdot B}$, $X_0 = 10$ and A varies from 1 to 10. The student can show that if K represents $A = 5$ and $B = 20$, and if L represents $A = 6$ and $B = 16.67$, then the RTS calculated for the arc KL is roughly -3.66. (Mathematically, RTS at point K is exactly -4: $\mathrm{MP}_a = 1$, and $\mathrm{MP}_b = 0.25$.)

In the real world the substitutability of one factor for another is of utmost importance. For example, following the rise of prices of energy resources during 1973 and 1974, economists asked two basic questions: (1) would nonenergy capital substitute with ease for energy resources? (2) Would nonfossil sources of energy substitute with ease for fossil resources? In order to answer these and similar questions, economists developed an apparatus known as the *elasticity of substitution* (between two factors). In Figure 5-9, when we move on the isoquant from point K to point K', the RTS declines from $\Delta B_o/\Delta A_0$ to $\Delta B_1/\Delta A_1$. The difficulty involved in substituting one factor for another is measured here by the fact that at point K the amount of A required to replace one unit of B is smaller than at point K'. Also, when we go in the opposite direction, we observe that at point L' the amount of B required to replace one unit of A is smaller than at point L.

Let us denote $\Delta B/\Delta A$ by r and B/A by R; then, the elasticity of substitution σ is

$$\sigma = \frac{\Delta R/R}{\Delta r/r} \tag{5-8}$$

where all Δs are very small (point K is very close to point L, etc.).

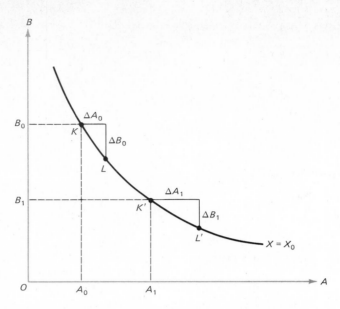

FIGURE 5-9   AN ISOQUANT: ILLUSTRATING RTS AND THE ELASTICITY OF
SUBSTITUTION
The curve $X = X_0$ is an isoquant enumerating all the combinations of A and B which could
produce a fixed amount of output equal to X_0. Going from point K to L along the isoquant
means increasing the use of A by ΔA_0 and reducing the use of B by ΔB_0. Likewise, moving
from K' to L' means increasing the use of A by ΔA_1 and reducing the use of B by ΔB_1. The
slope of the isoquant is $\Delta B/\Delta A$. This slope is equal to $- MP_a/MP_b$.

It is difficult to see intuitively why σ measures the ease with which two
factors are substituted for one another. The student can gain some feel for
the meaning of the elasticity of substitutions by observing that for the case in
which no substitution is possible, $\sigma = 0$; for the case in which substitution is
perfect, $\sigma = \infty$.[9] The real world is somewhere in between these two ex-
tremes. Consider Figure 5-10. In panel (*a*) the ray denoted by *m* represents a
fixed proportion between B and A. (The slope of *m* is the fixed proportion
B/A.) Thus, only points on *m* are feasible. Isoquants must be L-shaped with
a corner belonging to *m*. Deviating from the corner either rightward or
upward would not require any change in the amount of the other input used.
For illustration, if we add $\overline{FG}$ units of A to the process of production, we
cannot save on the amount of B used; moreover, $\overline{FG}$ units of A are idle. This
is a case of *fixed proportions* in which substitution is impossible: The elasticity of substitution is equal to zero. Panel (*b*) shows a regular isoquant with
an elasticity of substitution equal to unity. For example, the elasticity of
substitution of the production function $X = \sqrt{A \cdot B}$ is unity. Finally, panel
(*c*) shows a linear isoquant representing perfect substitution between the two

---

[9]The symbol ∞ represents infinity. For our purposes infinity is a very large number.

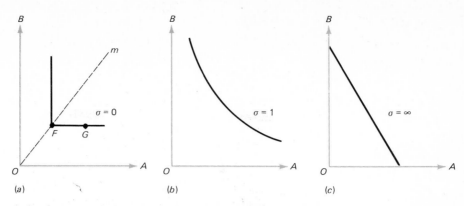

FIGURE 5-10 THREE ISOQUANTS REPRESENTING PAIRS OF INPUTS

In panel (a) the isoquant is L-shaped; this relects a case of fixed proportions: Only the combinations of inputs A and B on the ray m can be fully used in the production of the good. Any other combination must lead either to a surplus of A or a surplus of B. In panel (b) we show a normal case in which the isoquant is convex toward the origin and negatively sloped. In panel (c) the isoquant is linear, reflecting a case in which inputs A and B are perfect substitutes for one another.

factors. Here the elasticity of substitution is ∞. Needless to say, if the isoquant is linear, the two factors must be identical.

The convexity (toward the origin) of the isoquant should be mentioned here. Section 1.4c explained why, if utility can be measured cardinally, indifference curves must be convex toward the origin. Since production can always be measured cardinally, the law of diminishing marginal physical product (Section 5.3b) gives rise to convex isoquants. The proof is left as an exercise for the student.

5.4b An Example: Statistical Values of Elasticities of Substitution in Some Manufacturing Industries

Charles E. Ferguson estimated the elasticity of substitution between labor and capital for 19 American manufacturing industries.[10] He applied statistical methods to time-series data over the period 1949–1961. His results are given in Table 5-5.

As Table 5-5 indicates, the magnitudes of the elasticity of substitution varied from a low of 0.24 in food and transportation to a high of 1.30 in petroleum. In a statistical sense, however, in food, rubber, and transportation the estimated elasticity of substitution was not significantly different from zero. In furniture,

chemicals, petroleum, and primary metals the elasticity of substitution was significantly greater than unity. For the rest of the industries the elasticity of substitution was not significantly different from unity.

The so-called energy crisis of 1973–1974 has led to increased interest in the spectrum of characteristics of energy demand. In particular, the extent to which energy users would respond to energy prices became a very attractive point of interest. Atkinson and Halvorsen studied the degree of substitution among the various fuels, i.e., coal, oil, and natural

---

[10]Charles E. Ferguson, "Time-Series Production Functions and Technological Progress in American Manufacturing Industry," *Journal of Political Economy*, vol. 73, April 1965, pp. 135–147.

TABLE 5-5 **Statistical Values of Elasticities of Substitution for Various Industries**

Industry	Estimate of elasticity of substitution
Food and kindred products	0.24
Tobacco products	1.18
Textile mill products	1.10
Apparel and related products	1.08
Lumber and timber	0.91
Furniture and fixtures	1.12
Paper and allied products	1.02
Printing and publishing	1.15
Chemical and allied products	1.25
Petroleum and coal	1.30
Rubber and plastic	0.76
Leather and leather products	0.87
Stone, clay, and glass	0.67
Primary metals	1.20
Fabricated metal products	0.93
Machinery (except electrical)	1.04
Electrical machinery	0.64
Transportation equipment	0.24
Instruments	0.76

Source: Charles E. Ferguson, "Time-Series Production Functions and Technological Progress in American Manufacturing Industries," *Journal of Political Economy,* vol. 73, April 1965, pp. 135–147.

gas, which were used in electric-power generation in 1971. They concluded that substantial ex post substitution exists between fuels which are used in electric-power generation.[11]

5.4c Homogeneous Production Functions

When a firm increases the employment of all factors of production per unit of time, we can say that it is increasing its *scale* of operations. The change in scale is defined quantitatively only for cases where the amount of each factor used is varied at the same rate. Thus, to say that the amount of each factor used has doubled is equivalent to saying that the *scale* has doubled. Consider three firms. Let us assume that in each firm the amount of each factor used is raised K percent. Assume that this entails less than K percent increase in the level of output in the first firm, exactly K percent increase in output in the second firm, and more than K percent increase in output in the third firm. Then, the first firm is said to be governed by *decreasing returns to scale*, the second firm by *constant returns to scale*, and the third firm by *increasing returns to scale*. It is left for the student to show that the production function $X = \sqrt{A \cdot B}$ obeys constant returns to scale. (*Hint*: Multiply each factor by a

---

[11]Scott E. Atkinson and Robert Halvorsen, "Interfuel Substitution in Steam Electric Power Generation," *Journal of Political Economy,* vol. 84, October 1976, pp. 959–978.

positive number greater than unity. For example, to increase the scale by 20 percent, you should multiply each factor by 1.20.) In other terminology frequently used, the first firm is *homogeneous of a degree less than 1*, the second firm is *homogeneous of degree 1*, and the third is *homogeneous of a degree more than 1*.

From the purely logical viewpoint only the case of constant returns to scale is acceptable: In order to double its scale, the firm must erect a "twin" plant next to the existing plant. But this must result in doubling of output. If the "twin" plants together produce a little less than twice the production of the original plant, it implies that the management of the firm constitutes a fixed factor and we do not observe a *pure* doubling of the scale of the firm. Economists normally ignore this fine point and simply state that the firm obeys decreasing returns to scale.

If the production function is governed by constant returns to scale, then AP_a and MP_a are determined by the ratio of A/B rather than absolute magnitudes of the two inputs. In Figure 5-8 we derived the AP_a and MP_a curves under the assumption that $B = B_0$. Suppose instead of holding B constant at a level of B_0 we hold it constant at a level of $2B_0$ and double the amount of A used; namely, instead of A_1 we employ $2A_1$, instead of A_2 we employ $2A_2$, and so on. We also change the scale of the horizontal axis such that a new unit is half the length of the previous unit of A. The new AP_a and MP_a curves remain the same as they were prior to such a change. In other words, if the A axis in panel (*b*) of Figure 5-8 is replaced by an A/B axis, the curves AP_a and MP_a remain the same regardless of the absolute magnitudes of A and B, respectively.

To prove that under constant returns to scale marginal physical product and average physical product are determined by the ratio A/B, we need only to use our intuition: Consider a firm that owns only one plant which employs B_0 units of B and A_1 units of A, as illustrated in Figure 5-8. Total output of the firm is $\overline{A_1R}$, and the associated AP_a and MP_a, respectively, are $\overline{A_1G}$ and $\overline{A_1F}$. As noted before, to have a "pure" doubling of the scale of the firm means to have twin plants where each employs A_1 units of factor A and produces $\overline{A_1R}$ units of output. *Note:* Since at each of the "twin" plants B_0 units of the fixed factor are employed, it is clear that the firm (which now operates two plants) employs $2B_0$ units of the fixed factor and $2A_1$ units of the variable factor. Total output is $2 \cdot (\overline{A_1R})$, and AP_a at that level is $[2 \cdot (\overline{A_1R})]/2A_1 = \overline{A_1R}/A_1 = \overline{A_1G}$. AP_a is the same as it was before the scale of production was doubled. Next, the MP_a remains the same because the two total output curves of the two "twin" plants are identical. Hence the slope of the total output curve at point R is identical for both plants. Thus, adding one additional unit of A per unit of time to either the original plant or the second plant would result in the same additional amount of X. The conclusion is that MP_a is invariant to scale variations.

What is the geometric meaning of constant returns to scale? Figure 5-11 is a map of isoquants. If we send any ray from the origin, such as m, it will cut isoquants X_0, X_1, and X_2 at points like K, L, and M. Geometrically, along any ray which starts at the origin the ratio A/B is unchanged; in Figure 5-11,

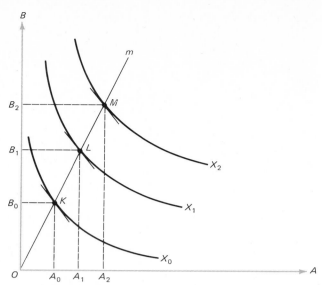

FIGURE 5-11 CONSTANT RETURNS TO SCALE
The isoquants X_0, X_1, and X_2 are sliced from a production hill generated by a production function obeying constant returns to scale. The ray m, which starts at the origin, represents pairs of A and B that are used in a fixed proportion: $A_0/B_0 = A_1/B_1 = A_2/B_2$, etc. Since a fixed proportion is maintained along the ray, and since the production function is homogeneous of degree 1, MP_a and AP_a as well as MP_b and AP_b are invariant along the ray. Since RTS $= -MP_a/MP_b$, it follows that the slope of the isoquants along the ray (at points like K, L, and M) is unchanged.

$A_0/B_0 = A_1/B_1 = A_2/B_2$. If we assume that the production function obeys constant returns to scale, then along the ray m marginal physical products of inputs A and B, respectively, are unchanged: MP_a is unchanged at points like K, L, and M; MP_b is unchanged at points like K, L, and M. Since by Equation 5-7 the slope of an isoquant (RTS) is equal to $-MP_a/MP_b$, it follows that the slope of all isoquants along the ray m (or any other such ray) is the same. In particular, the slope of the isoquants X_0, X_1, and X_2 is the same at points K, L, and M.

5.5 THE INDIVISIBILITY OF THE FIXED FACTOR (Optional)

When drawing the various curves in Figure 5-8, we assumed that the firm is stuck with B_0 units of some fixed factor. It should be stressed that in most cases B_0 is indivisible. For example, if a farm is stuck with a big tractor, and one day it sells most of its land (which in this case is the variable factor), the farmer cannot adjust this situation by using only a fraction of the tractor. As a result of the *indivisibility of the fixed factor*, its marginal physical product is negative. The puzzled student may wonder about the meaning of MP_b. The answer is that the marginal physical product of the fixed factor B is the additional amount of output that *would* have been obtained had the assump-

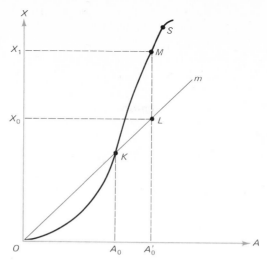

FIGURE 5-12 INDIVISIBILITY OF THE FIXED FACTOR

The amount of input A used is measured along the horizontal axis, and the amount of output X used is measured along the vertical axis. The curve is a portion of the total output curve shown in panel (a) of Figure 5-8. If B is kept constant (as it is along the total output curve), moving from A_0 to A_0' would lead us from point K to point L on the total output curve. Assume constant returns to scale. If we relax the assumption that B is held constant and we increase B equiproportionately, we move instead to point L, which lies on the ray that connects the origin with point K. Thus, adding more B to the process of production results in less output. In that zone MP_b is therefore negative.

tion of fixity been relaxed and the fixed input increased by a small amount. In the farm example, varying the size of the tractor by some relevant unit (horsepower) would illustrate a situation in which B is changed by ΔB.

The above intuitive discussion can be stated more vigorously as follows:

If the production function is governed by constant returns to scale, then MP_b is negative in the range of output where AP_a rises.[12]

The proof proceeds as follows: Part of panel (a) of Figure 5-8 is reproduced in Figure 5-12. Consider any point K on the output curve which lies to the left of point S. If we increase factor A from A_0 to A_0', and if at the same

---

[12]The assumption of constant returns to scale is too restrictive. For example, any production function obeying *decreasing*, *constant*, or *increasing returns to scale* will yield this result provided the following holds: Assume that we are at point K (Figure 5-12); we increase input A from A_0 to A_0'. We relax the assumption of the fixity of B and increase input B from B_0 to B_0', such that

$$\frac{B_0' - B_0}{B_0} = \frac{A_0' - A_0}{A_0}$$

Instead of KM (Figure 5-12) the total output curve in domain $\overline{A_0A_0'}$ will be some other curve KL. If we do not assume constant returns to scale, the new curve KL will be nonlinear. But so long as there is a gap between L and M such that M occupies a position higher than L, the marginal physical product of the fixed factor B will be negative in the range where AP_a is rising.

time we relax the assumption that B is fixed and increase factor B by the same proportion of $(A_0' - A_0)/A_0$, output will also increase proportionately. Geometrically, the firm will expand along the ray denoted by m sent from the origin to point K. The expansion will be from K to L. An output of X_0 units corresponds to point L. If we now divert the increment of factor B (ΔB) away from production, that is, we return to a fixed B, output will increase more than proportionately to $(A_0' - A_0)/A_0$. In fact, the firm will expand from K to M along the total output curve, gaining an output of $X_1 - X_0$. Thus the diversion of ΔB away from production gave rise to a gain in output. Since $\Delta X = X_1 - X_0$ is positive and ΔB is negative, $MP_b (= \Delta X / \Delta B)$ must be negative (in the domain extending from 0 to A_2).

If factor B were divisible, the firm could increase it (up to the amount in which it is fixed) proportionately to the increase in factor A, and MP_b would not be negative. It is left for the student to draw the two panels of Figure 5-8 under the assumption that factor B is divisible.

The three *zones* were discussed in Section 5.3b, along with the fact that in zone III marginal physical product of input A is negative. Now we have discovered that in zone I the marginal physical product of B is negative. This leaves only zone II with both marginal physical products positive. The reader interested in pursuing this point is referred to footnote 8.

5.6 THE SEMANTICS OF RELATING INPUTS TO EACH OTHER

Before the discussion on the theory of production is concluded, the student should be warned that there are two distinct methods of classifying pairs of factors of production vis-à-vis how they relate to each other. Economists use confusing terms to describe relationships between pairs of inputs. The two methods of classification are distinguished here in the hope of avoiding later confusion.

1. *Classification by substitutability.* Substitutability is defined as the relationship between any two factors of production when the level of output is held constant. If only two inputs are involved in the process of production, they must relate as substitutes toward one another. This is proved by simply recalling that the isoquant is negatively sloped. Similar cases were discussed in Section 3.3c with regard to a consumption process in which only two goods are involved. In economic jargon inputs that are substitutes for one another are called *competitive inputs*. Analogous to the theory of consumption, if the dimensionality of the production function is extended from two to n (n is at least three), a relationship of *complementarity* can exist between two factors. For example, energy and capital may be a pair of *complements* while energy and labor (or labor and capital) are a pair of *competitive* factors of production.[13]

---

[13]If more than two inputs are used in the process of production, the elasticity of substitution σ can be either positive or negative. This elasticity of substitution is known as *Allen's elasticity of substitution*. It is denoted by σ_{ij} for any pair of inputs i and j. If the two inputs are *competitive*, σ_{ij} is positive. If the two inputs are *complementary*, σ_{ij} is negative.

2. *Classification by marginal physical products.* This classification is based on the cross relationship between input A and the marginal physical product of B, and input B and the marginal physical product of A. Experience shows that if there is a positive relationship between A and MP_b, there will also be a positive relationship between B and MP_a; positive relationship simply means that, *ceteris paribus,* an increase in A leads to a rise in MP_b and an increase in B leads to a rise in MP_a. Conversely, negative relationship means that an increase in A leads to a fall in MP_b and an increase in B leads to a fall in MP_a.[14] Figure 5-13 illustrates this type of cross relationship. In panel (a) a positive relationship between A and B is assumed and the impact of an increase in the amount of B used on MP_a is demonstrated: The lower MP_a curve is drawn for a level of B which is kept constant at B_0. It is denoted by $B = B_0$. As the level of B rises to a higher level of B_1 owing to positive dependence MP_a is higher everywhere; hence the MP_a curve shifts to a higher level denoted by $B = B_1$. In panel (b) we assume a negative relationship between A and B. Initially the MP_a curve is the one denoted by $B = B_0$. After B increases from B to B_1, MP_a is lower everywhere; accordingly, the MP_a curve shifts downward to a position $B = B_1$.

5.7 AN EXAMPLE: EDUCATION AS AN INPUT IN THE PRODUCTION FUNCTION

Economists have estimated statistical production functions wherever and whenever the data were available. The main targets for such studies have been the agricultural and industrial sectors. However, economists have not stopped there; they have gone as far as estimating a production function for medical services associated with physicians. Regardless of the mathematical form that economists select in order to approximate the production function, they are mostly interested in the following parameters:

1. The elasticity of productions E_a as defined in Section 5.3c by Equation 5-5, for the various inputs.
2. A coefficient for returns to scale. If this coefficient is unity, the production function is governed by increasing returns to scale: A 10 percent increase in scale would result in a 10 percent increase in output. If this coefficient is greater than unity, the production function is governed by increasing returns to scale: For example, if this coefficient is estimated at 1.2, it

implies that a 10 percent increase in scale would result in a 12 percent increase in output. Finally, if the coefficient is less than unity, the production function is governed by decreasing returns to scale. If the returns-to-scale coefficient is 0.8, a 10 percent increase in scale will result in only an 8 percent increase in total output. The coefficient of returns to scale is thus an elasticity of production measuring the response of production to an equiproportional change in all inputs. It was mentioned in Section 5.4c that since the change in scale in reality is never pure, the returns-to-scale coefficient is normally either greater than unity or smaller than unity.
3. The elasticity of substitution σ as defined by Equation 5-8.

We feel that workers with a higher level of education are better agents of production. Can education be identified as a factor of production? We also know intuitively that research contributes to higher levels of

---

[14]MP_a is mathematically defined as $\partial X/\partial A$. The relationship between B and MP_a is revealed by examining the derivative $\partial(\mathrm{MP}_a)/\partial B$, which boils down to the second-order cross derivative written as $\partial^2 X/(\partial A \cdot \partial B)$. If this second-order (cross) derivative is positive, there is a positive relationship between A and B; if it is negative, there is a negative relationship between A and B.

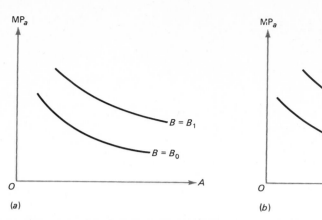

(a)

(b)

FIGURE 5-13 POSITIVE AND NEGATIVE RELATIONSHIPS BETWEEN A AND B

Panel (a): Along the horizontal axis we measure input A and along the vertical axis we measure MP_a. Initially $B = B_0$ and the MP_a curve occupies a lower position; as the amount of input B increases from B_0 to B_1, the MP_a curve shifts to a higher position, which reflects a positive relationship between A and B.

Panel (b): The axes are the same as in panel (a). Initially $B = B_0$. After B increases from B_0 to B_1, the MP_a curve shifts to a lower position because of a negative relationship between A and B.

output. Can research be treated as an input and be incorporated into a production function? Griliches estimated an agricultural production function in which he included education and research (and extension services).[15] He also estimated the elasticity of substitution and the coefficient for constant returns to scale. (The elasticity of subsitution was estimated

separately from the production function.) Education was estimated from a rough description of years of school completed by males in rural farm areas. A proxy for research and extension services was obtained by taking the sum of all expenditures by agricultural experiment stations and extension services. The results are given in Table 5-6.

5.7a An Application: What Do We Learn from Empirical Production Functions?

Note that smallness of production elasticity estimate does not imply that the coefficient is unimportant. During the relevant period the expenditures for research and extension services amount to $32 per farm. The average gross output per farm was $7205. Doubling the amount of money spent per annum on research and extension services would have yielded an additional output of $425 (5.9 percent of $7205). Thus, for each additional dollar spent on research and extension services farmers could expect $13 in additional output. This would have amounted to a huge rate of return of 1300 percent. Another interest-

ing result of the Griliches study is the estimate of the production elasticity of education of 0.40, which was only slightly less than 0.51, the estimate for labor. In fact this result roughly tells us that the labor force is two-dimensional: A rise in the level of schooling of farm workers by 10 percent would result in almost the same increase in output from a 10 percent increase in the number of workers. In developing countries the agricultural sector is substantial. The results of empirical agricultural production functions point out that investment in education may pay handsomely. Obtaining an estimate in excess of unity for the re-

[15]Zvi Griliches, "Research Expenditures, Education and the Aggregate Agricultural Production Function," *The American Economic Review*, vol. 54, December 1964, pp. 961–974.

TABLE 5-6 **Estimates of an Agricultural Production Function for 1949, 1954, 1959**

Production elasticities	
Other	0.37
Land buildings	0.15
Fertilizer	0.10
Machinery	0.16
Labor	0.51
Education	0.40
Research and extension services	0.06
Returns to scale	1.28
Elasticity of substitution	1

Source: Zvi Griliches, "Research Expenditures, Education and the Aggregate Agricultural Production Function," *The American Economic Review*, vol. 54, December 1964, pp. 961–974.

turns-to-scale coefficient implied that farmers were in disequilibrium in the sense that they could have benefited from expanding their scale of operation.

SUMMARY The analysis in this chapter was based on the assumption that a process of production can be summarized by a *production function*. Given a production function in which output depends on two inputs, the analysis started by considering the *production hill* both in a real example (corn) and in theory. The focus was on two *slices* of the production hill—the *vertical slice* and the *horizontal slice*.

The vertical slice yielded the *total output curve*. From the total output curve, the *average physical product* (AP_a) and the *marginal physical product* (MP_a) were derived for the case in which B is held constant at a certain level. We have seen that the MP_a curve cuts the AP_a curve at the maximum point of the AP_a curve. Moreover, MP_a exceeds AP_a between a production of zero and the point of intersection, and thereafter AP_a exceeds MP_a. Since the elasticity of production of output with respect to the variable input E_a is MP_a/AP_a, it was concluded that this elasticity is greater than unity between the origin and the point of intersection of AP_a and MP_a, and thereafter it is smaller than unity. The fact that total production curves are (in general) first convex downward and then concave downward was also discussed. The *point of inflection* separates the convex from the concave portions of the total output curve. Between its point of inflection and point of maximum, the total output curve has a positive slope, and it increases at a decreasing rate. Associated with these properties of the total output curve is a declining (but positive) MP_a. This phenomenon is known as the law of *diminishing marginal physical product*. The domain of A (for the case when B is held constant) was divided into three zones: In zone I, MP_a rises, reaches a maximum level, and then begins to fall; AP_a rises. The boundary of this zone is the point of intersection between MP_a and AP_a. (In this zone the MP_b is negative.) Zone II is known as the zone of production. Both MP_a and MP_b are falling. This zone ends where MP_a cuts the horizontal axis. In zone III, MP_a is negative. The firm would always avoid zone III, would most of the time avoid zone I, and would almost always produce in zone II.

The *horizontal slice* yielded the *isoquant*. The *isoquant map* was discussed and divided into four regions. It was concluded that only region I, in which both input A and input B are "goods," is of interest to the producer. We saw that the *marginal rate of technical substitution* (RTS), which is the slope of the isoquant, is equal to $-MP_a/MP_b$. We then focused on the ease with which two inputs can be substituted for one another: If the inputs are good substitutes, the isoquant is very flat, approaching in the limit a linear curve; if the inputs are poor substitutes, the isoquant is bulging toward the origin, approaching in the limit the L-shaped curve. *The elasticity of substitution* σ was defined, recalling the fact that it is used by economists to measure the ease with which inputs can replace one another.

All production functions were classified as obeying *decreasing returns to scale, constant returns to scale,* or *increasing returns to scale.* Pure logic dictates that only constant returns to scale are possible. Since in reality management (entrepreneurial capacity) is a fixed factor, however, we observe that production functions obey all possible returns to scale.

Finally we noted that pairs of inputs can be classified according to two distinct keys: First, they can be classified as to whether they are *competitive* or *complementary*, and second they can be classified as to whether there is a positive or negative relationship between the amount of one input and the marginal physical product of the other input.

GLOSSARY **Factors of production** Also known as *inputs*, these are resources transformed into output in the process of production.

Firm An agency engaged in transforming *inputs* into *outputs*.

Production function Given a firm, there is a maximum output that can be produced from any feasible combination of inputs; this is a *relation* between a combination of inputs and a level of output. The collection of all such possible relations is the production function. For the case of output X and two inputs A and B, the production functions is expressed as $X = f(A, B)$.

Production hill Given a two-dimensional production function $X = f(A, B)$, the production hill is obtained by drawing the production surface in a three-dimensional diagram, where output X is measured along the vertical axis which is perpendicular to the A,B plane.

Total output curve Obtained from a *vertical slice* of the production hill. It relates total output to one variable input when all other inputs are held constant.

Inflection point The point where the total output curve (or any other curve) ceases to be *convex downward* and begins to be *concave downward*.

Marginal physical product The change in total output over a small change in one input ($\Delta X/\Delta A$), when all other factors of production are unchanged.

The marginal physical product of factor A is denoted by MP_a. Geometrically, the marginal physical product is the slope to the total output curve.

Average physical product Total output divided by the total amount of an input used per unit of time (X/A). Geometrically, it is the slope of a line connecting the origin and a point on the total output curve. The average physical product of factor A is denoted by AP_a.

Isoquant Also known as a *production indifference curve*. Obtained from taking a horizontal slice of the production hill. It is the collection of all possible inputs capable of producing a fixed level of output. In the A,B plane the isoquant is a locus of points, each representing a pair of A and B which is required to produce a fixed level of output.

Isoquant map Obtained from slicing the hill at many "altitudes." Each slice yields an isoquant associated with a different fixed level of output. Formally, the isoquant map is identical with the *indifference map*.

Entrepreneurial capacity A term used to denote the *owner* in small firms such as *partnerships* and *single proprietorships;* in such small firms the assumption is made that the owner is also the manager. In large *corporations* this term denotes the combination of the *majority stockholder* (or if there is no majority stockholder, the board of directors representing the stockholders) and the *top management*.

Elasticity of production The relative change in output over a small relative change in one input, when all other inputs are held constant. This elasticity, which is denoted by E_a (for input A), is equal to MP_a/AP_a. Hence it is greater than unity between the origin and the point of intersection between MP_a and AP_a, and it is smaller than unity thereafter.

The law of diminishing marginal physical product The law states that if at least one factor of production is held constant, then when the firm varies one input (or more than one input), beyond a certain point the marginal physical product of the variable input falls. Geometrically, the marginal physical product begins to fall at the level of input where the inflection point occurs on the total output curve.

Marginal rate of technical substitution Known as the RTS, this is the slope of the isoquant ($\Delta B/\Delta A$). The RTS is also equal to $-MP_a/MP_b$.

The elasticity of substitution A technical measure designed to measure the ease with which two inputs can be substituted for one another. If only two inputs participate in the process of production, the elasticity of substitution is close to zero when the two inputs are poor substitutes, and it is close to infinity when the two inputs are very good substitutes. In many industries in the United States the elasticity of substitution between labor and capital is near unity. The elasticity of substitution is denoted by σ.

Homogeneous production functions Production functions are divided into three groups: Homogeneous of *degree less than 1,* of *degree 1,* and of *degree greater than 1. Scale of production* is defined as all inputs varying equiproportionately. Thus, if the production function is homogeneous of degree less than 1, increasing scale by K percent will result in less than K percent increase in output; this production function obeys the law of *decreasing returns to scale*. If the production function is homogeneous of degree 1, increasing scale by K percent will result in exactly K percent increase in output; this production function obeys the law of *constant returns to scale*. If the production function is homogeneous of degree higher than 1, increasing scale by K percent will result in more than K percent increase in output; this production function obeys the law of *increasing returns to scale*.

Indivisibility The property that the fixed factor cannot be used in amounts smaller than a certain size with which the firm is left. The indivisibility of the fixed factor is the reason why the total output curve of the variable factor is *convex downward* when small doses of the variable input are used.

Competitive factors Two inputs that are substitutes for one another. Substitutability is measured when production is restricted to an isoquant.

Complementary factors Two factors that are complementary to one another. Complementarity is measured when production is restricted to an isoquant. However, in order for complementarity to be feasible there must be more than two factors in the process of production.

Positive or negative relationship The relationship between input A and MP_b, and input B and MP_a.

PROBLEMS An asterisk indicates an advanced problem.

5-1. Table 5-2 shows how the consumption of fertilizers varies considerably from country to country. What is the lesson drawn from the data in Table 5-2?

5-2. Go to Table 5-3. Calculate the marginal physical product and average physical product of corn output with respect to nitrogen. Assume that phosphate is fixed at 160 pounds per acre. *Note:* The marginal physical product of nitrogen should be associated with 20, 60, 100 pounds, and so on. Draw the curves that you have calculated and describe the zones of production covered by this (corn) production function.

5-3. Do you agree with the following statement? AP_a must be greater than MP_a so long as MP_a is falling.

5-4. Prove that in domain $\overline{OA_2}$ (Figure 5-8) elasticity of output with respect to input $A(E_a)$ is greater than unity; is unity when A_2 units of A are used; and is smaller than unity beyond this point.

5-5. Prove that the production function $X = \sqrt{A \cdot B}$ obeys constant return to scale. How about the production function $X = A \cdot B$?

5-6.* Redraw the two panels of Figure 5-8 under the assumption that the fixed factor B is divisible. (This is equivalent to saying that factor B is variable, but it is limited to a maximum amount of B_0.)

5-7. Explain why, contrary to pure logic, production functions in reality may reveal increasing or decreasing returns to scale.

5-8. Calculate the RTS for $X_0 = \sqrt{A \cdot B}$, where $X_0 = 10$, between the points K $(A = 5, B = 20)$ and $L(A = 6, B = 16.67)$. Use the formula RTS $= -\text{MP}_a/\text{MP}_b$.

5-9. Why must the isoquant be convex toward the origin if the firm operates at the stage of production where the marginal physical product of the two inputs, respectively, diminishes?

5-10. Derive the two MP_a schedules from the production function $X = \sqrt{A \cdot B}$ first for $B_0 = 2$ units and then for $B_1 = 3$ units. A should vary with increments of 1 from 0 to 6 units.

5-11.* The estimates of the agricultural production function (Griliches) indicated that production elasticity with respect to fertilizer is 0.10. What information would you need in order to determine whether farmers' use of fertilizer is optimal?

MATHEMATICAL APPENDIX 5

M5.1 HOMOGENEOUS PRODUCTION FUNCTIONS

Mathematically, MP_a is defined as the partial derivative of output with respect to input A. In what follows the partial derivative will be denoted by $f_a(=\partial X/\partial A)$. Consider the production function $X = f(A, B)$. This function is said to be homogeneous of degree h if, given a positive parameter t, the following is satisfied:

$$t^h \cdot f(A,B) = f(tA,tB) \tag{m5-1}$$

Note that h is the degree of homogeneity. Thus, given a production function which is governed by decreasing, constant, or increasing returns to scale, h is less than, equal to, or greater than unity, respectively.

Differentiating both sides of Equation m5-1 with respect to input A gives

$$t^h \cdot f_a(A,B) = t \cdot f_{ta}(tA,tB)$$

where $ta = tA$. Dividing both sides of the above result by t gives

$$t^{h-1} \cdot f_a(A,B) = f_{ta}(tA,tB) \tag{m5-2}$$

Namely, the marginal physical product of A (or any input) is homogeneous of degree $h - 1$.

If we set $h = 1$, the production function is homogeneous of degree 1 (constant returns to scale). If $h = 1$, the power of t in Equation m5-2 is zero. Hence the marginal physical product is homogeneous of degree 0, or to put it differently, it is invariant with respect to equiproportional changes in all inputs: It is determined solely by the ratio A/B. It is easy to show that if $h = 1$, the average physical product is invariant to changes in the scale of production (Equation m5-1).

Consider a production indifference map as depicted by Figure 5-14. Recall that RTS (marginal rate of technical substitution) is defined as $-\text{MP}_a/\text{MP}_b =$

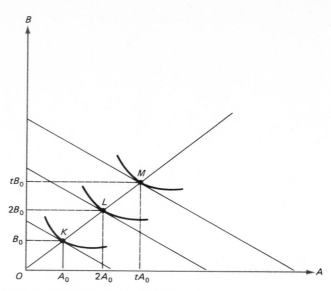

FIGURE 5-14   HOMOGENEOUS PRODUCTION FUNCTIONS

$-f_a/f_b$ (Equation 5-7). If we send a ray from the origin in any direction, then geometrically a movement on the ray means changing the inputs equiproportionately, that is, changing scale. For illustration we selected three points on the ray, namely, K, L, and M. Point L represents twice the scale of K and point M represents t times the scale of K. Given a production function homogeneous of any degree h, the RTS is the same at any point such as K, L, and M on the ray. Geometrically, the RTS is the slope of a line which is tangent to the isoquant at the relevant point. Therefore, the three lines which are tangent to the three isoquants at points K, L, and M, respectively, are parallel. Making use of Equation m5-2, we prove it as follows:

$$\text{RTS}(M) = -\frac{f_{ta}(tA, tB)}{f_{tb}(tA, tB)} = -\frac{t^{h-1} f_a(A,B)}{t^{h-1} f_b(A,B)} = -\frac{f_a(A,B)}{f_b(A,B)} = \text{RTS}(K)$$

That is, the RTS is invariant with respect to the scale of production as measured by t.

If $h = 1$, then, as we move from K to L output doubles, and as we move from K to M output increases t-fold. Moreover, since at K, L, and M, respectively, the ratio of inputs is maintained at the same level of A_o/B_o, as we move from point to point on the ray, MP_a, MP_b, AP_a, and AP_b are unchanged.

M5.2 EULER'S THEOREM (ADDING UP)

Euler's theorem states that for any homogeneous production function expressed as $X = f(A,B)$ the following is true:

$$h \cdot X = A \cdot f_a + B \cdot f_b \tag{m5-3}$$

To prove it, differentiate Equation m5-1 with respect to t to obtain

$$h \cdot t^{h-1} \cdot f(A,B) = A \cdot f_{ta}(tA,tB) + B \cdot f_{tb}(tA,tB)$$

Substituting $t^{h-1} \cdot f_a(A,B)$ for $f_{ta}(tA,tB)$ (as proved to be true by Equation m5-2) and so on, and dividing both sides by t^{h-1} yields the result as given in Equation m5-3.

It was demonstrated geometrically that if the production function is governed by constant returns to scale, then in the stage of production where AP_a is rising, MP_b (of the fixed factor) must be negative (Section 5-3d). It is left for the reader to prove it mathematically by making use of Euler's theorem. (*Hint:* Set h equal to 1 in Equation m5-3. Then divide both sides of the equation by A and recall that in the relevant stage of production $AP_a <$ MP_a.)

M5.3 THE MATHEMATICAL EXPRESSION FOR THE ELASTICITY OF SUBSTITUTION

It can be proved[16] that the elasticity of substitution can be expressed as follows:

$$\sigma = \frac{f_a \cdot f_b}{X \cdot f_{ab}} \tag{m5-4}$$

where $f_{ab} = \partial^2 X/(\partial A \cdot \partial B)$.

M5.4 MATHEMATICAL PRODUCTION FUNCTIONS

Economists have developed a variety of production functions. These functions are useful in empirical studies. Only two mathematical functions that are frequently used in econometric studies will be discussed.

M5.5 THE COBB-DOUGLAS PRODUCTION FUNCTION

For the case of two inputs the Cobb-Douglas production function is stated as

$$X = KA^{\alpha}B^{\beta} \tag{m5-5}$$

where α and β, respectively, are positive parameters. By taking logarithms ($\ln X = \ln K + \alpha \ln A + \beta \ln B$) and then taking the complete differential, we obtain

$$\frac{dX}{X} = \frac{dK}{K} + \alpha \frac{dA}{A} + \beta \frac{dB}{B} \tag{m5-6}$$

---

[16]The proof is lengthy. See Roy G. D. Allen, *Mathematical Analysis for Economists*, Macmillan, London, 1947, chap. 19.

that is, α and β, respectively, are the production elasticities. If $\alpha + \beta = 1$, the Cobb-Douglas function obeys constant returns to scale.

The interested student could easily show the following properties of the Cobb-Douglas function:

$$MP_a = \alpha \cdot \frac{X}{A} \qquad MP_b = \beta \cdot \frac{X}{B}$$

The Cobb-Douglas production function is governed by the law of diminishing marginal physical product. (It fits only zone II of Figure 5-8.) *Hint:* Prove that the second-order derivative (with respect to any factor) is negative.

There is a positive relationship between A and B. (*Hint:* Show that the second-order cross derivative is positive.)

The elasticity of substitution of the Cobb-Douglas production function is always equal to unity. (*Hint:* Utilize Equation m5-4.) This is why the convenient Cobb-Douglas production function is sometimes abandoned in favor of other functions in which the elasticity of substitution can also take on values different from unity.

M5.6 THE CES (CONSTANT ELASTICITY OF SUBSTITUTION) PRODUCTION FUNCTION

The CES function is written

$$X = K[\gamma A^{-\rho} + (1 - \gamma)B^{-\rho}]^{-h/\rho} \qquad \text{(m5-7)}$$

The advantage of the CES over the Cobb-Douglas function is that its σ is not constrained to unity. The CES production function obeys constant returns to scale when $h = 1$. The following comments will be confined to the case of homogeneity of degree 1 by setting h equal to unity.

The reader can easily prove that the marginal physical product of the CES function with respect to A is $(\gamma/K^{\rho}) \cdot (X/A)^{\rho+1}$ and similarly, with respect to B, is $[(1 - \gamma)/K^{\rho})] \cdot (X/B)^{\rho+1}$. Also, by utilizing Equation m5-4, it can be easily shown that

$$\sigma = \frac{1}{1 + \rho} \qquad \text{(m5-8)}$$

If $\rho = -1$, the CES function reduces to a linear production function. The isoquant associated with this case is linear [panel (c) of Figure 5-10]. The slope of the isoquant is $-\gamma/(1 - \gamma)$, and $\sigma = \infty$.

If ρ approaches zero, by taking the limit of Equation m5-7 it can be shown that the CES function approaches the Cobb-Douglas form, namely, $X = G \cdot A^{\alpha}B^{\beta}$. The isoquant has the regular curvature [panel (b) of Figure 5-10]. $\sigma = 1$.

If ρ approaches ∞, we obtain the case of fixed proportions [panel (a) of Figure 5-10]. σ approaches zero.

The main disadvantage of the CES function, as indicated by its name, is that its σ is constant.

In their search for a still more flexible production function, economists invented new forms of production functions. One such function is the *translog* (transcendental logarithmic) production, which is written as

$$\ln X = K + \alpha \ln A + \beta \ln B + \gamma \ln A \cdot \ln B + \delta (\ln A)^2 + \epsilon (\ln B)^2 \qquad \text{(m5-9)}$$

This function reduces to Cobb-Douglas if γ, δ, and ϵ vanish. In the translog function the elasticity of substitution varies with output. Note, however, the tradeoff between flexibility and econometric convenience: The more flexible the production function, the more difficult the statistical procedures of estimation become.

C H A P T E R

THE THEORY OF COST AND PRODUCTION

The theory of the *production function* was developed in Chapter 5. You will recall that the production function tells about the transformation of inputs into outputs. In the example of corn production in Iowa 91 different transformations of pounds of phosphate and nitrogen (per acre) into bushels of corn were enumerated. This chapter takes a step further to answer the following question: Suppose a farmer in Iowa is confronted in the marketplace with a price of phosphate and a price of nitrogen; what then is the *least-cost combination* of phosphate and nitrogen that will yield a certain level of output? If we can find a formula yielding the least-cost combination of inputs (phosphate and nitrogen) for a particular level of output (corn), we can apply this formula to each level of output, extending from zero to maximum output. Furthermore, if we multiply the inputs generated by this formula by their respective prices and add the results, we obtain the least total cost of production.

To further illustrate what we are up to, let us consider the flowchart presented in Figure 6-1. Let us denote the prices of the two inputs confronting the producer by P_a and P_b. In particular, the prices that currently prevail in the marketplace are P_{a0} and P_{b0}. Let the amounts of the two inputs used in the process of production be denoted by A and B; in particular, the least-cost combinations of A and B associated with a given level of output are $\overline{A}$ and $\overline{B}$. Let us define the total amount of money spent on the two (or more) factors as total cost, denoted by C. Our first step is to feed information into the first box. The information covers the production function $X = f(A,B)$, the prices of the inputs in the marketplace P_{a0} and P_{b0}, and a certain level of output X_0. After the information is fed into the box, the formula to determine the least-cost combination of inputs is applied; the result is the least-cost combination of $\overline{A}$ and $\overline{B}$ units of A and B, respectively. The final step is performed in the second box: The least-cost quantities of inputs are multiplied by the corresponding prices to calculate total cost. Once we have calculated total cost, we can calculate other relevant costs. Much of this chapter has to do with finding least-cost combinations of inputs and calculating associated costs.

FIGURE 6-1 A FLOWCHART OF THE LEAST-COST COMBINATION OF INPUTS MODEL
Going from right to left: The information required to find the least-cost combination of inputs is fed into the first box; this information covers the *production function*, the *prices of the inputs* in the marketplace, and a level of output. The first box represents a procedure which enables the entrepreneur to find the least-cost combination of the inputs. This result is fed into the second box, in which a simple multiplication operation yields the lowest cost incurred in the production of the given level of output.

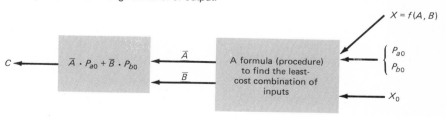

The student is reminded that this is the second in a series of four steps. Once we can derive the cost curves of the competitive firm, all we need is information about the price of output in order to determine the third step, the optimal level of production. Determining the optimal level of production will be taken up in the next chapter.

Before we start with the theory of cost, however, we must clarify some concepts relating to costs.

6.1 OPPORTUNITY COSTS, SOCIAL COSTS, AND PRIVATE COSTS

6.1a Opportunity Costs

A farmer in Iowa purchases phosphate and nitrogen. The price paid for these inputs in the marketplace times the quantities purchased constitutes a cost of production. Chapter 14 will show that the price paid for these fertilizers reflects an *opportunity cost*, which is simply the value of fertilizers in their next best alternative use on other farms. If you need some convincing, assume that vast rich lands hitherto unknown to us are discovered. This discovery will definitely lead to a rise in the price of fertilizers (at least in the short run). Why? Because the value of fertilizers in their next best use has increased. Consider the cost of the services rendered by an entrepreneur's capital. Assume that the entrepreneur invested money in a small furniture factory. What is the economic cost of the capital, that is, the entrepreneur's own money invested in machinery, inventories, and the like? Clearly, the only way to find out is to estimate the return on this capital had it been invested elsewhere in the economy in the next best possible project. Likewise, what is the cost of the services rendered by the entrepreneur? It is the income this entrepreneur could have earned had he or she been employed in the next best job available.

This subject will be considered again at the end of the next chapter when accounting versus economic costs is discussed.

6.1b Social Costs and Private Costs

Consider a paper mill that disposes of its wastes in a river. Since the river is not owned by anybody, water use does not cost the paper mill a penny. However, fishermen and swimmers downstream suffer losses which are not reflected in the cost of the paper mill. The *social cost* is the total cost incurred by the paper mill, including both the *private cost* incurred by using resources such as labor and capital and the damage suffered by fishermen and swimmers. Chapter 17 will return to this subject, known in economics as *externalities*. Most of the cost analysis covered in this book, however, deals only with private cost.

6.2 COST TERMINOLOGY

The most important cost functions will now be defined. *Total cost* is defined as the aggregate of total amounts of inputs used up in the process of production, multiplied by their respective prices. We must keep in mind that in some cases prices of inputs must be evaluated by estimating the value of the input in its next best use in the economy. Total cost, denoted by C, can be expressed as

$$C = P_a \cdot A + P_b \cdot B \tag{6-1}$$

P_a and P_b have already been defined as the prices of inputs A and B that are paid in the marketplace. You will recall that A and B are flows (quantities used per unit of time) of the factors A and B which are transformed into final output.

If in the process of production some inputs are variable and others are fixed, we may want to divide total cost into *total variable cost* and *total fixed cost*. Total variable cost is the cost incurred by using variable inputs in the process of production; total fixed cost is the cost incurred by using the fixed inputs in the process of production. If A denotes the variable factor and B_0 denotes the fixed factor, we can express total variable cost as

$$VC = P_a \cdot A \tag{6-2}$$

where VC stands for total variable cost, and we can express total fixed cost as

$$FC = P_b \cdot B_0 \tag{6-3}$$

where FC stands for total fixed cost.

Average cost, denoted by AC, is defined as total cost divided by total output, and is written as

$$AC = \frac{C}{X} \tag{6-4}$$

Average variable cost, denoted by AVC, is defined as total variable cost divided by total output, and is written as

$$AVC = \frac{VC}{X} \tag{6-5}$$

Average fixed cost, denoted by AFC, is defined as total fixed cost divided by total output, and is written as

$$AFC = \frac{FC}{X} \tag{6-6}$$

Since total variable cost plus total fixed cost is equal to total cost, we have a theorem that average variable cost plus average fixed cost is equal to average cost. We can prove this theorem more formally as follows:

$$AC = \frac{C}{X} = \frac{P_a \cdot A + P_b \cdot B_0}{X} = \frac{P_a \cdot A}{X} + \frac{P_b \cdot B_0}{X} = \text{AVC} + \text{AFC} \qquad (6\text{-}7)$$

Marginal cost is the change in total cost over a small change in output with which it is associated. Suppose a producer varies output by a small amount of ΔX. In order to achieve this change in output, a greater amount of the variable input (or inputs) must be employed. The additional cost associated with the variation in inputs is denoted by ΔC. Thus marginal cost, which we denote by MC, is

$$\text{MC} = \frac{\Delta C}{\Delta X} \qquad (6\text{-}8)$$

In Chapter 7 we shall see that the average cost curves are relevant for determining the profitable range of production and the marginal cost curve is relevant for pinpointing the unique level of output yielding maximum profit.

Before the main cost curves of the firm are derived, the student is reminded again of the importance of distinguishing between short-run and long-run cost curves.

6.3 THE SHORT-RUN AND LONG-RUN DICHOTOMY

It makes a lot of sense to distinguish between short-run and long-run cost curves because some factors of production either cannot be increased (or decreased) in the short run, or they can be increased in a short time only at an enormous cost. In Chapter 5 a firm that produces electric power was mentioned. Power stations cannot be built overnight, not even at an enormous cost. Fuel, on the other hand, can be increased or decreased continuously. In the short run the firm is stuck with a fixed number of structures and machinery; it responds to the needs of the market by varying the amount of fuel it burns per unit of time. In the long run the firm can respond to a rise in demand for electricity by adding more power stations. In the short run its options are limited; even if the price of fuel changes, the pattern of production is unchanged. In the long run the firm can respond to changes in the relative price of fuel by selecting different machinery, perhaps new power stations capable of converting fossil fuel more efficiently.

The loose description of an electric-power-producing firm can be illustrated geometrically. Consider the isoquant map in Figure 6-2. In the short run the firm is stuck with B_0 units of the fixed factor. If the firm wants to increase output from X_0 to X_1 and then to X_2 and X_3, it is restricted to a horizontal movement along the line B_0B_0, regardless of the relative prices of fuel. On the other hand, in the long run there are many possible routes that lead to higher elevations on the production hill; in Figure 6-2, L_1 and L_2 are examples of such routes. Climbing the production hill along L_1 involves a movement from K' to L' and then to M' and N'. Climbing the hill along L_2 involves a movement from K'' to L'' and then to M'' and N''. L_1 and L_2 and other similar long-run routes are not arbitrarily chosen: We shall see later

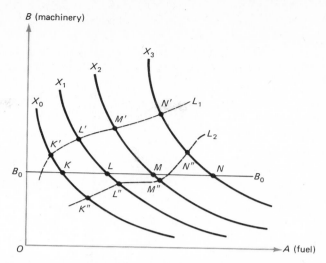

FIGURE 6-2 CLIMBING THE PRODUCTION HILL: SHORT RUN AND LONG RUN

We measured the amounts of two inputs used along the two axes. Four isoquants are shown. If one factor, say, B, is fixed at a level of B_0, the movements of the firm are restricted to the horizontal line B_0B_0, regardless of the input prices. However, if both inputs are variable, to each price ratio P_a/P_b there corresponds a unique route for climbing the production hill; examples are L_1 and L_2.

that for each price ratio P_a/P_b there corresponds a unique long-run route. Thus, for the electric-power-producing firm, selecting the long-run route is in reality *long-run planning* of the quantity and quality of machinery and equipment.

Short-run cost curves will be considered first.

6.4 DERIVING THE SHORT-RUN COST CURVES

6.4a Deriving the Variable Cost Curves

This chapter and the following chapters up to Chapter 11 will consider the *competitive firm*. The concept of *perfect competition* will be defined in Chapter 7. However, for the time being, perfect competition will mean an economic environment in which prices of both inputs and outputs are independent of the activities of the firm; the firm in perfect competition may discontinue production altogether or increase its production rate tenfold without having any appreciable influence over the prices of inputs and outputs.

We are now ready to derive the short-run variable cost curves. Consider Figure 6-3. Panels (*a*) and (*b*) are replicas of Figure 5-8. You will recall that in panel (*a*) we drew the total output curve denoted by $X(B = B_0)$. In other words, the total output curve is a vertical slice of the production hill at $B = B_0$. Recall (Equation 6-2) that total variable cost equals the price of the

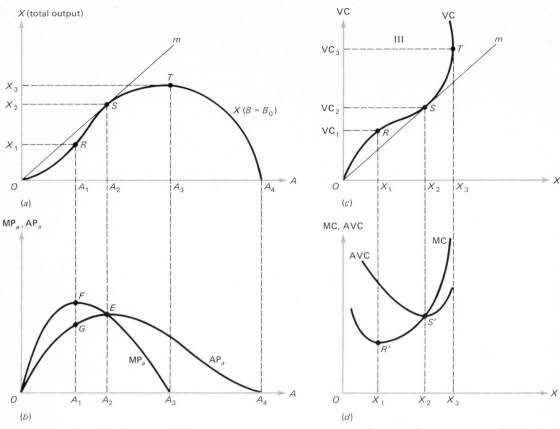

FIGURE 6-3   DERIVING THE COST CURVES OF THE FIRM IN THE SHORT RUN

(a) and (b): A replica of Figure 5-8. Recall that in panel (a) total output curve is displayed. In panel (b) AP_a and MP_a curves are drawn. The point of inflection R on the total output curve is associated with the maximum point on the MP_a curve F. The point of tangency between ray m and total output curve S is associated with the point of intersection between MP_a and AP_a (E).

(c): The total variable cost curve (VC) is the same as the total output curve in panel (a), except that the axes are transposed and VC = $1 · A$. If P_a is different from $1, we simply change the scale of the vertical axis in order to accommodate a different price; the VC curve is invariant to changes in P_a provided that the scale of the VC axis is adjusted.

(d): Average variable cost (AVC) and marginal cost (MC) curves are drawn. The minimum point on the MC curve R' corresponds to the inflection point R on the VC curve. The intersection between MC and AVC (S') corresponds to the tangency point S between ray m and the VC curve. MC approaches infinity (becomes increasingly high) when output approaches a level of X_3.

variable input times the amount of the variable input used up in the process of production, per unit of time. More formally, it is written as $VC = P_a · A$. We start with a price of A equal to $1 ($P_a = $1). In that case $VC = A$, and the horizontal axis of panel (a) measures the variable cost. In fact, the total output curve now tells us also how VC is related to output X; the only problem with panel (a) is that the axes are not pointed in convenient directions. To adjust the direction of the axes, we *transpose* them; we interchange the X axis with the A axis. Transposing the axes and redrawing the curve, we obtain the curve VC as a function of X in panel (c). Points R, S, and T in panel (c) are the same as points R, S, and T in panel (a). Because of the transposition, the VC curve is first concave downward and then becomes convex downward. Given the VC curve in panel (c), it is an easy matter to derive the average variable cost (AVC) and marginal cost (MC) curves. Let us first focus on the MC curve. The marginal cost was defined as a change in total cost over a small change in output. Between the origin and R in panel (c) VC is concave; that is, total cost is increasing at a decreasing rate, which results in a diminishing marginal cost. (Can you show why the change in total cost is the same as the change in total variable cost?) The result is a falling MC curve between the origin and point R' in panel (d). Beyond point R, VC is convex downward; that is, total cost increases at an increasing rate. In panel (d) this is translated into a rising MC curve. Thus MC attains its minimum at a level of output of X_1. Notice that X_1 is associated with A_1 in panel (b). In fact $X_1 = f(A_1, B_0)$. Ray m in panel (c) occupies the lowest position among all other rays connecting the origin with any point on the VC curve. The slope of a ray connecting the origin with a point on the VC curve equals AVC. For example, at point S in panel (c) AVC = $\overline{X_2S}/X_2$. This leads to the conclusion that AVC attains its minimum at a level of output of X_2 corresponding to point S. In Section 5.3a we saw that the marginal magnitude must cross average magnitude at the minimum or maximum points on the average magnitude. Accordingly, the MC curve must cut the AVC curve at the minimum of AVC denoted by S'. This occurs at a level of output of X_2.

We started out by assuming $P_a = \$1$. What if $P_a = \$2$? Nothing changes. We simply change the scale of the vertical axes in panels (c) and (d): If initially a dollar was represented by half an inch, now it should be represented by a quarter of an inch.

Note also that the MC and AVC curves in panel (d) may be derived from panel (b) rather than from panel (c).

First, we can develop the concept of AVC (Equation 6-5) as follows:

$$\text{AVC} = \frac{\text{VC}}{X} = \frac{P_a \cdot A}{X} = \frac{P_a}{X/A} = \frac{P_a}{AP_a} \qquad (6\text{-}9)$$

P_a, the price of the variable input, is independent of the rate of production of the competitive firm. Hence it is unchanged. Now, since in panel (b) AP_a rises from the origin to A_2 and then begins to fall, it must be (by Equation 6-9) that AVC in panel (d) falls to a level of X_2 [$=f(A_2, B_0)$], attains its minimum at X_2, and then begins to rise.

Second, we can develop the concept of MC (Equation 6-8) as follows:

$$\text{MC} = \frac{\Delta C}{\Delta X} = \frac{P_a \cdot \Delta A}{\Delta X} = \frac{P_a}{\Delta X/\Delta A} = \frac{P_a}{\text{MP}_a} \qquad (6\text{-}10)$$

Since MP_a in panel (b) rises in the range $\overline{OA}_1$ and then begins to fall, it must be (by Equation 6-10) that MC in panel (d) falls to X_1 $[= f(A_1, B_0)]$ and then begins to rise. Moreover, since AP_a and MP_a in panel (b) intersect where A equals A_2, AVC and MC in panel (d) must intersect at a rate of production of X_2.

6.4b A Summary of the Relationships between Total Magnitude and Average and Marginal Magnitudes

Section 2.2 explained why, if Y is any function of X, given any point on the curve $Y = f(X)$ [Figure 2-1], the slope of the curve measured by $\Delta Y/\Delta X$ equals the slope of a line which is tangent to the curve at that point. This relationship between total magnitudes and marginal magnitudes was again illustrated in Section 5.2e (Figure 5-5). We can summarize these findings as a general rule:

1. Given a curve representing any general function $Y = f(X)$, the slope of this curve measures its associated marginal magnitude. The marginal magnitude curve can be drawn by measuring the slope of Y with respect to X point by point.

Thus the MC curve in panel (d) of Figure 6-3 represents the slope of the VC curve in panel (c) of Figure 6-3.

2. Given the same curve representing $Y = f(X)$, the slope of a ray connecting the origin with any point lying on the curve is its associated, average magnitude. The average magnitude curve can be drawn by measuring the slope of such a ray point by point.

Thus the AVC curve in panel (d) of Figure 6-3 represents the slope of such rays that one could draw in panel (c) of Figure 6-3.

6.4c Adding the Fixed Cost to the Picture

Fixed cost is the price of the fixed factor times the amount of the fixed factor used per unit of time. In the case in which B_0 is the amount of the fixed factor used, fixed cost is $P_b \cdot B_0$ (Equation 6-3). Let us now shift our attention to Figure 6-4. Panel (a) of Figure 6-4 is similar to panel (c) of Figure 6.3, except that we add vertically to the VC curve a fixed cost equal to $\overline{OF}$ dollars. The vertical distance between the VC curve and the *total cost curve*, denoted by C, is $\overline{OF}$. We then send a ray (m') from the origin and rotate it counterclockwise about the origin until it just touches the C curve at point S_t. Geometrically, the new point of tangency S_t must lie to right of S; hence its associated level of output X_2^t must lie to the right of X_2. Let us now shift our focus to panel (b). The AC curve is derived by dividing total cost C by total output X (Equation 6-4). We have already seen that AC = AFC + AVC (Equation 6-7). That is, the AC curve in panel (b) occupies a position higher than the AVC curve. The vertical distance between these two curves is average fixed cost—AFC. Also, since S_t lies to the right of S, the intersection point between AC and MC (S_t') lies to the right of the intersection point between AVC and MC (S').

The (dashed) AFC curve (Equation 6-6) in panel (b) is fixed cost divided by total output. By its nature, this curve approaches the X axis asymptoti-

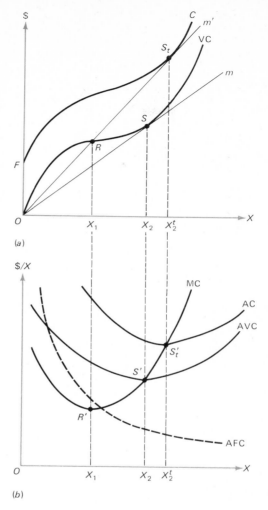

FIGURE 6-4 SHORT-RUN COST CURVES

Basically the same as the right-hand panels of Figure 6-3. To the VC curve in panel (*a*) we add a vertical segment of $\overline{OF}$ dollars which represents the fixed cost. Accordingly, the total cost curve *C* is higher than the VC curve by the amount of the fixed cost. In panel (*b*) the average fixed cost curve (AFC) is the dashed curve, which approaches infinity for very small levels of output and zero for relatively large levels of output. The average cost curve (AC) is derived by adding the AFC curve vertically to the AVC curve. The minimum point of the AC curve (S_t') lies to the right of the minimum point of the AVC curve (S').

cally as X increases significantly and approaches the vertical axis asymptotically as X decreases and approaches the origin.[1]

What have we learned so far? Mainly that short-run cost curves tend to

---

[1]The AFC curve is a *rectangular hyperbola*. AFC = FC/X; hence we can write AFC $\cdot X =$ FC. This is the formula of a rectangular hyperbola, since FC is fixed.

rise beyond a certain level of output. This is a limitation that can be overcome in the long run only by varying the fixed input. (See the next section.)

The shapes of the cost curves presented in Figure 6-4 are universal, regardless of the number of variable factors participating in the process of production. The only exception will be discussed later: the case of a production function which is governed by constant returns to scale.

The student might ask the following relevant question: In order to derive the cost curves in the case of a single variable factor, we did not engage in any process of cost minimization; what then is the meaning of the concept of *least-cost combination of factors* (A and B)? The answer is that if only one factor varies, cost minimization is trivial. Yet cost minimization is implied by the definition of the production function, namely, that for each combination of inputs, only the greatest feasible amount of output per unit of time is considered.

6.5 DERIVING THE LONG-RUN COST CURVES

We now turn our attention to the more interesting aspect of cost curves. In the short run entrepreneurs are restricted in their response to changes in the marketplace: they can employ more or less of the variable input A. In the long run, which is also the *planning run*, entrepreneurs have more options; they can vary all inputs involved in the process of production. Their main problem is summarized by the flowchart in Figure 6-1: They must find the least-cost combination of all inputs for any feasible level of output.

Lest the student conclude that the theory of least-cost combination of inputs is only another theoretical block in the theory of cost, note that an applied discipline known as *operations research* deals with practical aspects of least-cost combination of inputs (as well as other practical business problems). This field will be described in Chapter 18.

The definition of *long-run cost* is the cost of production when all inputs are varied in the process of production. Equation 6-1 would be short run if B is held constant and long run if both B and A are variable.

6.5a The Isocost

Recall the theory of the budget line developed in Chapter 1. The consumer had a fixed budget that was exhausted on goods X and Y in order to "produce" utility. Here the theory of the *isocost*, which formally is identical with the theory of the budget line will be developed. Consider a firm (producer) that purchases production factors A and B in order to produce some output X. If in Equation 6-1 we replace C by some fixed outlay, say, C_0, we obtain the isocost equation

$$C_0 = P_a \cdot A + P_b \cdot B \tag{6-11}$$

which is the same as an equation of a budget line $I_0 = P_x \cdot X + P_y \cdot Y$, as discussed in Section 1.4a. Such an isocost is presented in Figure 6-5. A movement along the isocost would be governed by the equation

$$\Delta A \cdot P_a + \Delta B \cdot P_b = 0 \tag{6-12}$$

which is formally identical with Equation 1-6 ($\Delta Y \cdot P_y + \Delta X \cdot P_x = 0$). If we subtract the expression $\Delta A \cdot P_a$ from both sides of Equation 6-12, we get

$$\Delta B \cdot P_b = -\Delta A \cdot P_a$$

Dividing both sides first by ΔA and next by P_b, we get the slope of the isocost as

$$\text{Slope} = \frac{\Delta B}{\Delta A} = -\frac{P_a}{P_b} \tag{6-13}$$

which is formally identical with the slope equation to the budget line as given by Equation 1-7.

Recall from Section 1.4a that the intercept of the budget line with either axis was obtained by dividing the price of the associated good into the budget; thus the intercept of the budget line with the X axis indicated the maximum amount of X that could be purchased with the entire budget. In exactly the same way we obtain the intercepts of the isocosts with the A and B axes; that is, these intercepts are C_0/P_a and C_0/P_b. Dividing the first intercept into the second and adding a minus sign gives the slope of the isocost curve as follows:

$$\frac{-(C_0/P_b)}{C_0/P_a} = -\frac{P_a}{P_b}$$

FIGURE 6-5 LEAST-COST COMBINATION OF INPUTS (A AND B)

In an isoquant map for a production hill, only four horizontal slices are shown: X_1, X_2, X_3, and X_4. An isocost for $C = C_0$ dollars just touches the isoquant $X = X_3$ at point W. Thus W represents the least-cost combination of inputs, and C_0 is the minimum cost that can be incurred to produce X_3 units of output.

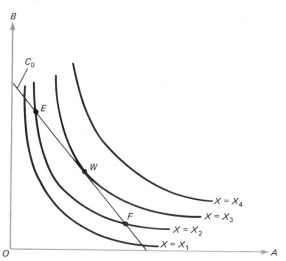

The rotations of the budget lines and isocosts follow the same rules: A decline in P_a will increase the intercept of the isocost with the A axis and rotate the budget line counterclockwise; a decline in P_b will increase the intercept of the isocost with the B axis and lead to a clockwise rotation of the isocost; a rise in either P_a or P_b will lead to opposite rotations.

We are now ready to discuss the least-cost combination of inputs.

6.5b The Least-Cost Combination of Inputs

In Figure 6-5 a map of isoquants (production indifference curves) is represented by four curves only: $X = X_1, X = X_2, X = X_3$, and $X = X_4$. At point W the isocost C_0 just touches the isoquant for $X = X_3$. This is interpreted as follows: If the firm is limited to spending at most C_0 dollars on inputs A and B, then points to the right of the line C_0 are unattainable. Points to the left of the isocost line, as well as points on the line itself, are attainable. W, the point of tangency between C_0 and the isoquant for $X = X_3$, represents the best attainable combination of A and B, that is, the combination that would yield the highest level of output. Another way to look at the same problem is to focus on the isoquant $X = X_3$ and to note that isocosts that occupy lower positions than C_0 are not sufficient for purchasing even a single combination of A and B with which X_3 can be produced. Isocosts that occupy positions higher than C_0 are sufficient for purchasing combinations of A and B with which X_3 can be produced, but why pay more than C_0 in order to produce X_3? So the conclusion is that point W represents the *least-cost* combination of A and B needed for the production of X_3.

The subsequent analysis is formally identical with the derivation of equilibrium conditions for the consumer in Section 1.4b. From geometry we know that at the point of tangency W the slope of the isoquant (RTS) [Section 5.4a] must be equal to the slope of the isocost. The equality of the slopes, respectively, can be expressed as follows:

$$\text{Slope of isocost} = -\frac{P_a}{P_b} = -\frac{\text{MP}_a}{\text{MP}_b} = \text{RTS} \qquad (6\text{-}14)$$

It is left as an exercise for the student to show that if producers are at point E (Figure 6-5) it will pay them to move in the southeasterly direction along the isocost. If, on the other hand, they happen to be at point F, it will be better to move in the northwesterly direction along the isocost.

Equation 6-14 can be rearranged to yield an equation stating that $P_a/\text{MP}_a = P_b/\text{MP}_b$. Recall that in the case where only one input varies, P_a/MP_a is the marginal cost of the firm (Equation 6-10). This result can now be extended to state that marginal cost at the least-cost-combination point W is calculated as either P_a/MP_a or P_b/MP_b as follows:

$$\text{MC} = \frac{P_a}{\text{MP}_a} = \frac{P_b}{\text{MP}_b} \qquad (6\text{-}15)$$

Equation 6-15 is very important: It tells us that when the least-cost input combination is achieved, the extra cost resulting from increasing output by one unit by employing more A (and holding B constant) is equal to the extra cost resulting from increasing output by one unit by employing more B (and holding A constant). To illustrate the meaning of Equation 6-15, we calculate the marginal physical products of A and B for the production function $X = \sqrt{A \cdot B}$, where A is equal to 8 units and B is equal to 2 units. (Recall from Section 5.2d that $MP_a = \Delta X/\Delta A$ and $MP_b = \Delta X/\Delta B$.) In order to obtain good approximations, the increment of both inputs is 0.1. The calculations are carried out in Table 6-1.

Equation 6-14 tells us that in order to attain the least-cost combination of A and B, the slope of the isocost must be equal to the slope of the isoquant: that is, the isocost is just tangent to the isoquant. Table 6-1 shows that the slope of the isoquant (RTS) is $-MP_a/MP_b = -0.25/1 = -0.25$. Any price ratio $-P_a/P_b$ which will be equal to -0.25 will yield the desirable result. For example, if $P_a = \$0.50$ and $P_b = \$2.00$, the slopes will be equal. But other pairs of P_a and P_b such as $\$1.00$ and $\$4.00$ will satisfy the condition for tangency. We can now use Equation 6-15 to calculate MC at point W in Figure 6-6: $MC = P_a/MP_a = P_b/MP_b = \$0.5/0.25 = \$2/1 = \$2$.

The result of finding a point of tangency between an isocost for $P_a = \$0.50$ and $P_b = \$2.00$ and an isoquant $4 = \sqrt{A \cdot B}$ for $A = 8$ and $B = 2$ is illustrated in Figure 6-6. The isoquant was drawn by finding pairs of A and B satisfying $4 = \sqrt{A \cdot B}$, such as 2 and 8 or 4 and 4. The isocost was found by calculating the least cost as being $\$8$ ($\$0.5 \cdot 8 + \$2 \cdot 2$) and then calculating the intercepts as follows: $\$8/\$0.5 = 16$ units of A; $\$8/\$2 = 4$ units of B. Tangency between the two curves occurs at point W.

In reality we are confronted with prices of inputs and a production function, for which we are supposed to find the least-cost combination of inputs. Let us focus again on Table 6-1 and Figure 6-6. Assume that the price of A rises from $\$0.5$ to $\$2.00$; the price of B remains unchanged at $\$2.00$. What is the new point of tangency? To find the solution requires mathematics beyond what we assume here. However, it is left for the student to confirm that for $X = 4$ units, the least-cost combination of inputs would be $A = 4$ and $B = 4$. (Apply procedures used in Table 6-1 to calculate MP_a and MP_b.) In real life production functions are not as easy to handle as $X = \sqrt{A \cdot B}$; economists and mathematicians are therefore engaged in operations research, as mentioned earlier.

TABLE 6-1 **Calculating MP_a and MP_b for $X = \sqrt{A \cdot B}$, $A = 8$, $B = 2$**

A	B	$\sqrt{A \cdot B}$	X	$MP_a = \Delta X/\Delta A$	$MP_b = \Delta X/\Delta B$
8	2	$\sqrt{8 \cdot 2}$	4		
8.1	2	$\sqrt{8.1 \cdot 2}$	4.025	$0.025/0.1 = 0.25$	
8	2.1	$\sqrt{8 \cdot 2.1}$	4.1		$0.1/0.1 = 1$

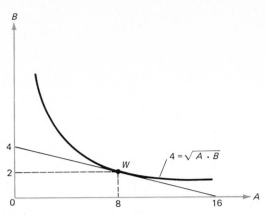

FIGURE 6-6   CALCULATING A TANGENCY POINT BETWEEN AN
ISOQUANT AND AN ISOCOST
An isoquant is drawn for $X = \sqrt{A \cdot B}$ where $X = 4$ units. At point $W(A = 8$ and $B = 2)$, MP_a
$= 0.25$ and $MP_b = 1$. Hence the slope of the isoquant at W is RTS $= -MP_a/MP_b = -0.25/1$
$= -0.25$. An isocost $C = \$0.5 \cdot A + \$2 \cdot B$ just touches the isoquant at W. The slope of the
isocost is $-P_a/P_b = -\$0.5/\$2 = -0.25$.

6.5c The Expansion Path

The parallelism between the theory of the consumer and theory of the producer continues. In Section 2.3b we derived the income consumption curve (ICC) by continuously increasing the budget of the consumer. Thus in Figure 2-2, as income increased, the budget line shifted outward and the consumer determined his or her equilibrium by locating points of tangency between budget lines and indifference curves. The income consumption curve was traced by passing a curve through all tangency points. If we view the consumer as a producer of utility and X and Y as the two inputs in the production of utility, we may view budgets as outlays, and thus budget lines may play the role of isocosts and indifference curves the role of isoquants. More specifically, if A and B are substituted for X and Y and *outlay* and *output* are substituted for *budget* and *utility*, the income consumption curve (ICC) in Figure 2-2 becomes the *expansion path* as depicted in Figure 6-7. In Section 2.3b it was stressed that points of tangency represent the highest level of utility for a given budget. Here the fact is stressed that in Figure 6-7 points of tangency represent least-cost combinations of inputs (A and B) yielding given levels of output. The difference is in focus rather than in substance: Tangency points like K, L, and M in Figure 2-2 could be viewed as least-cost combinations of goods (X and Y) yielding given levels of utility.

6.5d Longest-Run Cost Curves

The competitive firm, because of its small size, has no influence on the prices of inputs A and B; P_a and P_b are given to the firm. If A, B, and the entrepreneurial capacity are variable, these three factors can be varied

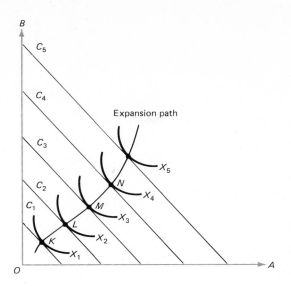

FIGURE 6-7   THE EXPANSION PATH
The isoquant map is represented by the isoquants X_1, X_2, and so on. This isoquant map is derived from horizontally slicing a production hill generated by a production function $X = f(A, B)$. Given the prices of A and B, all isocosts must have the same slope of $-P_a/P_b$. For each isoquant we find an isocost which is tangent to it. For example, C_1 is tangent to X_1 at K; C_2 is tangent to X_2 at L, and so on. The expansion path is the locus of all such tangency points (here these points are K, L, M, N, and so on). At each tangency point a least-cost combination of A and B is achieved.

equiproportionately. As explained in Section 5.4c (constant returns to scale), output would also vary in the same proportion. In Figure 6-8, along the expansion path, the ratio X_1/X_0 is the same as A_1/A_0 and B_1/B_0, respectively. X_2/X_1 is the same as A_2/A_1 and B_2/B_1, respectively, and so on.[2] In other words, as we move from the origin outward along the expansion path, total cost as defined by Equation 6-1 must increase in the same proportion as output. For example, if X_1 is twice X_0, A_1 is twice A_0, and B_1 is twice B_0. Then C_1, the cost of producing X_1 with A_1 and B_1, must be twice C_0. [$C_1 = P_a \cdot A_1 + P_b \cdot B_1 = P_a \cdot (2A_0) + P_b \cdot (2B_0) = 2(P_a \cdot A_0 + P_b \cdot B_0) = 2C_0$.] The total cost curve associated with such a production function which obeys constant returns to scale must be linear-homogeneous as depicted in panel (a) of Figure 6-9. This *long-run total cost* curve is denoted by LRC. (Linear-homogeneous is, in other words, a ray starting at the origin.) The *long-run marginal cost* (LRMC) is the slope of the total cost, namely, $\Delta C/\Delta X$. Since the long-run total cost curve (LRC) is linear, marginal cost is the same for all levels of output. Notice also that since the intercept of the

---

[2] If the production function obeys constant returns to scale, then, as explained in Section 5.4c (Figure 5-11) the slopes of the isoquants along a ray m starting at the origin are equal to each other. By implication, then, this ray is the expansion path. This is why the expansion path in Figure 6-8 is linear. In Figure 6-7 the expansion path represents a general production function.

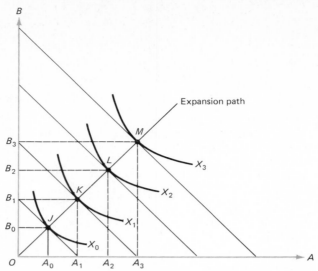

FIGURE 6-8   THE EXPANSION PATH: CONSTANT RETURNS TO SCALE

X_0, X_1, X_2, and X_3 represent the isoquant map. The fact that the expansion path is drawn as a ray indicates that along this expansion path inputs are increased in the same proportion: $A_1/A_0 = B_1/B_0$, etc. Points J, K, L, and M represent tangency points between isocosts and isoquants.

long-run total cost curve is zero, long-run marginal cost is equal to the *long-run average cost*. For example, at point I the ratio $\overline{GH}/\overline{IG}$, which is long-run marginal cost, is equal to the ratio $\overline{FI}/\overline{OF}$, which is long-run average cost. The slope of the long-run total cost curve (LRC) in panel (*a*) is equal to

FIGURE 6-9   THE LONGEST-RUN COST CURVES

(*a*): If the production function obeys constant returns to scale and all inputs are variable, total cost curve in the long run (LRC) is a ray starting at the origin.

(*b*): The long-run average cost curve (LRAC) and the long-run marginal cost curve (LRMC) are identical; moreover, the LRMC (which is also the LRAC) is a horizontal line. $\overline{OT}$, the intercept of this line with the vertical axis, is the slope of LRC in panel (a).

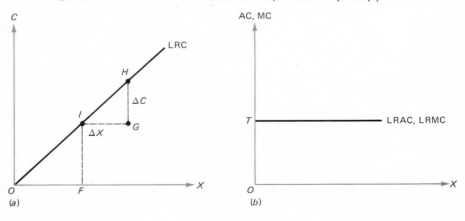

the segment $\overline{OT}$ in panel (b). We conclude that long-run marginal cost (LRMC) is identical with the long-run average cost curve (LRAC), and it is a horizontal line at the $\overline{OT}$ level.

> *In general, if all inputs (including the entrepreneurial capacity) are variable, the production function is assumed to obey constant returns to scale leading to a flat LRMC curve which is identical with the LRAC curve.*

Do we find horizontal long-run marginal cost curves in real life? Refuse collection is examined in the next section as an example of a cost function which appears to indicate constant returns to scale.

6.5e An Example: Cost Function of Refuse Collection

Cities may be viewed as multiple-plant firms providing a variety of services, such as fire and police protection and refuse collection. Accordingly, studying the cost functions of these plants could be revealing to the economist and relevant for policy makers. Werner Z. Hirsch studied the cost function (cost as related to production) of garbage collection based on data from 24 cities and municipalities in the St. Louis City–County area in 1960.[3] This is one of the few studies that traces a horizontal marginal cost curve apparently resulting from constant returns to scale. In Hirsch's study the size of the municipalities and cities varied from 200 to 225,000 trash pickup units.

Hirsch estimated an empirical average cost function for refuse collection by applying econometric (applied statistics and mathematics) methods to his data.[4] He found out that the long-run average cost curve of refuse collection is flat as in panel (b) of Figure 6-9. He defined his average cost as 1960 average annual residential refuse collection and disposal cost per pickup. The long-run average cost, which, being flat, is also the long-run marginal cost curve, was estimated at $6.16; in other words, in panel (b) of Figure 6-9, $\overline{OT}$ = $6.16. His study also showed that (1) increasing the frequency of collection from twice a week to three times a week would shift

---

[3]Werner Z. Hirsch, "Cost Functions of an Urban Government Service: Refuse Collection," *Review of Economics and Statistics*, vol. 47, February 1965, pp. 87–92.

[4]In Hirsch's study the variables were defined as follows:

X_1 = 1960 average annual residential refuse collection and disposal cost per pickup
X_2 = number of pickup units per city or municipality
X_3 = weekly collection frequency
X_4 = pickup location: curb is 0 and rear of house is 1
X_5 = number of residential pickups per square mile
X_6 = contractual arrangement, where municipal arrangement is 0 and private collection is 1
X_7 = type of fee, where general revenue financing is 0 and user charge is 1

The result of statistically estimating the average cost function is as follows:

$$X_1 = 6.16 + (0.000089X_2 - 0.000000000436X_2^2) + 3.61X_3 + 3.97X_4 - 0.000611X_5 - 1.87X_6 + 3.43X_7$$

The X_2 variable is the number of pickup units, and hence it is a good proxy for the level of output, or scale entered in the parabolic form $(aX_2 + bX_2^2)$, in order to test the presence of a U-shaped average cost curve. The coefficients of this variable are very small and statistically insignificant. This indicates that the average cost curve of refuse collection obeys neither economies nor diseconomies of scale. It is rather a flat curve which may shift up or down depending on other variables as follows: The significant (statistically) variables were X_3, X_4, and X_5. The coefficient of X_3 says that (in 1960) increasing the frequency of collection from twice a week to three times a week would shift the average cost curve upward by $3.61. The coefficient of X_4 tells us that switching collection from the curb to the rear of the house would have increased the average cost by $3.97. Finally, the coefficient of X_5 tells us that the higher the density, the lower the average cost of refuse collection: Increasing the density by 100 per square mile could have lowered the average cost curve by 6 cents.

the average cost curve upward by $3.61, and (2) switching collection from the curb to the rear of the house would increase average (marginal) cost by $3.97. This information could be used by a city administration contemplating either a change in collection frequency or a switching from curb to rear, or rear to curb, collection.

6.5f Long-Run Cost Curves

We now abandon the assumption that the entrepreneurial capacity is a variable factor of production. Instead, we realistically assume that the entrepreneurial capacity is a fixed factor. Notice, however, that the cost function (Equation 6-1) does not account for the cost of the entrepreneur. The firm does not enter into a contract with the entrepreneur to pay an agreed-upon rate per unit of effort performed. Rather, as mentioned earlier (Section 5.1a), the entrepreneur claims the residue, namely, the revenue minus contractual costs. This situation (of holding entrepreneurial capacity constant) is similar to having one fixed and one variable factor. However, instead of expanding along the A axis in panel (a) of Figure 5-8, we expand along the expansion path of Figure 6-8 (or Figure 6-7 for nonhomogeneous functions).

Consider Figure 6-8 again. Assume that between the origin and point L the production function obeys increasing returns to scale.[5] Inputs A and B are increased equiproportionately along the expansion path, causing output to increase in greater proportion. For example, $X_1/X_0 > A_1/A_0 = B_1/B_0$. Also, $X_2/X_1 > A_2/A_1 = B_2/B_1$. If inputs are increased equiproportionately, total cost (Equation 6-1) must also increase in the same proportion; given increasing returns to scale, output must increase in greater proportion. We have a situation in which the rate of change of output outstrips the rate of change of total cost. At point L the degree of homogeneity of the production function switches from more than unity to less than unity. Beyond point L the rate of change of total cost outstrips the rate of change of output. $X_3/X_2 < A_3/A_2 = B_3/B_2$.

A new concept known as the *elasticity of total cost with respect to output,* denoted by E_{cx}, is now defined as follows:

$$E_{cx} = \frac{\dfrac{\Delta C}{C}}{\dfrac{\Delta X}{X}} = \frac{\dfrac{\Delta C}{\Delta X}}{\dfrac{C}{X}} = \frac{MC}{AC} \tag{6-16}$$

As stated earlier, between the origin and point L the rate of change of output outstrips the rate of change of total cost. This can be written as an inequality $\Delta X/X > \Delta C/C$, which by Equation 6-16 implies that $E_{cx} < 1$ and hence that $MC < AC$. Beyond point L, $\Delta X/X < \Delta C/C$; hence $E_{cx} > 1$ and $MC > AC$. The above results (plus the analysis of Section 5.3a) lead to the derivation of the long-run cost curves in Figure 6-10. In panel (a), K depicts the point of

---

[5]Such a production function would be expressed as $X = f(A,B)$; that is, it excludes the entrepreneurial capacity as a third explanatory input. It amounts to pretending that the entrepreneurial capacity does not exist, which is convenient from the formal viewpoint.

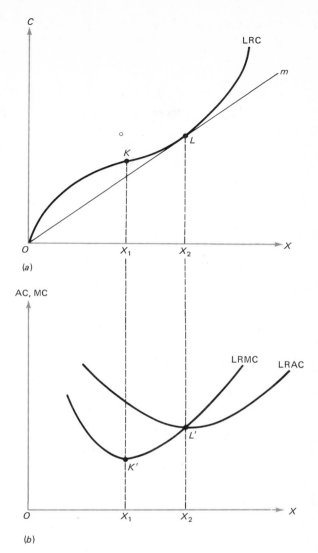

FIGURE 6-10 LONG-RUN COST CURVES

(a): Output X is measured along the horizontal axis and total cost C along the vertical axis. The long-run total cost curve (LRC) is concave downward up to point K and thereafter convex downward. K is the point of inflection. Ray m starting at the origin is tangent to LRC at L, where the rate of output is X_2 units.

(b): Output is measured along the horizontal axis. Long-run marginal cost (LRMC) and long-run average cost (LRAC) are measured along the vertical axis. LRMC attains its minimum at point K' associated with the point of inflection K on the LRC in panel (a). LRMC cuts the LRAC at its minimum point L', associated with the point of tangency L in panel (a). Between zero output and X_2 the production function obeys increasing returns to scale (scale economies); $E_{cx} < 1$. Thereafter, the production function obeys decreasing returns to scale (scale diseconomies); $E_{cx} > 1$. X_2 is a point of transition. At that point the production function obeys constant returns to scale; $E_{cx} = 1$.

inflection: Up to point K long-run total cost (LRC) increases at a decreasing rate. Beyond K, LRC increases at an increasing rate. Accordingly, in panel (b), up to a level of output of X_1 the long-run marginal cost curve (LRMC) is falling. When the firm produces X_1 units of output, LRMC reaches its minimum (K') and thereafter continues to rise. In panel (a), ray m, which is sent from the origin, just touches the LRC curve at point L. In panel (b) the associated point is L', at which LRMC cuts the long-run average cost (LRAC) from below going from left to right. Points L and L' correspond to output X_2.

In the domain of output ranging from zero to X_2 the production function obeys increasing returns to scale. In this range of output the long-run average cost curve is falling. The elasticity of total cost to output (E_{cx}) is less than unity. This is sometimes called the range of internal economies of scale. At X_2 the long-run average cost curve is level. This is the level of output at which the transition from increasing returns to scale to decreasing returns to scale occurs. Beyond X_2 the production function obeys decreasing returns to scale. The long-run average cost curve is rising. The elasticity of total cost to output is greater than unity. This is sometimes called the range of internal diseconomies of scale.

Note the similarity of AVC and MC in panel (d) of Figure 6-3 to LRAC and LRMC in panel (b) of Figure 6-10. However, along the LRMC Equation 6-15 is continuously satisfied, guaranteeing the least-cost combination of A and B at every point.

6.5g The Length of the Run in Reality

It has already been mentioned that in reality the length of the run is determined by the number of variable inputs: The longer the time the firm has for adjustment, the larger the number of variable factors. When market conditions improve, the firm will have an incentive to expand. (This issue will be discussed in the next chapter.) In the *shortest run* farmers would expand by applying more fertilizer per acre. In an *intermediate run* they would invest in better machinery, and in the *long run* they would attempt to add more land to the farm. Although increasing the amount of fertilizers can be achieved in a short period, increasing the amount of machinery may involve a longer period, especially if old machines must be worn out before they are replaced by bigger and better machines. (If all or most farmers want to replace their old tractors, the price of used tractors in the market is very low.) In industry the relationship between the short run and the long run is sometimes simple. For example, in cotton spinning output is determined by the number of spindles and the average hours worked per spindle. In the short run expansion or contraction of output will be achieved by increasing the number of hours per spindle, involving expansion or contraction of labor, energy, and raw materials. In the long run variation in output will be achieved by varying the number of spindles, which boils down to a variation in the volume of capital.[6] In the short run oil companies would pump faster in order to respond to improving market conditions. In the long run, given time needed for exploration and development, oil companies would develop new fields (offshore).

In Section 6.4 cost curves were derived for the case where A is variable and B is fixed. This approximates a situation in agriculture where more fertilizer is applied per acre, or in cotton spinning where average spindle hours are increased. Section 6.5 discussed the long-run cost curves where both input A and input B are variable. This approximates a situation in agriculture where both fertilizer and land are variable inputs, and in cotton spinning where the number of spindles as well as spindle hours are variable. The next section shows how the two are related.

6.6 THE GEOMETRY OF SHORT RUN AS RELATED TO LONG RUN

In panel (a) of Figure 6-11, OM is the expansion line. Three points of tangency (least-cost combinations of A and B) are shown, namely, F, E, and K. The respective levels of output for these points are X', X_0, and X^*. The isocost lines C', C_0, and C^* represent the respective least costs involved in producing X', X_0, and X^*: The three isocost lines mentioned above are tangent to the three levels of output at points F, E, and K, respectively. A long-run total cost curve is read off from this expansion line. This long-run total cost curve denoted by LRC is drawn in panel (b). We now return to panel (a) and note that the pair A_0 and B_0 represents the least-cost combination of inputs required to produce X_0.

If we fix the level of B at B_0 and allow only input A to vary, we are restricted to a movement along the horizontal line B_0B_0. As shown in the diagram, the production of the low-level output X' occurs where B_0B_0 cuts the isoquant X', that is, at point G. The isocost line C'', which passes through point G, represents a level of expenditures C'' which is higher than C'. This unfortunate result, namely, that short-run costs are higher than long-run costs, cannot be escaped by moving to the right (of point E) along the B_0B_0 line: The B_0B_0 line cuts the isoquant X^* at point L. The isocost line that passes through point L is denoted by C^{**}. It represents a higher level of cost than C^*. From examining panel (a) it is clear that except for point E, expansion along the short-run line B_0B_0 must give rise to a higher cost of production as compared with expansion along the expansion line OM. A short-run total cost curve is read off from the B_0B_0 line. This short-run curve denoted by SRC is drawn in panel (b): Except for the level of output of X_0, SRC is higher than LRC.

---

[6]Stigler carried out statistical measurements. He was able to show that the cotton-spinning industry responded by varying the number of hours per spindle when the industry benefited from a period of stability, and by varying the number of spindles when the industry declined. George J. Stigler, *The Theory of Price*, Macmillan New York, 1966, 3d ed., pp. 143–144).

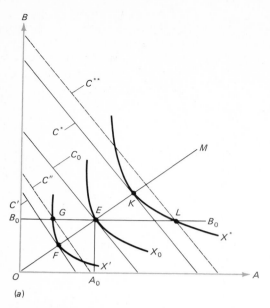

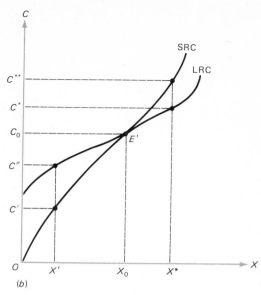

FIGURE 6-11 THE RELATIONSHIP BETWEEN LONG-RUN AND SHORT-RUN TOTAL COST CURVES

(a): A and B are two inputs measured along the two axes. At points F, E, and K tangency between isoquants X', X_0, and X^* and isocosts C', $C^°$, and C^*, respectively, occurs. Line M that connects these points is the expansion path. At point E, A_0 units of A and B_0 units of B are used in order to produce X_0 units of output. If input B were fixed at B_0, the firm would be restricted to move along B_0B_0. The horizontal line B_0B_0 cuts X' at point G, through which goes an isocost C''; $C'' > C'$. It then goes through point E and later cuts X^* at point L, through which goes an isocost C^{**}; $C^{**} > C^*$.

(b): Output X is measured along the horizontal axis and total cost is measured along the vertical axis. The short-run total cost curve (SRC) is read off from the B_0B_0 line in panel (a). The long-run total cost curve is read off from expansion line OM. the result is that SRC occupies a higher position relative to LRC except at E' [corresponding to E in panel (a)], where the two curves are tangent.

Point E' in panel (b) deserves special attention: It is the only point common to SRC and LRC. Since it takes the same amount of C_0 dollars to produce X_0 in the short run as in the long run, it must be true that at that point short-run average cost is equal to long-run average cost (both are C_0/X_0). Also, E' is a point common to the two curves but *not* an intersection point; rather it is a tangency point. The conclusion must be that the slopes of the two curves at E' are equal. Thus at E' the short-run marginal cost is equal to the long-run marginal cost.

Suppose B represents the size of the plant (number of spindles) which can be adapted to a varying level of output (spinned cotton). We can imagine starting the analysis with a very low level B_0B_0 line which is gradually lifted upward, generating an infinitely large number of SRC curves, each touching the LRC curve at one point only. Consider Figure 6-12. In panel (a) three such curves are presented: SRC_1, SRC_2, and SRC_3, representing plants adapted for *low*, *middle*, and *high* level of output, respectively. Since these curves lie above the LRC curve and each has a tangency point with it, the LRC is called the *envelope curve* of the SRC curves. We draw the associated marginal and average cost curves in panel (*b*). For similar reasons, the long-run average cost curve (LRAC) is the envelope of the short-run average cost curves (SRAC). At the point of tangency where a certain SRAC just touches the LRAC, the associated short-run marginal cost (SRMC) must intersect with the long-run marginal cost (LRMC).

In Figure 6-12, X_1, X_2, and X_3 represent low, middle, and high level of output, respectively. For the level X_1 the tangency between SRAC$_1$ and LRAC occurs at a point where the curves slope downward. For X_2, tangency between SRAC$_2$ and LRAC occurs where the two curves are level. For a level of output of X_3, tangency occurs at a point where the two curves slope upward.

As an exercise, it is left for the student to draw the envelope curves and the short-run curves for the production function which in the long run obeys constant returns to scale.

The importance of the relationship of short-run to long-run cost curves cannot be exaggerated. The theories developed in this section will be used in

FIGURE 6-12 ENVELOPE COST CURVES
(*a*): The long-run total cost curve LRC is the envelope of three short-run total cost curves SRC$_1$, SRC$_2$, and SRC$_3$ that just touch LRC at output levels of X_1, X_2, and X_3.
(*b*): The long-run average cost curve (LRAC) is the envelope of the short-run average cost curves (SRAC$_1$, SRAC$_2$, and SRAC$_3$). Tangencies between LRAC and SRAC curves occur at X_1, X_2, and X_3, as in panel (*a*). The short-run marginal cost curves (SRMC$_1$, SRMC$_2$, and SRMC$_3$) intersect with the long-run marginal cost curve (LRMC) at output rates of X_1, X_2, and X_3.

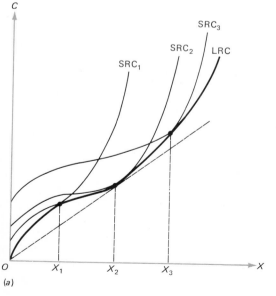

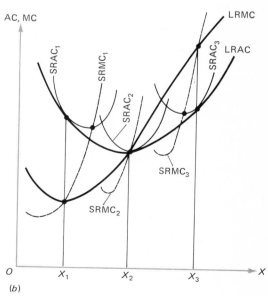

the following two chapters. For the time being the student can deduce intuitively from Figure 6-12 that in the short run the firm is rather limited in its ability to respond to market changes. On the other hand, in the long run the firm has the capacity to respond more flexibly.

It is also interesting to note that competitive firms (which have no appreciable influence over prices of inputs and outputs) will avoid the domain of output where LRAC is falling. Noncompetitive firms (which have some influence over the price of the output they sell in the marketplace) may produce in the domain where LRAC is falling.

6.7 EMPIRICAL COST CURVES

6.7a Some General Problems

The focus of empirical studies is on long-run cost curves. The structure of long-run average cost curves determines whether the market will accommodate many firms, thus creating competition, or accommodate a few firms, which will generate less competition. This issue will be discussed in Chapter 13. At this point it is sufficient to state that if the minimum point of the long-run average cost curve occurs at a level of output which is but a small fraction of the entire capacity of the industry, there is room in the market for many firms, and competition will result. On the other hand, if the minimum average cost occurs at a level of output which is relatively large, eventually a few firms will expand to the extent where they dominate the industry. An example is the automobile industry in the United States, which is dominated today by four firms.

In *single proprietorships* and *partnerships* (e.g., farms) the entrepreneurship is embodied in one person who is both the owner and the manager. Thus the profit of the entrepreneur, which is revenue minus cost, reward both *managerial effort* and *risk taking*. Risk arises because entrepreneurs could have invested their money in a safe (or at least safer) next best alternative. In corporations (e.g., large manufacturing firms) managers are paid contractual salaries which constitute a legitimate cost component, but they also receive bonuses which may be considered a fraction of a profit.

How then is cost defined in empirical studies? In the case of a large manufacturing firm, cost would usually include management; profit would by and large be a reward for undertaking risk. In the case of the family farm, cost would usually exclude management; profit would be a reward for both management (supervision and coordination) and undertaking risk. Agricultural economists sometimes report constant returns to scale, that is, long-run flat average cost curves. They are therefore puzzled that farms do not grow to infinity very rapidly. The answer might be that if the cost of supervision and coordination were properly included, the long-run average cost curve would be U-shaped. Consider Figure 6-13. $LRAC_1$ is flat beyond point A. It fails to include the cost of management properly. $LRAC_2$, which covers the

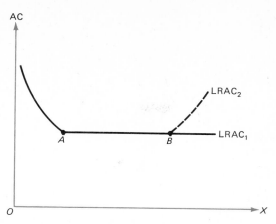

FIGURE 6-13 TWO VERSIONS OF AN EMPIRICAL LRAC CURVE
The long-run average cost curve denoted by LRAC$_1$ fails to include the cost of management properly; hence it is flat beyond point A. If the cost of management (supervision and coordination) is properly included, the long-run average cost curve begins to rise at a certain point B. In other words, because of the limitation of management we observe decreasing returns to scale beyond point B.

cost of management, departs from LRAC$_1$ at point B and thereafter rises. LRAC$_2$ rises because farmers who increase the scale of their farms beyond a one-person farm must hire nonfamily labor and expend the extra effort of supervising and coordinating the activities of hired hands.

Three examples of average cost curves follow: the *power-generating industry*, the *petroleum-refining industry*, and sample *farms*. Statistical methods are used for estimating the cost functions of the first industry. For example, data of cost and electric-power generation are collected for many firms across the country, and then an average cost curve (translog) is estimated by utilizing econometric methods. In the case of petroleum refining the *survivor method* is applied in order to estimate the rough shape of the average cost function. For example, if very small firms do not survive over time, it is interpreted that small firms are inefficient. Accordingly, small firms must either discontinue their operations or, if they can, expand their scale of output. In the case of farm cost curves the *economic-engineering* (known also as synthetic-firm) approach is applied to obtain an estimate of the average cost curve.

6.7b Example 1: Economies of Scale in Electric-Power Generation

The importance of empirical studies of cost functions of the electric-power-generation industry cannot be exaggerated. In the wake of the energy crisis it was proposed that firms generating electric power be vertically disintegrated by divorcing the generation of electricity from transmission and distribution. This proposal was based on the assumption that firms specializing only in generation would compete in the market and thus force prices down. The question to be answered was whether substantial scale economies would be sacrificed. To answer this question, cost curves of the electric-power industry had to be studied. Such a study was conducted by Laurits R. Christensen and William H. Greene.[7] To avoid confusion, the unit studied was the firm, as differentiated from plants or individual generating units. The study was based on two cross sections, the first for 1955 and the second for 1970, and was limited to investor-owned utilities with more than $1 million in annual revenues. These firms accounted for 77 percent of total power produced in the United States.

Section 6.5f showed that the falling part of the long-run average cost curve (LRAC) is associated with E_{cx} (elasticity of total cost) which is less than unity; the production function obeys increasing returns to scale. At the minimum point of the LRAC curve E_{cx} is equal to unity; the production function obeys constant returns to scale. Beyond the minimum point of the LRAC curve E_{cx} is greater than unity; here the LRAC curve is rising and the production function obeys decreasing returns to scale. Consider the following three possibilities: E_{cx} = 0.8, 1, and 1.2, associated with the falling segment, minimum, and rising segment of the LRAC, respectively [panel (b) of Figure 6-10]. In each of these three possibilities a 1 percent increase in output will entail 0.8, 1, and 1.2 percent increase in cost, respectively. These three cases are sometimes called *economies of scale, constant returns to scale*, and *diseconomies of scale*. Table 6-2 presents some estimates of E_{cx} for firms generating electric power as given in Christensen and Greene.[8]

First notice that for all firms in the sample E_{cx} increased; that is, scale economies declined from 1955 to 1970. In other words these firms increased their scale of operations between 1955 and 1970 and thus slid down the left-hand side of their U-shaped long-run AC curves. As a matter of fact, Commonwealth Edison passed the minimum point on its long-run AC curve. Community Public Service was on the higher portion of the left side of the long-run AC curve. Virginia Electric Power was on the portion of the long-run AC curve which is practically flat but had not yet reached the minimum point of the AC curve. Commonwealth Edison was also on the portion which is practically flat but had passed the minimum point.

Figure 6-14 shows the two long-run AC curves as given by Christensen and Greene. Note that from 1955 to 1970 the AC curve shifted downward, probably owing to technological innovations. This shift, which gave rise to a significant decline in the average cost of electricity and was coupled with a high increase in scale, was mistaken to indicate huge returns to scale in the power-generating industry. Notice also that beyond 15 billion kilowatthours the average cost curve is practically flat, although as indicated by the diagram, at about 30 billion kilowatthours (for 1970) the minimum AC is attained.

TABLE 6-2 **Estimates of Elasticities of Total Cost for Selected Firms in the Electricity-Generating Sector[8]**

Company	E_{cx}	
	1955	1970
Community Public Service	0.637	0.753
Atlantic City Electric	0.839	0.906
Virginia Electric Power	0.923	0.985
Commonwealth Edison	0.976	1.014

Source: Laurits R. Christensen and William H. Greene, "Economies of Scale in the U.S. Electric Power Generation," *Journal of Political Economy*, Vol. 84, August 1976, pp. 655–676.

---

[7]Laurits R. Christensen and William H. Greene, "Economies of Scale in U.S. Electric Power Generation," *Journal of Political Economy*, vol. 84, August 1976, pp. 655–767.

[8]Actually Christensen and Greene reported their results in terms of *scale economies* denoted by SCE; SCE = $1 - E_{cx}$. We used $E_{cx} = 1 - $ SCE.

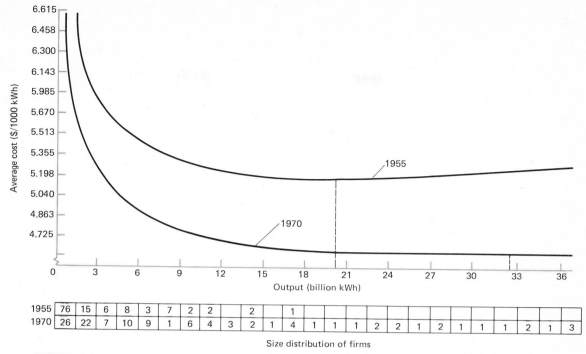

1955	76	15	6	8	3	7	2	2		2		1																
1970	26	22	7	10	9	1	6	4	3	2	1	4	1	1	1	2	2	1	2	1	1	1	2	1	3

Size distribution of firms

FIGURE 6-14 LRAC CURVES FOR FIRMS IN THE ELECTRICITY-GENERATING SECTOR
LRAC for 1970 is lower than that for 1955, reflecting technological innovations. Minimum points are achieved at a relatively large level of output; moreover, beyond the minimum point the LRAC curve is almost flat. (*Source:* Same as for Table 6-2.)

6.7c Example 2: The Survivor Technique—Petroleum Refining

The idea of applying the *survivor test* to determine the shape of the average cost curve is due to Stigler.[9] According to George J. Stigler, Mill suggested the method first but thought that it would be appropriate primarily in the case of competition. Instead, Stigler applied the method to cases of typical oligopoly (a form of an imperfect market to be discussed in Chapter 13). The survivor test does not reveal the precise shape of average cost curves. Rather, it provides the notion of the general shape of the long-run average cost curve: In what range of output is it (1) falling, (2) not changing, and (3) rising? In other words, in what range of output do we observe (1) economies of scale for the firm, (2) constant re-

turns to scale, and (3) diseconomies of scale? The test proceeds as follows: Firms in a certain industry are classified by size. The share of total output produced by each class is then calculated over time. If the share of a given class falls over time, the size of this class is inefficient.

In the case of refining petroleum Stigler found that small companies with a share in the range of 0.1 to 0.5 percent of refining capacity declined from 1947 to 1954. In other words, small firms in that range were inefficient. Companies in the range of 0.5 to 10 percent of total capacity either held their share or slightly increased it. The one large company with a share in excess of 10 percent (but less than 15 percent)

[9]George J. Stigler, "The Economies of Scale," reprinted with permission from the *Journal of Law and Economics,* vol. 1 (October 1958), pp. 54–71. Copyright 1958 by the University of Chicago Law School.

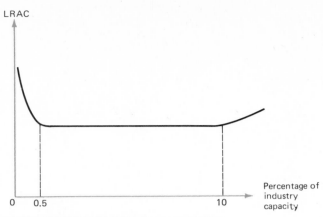

FIGURE 6-15 LRAC ESTIMATED BY THE SURVIVOR TECHNIQUE

A long-run average cost curve for refining petroleum is shown. The horizontal axis measures output as percentage of industry capacity. The long-run average cost curve is falling up to 0.5 percent capacity, horizontal between 0.5 and 10 percent capacity, and thereafter rising. The curve is drawn by applying Stigler's *survivor technique*. [*Source*: Reprinted with permission from the *Journal of Law and Economics*, vol. 1 (October 1958). Copyright 1958 by the University of Chicago Law School.]

slightly declined from a share of 11.65 percent in 1947 to 10.72 in 1954. Given these results, we can conclude that the shape of a typical average cost curve of a refinery is as illustrated in Figure 6-15. Note finally that the survivor analysis leading to Figure 6-15 was applied to companies (firms) and not to individual plants. It is likely that companies in the range of 0.5 and 10 percent were very efficient because of their ability to manage multiple plants.

6.7d Example 3: Irrigated Cotton Farms in Texas High Plains

This example is taken from an article by J. Patrick Madden.[10] In applying the *economic-engineering* method the assumption was made that the operator-manager and risk taker constituted the residual claimant, namely, the entrepreneur. Thus, the cost curves generated by this method do not reflect the cost of supervision and coordination of farm activities. Figure 6-16 presents the results of the study. The average cost of the one-person farm achieves its minimum at a level of output of $60,000 worth of output. At that point the LRAC is 71 cents. For a five-person farm the level of minimum AC was nearly $235,000 worth of output. The AC was only slightly higher than 71 cents. In acreage the sizes are 440 and 1720 for a one-person and five-person farm, respectively. Beyond a level of $60,000 output it seems that the envelope average cost curve (dashed) would be almost flat. Yet Madden reports that during the period 1954–1959 the number of farms with more than 1000 acres increased only moderately by 5 percent. The number of farms with less than 500 acres declined. The number of farms with 500 to 1000 acres increased by 10 percent. In other words, the economic-engineering method supplies only part of the relevant information. It hides the true nature of the average cost curve because it does not include the cost of the managerial effort. It seems that the survivor method indicates that the one- and two-person are the most efficient farms.

---

[10]J. Patrick Madden, "Economies of Size in Farming," *Economic Research Service, Agricultural Economic Report* 107, U.S. Department of Agriculture, February 1967.

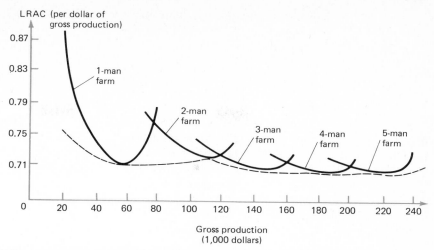

FIGURE 6-16 AVERAGE COST CURVES OF COTTON FARMS IN TEXAS

Gross farm production (in $1000) is measured along the horizontal axis. Average cost (dollar cost per dollar production) is measured along the vertical axis. Five average cost curves for cotton farms in Texas are shown. The "person" in this diagram is the fixed factor *B*, which varies from a one-person farm to a two-person farm, and so on. The envelope curve (dashed) is almost flat, indicating constant returns to scale, provided that "person" is varied along the other factors. (*Source*: J. Patrick Madden, "Economies of Size in Farming," *Economic Research Service. Agricultural Economic Report* 107, U.S. Department of Agriculture, February 1967.)

SUMMARY The analysis in this chapter started by stressing that in economics we define costs as *opportunity costs*, which are the values of inputs in their next best ues. It was also mentioned that there are situations in which *social cost* diverges from *private cost*.

The next step was to provide the *cost terminology*: *total cost, average cost, marginal cost*, and other related costs were defined.

The *short-run total variable cost curve* was then derived by showing that if the price of the variable input *A* is equal to $1, the *total variable cost* is simply the total output curve drawn in a diagram in which the axes are transposed, and the *A* axis is retitled the cost axis. From the total variable cost curve the *short-run marginal cost curve* and the *average variable cost curve* were derived. The *fixed cost curve* was added by shifting the total variable cost upward by the amount of the fixed cost. This allowed us to draw the short-run average cost curve by simply adding the average fixed cost vertically to the average variable cost.

Subsequently, the *long-run cost curves* were analyzed. First, *isocost lines* were defined as formally identical with *budget lines*. Then it was shown that the *least-cost combination of inputs* is obtained by seeking the point of tangency between an *isocost* and an *isoquant;* the locus of all such points was defined as the expansion curve of the firm. It was established that in order to increase output the firm must progress along the expansion path in the same way that a consumer with an increased income would expand along his or her income consumption curve (ICC). The next step was to prove that if the production function obeys constant returns to scale, the marginal cost curve and the average cost curve in the long run will be horizontal and identical. However, given the realistic assumption that entrepreneurial capacity is fixed, the long-run cost curves will assume a shape similar to the shape of short-run cost curves. The *elasticity of cost* E_{cx} was defined as the relative change in cost over a small relative change in output, when all factors (but the entrepreneurial capacity) vary equiproportionately. It was then shown that in the range of output where the production function obeys *increasing returns to scale* long-run average cost (LRAC) exceeds long-run marginal cost; in this range $E_{cx} < 1$ and LRAC is falling. There follows a range of output in which the production function obeys decreasing returns to scale; in this range $E_{cx} > 1$ and LRAC is rising. The transition from *scale economies* to *scale diseconomies* occurs where LRAC and LRMC intersect. At that point the production function obeys constant returns to scale, and $E_{cx} = 1$.

It was explained why any *short-run total cost curve* (SRC) must, except at a unique point of tangency, be higher than the *long-run total cost curve* (LRC). From this the property was derived that the LRC curve is the envelope of the SRC curves. Moreover, the long-run average cost curve (LRAC) is the envelope of the short-run average cost curves (SRAC).

Last, it was illustrated how economists estimate empirical long-run cost curves by applying various methods, and why such cost curves are relevant in policy making.

GLOSSARY **Opportunity costs** The value of inputs used in the process of production in their next best alternative.

Social cost In most cases social cost is identical with *private costs*. In some cases *social cost* covers both private cost and damage to the environment for which the producer may not be required to pay.

Total cost The aggregate of total amounts of inputs used up in the process of production multiplied by their respective prices. Where two inputs are used, $C = P_a \cdot A + P_b \cdot B$.

Total variable cost The portion of *total cost* incurred by the variable inputs only. If A is the only variable input, $VC = P_a \cdot A$.

Total fixed cost The portion of total cost incurred by the fixed factor only. If B is the only fixed factor, $FC = P_b \cdot B$.

Average cost Total cost divided by total output: $AC = C/X$.

Average variable cost Total variable cost divided by total output: $AVC = VC/X$.

Average fixed cost Total fixed cost divided by output: $AFC = FC/X$.

Marginal cost The change in total cost over a small change in output: $MC = \Delta C/\Delta X$.

Competitive firm A firm that has no appreciable influence either over the prices of inputs it uses in the process of production or over the price of the output it sells in the market.

Short-run cost curves Cost curves derived in order to describe the costs incurred by the firm in the short run. In the short run the firm cannot vary all the participating inputs.

Isocost The locus of points where each point represents a combination of inputs that can be purchased with a fixed total cost. If the fixed cost is denoted by C_0, then for the case of two inputs the equation of the isocost is given by $C_0 = P_a \cdot A + P_b \cdot B$. C_0, P_a, and P_b are the parameters; A and B are the variables. The slope of the isocost is $\Delta B / \Delta A = - P_a / P_b$.

Least-cost combination of inputs Given a certain level of output, the firm can widely vary the combinations of inputs in order to produce the given level of output. The combination of inputs that costs the firm the smallest amount of money is known as the *least-cost combination of inputs*. Geometrically, the least-cost combination is obtained by finding the tangency point between the isoquant representing the given amount of output and an isocost. For two variable inputs the following must be satisfied for least-cost combination to be achieved: $P_a / MP_a = P_b / MP_b$ (which is also the marginal cost at that level of output).

Expansion path The locus of all points satisfying the condition for least-cost combination of inputs. If there are only two variable inputs, the *expansion path* is the locus of all tangency points between isocosts and isoquants in the A, B space. The *expansion* path is formally identical with the ICC.

Longest-run cost curves Cost curves derived under the assumption that all factors of production are variable and the production function obeys *constant returns to scale*. Under such conditions LRAC and LRMC are horizontal and identical.

Long-run cost curves Cost curves derived under the assumption that all factors of production are variable. However, the production function first obeys increasing returns to scale; only when the scale of production increases beyond a certain point does the law of decreasing returns to scale take over. The shape of such long-run cost curves is similar to the shape of short-run cost curves.

The reason for the presence of increasing returns to scale (scale economies) first and decreasing returns to scale (scale diseconomies) next is the fixity of the entrepreneurial capacity.

Elasticity of total cost The relative change in total cost over a small relative change in output; the change in output results from an equiproportional change in all inputs. Formally, $E_{cx} = (\Delta C / C)/(\Delta X / X) = MC/AC$.

Envelope cost curves The *long-run total cost curve* (LRC) is the envelope of all *short-run cost curves* (SRC$_i$). Each SRC curve lies above the LRC curve, except for a single point of tangency. The *long-run average cost curve* (LRAC) is the envelope of all the *short-run average cost curves* (SRAC$_i$). Each SRAC curve lies above the LRAC curve, except for a single point of tangency.

PROBLEMS An asterisk indicates an advanced problem.

6-1.   A person who invested \$100,00 in a cabinet shop is the owner and the manager of the shop. Suppose the profit is $40,000 a year, how would you determine whether that person is successful or not?

6-2. A paper mill upstream discharges effluents into the stream. Assume that the cost of bargaining (and reaching agreement) between the paper mill and fishermen downstream is nil. Describe the agreement that might be reached if (1) the stream is owned by the fishermen and (2) the water is common property. What if the cost of bargaining is very high?

6-3. In Figure 6-4, the minimum of the AC curve lies to the right of the minimum of the AVC curve. Explain why.

6-4. Show that it will pay a producer who is at point E in Figure 6-5 to move in the southeasterly direction along the isocost (toward point W). Do not use the (evident) argument that such a movement means climbing the production hill. Rather compare the decrease in the amount of B by ΔB with the increase in the amount of A by ΔA. Apply similar analysis to point F.

6-5.* It was calculated in Section 6.5b that for $X = \sqrt{A \cdot B}$ for $A = 8$ and $B = 2$, $P_a = \$0.5$, $P_b = \$2$ and MC = $\$2$. Show that the best (least-cost) way to increase output from 4 to 5 units is to increase the inputs, respectively, by 25 percent. Draw the marginal cost curve for this case.

6-6. Consider the example in Section 6.5b (Figure 6-6). Assume that the price of A rises from $\$0.5$ to $\$2.00$; the price of B remains unchanged at $\$2.00$. Confirm that the new point of least-cost combination of A and B is achieved where $A = 4$ and $B = 4$. Calculate the new MC for that point.

6-7. Why in the shortest of all runs is the marginal cost vertical?

6-8. In panel (b) of Figure 6-11 LRC starts at the origin while SRC has a positive intercept (with the C axis). Explain why.

6-9. Between 1955 and 1970 the average cost of producing electric power declined significantly. There were two reasons for this sharp decline in (long-run) average cost. Can you distinguish the two reasons by using a diagram similar to Figure 6-14?

6-10.* The cost elasticity E_{cx} of an electric utility is 0.62. The utility is regulated such that the price is equal to LRAC. [Assume that by trial and error the management of the utility finds a price which (1) is equal to the long-run average cost curve and (2) equates total use of electricity with total production.] Would you expect the price to rise or to fall as a result of population growth? Management calculated that in order to meet the needs of a growing population long-run adjustments will be made and the cost elasticity E_{cx} will rise to 0.75.

6-11. Despite the fact that the *envelope* long-run average cost curve in

Figure 6-16 would tend to become flat as gross farm product increases, farm size does not tend to increase tremendously. Explain why.

6-12. The production of whatnots involves water pollution. In order to fight against pollution, the government imposed a tax of 5 cents per whatnot. Draw the MC curve of a whatnot-producing firm before and after the tax is imposed.

6-13. It is argued that it costs a firm less to expand in the short run than in the long run. The intuitive reason is that in the short run a smaller number of inputs must be varied as compared with the long run. Do you agree with this argument? (Examine Figure 6-11 before you answer.)

6-14. Draw the envelope (LRC and LRAC) curves and the short-run curves for the case in which the production function obeys constant returns to scale.

MATHEMATICAL APPENDIX 6

Some of the properties developed in this chapter will now be proved mathematically.

M6.1 LEAST-COST COMBINATION OF FACTORS

Let the production function of a competitive firm be

$$X = f(A_1, A_2, \ldots, A_n) \tag{m6-1}$$

where A_i stands for both factor i and its quantity used in the process of production. The firm has no influence over the prices of inputs. These prices are $P_1, P_2, \ldots, P_n$. The cost function is $C = P_1A_1 + P_2A_2 + \ldots + P_nA_n$.

We want to minimize the cost of producing a given output X_0. We thus form the Lagrange equation:

$$L = P_1A_1 + P_2A_2 + \ldots + P_nA_n + \lambda[X_0 - f(A_1, A_2, \ldots, A_n)] \tag{m6-2}$$

The necessary conditions for the least-cost combination of inputs are that partial derivatives be equal to zero; that is,

$$\frac{\partial L}{\partial A_1} = P_1 - \lambda \cdot f_1 = 0$$

$$\frac{\partial L}{\partial A_2} = P_2 - \lambda \cdot f_2 = 0$$

$$\vdots \tag{m6-3}$$

$$\frac{\partial L}{\partial A_n} = P_n - \lambda \cdot f_n = 0$$

which may be written as

$$\frac{P_1}{f_1} = \frac{P_2}{f_2} = \ldots = \frac{P_n}{f_n} = \lambda \qquad \text{(m6-4)}$$

Notice that either Equation m6-3 or Equation m6-4 is a set of n equations. These n equations together with the side relation (the production function) determine the respective amounts of the different factors used, and λ. The complete differential of total cost is

$$dC = P_1 \cdot dA_1 + P_2 \cdot dA_2 + \ldots + P_n \cdot dA_n \qquad \text{(m6-5)}$$

The complete differential of output is

$$dX = f_1 \cdot dA_1 + f_2 \cdot dA_2 + \ldots + f_n \cdot dA_n \qquad \text{(m6-6)}$$

Dividing Equation m6-6 into Equation m6-5 and taking advantage of Equation m6-3 gives

$$\frac{dC}{dX} = \frac{P_1 \cdot dA_1 + P_2 \cdot dA_2 + \ldots + P_n \cdot dA_n}{f_1 \cdot dA_1 + f_2 \cdot dA_2 + \ldots + f_n \cdot dA_n} = \lambda \qquad \text{(m6-7)}$$

Thus it was proved that λ in Equation m6-4 is the marginal cost—MC. Since $f_1 \, (\partial X / \partial A_1)$ is the marginal physical factor of A_1 and so on, if we substitute dC/dX, namely, MC, for λ in Equation m6-4, we obtain the proof for Equation 6-15. In general it can be written as

$$\frac{P_1}{\text{MP}_1} = \frac{P_2}{\text{MP}_2} = \ldots = \frac{P_n}{\text{MP}_n} = \text{MC} \qquad \text{(m6-8)}$$

M6.2 SECOND-ORDER CONDITIONS

The second-order conditions for minimum cost are that the determinants

$$\begin{vmatrix} 0 & f_1 \\ f_1 & f_{11} \end{vmatrix} \begin{vmatrix} 0 & f_1 & f_2 \\ f_1 & f_{11} & f_{12} \\ f_2 & f_{21} & f_{22} \end{vmatrix} \ldots \begin{vmatrix} 0 & f_1 & \ldots & f_n \\ f_1 & f_{11} & \ldots & f_{1n} \\ \vdots & & & \\ f_n & f_{n1} & \ldots & f_{nn} \end{vmatrix} \qquad \text{(m6-9)}$$

are alternately negative and positive.

Let us denote the last determinant in Equation m6-9 by F, the cofactor of f_i by F_i, and the cofactor of f_{ij} by F_{ij}. Differentiating the production function (Equation m6-1, $X = X_0$) and Equations m6-3 with respect to P_i, and then solving by Cramer's rule (this stage is left for the interested student) gives

$$\frac{\partial A_j}{\partial P_i} = \frac{1}{\lambda} \cdot \frac{F_{ij}}{F} \qquad \text{(m6-10)}$$

Since there are no restrictions on the sign of F_{ij}/F, $\partial A_j/\partial P_i$ may be either positive or negative, and accordingly, the pair of inputs A_j and A_i may be related to each other either as *competitive* or as *complements*. If $i = j$, Equation m6-10 becomes

$$\frac{\partial A_i}{\partial P_i} = \frac{1}{\lambda} \cdot \frac{F_{ii}}{F} \qquad \text{(m6-11)}$$

Since the order of arranging factors does not matter, we may require that $i = n$. Since the determinants in Equation m6-9 are alternately positive and negative, F_{ii}/F must be negative.

C H A P T E R

7

THE COMPETITIVE FIRM

The physical and technical aspects of the process of production were discussed in Chapter 5. In Chapter 6 the second step in the analysis of the firm added information about prices of inputs confronting the producer in the marketplace; this information, coupled with the theory of the production function, led to the derivation of cost curves. The theory of cost curves, while telling us what is the least-cost combination of inputs associated with each level of output, cannot tell us what is the level of output which would yield the maximum profit for the firm. This chapter takes the third step in the theory of the producer: incorporating information from the marketplace about output. In the case of a competitive firm this information boils down to the price of final output confronting the firm in the marketplace. Given its cost curves and the price of output, the firm can determine the level of output that will yield maximum profit.

For all practical purposes, we could assume that the individual consumer is too insignificant to have any appreciable impact on prices in the marketplace. We cannot say the same about all producers. In some market situations the individual producer (firm) has little or no influence on the price of the good it sells in the market, and it has no appreciable influence on the prices of the inputs it purchases. But there are situations in which an individual producer dominates the market for a good (even though it has no appreciable influence on the prices of inputs). We should therefore become familiar with the *four basic market situations*: *perfect competition*, *monopolistic competition*, *oligopoly*, and *monopoly*.

1. *Perfect Competition* (e.g., agriculture). Where there are (*a*) ease of entry and exit, (*b*) many sellers, and (*c*) a homogeneous good. Both (*b*) and (*c*) imply that the firm has no influence on the price of the good it sells in the market. (As we shall see later in this chapter, the firm is confronted with an infinitely elastic demand curve.)

2. *Monopolistic Competition* (e.g., retailing, soft drinks, beer). Where there are (*a*) ease of entry and exit, (*b*) many sellers, and (*c*) a slightly differentiated product, which implies that the individual producer has some influence on the price of the good sold in the market. (The firm is confronted with a demand curve with a finite slope.)

3. *Oligopoly*. Where (*a*) there are barriers to entry and (*b*) the market is dominated by a small number of producers. The product of an oligopoly may be either differentiated (e.g., automobiles) or homogeneous (e.g., steel). (The firm is confronted with a demand curve with a finite slope.)

4. *Monopoly* (e.g., telephone company). Where there are (*a*) difficulty of entry to the industry, (*b*) one seller, and (*c*) no close substitutes to the product or service. Both (*b*) and (*c*) imply that the firm has significant influence on the price of the good it sells in the market. (The firm is confronted with a negatively sloped demand curve for its product. This is the market demand curve.)

This chapter is devoted to the theory of the competitive firm, as defined in the first market situation. Chapter 8 deals with the behavior of a group of competitive firms. The perfect market situation is covered in Chapter 9.

Chapter 11 deals with the other extreme of the market spectrum, the monopoly. Monopolistic competition and oligopoly are discussed in Chapters 12 and 13, respectively.

Chapter 5 discussed the production function, and Chapter 6 added information about prices of inputs to the knowledge of the production function. This led to the theory of the least-cost combination of inputs required for the production of any feasible level of output. Here information is added about the price of the product made by the firm; given this price, the competitive firm can determine the optimal level of output. The optimal level of output is synonymous with the classical *profit maximization*. Since an attack was mounted (by Galbraith and others) against the concept of profit maximization, this issue will be discussed before the theory of the competitive firm is developed.

7.1 PROFIT MAXIMIZATION

7.1a The Challenge to the Classical Tradition

In what follows *economic profit* should be distinguished from *accounting profit*. The difference between the two concepts will be discussed in Section 7.5. For the time being it is sufficient to note that profit is revenue minus all contractual costs (Section 5.1a) incurred by the firm. The entrepreneur is the claimant of this residue, which, following tradition, is called profit. In the classical tradition it is assumed that (except for public utilities) firms always attempt to maximize their profits; this implies that when profit is maximized the firm has reached equilibrium. To put it in other words, the classical tradition asserts that the *profit motive* is the force which moves the free enterprise system. There is a difference between proprietorships and partnerships on the one hand and corporations on the other (Section 5.1a). In the first form of organization the residual claimant (owner) is also the manager. In the second form, especially in large corporations, management is separate from the stockholders, who are the residual claimants. The challenge to the tradition of profit maximization came from a group of economists, the most notable of whom are William J. Baumol and John Kenneth Galbraith. Baumol observed that some corporations tend to increase their sales beyond the level of output yielding maximum profit.[1] Galbraith reiterated Baumol's point that managers of large corporations pursue a goal of *increasing sales* rather than maximizing profits for the stockholders. To this Galbraith added another goal sought by managements of large corporations, namely, *stability*.[2] As the reader can see, the challenge to the classical tradition grew out of the fact that in large corporations managements are separate from stockholders and therefore would pursue goals which do not necessarily coincide with the aspirations of stockholders.

---

[1] William J. Baumol. *Business Behavior, Value and Growth,* Macmillan, New York, 1959.
[2] John Kenneth Galbraith, *The New Industrial State,* Houghton Mifflin, Boston, 1967.

(There is no argument among economists that profit maximization is the sole goal of stockholders.) Although the challenge to the classical tradition of profit maximization amounted to nothing more than a small storm, it will be presented here in geometric terms.

7.1b The Geometry of the Challenge

The conflict between stock owners and management arising from managerial discretion in large corporations can be illustrated further. Consider Figure 7-1, in which staff is measured along the horizontal axis and profit along the vertical axis. Staff can be narrowly interpreted as covering only secretaries and assistants, or it may be broadly interpreted as covering the entire work force. One way or the other, as staff increases, profit rises, reaches it maximum at point M, and declines thereafter. In proprietorships and partnerships point M is the goal of the manager-owner. But in large corporations, where managers are separate from stockholders, they are likely to expand the staff beyond the optimal level of S_0 up to a level of S_1 because profit (to stockholders) is not the only variable entering the utility function of managers. Clearly, higher profits would lead to higher salaries. But, the argument goes, experience may tell the manager that larger staffs also correlate with higher salaries. Since both profit and staff enter as two "goods" in the utility function of the manager, the resulting indifference curves must

FIGURE 7-1 AN ILLUSTRATION OF THE ALLEGED CONFLICT BETWEEN MANAGEMENT AND STOCKHOLDERS

Profit is presented as a function of staff: Increasing the staff beyond a level of S_0 results in a decline in profit. Stockholders are interested in a level of S_0. The indifference curves of management, however, are negatively sloped and convex toward the origin: Management considers both *profit* and *staff* as "goods." The point yielding maximum utility to management is N. Thus, management is interested in a staff of S_1. This is the alleged conflict between stockholders and management.

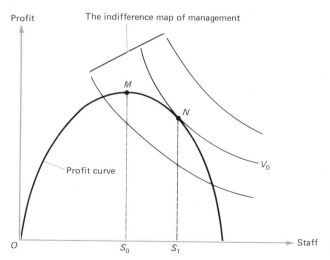

be convex toward the origin and negatively sloped. Moreover, tangency occurs at point N, which is optimal for the manager, rather than at point M, which yields the maximum profit to stockholders.

7.1c Profit Maximization Survives

The argument that the principle of profit maximization should be retained in the theory of the firm proceeds in the three steps: First, we see that a significant fraction of all firms in the United States are organized as proprietorships and partnerships. Second, we see that a significant fraction of all remaining firms which are organized as corporations are very competitive and that thus, in order to survive, they must maximize profit. Third, the remaining group of firms which are organized as corporations but are not continuously exposed to the process of competition are not necessarily owned by naive stockholders. Before proceeding, the student should note that economists, by and large, would agree that managements of regulated public utilities do pursue goals that are in accord with maximizing their own utility function. Since these public utilities (electricity, water, natural gas) normally enjoy a protected market, they can easily earn the maximum allowable profit and increase their staffs. As shown by Alchian and Kessel, they not only increase their staffs numerically, they (more than nonutilities) also discriminate against religious and racial groups in order to enhance their own utility in the office.[3] For example, if competition is keen, a manager will hire a black engineer rather than a white engineer if the black is better qualified. A manager of a public utility, however, may hire white engineers, who are less qualified because the manager can afford to put prejudice above the profit of the corporation.

Table 7-1 presents data concerning the distribution of firms by form of organization as well as the aggregate net profit earned by the various groups of firms. In 1960 and 1970 proprietorships and partnerships accounted for over 80 percent of all firms in the United States. As the data about net profit show, proprietorships and partnerships accounted for about 40 percent of total net profit.

What about the corporations? For example, in 1970, 1,665,000 corporations operated in the United States. Most economists would agree that in industries where competition prevails the struggle to survive is keen. Firms that fail to adhere to the principle of profit maximization are eliminated by the process of "natural selection." Let us see what is the rough division between the competitive and the less competitive corporations. In 1970, public utilities numbered 67,000. This number subtracted from 1,665,000 gives 1,598,000. The number of corporations in competitive industries in 1970 was apportioned as shown at the top of the next page.

---

[3]Armen A. Alchian and Reuben A. Kessel, "Competition, Monopoly, and the Pursuit of Pecuniary Gain," in *Aspects of Labor Economics,* National Bureau of Economic Research, Princeton, 1962.

Agriculture	37,000
Retail trade	351,000
Services	281,000
Finance, insurance, and real estate	406,000
Contract construction	139,000
Total	1,214,000

Thus competitive corporations accounted for roughly 70 percent of the total number of corporations. The other 30 percent (excluding the public utilities) were mining and manufacturing industries and wholesale trade. While wholesale trade is probably competitive to a large extent, some of the corporations in the services and financial sectors are probably not struggling to survive. It would be reasonable to assume that 70 percent of corporations accept the hypothesis of profit maximization.

What about the remaining 30 percent of the corporations in mining, manufacturing, and wholesale industries? Some of these corporations are oligopolies. Oligopolies will be discussed in Chapter 13. (Most of the monopolies in the United States are public utilities. Monopolies will be discussed in Chapter 11.) It is true that for some established corporations, because of barriers to entry into the industry, the struggle to survive is less than keen. Yet we should not conclude that the behavior of these corporations is not governed by the principle of profit maximization for the following reasons:

1. Stockholders can employ experts (accountants) in order to police the corporation and detect deviations from profit-maximization procedures. The smaller the diffusion of stockholders, the lower will be the cost of policing and detection. In cases in which one family owns a relatively large block of stocks, it is unlikely that managements will get away with deviating from point M in Figure 7-1.

2. Even if stockholder diffusion is wide, stockholders can adopt policies of remunerating managers (partially or wholly) with bonuses. If such bonuses are highly correlated with profit (say, they are a certain percentage of profit), the utility function of managers will become nearly horizontal and tangency

TABLE 7-1

Proprietorships, Partnerships, and Corporations, Number and Profit

	Total		Proprietorships		Partnerships		Corporations	
Year	Number (1000)	Net profit ($ billion)	Number (1000)	Net profit ($ billion)	Number (1000)	Net profit ($ billion)	Number (1000)	Net profit ($ billion)
1960	11,171	73	9090	21	941	8	1140	44
1970	12,000	109	9399	33	936	10	1665	66

Source: U.S. Bureau of the Census, *Historical Statistics of the United States, Colonial Times to 1970,* Washington, 1975, part 2, p. 911.

in Figure 7-1 will occur near or at point M. This is left as an exercise for the student.

3. Suppose that ownership is widely dispersed and it does not occur to the board of directors to link the salaries of their top managers to the profitability of the corporation. Even under such unlikely circumstances, the management cannot isolate itself from potential *raiders*, who would soon offer their managerial services to the board of directors. If the president of Ford was not fired for failing the maximize the profits of the stockholders, why was he fired?

4. A group of outside investors may sense that better policing will increase profitability tremendously. Hence they will attempt to *take over* the corporation by purchasing a significant block of stocks. *Takeovers* cannot be ignored by the current management.

7.2 THE THEORY OF THE FIRM

7.2a The Demand Curve Confronting the Individual Firm

When a large number of small firms are engaged in the production of a certain homogeneous product, the firms are said to be competitive, provided that the following holds:

1. Each individual firm has no appreciable influence on the price of the product it sells in the market.
2. The firm does not exert any appreciable influence on the prices of factors of production.

The statement about the negligible influence of the individual firm on the price of the product it sells can be illustrated by the following example: Consider a product which is produced by 10,000 firms. On average the individual firm shares 1/10,000 of total production. Assume that the aggregate demand curve facing the industry has an elasticity of $-1/2$. By its decision to double the rate of production the firm will increase the total output of the entire industry by 1/10,000. By applying the formula for price elasticity [$\eta = (\Delta X/X)/(\Delta P/P)$], we have

$$-\frac{1}{2} = \frac{0.01 \text{ percent}}{\text{percentage change in price}}$$

And thus the change in price is -0.02 percent. For example, if the original market price was \$10, after the individual firm has doubled its production, the new market price is \$9.998. The inability of the firm to exert any significant influence on the market price means that the firm is faced with a horizontal demand curve for its product. Consider Figure 7-2: This demand curve, which is shown in panel (*b*), is sometimes called the *price line*.

Revenue received by the firm is the price confronting the firm times output. Namely, revenue is $R = P \cdot X$, which is represented by the homogeneous linear curve denoted by R in panel (*a*).

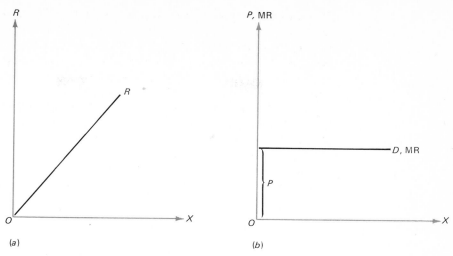

FIGURE 7-2 REVENUE, DEMAND, AND MARGINAL REVENUE CURVES OF A
COMPETITIVE FIRM

(a) The *total revenue curve* is a ray sent from the origin. In fact, it is $R = P \cdot X$.

   (b) The *demand curve* D and the *marginal revenue* MR are identical. The intercept of this line with the vertical (P) axis is equal to the price, which is the slope of the curve R in panel (a).

7.2b Marginal Revenue of the Firm

Marginal revenue is defined as the change in total revenue over a small change in total production or simply the extra revenue resulting from the production of one additional unit. The assumption is made here that each additional unit produced is eventually sold in the market. Now, since the demand curve confronting the competitive firm is flat, marginal revenue is identical with the demand curve. One way to prove it is to recall Equation 3-4, i.e., $MR = P(1 + 1/\eta)$. Since the demand curve D in panel (b) of Figure 7-2 is infinitely elastic, $\eta = -\infty$ and Equation 3-4 reduces to $MR = P$. An alternative way to look at it is to use the definition of MR as follows:

$$MR = \frac{\Delta R}{\Delta X} = \frac{P \cdot \Delta X}{\Delta X} = P$$

7.2c The Optimum Level of Output in the Long Run

The profit of the firm is revenue minus all costs. If profit is denoted by π, we can write the profit equation as

$$\pi = R - C \tag{7-1}$$

We then see that profit is maximized at the level of output where marginal revenue is equal to marginal cost as follows:

$$MR = MC \tag{7-2}$$

The total revenue as presented in panel (a) of Figure 7-2 is drawn together with the long-run total cost curve [panel (a) of Figure 6-10] in Figure 7-3. Notice that between the origin and the level of output of X_1^b total cost is in excess of total revenue. Within this range the vertical distance between the two curves measures the loss to the firm at each level of output. Between output levels of X_1^b and X_2^b the revenue curve occupies a higher position than the total cost curve; the vertical distance between the two curves measures the profit of the firm. Beyond point X_2^b the firm again incurs losses. The levels of output separating the profitable and the nonprofitable domains of output are known as *break-even* levels of output. In Figure 7-3 the *first break-even level* of output is X_1^b and the *second break-even level is* X_2^b; the associated two *break-even points* are F and H. Maximum profit must occur between the points X_1^b and X_2^b. At any point on the LRC curve between F and G the slope of the LRC curve ($\Delta C/\Delta X$) is smaller than the slope of the R curve ($\Delta R/\Delta X$). This means that increasing output by ΔX would increase revenue by ΔR and cost by ΔC. Since ΔR is greater than ΔC, profit to the firm would increase by $\Delta R - \Delta C$. From this we deduce that it will pay the firm to expand from output level X_1^b to a level of X_0. The point on the LRC curve associated with X_0 units of output is denoted by G. At that point the slope of the LRC curve is equal to the slope of the R curve: Additional revenue due to expanding output by ΔX is equal to additional cost. Beyond G the slope of LRC is greater than the slope of R: Expanding output by ΔX

FIGURE 7-3 DETERMINING THE LEVEL OF OUTPUT YIELDING MAXIMUM PROFIT

The long-run total cost curve (LRC) is first concave downward and then convex downward. This curve and the *total revenue curve R* start at the origin. The LRC curve cuts the R curve at points F and H, known as the *break-even points*. The profitable domain of output extends from X_1^b, to X_2^b. Maximum profit is achieved at a level of X_0 where the slope of LRC (MC) is equal to the slope of R (MR = P). At a level of output of X' the slopes of R and LRC are also equal; however, this is the level of output where loss is the highest.

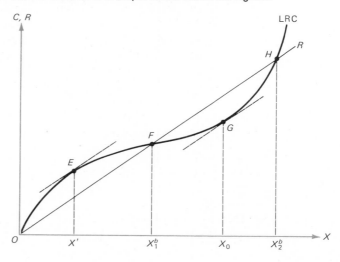

would decrease profit by $\Delta C - \Delta R$. We conclude that maximum profit occurs at a level of output of X_0 units where the slope of the revenue curve is equal to the slope of the total cost curve. But what about point E at which equality between the slope of the total cost curve and the revenue curve also occurs? It is evident that when output is increased from the origin toward X' the loss to the firm increases. The loss attains its highest level at a level of output of X' and thereafter it subsides. The slope of the total cost curve is the marginal cost for the associated level of output. The slope of the revenue curve is the marginal revenue for the associated level of output. Around point E, LRC is concave downward: Cost is increasing at a decreasing rate, and accordingly, marginal cost is falling. Around point G, the cost curve is convex downward: Cost is increasing at an increasing rate, and marginal cost is rising. The above geometric discussion can now be summarized as follows:

1. The necessary condition for profit maximization is that the slope of the total cost curve be equal to the slope of the total revenue curve. This is equivalent to requiring that marginal cost be equal to marginal revenue as stated in Equation 7-2.
2. The sufficient condition for profit maximization is that marginal cost would be rising at the level of output where marginal cost is equal to marginal revenue. This condition excludes point E from being considered as representing an optimum rate of production.

We now turn our attention to the MC, AC, and MR curves. Long-run average and marginal cost curves were derived from the long-run total cost curve in Figure 6-10. Such LRMC and LRAC, which are derived from the long-run cost curve in Figure 7-3, are presented in panel (a) of Figure 7-4. The marginal revenue curve, which is the slope of the total revenue curve R in Figure 7-3, is the flat line in panel (a) of Figure 7-4. It is both the marginal revenue curve and the demand curve confronting the firm. [Only the horizontal scale is the same for Figure 7-3 and panel (a) of Figure 7-4.] The associated profit curve denoted by π is drawn in panel (b) of Figure 7-4. The two break-even levels of output, X_1^b and X_2^b, are associated with points F' and H', where the LRAC curve intersects with the demand curve confronting the firm. Correspondingly, in panel (b) profit is zero at these break-even levels of output. Profit is negative between the origin and X_1^b and positive between X_1^b and X_2^b. In panel (a) the LRMC curve intersects with the MR curve (which is identical with the D curve under the assumption of perfect competition) at points E' and G'. These points are associated with levels of output of X' and X_0, respectively. Notice in panel (a) that at point G' the second-order condition is satisfied: The marginal cost curve is rising. Hence, as shown in panel (b), when output is produced at a rate of X_0 units per unit of time, profit is maximized. At point E', on the other hand, the marginal cost curve is falling. The second-order conditions are not satisfied. Hence at the associated level of output, profit is at its lowest level. Since profit is actually negative there, we may say that at a level of output of X' the loss is the greatest.

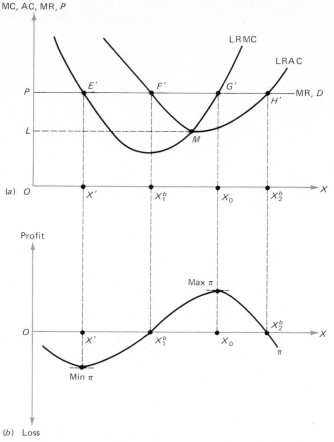

FIGURE 7-4 PROFIT MAXIMIZATION AND THE LONG-RUN SUPPLY CURVE OF THE COMPETITIVE FIRM

In both panels X', X_1^b, X_0, and X_2^b represent the same levels of output as in Figure 7-3. Panel (*a*). At output levels of X' and X_0 the long-run marginal cost curve (LRMC) cuts the price line. E' is the point of maximum loss and G' is the point of maximum profit; only at G' are the second-order conditions for profit maximization satisfied. At the *break-even points* X_1^b and X_2^b, the long-run average cost curve (LRAC) cuts the price line.

Panel (*b*). The profit is negative between the origin and the first break-even point; it is positive between the two break-even points. The negative profit (loss) is highest at X' and the profit is highest at X_0.

7.2d The Supply Curve of the Firm in the Long Run

The *supply curve* of the competitive firm tells us how much the firm will produce per unit of time at a given price. The response of the firm to price changes in the long run is illustrated by focusing again on panel (*a*) of Figure 7-4. First, a long-run price is a price which is believed by the firm to last for a long time period. In fact, the length of the period should be sufficient to justify investment in fixed factors such as tractors and land in farming, spindles in cotton spinning, and rigs in crude oil production (Section 6.5g). The long-run price does not have to be stable from day to day. The price of farm output may vary from season to season; it may even fluctuate from year to year. Farmers will consider some moving average of price over time as an indicator of the long-run price level. In some cases the long-run price is actually stable from day to day: The price of "old oil" in the United States in the late 1970s was regulated, while the price of "new oil" was practically determined by OPEC.

Now, if the long-run price is lower than minimum point M on the LRAC curve, a potential firm will not enter the industry and a firm in the industry will discontinue production. This can be summarized by noting that the first segment of the long-run supply curve of the firm is vertical segment $\overline{OL}$: The firm produces zero as the price level rises from zero to $\overline{OL}$. As the price rises just a little above $\overline{OL}$, there is a jump from zero output to $\overline{LM}$ units of output per unit of time. Above that level, the firm would, in the long run, supply quantities as indicated by the LRMC curve because it would maximize profit at levels of output where the flat demand curve cuts the LRMC curve. For example, at a price of P [panel (a) of Figure 7-4] the intersection between the price line (the demand curve confronting the firm) and the LRMC curve occurs at point G'. Hence at that price the firm will supply $\overline{PG'}$ ($= X_0$) units of output per unit time. The results of the above analysis can be summarized as follows:

> The long-run supply curve of the firm is the portion of the LRMC curve above the minimum of the LRAC curve. More precisely, it is composed of the vertical segment $\overline{OL}$, the horizontal (dashed) segment $\overline{LM}$, and the LRMC curve above point M.

7.2e An Example: Business Formations and Business Failures

In a static economy one would expect that over time the number of business failures would be roughly equal to the number of business formations. In a dynamic growing economy, the number of potential entrepreneurs who believe that the long-run price of a certain product will rise to a level higher than the minimum LRAC curve is greater than the number of entrepreneurs who happen to experience a drop in the long-run price to a level below the minimum point of their LRAC curves. Table 7-2 presents data on business formations and business failures for 1950, 1960, and 1970. Some businesses such as finance, insurance, real estate, professionals, and farmers are not covered by Table 7-2. It is interesting to note that the ratio of new business formations to business failures rose from 1950 to 1970. The business failure rate, which is the number of failures per 10,000 existing firms, is surprisingly low, probably indicating that entrepreneurs avert risk.

7.2f Constant Returns to Scale

The cost curves for the case in which the production function obeys constant returns to scale and all factors of production are variable were analyzed in Secton 6.5d. The resulting LRC curve was drawn in panel (a) of Figure 6-9, and LRMC, which is identical with the LRAC curve, was drawn in panal (b) of Figure 6-9. Earlier in this chapter we derived the demand curve which

TABLE 7-2 **Business Formations and Business Failures for 1950, 1960, and 1970***

Year	New business formations	Business failures	Business failure rate
1950	93,092	9,162	34
1960	182,713	15,444	57
1970	264,209	10,748	44

*Some firms such as finance, insurance, real estate, professionals, and farmers are not included.
Source: U.S. Bureau of the Census, *Historical Statistics of the United States, Colonial Times to 1970*, Washington, 1975, part 2, p. 912.

confronts the competitive firm as well as the total revenue curve. These curves are drawn in Figure 7-2. When this figure is compared with Figure 6-9, Figure 7-5 can be drawn. In Figure 7-5 total revenue and long-run total cost curves are presented in panel (a). Marginal revenue and long-run marginal cost curves are presented in panel (b). If the price confronting the firm is P_1, except at the origin, in panel (a) the associated R_1 curve is lower than the LRC_0 curve. In panel (b) the associated MR_1 curve is lower than the $LRMC_0$ curve throughout. The conclusion is that the firm will produce zero output, because losses will be incurred at any other level of output. In panel (a) the loss would be the vertical distance between the LRC_0 curve and the R_1 curve for any level of output. In panel (b) the loss would be the area of the rectangle circumscribed by the vertical axis, the $LRMC_0$ curve, the MR_1 curve, and a vertical line which is perpendicular to the horizontal axis at the rate of production level. An intermediate case would be one in which the price confronting the firm, P_0, is identical with the long-run marginal cost $LRMC_0$. The cost and revenue curves are identical, and the firm will incur neither a loss nor a profit regardless of the rate of production. Finally, if the price confronting the firm, P_2, is higher than $LRMC_0$, the firm will produce infinity output: In panel (a) profit, which is the vertical distance between the R_2 curve and the LRC_0 curve, will increase with output. In panel (b) profit, which is the rectangle circumscribed by the vertical axis, the MR_2 curve, the $LRMC_0$ curve, and the vertical line at the level of output, will also increase with output. In fact, profit would simply be equal to $X \cdot (P_2 - LRMC_0)$ and thus will increase proportionately to output.

The above analysis implies that firms will produce either zero or infinity. Moreover, it implies that if the LRMC curves of firms are not all identical (at the same horizontal level) the firm with the lowest LRMC curve will become a monopoly (sole producer). It is left as an exercise for the student to show that under such conditions there is a price that would eliminate all firms but the one with the lowest LRMC curve. If all firms have identical LRMC curves, chaos will prevail.

Note: The case of constant returns to scale is consistent with noncompetitive markets. For example, an empirical study was presented in Chapter

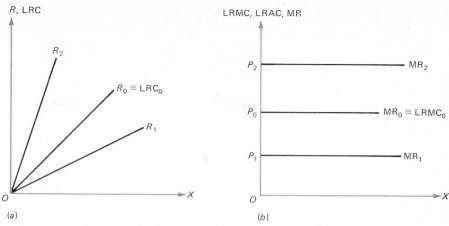

FIGURE 7-5 COST AND REVENUE CURVES: CONSTANT RETURNS TO SCALE AND PERFECT COMPETITION

To the three total revenue curves R_1, R_0, and R_2 in panel (a) there corresponds three marginal revenue curves MR_1, MR_0, and MR_2 in panel (b). The long-run total cost curve (LRC_0) in panel (a) is identical with R_0. Correspondingly, the long-run marginal cost curve ($LRMC_0$) in panel (b) is identical with MR_0. Such cost curves are possible if the production function of the firm obeys constant returns to scale. Such a hypothetical firm will produce zero if $R = R_1$ (and $MR = MR_1$), will produce an infinitely large amount if $R = R_2$ (and $MR = MR_2$), and will be indifferent as to the level of output if $R = R_0$ (and $MR = MR_0$).

6 which points out that refuse collection is governed by constant returns to scale. In most cases refuse collection is a local monopoly which is owned and run by the city (Section 6.5e).

7.2g The Optimum Level of Output in the Short Run

The theory of the short-run cost curves as related to long-run cost curves was discussed in Section 6.6. The optimum level of output in the short run will now be considered. The issue might arise in one of two situations:

1. The market price for a good is relatively stable over time. The firm selects a long-run size for its plant which is tailored for some expected long-run price. If, later, the realized price happens to be different from the expected price, the firm will either contract or expand along its short-run marginal cost curve.

2. The market price fluctuates all the time. The firm will formulate its long-run price expectation based upon some moving average, a trend line, or more sophisticated forecasting models. The size of the firm will be tailored to this long-run expected price. However, in the short run the firm will respond to price fluctuations by moving along its short-run marginal cost curve.

Consider Figure 7-6. The long-run price is P_0. If we extend a horizontal line at the $\overline{OP_0}$ level to the right, it will intersect with the LRMC curve at

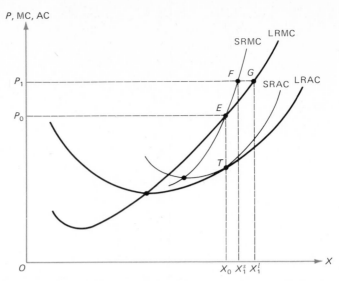

FIGURE 7-6 THE LONG-RUN AND SHORT-RUN SUPPLY CURVES OF THE COMPETITIVE
FIRM
Currently, the price is P_0 and it intersects with the long-run marginal cost curve (LRMC) at
point E. The long-run quantity produced by the firm is X_0. If the price were to rise from P_0 to
P_1, the firm would first expand along the short-run marginal cost curve (SRMC) to point F.
The quantity supplied by the firm would rise to X_1^s. If the firm believes that the price is going
to remain permanently at P_1, it will expand to point G on the LRMC, and quantity supplied will
rise to X_1^l.

point E. Accordingly, the firm will plan an optimal-size plant for the production of X_0 units of output: At the rate of production of X_0 units per unit of
time the SRAC curve is tangent to the LRAC curve (point T). Suppose the
price rises from P_0 to P_1. This rise might reflect a fluctuation, or it might
simply represent an unanticipated price movement. One way or the other, it
will pay the firm to increase its output. However, since some factors cannot
vary in the short run, the firm will expand along the short-run marginal cost
curve. The short-run solution will be determined by extending a horizontal
line at the $\overline{OP}_1$ level to the right until it intersects with the SRMC curve at
point F. The short-run level of output will be X_1^s, and the change in the rate of
production in the short run is $X_1^s - X_0$. It is important to stress again that so
long as the price is above the marginal cost, be it in the long run or the short
run, it pays the firm to increase its rate of production. In the short run
equilibrium will be achieved where the price line intersects with the short-
run marginal cost curve. In the long run equilibrium will be achieved where
the price line intersects with the long-run marginal cost curve. Indeed, if the
rise in the price from P_0 to P_1 is viewed as permanent by the firm, it will
eventually vary the size of its plant to fit the higher price; the firm will
accordingly move from point F to point G and expand its output from X_1^s to
X_1^l. On the other hand, if the price movement from P_0 to P_1 was temporary,

as the price returns to P_0, the firm will contract along the short-run marginal cost curve from point F back to point E.

We do not show in Figure 7-6 a downward movement in the price. However, the analysis is the same: Given a decline in the price, the firm would first contract along the SRMC curve. Only if the fall in the price is viewed by the firm as permanent will the firm retreat to the LRMC curve.

7.2h The Supply Curve of the Firm in the Short Run

The short-run supply curve of the firm tells how the firm will respond in the short run to price changes. Following the analysis of Section 7-2g, we conclude that *the short-run marginal cost curve of the firm denoted by SRMC is the short-run supply curve of the firm.* Notice, however, that while for a given production function and prices of inputs there is only one long-run supply curve, namely, the LRMC curve (above the minimum point of the LRAC curve), there are many short-run supply curves. In fact, through each point on the long-run marginal cost curve we can pass a short-run marginal cost curve which is the short-run supply curve for a certain size of the firm.

Recall that the long-run supply curve of the firm was defined to be the long-run marginal cost curve above the minimum point of the long-run average cost curve (Section 7.2d). The issue of the minimum point of the short-run supply curve of the firm is a bit more involved. Consider again Figure 7-6. Assume that the price falls to a level which is lower than the minimum point of the SRAC curve. Should the firm continue to produce in the short run? To answer this question, we redraw the short-run curves of Figure 7-6 plus an AVC curve in Figure 7-7. Suppose the price declines from a level of P_0 (Figure 7-6) to a lower level of P_2, as shown in Figure 7-7. Notice that the price P_2 is lower than the minimum point of the SRAC curve but is above the minimum point of the AVC curve. Since the price line is everywhere lower than the SRAC curve, the best the firm can hope to do is minimize its loss. If the firm continues to produce, loss will be minimized at a rate of production of X_2^s units, where the price line (which is the marginal revenue curve) intersects with the SRMC curve. Total fixed cost is the vertical distance between SRAC and AVC times the level of output of X_2^s; geometrically, this is the shaded rectangle. The part of this rectangle which lies above the price line is the loss to the firm; it is the uncovered portion of the fixed cost. If the fixed cost is *unavoidable*, the firm should continue to produce X_2^s units so long as the price remains at the level of P_2. If the fixed cost is *avoidable*, the firm should discontinue production and by so doing avoid the fixed cost and have neither a loss nor a profit. This is better than incurring a loss which is equal to the portion of the rectangle above the price line (marked by diagonal stripes). In reality, fixed costs are likely to be unavoidable. The reason is that when the price declines to a very low level, everybody will attempt to get rid of fixed factors, thus driving down their prices. Moreover, in most cases fixed inputs like heavy machinery are adapted to a specific environment prevailing in a specific firm, rendering its sale in the market practically impossible. If the price declines further to a level lower than the minimum

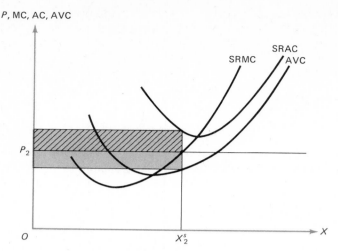

FIGURE 7-7 SHORT-RUN COST CURVES OF THE COMPETITIVE FIRM ARE SHOWN
The price line P_2 happens to lie below the minimum point of the short-run average cost curve (SRAC) and above the average variable cost curve (AVC). If the firm were to produce X_2^s units (where the price line cuts the short-run marginal cost curve), total fixed cost would be the shaded rectangle; total revenue minus total variable cost is the portion of the shaded rectangle below the price line; the loss to the firm would be the portion of the shaded rectangle lying above the price line which is marked by diagonal stripes. If the fixed cost is *unavoidable*, producing zero would result in a loss equal to the entire shaded rectangle. The firm should prefer to produce X_2^s, where the loss is only the rectangle marked by diagonal stripes. If the fixed cost is *avoidable*, the firm should discontinue production and neither enjoy a profit nor suffer a loss, which is preferable to a loss amounting to the rectangle marked by diagonal stripes.

point of the AVC curve, the firm should discontinue production. It is left as an exercise for the student to show that there might be situations in which the firm might discontinue production in the short run but resume production in the long run, even if the price remains at a very low level in the long run.

7.2i An Example: The Smart Farmer and the Not-So-Smart Farmer

The following two examples from *The Wall Street Journal* illustrate how the smart farmer and the not-so-smart farmer behave in the face of price fluctuation.

[*The smart farmer*] Food prices may rise some 8% next year on top of this year's expected 10% jump partly because of the way farmers like Randall Matson raise pigs.

Mr. Matson, of Ames, Iowa, has been getting good prices for his animals, but he isn't rushing out to produce lots more of them—a move that would help keep meat prices down next year. That is because Mr. Matson, like a growing number of pork producers, raises his hogs in indoor facilities, which means that boosting production involves a lot more than mating a sow to a boar.

"We used to just raise pigs under the oak trees, but now expanding means capital investment, maybe $200,000 or so for new buildings," he explains. "It's like factory production, like General Motors making cars. You don't just rush into expansion because prices are good for the moment."[4]

---

[4]*The Wall Street Journal*, November 7, 1978.

The not-so-smart farmer together with other similar farmers attempted to correct their errors in interpreting short-run price movements as long-run price movements by leading a "tractor protest" in Washington in early 1979:

The Washington protest has been organized by the American Agricultural Movement, a loosely organized group that led a similar protest in the capital last year. Last year's effort was partly successful, which helps to explain why the tractors are back.

Mr. Bergland has often stressed that net farm income last year rose $8 billion to $28.1 billion, a fact that surely indicates that the average farmer is better off than he was a year ago. Why, then, are some farmers in trouble?

The answer, to some extent, is speculation—not by foreign investors but by American farmers themselves. Earlier in the current decade, the farmers watched the prices of their products soar. Barley went from a little more than $1 a bushel in 1971 to more than $4 in 1974. No. 3 yellow corn at Chicago went from $1.39 a bushel in 1971 to $3.22 in 1974.

Some farmers thought that prices would keep on going up, or at least would maintain the high 1974 levels. So they borrowed heavily to buy more machinery and land. Agriculture, however, is like the stock market: Prices tend to fluctuate. Prices now are still high in relation to the beginning of the decade, but they're below the peak 1974 level.

As Mr. Bergland put it, the government shouldn't take responsibility for the business problems of some farmers who made poor investment in land and equipment.[5]

7.3 AN APPLICATION: THE MULTIPLANT FIRM

A firm may operate many plants. A typical example would be a firm that operates several electricity-generating plants interconnected by a network of transmission lines, such that electricity can be generated by all or some of the plants. During the day the demand for electricity fluctuates. In January peak demand could occur at 7 P.M., and minimum demand could occur, say, at 3 A.M. The minimum could be 70 percent of peak demand. In August peak demand could occur at 4 P.M. and minimum demand at 4 A.M. Minimum demand could be as low as 60 percent of the peak demand. In the short run the number of plants is fixed. The firm responds to the intraday fluctuations in demand by varying the amount of fuel used. Thus the short-run marginal cost curve of any plant is given by the price of fuel (it could be specified as dollars per Btu) divided by the marginal physical product of fuel, derived from the production function of that particular plant (Equation 6-10). The marginal physical product of fuel declines up to a certain level at which the production of power for that plant reaches its maximum. (In Figure 5-8, such a level was A_3, at which total output reached its maximum and MP_a was zero.) Accordingly, the short-run MC curves of a typical plant would slope positively up to the point of maximum capacity, where they would become vertical [X_3, panel (d) of Figure 6-3]. The electricity-generating plants are not identical: As the scale of the

firm increases over time, more plants are added. The new plants are technologically more advanced than old ones. The firm does not scrap the old plants; they are left to operate during peak demand hours. The question is: What is the least-cost allocation of demanded electricity among the various plants? To simplify the problem, the cost of transmission is discarded. The answer is that at each moment during the day production of power must be allocated such that the various short-run marginal costs of the various plants are equated. This is true because if, say, MC_1 (the short-run marginal cost of the first plant) is higher than MC_2 (the short-run marginal cost of the second plant), it would pay the firm to reduce output in the first plant and increase output in the second plant. The approximate gain by shifting the first unit is $MC_1 - MC_2$. This process of shifting production from Plant 1 to Plant 2 will continue until $MC_1 = MC_2$.

Suppose an electric company operates two plants. Plant 1 is modern and Plant 2 is old. The short-run marginal cost curves of the two plants are plotted in panel (a) and panel (b), respectively, of Figure 7-8. The two short-run marginal cost curves are horizontally aggregated in panel (c). X_1, X_2, and X_t measure power generated by Plant 1, Plant 2, and aggregate power, respectively. Suppose the demand for electric power at 2 P.M. is X'_t. To allocate X'_t between the two plants, we measure X'_t units along the

---

[5]*The Wall Street Journal,* February 27, 1979.

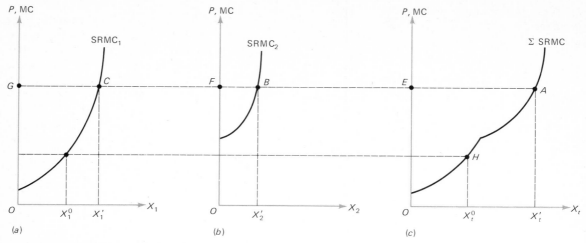

FIGURE 7-8 A MULTIPLANT FIRM

$SRMC_1$ [panel (a)] and $SRMC_2$ [panel (b)] are the short-run marginal cost curves of two plants belonging to a firm. $\Sigma SRMC$ is the aggregate of the two SRMC curves. An amount X'_t is allocated in the least-cost way between the two plants by tracing a vertical line from X'_t in panel (c) to point A on the $\Sigma SRMC$ curve, and then extending a horizontal line at the level of point A back to panel (a) and panel (b). The points of intersection between this line and the two short-run marginal cost curves tell the manager how to allocate the output between the two plants. Such an allocation implies $SRMC_1 = SRMC_2$.

horizontal axis of panel (c). A vertical line is extended from X'_t upward until it hits the aggregate $\Sigma SRMC$ curve at point A. Then a horizontal line at the $\overline{X'_t A}$ level is extended from panel (c) back to panels (a) and (b). This line cuts $SRMC_1$ and $SRMC_2$ at points C and B, respectively. At this point $SRMC_1$ is equal to $SRMC_2$. The associated levels of production are $\overline{GC}$ units by Plant 1 and $\overline{FB}$ units by Plant 2. From the way in which $\Sigma SRMC$ was constructed, it must be true that $\overline{GC} + \overline{FB} = \overline{EA}$. Or, what is the same, $X'_1 + X'_2 = X'_t$. Suppose at 4 A.M. the demand for electric power falls from X'_t to X^0_t. If we apply a similar procedure, we find that if a horizontal line at the $\overline{X^0_t H}$ level is ex-

tended back to panel (a) and panel (b), respectively, it completely misses $SRMC_2$. Thus the firm shuts down Plant 2, and the entire production of power is allocated to Plant 1. In this case $X^0_t = X^0_1$.

The above analysis can be extended to the case of n plants, as well as a multiplant firm facing a price of P_0 for its output. If P_0 is $\overline{OE}$, we extend a horizontal line at the $\overline{OE}$ level back to panels (a) and (b). The intersection of this line with $SRMC_1$ and $SRMC_2$, respectively, will determine how to allocate production among the two (or n) plants in order to maximize profit.

7.4 THE PRODUCER'S SURPLUS

The concept of the *consumer's surplus* was developed in Chapter 2. A parallel concept in the theory of the producer is the *producer's surplus*. Both these concepts are useful in welfare analysis. In particular, these concepts will prove very useful in discussion of welfare loss due to monopolistic pricing (Chapter 11) as well as due to taxation (Chapter 10)

The analysis shows first that the area under the marginal cost curve is equal to total variable cost. Consider Figure 7-9. First, note in panel (a) that when there is no production only total fixed cost exists. When the first unit is produced, the additional variable cost involved is one unit times the corresponding MC, or the rectangle with the diagonal stripes. When the second unit is produced, the additional variable cost is one unit times the marginal cost associated with the second unit, which is indicated by the shaded rectangle. Likewise, the additional variable cost from adding the third unit is the rectangle marked by crisscrosses. We can continue to estimate total variable cost by adding more rectangles as output increases. These rectangles approximate the area under the marginal cost curve: The smaller the units of output, the better the approximation. If we allow the units to approach a size of zero, we obtain the result that the area under the marginal cost curve is equal to the total variable cost.

Panel (b) of Figure 7-9 shows the same marginal cost curve. The price confronting the firm is P_0, and the firm supplies X_0 units of output per unit of time. Price times output is total revenue, namely, the rectangle denoted by OP_0GX_0. If we subtract the striped area lying under the marginal cost curve, we are left with the shaded area lying above the marginal cost curve but under the price line. This shaded area is the *producer's surplus*; defined as total revenue minus total variable cost, it boils down to returns on fixed factors. Since in the long run entrepreneurial capacity is the only fixed factor, the producer's long-run surplus is equal to the returns to the entrepreneur.

From examining Figure 7-9, panel (b), it becomes evident that the producer's surplus arises because the MC curve of the firm slopes positively.

FIGURE 7-9 THE PRODUCER'S SURPLUS

In panel (a) we illustrate why the area under the marginal cost curve equals total variable cost. In panel (b) the rectangle OP_0GX_0 has an area which is equal to total revenue. If we subtract from it the area shaded with diagonal stripes under the marginal cost curve, we are left with the shaded area, which is known as the *producer's surplus*.

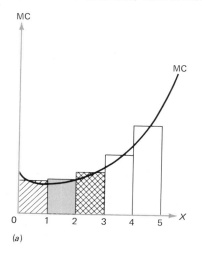

(a)

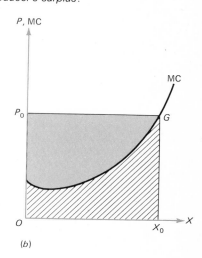

(b)

We recall that if in the long run all factors (including entrepreneurial capacity) were variable, then the long-run marginal cost curve would be horizontal and there would be no producer's surplus (Section 6.5d). Hence in the long run the producer's surplus is attributed to the limited supply of entrepreneurial capacity.

7.5 ACCOUNTING VERSUS ECONOMIC COSTS

The economic profit (sometimes called rent) differs from net earnings as computed by accountants. The difference arises primarily because the economist is interested in one thing and the accountant in another. The profit as calculated by the economist tells entrepreneurs whether they are doing at least as well as they could do by investing their capital elsewhere, in the next best project, and hiring themselves out for the available next best job. This approach is in accord with the economic definition of *opportunity cost*, which is simply the opportunity sacrificed because some action was taken. When a young person acquires schooling at a university, its cost should include, on top of tuition, income forgone while attending the university. A worker who decides to work one additional hour sacrifices one hour of leisure. It has already been mentioned that workers might perform less work when their income rises simply because they value leisure more after income rises (Section 1.6). When a municipality purchases water rights from a farmer in the semiarid southwestern United States, the city pays for the forgone opportunity to grow alfalfa. The opportunity cost of capital is simply the rate of return that a certain capital could have earned elsewhere in the economy, in the next best opportunity. For example, if this capital were invested in treasury bills, it could have earned 5 percent without bearing any risk. Entrepreneurs could have hired themselves out or could have devoted their time to fun; that is, they could have had more leisure. Net earnings as calculated by the accountant indicates what is left for the owner as taxable income after all expenses are paid. With proper adjustment, the data provided by the accountant may be used in economic analysis.

To illustrate, consider a carpenter who is the proprietor of a small furniture shop. Investment in all assets amounts to $200,000. Let us assume that the carpenter can be employed in a furniture factory for $16,000 a year. The carpenter invested $120,000 and borrowed $80,000 from the bank at a going interest rate of 5 percent. During the year sales amount to $90,000 (1000 units at a price of $90), the cost of materials was $14,000, payments to hired labor amounted to $28,000, and depreciation and maintenance were $26,000. The accountant prepared the following income statement:

Net sales		$90,000
Less: Materials	$14,000	
Labor cost	28,000	
Depreciation and maintenance	26,000	
Interest charges (5 percent on $80,000)	4,000	
Total costs		72,000
Net earnings		$18,000

The economist adjusted the income statement as follows:

Net sales		$90,000
Less: Materials	$14,000	
Labor: (1) Hired	28,000	
(2) Self	16,000	
Depreciation and maintenance	26,000	
Interest on capital (5 percent on $200,000)	10,000	
Total economic costs		94,000
Economic profit (rent)		−$ 4,000

In the above example, even though net earnings as estimated by the accountant amounts to $18,000, the economist shows that the carpenter would have done better to invest capital ($120,000) elsewhere and hire out; in fact, as indicated by the result calculated by the economist, the carpenter would have been $4000 better off by seriously considering other next best alternatives.

Suppose, for the sake of illustration, that the furniture shop is organized as a corporation. The intitial investment was financed by issuing $80,000 in bonds paying 5 percent interest and 12,000 common shares at $10 each. The carpenter is hired as the manager at a salary of $16,000 per annum. The income statement of the corporation is as follows:

Net sales		$90,000
Less: Materials	$14,000	
Labor	44,000	
Depreciation and maintenance	26,000	
Interest (on bonds)	4,000	
Total costs		88,000
Net earnings		$ 2,000

If the corporation decides to pay the net earnings to stockholders, the dividend will amount to $0.17 per share ($2000/12,000), a return of only 1.7 percent. For the stockholders, the opportunity sacrificed was to earn 5 percent on their investment by investing it in bonds. Had they done so, they could have earned 5 percent on $120,000, or $6000. Their loss, as calculated by the economist, is $4000.

The predicament of the furniture shop is illustrated geometrically in Figure 7-10.

SUMMARY This chapter started with the postulate of profit maximization. After the criticism leveled at the classical tradition was discussed, it was demonstrated that by and large the major force that moves the free enterprise economy is profit maximization, and the classical tradition escaped the attack without a scar.

The next step was to investigate the *demand curve* confronting the competitive firm. The competitive firm was defined as a firm that has no appreciable influence on either the prices of inputs or the price of the final good it

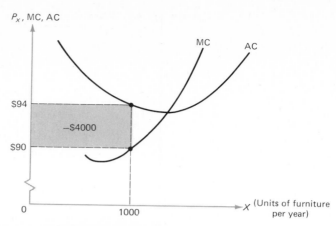

P_x, MC, AC

$94

−$4000

$90

0   1000   X (Units of furniture per year)

FIGURE 7-10 ACCOUNTING VERSUS ECONOMIC COSTS
At a price of $90 the firm sells 1000 units. The *economic* average cost of the firm is $94.
Thus the economic loss of this firm is the shaded rectangle amounting to $4000.

produces. We saw that the demand curve confronting such a competitive firm is horizontal and cuts the vertical axis at the level of the price of the good currently prevailing in the marketplace. It was shown that this demand curve is identical with the *marginal revenue curve* of the firm.

It was then proved that in the long run the firm will maximize its profit by producing where the price (which is identical with marginal revenue) is equal to the long-run marginal cost curve (LRMC). It was also established that a second-order condition for profit maximization is for the LRMC curve to cut the price line from below, going from left to right. The analysis led to the definition of the *long-run supply curve* of the competitive firm as being zero (production) for prices lower than the minimum point of the long-run average cost curve, and being identical with the LRMC for prices higher than the minimum point of the LRAC. We also saw that the supply curve of the firm in the longest run, where all inputs are variable and the process of production obeys constant returns to scale, is horizontal; we concluded that this case is inconsistent with equilibrium because the size of the firm is indeterminate.

The next major step in the chapter was to show that in the short run the firm will expand and contract along its short-run marginal cost curve (SRMC). Thus the *supply curve* of the competitive firm in the *short run* is identical with the SRMC curve, and short-run supply curves are consequently steeper than the long-run supply curve. We noted that in the short run the firm will always produce when the price is above the minimum point of the short-run average cost curve (SRAC), will not produce when the price is below the minimum point of the average variable cost, and may or may not produce if the price is between the two minimum points of the average cost curves, respectively.

A special application, the multiple-plant firm, was discussed. We concluded that in the short run the multiple-plant firm should allocate production among the various plants by adhering to the principle of equating the marginal costs of all the plants.

The *producer's surplus* was defined as total revenue R minus total variable costs VC. Since the area under the marginal cost curve is equal to total variable cost, the producer's surplus is $R - VC$, which is the area above the marginal cost curve and under the price line (demand curve).

Lastly we considered *accounting* versus economic costs. While accountants are interested in costs to calculate *taxable income,* economists are interested in *opportunity costs,* defined as the value of inputs in their next best use. In order to transform accounting costs into economic costs, we must redefine the cost of *capital* and the cost of the *entrepreneurial capacity.*

GLOSSARY   **Perfect competition** A market situation in which there is ease of entry and exit, many sellers and buyers, and a homogeneous good. In this situation the firm is a *price taker*; it has no appreciable influence either on prices of inputs it uses up in the process of production or on the price of output it produces.

Perfect market A market in which *perfect competition* prevails.

Competitive firm A firm buying its inputs and selling its output in *perfect markets.*

Demand curve confronting the competitive firm A horizontal line in a diagram in which output is measured along the horizontal axis and price is measured along the vertical axis. This line intersects with the vertical axis at the prevailing price level.

Marginal revenue curve of the competitive firm A horizontal line identical with the demand curve confronting the competitive firm.

Break-even point A level of output where total revenue equals total cost.

Equilibrium of the competitive firm The level of output of profit maximization is known as the equilibrium output of the firm. The first-order condition for profit maximization is that the price (marginal revenue for the competitive firm) be equal to the marginal cost; the second-order condition is that the marginal cost cut the price line from below, going from left to right.

Long-run supply curve of the competitive firm Quantity supplied is zero for prices lower than the minimum of the long-run average cost curve (LRAC). Quantity supplied is determined by the long-run marginal cost curve (LRMC) for prices higher than the minimum of the LRAC.

Longest-run supply curve of the competitive firm The longest-run marginal cost curve for *constant returns to scale* is a horizontal line. This horizontal line is the longest-run supply curve of the firm. Such supply curves are drawn only to show that they are inconsistent with perfect competition.

Short-run supply curve of the competitive firm Quantity supplied in the short run is determined by the short-run marginal cost curve (SRMC). The short-run supply curve is steeper than the long-run supply curve. We can pass a short-run supply curve through each point on the long-run supply curve (above the minimum of LRAC). If the price is lower than the minimum point of the average variable cost (AVC), the quantity supplied is zero. If the price is higher than the minimum point of the short-run average cost curve (SRAC), the firm should produce. If the price is between the two minimum points, respectively, the firm should produce if the fixed cost is unavoidable, and discontinue production if the fixed cost is avoidable.

Multiplant firm A firm operating more than one plant. The rule of optimal operation is to equate the marginal costs in all the plants.

Producer's surplus Total revenue R minus total variable cost VC. It is the area under the price line and above the marginal cost curve. In the short run it is equal to returns to fixed inputs. In the long run it is equal to returns to the entrepreneurial capacity.

Accounting costs Costs prepared by the accountant to calculate taxable income. The main difference between *accounting* and *economic* costs lies in *capital costs* and the cost of the *entrepreneurial services*.

PROBLEMS   An asterisk indicates an advanced problem.

7-1.   Suppose that the stockholders of Corporation Z do not enjoy maximum profit because management selected point N rather than point M in Figure 7-1. By applying geometric analysis, discuss the following two proposals raised in the meeting of the board of directors:

(a) Pay top managers a bonus instead of a salary. The bonus should be equal to a certain fixed percentage of profit.

(b) Spend money on policing and detection.

7-2.   Baumol argued that some large corporations pursue a goal of sales maximization subject to the constraint of earning a certain fixed minimum profit.

(a) Illustrate the behavior of such a (competitive) corporation by drawing its cost curve (AC and MC) and the demand confronting the corporation.

(b) What would be the impact of imposing a fixed tax (like $10,000 per annum) on the behavior of the firm?

7-3.   Show that if the production functions of all the firms which produce good X are governed by constant returns to scale, and if all factors of production are variable, then, if cost functions are not identical (because production functions are not identical), a monopoly will emerge.

7-4.   Farmer Matson explained why he would not rush into new investments (Section 7.2i). Would you, however, expect some response in output from Mr. Matson?

7-5.   Read Section 7.2i again. In your opinion, was the Secretary of Agriculture (Mr. Bergland) absolutely correct in the statement he made?

7-6. Assume that only inputs A and B are used by a competitive firm; B is a fixed input. Would the firm produce in the stage of production where AP_a is rising $(\overline{OA_2}$, Figure 5-8)?

7-7.* The following table describes a firm which produces electric power. As indicated by the table, the firm operates only two plants.

Marginal fuel used (10^6 Btu) per megawatt-hour: $1/MP_a$	Associated level of output, megawatthours	
	Plant 1	Plant 2
1	0	0
5	0	0
10	50	0
15	80	0
20	100	20
25	110	50
30	115	70
35	115	80
40	115	80

The cost of fuel is \$2.5 per 10^6 Btu for the first plant and \$2 per 10^6 Btu for the second plant. (a) How would you allocate power production among the two plants if demand is 150 megawatthours per hour? (b) The same as (a), but the demand is only 50 megawatthours per hour? (c) What is the maximum capacity of the two plants?

7-8. Consider again the example of the furniture shop (Section 7.5). Should the firm continue to produce in the short run if the fixed costs are unavoidable?

7-9. A competitive firm produces X and Y in fixed proportions; one unit of X with one unit of Y. The marginal cost of a joint unit of X and Y (e.g., beef and leather) is given by the equation $MC = 1 + 2Z$, where Z is a joint unit. How many joint units should the firm produce if the market price of X is \$2 and of Y is \$3?

7-10. A competitive firm produces 100 units per month of a certain product. The price is \$12. If the firm decided to increase output to 106 units per month, extra cost would be:

Labor	\$15
Raw materials	35
Electricity	8
Other items	2

(a) Estimate MC in the range extending from 100 to 106 units.
(b) Should the firm increase its production to 106 units per month, and if so, what would be the (rough) change in the producer's surplus?

7-11. Discuss the following two statements as being *true, false,* or *uncertain*:

    (a) Since by definition there is only one price under competition, quantity discounts indicate the absence of competition.

    (b) A firm in a competitive industry does not have to know its marginal cost schedule to maximize profits.

7-12.* Should a competitive firm prefer a stable price of P_0 year in and year out over a price fluctuation in which one year the price is $P_0 - \Delta P$ and the next year the price is $P_0 + \Delta P$? *Note:* A is the only variable factor; storage is not feasible; the size of ΔP does not change from year to year.

MATHEMATICAL APPENDIX 7

Some mathematical derivations relevant to profit maximization will now be presented.

M7.1 FIRST- AND SECOND-ORDER CONDITIONS FOR PROFIT MAXIMIZATION

Let P stand for the price of good X, which is sold in a competitive market. Let $C = C(X)$ represent the cost function. The profit π is

$$\pi = P \cdot X - C(X) \qquad \text{(m7-1)}$$

Differentiating profit with respect to output and equation to zero, we get

$$\frac{d\pi}{dX} = P - \frac{dC}{dX} = 0 \qquad \text{(m7-2)}$$

Shifting dC/dX to the right of the equality sign, we obtain the first-order condition, namely,

$$P = \frac{dC}{dX} \qquad \text{(m7-3)}$$

Equation m7-3 is the familiar equality between price and MC (dC/dX), which is the first-order condition for profit maximization in perfect competition. The second-order condition is obtained by differentiating Equation m7-2 with respect to X and setting it as an inequality as follows:

$$\frac{d^2\pi}{dX^2} = 0 - \frac{d^2C}{dX^2} < 0 \qquad \text{(m7-4)}$$

which can be written as $d^2C/dX^2 > 0$. But this inequality can be written as $d(\text{MC})/dX > 0$. In other words, we obtain the conditions that MC must be rising where it intersects with the price line in order to guarantee that the optimum is a point of profit maximization rather than a point of profit minimization.

If we combine the result of Equation m7-3 with Equation m6-8, we obtain the general result, namely,

$$\frac{P_1}{MP_1} = \frac{P_2}{MP_2} = \ldots = \frac{P_n}{MP_n} = MC = P \qquad \text{(m7-5)}$$

Another approach would be to differentiate the profit function directly with respect to the inputs. If $X = f(A,B)$, we can set the profit function as

$$\pi = P \cdot f(A,B) - P_a \cdot A - P_b \cdot B \qquad \text{(m7-6)}$$

Let us denote $\partial X/\partial A$ by f_a and $\partial X/\partial B$ by f_b. Differentiating with respect to A and B, respectively, and equating to zero gives the first-order conditions for profit maximization:

$$\frac{\partial \pi}{\partial A} = P \cdot f_a - P_a = 0$$

$$\frac{\partial \pi}{\partial B} = P \cdot f_b - P_b = 0 \qquad \text{(m7-7)}$$

Equation m7-7 can be rearranged to yield

$$\frac{P_a}{f_a} = \frac{P_b}{f_b} = P \qquad \text{(m7-8)}$$

which is the same result as given in Equation m7-5. The second-order conditions are that

$$f_{aa} \qquad \begin{vmatrix} f_{aa} & f_{ab} \\ f_{ba} & f_{bb} \end{vmatrix} \qquad \text{(m7-9)}$$

and are alternatively negative and positive. This implies that

$$f_{aa} < 0 \qquad f_{bb} < 0$$

$$f_{aa} \cdot f_{bb} - f_{ab}^2 > 0 \qquad \text{(m7-10)}$$

CHAPTER

8

PRODUCTION AND THE THEORY OF SUPPLY

Chapter 7 proved that in order to maximize its profit the competitive firm must operate where price equals marginal cost. This implied that the marginal cost curve of the competitive firm is also its supply curve; indeed, the supply curve was defined as being its marginal cost curve (Sections 7.2d and 7.2h). The supply curve tells what quantities will be produced by the firm at different prices. In this chapter we take the fourth step in the theory of production and supply: We shall derive the supply curve of the industry by aggregating all the marginal cost curves of the firms in the industry. In Chapter 9 the theory of the aggregate demand curve (Chapter 3) will be integrated with the theory of the aggregate supply to obtain the theory of competitive markets.

At this stage we should recall the distinction made in Section 3-3 between a *change in demand*, which resulted from demand shifts unaccompanied by a change in the price of the good, and a *change in quantity demanded*, which resulted from a change in the price of the good and thus implied a movement along the demand curve. Likewise, in what follows, a shift in the supply curve will result in a *change in supply*, while a change in price will result in a change in *quantity supplied*, implying movement along the supply curve.

It is also worthwhile to recall that in the theory of demand price is taken to be *exogenous* for the individual consumer; since there are many small consumers, none has any appreciable influence on the price in the marketplace. Since aggregate demand is the sum of all individual demand curves, in the theory of aggregated demand price appears as an exogenous variable. The same holds true for firms in a competitive industry. The individual (relatively) small firm has no appreciable influence on the price in the marketplace. For example, one farmer in Iowa has no influence on the price of corn. Such a farmer is a *price taker* who may discontinue production altogether or double output without affecting the price. This will not change when we aggregate the supply curves of all corn farmers in Iowa or in the world. The price of corn is independent of the activities of each individual farmer; the price is exogenous for the individual firm. This phenomenon of competitive markets allows us to say, ''Assume the price confronting corn producers goes up; this induces them to increase their quantity of corn supplied.'' Of course, the price of corn cannot just rise miraculously. A change, such as a rise in the demand for popcorn, must have taken place in the market to trigger a rise in the price of corn. But individual corn growers do not really care what caused the rise in the price; they read the signals in the marketplace and adjust production accordingly. Hence it is correct from their viewpoint to state that the price of corn rose and farmers reacted by increasing their quantity supplied.

How is the price of corn or any other good determined in a competitive market? This will be the topic of Chapter 9, which will show that it takes two blades of the scissors, supply and demand, to cut the price.

To summarize here, in demand analysis the price is treated as an exogenous variable. In supply analysis, where perfect competition is assumed, price is treated as an exogenous variable, too. However, when supply and demand are brought together into the marketplace, price becomes an endogenous variable.

8.1 THE INDUSTRY

The production sector of the economy could be viewed as the set of all firms engaged in the production of goods. (See the "firms" box in Figure I-2.) A subset of firms specializing in the production of a certain good X is known as an *industry*. For example, all the firms specializing in the production of shoes is a subset known as the shoemaking industry. Sometimes an industry specializes in more than one good: Refineries specialize in the production of a subset of closely related goods such as gasoline, diesel fuel, and jet fuel. In agriculture the composite commodity produced by the subset of farms is defined as food. On the other hand, a subset of the farm industry could be all farms that specialize in grains. If an industry specializes in the production of closely related goods, these goods can be aggregated into a composite good by means of quantity indices, and the prices of the various goods can be unified into one composite price by means of price indices (Section 4.1). In some cases an industry will specialize in the production of joint products which are unrelated in consumption. For example, cattle ranchers sell both meat and hides. These two goods, while produced jointly, are not related in consumption. (Joint products will be discussed in Chapter 10.)

Chapters 12 and 13 will return to the problem of what constitutes an industry when products are close but imperfect substitutes. Chapter 12 will focus on the issue of *imperfect competition* (introduction to Chapter 7) arising from imperfect substitution of products, as in different brands of beer.

8.2 THE INDUSTRY SUPPLY CURVE

8.2a The Long-Run Industry Supply Curve

In Chapter 7 we explained that the portion of the long-run marginal cost curve of the firm lying above the minimum point of the long-run average cost curve is its long-run supply curve (Section 7-2d). *The long-run industry supply curve is, accordingly, derived by horizontally adding the long-run marginal cost curves of all the firms in the industry.* The process of aggregating the marginal cost curves is formally the same as aggregating individual demand curves in order to obtain the market demand curve (Section 3.1). The long-run industry supply curve is distinguished from the short-run supply curve (to be discussed shortly) not only by the length of the run but also by the fact that the number of active firms in the industry is not fixed: As the price of the product produced by the industry rises (say, because of an increase in demand), more firms will enter the industry. As the price falls (say, because of a fall in demand), firms will exit the industry. As explained in Section 7.2d, changes in price are interpreted by firms to be long run in nature if firms believe these changes will last for a relatively long time. Figure 8-1 illustrates the process of deriving the long-run marginal cost curves (above the respective minimum points of the LRAC curves). For the sake of geometric simplicity the horizontal sum of only three firms is derived. In reality, if only three firms were active in an industry, oligopoly would prevail (Chapter 13), and the concept of an industry supply curve would not be relevant.

Panel (a) of Figure 8-1 presents the long-run marginal cost curves (LRMC) of three firms, 1, 2, and 3, and their associated minimum points on the long-run average cost curves (LRAC), B, E, and G. The aggregation of these three curves is carried out in panel (b). The fact that the minimum points (B, E, and G) on the LRAC curves are dispersed is explained by considering the following three examples: (1) For various reasons firms may be located at different distances from the market. (Dairy farms, for instance, may be located at different distances from the city.) Thus the cost of shipping may be relatively high for faraway firms and very low for firms near the marketplace. (2) The cost of coal extraction will increase with the depth of the seam and decrease with the thickness of the seam. Thus a firm mining a shallow thick coal seam will show a low minimum LRAC as compared with a firm mining a relatively deep thin coal seam. (3) The cost of oil exploration and drilling is higher offshore than on dry land. The minimum LRAC of offshore crude oil production is thus higher than the minimum LRAC of

FIGURE 8-1 DERIVING THE LONG-RUN SUPPLY CURVE

Here we illustrate how the *long-run supply curve* of the industry is derived by aggregating the long-run marginal cost curves of the individual firms. Panel (*a*) shows the long-run marginal cost curves (LRMC) of three firms. The minimum points on the long-run average cost curves (LRAC) of the three firms are *B, E,* and *G.* As the (long-run) price rises from zero to some high level, a firm would join the industry only when the price is a cut above the minimum point on its LRAC. Thus the first firm joins only after the price is a cut above $\overline{OA}$, and then it expands along the LRMC$_1$ curve, and so on. The result of this process of aggregation is the curve *OKLNRTUV* in panel (*b*), which is the aggregate long-run supply curve of the three firms.

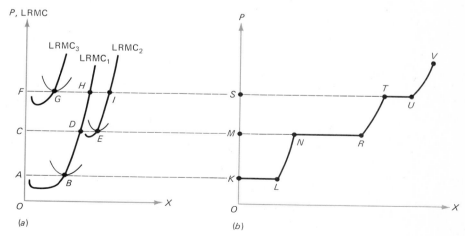

(a)   (b)

crude oil production on dry land. Even if physical conditions of production were identical, entrepreneurs are not born with identical managerial talents. The fact that entrepreneurs are widely diverse in their ability is sufficient to give rise to a dispersion of the minimum points of the LRAC curve, as illustrated in panel (a).

If the price is less than $\overline{OA}$ in panel (a), output supplied will be zero. At a price of $\overline{OA}$, Firm 1 would supply $\overline{AB}$ units, which is equal to $\overline{KL}$ in panel (b). As the price rises from $\overline{OA}$ to $\overline{OC}$, Firm 1 will expand along its long-run marginal cost curve LRMC$_1$ from point B to point D. The associated expansion in panel (b) is from point L to point N. Now, the minimum point of the LRAC curve of Firm 2 occurs at an $\overline{OC}$ price level. Accordingly, there will be a sudden supply increase of $\overline{CE}$ units due to the entry of Firm 2. In panel (b) this will be represented by a sudden increase in the quantity supplied amounting to $\overline{NR}$ units [which is equal to $\overline{CE}$ units in panel (a)]. As the price continues to rise from $\overline{OC}$ to the $\overline{OF}$ level, Firm 1 will expand from point D to point H, while Firm 2 will expand from point E to point I. The combined expansion of the two firms in panel (b) will be represented by a movement from point R to point T. As the price finally climbs to a level of $\overline{OF}$, Firm 3 will enter. The initial contribution of Firm 3 will be $\overline{FG}$ units [$\overline{TU}$ in panel (b)]. As the price continues to rise above the level of $\overline{OF}$, the combined expansion of the three firms along their respective long-run marginal cost curves is represented by UV in panel (b). In panel (b), the curve traced by $OKLNRTUV$ is the long-run industry supply curve. If the price were to fall (from a level higher than $\overline{OF}$ dollars), the industry would contract along the long-run supply curve in panel (b). The order of leaving the industry would be reversed: Firm 3 will exit first (at a price of $\overline{OF}$), then Firm 2 (at a price of $\overline{OC}$), and finally Firm 1 (at a price of $\overline{OA}$). This particular industry would come to an economic end.

Since the supply curve is obtained by a horizontal summation of all MC curves of all the firms in the industry, we can symbolically denote the supply curve as

$$S = \sum_{i=1}^{n} MC_i \tag{8-1}$$

What would be the shape of the long-run supply curve of the industry if all firms were identical? The answer is that the supply curve would be a horizontal straight line at the minimum of LRAC level. This topic is covered in Section 10.4.

8.2b Supply Elasticity

The supply curve in panel (b) of Figure 8-1 has kinks and flat segments. This is a result of the fact that the process of horizontal aggregation was illustrated with a small number of firms. Had the aggregation been carried out over a large number of firms, the result would be a supply curve which was smooth for all practical matters. Such a supply curve is shown in Figure 8-2.

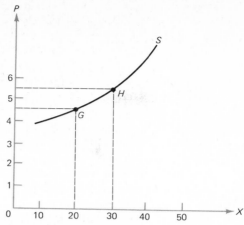

FIGURE 8-2 ILLUSTRATING SUPPLY ELASTICITY

The curve denoted by S is the (long-run) supply of an industry. As a result of exogenous changes in the marketplace (say, an increase in demand) the price confronting producers rises from $4.5 to $5.5. Producers respond by increasing their quantity supplied from 20 to 30 units per unit of time. The elasticity of supply between G and H is $\epsilon = (\Delta X/X)/(\Delta P/P) = (10/25)/(1/5) = 40$ percent/20 percent $= 2$.

We use this supply curve to illustrate the concept of supply elasticity. The *price elasticity of supply* measures the responsiveness of an industry to price changes. The concept of price elasticity of supply is formally identical with the price elasticity of demand (Section 2.4f). It is denoted by ϵ (epsilon) and defined as the relative change in quantity supplied over a small relative change in price. This is equivalent to the percentage change in quantity supplied by the industry per 1 percent change in price. It can be written as

$$\epsilon = \frac{\dfrac{\Delta X}{X}}{\dfrac{\Delta P}{P}} = \frac{\text{percentage change in quantity supplied}}{\text{percentage change in price}} \tag{8-2}$$

For example, S in Figure 8-2 represents a supply curve of a certain industry producing good X. When the price rises from $4.5 to $5.5, the quantity supplied by the industry increases from 20 to 30 units. The supply elasticity in the neighborhood of GH can be estimated by applying Equation 8-2. [The *arc* elasticity is calculated as in Section 2.2. Recall that we have the option to choose $\overline{X} = (X_0 + X_1)/2$, etc. Recall also (Section 2.2) that $\overline{X}$ is preferred to the endpoints X_0 and X_1 in Figure 2-1.]

$$\overline{X} = \frac{20 + 30}{2} = 25$$

$$\Delta X = 30 - 20 = 10$$

$$\overline{P} = \frac{5.5 + 4.5}{2} = \$5$$

$$\Delta P = 5.5 - 4.4 = \$1$$

Then,

$$\epsilon = \frac{\dfrac{10}{25}}{\dfrac{1}{5}} = \frac{40 \text{ percent}}{20 \text{ percent}} = 2$$

In the above example, a 20 percent change in price induced a 40 percent change in the quantity of X supplied by all the firms in the industry. An elasticity of 2 is valid only for the price range between \$4.5 and \$5.5. As in the case of demand (Section 2.4f), it would be incorrect to extrapolate and assume that supply elasticity is constant throughout. If economists sometimes assume that constant elasticity prevails throughout, they are motivated by mathematical convenience.[1]

8.2c An Example: Long-Run-Supply Elasticity of Natural Gas

Estimates of long-run-supply elasticity become crucial when shortages arise. [A shortage will be defined precisely in Chapter 9, but for the time being it means a situation in which the price is artificially fixed (by the government) at a level lower than the price at which consumers buy what producers produce.] Most economists would argue that given a shortage the price should be deregulated and allowed to climb to a relatively higher level. Such a rise in the price would induce the industry to respond by expanding its capacity and thus would increase its quantity supplied. Those who oppose deregulation would argue that if the supply curve is inelastic a rise in the price will induce only a small response. Naturally, if good estimates are not available, this would lead to debates on the magnitude of supply elasticity.

In 1977 and the beginning of 1978, the "to regulate or deregulate" debate was very hot. The federal administration wanted to continue the regulation of natural gas. The economic profession, almost without exception, recommended deregulation. The majority of senators opposed the administration. The result was a compromise which amounted to a gradual phasing out of regulation as it existed in 1977. The Wall Street Journal published an interesting article accompanied by a diagram with three supply curves of (conventional) natural gas.[2] This diagram is reproduced in Figure 8-3.

A group of ERDA (Energy Research and Development Administration) experts in the Market-Oriented Program Planning Study (MOPPS) approached the question three times. The result is known as the MOPPS Study. On April 1, 1977, the group came up with "estimate 1." It was "embarrassingly" high. As The Wall Street Journal reported, they tried again, and on April 6 they found less gas and came up with "estimate 2," which is a less elastic supply curve. Finally on June 3 the group published its most pessimistic supply curve of natural gas, which is denoted "estimate 3." It is the least elastic of the three estimates.

What is the supply elasticity which is implied by "estimate 3" in Figure 8-3? It is roughly estimated at 1.11 as follows:

$$\epsilon = \frac{\dfrac{520 - 260}{390}}{\dfrac{3.25 - 1.75}{2.5}} = 1.11$$

---

[1] The mathematical equation of the constant-elasticity supply curve is

$$X = H \cdot P^{\epsilon}$$

where H is a coefficient and ϵ is the constant elasticity of the supply curve. The logarithmic form of this supply curve is $\ln X = \ln H + \epsilon \cdot (\ln P)$. Differentiating, $dX/X = dH/H + \epsilon \cdot (dP/P)$. If $dH = 0$, we obtain the result that $\epsilon = (dX/X)/(dP/P)$. If $\epsilon = 1$, the supply equation reduces to $X = H \cdot P$, which is a ray sent from the origin.

[2] The Wall Street Journal, June 14, 1977.

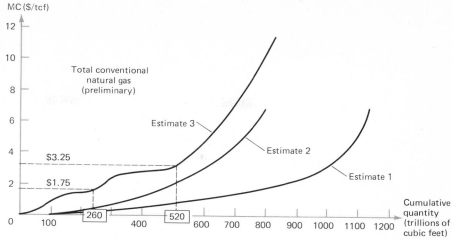

FIGURE 8-3 LONG-RUN SUPPLY OF NATURAL GAS
The cumulative supply of natural gas is measured along the horizontal axis. The student is reminded that *cumulative* supply indicates a *stock* rather then a *rate of production*. The price of natural gas is measured along the vertical axis. The three supply curves of natural gas reflect three estimates of elasticity. For *estimate 3* an elasticity of 1.11 was calculated. (*Source*: *The Wall Street Journal*, June 14, 1977.)

[Note that the quantities are given in trillions of cubic feet (TCF) while prices are in dollars per thousand cubic feet.] In other words, a 10 percent increase in the price of natural gas would lead to an 11 percent increase in the *cumulative*[3] quantity of available natural gas. (This estimate does not include the change in the supply of gas from nonconventional sources such as geopressurized methane.) According to *The Wall Street Journal*, Mr. White, MOPPS chairman, told the *Washington Post* that the original estimate ("estimate 1") might have been a "pretty good estimate."

The upshot of all this is that when the energy crisis erupted, economists should have attempted to estimate the long-run supply elasticity of energy resources such as natural gas. Failure to do so diminished the force of their arguments. We also learn from the "natural gas story" that our ability to estimate empirical elasticities of supply falls short of our ability to estimate empirical elasticities of demand.

8.2d Short-Run Supply Curves

The short-run industry supply curve is related to the long-run industry supply curve as the short-run marginal cost curve of the firm is related to the long-run marginal cost curve of the firm. As explained in Section 7.2g, firms formulate their expectations regarding the long-run price. Based on these expectations, they select a long-run plant size. If firms later realize that the long-run price either exceeded or fell short of their expectations, they vary their output along their respective short-run marginal cost curve. The possibility also exists that prices may fluctuate during a year or from year to year,

---

[3]Cumulative means a *stock* to be distinguished from a *flow*. The topic of *stocks* versus *flows* was discussed in Sections 2.1 and 5.1. Note that unlike land, which is a permanent stock, natural gas is nonrenewable.

or both. Firms will then select plant sizes to fit some average price. They will respond to temporary price fluctuations by moving up and down along their short-run marginal cost curves. Such a short-run marginal cost curve was illustrated in Figure 7-6. The long-run price was assumed to be P_0, and accordingly a short-run marginal cost curve intersected with the long-run marginal cost at that price level. (E was the point of intersection.) Hence, given a long-run price, we can in principle draw the short-run marginal cost curves for all the firms in the industry (which intersect with the associated long-run marginal cost curves at that price level). *The short-run industry supply curve is derived by horizontally aggregating all short-run marginal cost curves.* From the above analysis two points emerge:

1. To each point on the long-run industry supply curve there corresponds a short-run industry supply curve. The short-run supply curve is less elastic than the long-run supply curve.

2. In the short run the number of firms is fixed. This is true because the number of firms is determined by the long-run price and not by the short-run price.

The short-run and long-run industry supply curves are presented in Figure 8-4. The short-run industry supply curve is denoted by SRS, and the long-run supply curve is denoted by LRS. The long-run price is P_0. If the price remained stable at a level of P_0 for a long period, the industry would supply a quantity of X_0 units per unit of time. If in the short run the price sometimes rose to a level of P_1 and sometimes fell to a level of P_2 (say, because of seasonal demand changes), the industry would respond by moving along the SRS curve, sometimes expanding output to a level of X_1^s and sometimes contracting to a level of X_2^s. However, should the price rise to a level of P_1 and stabilize there, and should the firms in the industry perceive this as a permanent change, the industry would first expand along the SRS curve and increase its output to a level of X_1^s. Then, given some time for adjustment, firms would adjust the size of plants and move to the point where the price line P_1 cuts the long-run supply curve LRS. Output would increase to a level of X_1^l. At that point the number of firms in the industry may have increased. If the price were to fall to a level of P_2 and stabilize there, in the short run the industry would contract along the SRS curve to a level of output of X_2^s. However, given time for adjustment, firms will decrease the size of their plants and the industry will retreat to its LRS curve; output will shrink to a level of X_2^l units per unit of time. The number of firms in the industry may also shrink.

The above analysis can now be summarized as follows:

To each point on the long-run supply curve of the industry there corresponds a short-run supply curve. The short-run supply curve is less elastic than the long-run supply curve.

For simplicity of exposition we pretended that only one short-run supply curve is associated with each point on the long-run supply curve. Section 6.5g demonstrated that there exists as many "runs" as there are variable

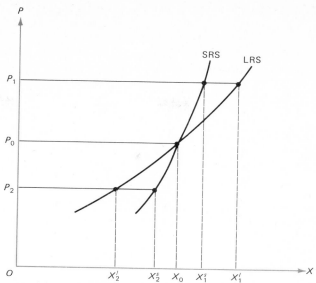

FIGURE 8-4 SHORT-RUN AND LONG-RUN SUPPLY CURVES
LRS is the long-run supply curve. The industry reaches equilibrium when it produces
(supplies) a quantity of X_0 units in response to a price of P_0. If in the short run the price were
to fluctuate between P_1 and P_2, the industry would respond by expanding along the short-run
supply curve (SRS), producing X_1^s at a price of P_1 and X_2^s at a price of P_2. If the price were to
rise to a level of P_1 and stay there permanently, the industry would first expand along SRS
and increase its output to a level of X_1^s. Given time for adjustment, the firms in the industry
would adjust their size and increase output to a level of X_1^l. If the price confronting the firms
were to fall to a level of P_2 and remain at that low level permanently, firms would first contract along the SRS curve, and the quantity supplied would first shrink to a level of X_2^s; in the
long run firms would adjust their size, and quantity supplied would shrink further to X_2^l. In
summary, SRS is less elastic than LRS.

factors involved in the process of production. In the shortest of all short runs
firms in the industry may be able to vary only raw material and energy; the
short-run supply curve is very inelastic. Given some additional time for
adaptation, the firms may be able to vary the amount of labor; the intermediate short-run supply curve is thus more elastic. The longest of all short-
run supply curves may represent a situation in which all firms vary all
variable inputs but the number of firms in the industry is fixed.

8.2e An Example: Supply of Agricultural Commodities

The theory of industry supply predicts that firms respond to a higher price by producing more. In the
case of farming, an interesting question arises: What
price? Definitely it would be wrong to claim that farmers respond to the currrent price. The price of corn in
the fall is a result of the acreage that was seeded with
corn in the spring. To correct for this, economists
used to estimate the supply of agricultural crops by
lagging the price one year, that is, by assuming that
the quantity supplied this year is a response to the
price of last year. This method did not yield satisfac-
tory results; price elasticities seemed to be too low. A

study by Marc Nerlove introduced a breakthrough in the method of estimating supply functions.[4] In estimating his supply function, Nerlove used acreage as a proxy for supply. For example, if acreage seeded with corn increased by 10 percent from one year to the next, he assumed that quantity supplied roughly increased by 10 percent. He formulated an idea of expected price, which he illustrated as follows: Suppose farmers expect this year a price of $2.00 per bushel of wheat. They realize a price of $1.90 in the market. Should they conclude that next year the price would be $1.90? Nerlove said that farmers would revise their expectations downward, but not all the way. If they revise their expectations downward to $1.94, their *expectation coefficient* is 0.6 (60 percent). It is surprising to note that if farmers, say, at the end of 1949, knew the price of wheat in 1949 and in previous years, they could (intuitively) formulate a forecast of the 1950 price as follows:

$$P_{1950} = 0.6 \cdot P_{1949} + (0.4)(0.6) \cdot P_{1948} + (0.4)^2(0.6) \cdot P_{1947} + \cdots$$

which means that farmers formulate their expected price for next year by taking a weighted average of past prices, where the weights decline more the farther the past year is from the present.

Nerlove formulated a method by which he could estimate both the supply elasticity and the expectation coefficient. His results for the period 1909–1932 are given in Table 8-1.

Since the study by Nerlove was published, a variety of supply curves have been estimated successfully. The upshot of all this is that producers do not just look at the price in the previous season but rather account for several seasons in order to forecast the price next season.

8.3 A CHANGE IN THE PRICE OF A FACTOR

8.3a One Variable Factor

When the price of a factor of production rises, the marginal cost also increases; or in other words, *ceteris paribus*, a rise in the price of an input entails an upward shift in the MC curve, while a decline in the price of an input gives rise to a downward shift in the MC curve. Consider the case in which only one input is variable. Let the production function be $X = f(A, B)$, where B is the fixed factor and A is the variable factor. Recall that under such conditions the marginal cost curve is $MC = P_a/MP_a$ (Equation 6-10). Notice also that if only one input is variable the firm cannot mitigate the impact of a rise in the price of A by using less A and more of another variable input. This situation in which only one factor is variable is typical of the short run and atypical of the long run. For example, oil may be the only variable input in the process of generating electric power in the short run. Thus a 10 percent rise in the price of oil will result in a 10 percent upward shift in the short-run marginal cost of electricity. As an example consider the production function $X = \sqrt{B \cdot A}$. Assume that $X = 10$ units of output, $A = 10$ worker-hours, and $B = 10$ machine-hours. Assume that the price of one worker-hour is $4. Applying the method of Section 5.2e, we can calculate MP_a at that point as equal to 0.5. [For example, if ΔA is 0.01, the calculation is carried out as follows: $0.5 = (\sqrt{10 \cdot 10.01} - \sqrt{10 \cdot 10})/(10.01 - 10)$.] Then marginal cost for $X = 10$ is calculated to be $MC = \$4/0.5 = \$8$. If the price of

---

[4]Marc Nerlove, "Estimates of the Elasticities of Supply of Selected Agricultural Commodities," *Journal of Farm Economics*, vol. 33, May 1956, pp. 496–509.

TABLE 8-1 Long-Run-Supply Elasticities of Farm Commodities

Crop	Long-run elasticity (with respect to expected price)	Coefficient of expectation
Cotton	0.67	0.51
Wheat	0.93	0.52
Corn	0.18	0.54

Source: Marc Nerlove, "Estimates of the Elasticities of Supply of Selected Commodities," *Journal of Farm Economics,* vol. 33, May 1956, pp. 496–509.

labor were to rise by 10 percent, the new marginal cost would be MC = $4.4/0.5 = $8.8. We can summarize the above results as follows:

> *If (in the short run) firms in a certain industry use only one variable input, a rise in the price of that input would lead to an equiproportionate rise in the marginal cost of each firm. A fall in the price of that input would lead to an equiproportionate fall in the marginal cost curve of each firm. Since the supply curve is the horizontal aggregate of all marginal cost curves, the supply curve of the industry will shift vertically equiproportionately to the change in the price of the variable input.*

So far we have not mentioned the impact of industry expansion (contraction) on factor prices. We have assumed that the industry supply curve is the sum of all firms' MC curves; MC curves (for a single input) were defined as P_a/MP_a, where P_a is fixed. This formulation of the industry supply is only a first approximation to the extent that the elasticities of supply of the variable factors are less than infinite. If the supply of factor A confronting the industry is positively sloped, an expansion along the supply curve of the industry must imply an increase in the employment of input A and thus a rise in the price of A. Since MC = P_a/MP_a, a rise in the price of A must displace the marginal cost curve of every firm in the industry in the upward direction. Thus, while it is always true that the industry supply curve is the sum of all firms' MC curves, if the supply of the input confronting the industry is positively sloped, the MC curves are displaced as the individual firms expand (contract) along these curves. This issue will be discussed in Chapter 9.

The results obtained for the case of a single variable input can easily be extended to the case of two or more variable factors of production; it is intuitively clear that if A and B are variable inputs, the impact of a rise in the price of A will be mitigated by substituting B for A; hence a 10 percent rise in the price of A will lead to a less than 10 percent upward shift in the MC curve. The student who is interested in a more formal approach to the case of two or more variable inputs is referred to the next section.

8.3b More Than One Factor Is Variable (Optional)

Let us assume that the production function is $X = f(A,B,H)$; A and B are variable inputs and H is fixed. Factors A and B are *competitive* with one another (Section 5.6). Figure 8.5 illustrates the impact of a rise in the price of A on MC. First, in panel (a), C_0 represents an isocost with the slope of $-P_{a0}/P_{b0}$. This isocost is tangent to an isoquant for $X = X_0$ at point R. Thus the least-cost combination of factors is A_0 units of A and B_0 units of B, respectively, per unit of time (Section 6.5b). As shown in panels (b) and (c), the associated marginal physical products are MP_{a0} and MP_{b0}, respectively.[5] In panel (d), MC_0 is the marginal cost curve corresponding to $P_b = P_{b0}$ and $P_a = P_{a0}$. In particular, when the least-cost combination of A_0 and B_0 is used to produce X_0 units of output, the marginal cost is mc_0 as follows (Equation 6-15):

$$mc_0 = \frac{P_{a0}}{MP_{a0}} = \frac{P_{b0}}{MP_{b0}}$$

Segment mc_0 in panel (d) is the vertical distance between the horizontal axis and the MC_0 curve at $X = X_0$. Suppose the price of A rises 10 percent, namely, $P_{a1} = 1.1 \cdot P_{a0}$. As a result, the isocost in panel (a) rotates to a new position depicted by C', with a new slope $-P_{a1}/P_{b0}$. The new point of tangency is S, where the least-cost combination for the production of X_0 is A_1 units of A and B_1 units of B: The firm has substituted B for A. In panel (b) the fall in the amount of A leads to an increase in MP_a from MP_{a0} to MP_{a1}. In panel (c) the increase in the amount of B gives rise to a decline in MP_b from MP_{b0} to MP_{b1}. The new marginal cost associated with the production of X_0 will be

$$mc_1 = \frac{P_{a1}}{MP_{a1}} = \frac{P_{b0}}{MP_{b1}}$$

Consider the above equation for mc_1. First we see that mc_1 exceeds mc_0 by focusing on factor B. The inequality

$$mc_1 = \frac{P_{b0}}{MP_{b1}} > \frac{P_{b0}}{MP_{b0}} = mc_0$$

holds because as indicated by panel (c) MP_{b1} is smaller than MP_{b0}. Thus mc_1 must be greater than MC_0. Second, we see that mc_1 changes less in proportion to the change in the price of A. Since in the example $P_{a1} = 1.1 \cdot P_{a0}$, we should be able to show that $mc_1 < 1.1 \cdot mc_0$, namely, that mc has increased by less than 10 percent. To prove it, we now focus on factor A in the mc_1 equation. The inequality

$$mc_1 = \frac{P_{a1}}{MP_{a1}} = \frac{1.1 \cdot P_{a0}}{MP_{a1}} < 1.1 \frac{P_{a0}}{MP_{a0}} = 1.1 \, mc_0$$

holds because, as indicated by panel (b), MP_{a1} exceeds MP_{a0}. Thus mc_1 is less than $1.1 \cdot mc_0$. Since what was proved for X_0 can apply to any level of

---

[5] To simplify the presentation, the cross relationship between MP_b and the amount of A employed and MP_a and the amount of B employed (Section 5.6) was not specified. If the common positive relationships are assumed, the MP_b curve would shift downward and the MP_a curve would shift upward. This would not change our previous results.

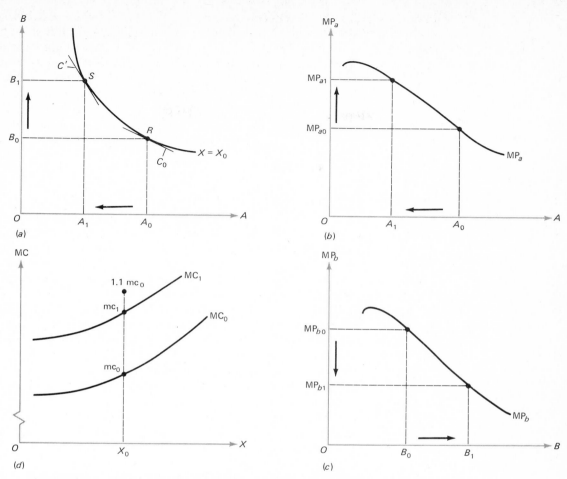

FIGURE 8-5 THE IMPACT OF A RISE IN THE PRICE OF A FACTOR ON
THE SUPPLY CURVE

Originally $P_a = P_{a0}$, $P_b = P_{b0}$. Given a production function $X = f(A, B, H)$, where A and B are variable and H is fixed, the marginal cost is mc_0. This initial situation corresponds to the following points in the diagrams: Panel (a): The isocost C_0 just touches the isoquant $X = X_0$ at point R. The firm employs A_0 units of A and B_0 units of B. Panel (b): As indicated by the MP_a curve, MP_{a0} is associated with A_0 units of input A. Panel (c): As indicated by the MP_b curve, MP_{b0} is associated with B_0 units of B. Panel (d): The firm produces $X_0 = f(A_0, B_0, H)$ units. The marginal cost is $mc_0 = P_{a0}/MP_{a0} = P_{b0}/MP_{b0}$. The initial (partial) equilibrium is disturbed by a rise in the price of A by 10 percent: $P_{a1} = 1.1P_{a0}$. The resulting changes in the diagrams: Panel (a): The point of tangency travels along the isoquant in the northwesterly direction (from R to S); the amount of A employed reduces from A_0 to A_1; the amount of B employed increases from B_0 to B_1. Panel (b): As A shrinks from A_0 to A_1, as indicated by the MP_a curve, MP_a rises from MP_{a0} to MP_{a1}. Panel (c): As B increases from B_0 to B_1, as indicated by the MP_b curve, MP_b diminishes from MP_{b0} to MP_{b1}. Panel (d): The new marginal cost for X_0 is $mc_1 = P_{a1}/MP_{a1} = P_{b0}/MP_{b1}$. Note that mc_1 is higher than mc_0 because $P_{b0}/MP_{b1} > P_{b0}/MP_{b0}$; as explained in the text mc_1, is smaller than $1.1 mc_0$.

output, we reach the conclusion that the MC curve shifted upward, but by less than 10 percent. Also, since the marginal cost curve of each firm in the industry will shift upward by less than 10 percent, the industry supply curve will shift upward by less than 10 percent. The findings of Sections 8.3a and 8.3b can be summarized as follows:

A rise in the price of a variable factor of production will lead to an upward shift in the industry supply curve; a fall in a price of a variable factor will lead to a downward shift in the industry supply curve. The supply curve will shift less in proportion to the change in the price of the variable input.

8.4 TECHNOLOGICAL PROGRESS: A SPECIAL CASE

Technological progress is achieved through better organization and management, through changing the technical process of production, or by educating and training labor power. The simple but useful case known as the *neutral shift in the production function will be discussed. A neutral technological progress can be defined as a change in the process of production enabling the firm to produce more by employing the same set of inputs that were employed before the change.* A neutral technological change raises the MPs of all factors by the same percentage. For example, after farmers adopted use of hybrid corn seeds, their crops increased significantly. Employing the same combination of land, fertilizers, machinery, and labor, a farmer would obtain a greater crop by switching to hybrid corn seeds. This example will be discussed in more detail in the next chapter.

Technological progress is relevant to supply because it leads to a reduction in the cost of production. In particular, it results in a downward shift in the marginal cost curve of the firm and hence a downward shift in the entire industry supply curve. The impact of neutral technological progress on the MC curve can be illustrated by considering again the simple production function $X = \sqrt{B \cdot A}$, where B is held constant at 10 units. Assume that the price of the variable input A is \$4. As shown in Section 8.3a, when 10 units of A are employed, output is 10 units per unit of time and marginal cost is \$8 (= \$4/0.5). If the use of A is increased to 12.1 units, output will rise to 11 units per unit of time. The marginal physical product of the variable input A will fall to 0.454 [$\sqrt{10 \cdot 12.11} - \sqrt{10 \cdot 12.1})/(12.11 - 12.1)$]. The marginal cost will be \$8.8 (= \$4/0.454). The marginal cost curve that passes through these two points is denoted by MC_0 (Figure 8-6). Let us now introduce a coefficient K, which will reflect the change in technology. We may express the general production function as

$$X = K \cdot f(A,B) \tag{8-3}$$

For the particular production function, we write $X = K \cdot \sqrt{B \cdot A}$. In the example, before the technological progress, $K = 1$, $A = 10$, $B = 10$, and $X = 10$. Assume that a technological innovation is introduced such that productivity increases 10 percent: Employing the same set of inputs will result in producing 10 percent more than originally.

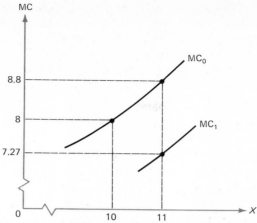

FIGURE 8-6 AN ILLUSTRATION OF THE IMPACT OF TECHNOLOGICAL PROGRESS ON THE MC CURVE

MC_0 is a marginal cost curve derived from a production function $X = \sqrt{A \cdot B}$, where B is held fixed at 10 units, and assuming that P_a, the price of the variable input, is $4. When 10 units are produced, marginal cost is $8. A 10 percent shift in the production function (K increases from 1 to 1.1) would increase output from 10 to 11 units. Also, such technological progress would increase MP_a by 10 percent (from 0.5 to 0.55), resulting in a fall in the marginal cost from $8 to $7.27 ($8 = $4/0.5, $7.27 = $4/0.55). In principle, the new MC_1 curve can be drawn by applying this procedure point by point.

In the example, the new level of technology is achieved by increasing K from 1 to 1.1, namely, by revising the production function to be $X = 1.1\sqrt{B \cdot A}$. In particular, when 10 units of A and 10 units of B are employed, output is 11 units per unit of time as follows:

$$X = 1.1\sqrt{10 \cdot 10} = 11$$

However, the new marginal physical product of input A increases as follows:

$$\text{New } MP_a = \frac{1.1\sqrt{10 \cdot 10.01} - 1.1\sqrt{10 \cdot 10}}{10.01 - 10}$$

$$= 1.1 \frac{\sqrt{10 \cdot 10.01} - \sqrt{10 \cdot 10}}{10.01 - 10}$$

$$= 1.1 \cdot 0.5 = 0.55$$

The new marginal cost associated with 11 units of output will be $7.27, which is calculated by dividing a marginal physical product of 0.55 into the price of A, namely, $4. *Note:* The new marginal cost of $7.27 is lower than the marginal cost of $8, which corresponded to a lower level of output. Since only the upward-sloping portion of the marginal cost curve is relevant for purposes of deriving the supply curve (Section 7.2c, sufficient condition for profit maximization), technological progress as described above must lead to a downward shift in the industry supply curve.

The above results can be generalized as follows: The marginal physical product of any factor of production (say, factor A) is

$$\text{MP}_a = \frac{\Delta X}{\Delta A} = \frac{X_1 - X_0}{A_1 - A_0}$$

Let us denote MP_a, ΔX, and X after the technological improvement is absorbed by the firm by $\overline{\text{MP}_a}$, $\overline{\Delta X}$, and $\overline{X}$. Then (for a 10 percent shift)

$$\overline{\text{MP}}_a = \frac{\overline{\Delta X}}{\Delta A} = \frac{\overline{X_1} - \overline{X_0}}{A_1 - A_0} = \frac{1.1 X_1 - 1.1 X_0}{A_1 - A_0}$$

$$= \frac{1.1(X_1 - X_0)}{A_1 - A_0} = \frac{1.1 \Delta X}{\Delta A} = 1.1 \cdot \text{MP}_a$$

Therefore, if the effect of the technological change is to increase the productivity of the firm by 10 percent, the marginal physical product of any factor will also increase by 10 percent. If K is originally unity and then, to represent a 10 percent technological change, it rises to a level of 1.1, the marginal cost for a level of output of $1.1 \cdot X_0$ units is given by (Equation 6-15)

$$\overline{\text{mc}} = \frac{P_a}{1.1 \text{MP}_a} = \frac{P_b}{1.1 \text{MP}_b} = \cdots = \frac{P_n}{1.1 \text{MP}_n} = \frac{\text{mc}_0}{1.1}$$

where mc_0 is associated with X_0 units of output.

This can be summarized as follows:

Technological progress in the form of a neutral technological innovation will result in a downward shift of the industry supply curve.

To appreciate the full impact of technological progress, market (supply and demand) analysis is required. Accordingly, the discussion of some examples of technological innovation will be postponed to the next chapter.

8.5 DO PEASANTS IN DEVELOPING COUNTRIES RESPOND TO CHANGES IN CROP PRICES?

Section 2.4e discussed briefly the alleged *vicious circle* of underdeveloped countries and argued against the allegation that people in developing countries have fixed wants and that when their earnings rise they reduce the amount of work performed. Another allegation, prevalent in the economic literature on developing countries, is that peasants in the traditional milieu do not respond to prices of crops. The usual conceit is either that peasants respond inversely to changes in prices of crops, or that supply curves of crops are inelastic and thus economic policies for developing countries should not rely heavily on market mechanism.

Whether or not peasants in developing countries respond to prices of crops is an empirical issue which must be settled empirically. In fact, if peasants respond positively to price changes, the supply curves of farm products should slope positively. On the other hand, if farmers are apathetic to prices or if they respond inversely to price changes, supply curves should be vertical or slope negatively, respectively. The following example illustrates how the hypothesis that peasants lack sensitivity (or display inverse sensitivity) to changes in crop prices was tested and rejected.

8.5a An Example: Farm Supply Response in the Punjab

Until Raj Krishna completed his study, the proposition that peasants in developing countries are apathetic to crop price changes was almost universally accepted by Indian economists. Krishna wrote: "For all we know, many of the prevailing views about peasants' responses may, in fact, be true. The point emphasized here is simply that they have not been, but they must be, subjected to adequate empirical tests before they are accepted or rejected."[6] Krishna studied the response of the Punjab peasants to changes in prices of cotton (and wheat). Following Nerlove (Section 8.2e), he formulated a supply of "American" (long-staple) cotton in the Punjab based on data from 1922 to 1944. Planted irrigated acres were used as a proxy for the quantity of cotton supplied. To obtain a *relative price* for "American" cotton, Krishna deflated the postharvest price index of "American" cotton by an index of the prices of six alternative competing summer crops (including the local variety of cotton). The result of the study was that the long-run elasticity of the supply of "American" cotton in the Punjab was 0.75. This compares favorably with a long-run elasticity of 0.67 for cotton in the United States obtained by Nerlove (Section 8.2e). The conclusion reached by Krishna was: "It appears that cotton farmers in the Punjab were at least as sensitive to price incentives as their counterparts in the U.S.A."

Thus policy makers in developing countries cannot base their policies on the proposition that peasants are insensitive to crop prices. The least they should do is follow Raj Krishna and study the supply functions of crops.

SUMMARY   The *long-run supply curve of the industry* was defined as the aggregate of all *long-run marginal cost curves* of the active and potential firms in that industry. The process of aggregation was performed by adding horizontally all long-run marginal cost curves of all firms where the lowest price at which a firm would begin production is the minimum of the long-run average cost curve. Symbolically, the supply curve (short-and long-run) was defined as

$$S = \sum_{i}^{n} \text{MC}_i.$$

Supply elasticity was defined as the relative change in the quantity supplied over a small relative change in the price. It was stressed that knowledge of supply elasticity is extremely important in practical application; as an example the debate on the issue of deregulation of natural gas in the mid and late 1970s was described. Knowledge of the size of supply elasticity would have told policy makers whether or not producers of natural gas would respond with large discoveries of gas to relatively small increases in the price of natural gas in the marketplace.

Next, *short-run supply curves* were defined as the aggregate of *short-run marginal cost curves* of all firms in an industry. It was concluded that since to each point on the long-run marginal cost curve of a firm (above the

---

[6] Raj Krishna, "Farm Supply Response in the Punjab (India-Pakistan), A Case Study of Cotton," unpublished Ph.D. dissertation, Department of Economics, Univerisity of Chicago, Chicago, 1961.

minimum of the LRAC) there corresponds a short-run marginal cost curve, it must be true that to each point on the long-run supply curve of an industry there also corresponds a short-run supply curve. The short-run supply curve is less elastic than the long-run supply curve. If prices fluctuate around some average price, either from season to season or from year to year, firms in the industry would tailor their size in the long run to fit this average price, as indicated by their long-run supply curves. Firms would respond to these price fluctuations by expanding and contracting (together) along the short-run supply curve. A permanent change in price would induce firms in an industry to first move (together) along their short-run supply curve, and only in the long run adjust by varying their sizes, thus moving to the optimal point on the long-run supply curve. What this means is that a change in price in the short run will lead to a smaller change in quantity supplied than in the long run.

In conjunction with this topic, it was mentioned that given seasonal production, as in agriculture, the current price observed in the market is not normally the price which guides producers when making decisions about the future. Producers are likely to formulate their expectations based on some weighted average of past prices, where the weights increase from the past to the present.

Next the case of a change in a price of a variable input was analyzed. It was concluded that a rise in the price of a variable input will lead to an upward shift in the supply curve, and conversely, a decline in the price of a variable input will lead to downward shift in the supply curve.

Then a special case in *technological progress* known as a *neutral shift in the production function* (e.g., hybrid corn in agriculture) was analyzed. The conclusion was reached that the main impact of such technological progress is to lower marginal cost, that is, to shift downward the supply curve of the industry benefiting from the innovation.

Finally, the issue was investigated of whether or not peasants in developing countries respond to price changes as do producers in developed countries. It was concluded that in order to test whether peasants in developing countries do or do not respond to price changes, elasticity of the relevant supply curve must be evaluated. An example is a study of farm supply response to price changes in the Punjab (India). This study showed that Punjab peasants are at least as sensitive to price variations in agricultural crops as are farmers in the United States.

GLOSSARY **Industry** A subset of firms engaged in the production of a good X (e.g., pencils) or a variety of goods that are substitutes in consumption (e.g., soft drinks). Sometimes an industry may be engaged in the production of a variety of products that are joint products in the process of production but are not closely related in consumption (e.g., the petroleum refining industry produces both energy products and medical commodities).

The industry supply curve A curve (or function) telling how much an industry would produce per unit of time at a given price. The industry supply curve is obtained by aggregating all marginal cost curves of all firms in the industry; formally, it is written as

$$S = \sum_{i}^{n} MC_i.$$

The long-run supply curve of the industry, which relates long-run quantities supplied to long-run prices, is derived by aggregating the long-run marginal cost curves of the firms in the industry. The short-run supply curve of the industry relates quantities supplied by the industry to price fluctuations around some average price, or the short-run response of an industry to a long-run (permanent) change in price. Short-run supply curves are less elastic than long-run supply curves. *Ceteris paribus* (technology and prices of inputs are fixed), only one long-run supply curve is associated with each competitive industry; through each point on the long-run supply curve there passes at least one short-run supply curve.

Supply elasticity A relative change in the quantity supplied over a small relative change in price. Formally $\epsilon = (\Delta X/X)/(\Delta P/P)$.

Expected price When production is seasonal, producers (farmers) formulate their price expectation by taking a weighted average of past prices, where the weight increases with time going from the past to the present.

Neutral technological progress A change in the process of production enabling the firm to produce more without changing either the amount of inputs (scale) or the mix of the factors. Formally, the production function can be expressed as $X = K \cdot f(A, B)$; a neutral technological progress would be embodied in the coefficient K. For example, a neutral technological progress leading to 10 percent additional output without any change in inputs could be expressed by increasing K from 1 to 1.1. Neutral technological progress results in a downward shift in the supply curve of the industry.

PROBLEMS An asterisk indicates an advanced problem.

8-1. The supply elasticity is equal to 3. By how much will production increase as a result of a 10 percent rise in price?

8-2. It is believed that, *ceteris paribus*, raising the salaries of teachers by 15 percent will entail a 30 percent increase in the number of people who apply for openings in schools. Estimate the supply elasticity of teachers.

8-3. The supply elasticity is ½. $P_0 = 10$ cents. What is the necessary (absolute) change in the price that will induce a 10 percent increase in the quantity supplied?

8-4. Currently the quantity supplied by industry X amounts to 100 units. The prevailing price is $10, and elasticity is estimated at 2. Estimate the additional producer's-surplus and additional total variable costs resulting from a $1 rise in the market price. (Use P_0 and X_0 to estimate ΔX.)

8-5.* Would the results of Section 8.3b change if the law of positive relationship were added to the law of diminishing marginal physical product?

8-6. Labor and electricity are the only variable inputs used in the production of whatnots. Currently the wage rate is $4 per hour. If the wage rate increases by $1, would the long-run supply curve shift by less than 25 percent, exactly 25 percent, or more than 25 percent? What would your answer be regarding the short-run supply of whatnots (in the short run only labor is varied)?

8-7. The whatnot industry is benefiting from technological progress, which may be summarized as being equivalent to a 15 percent neutral shift in the production function of whatnots.
(a) How would the supply of whatnots shift?
(b) Explain why it is impossible to calculate the precise percentage shift in the supply curve.

8-8. Imposing a fixed tax (a tax not related to output) of $5000 per annum on each firm in industry X is contemplated by the government. Is it true that since the fixed tax does not affect the marginal cost curves of the firms in the industry, the industry supply curve would not be affected?

8-9. Prove that if the supply curve is a straight line starting at the origin, supply elasticity always equals 1.

8-10. If the supply of a variable input (A) confronting an industry is positively sloped, the MC curves should be adjusted before we sum them to derive the industry supply curve. Explain.

MATHEMATICAL APPENDIX 8

M8.1 THE MARGINAL COST CURVE ASSOCIATED WITH THE COBB-DOUGLAS PRODUCTION FUNCTION

Recall that the Cobb-Douglas production function is $X = K \cdot A^\alpha B^\beta$ (Section m5.5). Also recall that for the Cobb-Douglas case $\mathrm{MP}_a = \alpha(X/A)$ and $\mathrm{MP}_b = \beta(X/B)$. Since $MC = P_a/\mathrm{MP}_a = P_b/\mathrm{MP}_b$, we can substitute in the production function and obtain

$$X = K \cdot \left(\frac{\alpha \cdot X \cdot \mathrm{MC}}{P_a} \right)^\alpha \cdot \left(\frac{\beta \cdot X \cdot \mathrm{MC}}{P_b} \right)^\beta$$

The solution for MC is

$$\mathrm{MC} = G \cdot [K^{-1} \cdot X^{1-(\alpha+\beta)} \cdot P_a^\alpha \cdot P_b^\beta]^{1/(\alpha+\beta)} \qquad (m8\text{-}1)$$

where G is a coefficient involving α and β. To have a rising MC curve $(\alpha + \beta) < 1$. Notice the following:

1. The powers of P_a and P_b, respectively, are smaller than unity. Hence, when the price of a variable factor (either P_a or P_b) rises, the MC curve shifts upward less than proportionately.

2. The power of the coefficient K (the production function shifter) is negative. Also, in absolute value it is greater than unity [$(\alpha + \beta) < 1$]. Hence a neutral technological innovation (which increases K) must lead to a downward shift in the MC curve.

3. The power of X is positive and less than unity. This implies a rising MC curve.

PART THREE

PERFECT COMPETITION, THE THEORY OF SUPPLY AND DEMAND

The first four chapters focused on consumers. Since consumers are too insignificant to have any appreciable influence on the market price, they are price takers. In other words, in the theory of the consumer (demand), price enters as an *exogenous* variable. The next four chapters considered competitive producers (firms). Like consumers, competitive producers are too insignificant to have any appreciable influence on the market price; like consumers, they are price takers. Accordingly, in the theory of the producer (supply), price enters as an *exogenous* variable. The unanswered question remains: If both consumers and competitive producers are price takers, how is the price determined in the marketplace? If the theory of the consumer (demand) or the theory of the competitive producer (supply) when considered alone is comparable with a single blade of a scissors, it is clear that two blades are required to cut the price. Indeed, a major task in Chapter 9 will be to show how, when demand and supply are brought together, the price is determined by what are called the supply and demand forces. Moreover, when demand and supply are considered simultaneously, the price becomes an *endogenous* variable of the market system.

Chapter 9 is the culmination of the first eight chapters; in it we finally see how the "invisible hand" of the market provides signals to millions of producers who interact in the marketplace with millions of consumers who purchase from the producers thousands of commodities and services.

The special problems that arise in competitive markets are numerous and interesting; *indirect taxes*, *foreign trade*, and the economics of *market regulation* are just a few. Chapter 10 contains supply and demand analysis of some of these special topics. The organization of Chapter 10, which is optional, allows readers to select whatever topic they may find interesting. A reader in a rush to cover as much basic theory as possible may skip Chapter 10 altogether.

At this point the student will benefit from reviewing the *circular flow model* as illustrated in Figure I-2. In particular, observe the role of the markets-for-finished-goods box in that model.

CHAPTER

9

THE COMPETITIVE MARKET

The demand and supply theories considered separately in previous chapters can now be brought together. In this chapter we shall first see how market equilibrium is determined by the forces of supply and demand. The next step will be to examine how changes in exogenous factors give rise to either demand shifts or supply shifts, leading to changes in market equilibrium. In particular, focus will be on some cases of supply shifts that are unique, e.g., technological progress. Chapter 8 just touched on the issue of external diseconomies; in this chapter we shall have a chance to explore this interesting topic further. We shall then turn our attention to price movement over time, a topic that will be discussed again in Chapters 10 and 16. The final major step in this chapter will be to examine the issue of rent and the zero-profit theorem.

9.1 THE DICHOTOMY BETWEEN CONSUMERS AND PRODUCERS

Because consumers and producers are two separate groups that interact in the marketplace, it seems appropriate here to devote some thought to the consumer-producer dichotomy. Consider Figure 9-1. Let circle A represent all consumers of shoes and circle B represent all shoe producers. Circle B is smaller than circle A to remind us that in real life there are many more consumers than producers. Thus there are in the diagram[1] two sets: a set of consumers and a set of producers. The intersection of the two sets A and B is the shaded area. An intersection symbolizes a person who is employed in the shoemaking industry and who also wears shoes. The assumption underlying modern microeconomic analysis is that the intersection of consumers and producers is a negligible share of the entire population. As an example, suppose tastes change and people want to wear more shoes than before. The result is that shoe producers would produce more shoes and thus their income would increase; this, however, has no appreciable impact on the income of the entire population.

Let us now see how the interaction between consumers and producers in the market results in market equilibrium.

9.2 MARKET EQUILIBRIUM

9.2a The Intersection between Supply and Demand

Before the determination of the price in the marketplace is discussed, we should be aware of the distinction between a *stable* and an *unstable* equilibrium. Consider this example: If you place a ball at the bottom of a valley, it is in a stable equilibrium; if you kick it, it will return to its original position by gravitational forces. However, if you place a ball at the top of a hill, it is not in a stable equilibrium; if you kick it, it will not return to its orginal position.

---

[1]This type of "set geometry" is known as a *Venn diagram*.

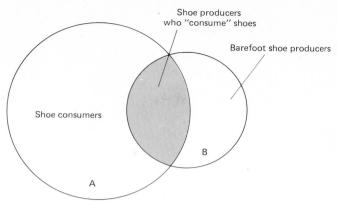

FIGURE 9-1   AN ILLUSTRATION OF THE DICHOTOMY BETWEEN CONSUMERS AND PRODUCERS

Shoe consumers are represented by circle A. Shoe producers are represented by circle B. The intersections between circle A and circle B represent shoe consumers who are also employed by the shoemaking industry. This intersection account for a small minority of consumers.

In the first instance, the disturbance caused the ball to deviate from its original position only temporarily. In the second instance, the disturbance caused the ball to depart permanently from its original equilibrium.

In Figure 9-2, demand and supply are brought together for the first time. The demand and supply curves for good X are denoted by D_0 and S_0, respectively. The two curves cross one another at point T. Point T represents *market equilibrium* in the sense that there is harmony between consumers and producers: Producers bring to the marketplace X_0 units of output per unit of time. This exact amount is taken off the market by consumers. In other words, at a price of P_0, producers produce X_0 and consumers consume X_0. Does point T represent a *stable market equilibrium*? To test it, we should in principle perform an experiment which is equivalent to kicking the ball and then observing whether the ball returns to its initial position or instead ends up resting at another spot. First, we upset the market equilibrium by raising the price above P_0, say, to a level of P_1. Producers will supply X_s^1 units, but consumers will demand only X_d^1 units, leaving on shelves an excess of supply over demand equal to X_s^1 minus X_d^1. Note that this excess of supply over demand is a surplus per unit of time, indicating that unless producers begin reducing prices they will soon face a problem of cumulative surpluses. Cumulative surpluses are costly; they involve storage and, in the case of some commodities like vegetables, spoilage. They also involve an interest loss, because a delay in selling implies a delay in inflows of cash. To avoid these costs, producers will cut back on prices. In other words, there are downward pressures on prices indicated by the arrow pointing in that direction. This pressure to move toward P_0 must continue until point T is achieved again. In economic jargon, we say that the market forces restore equilibrium.

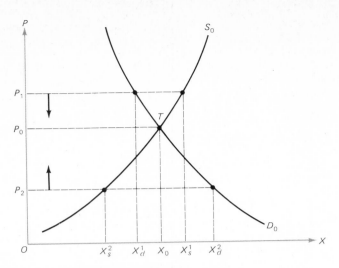

FIGURE 9-2 SUPPLY, DEMAND, AND MARKET EQUILIBRIUM
The supply curve S_0 intersects with the demand curve D_0 at point T. If the price is higher than the equilibrium price of P_0, say, P_1, excess of supply over demand $(X_s^1 - X_d^1)$ will induce producers to lower the price in order to get rid of excessive inventories. If the price is lower than P_0, say, P_2, excess demand over supply $(X_d^2 - X_s^2)$ will induce producers to raise the price in order to build up their dwindling inventories.

Next, consider any price below P_0, say, P_2. At that price the quantity supplied is X_s^2, while the quantity demanded is X_d^2. The quantity supplied is short of the quantity demanded by X_d^2 minus X_s^2. This means that inventories on shelves and in warehouses are depleted. As soon as sellers discover that this depletion of inventories is neither local nor temporary, they raise prices, without losing customers, in order to build up their inventories to a desirable level. This is indicated by the upward-pointing arrow showing that there are market forces that push the price up toward P_0. The rise in the price toward P_0 prevents a temporary decline in inventories from deteriorating into a shortage.

The above analysis shows that markets, in which the supply curve slopes positively and the demand curve slopes negatively, always adjust toward the point where the quantity supplied is equal to the quantity demanded. Such markets are known to be stable. A surplus or a shortage can arise in the marketplace only if the government (or another organization, e.g., a union or a cartel) interferes by fixing prices. These situations might be denoted as permanent disturbances. In the following section, two permanent disturbances are discussed.

9.2b An Example of a Permanent Surplus: Farm Price Support

Farm price support, which in essence means that the government sets a floor for the price (below which the price cannot fall), is related to the concept of *parity* price. The parity price for a farm commodity is the number of current dollars the farm will have to receive per unit of this commodity in order to be able to purchase with dollars as many units of goods, services, and inputs as could have been purchased by another farmer selling a unit of the same commodity during the base (prosperous) period of 1910–1914.[2] Recall (Section 3.2b) that in good years such as 1973 and 1974, when crops were modest and exports were significantly high, farmers reaffirmed their belief in the market forces. At the end of 1977 and early 1978, when bumper crops of wheat and corn depressed farm prices, farmers went on strike demanding 100 percent parity prices. The *support price* is a political mechanism designed to achieve some percentage of parity for farmers. An agency of the federal government, the Commodity Credit Corporation (CCC) is in charge of the program of price support. The price support works as illustrated by the following example: In 1977, the national average "loan rate" per bushel of wheat was $2.25. If the market price rose above the loan rate, the farmer would sell the wheat and pay the CCC the loan (plus interest). If the market price failed to rise above $2.25, the farmer would default on the loan and turn the wheat over to the CCC. This is how the government would get stuck with a surplus of wheat.

The price support program is illustrated in Figure 9-3. Without governmental intervention supply and demand intersect at point T; thus, without governmental intervention P_0 would have been the equilibrium price at which X_0 would have been cleared by the market. If the government sets a floor at a level of P_1, then at such a high price the quantity supplied is X_s; recall that X_s is determined by the intersection of the price with the supply curve. But at such a high level of price, the quantity demanded is only X_d; again, the quantity demanded is determined by the point of intersection between the price and the demand curve. The gap between the quantity supplied and the quantity demanded is $X_s - X_d$, and it is a *surplus* that must be taken off the market by the government, or else the price will fall back to a level of P_0. This program is costly to taxpayers: they pay a higher price for all products made of wheat (e.g., bread). They also have to pay more taxes to finance the program. For example, according to government documents, the total net loss from all the CCC operations in 1971 amounted to $4.083 billion.[3]

9.2c An Example of a Permanent Shortage: Price Control of Natural Gas

Until 1978, the Federal Power Commission (FPC) had the authority to regulate the price of natural gas. It divided the United States into five areas and imposed price ceilings separately on natural gas in each area. According to the *Economic Report of the President* (1976), the average regulated price paid by interstate pipelines rose from 27 cents per thousand cubic feet (tcf) in September 1974 to 37 cents per tcf in September 1975. Price regulations applied only to interstate flows of gas. During the same period, prices paid in intraproducing states reached a level of close to $2 per tcf. The impact of the price regulation of natural gas is illustrated in Figure 9-4. At a ceiling price of P_2, as indicated by the supply curve, producers are reluctant to produce more than X_s units of gas. At that low price, however, consumers would like to buy X_d units in the marketplace. Thus, at a ceiling

price of P_2, the quantity demanded X_d exceeded the quantity supplied X_s, and a shortage of $X_d - X_s$ arose in the market. Indeed, studies by the FPC indicated that natural gas shortfalls amounted to 3 to 6 percent in 1971, 5 percent in 1972, and over 10 percent in 1975.

Deregulation of the price of natural gas would cause the price to rise from P_2 to the equilibrium price of P_0. Quantity demanded will shrink in the long run from X_d to X_0. Consumers will switch from gas to other sources of energy such as solar energy. They will also invest in better insulation (Section 2.4j). At a higher price producers will increase their production rate from X_s to X_0. As discussed in Section 8.2c, the more elastic the supply curve, the larger the supply reaction will be.

---

[2]The parity price formula does not take into account the increase in farm productivity. For instance, the index of farm productivity has risen from 101 in 1968 to 112 in 1976, about a 1.5 percent increase in productivity per year. Those who like the parity price, if they accept economic logic, should agree to reduce the parity price by 1.5 percent per year.
[3]*Report of the President of the CCC*, 1971.

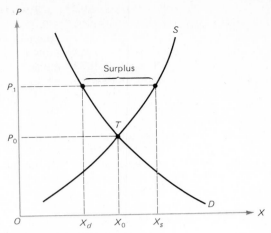

FIGURE 9.3 THE PRICE SUPPORT PROGRAM

Equilibrium occurs at point T where X_0 units are produced and sold at a price of P_0, per unit of time. If the government wants to provide producers a floor at a level of P_1, the government must take the surplus of $X_s - X_d$ off the market.

9.3 DEMAND AND SUPPLY SHIFTS

9.3a Exogenous and Endogenous Variables

Exogenous means originating from external causes. *Endogenous* means originating from internal causes. When consumers are considered separately from producers, income, prices of other goods, tastes, and the price of the

FIGURE 9-4 A PRICE CEILING ON NATURAL GAS

Equilibrium occurs at point T where X_0 units of natural gas are produced and sold at a price of P_0, per unit of time. If the government imposes an effective ceiling on prices at a level of P_2, a shortage of $X_d - X_s$ is created.

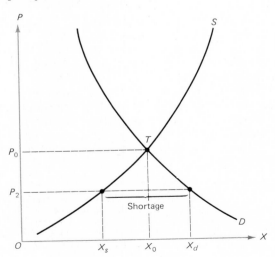

good under consideration are all exogenous. The quantity demanded is endogenous. When producers are considered separately from consumers, technology (the production function), prices of inputs, and the price of the good under consideration are all exogenous; the quantity supplied is endogenous. But when demand and supply are brought together, the price (and the quantity) is determined at the point of intersection of the demand and supply curves, and hence the price of the good under consideration becomes endogenous.

As we saw in Chapter 3, variations in the *exogenous* variables such as *income, tastes,* and *prices of other goods* lead to demand shifts. Demand shifts in turn give rise to a new point of intersection with the supply curve, resulting in a new price and a new quantity. As we saw in Chapter 8, variations in the *exogenous* variables such as *technology* and *price of inputs* lead to supply shifts. Supply shifts in turn give rise to a new point of intersection with the demand curve, resulting in a new price and a new quantity. The above discussion can be summarized as follows:

> In the supply-demand model of perfect competition, changes in exogenous variables lead to either demand shifts or supply shifts or both; the result is a change in the endogenous variables price and quantity.

9.3b Demand Shifts

Chapter 3 demonstrated how the (market) demand curve shifts as a result of changes in income per capita, population, prices of other goods, and tastes. Figure 9-5 combines demand shifts with the (industry) supply curve in order to demonstrate how demand shifts alter the equilibrium in the marketplace. Initially, market equilibrium is achieved at point G where the long-run supply curve S_0 cuts the demand curve D_0. Following the theory as developed in Figure 8-4, a less elastic short-run supply curve S_r also passes through G. The price and quantity of the initial equilibrium are P_0 and X_0, respectively. Now, suppose there is a change in an exogenous variable leading to a rightward shift in the demand curve to a new position D_1. (Such a shift could have resulted from a rise in income, if X is normal, from a rise in the price of a substitute, or from a change in tastes or population growth.) The industry first expands along its short-run supply curve S_r to point K; temporarily the price is P_1', and the quantity sold in the marketplace is X_1'. After time is allowed for adjustment, the industry varies its fixed factors and moves to point L where S_0 intersects with the new demand curve D_1; the long-run price is P_1 and the long-run quantity sold in the marketplace is X_1. Note that the long-run price is lower than the short-run price and the long-run quantity is larger than the short-run quantity. If the demand curve were to shift to the left, from D_0 to D_2 (income falls, the price of a substitute declines, population decreases, etc.), the analysis would be similar, except in the opposite direction. First, the industry will contract along its S_r curve to point M; temporarily the equilibrium price and quantity will be P_2' and X_2'. Given the time needed for fixed capital to be worn out, the industry will adjust by moving to point N where S_0 and D_2 intersect. A permanent equilibrium with a price of

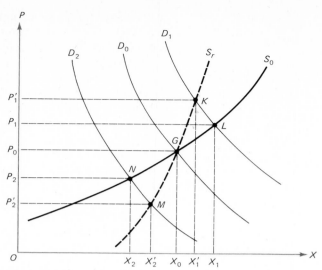

FIGURE 9-5 DEMAND SHIFTS

Originally equilibrium occurs at point G. Supply and demand are denoted by S_0 and D_0. A short-run supply curve S_r passes through G. An increase in demand leading to a rightward shift from D_0 to D_1 results in a short-run expansion along S_r to point K, and only in the long run a movement to point L. A decrease in demand leading to a leftward shift in demand from D_0 to D_2 results in a short-run contraction along S_r to point M, and only in the long run a movement to point N.

P_2 and a quantity of X_2 will be established. Note here that the long-run price is higher than the short-run price; the long-run quantity is smaller than the short-run quantity. We can summarize:

> *An increase in demand leading to a rightward shift in the demand curve will result in a higher price and a larger quantity. A decrease in demand leading to a leftward shift in the demand curve will result in a lower price and a smaller quantity. In the short run, most of the burden of the adjustment is borne by the price; in the long run, most of the burden of the adjustment is borne by the quantity.*

9.3c Supply Shifts

Chapter 8 demonstrated how the supply curve shifts as a result of changes in prices of inputs or technological progress. Figure 9-6 combines supply shifts with the market demand curve in order to demonstrate how supply shifts alter the equilibrium in the marketplace. Initially market equilibrium is achieved at point G, where the long-run supply curve S_0 cuts the long-run demand curve D_0. Following the theory as developed in Figure 2-12, a less elastic short-run demand curve D_r also passes through G. The price and quantity of the initial equilibrium are P_0 and X_0, respectively. Now suppose there is a change in an exogenous variable leading to a rightward shift in the supply curve to a new position S_1. (Such a shift could have resulted either

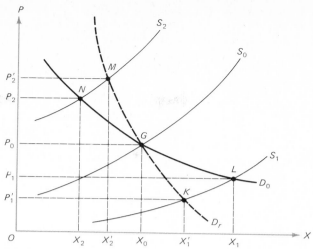

FIGURE 9-6   SUPPLY SHIFTS

Originally equilibrium occurs at point G. Supply and demand are denoted by S_0 and D_0. A short-run demand curve D_r passes through G. An increase in supply, leading to a rightward shift from S_0 to S_1, results in a short-run expansion along D_r to point K, and only in the long run a movement to point L. A decrease in supply, leading to a leftward shift from S_0 to S_1, results in a short-run contraction along D_r to point M, and only in the long run a movement to point N.

from technological progress or from fall in the price of an input.) The industry first expands along its short-run demand curve D_r to point K; temporarily the price is P_1' and the quantity sold in the marketplace is X_1'; after time is allowed for adjustment, consumers move to point L, where the long-run quantity X_1 is larger than the short-run quantity X_1', and the long-run price P_1 is higher than the short-run price P_1'. If the supply curve were to shift to the left from S_0 to S_2 (a price of a variable input rises), the industry would first contract along D_r to point M, where the temporary equilibrium price and quantity will be P_2' and X_2', respectively; given time for adjustment, consumers will move to point N on the long-run demand curve. The permanent price P_2 will be lower than the temporary price P_2', and the permanent quantity X_2 will be smaller than the temporary quantity X_2'.

The difference between short-run and long-run demand curves is not as evident as the difference between long-run and short-run supply curves. Let us return to the example given in Section 2.4j. After prices of gasoline started to rise in the wake of the energy crisis, consumers started to reduce the consumption of gasoline by switching to more efficient cars. Indeed, according to the *Economic Report of the President* (1976), 1974 model automobiles averaged an estimated rate of 13.9 miles per gallon, while the 1975 model automobiles had an estimated average of 15.6 miles per gallon. Because drivers are reluctant to replace *new* heavy cars by compacts, in the short run, only *old* (heavy) cars are replaced by compacts. Thus in the short run, only a small portion of the fleet is replaced; this is why the short-run demand for gasoline is very inelastic relative to the long-run demand. A Rand study confirmed the theory that the long-run demand for gasoline should be more elastic than the short-run demand.[4] The study concluded that in the first year the price elasticity of the demand for gasoline is in the range of −0.1 to −0.3; in the long run the elasticity rises to the range of −0.65 to −0.85. This finding is relevant for policy makers who might be tempted to base their policies on short-run observation. Economists always suspected that politicians who advocated gasoline rationing confused short-run with long-run demand curve and concluded that a rise in the price of gasoline would not induce consumers to reduce their gasoline consumption significantly.

The summary of this section is as follows:

An increase in supply leading to a rightward shift in the supply curve will result in a lower price and a larger quantity. A decrease in supply leading to a leftward shift in the supply curve will result in a higher price and a smaller quantity. In the short run, most of the burden of the adjustment is borne by the price; in the long run, most of the burden of the adjustment is borne by the quantity.

9.3d Exogenous and Endogenous Variables: Comparative Statics and Dynamics (An Example: Coffee)

As explained in Section 9.3a, a change in the market takes place when an exogenous factor such as population or income per capita changes, giving rise to a change in demand, or when an exogenous factor such as technology or a price of a factor of production changes, giving rise to a change in supply. As a result of these changes, the endogenous variables, namely, equilibrium quantity and price, change. Figure 9-7 illustrates this case by considering the case of coffee.

In July 1975 frost significantly reduced the 1976 Brazilian coffee harvest. As Table 9-1 shows, the 1976–1977 world exportable production was 18 percent below the 1975–1976 level. In Figure 9-7, this is summarized by a leftward supply shift from S_0 to S_1. The exogenous variable shifting the supply curve to the left is the 1975 frost, which may be considered a negative technological "innovation." As a result an excess demand over supply amounting to $\overline{GA}$ was created in the market. This gave rise to shrinking inventories and hence rising prices and falling quantities—the two endogenous variables. In the diagram

this is represented by a movement from point A where equilibrium price and quantity are, respectively, P_0 and X_0, to point B, where the new equilibrium price and quantity are, respectively, P_1 and X_1.

How does it look in reality? Figure 9-8 shows the actual prices of coffee as recorded weekly in the New York Exchange. From a level of 80 cents per pound in 1975, coffee prices rose to a level of about $3 per pound in 1977. In Figure 9-7, point A represents the 1975 situation before the frost, and point B represents the high price during 1977 after the adjustment had taken place. The comparison of point A with point B is known in microeconomics as *comparative statics*. In this book we are mainly interested in comparative statics. The analysis concerned with the time path of X and P from point A to point B is known as *dynamics*; because it requires advanced mathematics, it will not be discussed in this book.[5] A consumer boycott, if it were successful, would have been an example of an exogenous factor giving rise to a demand shift. Consider Figure 9-7 again: If the

---

[4]Sorrel Wildhorn, Burke K. Burright, John H. Enns, and Thomas F. Kirkwood, "How to Save Gasoline," R-1560-NSF, October 1974, Rand.

[5]*Comparative statics* means a comparison of two static situations: Figure 9-7 compares point B with point A; more specifically, it compares the new equilibrium price and quantity P_1 and X_1 with the old equilibrium price and quantity P_0 and X_0; for example, we may be interested in the percentage increase of P_1 over P_0. *Dynamics*, on the other hand, is involved in describing the behavior of price and quantity over time between point A and point B; for example, the equation describing the behavior of price over time between A and B may have the form $P(t) = P_0 + f(t)$.

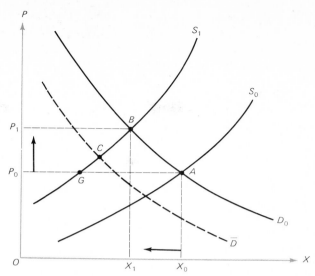

FIGURE 9-7 THE IMPACT OF THE 1975 FROST ON THE MARKET FOR COFFEE
Initially equilibrium occurs at point A where demand curve D_0 intersects with supply curve S_0. The frost in Brazil causes the supply curve to shift leftward to S_1; less coffee is produced, and it is sold at a higher price. Point B represents this new situation. If the boycott of consumers were successful, the demand curve would have shifted to the left to a new position $\overline{D}$. Point C would have represented the new equilibrium.

boycott were successful, the demand curve would have shifted to the left, say, to position $\overline{D}$, and the point of its intersection with S_1 would have been C. The resulting price would have been lower than P_1 (not shown in the diagram). Boycotts normally do not work; consumers usually encourage other consumers to boycott, hoping that the boycotting by others will cause the price to go down. Organizers of the boycott are also known later to claim victory by insisting that the reduction in consumption from X_0 to X_1 was due to the boycott.

9.4 A CHANGE IN THE PRICE OF A FACTOR OF PRODUCTION

9.4a Supply and Demand Analysis

Section 8.3 analyzed the impact of a change in the price of an input on the supply curve of the industry and concluded that the supply curve will shift in

TABLE 9-1 **World Green Coffee (Exportable) Production**

In 1000 bags

Crop year	Brazil	Total world
1974–1975	19,500	62,434
1975–1976	15,000	55,282
1976–1977	2,500	45,474

Source: 1977 Commodity Year Book, p. 115.

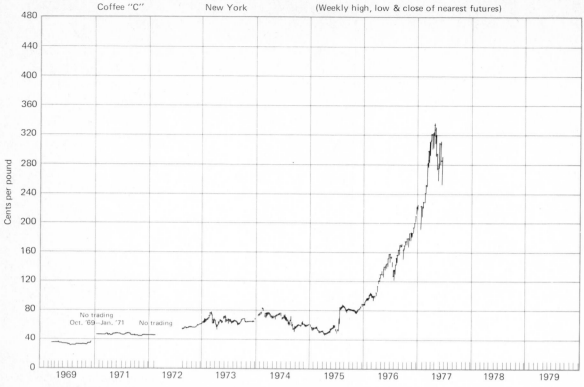

FIGURE 9-8 PRICES OF COFFEE, 1969–1977, CENTS PER POUND

A chart showing the movement of coffee prices. (*Source:* Prepared by Commodity Research Bureau, Inc., One Liberty Plaza, New York, N.Y. 10008. Printed in *1977 Commodity Year Book*, p. 115.)

the direction of the input price change: A rise in the price of an input will result in an upward shift in the supply curve, and a fall in the price of an input will result in a downward shift in the supply curve. In the trivial case where only one variable input is employed by the industry, the upward displacement of the supply curve will be proportional to the rise in the price of the variable input; in the more realistic case where more than one variable input is employed, the impact of the rise in the price of a single input will be mitigated by substitution: Producers will substitute other factors for the factor whose price rose. If the price of a single factor falls, the supply curve will shift downward by less than an amount proportional to the decline in the price of the variable input.

Let us now focus on Figure 9-9. In panel (a), initially the marginal cost curve of the individual (typical) firm is MC_0. In panel (b) the initial supply curve S_0 is the sum of all MC_0 curves. This supply curve intersects with the demand curve D_0 at point E. The associated initial total output and price are

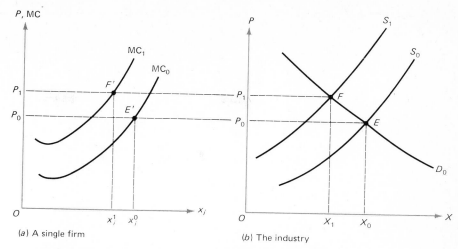

(a) A single firm   (b) The industry

FIGURE 9-9 A CHANGE IN THE PRICE OF A FACTOR OF PRODUCTION
First, in panel (a) as the price of a factor rises, the MC curve shifts upward from MC_0 to MC_1; in panel (b) the supply is the sum of all MC curves, and following the displacement in panel (a) the supply curve shifts upward from S_0 to S_1. Equilibrium in the market changes from E to F. In panel (a) the individual firm is now confronted with a higher price P_1; the equilibrium of the individual firm changes from E' to F'.

X_0 and P_0, respectively. The contribution of the individual firm in panel (a) is x_i^0 units of output; in fact for n firms we have

$$X_0 = \sum_{i=1}^{n} x_i^0.$$

Suppose the wage rate confronting the coal-mining industry rises. As a result, the MC curve of each firm will shift upward from MC_0 to MC_1; this is shown in panel (a). In panel (b) the supply curve, being the sum of all MC curves, will follow and shift upward from S_0 to S_1. The equilibrium of the industry will shift from E to F: The quantity of coal mined will decline from X_0 to X_1, and the price will rise from P_0 to P_1. In panel (a) the individual firm will move from an equilibrium denoted by E' to a new equilibrium denoted by F'.

Would it be possible for the new price P_1 to be so high as to induce the firm to produce more coal than was produced initially? In other words, would it be possible for F' to lie to the right of E', such that $x_i^1 > x_i^0$? Answering this question is left for the student.

9.4b An Example: The Bituminous Coal Industry

A major union drive to raise wages of coal miners started in the 1940s. This union drive resulted in raising real wages of coal miners and thus created a classic example of industry response to a rise in the price of a variable factor of production. Table 9-2 presents data drawn from the bituminous coal industry. As may be calculated from the first row of the table, real annual payments per employee increased by

TABLE 9-2 Historical Data of the Bituminous Coal Industry in the United States

	1919	1929	1939	1954
Annual earnings: real wages, deflated by CPI	$2463	$2520	$2877	$5024
Index of coal production	100.0	116.6	85.2	84.1
Index of employment	100.0	82.0	68.4	36.8
Index of horsepower used	100.0	145.6	155.0	284.1

Source: Real earnings: *Historical Statistics of the U.S. Colonial Times to 1970*, U.S. Department of Commerce Bureau of the Census, part I, p. 166.

Indices: G. S. Maddala, "Productivity and Technological Change in the Bituminous Coal Industry, 1919–54," *The Journal of Political Economy,* vol. 73, June 1965, no. 3, pp. 352–356.

some 5 percent per annum between 1939 and 1954. As a result of the change in the price of labor relative to capital, the index of labor employment in the bituminous coal mines declined from 68.4 in 1939 to 36.8 in 1954.[6] During the same period the use-of-horsepower index increased from 155.0 to 284.1. In the coal-mining industry horsepower is viewed as a good proxy for capital. Note that the decrease in the production of coal (from 100 in 1919 to 84.1 in 1954) may have also been influenced by the cheapening of substitutes such as crude oil. It is interesting to learn that Maddala, who studied the bituminous coal industry, reports no significant change in the structure of the aggregate production function of bituminous coal over the period 1919–1954.[7] Put another way, the data in Table 9-2 reflect the industry reaction to the rise in the relative price of labor.[8]

---

[6]See Section 4.1.

[7]G. S. Maddala, "Productivity and Technological Change in the Bituminous Coal Industry, 1919–1954," *The Journal of Political Economy*, vol. 73, June 1965, no. 3, pp. 352–356.

[8]As the individual firm depicted in panel (*a*) of Figure 9-9 is all of a sudden confronted with a higher price of labor, it will substitute capital for labor. Consider the following figure: Labor (*L*) is measured along the horizontal axis and capital (*K*) is measured along the vertical axis.

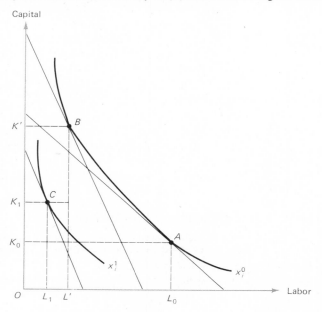

9.5 TECHNOLOGICAL CHANGE

9.5a The Supply Shift due to Technological Change

The impact of a change in technology on the MC curve, and hence on the supply curve, was discussed in Section 8.4. It was argued that since MC is defined as the price of the variable factor over its marginal physical product, and since a neutral technological innovation increases the marginal physical product of the factors, the marginal cost curve of the firm falls as a result of a technological innovation. Since the MC curve of the firm shifts downward, the entire supply curve of the industry shifts downward. The most amazing technological innovation currently under way is the new development in microelectronics. Robert N. Noyce provides a summary of the technological progress in the field.[9] He reports that as a result of the development of integrated circuits, a minicomputer in 1977, priced at only \$300 and ordered by mail, is 20 times faster, is thousands of times more reliable, has a far larger memory, takes the power of only a light bulb to operate, occupies 1/30,000 of the volume, and costs only 1/10,000 as much as the ENIAC, the first large electronic computer built in the 1940s. In the same article Professor Noyce reports that the cost of hand-held calculators has declined by a factor of 100 in the past decade. He attributes this decline in the cost to the "learning curve," according to which experience is approximated by output: Most industries reduce their real costs by 20 to 30 percent each time their cumulative outputs double. For example, the real cost of integrated circuits has declined 28 percent each time the cumulative output doubled.

Figure 9-10 illustrates the case of a technological change. Because of the technological change the supply curve shifted downwards from S_0 to S_1, and as a result the equilibrium point changed from A to B. Price has declined from P_0 to P_1, and quantity has increased from X_0 to X_1. The concepts of consumer and producer surplus were discussed in Sections 2.7 and 7.4, respectively. These concepts can now be utilized. The benefit to society from a technological innovation is unambiguous: Originally the consumer's surplus was the striped area denoted by FP_0A. After the technological innovation takes place, it is the area denoted by FP_1B; specifically, it increases by the shaded area denoted by P_0P_1BA. For producers (owners of fixed factors) the case is not so clear-cut. Originally the producer's surplus is

---

Initially the firm is producing x_i^0 units of coal per annum. The isoquant x_i^0 just touches an isocost (reflecting input prices in 1940) at point A. If wages rose as indicated by Table 9-2 but the firm was forced to stay on the same isoquant of x_i^0 units, it would move along the initial isoquant in the northwesterly direction to point B. The movement from A to B is known as the *substitution effect*. The substitution effect entails decreasing the employment of labor from L_0 to L' and increasing the application of capital (horsepower) from K_0 to K'. We noted in panel (*a*) of Figure 9-9 that output actually fell from x_i^0 to x_i^1; accordingly, to find the final point of equilibrium of the firm, the isocost that touches x_i^0 at B is shifted parallel to itself until it just touches the isoquant x_i^1 at point C. The movement from B to C is known as the *expansion effect*. Because of the expansion effect the firm decreases its labor employment further from L' to L_1; it modifies its capital application from K' back to K_1.

[9]Robert N. Noyce, "Microelectronics," *Scientific American*, vol. 237, no. 3, September 1977, pp. 63–69.

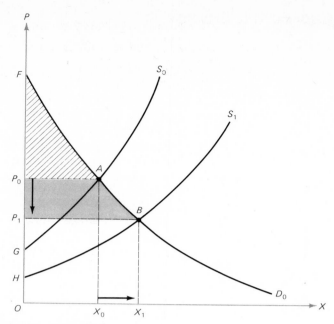

FIGURE 9-10 TECHNOLOGICAL PROGRESS
Originally equilibrium in the market is at point *A*. As a result of technological progress, the supply curve shifts down from S_0 to S_1. The consumer's surplus increases by the shaded area.

P_0GA. After the innovation takes place, it becomes P_1HB. For all practical purposes GA and HB could be considered as linear. Then we can compare the area of two triangles. The original triangle is $1/2 \cdot (\overline{P_0A}) \cdot (\overline{P_0G})$, and the posttechnological change triangle is $1/2 \cdot (\overline{P_1B}) \cdot (\overline{P_1H})$. Clearly, so long as the demand curve is not vertical, $\overline{P_1B}$ must be larger than $\overline{P_0A}$. But $\overline{P_1H}$ will exceed $\overline{P_0G}$ only if $\overline{GH}$ exceeds $\overline{P_0P_1}$. If S_0 and S_1 are vertically parallel, this would be the case and producers would benefit from the innovation; otherwise, it is ambiguous. It is left for the reader to show that even if the producer's surplus were to decline, the gain to consumers would be sufficient to offset the loss to producers.

9.5b An Example: Hybrid Corn

The gain to society from technological innovations can be empirically estimated. Zvi Griliches estimated the net gain to society from hybrid corn, a typical case of a neutral shift in the production function.[10] The topic of interest, capital, and benefit-cost ratios will be discussed in Chapter 16. Here only the result will be stated—namely, that as of 1955, for every dollar invested in hybrid corn research, society reaped a return of $7 in perpetuity. This return is in the form of a positive change in the consumer's surplus.

---

[10]Zvi Griliches, "Research Costs and Social Returns: Hybrid Corn and Related Innovations," *Journal of Political Economy*, vol. 66, October 1958, pp. 419–431.

9.6 EXTERNAL DISECONOMIES AND ECONOMIES

9.6a The Theory

Section 6.5f explained that even in the long run firms with U-shaped long-run average cost curves (LRAC) are observed. The U shape arises because of the fixity of entrepreneurial capacity. We saw that up to the minimum point of the LRAC, the firm obeys increasing returns to scale known as the range of *internal economies*; beyond that point, the firm obeys decreasing returns to scale known as the range of *internal diseconomies*. The long-run marginal cost curve (LRMC) is also rising beyond the minimum point of the LRAC curve; this shape of the LRMC curve is also attributed to the fixity of the entrepreneurial capacity; the long-run supply curve of the firm is that relevant portion of the LRMC curve. We can say that the long-run supply curve of the firm rises because of *internal diseconomies*. You will recall from Section 6.5d that in the absence of fixed factors the LRMC curve is horizontal; there are neither internal economies nor internal diseconomies. The term *internal* implies a certain property of the structure of the firm, and in particular the fixity of a certain factor is the reason why the supply curve of the firm is rising (beyond a certain point). The problem of internal diseconomies intensifies in the short run because more factors of production are held fixed relative to the long run. In consequence, in the short run the marginal cost (supply) of the firm is rising faster than in the long run.

External diseconomies were mentioned in Section 8.3a in conjunction with a rise in the price of an input as a result of an increase in the total output of the entire industry. Here, while the individual firm has no appreciable influence on the price of an input, if the entire industry faces a rising supply curve of a variable input, the industry as a whole might have an appreciable influence on the price of a variable input. This case of external diseconomies is classified as *external pecuniary diseconomies*.

9.6b The Geometry of External Diseconomies and External Economies

To illustrate the case of external diseconomies, consider a case in which an industry is faced with a positively sloped supply curve of labor. The common sense of this situation is the following: If the industry as a whole should expand, it would need to employ more labor, but in order to attract more labor to the industry, wages would have to be raised. When one firm or a few firms decide to expand, they cannot exert influence on wages simply because the amount of labor employed by one firm or a few firms is negligible. But when all firms decide to expand their level of production, they have to attract a significant additional amount of labor. They can do it only by raising wages. This situation is illustrated in Figure 9-11. Currently the single firm produces X_0 units of output. (The price P_0 which induces the firm to produce X_0 is not shown in the diagram in order to keep the diagram simple. Such a price would be represented by a horizontal line passing through point K.) If the wage rate is given to the firm, then MC_0 is the relevant marginal cost curve, which is the supply curve of the firm. Put differently, if the firm were

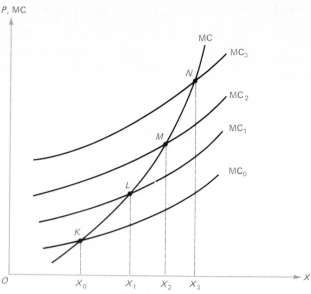

FIGURE 9-11 EXTERNAL DISECONOMIES: THE INDIVIDUAL FIRM

MC_0 is the marginal cost curve as seen by the firm; as the price rises (say, owing to an increase in demand), all firms attempt to expand along an MC curve like MC_0. But if the industry is confronted with a rising supply of a variable input, as the industry uses more of that input, its price will rise, leading to a displacement of MC from MC_0 to MC_1. The firm finds itself expanding from point L, and so on.

the only one to expand, then as the price of output rises (say, because demand increases), the single firm would expand along the MC_0 curve. However, assume that when the price rises all firms in the industry expand. As a result, the wage rate rises. As explained in Chapter 8, a rise in the price of a variable factor of production leads to an upward shift in the MC curve (Section 8.3). Assume that the MC curve shifted from MC_0 to MC_1. If the price is represented by a horizontal line going through point L, the firm would now produce X_1 units of output. Given that L is the new point of equilibrium, if the price of output were to rise again, the single firm might plan to expand along the MC_1 curve, but if all other firms increase their level of output, the MC curve of the firm would shift, this time from MC_1 to MC_2. The firm would find itself at point M, through which passes a new MC curve denoted by MC_2. The conclusion is that if the industry as a whole is faced with a positively sloped supply of a variable factor of production, then as the price of output rises the marginal cost curve of each firm shifts upward, reflecting the external diseconomy, namely, the rise in the price of the variable factor of production. As demonstrated in Figure 9-11, connecting points $K, L, M,$ and N yields the less elastic MC curve which reflects the externality. This is known as *pecuniary external diseconomy*. External diseconomies might be *technical* rather than *pecuniary*. For example, consider firms using water pumped from the same lake and discharging the polluted water back to the lake. If one firm were to increase its level of production, its additional pollution would be negligible. But if all firms expand, the additional pollution in the lake may be significant, thus requiring each of them to spend additional money on cleaning water before using it. This would give rise to the same upward shifting of the MC curve of each firm as the aggregate output of the industry increases.

Figure 9-12 shows the difference between industry response to an increase in demand without and with external diseconomies, respectively. Original equilbrium is denoted by K. There the demand curve D_0 cuts the supply curve ΣMC_0. A demand shift from D_0 to D_1 would, if there are no externalities, lead to a new point of equilibrium denoted by L'. Output and price would increase from X_0 and P_0 to X' and P', respectively. But if external diseconomies are present, as the industry expands, the supply gradually shifts from ΣMC_0 to ΣMC_1 and the final point of equilibrium is L instead of L'. The new price under external diseconomies is P_1, which is higher than P', and the new quantity X_1 is lower than the new quantity in the absence of externality, X'. In summary, with external diseconomies the supply curve S_0 is less elastic than in the case of no externalities (ΣMC_0).

How about external economies? While it would be hard to find a case of external pecuniary economies, one could find examples of external technical economies. According to the learning curve, mentioned in Section 9.5a, if all firms expand simultaneously, they learn more from the experience of each other; for example, if all timber cutters produce more, they can economize

FIGURE 9-12   EXTERNAL DISECONOMIES: THE INDUSTRY
Initial equilibrium occurs at point K where D_0 cuts the sum of all MC curves denoted by ΣMC_0. In the absence of external diseconomies an increase of demand leading to a shift to D_1 would have led the industry to expand along the ΣMC_0 curve to point L'. If external diseconomies are present, as the industry expands the sum of all MC curves slowly shifts up to ΣMC_1 and the industry ends up at point L. The true supply curve reflecting external diseconomies is the S_0 which passes through points like K and L.

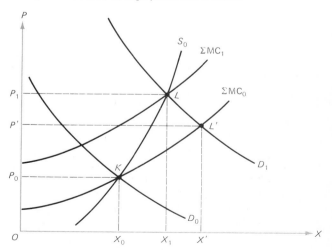

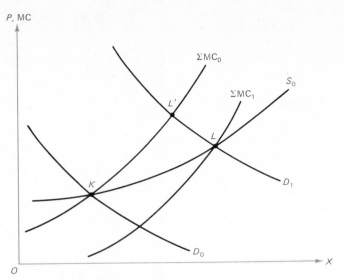

FIGURE 9-13 EXTERNAL ECONOMIES: THE INDUSTRY
Initial equilibrium occurs at point K where D_0 intersects with ΣMC_0. In absence of external economies an increase of demand leading to a demand shift to D_1 will result in an expansion along the ΣMC_0 curve from point K to point L'. But if external economies are present, as the industry expands, the sum of the marginal cost curves will shift downward from ΣMC_0 to ΣMC_1. The industry will end up at point L. The true supply curve will be S_0 that passes through points like K and L.

on shipping costs. The case of external economies is illustrated in Figure 9-13. As the industry expands, the supply curve drops gradually from ΣMC_0 to ΣMC_1; thus, instead of moving from point K to L', which would be the case without external economies, the industry moves to point L. Connecting points like K and L, we obtain the more elastic supply curve denoted by S_0.

Under conditions of external economies, could the supply curve of the industry be negatively sloped? This is left as a problem for the reader to solve.

9.6c An Example of Technical Externalities: The Pecos River Basin

Farmers in the Pecos River Basin in New Mexico use mainly groundwater for irrigation. According to a study by Micha Gisser and Abraham Mercado, in the aggregate, farmers already pump more water than the natural recharge.[11] Thus the supply curve of farm ouput of the Pecos farmers is shifting upward over time. If one farmer alone increases his level of output, the impact on the water table is infinitesimal. But if all

---

[11]Micha Gisser and Abraham Mercado, "Integration of the Agricultural Demand Function for Water and the Hydrologic Model of the Pecos Basin," *Water Resources Research*, vol. 8, no. 6, December 1972, pp. 1373–1384.

Groundwater must be lifted from the water table to the surface where the well is located. The lower the water table the more it costs to lift the water to the surface. Natural recharge is the natural supply of water to the aquifer; an example would be the rain over the aquifer that percolates downward until it reaches the aquifer.

farmers increase their production, and hence their water use, the water table will fall faster as a result. The fall of the water table due to increasing pumping can be calculated by applying hydrologic formulas. In 1970, a fall of the water table by 1 foot entailed a rising cost of 3 cents per acre-foot pumped. With a rise in the cost of energy, the impact of these external diseconomies would be more severe.

9.7 PRICE DISPERSION

In competition, the market price tends to be set at about the same level adjusted for geographical location. There are always economic forces that will tend to equate the prices in different geographical locations. For example, if it costs 1 cent to ship one orange from Florida to Chicago, then on the average the price differential between Chicago and Florida can only temporarily exceed 1 cent. If, temporarily, the Chicago price is 13 cents and the Florida price is 10 cents, there is an incentive to divert oranges away from the market in Florida to Chicago. The net gain of shipping the first load to Chicago is 2 cents per orange. The process of shipping oranges to Chicago will lower the Chicago price and raise the Florida price just until the price differential amounts to 1 cent.

Price dispersion may arise because of the difference in service that is added to the product. For example, even though cleaners are competitive, one cleaner may charge 25 cents per shirt while a neighbor charges 24 cents. The first cleaner may be relatively closer to a parking lot or a shopping center.

Price differentials may also arise because of the relatively high cost of obtaining information about the market, time spent being a major factor. If such a cost did not exist, it would benefit the consumer to call all the sellers in order to select the one who offers the lowest price. Thus, if information were absolutely costless, price dispersion of homogeneous commodities would be present only if heterogeneous services were attached to the product. In reality, however, information is not costless, and thus consumers will devote only a limited amount of time to inquiring about the market prices. George Stigler has shown that returns to obtaining information diminish very rapidly.[12] Following Stigler, let sellers be divided into two groups, one in which sellers ask a certain low price, and one in which they ask a certain high price. Then, if only one seller is canvassed, the probability of paying the low price is 0.50. For canvassing four sellers, it becomes 0.9375. Clearly, if the item is very expensive, it will take the canvassing of a relatively large number of sellers before the marginal cost of obtaining information is equated with its marginal gain. On the other hand, if the item is relatively cheap, the 10 cents that it costs to make one phone call may exceed the expected reduction in price.[13] Accordingly, price dispersion due to imperfect

---

[12]George J. Stigler, "The Economics of Information," *The Journal of Political Economy*, vol. 69, June 1961, pp. 213–225.

[13]Suppose sellers are divided into two equal groups: The first group charges a high price of $2, and the second group charges a low price of $1. A potential buyer wants to canvass the market; he or she spends $0.10 per phone call. We assume that the time wasted is not consid-

knowledge will be relatively low in markets for expensive commodities and relatively high in markets for inexpensive commodities.

Note that price dispersion does not render the supply-demand model unusable. The only revision that it needs is that the point of intersection of supply and demand determines the *average* market price rather than a unique market price. For example, an increase in supply leading to a rightward supply shift will lead to a lower average market price. This means that the various prices of the same commodity will be set at lower levels.

9.8 SHORT-RUN PRICE MOVEMENTS OVER TIME

There are two types of short-run price movements over time. First, there are seasonal demand or supply movements; for example, prices of toys increase during the month of December. Also, the quantity of toys sold increases during the month of December. The reason for this, of course, is that demand for toys increases drastically before Christmas. Another example is the seasonal price changes of perishable fruit: The price of peaches may go down from $1 per pound in January to 30 cents in August. This is true because fresh peaches can be stored only for a relatively short time, and accordingly the summer crop is practically dumped in the market daily and clears at whatever price the market will alow. In January, the supply of peaches is very limited; hence the supply curve occupies a very high position, reflecting the high cost of importing peaches from remote warm areas where the climate allows picking peaches in January. But, as temperatures begin to rise in May, local orchards begin to yield their own crops, and the supply curve of peaches begins to shift to the right. With the seasonal increase in supply, its point of intersection with demand falls, and accordingly the price falls. As a rule, the more perishable the commodity, the more marked will be the seasonal price and quantity movements. The case of potatoes, which are far less perishable than peaches, provides a sharp con-

ered as a loss. The following table shows that it actually pays the potential buyer to make three calls:

Number of sellers canvassed, n	Probability of paying the high price of $2, $p = 0.5^n$	Probability of paying the low price of $1, $1 - p$	Expected price, $2 \cdot p + 1 \cdot (1 - p)$, $	Marginal saving due to search, $	Marginal cost of canvassing, $
1	0.5	0.5	1.50	0.00	0.10
2	0.25	0.75	1.25	0.25	0.10
3	0.125	0.875	1.12	0.13	0.10
4	0.0625	0.9375	1.06	0.06	0.10
5	0.0312	0.9688	1.03	0.03	0.10

The third call would cost him or her an additional $0.10, but the expected marginal saving (in price reduction) would be $0.13. It does not pay the buyer to make the four calls because the marginal gain of $0.06 is short of the marginal cost of $0.10.

trast. Although more than half the crop of potatoes is harvested in the fall, the seasonal price deviation from some annual average is normally not in excess of 30 percent.

When we deal with nonperishables or slightly perishable commodities such as wheat, the quantity supplied in a period of time equals stocks carried into the period plus current production minus stocks carried out of the period. The decision on how much to carry out of the period will affect the price this period and the price the next period: the larger the amount carried out of this period to the next period, the smaller will be the supply in this period and the larger the supply the next period. Accordingly, the higher will be the price this period and the lower will be the price the next period. In other words, the price differential between this period and the next period will be smaller, the larger the amount carried out. If the difference between the expected price next period and the price this period is larger than the marginal cost of storage, it benefits producers to carry stocks out of this period to the next period. The marginal cost of storage is the extra cost of warehouses, loading, the interest charges, minus the extra convenience of stocks per one additional unit of output stored.

Carrying out stocks from one period to the next tends to smooth prices over a long period of time. This is true because the amount carried out of this period is negatively related to the price differential between this period and the next. Commodities such as grains, which are produced periodically, are traded in *futures markets*, in which legal commitments are made either to deliver or to purchase in the future a certain amount of a commodity at a prefixed price; they will be analyzed in Chapter 10. Futures markets accommodate the movement of commodities from one period to the next, and thus they fulfill a very important function in the modern economy.

9.9 LONG-RUN PRICE MOVEMENTS OVER TIME: THE CASE OF EXHAUSTIBLE NATURAL RESOURCES

Given an exhaustible natural resource, say, light crude oil, it can be shown that the price of this natural resource must rise over time such that at the time of exhaustion a new resource appears in the market. The theory goes further to assure us that at the time of switching, the new resource will be sold at the last price of the old resource. The logic of this theory is as follows: Let *royalty* be defined as the price minus the marginal cost of mining; if the value of royalty is rising over time at a rate smaller than the rate of interest, it pays miners to increase production rate. This is equivalent to switching their wealth from the mines to the banks. Such an increase, however, depresses the present price of the mineral in the marketplace; this process of dropping the current price must continue just until the growth rate of royalties is equal to the interest rate. Now if royalties grow over time at a rate exceeding the rate of interest, it will benefit miners to slow down production because the mineral in the ground is worth more than money in the bank; a slowdown will lift present prices, and this process will continue until the rate of growth of royalties is in step with the interest rate.

This topic of intertemporal price movement of exhaustible resources gained prominence after the sharp increase in oil prices in the mid-1970s. Part of Chapter 16 is devoted to the theory of exhaustible natural resources.

9.10 ECONOMIC RENT

9.10a The Theory

Section 7.5 explained the difference between *accounting* and *economic costs*. The economic *rent* is obtained by subtracting total economic costs from total revenue. In particular, it was stressed that economic costs include, among other things, the alternative cost of capital, a concept which will be discussed in Chapter 16, and the alternative cost of the entrepreneurial capacity. Recall from Section 7.5 that the cost of the entrepreneurial capacity is the income the entrepreneur could have earned in the next best alternative; by implication, then, in the long run total revenue minus total (economic) cost is "gravy" for the entrepreneur: it is income over and above the *reservation price*, which is the minimum price (or income) that would barely induce an entrepreneur to leave the next best alternative. Because economic rent is "gravy," we say that it is *price-determined* rather than *price-determining*. Put another way, any payment to entrepreneurs over and above their reservation price will not affect their decision concerning their current employment.

Consider now Figure 9-14. In panel (*c*) the supply is the sum of all the long-run marginal cost curves. Panels (*a*) and (*b*) present the long-run marginal cost curves (LRMC) and the long-run average cost curves (LRAC) of two typical firms in the industry. Note that the entrepreneur of the first firm in panel (*a*) is more capable: His or her minimum LRAC is lower than the minimum LRAC of the second firm in panel (*b*). If at a price of P_0, there are no potential firms intending to enter the industry, the industry has reached long-run equilibrium.

The shaded area in panel (*a*) represents the rent received by the entrepreneur; this rent is a return to the scarcity of entrepreneurial capacity. First, it is due to the fact that very talented entrepreneurs as depicted by panel (*a*) are hard to find. Even if the supply of less talented entrepreneurs were unlimited, the price could not fall below P_0, guaranteeing a rent to the entrepreneur who is depicted by panel (*a*). Second, it is due to the scarcity of entrepreneurial capacity in general. Suppose all entrepreneurs were clones managing firms as depicted by panel (*b*). Even if the demand were increasing constantly, the long-run price would never rise above P_0, making it impossible for any rent to be generated.

Section 7.2h discussed some short-run problems that are faced by the competitive firm. In particular it was mentioned that if the price lies between the minimum points of the average variable cost (AVC) and the short-run average total cost (SRAC), the firm would continue to produce in the short run provided that the fixed cost is unavoidable. The shaded area in Figure 7-7 which is not covered by diagonal stripes is known as *quasi-rent*. It is a

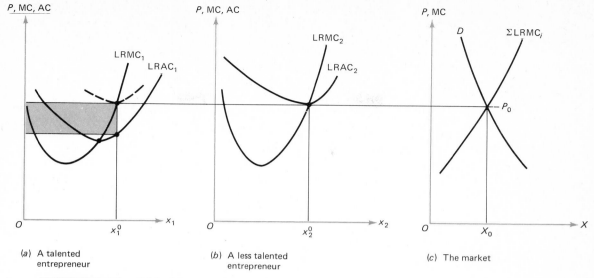

(a) A talented
entrepreneur

(b) A less talented
entrepreneur

(c) The market

FIGURE 9-14   ECONOMIC RENT
In panel (c) equilibrium occurs at the point of intersection between $\Sigma LRMC_i$ and D. A firm managed by an efficient entrepreneur is depicted by panel (a); for this firm the shaded area is the rent. A firm managed by an entrepreneur who barely makes it is depicted by panel (b); the price line just touches the minimum point of the LRMC curve; rent is zero.

quasi-rent because it boils down to remunerating fixed factors of production which in the short run have no alternative use and hence have a zero reservation price (alternative cost). In Figure 7-7, regardless of the size of the quasi-rent (provided it is positive), in the short run the firm will continue to produce. In other words, in the short run the quasi-rent is price-determined rather than price-determining.

Rents may arise as a result of factors that have nothing to do with the ability of the entrepreneur. As an example, consider the case of natural gas. Figure 9-4 showed that deregulation of the price of natural gas will raise the price from P_2 to P_0. Given that the supply of natural gas is not perfectly elastic (Figure 8-3), the price would rise and lead to positive rents to firms depicted by panel (b) and to larger rents to firms depicted by panel (a). During the Vietnam War prices of copper went up. Rents accruing to owners of copper mines increased for the duration of the war. A Georgia peanut processor found out that because of the unexpected rise of his brother to prominence, he could make $5000 a day appearing at stock car races; but, if the famous brother had a million brothers, the rent of the peanut processor from Georgia would have been much less.

9.10b An Example: Old Oil

The firm depicted by panel (a) of Figure 9-14 could be a company owning a field of "old" oil wells. What is the difference between "old" oil and newly discovered oil? The story is that a geologist named A. D. Zapp noted that by 1961, 1.1 billion feet of drilling yielded a discovery of 130 billion barrels of crude oil. On average, up to that point, 1 foot of exploratory drilling yielded 118 barrels of discovered oil. Zapp also estimated that the remaining exploratory drilling in the United States amounted to 3.9 billion feet. He multiplied it by 118 barrels per (exploratory) foot and arrived at the optimistic conclusion that 460 billion barrels is the additional potential of oil to be discovered in the United States. Another geologist, named M. K. Hubert, knew more about the difference between marginal and average values. He noted that while at the beginning of the century oil was discovered at a rate of 200 barrels per exploratory foot, in 1965 this rate had dropped to 35 barrels per (exploratory) foot. Assuming that the rate would continue to decline, Hubert concluded that future discoveries would amount to 30 to 40 billion barrels of oil. We can summarize this by saying that from the beginning of the century to 1965, the exploratory component in the marginal cost of oil rose from 0.005 to 0.029 foot per barrel. Even if all other components in the marginal cost of producing oil remain unchanged over time, in order to induce the oil companies to discover new oil, the price must rise in order to cover the additional cost of exploratory drilling per expected barrel of oil. The rent in panel (a) of Figure 9-14 may be viewed as returns to the ease with which old wells were discovered (0.005 foot per barrel), relative to new fields that are discovered at a higher cost (0.029 foot per barrel). Panel (b) of Figure 9-14 illustrates the economics of a new oil well. The relatively high price of P_0 barely induced a discovery of a new oil field; presently the P_0 line just touches the minimum of the $LRAC_2$ curve. In the future, if the cost of exploration rises, following an increase in demand the price of crude oil will increase and the owner of the "new" oil well depicted by panel (b) of Figure 9-14 will receive an economic rent.

9-10c The Zero-Profit Theorem

The *zero-profit theorem* states that in the long run all rents are dissipated. This theorem, unless carefully explained, may be misleading rather than helpful in clarifying the problem. Consider panel (a) of Figure 9-14 again. Suppose P_0 is expected to prevail for a very long time. Then the shaded area is an expected future flow of an economic rent. The present value of this future income stream represents wealth.[14] This wealth is reflected in the price of the stock of the lucky corporation. If you purchase the firm described in panel (a) of Figure 9-14, you will have to pay for this wealth. Indeed, by having paid for the wealth, your economic rent will by definition be zero. Your AC curve will climb to the dashed LRAC curve.

That price of stocks reflects the capitalization of expected earnings of firms was demonstrated by Victor Neiderhoffer and Patrick Regan.[15] They examined the performance of 650 stocks for the 5-year period ending in 1970. The median changes in stock prices and earnings per share were as follows: The top (median) 50 corporations recorded advances between 182 and 199

---

[14] Wealth is the present value of all future income streams. A person who expects a rent of R_1 in the next year, R_2 in the second year, and so on, can, if no risks are involved, go to any bank and convert the expected future income streams into wealth worth W; W is determined as follows:

$$W = \frac{R_1}{1+r} + \frac{R_2}{(1+r)^2} + \frac{R_3}{(1+r)^3} + \cdots + \frac{R_i}{(1+r)^i} + \cdots$$

where r denotes the going interest rate; W, the wealth, is equal to the present value of all expected future income streams. This topic will be covered in detail in Chapter 16.

[15] Victor Neiderhoffer and Patrick J. Regan, "Earnings Changes, Analysts Forecasts and Stock Prices," *Financial Analysts Journal*, vol. 28, May–June 1972, pp. 65–71.

percent, while the bottom (median) 50 finished with declines between 62 and 61 percent. The correlation is very high indeed.

9.11 AN APPLICATION: CRIME (OF THE RUSSIANS) AND PUNISHMENT (BY PRESIDENT CARTER)

In December 1979 the Russians invaded Afghanistan; to punish the Russians, President Carter imposed an embargo on wheat shipments from the United States to the Soviet Union. Suppose you are an economist and President Carter asked for your advice. You refer the President to Figure 9-15. Since wheat is an international commodity, we can conceive of D_0 and S_0 as the world demand and supply curves of wheat. Initially point A denotes the equilibrium in the world wheat market; X_0 bushels of wheat are cleared at a price of P_0. The President tells you that he intends to withdraw the amount of wheat that was initially earmarked for export to the Soviet Union; this wheat will be used to produce alcohol to help alleviate the energy crisis. You tell the President that as a result the supply of wheat (in the nonenergy

market) will shift to the left from S_0 to S_1. Assuming that the Russians will continue to purchase wheat through proxies (Eastern Bloc states), the position of the demand curve will not be affected. The new equilibrium point will he depicted by B, where a smaller quantity X_1 will be cleared at a higher price of P_1. You summarize it for the President as follows:

1. The punishment intended solely for the Russians will be borne by all wheat consumers in the world. The punishment will be nothing more than a rise in the price of wheat from P_0 to P_1.
2. Farmers in the United States should be advised to praise the President: They will end up gaining from the scheme and will receive a higher price.
3. Economic embargoes are tricky.

FIGURE 9-15 PUNISHING THE RUSSIANS: THE WORLD MARKET FOR WHEAT
The initial equilibrium in the world wheat market is depicted by point A. Initial quantity and price are X_0 and P_0. If President Carter takes the amount of wheat that was earmarked for export to Russia off the food (and feed) market and converts it into energy (alcohol), supply will shift to the left to position S_1, resulting in a higher price (for Russians and non-Russians) of P_1 and a lower quantity of X_1. This model is based on the assumption that the Russians can continue to buy wheat through proxies.

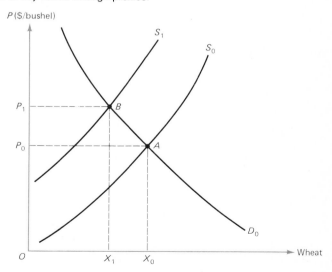

9.12 GROWTH, OR LONG-RUN SHIFTS OF SUPPLY AND DEMAND [AN EXAMPLE: THE FARM SECTION (Optional)]

Let us now gloss over the seasonal and year-to-year changes in prices and quantities in competitive markets. Let us concentrate on long-run shifts in supply and demand. In the case of supply, long-run shifts are determined mainly by technological innovations and changes in prices of factors of production. In the case of demand, long-run shifts are determined mainly by population growth and changes in income per capita. If aggregates like farm output are discussed, there is no need to worry about the price of substitute goods. But if beef is studied, the price of a close substitute such as poultry becomes crucial. As shown in Equation 3-6, the long-run shift in the demand curve can be summarized as follows:

$$\frac{\Delta X_1}{X_1} = \frac{\Delta \Pi}{\Pi} + \alpha \frac{\Delta I}{I} + \eta_{12} \frac{\Delta P_2}{P_2} \qquad (9\text{-}1)$$

Namely, the percentage change in demand is proportional to the change in population Π, to the percentage change in income per capital I times income elasticity α, and to the percentage change of the price of a closely related good P_2 times the cross-elasticity η_{12}. As for the supply curve, it is more difficult to quantify the shift over time, but it can be estimated in a rough manner.

Yeh provided some interesting estimates of long-run supply and demand shifts for the farm sector.[16] His estimates were as follows:

Demand:
Price elasticity, long run	−0.214
Price elasticity, short run	−0.15
Income elasticity	0.15

Supply:
Price elasticity, long run	1.00
Price elasticity, short run	0.20

The problem of short-run price elasticities, which draws on dynamics, will be ignored here. The information given by Yeh concerning the demand curve is as follows: Between 1967 and 1974, United States population increased at a rate of 0.97 percent per annum. During the same period real per capita disposable income grew at an average rate of 2.05 percent per year. Domestic demand accounted for 85 percent of total demand for farm output, and exports, which accounted for the remaining 15 percent, increased by 38 percent during the entire period. Exports grew at an annual rate of 4.7 percent $[(1.047)^7 = 1.38]$. The annual demand growth accounted for by population and export growth was then

$$0.85 \cdot 0.97 + 0.15 \cdot 4.7 = 1.53$$

---

[16]Chung J. Yeh, "Prices, Farm Output, and Income Projections under Alternative Assumed Demand and Supply Conditions," *American Journal of Agricultural Economics*, vol. 58, no. 4, November 1976, pp. 703–711.

In other words, because of population and exports growth alone, the aggregate demand for farm output shifted at a rate of 1.53 percent per annum. Income elasticity α was estimated at 0.15. It is adjusted here for the fact that the domestic component accounted for only 85 percent of the aggregate demand by multiplying α by 0.85: $0.85 \cdot 0.15 = 0.13$. The horizontal supply shift is obtained by multiplying the vertical supply shift by the (long-run) supply elasticity. Since in Yeh's study supply elasticity is unity, the downward 1 percent shift in the supply due to technological progress is translated into a rightward shift of 1 percent.

Finally the reader should note a development in Mathematical Appendix 9 in which supply and demand equations are reduced to two equations showing the percentage change in the endogenous variables, quantity and price, as functions of the exogenous variables. Let us denote supply elasticity by ϵ, demand shift by K, and supply shift by H. Let us agree to denote the percentage change in K by $\Delta\%K$, etc. The two equations then become

$$\Delta\%P = \frac{1}{\epsilon - \eta} \Delta\%K - \frac{1}{\epsilon - \eta} \Delta\%H + \frac{\alpha}{\epsilon - \eta} \Delta\%I \qquad (9\text{-}2)$$

$$\Delta\%X = \frac{\epsilon}{\epsilon - \eta} \Delta\%K - \frac{\eta}{\epsilon - \eta} \Delta\%H + \frac{\epsilon\alpha}{\epsilon - \eta} \Delta\%I \qquad (9\text{-}3)$$

Accordingly, the annual changes in price and quantity are obtained as follows:

$$\frac{\Delta P}{P} \cdot 100 = \frac{1}{1.214} \cdot 1.53 - \frac{1}{1.214} \cdot 1 + \frac{0.13}{1.214} \cdot 2.05 = 0.66 \text{ percent}$$

$$\frac{\Delta X}{X} \cdot 100 = \frac{1}{1.214} \cdot 1.53 - \frac{-0.214}{1.214} \cdot 1 + \frac{1 \cdot 0.13}{1.214} \cdot 2.05 = 1.66 \text{ percent}$$

Figure 9-16 illustrates this result: Supply shifts 1 percent a year; demand shifts 1.53 percent (population and exports) plus 0.27 percent (due to income: $0.13 \cdot 2.05$), a total of 1.8 percent per year. As a result the two endogenous variables, price and quantity, increase by 0.66 and 1.66 percent, respectively.

SUMMARY   In this chapter supply and demand curves were brought together. It was explained why equilibrium in competitive markets occurs at the point of intersection between supply and demand. Equilibrium is stable because a price deviation from *equilibrium* will generate either a temporary surplus or a temporary shortage that will in turn generate market forces pushing the price back to its equilibrium level. A permanent surplus will result from the establishment of a price floor. A *price floor* can be effective only if an agency (like the government) is willing to purchase the surplus at the floor price. A *permanent shortage* will result from the establishment of a price ceiling by the government.

Next we saw that changes in *exogenous variables* lead to either demand or supply shifts. The major exogenous variables are population, income per

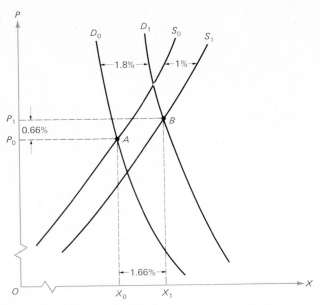

FIGURE 9-16 CHANGES IN EXOGENOUS FACTORS AND RESULTING CHANGES IN ENDOGENOUS VARIABLES

Following changes in *exogenous variables* demand increases by 1.8 percent and supply increases by 1 percent. Utilizing equations 9-2 and 9-3, we calculate that the *endogenous variables* change as follows: Prices rise by 0.66 percent; quantity increases by 1.66 percent.

capita, prices of other goods, and tastes affecting the demand and prices of inputs and technology affecting the supply. As a result of demand or supply shifts the two *endogenous variables*, price and quantity, change. We saw that an increase in demand will lead to an increase in both price and quantity. An increase in supply will lead to a decrease in price and an increase in quantity. In the short run the burden of the adjustment falls mainly on price; in the long run the burden of adjustment falls mainly on quantity.

Some major cases of supply shifts were then illustrated by considering the impact of the frost in Brazil on the coffee market, the rise in the wages of coal miners on the coal market, and the innovation of hybrid corn on the corn market.

Next the issue of *external economies* and *diseconomies* was discussed. The difference between *internal* and *external* economies and diseconomies was explained. It was concluded that the main cause of external (pecuniary) diseconomies is a situation in which the industry faces a rising supply curve of a variable factor of production; as the industry expands, the price of this variable input must rise, leading to an upward shift of the supply curve (sum of the firms' MC curves). It was concluded that if external diseconomies are present, the supply curve will be steeper. Conversely, the presence of external economies will lead to a more elastic supply curve. The possibility of *technical* (rather than pecuniary) *externalities* was mentioned.

Price dispersion was then discussed and it was concluded that price dispersion may result from a variety of situations. An example of this would be price dispersion due to variations of distance of markets from centers of production, in the case of a relatively cheap commodity, due to the cost of market searching (canvassing sellers).

The next topic was price movement over time. In the short run price may vary over time as a result of seasonal supply and demand changes. If production is cyclical (as in the case of most agricultural commodities), prices will vary over time first because commodities are stored in warehouses from harvest to harvest, and second because the harvest will vary owing to variations in weather conditions. The price of exhaustible resources constantly increases over time because owners of these resources have the option of storing their wealth either in the ground or in the bank.

The *economic rent*, which was viewed as "gravy" received by entrepreneurs, was then analyzed. Economic rent results from scarcity of either entrepreneurial talent or other factors such as convenient location or high-grade natural resources (old oil). The economic rent is either a return to entrepreneurial capacity in excess of the reservation price of the entrepreneur or a return to other scarce resources.

The last topic was the impact of long-run changes in exogenous factors on endogenous variables. It was demonstrated how, given a simultaneous shift in supply and demand curve, we can solve for the resulting changes in price and quantity.

GLOSSARY   **Market equilibrium** A price at which what producers produce consumers consume; geometrically in perfect competition equilibrium occurs at the point of intersection between supply and demand.

Floor price The lowest price allowed by an agency (usually the government). A floor price can be effective only if the agency is willing to back it up by taking the *surplus* off the market.

Ceiling price The highest price allowed by an agency (usually the government). Price ceilings are difficult to enforce.

Exogenous variables Variables that originate from external causes. In demand-supply analysis such variables are population, income per capita, prices of other goods, and tastes that shift the demand curve and prices of inputs and technology that shift the supply curve.

Endogenous variables Variables that originate from internal causes. In demand-supply analysis such variables are price and quantity.

Comparative statics An analysis which focuses on the comparison of two different equilibria.

Dynamics An analysis which focuses on the time path between one equilibrium and the next.

External (pecuniary) diseconomies A state of an industry where if only one firm expands its rate of production prices of inputs are unaffected; if, however, all firms expand, prices of one or more inputs will rise, leading to an upward shift of the MC curve of each firm. As a result, in the presence of external diseconomies industry supply is steeper. A *technical* (rather than a pecuniary) external diseconomy would arise if the upward displacement of the MC curves resulted from an industry-wide expansion leading to worsening technical conditions (e.g., water pollution).

External economies The same as *external diseconomies*, except that industry-wide expansion in production would lead to downward shifts in the MC curves of all the firms. External economies are rare and are usually technical.

Economic rent Total revenue minus total *economic* costs. In the long run rent is "gravy" received by entrepreneurs. It is a return to entrepreneurial capacity over and above their reservation price, i.e., over and above their return at the next best alternative.

Quasi-rent In the short run fixed factors of production have no alternative uses; hence their reservation price (remuneration at the next best alternative) is zero. Accordingly, if the price is equal to or lower than the *minimum* of the short-run average cost, total revenue minus total variable cost is a short-run rent for fixed factors, which is termed *quasi-rent*.

Zero-profit theorem In the long run all rents are dissipated. This is a result of the fact that if a firm is sold, the buyer must pay for the present value of all expected future rents.

PROBLEMS   An asterisk indicates an advanced problem.

In solving problems 9-1 to 9-8, you should start from an assumption that the market is in initial equilibrium. This equilibrium is upset as described in each problem. The disturbance brings about a shift in either the demand curve, the supply curve, or both. Indicate what is the nature of the shift by drawing a new curve. Then indicate what is the new price and the new quantity at the new point of market equilibrium.

9-1.   The union of workers in industry A raises wages.

9-2.   There is a change in tastes; people like more tea and less coffee (draw two panels).

9-3.   Crops of coffee happened to be exceptionally good. Analyze the market for tea. Assume that coffee and tea are substitutes (draw two panels).

9-4.   After hybrid corn was adopted by farmers, corn crops increased enormously.

9-5.   The city of Chicago is going to increase the number of buses that are operated in the area. Analyze the market for cab services.

9-6.*   Because the Suez Canal has been closed by Egypt (1967), the cost of transporting oil via the sea has increased. Analyze the domestic oil market in a country where part of the oil consumption is supplied by domestic wells and part is imported from the Middle East.

9-7.   There is a severe frost in Florida. Analyze the market for oranges.

9-8. Duties on cars are eliminated in country X. Analyze the market for gasoline. (Draw two panels.)

9-9. In Figure 9-9 is it possible that P_1 will be so high that x_i^1 will be larger than x_i^0?

9-10.* Following a technological change there is a change in both consumer's and producer's surplus. Show that even if producer's surplus declines, the increase in consumer's surplus exceeds the decline in producer's surplus.

9-11.* Griliches assumed a horizontal supply curve of corn and a price elasticity of demand of -0.5. The current price (1955, after the hybrid corn was adopted) was $1 per bushel and total harvest was 2700 million bushels. The annual current expense to produce the hybrid seeds was estimated at $93 million. (The supply curve shifted downward by 13 percent because of the hybrid corn.) Estimate the net annual gain to consumers. (For reference to Griliches, see Section 9.5b.)

9-12. If it is not certain that the producer's surplus increases as a result of technological innovation, why do producers in the field of microelectronics invest in research?

9-13. Could the supply curve S_0 in Figure 9-13 slope negatively?

9-14. In the United States during the period 1973–1974, exports were high and production of farm output was about normal. Farmers praised the free market. During the period 1976–1977, exports were relatively low, but farm output, mainly wheat and feed grains, exceeded the normal level. Farmers threatened that unless they got 100 percent parity prices from the federal government, they would go on strike. Explain.

MATHEMATICAL APPENDIX 9

M9-1 STRUCTURAL EQUATIONS AND REDUCED FORMS

In the text the effects of demand and supply shifts in the long run were discussed. Equations 9-2 and 9-3 were provided to illustrate how the percentage changes of the endogenous variables are calculated. The equations called *reduced forms*, which are reduced from the supply and demand equations known as the *structural equations*, are now derived. Consider Figure 9-17.

The demand curve may shift because of changes in income, in prices of

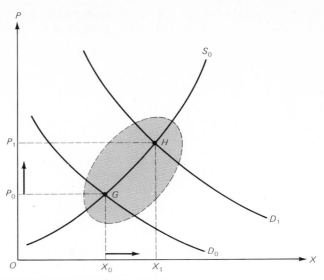

FIGURE 9-17   AN ILLUSTRATION OF A DEMAND SHIFT.
A change in an exogenous variable leads to a demand shift from D_0 to D_1. As a result the price rises from P_0 to P_1 and the quantity rises from X_0 to X_1.

other commodities, or in tastes. The supply curve may shift because of technological changes or because factors of production are becoming either cheaper or dearer. For simplicity, assume that the demand curve shifts rightward as a result of a change in income per capita. Tastes of consumers and the number of consumers are unchanged. The supply curve does not shift at all. This is illustrated by Figure 9-17. If we knew the mathematical functions of S_0, D_0, and D_i, we would be able to determine the coordinates of point G and point H, respectively. In reality, we have only a rough idea of the order of magnitudes of elasticities, and we have to make some use of it. If we are ready to make the assumption that elasticities are fixed in the shaded area in Figure 9-17, we can provide a crude estimate of the respective changes in the price and the quantity. The smaller the shaded area in Figure 9-17, the more realistic is the assumption of fixed elasticities.

At the point of intersection between supply and demand the following hold:

$$X_D = K + \eta \cdot P + \alpha \cdot I \qquad \text{(m9-1)}$$

$$X_s = H = \epsilon \cdot P \qquad \text{(m9-2)}$$

$$X = X_s = X_D \qquad \text{(m9-3)}$$

where the subscripts D and S denote demand and supply, respectively; η is price elasticity of demand; α is income elasticity; ϵ is price elasticity of supply; and X, I, and P are the *logarithms* of quantity, income per capita, and price, respectively. (Since the variables are in logarithms, η, α, and ϵ are elasticities.) Equation m9-1 is known as the *demand structural equation*, and

Equation m9-2 is known as the *supply structural equation*. The variables X and P are endogenous: they are determined by Equations m9-1, m9-2, and m9-3.

Solving for P and X gives the *reduced forms*

$$P = \frac{K - H}{\epsilon - \eta} + \frac{\alpha}{\epsilon - \eta} \cdot I \qquad \text{(m9-4)}$$

and

$$X = \frac{\epsilon K - \eta H}{\epsilon - \eta} + \frac{\epsilon \alpha}{\epsilon - \eta} \cdot I \qquad \text{(m9-5)}$$

For example, the coefficient of I in Equation m9-4 is the elasticity of the price with respect to income per capita, and the coefficient of I in Equation m9-5 is the elasticity of the quantity with respect to income per capita.

Finally consider the short run versus the long run: Let X^* denote the desired level of output (demanded or supplied). The relationship between X^* and P is as follows:

$$X^* = a + bP \qquad \text{(m9-6)}$$

where coefficient a could stand for either the demand shifter or the supply shifter and coefficient b could stand for either long-run price elasticity of demand or long-run price elasticity of supply. X and P are in logarithm form. Otherwise Equation m9-6 is in a linear form. Let k stand for the adjustment coefficient. Mathematically this means

$$X_{t+1} = X_t + k(X_t^* - X_t) \qquad \text{(m9-7)}$$

Rearranging and substituting, we obtain

$$X_{t+1} = (1 - k)X_t + ka + kbP_t \qquad \text{(m9-8)}$$

For example, consider the linear form of Equation m9-6. If $a = 2$ and $b = 0.5$, then X^* is 3 if P is 2. Assume that $X_0 = 2$, then, given an adjustment coefficient of 0.7 over time, X will approach its optimum (X^*) as follows:

t	X
1	2.70
2	2.91
3	2.97
4	2.99
5	3.00
6	3.00

C H A P T E R

10

SPECIAL ISSUES IN THE COMPETITIVE MARKET

(optional)

The theory of supply and demand can be applied to numerous real-world problems. This chapter will examine the theory of competitive markets in some of its most significant applications. At this stage the student may wish to review Section 8.1, in which the concept of the *industry* was discussed. The student may also benefit from reviewing Sections 9.1, 9.2, and 9.3, where the basic ideas of *supply and demand* analysis were considered. This chapter will gloss over the issue of short run versus long run. Unless otherwise stated, supply and demand will mean long-run supply and long-run demand.

The topics included in this chapter do not appear in their order of importance. The student or professor may select one or more topics for study, depending on personal inclination and need. The purpose of this chapter is simply to reinforce Chapter 9 by providing the interested reader with some theoretical applications to real-world problems. The reader who is in a rush to grasp as much theory as possible in a short time may opt to skip this chapter and go directly to Chapter 11.

10.1 EXCISE TAXES

10.1a Definitions

An *excise tax* is a tax which (1) is levied on sellers and (2) is positively related to the volume of sales. An excise tax may be levied in two distinct forms: *unit* and *ad valorem*.

A *unit tax* (sometimes called *specific* tax) is assessed as a given amount of money per unit of output. For example, if a unit tax of $2 per quart of whiskey is imposed, $2 is paid to the government on each quart of whiskey sold in the marketplace, regardless of the price of whiskey and regardless of the amount of whiskey sold.

An *ad valorem* tax is assessed as a percentage of the sales price. For example, if an ad valorem tax of 50 percent is imposed on whiskey, the tax on a $6 bottle is $3 and the tax on an $8 bottle is $4.

A *subsidy* is a negative tax that the government pays the producer as either a specific or an ad valorem subsidy. In some developing countries, bread is subsidized.

10.1b The Impact of Unit Taxes on the Supply Curve

Suppose you are a producer of whiskey and the government imposes a unit tax of $1 per quart of whiskey sold. Such a tax must shift your marginal cost curve upward by $1. The explanation for this is that in addition to paying for the variable inputs required to produce one additional quart, you must now pay an additional dollar to the government. Let us denote the unit tax by T. In Figure 10-1, MC_0 depicts your pretax marginal cost curve. For instance, when you produce X_0 quarts of whiskey, you pay mc_0 dollars for additional variable inputs used in producing the last unit. Suppose mc_0 is $5. After the tax is imposed, your actual additional payment is $5 + $1 = $6. In general terms the actual additional payment is $mc_0 + T$. Put another way, your actual marginal cost is depicted by point B rather than point A. If you apply this procedure to each feasible level of output, you find that your entire marginal cost curve is displaced by T dollars upward: Instead of MC_0 the marginal cost curve after tax is MC_1.

Since the supply curve of the industry is the sum of all the MC curves of all individual firms (Section 8.2a), imposing a unit tax T will cause the industry supply curve to shift upward by T dollars. In the example, your MC curve, as well as the MC curve of each whiskey producer, will shift upward by $1, leading to an upward shift of the whiskey supply curve by $1.

10.1c The Effect of a Unit Tax on Output and Price

Consider Figure 10-2. Before the tax is imposed, initial demand curve D_0 intersects initial supply curve S_0 at point E. Equilibrium price and quantity are P_0 and X_0. After the tax is imposed, the supply curve shifts upward by T dollars from S_0 to S_1. At the new point of equilibrium G, the market clears X_1 units at a price of P_1. Since by construction (of S_1) the vertical distance between S_0 and S_1 is T dollars, the segment $\overline{FG}$ is equal to T dollars. The new price paid by consumers in the marketplace is $\overline{X_1G}$; we denote it by P_1 on the price axis. The price received by producers net of the tax is $\overline{X_1F}$; we denote it by P_2. The revenue collected by the government is $T \cdot X_1$, which is the shaded rectangle indicated by P_2FGP_1. The imposition of the tax leads to a

FIGURE 10-1   THE IMPACT OF A UNIT TAX ON THE MARGINAL COST CURVE

Quarts of whiskey are measured along the horizontal axis; price (dollars per quart) is measured along the vertical axis. The original marginal cost curve is depicted by MC_0; at a level of X_0 the marginal cost is mc_0. After a unit tax of T dollars is imposed, the marginal cost rises to $mc_0 + T$. Applying similar analysis to each feasible level of output yields the MC_1 curve, which is T dollars higher than the MC_0 curve.

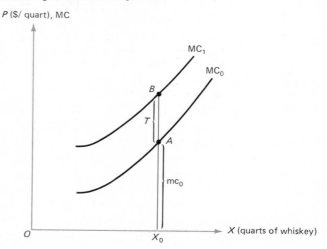

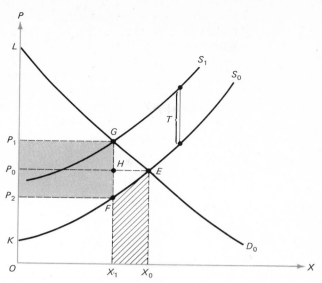

FIGURE 10-2 THE IMPACT OF A UNIT TAX ON THE INDUSTRY

The initial demand curve D_0 intersects with the initial supply curve S_0 at point E. After a unit tax of T dollars is imposed, the supply curve shifts upward to the position S_1. As a result, output shrinks from X_0 to a new level of X_1. The price to consumers rises to P_1. The price received by producers net of the tax is P_2. The shaded area is the revenue collected by the government; the striped area is market value of variable resources that had to find employment elsewhere in the economy; the burden of the tax borne by consumers is $\overline{HG}/T$, and by producers $\overline{HF}/T$. The welfare loss to society is the area of the triangle GFE.

fall in production from X_0 to X_1. Variable inputs whose worth to society falls within the striped area X_1FEX_0 (Section 7.4) must find employment elsewhere in the economy.

10.1d The Incidence of the Unit Tax

Who bears the burden of the tax? Because unit taxes are imposed on producers, laypeople tend to deduce that producers can shift the tax forward to consumers. This is a fallacy that can be exposed with the aid of supply and demand apparatus. Consider Figure 10-2 again. After a tax of T dollars $(\overline{FG})$ is imposed, the price to the consumer rises from P_0 to P_1, an increase of $\overline{HG}$ dollars. The price received by the producer, net of the tax, falls from P_0 to P_2. This amounts to a decline of $\overline{HF}$ dollars. The incidence of the tax to the consumer is defined as the ratio of the (positive) change in the price which the consumer must pay to the tax:

$$\text{Incidence of tax} = \frac{\Delta P_{consumer}}{T} = \frac{\overline{HG}}{\overline{FG}} \tag{10-1}$$

Since the change in the price to the consumer plus the change in the price to the producer must be equal to the excise tax $(\overline{HG} + \overline{FH} = \overline{FG})$, the incidence of the tax to the consumer plus the incidence of the tax to the producer ($\overline{HF}/\overline{FG}$) must add up to unity.

Consider the vicinity of point E in Figure 10-2. The (negative) change in quantity is $\Delta X = \overline{EH}$. The (positive) change in the price paid by consumers is $\Delta P_d = \overline{HG}$; the (negative) change in the price received by producers is $\Delta P_s = \overline{HF}$. Let us denote the slope of the demand curve by d and the slope of the supply curve by s. Around point E the two slopes can be expressed as

$$d = \frac{\Delta P_d}{\Delta X} = \frac{\overline{HG}}{\overline{EH}} \qquad s = \frac{\Delta P_s}{\Delta X} = \frac{\overline{HF}}{\overline{EH}}$$

And we can write

$$\text{Incidence} = \frac{\overline{HG}}{\overline{FG}} = \frac{\overline{HG}}{\overline{HG} + \overline{FH}} = \frac{\overline{HG}}{\overline{HG} - \overline{HF}}$$

$$= \frac{\overline{HG}/\overline{EH}}{\overline{HG}/\overline{EH} - \overline{HF}/\overline{EH}} = \frac{d}{d - s}$$

If we multiply the numerator and the denominator of the above expression by X/P [recall (Section 2.2) that the slope here is $\Delta P/\Delta X$, which should not be confused with $\Delta X/\Delta P$ appearing in the formula of elasticity], we obtain

$$\text{Incidence} = \frac{1/\eta}{1/\eta - 1/\epsilon} = \frac{1}{1 - \eta/\epsilon} = \frac{1}{1 + |\eta|/\epsilon} \qquad (10\text{-}2)$$

where η is demand elasticity (Section 2.4f) and ϵ is supply elasticity (Section 8.2b). If the supply curve is very elastic, ϵ is very large and $|\eta|/\epsilon$ approaches zero. Thus the incidence is unity and the entire burden of the tax is borne by consumers. On the other hand, if the demand curve is very elastic, $|\eta|$ approaches infinity, and the incidence in Equation 10-2 is zero. The entire burden of the tax is borne by producers. These two extreme cases are illustrated geometrically by Figure 10-3: In panel (a) the supply curve is infinitely elastic and the price to the consumer rises by the entire amount of the tax: P_1 is by $\overline{FG}$ higher than P_0. In panel (b) the demand curve is infinitely elastic. The price to the consumer does not change. The net price received by the producer is P_2, which is by the amount of the tax ($\overline{FG}$) less than the original price P_0.

Hence the question ''Who bears the burden of the tax, the consumer or the producer?'' depends on the relative magnitudes of supply and demand elasticities. For example, if supply elasticity is equal to demand elasticity, the burden of the tax is borne equally by producers and consumers.

10.1e Welfare Loss due to Unit Taxes

Section 2.7 argued that the area under the demand curve and above the price line represents the consumer's surplus. Section 7.4 also argued that the area lying above the marginal cost curve and under the price line is the producer's surplus. These concepts of consumer's and producer's surplus will now be utilized to show how welfare loss due to excise taxes is estimated.

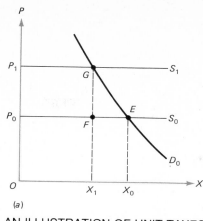

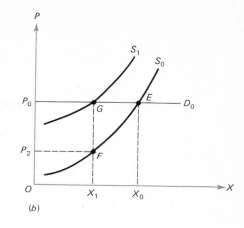

(a)

(b)

FIGURE 10-3 AN ILLUSTRATION OF UNIT TAXES

(a) Initial supply curve S_0 is horizontal. A unit tax amounting to $\overline{FG}$ dollars shifts the supply curve to S_1. The entire burden of the tax is borne by the consumers: P_1 is by $\overline{FG}$ higher than P_0.

(b) Initial demand curve D_0 is horizontal. A unit tax amounting to $\overline{FG}$ dollars shifts the supply curve from S_0 to S_1. The entire burden of the tax is borne by producers: P_2 is by $\overline{FG}$ lower than P_0.

Consider Figure 10-2 again. Before the imposition of the tax, equilibrium occurs at point E. The consumer's surplus is the area denoted by P_0EL and the producer's surplus is the area denoted by P_0EK. After a unit tax T is imposed, the price to consumers rises to a level of P_1, and the consumer's surplus accordingly shrinks to P_1GL. The loss to consumers is area P_0EGP_1.

Next, we turn our attention to producers and find that after the tax is imposed the net price received by producers falls to P_2. The new producer's surplus area is P_2FK and the loss to producers is P_0EFP_2. The combined loss to producers and consumers is area P_1GEFP_2. However, since the government gains rectangle P_1GFP_2, the net loss is the area represented by GEF. If we assume that the demand curve and the supply curve are linear in the range EG and EF, respectively, the welfare loss is the area of triangle GFE. This welfare loss is sometimes called *deadweight loss to society*.

The following points are relevant here:

1. In estimating the welfare loss to society, we followed convention and assumed that society values the services rendered by the government as equal to rectangle P_1GFP_2.

2. The deadweight loss to society is very small. Indeed, triangle GEF has an area equal to $\frac{1}{2} \cdot \Delta X \cdot T$. Let us for simplicity imagine that the supply curve of X is perfectly elastic [panel (a) of Figure 10-3] and that in equilibrium 100 units are sold at a price of $100. If price elasticity is unity, an excise tax of $5 will lead to a loss of 0.12 percent of the total value of X. This is calculated as follows: First, a 5 percent rise in the price of X would lead to a 5 percent decline in the quantity sold on the market. Thus $\Delta P = \$5$ and $\Delta X = -5$ units. The welfare loss is then

$$\text{Welfare loss} = \frac{1}{2} \cdot 5 \cdot 5 = 12.5 \text{ dollars}$$

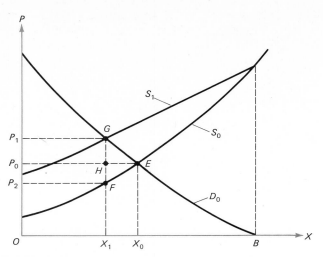

AN AD VALOREM TAX

The tax is assessed as a percentage of the market price; in other words it is assessed as a percentage of the demand price. Since the demand price is inversely related to output marketed, the tax decreases with output until it completely vanishes when demand curve D_0 cuts the output axis at point B. As a result of the ad valorem tax the supply curve shifts from S_0 to S_1; except for the fact that S_1 is not parallel to S_0, the results are similar to the case of a unit tax: Output falls from X_0 to X_1; price to consumers rises from P_0 to P_1; price net of the tax to producers falls from P_0 to P_2. Revenue collected by the government is the area of rectangle P_1P_2FG; the incidence to consumers is $\overline{HG}/T$ and to producers $\overline{HF}/T$. The welfare loss to society is the area of triangle FGE.

This is 0.12 percent of total revenue, namely, of $10,000 (= $100 \cdot 100$).

3. The analysis presented above ignores *general equilibrium*. Economists call it partial-equilibrium analysis. Measuring the deadweight loss to society in a framework of general equilibrium will be discussed again in Chapter 17. For the moment, it is stressed that partial-equilibrium estimates are rough and that the entire issue of welfare loss measurements is not entirely settled.

10.1f Ad Valorem Tax

You will recall that an ad valorem tax is assessed as a percentage of the sales price (Section 10.1a). Accordingly, an ad valorem tax will differ from a unit tax in the manner in which the supply curve is displaced. We saw that a unit tax results in a new supply curve which is T dollars higher than the initial supply curve. Let us now see how the supply curve will shift because of the imposition of an ad valorem tax. Consider Figure 10-4. Let S_0 and D_0 represent the initial supply and demand curves, respectively. The demand curve intersects with the X axis at a level of output of $\overline{OB}$. Since at that level the demand price is zero, the ad valorem tax will also be zero. If we denote the ad valorem rate by t (if the rate is 10 percent, $t = 0.1$) and the price as indicated by the demand curve by P_d, the tax per unit is $t \cdot P_d$. In the case of a unit tax the upward shift in the supply curve is T dollars. In the case of an ad valorem tax, the shift is $t \cdot P_d$, which increases as output decreases. If P_s denotes the supply price, then in the case of a unit tax the new supply is related to the original supply curve by the equation $P_{s1} = P_{s0} + T$. In equilibrium, since $P_d = P_{s1}$, we have to satisfy the equation $P_d = P_{s0} + T$. (In Figure 10-2 this is equivalent to $\overline{X_1 G} = \overline{X_1 F} + T$.) In the case of an ad valorem tax, the new supply curve is related to the original supply curve by the equation $P_{s1} = P_{s0} + t \cdot P_d$. In equilibrium, since $P_d = P_{s1}$, we have to satisfy the equation $P_d = P_{s0} + t \cdot P_d$. This can be rearranged and written as $P_d(1 - t) = P_{s0}$ or as $P_d = P_{s0}/(1 - t)$. [In Figure 10-4 this is equivalent to $\overline{X_1 G} = \overline{X_1 F}/(1 - t)$.]

As in the case of a unit tax, the welfare loss resulting from an ad valorem tax will be the area of triangle GFE, and the revenue gained by the government will be the area of rectangle $P_1 GFP_2$. Output produced by the industry will fall from X_0 to X_1, and variable inputs valued by area $X_1 FEX_0$ will find employment elsewhere in the economy. Section 10.1i will point out a difference between the impact of unit tax and ad valorem tax on qualitative changes in the taxed good.

10.1g An Example: The Impact of Increasing Sales Taxes in New York City and Alabama

Imposing excise taxes on items for which demand is elastic leads to a significant decline in the quantity marketed [panel (b) of Figure 10-3]. In other words, in the case of elastic demand curves, consumers avoid paying a part of the tax by shifting purchasing power away from the taxed commodity to other goods. Accordingly, taxes which are placed on items with elastic demand curves are sometimes called "demand-shifting taxes." Sometimes the shifting of the tax occurs across the border of a state: A state government which imposes a sales tax (assessed as a percentage of the sales value) may find that its citizens who live near the state's border will avoid the tax by shopping in the next state. For a local government the most important practical aspect of imposing a sales tax is the demand elasticity for the taxable good. If raising the tax will result in a smaller revenue for the government, why do it to begin with?

William Hamovitch studied the effects of rate increases in New York City and the state of Alabama.[1] The two cases were chosen because both governments raised sales tax rates from 2 to 3 percent in 1951 and from 3 to 4 percent in 1963. New York City was surrounded by shopping areas in sales tax–free counties in both New York State and New Jersey. Alabama, on the other hand, was surrounded by sales tax states. Moreover, the distances for most shoppers in Alabama from residential areas to neighboring states were relatively long.

Hamovitch estimated statistically the impact of a change in sales tax rates on taxable sales. In New York City he found that a change of the tax rate by one percentage point gave rise to a loss of 575 million dollars per annum in taxable sales. It is important to note that this loss was not recouped later. The loss in taxable sales was permanent. In Alabama, the statistical study showed no significant relationship between raising the tax rate and taxable sales.

After the sales tax rate was rasied one percentage point in 1950–1951 taxable sales fell by 334 million dollars. (This is short of 575 million dollars because disposable personal income increased during the same period.) Even without resorting to sophisticated statistical studies, it was clear that in New York City tax avoidance resulting from the rise in the rate was great.

[1]William Hamovitch, "Sales Taxation: An Analysis of the Effects of Rate Increases in Two Contrasting Cases," *National Tax Journal*, vol. 19, December 1966, pp. 411–420.

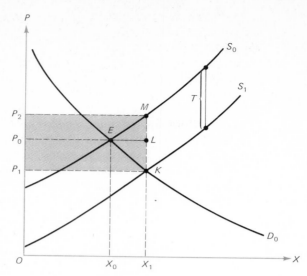

FIGURE 10-5   A SUBSIDY

Initially the supply and demand curves are S_0 and D_0, respectively. After a unit subsidy of T dollars is extended to producers, the supply curve shifts downward by T dollars to S_1. As a result output increases from X_0 to X_1. The price received by producers rises from P_0 to P_2 and the price paid by consumers falls from P_0 to P_1. The cost of the subsidy to the government is the shaded rectangle. The (negative) burden on producers is $\overline{LM}/T$ and on consumers $\overline{LK}/T$.

10.1h Subsidy

Consider the case where the government extends a subsidy of T dollars per unit of a good sold in the market. For example, instead of a price support to farmers (Section 9.2b) the government can extend a subsidy of $0.50 per bushel of wheat or grains. The advantage of such a program would be to eliminate surpluses. However, as will be shown soon, a subsidy gives rise to a deadweight loss to society similar to the loss due to taxes. A subsidy is illustrated in Figure 10-5. Originally the point of intersection between supply S_0 and demand D_0 is E, where the price is P_0 and the quantity cleared is X_0. After a subsidy (of T dollars) is extended, the MC curve of each firm in the industry shifts downward by T dollars (Section 10.1b). Hence the supply curve of the industry shifts downward by T dollars to a new position S_1. The new point·of intersection between S_1 and D_0 is K. There, X_1 units are produced. Thus a unit subsidy results in a greater level of production. The cost of the program to the government is $X_1 \cdot T$ dollars, which is the area of the shaded rectangle indicated by P_1KMP_2. Consumers now pay a lower price of P_1 ($\overline{X_1K}$) and producers receive a higher price of P_2 ($= \overline{X_1M}$). The welfare loss is calculated as follows: The gain to consumers is the area indicated by P_0EKP_1, the increment in the consumer's surplus. The gain to producers is the area indicated by P_0EMP_2, the increment in the producer's surplus.

Subtracting these two gains from the shaded rectangle P_1KMP_2 (the loss to the government) leaves us with an uncovered loss of EKM, the familiar "triangle" known as the deadweight loss to society. The three points made in Section 10.1e with regard to welfare loss due to unit taxes apply in the case of excise subsidies with the same force.

10.1i Quality Changes due to Unit Taxes

A gasoline tax is often regarded as a means to combat air pollution. However, if the tax is imposed per gallon of gasoline rather than per unit of pollution, the market might induce substitution toward high-octane gasoline.[2] Higher octane rating is achieved by adding lead to gasoline. Lead is believed to be a major air pollutant. Thus, by imposing a tax on gasoline, we may cause more pollution and definitely more lead pollution. In this example a specific tax resulted in a quality change of the taxed commodity. The reason for the quality change in the example is that gasoline has a few attributes, one of which is the octane rating. Since octane rating was not subject to the tax, producers increase the amount of the untaxed attributes relative to the taxed attributes. Yoram Barzel formalized the theory of quality changes due to excise taxes.[3] He illustrated how a specific tax will increase the durability of light bulbs as follows: In Figure 10-6 along the X axis, we measure months of service rather than light bulbs. The price is dollars per unit of service (months of light) rather than dollars per light bulb. It is realistic to assume that so long as the lifetime of a light bulb is not too short, consumers are interested in the service they get rather than in the source of the service. Suppose that originally manufacturers produce light bulbs with 2 months' durability. [There are different costs of production for different durabilities, but competition forces manufacturers to select the durability which would entail the lowest marginal cost curve (per unit of service). In this example 2 months is supposed to be the optimal durability.] The supply curve is $S(2)$; the number in parentheses indicates the durability. Demand and supply intersect at point E, where $X(2)$ units of service (months of light) are purchased. After a specific tax per light bulb is imposed, the supply curve shifts upward by the amount of the tax per unit of service (tax per light bulb divided by 2 months). For a while, the new supply curve is $S_t(2)$. The price per unit of service to the consumer is $\overline{X_t(2)G}$, the price received by producers net of the tax is $\overline{X_t(2)F}$, and the tax per unit of service is $\overline{FG}$. If producers were to increase durability, the tax would be reduced. In fact, we can write

$$\text{Tax per unit of service} = \frac{\text{tax per light bulb}}{\text{durability}}$$

---

[2] High-octane gasoline yields better results in high-compression engines.

[3] Yoram Barzel, "An Alternative Approach to the Analysis of Taxation," *Journal of Political Economy*, vol. 84, February–December 1976, pp. 1177–1197.

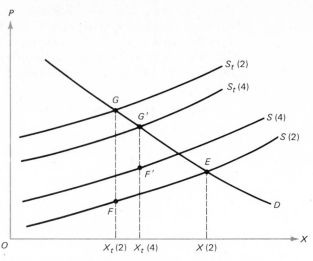

FIGURE 10-6   THE IMPACT OF SPECIFIC TAXES ON DURABILITY

Along the horizontal axis we measure the *service* rendered by a *durable good*; in the example this service is months of light; by assumption the lowest MC curve of every individual firm is associated with 2 months' durability; we denote the sum of such MC curves by $S(2)$. $S(2)$ intersects with the demand curve for months of light at point E. Output is $X(2)$ months of light. After the tax is imposed, the supply curve shifts by the tax (the tax on light bulbs divided by 2) to a new position $S_t(2)$. The new supply curve cuts the demand curve at point G. Output falls to a level of $X_t(2)$. The tax per month of light is $\overline{FG}$. Given some time for adjustment, producers begin to produce light bulbs with 4-month durability. The supply curve shifts slightly upward to $S(4)$, but since now the tax is half of what it used to be (the tax on light bulbs divided by 4), the new supply curve after the tax, $S_t(4)$, lies below $S_t(2)$; it intersects with the demand curve at point G'. The new level of output, $X_t(4)$, is higher than $X_t(2)$.

and thus in Figure 10-6 when durability increases from 2 to 4 months, the tax per month of light is cut by a half. However, since by assumption it is cheaper to produce 2-month light bulbs than light bulbs with any other durability, an increase in durability entails an upward shift in the (before-tax) supply curve from $S(2)$ to $S(4)$. In Figure 10-6 the tax savings (half of $\overline{FG}$) is in excess of the additional cost resulting from the switch to higher durability [the vertical distance between $S(2)$ and $S(4)$]. As a result we have a new supply curve $S_t(4)$, that is, $S(4)$ displaced upward by a quarter of the unit tax on light bulbs. This new supply curve intersects the demand curve at point G'. The amount of services sold increases from $X_t(2)$ to $X_t(4)$, and both consumers and producers benefit: Consumers pay a lower price of $\overline{X_t(4)G'}$ [relative to $\overline{X_t(2)G}$], and producers receive a higher price net of the tax $\overline{X_t(4)F'}$ [relative to $\overline{X_t(2)F}$]. The above analysis (Barzel law) can be summarized as follows:

> As long as the tax saving due to varying the quality of the taxed good exceeds the additional cost resulting from the quality change, producers will continue to change the quality.

Note: The impact of an ad valorem tax on market behavior is completely different. For example, if an ad valorem tax were to be imposed on cars but not on their components, it might pay buyers to buy car components separately and to then assemble a car by themselves. This might not work, however. The tax savings are small relative to the additional costs of self-assembly.

10.1j An Example: Quality Changes due to a Tax on Cigarettes

The conventional theory as developed in Section 10.1d states that after the unit tax is imposed the market price will rise at most by the amount of the tax. [This would occur when the supply is infinitely elastic as illustrated by panel (a) of Figure 10-3.] The supply of cigarettes in regional markets is infinitely elastic for all practical matters. Suppose a tax of 20 cents is imposed per package of cigarettes. Increasing the durability of cigarettes by 20 percent (say, by increasing length) would save the smoker 3.33 cents in taxes per package. If the additional cost of producing 20 percent longer cigarettes is less than 3.33 cents, producers would go ahead and lengthen cigarettes. In our example, the price per package would rise by 20 cents plus the additional cost of switching to longer cigarettes. Indeed, Barzel tested this theory and found that for the period 1954–1972, on average, a 1-cent increase in taxes would raise the retail price of cigarettes by 1.065 cents.[4]

10.1k The Laffer Curve

The *Laffer curve* relates the total revenue collected by the government to the rate of the tax. Although the Laffer curve is invoked in arguments surrounding tax issues in general, it can be applied to excise taxes as well. (The curve is named after Arthur B. Laffer, who made the idea popular among politicians. Some economists claim that the Laffer curve is something a congressman can digest in about 30 seconds and then talk about for months, which is why it is so popular.) The Laffer curve begins with the idea that when the rate of the tax is zero no revenue is collected by the government. If the rate of the tax is extremely high, the effort that goes into production is zero, and again no revenue is yielded. The conclusion is that as the rate rises from zero to some extremely high level, revenue must rise, reach its maximum, and then fall. Figure 10-7 illustrates a Laffer curve which is associated with an excise tax. In panel (a), supply cuts demand at point E where the rate of production is X_0 units. If no tax is imposed on commodity X, revenue to the government will be zero. But imagine a situation in which a very small unit tax is imposed and then the tax is gradually increased until it reaches a level of $\overline{KL}$ in panel (a). As the tax increases, the rate of output must decline because the unit tax must fit vertically between supply curve S and demand curve D (Section 10.1c). As the rate of output is decreased from X_0 to zero, the revenue, which is $T \cdot X$, rises, reaches its maximum level when output is X^*, and then falls until at a level of output of zero it vanishes.

---

[4]Ibid.

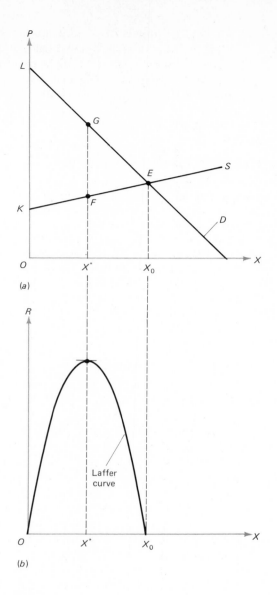

FIGURE 10-7 THE LAFFER CURVE

Panel (a) displays a supply curve and a demand curve. Along the vertical axis of panel (b) we measure R, the revenue collected by the government from a unit tax; $R = T \cdot X$, where in equilibrium, T, the unit tax, must fit vertically between the supply curve and the demand curve shown in panel (a). When output is X_0, demand and supply curves intersect. The tax is zero and hence revenue is zero. When output is zero (which will result from a tax of $T = \overline{KL}$ dollars), revenue collected by the government is zero. When the tax is $\overline{FG}$ dollars, revenue ($R = X^* \cdot \overline{FG}$) is maximized. At that level of output (of X^* units) the Laffer curve attains its maximum.

The revenue curve $(T \cdot X)$, which is the Laffer curve, is shown in panel (b).[5]

Politicians like the "free lunch economics" implied by the Laffer curve: If the rate of the tax is in excess of $\overline{FG}$ in panel (a), lowering the rate of the tax (up to $\overline{FG}$) will cause output as well as revenue to the government to increase.

10.2 IMPORTS AND EXPORTS

The importance of international economics cannot be exaggerated. Just think of the reliance of the United States, Western Europe, and Japan on imported oil. The discussion here, however, will not include welfare gain of nations from free trade but instead will be limited to supply-demand analysis and some specific issues related to the international oil market.

10.2a The Supply-Demand Geometry

American consumers purchase some of the sugar they consume from domestic sources and import the rest from abroad. This situation is also typical of wine, oil, and cars. American producers produce more wheat than is consumed domestically. The excess of production over domestic consumption is exported. This section will develop a simple geometric model which is useful in the analysis of problems involving imports or exports.

Assume that good X is produced both domestically and abroad. In Figure 10-8 the domestic market is depicted by panel (a), and the foreign market in panel (b) can be seen as aggregates of a few countries. Suppose international trade is absent because of high tariffs or administrative protectionism. Equilibrium in the domestic market occurs at point V where supply S_d intersects with demand D_d. Equilibrium in the foreign market occurs at point W where supply S_f intersects with demand D_f. The price in the foreign country (at point W) is lower than the domestic price (at point V). If restrictions on trade are lifted, foreign producers will begin to sell some of their output in the domestic market, thus raising the foreign price and depressing the domestic price. This will continue until the following conditions are met:

1. Excess supply over demand in the foreign market $\overline{LM}$ is equal to exports.
2. Excess demand over supply in the domestic market $\overline{BC}$ is equal to imports.

---

[5]If the demand price is denoted by P_d and the supply price by P_s, then $T = P_d - P_s$ and the revenue collected by the government is $(P_d - P_s) \cdot X$. If demand and supply curves are linear, namely,

$$P_d = a + bX$$

$$P_s = \alpha + \beta X$$

then the revenue collected by the government R_g is

$$R_g = (a - \alpha)X + (b - \beta)X^2$$

The level of output yielding the maximum revenue for the government is

$$X^* = \frac{a - \alpha}{2(\beta - b)}$$

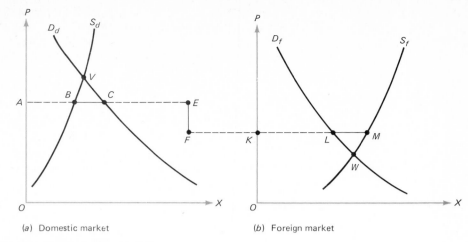

(a) Domestic market   (b) Foreign market

FIGURE 10-8   EXPORTS AND IMPORTS

Panel (a) shows the supply and demand for a good in the domestic market; panel (b) shows the supply and demand for a good in the foreign market. In equilibrium, excess supply over demand in one market (foreign), namely, $\overline{LM}$, must be equal to the excess demand over supply in the other market (domestic), namely, $\overline{BC}$. Segment $\overline{LM}$ is exports and segment $\overline{BC}$ is imports. Also, the price in importing country $\overline{OA}$ must exceed the price in exporting country $\overline{OK}$ by segment $\overline{FE}$, representing the unit shipping cost plus duty.

3. Exports of the foreign market are equal to imports into the domestic market: $\overline{LM} = \overline{BC}$.

4. The domestic price minus the unit cost of shipping is equal to the price in the foreign market. In Figure 10-8 this is stated as $\overline{OA} - \overline{FE} = \overline{OK}$, where $\overline{FE}$ is the cost of shipping. *Note:* If a duty[6] is imposed, $\overline{FE}$ is the unit cost of shipping plus the duty.

It is evident from Figure 10-8 that if a duty were imposed (or an existing duty were increased), the segment $\overline{FE}$ would increase, thus shrinking imports from the foreign to the domestic market. In fact, if the cost of shipping plus the duty were to grow to a level equal to the vertical distance between point W [panel (b)] and point V [panel (a)], international trade in good X would cease.

10.2b An Application: Some Welfare Considerations of Duties

Imposing a duty gives rise to a welfare loss. Although in most cases duties are imposed because of political pressures from domestic producers and unions, sometimes duties are justified by legitimate goals. As an example, in the late 1970s, duties on imported oil were advocated by those who were worried about overreliance on unstable foreign sources of oil. Until 1973, oil was traded in a free market; panel (a) of

Figure 10-8 roughly approximates the situation in the United States relative to the rest of the world at that time. In 1973, OPEC countries established a cartel and raised the price of crude oil significantly. Since the issue of the OPEC cartel will be discussed in the next chapter, let us for the moment assume that the United States is confronted with an OPEC price for imported oil over which it has no influence. In Figure

---

[6]A *duty* is an excise tax (unit or ad valorem) collected by the government on imported goods.

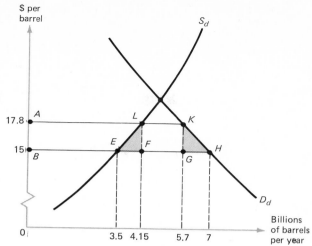

FIGURE 10-9 WELFARE LOSS DUE TO DUTIES ON OIL
Supply and demand curves for crude oil are shown; it is assumed that the price of $15 per barrel is determined by OPEC. Initially domestic quantity supplied is 3.5 billion barrels, and quantity demanded is 7 billion barrels. The difference of 3.5 billion barrels is imported. A duty of $2.8 per barrel will increase domestic production to 4.15 billion barrels and decrease domestic quantity demanded to 5.7 billion barrels. The loss to consumers will be the area of *ABHK*; the gain to the government will be *LFGK*, and to producers *ABEL*. This leaves the area of the two triangles *LEF* and *KGH* as deadweight loss to society.

10-9, S_d is the supply curve of domestic producers. D_d is the demand curve of domestic consumers. Assume that at a current price of $15 per barrel, consumption is 7 billion barrels per annum, half of which is imported. Suppose we want to reduce the reliance on foreign sources by about half the current imports, namely, by 1.75 billion barrels. If supply and demand curves have unitary elasticity ($\epsilon = 1, \eta = -1$), it would take a duty of $2.80 to achieve that goal. Domestic oil production would increase from 3.5 to 4.15 billion barrels and annual consumption would fall from 7 to 5.7 billion barrels. The consumer's surplus loss (Section 2.7) is area *ABHK*, which is [(7 + 5.7)/2] · ($17.8 − $15) = $17.78 billion. The producer's surplus gain is area *ABEL* (Section 7.4), which is equal to [(4.15 + 3.5)/2] · ($17.8 − $15) = $10.71 billion. The gain to

the government is simply imports ($\overline{LK}$) times the duty, which is the area of rectangle *LFGK*. This is equal to (5.7 − 4.15) · ($17.8 − $15) = $4.34 billion. The deadweight loss to society is calculated as follows:

Consumer's surplus decrement	$17.78 billion
Producer's surplus increment	−$10.71
Gain to government from duties	−$ 4.34
Net loss	$ 2.73 billion

The sum of $2.73 billion is deadweight loss to society. It is equal to the shaded areas of the two triangles *LEF* and *KGH*.

A decision to impose a duty of $2.80 per barrel of oil should be based on a "benefit-cost analysis" where the benefit is supply stability and the cost is a deadweight loss of $2.73 billion per annum.

10.3 JOINT PRODUCTS PRODUCED IN FIXED PROPORTIONS

In real life there are instances in which commodities are produced in fixed proportions. As an example, cottonseed and cotton fiber are produced in a fixed proportion of 2 to 1 (pounds). This section analyzes the markets for such goods.

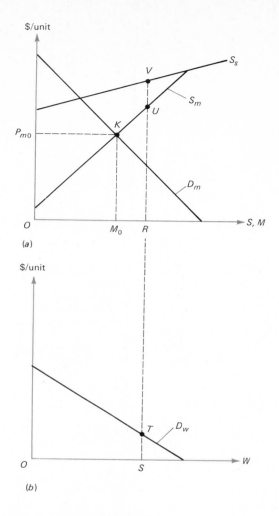

FIGURE 10-10   JOINT PRODUCTS AT THE INDUSTRY LEVEL

Mutton (*M*) and wool (*W*) are produced in fixed proportion: One sheep (*S*) results in a fixed amount of *M* and *W*. Panel (*a*) measures units of *S* and *M* along the horizontal axis. One unit of *M* is the amount of mutton produced from one average sheep. Panel (*b*) measures *W* along the horizontal axis; one unit of *W* is the amount of wool produced from one average sheep. In panel (*a*), S_s is the sum of all MC curves of sheep producers. In panel (*b*), D_w is the demand curve for wool. In panel (*a*), S_m, the supply of mutton, is derived by subtracting vertically D_w in panel (*b*) from S_s in panel (*a*); the demand for mutton, D_m intersects with the supply of mutton S_m at point *K*. $\overline{OM}_0$ units of *S*, *M*, and *W*, respectively, are produced. In equilibrium, MC (of sheep) $= P_m + P_w$.

An example of two joint products produced in fixed proportions would be wool and mutton. On the average, a sheep yields wool and mutton in fixed proportions. In this case it is meaningless to speak about the conventional marginal cost of wool or the conventional marginal cost of mutton. There is only the conventional marginal cost of sheep. Let us define one unit of wool as the amount of wool obtained from one sheep and one unit of mutton as the amount of mutton obtained from one sheep. For simplicity of notations, let W, M, and S stand for wool, mutton, and sheep.

Let us now turn to Figure 10-10. In panel (a), the supply curve of sheep, which is denoted by S_s, is the aggregate marginal cost of sheep (Section 8.2a). We can define the marginal cost of mutton by subtracting the price of wool from the marginal cost of sheep. For example, if the extra cost of raising one sheep is \$50 and the wool obtained from one sheep can be sold on the market for \$20, the marginal cost of mutton can be defined to \$30 = \$50 − \$20. The demand curve for wool D_w in panel (b) tells us what will be prices of wool if different quantities will be dumped in the market. Thus, if we subtract vertically the demand curve D_w from the supply curve S_s, we obtain the supply (aggregate marginal cost) curve of mutton, which is denoted by S_m. To illustrate this, if $\overline{OR}$ sheep are produced, the marginal cost is $\overline{RV}$. Associated with $\overline{OR}$ sheep are $\overline{OS}$ units of wool: $\overline{OR} = \overline{OS}$. If $\overline{OS}$ units of wool are dumped in the market, the price of wool is $\overline{ST}$. If we subtract $\overline{ST}$ from $\overline{RV}$, we are left with $\overline{RU}$, which is the marginal cost of mutton when output amounts to $\overline{OR}$ joint units. The supply curve of mutton thus derived cuts the demand curve for mutton D_m at point K. It is left for the student to show that in equilibrium (point K) the following must hold:

$$\text{MC}_s = P_m + P_w \qquad (10\text{-}3)$$

In other words, the marginal cost of sheep equals the price of mutton plus the price of wool.

10.4 IDENTICAL FIRMS

It is sometimes convenient to assume that all firms in an industry are identical. The convenience stems from the fact that under such conditions total output of the industry can be expressed as a product $X_t = n \cdot X$, where X_t is total output, n is the number of firms, and X is output produced by a single firm per unit of time. In what follows it is assumed that there are many (an infinitely large number) identical potential and active firms. The long-run average cost curves of the firms are U-shaped (Figure 6-10). It is evident that under such conditions the long-run supply curve of the industry must be a horizontal line with an intercept equal to the minimum of the long-run average cost. To see why this is the case, consider Figure 10-11. Panel (a) depicts the long-run average and marginal cost curves of the firm; panel (b) depicts the supply and demand curves of the industry as a whole. The analysis begins by assuming away externalities (Section 9.6b): In particular it is assumed that by expanding or shrinking its level of output, the industry cannot give rise to changes in prices of inputs. (The industry is confronted by flat supply curves of factors of production.)

Currently there are n firms in the industry. The price P_0 is equal to the minimum long-run average cost, which is $\overline{X_i^* K}$ in panel (a). In panel (b) it is shown that P_0 is determined by the intersection of the demand curve D_0 with the aggregate long-run marginal cost curve of n firms denoted by

$$\sum_{}^{n} \text{LRMC}_i$$

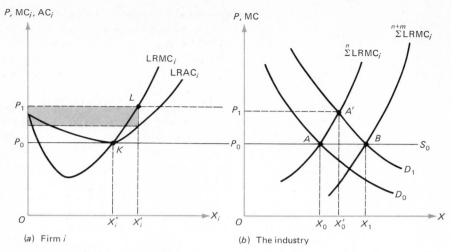

P, MC$_i$, AC$_i$

LRMC$_i$

LRAC$_i$

L

P_1

P_0

K

O

X_i^* X_i'

X_i

(a) Firm i

P, MC

$\sum\limits^{n+m}$LRMC$_i$

$\sum\limits^{n}$LRMC$_i$

A'

P_1

A   B

P_0 S$_0$

D$_1$

D$_0$

O

X_0 X_0' X_1

X

(b) The industry

FIGURE 10-11   IDENTICAL FIRMS

All firms in the industry, as well as potential firms, are identical. Long-run curves LRMC$_i$ and LRAC$_i$ of the single firm are depicted by panel (a). Initially, demand curve D$_0$ intersects with the sum of n MC curves ($\overset{n}{\Sigma}$LRMC$_i$) at point A, as shown in panel (b); the initial price is P$_0$; P$_0$ is equal to the minimum long-run average cost.

After the demand increases from D$_0$ to D$_1$, equilibrium shifts to point A' and the price rises to P$_1$. In panel (a) equilibrium of the individual firm shifts to point L. Rent received by the individual firm is now positive, and it amounts to the area of the shaded rectangle. This rent attracts potential entrepreneurs who are induced to form new (identical) firms; as the number of active firms increases, the supply shifts to the right. Finally, after m new firms enter the industry, the supply curve shifts to $\overset{n+m}{\Sigma}$LRMC$_i$. This new supply curve cuts the demand curve at point B, and the price of P$_0$ is restored. The horizontal long-run supply curve is obtained by connecting points like A and B.

At the point of intersection A, aggregate output is X_0 and it is equal to $n \cdot X_i^*$, where X_i^* is the rate of output per firm associated with the minimum average cost (point K). Suppose the demand for good X increases, leading to a shift in the demand curve from D_0 to D_1. To the first approximation the number of firms remains fixed at n. Each firm individually follows its LRMC$_i$ curve and moves from point K to point L. The n firms together expand along the aggregate long-run marginal cost curve from point A to point A'. As a result, each firm increases its rate of production from X_i^* to X_i', and all n firms aggregately increase the rate of production from X_0 $(= n \cdot X_i^*)$ to X_0' $(= n \cdot X_i')$. Let us now focus on panel (a). Before the demand increased, the price P_0 exactly covered the minimum average cost of the firm. Rent (economic profit, Section 9.10a) was zero and potential firms outside the industry were not attracted to join, nor had firms inside any incentive to leave. But as the price rises to P_1, economic rent of firms inside the industry grows to a level indicated by the area of the shaded rectangle in panel (a), which is output times price minus average cost (Section 7.5): $X_i' \cdot (P_1 - AC)$. Since there are many potential firms with cost curves identical to those depicted by panel (a), it is now attractive for such firms to enter the industry. As more and more firms enter the industry, the long-run aggregate marginal cost curve shifts farther rightward. Finally, after m new firms have entered, the new long-run aggregate marginal cost curve,

$$\sum^{n+m} \text{LRMC}_i,$$

will intersect the new demand curve at point B, which represents a price of P_0. Rent will be completely dissipated and new output will be $X_1 [= (n + m) \cdot X^*_i]$. We have seen that the long-run supply curve of an industry with identical firms must go through points A and B in panel (b); namely, it must be horizontal. We can summarize:

> If an industry is dominated by identical firms, and if many potential firms are waiting to enter the industry at the slightest sight of a positive rent, the long-run supply curve of the industry is flat.
>
> Since the position of the long-run supply curve is determined by the long-run minimum average cost, the supply shifts will follow familiar patterns as follows:
> 1. A change in the price of a variable input will shift the long-run horizontal supply curve in the same direction (Section 8.3).
> 2. A neutral technological innovation will shift the long-run horizontal supply curve downward (Section 8.4).
> 3. If external diseconomies are present, an increase in demand will be accompanied by an upward shift in the long-run marginal and average cost curves. Since this shift is conditional on the expansion of the industry, the supply curve may be viewed as being positively sloped (Section 9.10a)
> 4. A specific tax will shift the long-run horizontal supply curve upward by the amount of the tax (Section 10.1c). An ad valorem tax will shift the long-run supply curve upward by the rate of the tax times the demand price (Section 10.1b).

To determine that the above statements are correct, simply note that the long-run average cost curve follows the shifts of the long-run marginal cost curve.

10.5 THE ECONOMICS OF REGULATION

Governments tend to intervene in markets for reasons that cannot be enumerated here. Suffice it to say that when market forces are ignored, the results are not in accord with the written word in the law books. Three examples of market regulation follow.

10.5a Property Rights and Timber

Three major laws dominated the claiming of forest lands during the last quarter of the nineteenth century in the northwest regions of the United States: the Homestead Act, the Pre-emption Act, and the Timber and Stone Act. Basically these three acts allowed only bona fide settlers to claim no more than 160 acres for a certain fee per acre. Libecap and Johnson studied the economic aspects of the large-scale evasion of the federal laws which followed.[7] Because timber cutting was dominated by economies of scale,

---

[7]Gary D. Libecap and Ronald N. Johnson, "Property Rights, Nineteenth Century Timber

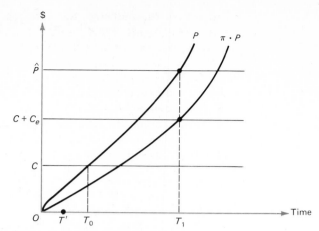

FIGURE 10-12 TRANSACTION COSTS OF LAW EVASION
Time is measured along the horizontal axis, and the dollar value of 1 acre of stumpage is measured along the vertical axis. The curve denoted by P shows the rise in the value of 1 acre of forest. The rise in P reflects both tree growth and a rise in the price of stumpage. π is the probability of successfully evading the law. The curve $\pi \cdot P$ is derived by multiplying P values by π. C is the government fee per acre and C_e is fraudulent money spent per acre. Equilibrium occurs at T_1 when $C + C_e = \pi \cdot P$.

large tracts of forest land, in excess of 160 acres, were required for efficient logging operations. Gary Libecap and Ronald Johnson write that, to evade the law, "prospective buyers contracted with agents for the locating and the securing of land. The agents hired cruisers to select desirable plots and entrymen to stake the claims under federal law. As soon as those entrymen received certificates of ownership from the Land Office, they passed them to the agent who deeded the land to the final purchaser. In exchange the purchaser paid the agent an agreed upon price for the land."[8] This was nothing more than a costly fraudulent activity which caused a delay in transferring property rights to private hands as well as higher transaction costs. Figure 10-12 (based on Libecap and Johnson)[9] illustrates the above analysis geometrically. C is the price of an acre ($2.50 or $1.25, depending on the law applied) and P is the value of an acre of forest land with secure property rights. The P curve rises over time, reflecting both the rise in stumpage prices and tree growth. Had the government determined a fee of C dollars per acre at time T' which was either equal to T_0 or slightly less than T_0, without any restrictions on the number of acres purchased, then at time T_0 timber companies would have purchased forest land with curves like P in Figure 10-12. π is the probability of successfully securing title to the land (Section 4.2a). C_e is the amount of fraudulent money spent by the purchaser

---

Policy, and the Conservation Movement," *Journal of Economic History*, vol. 39, no. 1, March 1979, pp. 129–142.
   [8]Ibid.
   [9]Ibid.

(over and above C) in the process of evading the law.[10] In equilibrium, the market value of an acre times the probability of success should be equal to government fee C plus the fraudulent money for evasion C_e. For example, if C is \$2.50 and C_e is another \$2.50 and if π is 0.5, then the market price must rise to \$10 in order to induce land claiming. The equation $0.5 \cdot \$10 = \$2.50 + \$2.50$ must be satisfied or else land would not be claimed. To put it more formally, the following equality must hold in order for land to be claimed:

$$\pi \cdot P = C + C_e \qquad (10\text{-}4)$$

In Figure 10-12 equilibrium occurs when the market value of an acre rises to $\hat{P}$. Time of claiming is postponed from T_0 to T_1 and transaction costs for securing the property rights of 1 acre increase from C to $\hat{P}$.

Libecap and Johnson cite many land fraud cases which occurred at the turn of the century.[11] As an example, the California Redwood Company acquired 57,000 acres of redwood under the Timber and Stone and Pre-emption Laws in 1883. About 400 entrymen were used in this act. While the fee to the government was \$2.50 per acre, the actual market price was \$7 per acre. The difference between \$7 and \$2.50 is the added transaction cost which was paid to agents and entrymen.

---

[10]π is functionally related to C_e. We can write it as $\pi = f(C_e)$: The larger the amount of fraudulent money spent, the larger would be the probability of success.

[11]Libecap and Johnson, op. cit.

FIGURE 10-13 RENT CONTROL

Along the horizontal axis we measure apartments; along the vertical axis we measure rent. Initially the supply of apartments S_0 intersects with the demand for apartments D_0 at point A, where X_0 apartments are rented (including self) at a rent of P_0. Over time demand increases to D_1; since rent is controlled at a ceiling of P_0, quantity supplied is frozen at X_0 units. A shortage of $X_1 - X_0$ apartments arises. As indicated by D_1, if the controls were lifted, in the short run rent would zoom to P_1.

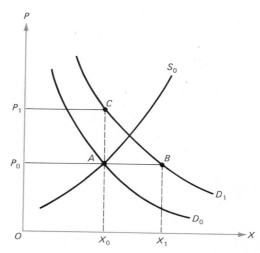

10.5b Rent Control

Residents of New York City and inhabitants of Britain, France, Israel, Sweden, and Austria, to mention just a few countries, at one time or another suffered from rent controls. While the intention of lawmakers was noble, namely, to provide the poor with inexpensive apartments, the results were disappointing, to say the least. The theory of rent control is simple, as illustrated by Figure 10-13. Population size, income per family (or individual), and tastes determine the position of the aggregate demand curve, while the level of technology and prices of inputs determine the supply curve of housing units. Consider a situation in which historically the supply of housing was S_0, demand was D_0, and equilibrium was at point A at which X_0 units were rented at a monthly rent of P_0. *Note*: Homeowners are both suppliers and demanders. If the government decides to regulate rent by imposing a ceiling of P_0, the demand for housing will continue to shift to the right because of population and income growth. With a frozen rent, though, supply will remain frozen at X_0 because investors will not have the incentive to invest additional moneys in housing unless the rent can rise above P_0. When rent controls are set artificially at a low level, shortages occur. The shortage, by the way, does not mean that the market does not clear. It clears by criteria other than price. For example, it clears partially by a huge amount of effort that goes into waiting for an apartment to be vacated. As Bertrand de Jouvenel wrote in 1948 about the Parisian plight resulting from rent control: "Young couples must live with in-laws, and the wife's major activity consists in watching out for deaths. Tottering old people out to sun themselves in public gardens will be shadowed back to their flat by an eager young wife who will strike a bargain with the janitor, the *concierge*, so as to be first warned when the demise occurs and to be first in at the death. Other apartment-chasers have an understanding with undertakers."[12]

Notice in Figure 10-13 that since the demand has grown to D_1 but only X_0 apartments are available, the rental value of an apartment should be P_1 dollars per unit of time. Indeed, in Israel, where the law allows it, when an apartment becomes vacant, huge amounts of money are paid in the "free market" as *key money* for the right to rent the apartment. As a matter of fact, one can assume that, roughly, the *key money* is equal to the present value of future benefits which amount to $\overline{AC}$ dollars per unit of time: The criteria that clear the market are effort spent on queuing (young wife shadowing old men to their flats) and *key money*. If the government intended to provide relief to the poor, it completely failed. The relief has been dissipated in the process of clearing the controlled market.

A shortage is an economic phenomenon, not a physical one. The analysis here predicts that since an important criterion of clearing a controlled market is allocation by waiting, vacancy rates should be smaller in controlled markets. Or, shortage is inversely related to vacancy rate. Olsen shows that this phenomenon is verified by the history of American cities (Table 10-1).

---

[12]Bertrand de Jouvenel, "No Vacancies," printed in Friedrich A. von Hayek, Milton Friedman, et al., *Rent Control: A Popular Paradox*, The Fraser Institute, Vancouver, British Columbia, 1975, ISBN 0-88975-007-6, pp. 106, 107.

TABLE 10-1 Vacancy Rates in American Cities

	New York City	Other cities
1940	7.3	4.7
1950	1.1	1.4
1960	2.0	4.0

Source: Edgar O. Olsen, "Questions and Some Answers about Rent Control: An Empirical Analysis of New York's Experience," in Hayek, Friedman, et al., op. cit., p. 147.

Note: In 1940, when neither New York City nor other American cities had rent control ordinances, the average vacancy rate in New York City far exceeded the rate in other cities. In 1950, when practically all cities were covered by rent control laws, the vacancy rates were very low relative to the 1940s in all cities. In 1960, only New York City remained covered by rent controls. Its vacancy rate was half the average rate of all other cities.

10.5c Regulation by Vintage

An example of regulation by vintage would be a price control imposed on old oil or old natural gas. In 1977, output from wells that were operational before a certain date was under price control. For example, in 1977, oil in the United States was under three price tiers: Old oil sold at $5.25 per barrel, new but controlled oil sold at $11.30 per barrel, and imports and stripper oil were under no control. As explained earlier (Section 8.2c), the reason given by policy makers was that supply of old oil (or gas) was inelastic and thus an uncontrolled rise in the price would place a bonanza in the pockets of oil companies. Whether the supply of old oil and natural gas is very elastic or relatively inelastic is an empirical question (Section 8.2c). The demand curve for gasoline in the United States is depicted by curve D in panel (*a*) of Figure 10-14. If for simplicity we assume that in 1977 the market was under two price tier systems—namely, old oil was regulated at $5.25 and new oil was sold at the OPEC price (to be explained in Chapter 11)—then the marginal cost of gasoline P_a was determined according to the following formula:[13]

$$P_a = W_1 \cdot P_r + W_2 \cdot P_{0p} + R$$

---

[13]This formula is based on the assumption that the weights W_1 and W_2 are adjusted continuously to the true ratios of regulated (domestic) oil to total domestic oil consumption (W_1), and imported unregulated OPEC oil to total domestic oil consumption (W_2). As an example, if initially $W_1 = 0.60$, $W_2 = 0.40$, $P_r = \$5.25$, and $P_{0p} = \$14$, the marginal cost (without the fixed R component) is

$$0.60 \cdot \$5.25 + 0.40 \cdot \$14 = \$8.75$$

If consumption of oil increases, leading to a change of ratios such that the new ratios are $W_1 = 0.58$ and $W_2 = 0.42$, the new marginal cost (again without R) will be

$$0.58 \cdot \$5.25 + 0.42 \cdot \$14 = \$8.92$$

That is, marginal cost increases by $0.17.

If W_1 and W_2 do not adjust continuously, but rather each refinery gets from the government an *entitlement* to purchase a *fixed* number of cheap regulated barrels of old oil, then the marginal cost of gasoline is P_{0p} (plus R); or in the example it is $14 (plus R), and deregulation cannot change the market price.

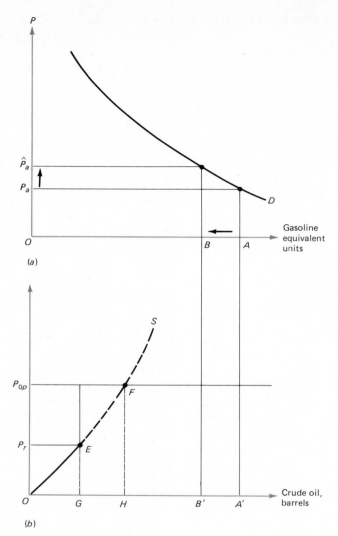

FIGURE 10-14 REGULATION OF OLD OIL

In panel (a) gasoline is measured along the horizontal axis and price of gasoline along the vertical axis. A unit of gasoline is the amount refined from 1 barrel of crude oil. The domestic demand for gasoline is depicted by D. In panel (b) crude oil (barrels) is measured along the horizontal axis and price of crude oil along the vertical axis. The domestic supply of oil is depicted by curve S. Since domestic oil (old oil) is regulated at a price ceiling of P_r, domestic producers produce only $\overline{OG}$ barrels. Back in panel (a), $P_a = W_1 \cdot P_r + W_2 \cdot P_{op} + R$ is the marginal cost of gasoline, where P_{op} is OPEC price and R is the marginal cost of refining 1 barrel of crude. The price line P_a cuts the domestic demand curve at a level of $\overline{OA}$ barrels. The associated amount in panel (b) is $\overline{OA}'$, and imported oil is $\overline{GA}'$ ($= \overline{OA}' - \overline{OG}$). Deregulation will raise the price of gasoline to $\hat{P}_a = P_{op} + R$; quantity demanded will fall to $\overline{OB}$ units [in panel (a)]. The associated amount in panel (b) will be $\overline{OB}'$. Domestic production will rise to $\overline{OH}$, where the higher price P_{op} cuts the domestic supply curve S. Imported oil will fall to $\overline{HB}'$ ($= \overline{OB}' - \overline{OH}$).

where P_r is the control price of old oil ($5.25 per barrel), P_{0p} is the OPEC price ($14 per barrel), and W_1 and W_2 are the shares of old and imported oil, respectively. Thus, if imported oil amounted to 40 percent of total domestic consumption, $W_1 = 0.6$ and $W_2 = 0.4$. R is the marginal cost of refining 1 barrel of oil. For simplicity we assume that the marginal cost curve of refining is horizontal. In accord with Section 10.3, since gasoline and other by-products are produced in fixed proportions, R is properly defined as the additional cost of refining 1 barrel of oil minus the additional revenue from selling the by-products of gasoline (from 1 barrel) on the market. It is important to note that gasoline is measured along the horizontal axis of panel (*a*) in "equivalent units," where a unit is the average amount of gasoline derived from 1 barrel of crude oil. We can now associate quantities in panel (*a*) with quantities in panel (*b*). At a price of P_a, $\overline{OA}$ equivalent units of gasoline are sold domestically per unit of time. In panel (*b*) this is associated with refining of $\overline{OA'}$ barrels of crude oil per unit of time.

The domestic supply curve of old oil is depicted by S in panel (*b*). Since a price ceiling of P_r ($5.25) is imposed on old oil, only $\overline{OG}$ barrels of old oil are produced domestically per unit of time. In summary, $\overline{OA'}$ barrels are consumed domestically, of which only $\overline{OG}$ are produced domestically; the rest, namely, $\overline{GA'}$, are imported. A price decontrol in 1977 would have allowed old oil to sell at the OPEC price. Thus the new marginal cost of an equivalent unit of gasoline would be

$$\hat{P}_a = P_{0p} + R$$

which is by $W_1(P_{0p} - P_r)$ higher than P_a.[14] In the example the change in marginal cost would be $0.6 \cdot (\$14 - \$5.25)$. As indicated in panel (*a*), the rise in the marginal cost of refining would lead to a cutback in consumption from $\overline{OA}$ to $\overline{AB}$ barrels. In panel (*b*) the associated reduction is from $\overline{OA'}$ to $\overline{OB'}$. Domestic producers of oil would expand along their supply curve S from point E, corresponding to the control price P_r, to point F, corresponding to the OPEC price P_{0p}.

In summary, the decontrol of old oil in 1977 would have led to a reduction in consumption of $\overline{B'A'}$ barrels and an increase in domestic production of $\overline{GH}$ barrels. The reliance on foreign oil would have declined from $\overline{GA'}$ to $\overline{HB'}$ in panel (*b*). Since the declared policy of the government was to reduce the reliance of American consumers on unstable foreign sources, it is evident that the regulation of old oil was at odds with the declared policy of the government. Moreover, it favored foreign over domestic oil producers.

10.6 THE FUTURES MARKET

10.6a Stable Demand and Production Conditions

Most agricultural commodities are produced periodically. Oranges are picked during the winter, wheat is harvested in May, and potatoes are dug

---

[14]See footnote 13.

out mainly in the fall. Stocks of such periodically produced commodities must be stored in the interim between harvests. To show how the market mechanism would have solved the problem of storage under stable demand and production conditions, consider Figure 10-15. For simplicity we assume that commodity X is harvested every second period. The demand curve does not change from one period to the next, and the crop is stable at X_0 units. Assume that if the crop were divided equally between the two periods the price would be \$3 per bushel. But if it cost 10 cents to hold a bushel in storage from one period to the next, it would benefit a farmer to sell everything now rather than pay for storage and sell in the next period. However, selling more than half the crop duing the harvest period would cause a deprivation in the following period and give rise to a price differential. The current price would fall and the price next period would rise. As a matter of fact, when the price differential in this example reaches 10 cents, farmers would become indifferent between the two periods.

The theory depicted in Figure 10-15, however, is somewhat different in reality. The demand schedule is anything but stable, mainly as a result of the export component. In 1972, the Russians "cornered" the American market for wheat. After the magnitude of the Russian operation was discovered, prices of wheat skyrocketed. Crops are even less stable. In 1975–1976 the production of coffee in Brazil amounted to 15 million bags. Then, because of the frost, the production of 1976–1977 declined to a level of 2.5 million bags. The instability of the markets for such commodities renders them similar to gambling casinos. *Producers* as well as *processors* of such commodities who are risk averters shift the risk to *speculators* who specialize in predicting future demand and production conditions. (More formal explanation is given in Section 10.6b.) Speculators function in *futures markets*, which are geographically located in centers known as *commodities exchange markets*. The *New York Coffee and Sugar Exchange* and the *Chicago Board of Trade* are two such commodities exchange markets. Commodities like coffee, sugar, wheat, soybeans, feed grains, and frozen orange juice, and nonagricultural commodities like silver and copper are traded in futures markets. The following section describes these markets.

10.6b The Market for Futures

The following is a list of new concepts which you should learn in order to understand the futures market.

A future, or future contract A legal commitment to deliver a certain amount of a certain commodity at a certain date in the future for a predetermined price. Thus, if A sells a contract to B, A sells B a future commodity at a predetermined price.

A short hedger A person or a firm that purchases the commodity in a spot market and simultaneously sells an equal amount of futures. A typical short hedger would be a firm that buys wheat from farmers in the spot market, stores the wheat, and sells an equal amount of futures of wheat.

A long hedger A person or a firm that sells the processed commodity for-

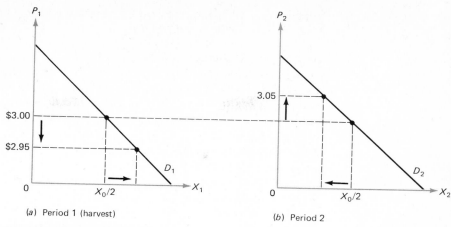

FIGURE 10-15 PERIODIC PRODUCTION

In panel (a), D_1 depicts the demand curve for commodity X in period 1; in panel (b), D_2 depicts the demand for commodity X in period 2. The two demand curves are identical. The harvest occurs at the start of period 1. if the harvest is X_0, then more (than $X_0/2$) will be consumed in period 1 and less (than $X_0/2$) in period 2, such that the price differential will cover the cost of carrying over one unit of X from period 1 to period 2. In the example the price differential is $0.10, the amount needed to cover the (unit) carry-over cost.

ward and buys futures of that commodity. An example would be millers who sell flour forward and buy wheat futures to cover themselves.

A short speculator A person or a firm that commits itself to deliver a certain amount of a certain commodity at a certain date in the future for a predetermined price. A short speculator sells futures hoping that the futures price will exceed the realized spot price. Consider the following example: A short speculator sold a long hedger 100,000 bushels of wheat futures at a price of $3 per bushel. Assume that the realized spot market happened to be $2.80 per bushel. The long hedger pays the farmer $2.80, and pays the short speculator $0.20. The profit of the short speculator is $20,000. Had the realized spot price been $3.20, the long hedger would have had to pay the farmer a price of $3.20, but the short speculator would have had to pay the long hedger $0.20 per bushel, with a loss of $20,000.

A long speculator A person or a firm that commits itself to buying a certain amount of a certain commodity at a certain date in the future for a predetermined price. A long speculator bets that the realized spot price would exceed the futures price. Thus a long speculator who purchased 100,000 bushels of wheat futures from a short hedger for $3 per bushel when the realized spot price was $3.20 would make a profit of $20,000.

Let us now see how the futures price is determined. First, we should explain the net demand of speculators. Speculators specialize in forecasting supply and demand conditions in the future. For example, a speculator in frozen orange juice should know a lot about weather forecasts in Florida, Texas, and California, about the stocks of frozen oranges, and so on. It is unlikely that all speculators would expect the same spot price in the future. If the futures price is very high, speculators would assume a short position and sell contracts. But as the price of futures declines, some will switch from short to long positions. It is conceivable that at a very low futures price all speculators would assume long positions. Consider the following example: Three speculators want to speculate on 1000 bushels of May wheat. It is now January, 4 months from May. The first speculator expects the spot price in May to be $3, the second expects it to be $2.50, and the third expects it to be $2. If the futures price is $4, they all assume a short position and sell futures. If the futures price is somewhere between $3 and $2.50, the first assumes a long position, and the other two remain in a short position. Their total net position is 1000 bushels short. If the futures price is between $2.50 and $2, their net position is 1000 bushels long. Finally, if the futures price is less than $2, their net position is 3000 bushels long. As the price of futures declined from over $3 to less than $2, the net position of the group changed from 3000 net short to 1000 net short, then to 1000 net long, and finally to 3000 net long. This implies a negatively sloped net demand curve for contracts by speculators.

Let us now consider the net supply of contracts by hedgers. If the futures price is very low, processors who are long hedgers would like to buy a relatively large quantity of futures. On the other hand, those who are in the business of storage would not be encouraged to sell many futures at a low price. The net position of hedgers would be long. But as the price of futures climbs, short hedgers increase their offers to sell contracts, and long hedgers decrease their demand to purchase contracts. The net supply of hedgers rises with the price. Figure 10-16 shows the net supply of hedgers, the net demand of speculators, and the equilibrium point B. In the case depicted in Figure 10-16, $\overline{OA}$ is the net amount of futures sold by short hedgers to long speculators. The net demand of speculators could conceivably cut the net supply of hedgers on the left side of the vertical axis. This situation would indicate that hedgers are in a net long position and speculators in a net short one.

10.6c An Example: The Russians Corner the Wheat Market

The *Commodity Year Book* of 1972 reported that "uncertain crop conditions exist for 1972 because of 'winter kill' not only in the USSR but also in the East European countries...."[15] The *Commodity Year Book* of 1973 reported that "the past year has been featured by the most extensive price rise in wheat since the 1947–1948 post-World War II boom. Much of this explosive advance took place in the second half of 1972. It was touched off by extensive Russian purchases of wheat in the summer of 1972, necessi-tated by crop reversals and deficit wheat production in the Soviet Union."[16]. Let us now consider the prices of May 1973 wheat futures (Table 10-2).

The average spot prices of wheat in May 1973 were No. 2 Softred at Chicago $2.71, No. 1 Hard Winter at Kansas City $2.69, and No. 1 Dark Northern Spring at Minneapolis $2.57. A speculator who took a long position in June 1972 on May 1973 wheat made a profit of roughly $1 per bushel.

---

[15]*Commodity Year Book*, 1972, p. 358.
[16]*Commodity Year Book*, 1973, p. 360.

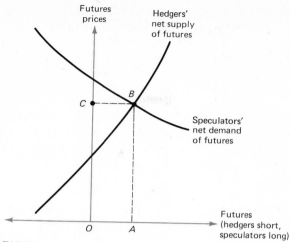

FIGURE 10-16 FUTURES MARKET

Along the horizontal axis we measure futures; along the vertical axis we measure future prices. Hedgers' net supply of futures intersects with speculators' net demand for futures at point B; the future price is accordingly $\overline{OC}$; $\overline{OA}$ is the net amount of futures sold by short hedgers to long speculators.

SUMMARY

This chapter discussed several special issues which relate directly to perfect competition. The issues are not related to one another; they are separate topics that the reader might find interesting in and of themselves. These topics have been useful in reinforcing the theory presented in Chapter 9.

TABLE 10-2 **Prices of May 1973 Wheat Futures**

	High	Low
1972:		
June	151¼	146⅞
July	166	153¼
August	200½	164¾
September	228½	198⅝
October	223½	205½
November	239¾	218
December	269½	240⅝
1973:		
January	266¾	233½
February	257	217
March	249	211
April	254	223½
May	275¼	235

Source: Commodity Year Book, 1974, p. 371.

Excise taxes We saw that an excise tax, either in the form of a *unit tax* or in the form of an *ad valorem tax*, would cause the supply curve to shift upward, thus leading to a higher price and a smaller quantity marketed. The burden of the tax falls partly on consumers and partly on producers, depending on the elasticity of demand relative to the elasticity of supply. The welfare loss due to excise taxes is relatively small. Unit taxes lead to qualitative changes in the taxed goods; this result (Barzel law) was explained by noting that untaxed traits are enhanced in the taxed good. Finally the Laffer curve was mentioned; it explains how it would sometimes be possible, by cutting back on the rate of the tax, to increase both revenue collected by the government and output.

Imports and exports In order to explain the market forces involved in determining equilibrium in international markets, a dual model was developed in which excess of supply over demand in one country is export; this export is equal to excess of demand over supply, which is import, of the other country. In a free market, the price in the importing country must be equal to the price in the exporting country plus the unit shipping cost and the tariff. The higher the tariff, the smaller will be the quantity exported from country to country. This section also discussed the issue of welfare loss due to the imposition of duties.

Joint products produced in fixed proportions Sometimes the nature of the production function is such that two or more commodities are produced in fixed proportions. Examples are fiber and cottonseed produced from cotton, or wool and mutton produced from sheep. We saw that if X and Y are produced in fixed proportions, the supply curve of X is obtained by subtracting vertically the demand for Y from the sum of the marginal cost curves of the joint commodity. The resulting equilibrium is one in which the marginal cost of the joint unit equals the price of X plus the price of Y: $MC_{joint\ unit} = P_x + P_y$.

Identical firms Chapter 9 derived the long-run supply curve under the realistic assumption that firms are unlikely to be identical. Still it is sometimes useful to consider the case of an infinitely large number of identical firms. This case was analyzed with the conclusion that the long-run supply curve for an industry that approximates this situation has the shape of a horizontal line at the level of the minimum point of the long-run average cost curve.

The economics of regulation Governments intervene in the marketplace on behalf of the poor. The intention of governments is noble; yet the results of interventions, which normally take the form of regulations, are in most cases the opposite of the original intention of governments. The economics of regulation was illustrated by three examples: *property rights and timber*, *rent control*, and *regulation by vintage*.

The futures market Futures markets arise in markets for goods that are produced periodically. We saw that even if demand and production were stable, periodic production would have resulted in a market for future commitments (to deliver commodities at a prefixed price). Given the uncertainty that surrounds the production of goods such as wheat, orange juice, corn, and similar commodities, a market for future commitments developed where one can either avoid risk at a price or undertake risk at a profit. This section explained the roles of *hedgers* and *speculators*, and how the interaction of the two groups in the marketplace leads to an equilibrium in the market for futures.

GLOSSARY

Excise tax A tax which is levied on sellers and is positively related to the volume of sales. It may be levied in the form of either a *unit* tax or an *ad valorem* tax.

Unit tax A tax which is assessed as a given amount of money per unit of output.

Ad valorem tax A tax which is assessed as percentage of the sales price.

Subsidy A negative tax.

Tax incidence The incidence of an excise tax on the consumer is the increase in the price to consumers (as a result of the tax) divided by the tax. The incidence of an excise tax on the producer is the decrease of the price received by producers divided by the tax. For excise taxes incidence to consumers equals $1/(1 + |\eta|/\epsilon)$, where η is demand elasticity and ϵ is supply elasticity.

Welfare loss due to an excise tax The loss in the consumer's surplus plus the loss in the producer's surplus minus the revenue from the tax collected by the government.

Sales tax A tax assessed as a percentage of the sales value.

Barzel law A law that states that a unit tax will lead to production changes, mostly in the form of qualitative improvement in the taxed commodity.

Laffer curve The original Laffer curve is a bell-shaped curve in which the tax rate is measured along the horizontal axis and revenue collected by the government along the vertical axis. Revenue is zero at the end points of the bell, namely, when the rate of the tax is zero and 100 percent, respectively. The revenue collected by the government reaches maximum at some intermediate rate of tax. The Laffer curve was adapted to the case of an excise tax, where the right end point is where supply and demand intersect and the left end point is where output is zero.

Rent control A ceiling imposed on rent that can be charged as a fee for apartment leasing.

Future A legal commitment to deliver and accept a certain amount of a certain commodity at a certain date in the future for a predetermined price. The commitment is dual: One party commits to sell in the future, and the other party commits to buy in the future.

Short hedger A person or a firm that purchases a certain amount of a certain commodity in a spot market and simultaneously sells an equal amount of futures.

Long hedger A person or a firm that sells the processed commodity forward and buys futures of that commodity.

Short speculator A person or a firm that commits itself to deliver a certain amount of a certain commodity at a certain date in the future for a predetermined price.

Long speculator A person or a firm that commits itself to buy a certain amount of a certain commodity at a certain date in the future for a predetermined price.

PROBLEMS An asterisk indicates an advanced problem.

10-1. By applying formula 10-2 analyze the incidence of an excise tax on consumers under the following assumptions:
(a) The demand curve is perfectly inelastic.
(b) The supply curve is perfectly inelastic.

10-2. Currently the market price is $10. Would imposing a unit tax of $1 or (alternatively) an ad valorem tax of 10 percent result in the same new market price?

10-3. Is it correct to assume that the proportion of the unit tax passed on to consumers is greater, the smaller the elasticities of the supply and demand curves?

10-4. Is it always true that by increasing the unit tax on good X the government will increase the revenue collected from the tax?

10-5. A unit tax on cigarettes will lead producers to produce longer cigarettes. Explain why cigarettes will not be 2 feet long.

10-6. Rich people save a larger share of their income. Does that mean that a sales tax would be regressive or progressive?

10-7. Would a switch from a unit tax to an ad valorem tax on gasoline increase the tendency of gas stations to open more self-service islands?

10-8. In 1967, the Suez Canal was closed by Egypt. As a result the cost of transporting oil via the sea increased. By applying diagrammatic analysis as in Figure 10-8 explain who benefited from it and who suffered, in a country where part of the oil is produced domestically and part is imported from the Middle East.

10-9.* Would the welfare (deadweight) loss to society resulting from duties on oil increase or decrease if the demand curve (or supply of domestic oil) were less elastic? Use Figure 10-9 for your analysis.

10-10. Consider Figure 10-9. Would you advise your government to impose an import quota of $\overline{LK}$ billions of barrels of oil instead of imposing a duty of $2.8 per barrel of oil?

10-11. Mutton and wool are produced in fixed proportions. How would the imposition of a unit tax on mutton affect the price of wool?

10-12. The supply curve of an industry with identical firms (with U-shaped long-run average cost curves) is flat. Yet the industry is stable. On the other hand, an industry with firms governed by constant returns to scale is said to be unstable. Explain.

10-13. Consider Figure 10-12 again. How would timber companies have behaved if there were no restrictions on the number of acres of forest land one could claim, and if at time T' the government charged a fee of C dollars?

10-14. The Homestead Act led to waste of resources. Explain.

10-15. Do you agree with the following statement: If the true goal of the government is to provide the poor with inexpensive apartments, an excise subsidy is preferable to rent control.

10-16. "Rent control or no rent control, the market always clears." Explain.

10-17. How would the price of futures wheat change as a result of drought forecast by the weather bureau? (Where would you shift the net demand curve of speculators and the net supply curve of hedgers?)

MATHEMATICAL APPENDIX 10

M10-1 Welfare Loss

The text (Section 10.1e) argued that the deadweight loss to society is equal to the area of the small triangle GEF in Figure 10-2. Let us adopt the following symbols:

$$\overline{HG} = \Delta P_d \qquad \overline{HF} = \Delta P_s \qquad \overline{FG} = \Delta P = T$$

and

$$\overline{FG} = \Delta P = \overline{HG} + \overline{FH} = \Delta P_d - \Delta P_s$$

From the formulas of elasticities we know that

$$\Delta P_d = \frac{(\Delta X/X) \cdot P}{\eta}$$

and

$$\Delta P_s = \frac{(\Delta X/X) \cdot P}{\epsilon}$$

Hence we obtain

$$\Delta P = \Delta P_d - \Delta P_s = \frac{\Delta X}{X} \cdot P \cdot \left(\frac{1}{\eta} - \frac{1}{\epsilon} \right)$$

and, rearranging, we obtain

$$\Delta X = \frac{\Delta P}{P} \cdot X \cdot \frac{1}{1/\eta - 1/\epsilon} \qquad \text{(m10-1)}$$

Multiplying Equation m10-1 by $\frac{1}{2}\Delta P$, we obtain the formula of the area of triangle GEF in Figure 10-2. If we now recall that tax T is equal to ΔP (which is $\overline{FG}$ in Figure 10-2), and if we define the ratio of the tax to the price as T^*, where

$$T^* = \frac{\Delta P}{P} = \frac{T}{P}$$

we obtain the formula for deadweight loss to society due to excise taxes as follows:

$$\text{Loss} = \frac{1}{2} \cdot (T^*)^2 \cdot R \cdot \frac{1}{1/\eta - 1/\epsilon} \qquad \text{(m10-2)}$$

Sometimes we are justified in making the simplifying assumption that the supply curve is horizontal, implying that $\epsilon = \infty$. In that case the deadweight loss to society formula simplifies to

$$\text{Loss} = \frac{1}{2} \cdot (T^*)^2 \cdot R \cdot \eta \qquad \text{(m10-3)}$$

The reader is reminded that Equations m10-2 and m10-3 are derived from partial-equilibrium analysis, and thus at best they provide a very rough order of magnitude.

PART FOUR

MONOPOLY AND IMPERFECT COMPETITION

The previous two chapters discussed firms that sell their output in *competitive markets*. These firms are price takers in the sense that they have no appreciable influence on the price of the good which they make and sell in the marketplace. The introduction to Chapter 7 briefly summarized the spectrum of market situations and mentioned three that differ from *perfect competition: monopoly, oligopoly,* and *monopolistic competition*. In perfect competition firms are *price takers*; in the other three market situations firms have some influence on the price of the good they sell.

We already know that perfect competition arises when a large number of small firms produce a homogeneous product such as wheat. What determines the number of firms in an industry? Put another way, what determines the size of the firm relative to aggregate demand? In most cases the answer lies in the internal economies of scale prevailing in an industry. You will recall from Section 6.5f that internal economies of scale determine the range of production over which the long-run average cost curve is falling. If this range is small relative to aggregate demand, a large number of firms will survive in an industry; if this range is large relative to aggregate demand, only a small number of firms will survive in an industry. In the extreme case where internal economies of scale are dominant, a *natural monopoly* will emerge. Bell Telephone is a prime example of a natural monopoly. However, monopolies might arise for various other reasons. For example, the chain of restaurants in Yellowstone National Park is a monopoly that was created by an exclusive franchise granted by the federal government; local public utilities are the legal creations of state and municipal governments. *Oligopolies* would normally arise when internal economies of scale are dominant, making room for only a small number of firms to survive. The production of automobiles is governed by scale economies; this explains why only four auto manufacturers have survived in the United States. Chapter 13 will analyze the airline oligopoly in the United States, which was created and sheltered by the federal government during the period 1938–1978. Oligopoly or monopoly could arise as a result of a scarce resource being dominated by a few firms or a single firm. In the 1960s International Nickel and Falconbridge dominated 90 percent of the proved nickel ore reserves in the United States. So long as no substitutes were found for nickel in the production of stainless steel, this concentration of control guaranteed an oligopolistic market situation. Oligopolies might arise because of ownership of a patent. The drug industry is to some extent oligopolistic because ownership of a patent entitles a firm to be the sole producer of a drug; other firms may produce the drug but must pay for a license or for research and development.

Market imperfection arises not only from the fact that an industry is dominated by a small number of producers. If a relatively large number of firms survive in an industry but the product of each firm is slightly differentiated from the product of other firms, each firm will have some limited influence on the price of the product it makes. Supermarkets are an example. The service of each supermarket is slightly differentiated; hence a single supermarket can lower its price and lure many customers from other stores in town. Or it may raise its price and lose a great number of customers to all the other supermarkets. This is true because services rendered by supermarkets are close substitutes for one another. Such a market situation, in which close substitutes are produced by many firms, is known as *monopolistic competition*. Monopolistic competition is so close to perfect competition that many economists advocate analyzing monopolistically competitive markets in the framework of perfect competition.

Chapter 11 analyzes the market situation of *monopoly*. The theory of monopoly is crucial to understanding monopolistic competition and oligopoly because it is the basis for analyzing profit maximization when the firm is not a price taker. Chapter 12 covers the theory of *monopolistic competition*. Theoretically, firms in monopolistic competition may be viewed as monopolies confronted with extremely elastic demand curves, almost to the point that they may be considered competitive firms for all practical purposes. Chapter 13 discusses the market situation of *oligopoly*. There is no unique theory of oligopoly. In perfect competition the individual firm takes the market price as given and proceeds to maximize its profit. The monopolistic firm takes the market demand as given and proceeds to maximize its profit. The single oligopolistic firm can take neither the price nor the market demand as given; its behavior in the marketplace is determined to a large extent by the behavior of its rivals.

Chapters 12 and 13 are optional for students in a one-semester course.

Before proceeding, the student will benefit from reviewing the circular flow diagram in Figure I-2, in particular the box representing the market for goods.

C H A P T E R

MONOPOLY

Monopoly is a market situation in which a single firm is the sole producer of a good for which no close substitutes exist. This single firm is also known as a monopoly. The monopoly constitutes the entire industry and thus faces the market demand curve. You will recall that the demand curve confronting the individual competitive firm is horizontal (Section 7.2a); moreover, because it is horizontal, it coincides with the marginal revenue curve. The market demand curve, being negatively sloped, does not coincide with the marginal revenue curve. Much of the new theory of this chapter will focus on this divergence between the demand curve and the marginal revenue curve.

In the United States most monopolies are found at the local level, for example, public utilities producing electric power, selling natural gas, and pumping and distributing water. Sometimes a whole industry organizes as a monopoly known as a *cartel* that might succeed for only a short time unless it is supported by the government. Physicians have been accused of organizing local monopolies. These problems for policy makers will be discussed, but first the theory of monopoly must be understood.

11.1 THE THEORY OF PRICE DETERMINATION BY A MONOPOLY

11.1a A Numerical Illustration

Suppose you are the manager of a monopolistic firm. The following information is provided by your marketing department about the market demand: At a price P of $10 you could sell only one unit of X per unit of time; at a lower price of $9 you could increase your sales to two units; at a price of $8 you could sell three units; and so on. This marketing information is illustrated by columns 1 and 2 in Table 11-1. With this information about the market demand function you can calculate total revenue R in column 3. Recall that total revenue is the product of the quantity marketed times the price: $R = P \cdot X$. For simplicity, assume that your fixed cost (FC) is $6 and marginal cost is unchanged at $4. Your calculation of profit is carried out in column 5, where you subtract total cost C from total revenue R to obtain profit; profit attains its maximum of $6 when the rate of production is 4 units per unit of time. (As a matter of fact the same profit is also attained when 3 units are produced, and thus the production of the fourth unit is optional. We assume that you decide to go ahead with the production of the fourth unit.) You recall from Section 3.2a, Equation 3-3, that marginal revenue is defined as the change in total revenue over the change in output, that is, $MR = \Delta R / \Delta X$. For example, marginal revenue of the third unit produced is $MR = (\$24 - \$18)/(3 - 2) = \$6$. MR is calculated and recorded in column 6; note that if the production rate is less than 4 units, MR exceeds MC; if output is in excess of 4 units, MC exceeds MR. Your profit is maximized at a level of 4 units when marginal revenue equals marginal cost which is equal to $4. We can summarize it as

$$MR = MC \tag{11-1}$$

Equation 11-1 is identical to Equation 7-2 as applied to a competitive firm

TABLE 11-1 Monopoly

X (1)	P (2)	R (3)	C (4)	Profit (rent) (5)	MR (6)	MC (7)
1	$10	$10	$10	$ 0	$10	$4
2	9	18	14	4	8	4
3	8	24	18	6	6	4
4	7	28	22	6	4	4
5	6	30	26	4	2	4
6	5	30	30	0	0	4
7	4	28	34	−6	−2	4
8	3	24	38	−14	−4	4
9	2	18	42	−24	−6	4

(Section 7.2c), but it conceals a major difference: since the monopolistic firm faces a negatively sloping demand curve, price diverges from marginal revenue.

Before we proceed, we note the following: If cost is defined properly so that it includes the alternative returns to entrepreneurial capacity and capital (Section 7.5), the profit is identical with rent (Section 9.10). What follows will follow tradition and denote total revenue minus total cost as profit, having in mind economic rent.

11.1b The Marginal Revenue of a Monopoly

Table 11-1 provides an intuitive feel for the concept of marginal revenue confronting a monopoly. We notice that when the price was set at $9, marginal revenue is $8; when the price is set at $8, marginal revenue is $6; and so on. It is intuitively evident that because the monopoly is confronted with a negatively sloping demand curve, the marginal revenue is less than the price. It has been shown formally that the marginal revenue of the aggregate demand curve is related to the demand price as follows (Equation 3-4):

$$MR = P\left(1 + \frac{1}{\eta}\right) \tag{11-2}$$

Since the price elasticity of demand is negative, marginal revenue must be smaller than the price. For example, if the monopoly is confronted with a demand curve which (in the relevant domain of output) has an elasticity of −2, then for a price of $10 the associated marginal revenue must be $5 as follows:

$$MR = \$10\left(1 + \frac{1}{-2}\right) = \$5$$

At this point it is important to elaborate on the concept of marginal revenue and see why, when the demand curve confronting a firm is negatively sloped, the marginal revenue curve lies below the demand curve. In order to do so, we recall (Section 3.2a) that if the price is lowered by some ΔP, leading to output expansion of ΔX, then the additional revenue is

$$\Delta R = X_0 \cdot \Delta P + \Delta X \cdot P_0 + \Delta X \cdot \Delta P \qquad (11\text{-}3)$$

Thus there are three components which make up ΔR. This expression may be simplified to the following:

$$\Delta R = X_0 \cdot \Delta P + \Delta X(P_0 + \Delta P) = X_0 \cdot \Delta P + \Delta X \cdot P_1 \qquad (11\text{-}4)$$

(Recall that $P_0 + \Delta P$ is equal to P_1.) Now, by examining Figure 11-1 (a replica of Figure 3-2), we can explain why the marginal revenue is less than the price. The first component in Equation 11-4, namely, $X_0 \cdot \Delta P$, is negative. It is the shaded rectangle in the diagram. It tells what is the loss in revenue to the monopoly because the entire output flow of X_0 units must now (after an expansion by ΔX) sell at a price of P_1, which is by ΔP lower than the original price of P_0. The second term, namely, $\Delta X \cdot P_1$, is positive. It is the rectangle marked by the diagonal lines. It tells what is the gain to the monopoly resulting from the expansion of output. Finally, we note that if ΔX is one unit of output, then ΔR is marginal revenue and Equation 11-4 becomes

$$MR = X_0 \cdot \Delta P + P_1 \qquad (11\text{-}5)$$

Equation 11-5 tells why the marginal revenue confronting the monopoly is less than the price: There is a tradeoff; when it expands, the monopoly gains P_1 dollars (namely, the price) but it loses $X_0 \cdot \Delta P$ (namely, the fall in the price of the current flow of output).

FIGURE 11-1   THE DIVERGENCE BETWEEN PRICE AND MARGINAL REVENUE

As the monopoly lowers the price by ΔP, it loses the shaded area because the initial X_0 units now sell for a lower price (P_1 instead of P_0). It gains the striped area on account of selling ΔX additional units (albeit at a lower price of P_1 dollars).

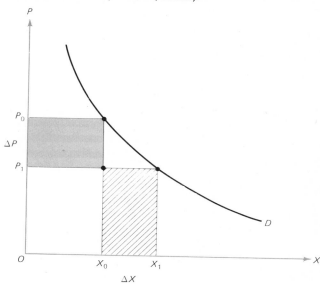

Let us illustrate Equation 11-5 with the aid of Table 11-1; let $X_0 = 2$. Since $\Delta X = 1$, we can apply Equation 11-1 directly as follows:

$$\text{MR} = X_0 \cdot \Delta P + P_1 = 2 \cdot (\$8 - \$9) + \$8$$

$$= 2 \cdot (-\$1) + \$8 = \$6$$

Marginal revenue curves may be derived from demand curves point by point by applying Equation 11-2. As explained in Mathematical Appendix 11, if the demand curve is linear, the associated marginal revenue curve is drawn by stretching a line between the intercept of the demand curve with the price axis and the midpoint between the origin and the intercept of the demand curve with the quantity (X) axis.

11.1c The Geometry of Price Determination by Monopolies

Section 7.2c described in detail the geometry of profit maximization in perfect competition. Before the geometry of profit maximization is illustrated by a monopoly, we note that the cost curves of a monopoly are shaped exactly like the cost curves of a typical competitive firm. The monopoly has influence on the price of the good it sells in the marketplace, but like any other competitive firm, it has no appreciable influence on the prices of inputs it purchases in the factor market. There are two main geometrical differences between a monopoly and a firm in perfect competition: First, recall that the total revenue (R) curve of a competitive firm is linear; in fact, it is a ray sent from the origin, reflecting the inability of the competitive firm to influence the price of the good it produces [panel (a) of Figure 7-2]. The R curve of a monopoly is nonlinear, reflecting the influence the monopoly exerts on the price of the good it produces. Second, recall that the demand curve facing the firm in perfect competition is horizontal and coincides with the marginal revenue curve [panel (b) of Figure 7-2]. As was argued in the previous section, the marginal revenue associated with a negatively sloped demand curve must occupy a lower position than the demand curve.

Figure 11-2 illustrates the process of selecting the price (and quantity) yielding maximum profit for the monopoly. Panel (a) displays the monopolistic solution in terms of total revenue and total cost; the monopoly seeks the level of output which would yield the greatest vertical distance between the total revenue curve (R) and the total cost curve (C). (Note: Depending on the length of the run, C could represent either a long-run or a short-run total cost curve.) This level of output is X_0 units, where the greatest distance between R and C is depicted by segment $\overline{GG^*}$. The C curve crosses the R curve once at point F and the second time at point H; correspondingly, the two break-even levels of output are X_1^b and X_2^b (Section 7.2c). For levels of output less than X_0 the slope of the R curve (MR) exceeds the slope of the C curve (MC); beyond the level of X_0 the slope of the C curve (MC) exceeds the slope of the R curve (MR). At the level of output of X_0 the two slopes are equal, namely, we confirm Equation 11-1 again: The two slopes are represented by the two lines, one tangent to the C curve at point G

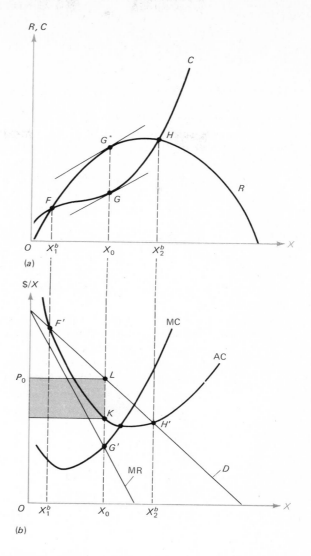

FIGURE 11-2 MONOPOLY EQUILIBRIUM.

In panel (a) total revenue curve R cuts total cost curve C at points F and H. Correspondingly, X_1^b and X_2^b are the two break-even rates of production. Maximum profit is attained at output X_0, where the vertical distance between the R curve and the C curve is the greatest ($\overline{GG}^*$). The vertical distance between the R and C curves measures profit. Associated with X_0, the slope of R at G^* is equal to the slope of C at G. In panel (b) the average cost curve AC cuts the demand curve D at points F' and H'. Correspondingly, X_1^b and X_2^b are the two break-even rates of production. Profit is maximized at point G', where the marginal revenue curve (MR) intersects with the marginal cost curve (MC). As in panel (a), X_0 is the associated level of output. The shaded area is the profit: $(P_0 - \text{AC}) \cdot X_0$.

and the other tangent to the R curve at point G^*. Panel (b) displays the monopolistic solution in terms of the per-unit-of-output curves, namely, average and marginal cost curves denoted by AC and MC, respectively, and average and marginal revenue curves deonted by D and MR, respectively. (Since the price is equal to the average revenue, the demand curve is also the average revenue curve.) Associated with the equality of the slopes of the C and R curves [in panel (a)], the MC and MR curves intersect at the same level of output of X_0. Also, associated with the intersection of the C curve with the R curve [in panel (a)], the AC curve cuts the D curve at output levels of X_1^b and X_2^b. Let us focus again on the maximum profit equilibrium. The MR curve cuts the MC curve at G'; we know that G' is the point which determines maximum profit; but can we measure maximum profit geometrically? At X_0 the price is P_0 (which is also the segment $\overline{X_0 L}$); as indicated by the AC curve, average cost is $\overline{X_0 K}$. The difference between price and average cost is segment $\overline{KL}$; this segment multiplied by output X_0 gives maximum profit, which is the shaded rectangle.

Table 11-1 cannot exactly fit Figure 11-2 because the associated marginal cost curve would be a horizontal line at \$4. Still, you can verify that in Table 11-1, $X_1^b = 1$, $X_2^b = 6$, and $X_0 = 4$. The maximum profit (shaded rectangle in Figure 11-2) is equal to \$6.

We should mention the *sufficient conditions* for profit maximization. The equality of the slope of the C curve with the slope of the R curve is the *necessary condition* of profit maximization. The fact that the slope of R exceeds the slope of C up to the level of output of X_0 and that thereafter the slope of the C curve exceeds the slope of the R curve is the sufficient condition for profit maximization. We can summarize:

1. The necessary condition for profit maximization by a monopoly is the intersection of the MC with the MR curve.
2. The sufficient condition for profit maximization by a monopoly is that the MC curve must cross the MR curve from below, going from left to right.

Note that the above conditions are formally identical with the conditions set for profit maximization by the competitive firm (Section 7.2c).

11.2 WELFARE LOSS DUE TO MONOPOLIES

11.2a Deadweight Loss to Society

In competitive markets firms equate their marginal costs with the price. Intuitively, this means that when the consumer pays a certain price for a good that is produced competitively, the price covers the additional cost of producing the good. As noted in the previous section, monopolistic pricing leads to a different solution: The price exceeds the marginal cost; in Figure 11-2 the price P_0 ($\overline{X_0 L}$) is in excess of the marginal cost, which is $\overline{X_0 G'}$. Consumers pay the monopoly more than the additional cost required to produce an additional unit of the good. Consider Figure 11-3. Under competition, output would have been determined at point E where the MC curve

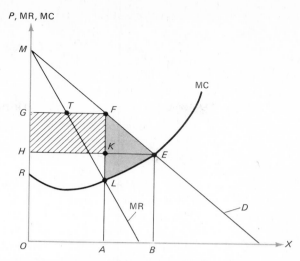

FIGURE 11-3 WELFARE LOSS DUE TO MONOPOLISTIC PRICING
The demand curve faced by the monopoly is denoted by *D*. MR is the associated marginal revenue curve and MC is the marginal cost curve. The shaded area (triangle) is the welfare loss to society. The striped rectangle is the transfer from consumers to owners (stockholders) of the monopoly.

cuts demand curve D. The associated level of output and price would have been $\overline{OB}$ and $\overline{OH}$. However, the monopolistic solution is depicted by the intersection of the MC curve with the MR curve at point L, where the level of output is only $\overline{OA}$ units. We conclude that in order to create the divergence between the price and the marginal cost, monopolies produce less than what would have been the level of output under a competitive solution. Thus the economic inefficiency of monopolistic pricing is reflected in a relatively lower level of output. It should be stressed that, like competitive firms, monopolies combine factors of production efficiently: Along the MC curve of a monopoly the *least-cost rule* of combining inputs (Equation 6.15) is satisfied.

The area lying under the demand curve and above the price line represents the consumer's surplus (Section 2.7). The area lying above the marginal cost curve and under the price line is the producer's surplus (Section 7.4). Hence, if a competitive solution is assumed, the consumer's surplus will be the area indicated by *MHE* and the producer's surplus the area indicated by *HRLE*. If the monopolistic solution is assumed, the price rises to $\overline{OG}$, the consumer's surplus shrinks to the area indicated by *MGF*, and the producer's surplus increases to the area depicted by *GRLF*. The rectangle with the diagonal stripes indicated by *GHKF* is a transfer from the consumers to the monopolistic firm. There is very little economists can say about this transfer, for two reasons: First, because of the impossibility of the interpersonal comparison of utility, they cannot even indicate whether such a transfer entails a loss or a gain in welfare. Second, conceivably some of the consumers of the monopolized good are holders of stocks issued by the monopolistic firm. Under the assumption of competition, the combined consumer's and producer's gain is the area indicated by *MRLE*. On the other hand, if a monopolistic solution is assumed, the combined surplus shrinks to *MRLF*. There is a net loss to society equal to the area (shaded) of triangle *FLE*. (*FLE* is a triangle if we assume that the segments connecting the pair of points *L* and *E* and the pair of points *E* and *F* are linear.) This welfare loss is known in economic jargon as *deadweight loss to society*. However, the above estimate of welfare loss is based on what economists call *partial analysis*. Controversy has surrounded the issue of *partial versus general analysis*. Chapter 17 will apply general analysis to display the welfare loss to society resulting from monopolistic pricing. No attempt will be made to reconcile the two approaches.

Let us again focus on Table 11-1. Assume that the fixed cost is zero; the monopoly could produce 7 units per unit of time and cover all its costs. At a rate of production of 7 units, $P = \text{MC} = \$4$; namely, it is a rate of production consistent with perfect competition. Consumer's surplus would have amounted to \$21 $(= \$10 - \$4 + \$9 - \$4 + \$8 - \$4 + \$7 - \$4 + \$6 - \$4 + \$5 - \$4 + \$4 - \$4)$. Under monopolistic pricing, consumer's surplus amounts only to \$6 $(= \$10 - \$7 + \$9 - \$7 + \$8 - \$7 + \$7 - \$7)$. The net loss to consumers is $\$21 - \$6 = \$15$. The transfer from consumers to producers is $(P - \text{MC}) \cdot X_0$, which is $(\$7 - \$4) \cdot 4 = \$12$. The *deadweight loss* to society is thus $\$15 - \$12 = \$3$. This loss amounts to 10.7 percent (\$3/\$28) of total value of output produced by the monopoly. This result is not indicative of the welfare loss resulting from monopolistic pricing in real life, which will be discussed in Section 11.2c.

11.2b The Lerner Formula

Intuitively, we feel that the power of a monopoly in the marketplace will diminish the more elastic the (market) demand curve confronting it; in fact, in the extreme case of perfect competition the demand curve is perfectly elastic and monopoly power diminishes completely. The elasticity of the demand curve is affected by the presence of substitutes in the marketplace. Thus the demand curve facing the producer of a certain brand of beer is very elastic, owing to the availability of many other brands of beer in the marketplace. This is the reason we do not classify the beer industry as a monopoly, but as *monopolistic competition*. (Some economists might classify it as an *oligopoly*.) The need to quantify the relationship between monopoly power and demand elasticity led to *Lerner's formula*, which we now consider.

Marginal revenue is related to the price by Equation 11-2. Since in monopolistic equilibrium marginal revenue equals marginal cost, it can be said that

$$\text{MC} = P\left(1 + \frac{1}{\eta}\right) \tag{11-6}$$

The more elastic the demand curve confronting the monopoly, the closer the

TABLE 11-2   Lerner's Formula

Price elasticity	Lerner's ratio	Monopoly power
-2	0.5	High
-4	0.25	Intermediate
-10	0.1	Low
$-\infty$	0	None

monopolistic solution would be to the competitive one. When the demand curve confronting the monopolistic firm is perfectly elastic ($\eta = -\infty$), we obtain the competitive solution, namely, $MC = P$. Abba P. Lerner suggested measuring the power of the monopolistic firm by the ratio of the divergence between the price and MC to the price.

$$\text{Lerner's ratio} = \frac{P - MC}{P}$$

$$= \frac{P - P(1 + 1/\eta)}{P} = -\frac{1}{\eta} \qquad (11\text{-}7)$$

As demonstrated in Table 11-2, Lerner's ratio declines as elasticity grows. Notice, however, that Lerner's formula is not always reliable: Figure 11-4

FIGURE 11-4   LERNER'S FORMULA AND WELFARE LOSS

By assumption, two different monopolies with an identical marginal cost curve (MC) operate in two different markets with demand curves depicted by D_1 and D_2. Curves D_1 and D_2 are tangent to one another at point A. Correspondingly, the two associated marginal revenue curves cross one another at point B. If MC passes through B, both monopolies achieve equilibrium at a rate of production of X_0. This implies that Lerner's ratio is the same for both monopolies, but the welfare loss of the monopoly facing D_2, is by the shaded area greater than the welfare loss of the other monopoly.

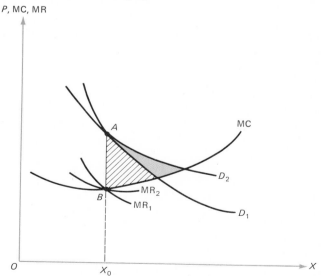

displays a situation in which two demand curves, D_1 and D_2, are tangent to each other at point A. Accordingly, the two associated marginal revenue curves, MR_1 and MR_2, must intersect at the same level of output X_0; the point of intersection is B. [The D_1 curve is related to the D_2 curve as an *envelope-long-run AC curve* is related to an *envelope-short-run AC curve*. This relationship was discussed in Section 6.6, and Figure 11-4 is formally identical with panel (*b*) of Figure 6-12. At point A the two demand curves must have the same elasticity: $\eta = (\Delta X/X)/(\Delta P/P)$. This can be rearranged as follows: $\eta = (P/X)/(\Delta P/\Delta X)$. Since $\Delta P/\Delta X$ is the slope of the demand curve, we can write $\eta = (P/X)/(\text{slope})$. At point A the two demand curves have the same slope by tangency, and also they have the same quantity (X_0) and the same price ($\overline{X_0 A}$)]. Now if we imagine two monopolistic firms with identical MC curves as displayed in Figure 11-4, one confronted with a demand curve D_1 and the other with a demand curve D_2, each of the two firms will reach equilibrium at point B. Although Lerner's ratio will be the same for both, the welfare loss due to the firm selling where the demand curve is D_1 will amount only to the area with the diagonal stripes. The welfare loss due to the firm selling where the demand curve is D_2 will amount to this area plus the shaded area.

11.2c Should We Fight Fires and Termites?

We saw that the welfare loss resulting from monopolistic pricing amounts to the shaded area in Figure 11-3. Should we be concerned about this welfare loss? To answer this, economists had to measure the welfare loss in real life. Arnold Harberger was the pioneer in attempting to measure the welfare loss due to monopolistic pricing in the United States.[1] Harberger estimated the welfare loss due to monopolistic pricing in manufacturing industries in the late 1920s. Although he made some simplifying assumptions, he basically measured the areas of triangles like *FLE* in Figure 11-3, and aggregated them. He concluded that the deadweight loss to society amounted to about one-tenth of 1 percent of gross national product, enough to treat every person in the United States to a good steak dinner once a year. Professor Stigler is alleged to have commented that if these findings were correct then "economists might serve a more useful purpose if they fought fires and termites instead of monopoly." George Stigler also dissented from Harberger's findings because reported profit rates for monopolistic firms may omit monopoly returns in the form of disguised "cost" items such as patent royalties and executive salaries (Section 7.1).[2] More recently, in 1963, John Siegfried and Thomas Tieman estimated that welfare loss due to monopolistic pricing was $354 million, a mere 0.0734 percent of national income.[3] They

---

[1]Arnold C. Harberger, "Monopoly and Resource Allocation," *American Economic Review*, vol. 44, May 1954, pp. 77–87.

[2]George J. Stigler, "The Statistics of Monopoly Merger," *Journal of Political Economy*, vol. 64, February 1956, pp. 33–40.

[3]John J. Siegfrid and Thomas K. Tieman, "The Welfare Cost of Monopoly: An Inter Industry Analysis," *Economic Inquiry*, vol. 12, June 1974, pp. 190–202.

confirmed Harberger's result. According to their report, five industries—plastics, drugs, petroleum refining, office and computing machinery, and motor vehicles—accounted for the lion's share (67 percent) of the total estimated welfare loss. The motor vehicle industry alone is responsible for almost a half (44 percent) of the loss.

The controversy surrounding the issue of welfare loss due to monopolistic pricing is not over. For example, Dean Worcester argued that the "maximum defensible" estimate of welfare loss due to monopolistic pricing is in the range of 0.5 percent of national income.[4] It is important to note that a reasonable explanation for the relatively small welfare loss due to monopolistic pricing might lie in the fact that Harberger and those who followed were looking at *oligopoly* rather than strict *monopoly*. Even the auto industry, which according to Siegfrid and Tieman in 1963 accounted for the lion's share of the welfare loss, is a typical oligopoly.[5]

11.3 PUBLIC UTILITIES

11.3a Natural Monopolies

Public utilities are firms supplying services such as electricity, gas, water, and local transportation. Utilities usually produce and market under conditions known in economic jargon as *natural monopolies*. They are firms which benefit from large (internal) *economies of scale*. The term economies of scale means geometrically (Section 6.5f), that the average cost curve is very high as a low rate of output and falls over a long range of output. The position of the demand curve relative to the AC curve is also relevant. Consider Figure 11-5. The market demand curve is denoted by D. The average cost curve of a typical utility is AC. Notice that AC is falling over a wide range of output. It reaches its minimum at point M, which represents a large percentage of the total market. If two firms attempted to produce for the same market, each firm would be confronted with half the total demand curve denoted by $1/2D$. In this case the AC curve would lie entirely over the $1/2D$ curve, and neither of the firms would be able to break even. The position of the demand curve relative to the AC curve is also relevant in creating market conditions conducive for natural monopolies: If the market demand curve were to be rotated clockwise from position D to position D', room would be made for additional firms to enter the market and produce profitably. We can summarize as follows:

If, because of (internal) economies of scale and the relative position of the de-

---

[4]Dean A. Worcester, Jr., "New Estimates of the Welfare Loss to Monopoly: U.S. 1956–69." *Southern Economic Journal*, vol. 40, October 1973, pp. 234–246.

[5]Chapter 13 will present Stigler's extension of Lerner's formula for oligopolies as Ratio = $-1/(n \cdot \eta)$, where n is the number of oligopolistic firms assumed to be identical, η is price elasticity of aggregate demand, and Cournot is the oligopolistic mode of behavior. Following Harberger in assuming $\eta = -1$ if $n = 5$, the extended Lerner's ratio is then 0.20 rather than unity, if we assumed strict monopoly.

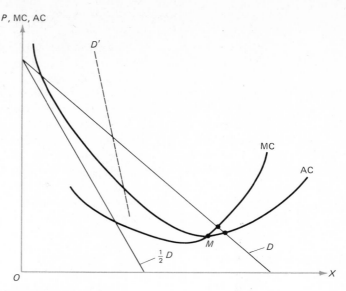

FIGURE 11-5 NATURAL MONOPOLY
The average cost of a typical firm is depicted by AC. The market demand curve is denoted by D. If the market demand curve is divided into two equal segments, $\frac{1}{2} D$ represents one such segment. The AC curve lies entirely above the curve denoted by $\frac{1}{2} D$. This indicates that there is room for only one firm—the natural monopoly. However, if the demand curve were to rotate clockwise, say, to position D', room would be made for additional firms.

mand curve, only a single firm can survive in the market, a natural monopoly will result.

11.3b Regulation of Utilities

At the turn of the century in state after state throughout the country public utilities commissions were established with the responsibility to regulate the utilities. The consensus was that public utilities are natural monopolies and unless regulated would charge the public monopolistic prices. The next section will present a minority challenge to public utilities regulation.

Consider Figure 11-6, displaying a natural monopoly. If the natural monopoly is unregulated, it will select a rate of output X_0 and a price P_0 corresponding to the point of intersection between the MC and the MR curves. If the public utilities commission regulates the utility by imposing a price P_1, associated with the intersection of the MC curve with demand curve D, the utility will produce at a rate of X_1 units per unit of time. In practice, the public utilities commissions regulate the utilities by requiring them to fix prices such that their revenues are just sufficient to cover all current costs, interest on loans, depreciation on buildings, equipment, and machinery, and a normal rate of return on equity. Since this boils down to equating revenue with economic cost (Section 7.5), this regulatory policy in fact sets a price P_2, where the AC curve cuts the demand curve. The rate of

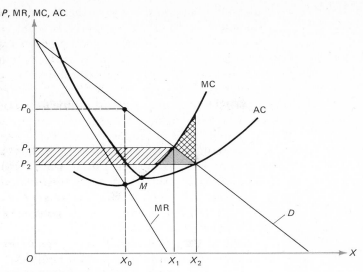

FIGURE 11-6 REGULATION OF PUBLIC UTILITIES
Here, if the natural monopoly were unregulated, it would charge a price of P_0 and produce at a rate of X_0, as indicated by the point of intersection between its marginal revenue curve (MR) and marginal cost curve (MC). If the monopoly were regulated where MC intersects with the demand curve D, it would charge a price P_1 and produce at a rate of X_1, and there would be no welfare loss. If the monopoly is regulated at the point where the average cost curve (AC) cuts the demand curve, it would charge a price P_2 and produce at a rate of X_2. The monopoly's loss would be the striped area plus the shaded area plus the crosshatched area; the increment in the consumer's surplus would be the striped area plus the shaded area. This would leave the crosshatched area as a (net) welfare loss.

production rises to X_2 and the crosshatched triangle is a deadweight loss to society as follows: The gain to the consumer is the area with the diagonal stripes plus the shaded triangle; the loss to the producer is the area with the **diagonal stripes plus the shaded triangle plus the triangle with the crosshatch design. The crosshatched area thus represents a net loss to society.**

11.3c Why Regulate the Utilities?

The conventional theory that public utilities are natural monopolies and thus should be regulated has been challenged by Harold Demsetz.[6] Demsetz claims that the history of public utility development indicates rivalry among a relatively large number of producers, rather than a natural monopoly. For example, six electric light companies were organized in 1887 in New York. At the turn of the century 45 electric light enterprises had the legal right to **operate in Chicago. These data show that the production of electric light was not necessarily governed by huge-scale economies.**

---

[6]Harold Demsetz, "Why Regulate the Utilities?" *Journal of Law and Economics*, vol. 11, April 1968, pp. 55–73.

There are two alternatives to regulation of utilities: First, if indeed there are no economies of scale, a few rivals could produce electricity and natural gas. When the time for a new contract comes, individuals would consider the cost of having the rival company run a new trench through their gardens versus the benefit of getting natural gas or electricity at lower prices. In other words, it is not necessarily true that duplications of parts of the distribution system will give rise to a higher price. But, claims Demsetz, even if it is clear that significant economies of scale lead to natural monopolies in the area of public utilities, it does not imply that we must regulate. As an example of a second possibility, in the case of electricity, the public could own the distribution system and generators. The city or state could put the generation of electricity out for bids and contract with the bidder offering the lowest price per kilowatthour.[7] In the case of garbage collection, in which the life of capital is relatively short (garbage trucks do not last as long as electric generators), a city could define a contract period as equivalent to the economic lifetime of the machinery and equipment used and put out for bids for a comparable time period. The contract would specify frequency and other terms of garbage collection. The bidder would have to provide equipment, labor, and management. [Suffice it to say that fixing the rate at which the capital owned by the city (or state) should be rented to the franchisees is a complex issue.] The theory as developed by Demsetz suggests that it is feasible to put out for bids goods and services currently provided by regulated public utilities. Only if a large number of local governments dare to experiment will we be able to determine whether such a system will work.

11.4 PRICE DISCRIMINATION

We sometimes observe that in perfect competition different prices are paid for what may seem to be the same good. For example, oranges cost more in Chicago than in Miami Beach; the difference is a result of the difference in transportation cost. A New York City butcher shop patronized by movie stars and other celebrities charges more for its meat; the higher price is paid not for the meat but for the company. In the supermarket, milk in a large container would cost less (per ounce) than milk in a small container; in a small container you get more "container" per ounce of milk. The consumer

---

[7]To bid means to offer a price. In secret bidding the bidders offer their prices in sealed envelopes to be opened at a prefixed date. In the case of a homogeneous good the buyer would accept the lowest bid. In the scenario set by Demsetz the rival who offers the buyers the most favorable terms will obtain their patronage. The two conditions required to guarantee a fair process of bidding are: (1) Inputs required to enter production must be available to a large number of potential bidders at prices determined competitively. An example would be coal for electric utilities. (2) The cost of colluding by bidders is prohibitively high. If there are many bidders, collusion would almost automatically become costly. If a group of bidders establishes a *cartel* (an organization of firms for the purpose of fixing prices; see Section 11.9), new bidding rivals will be paid to join in the collusion. In return for agreeing to join the cartel, they will be paid their pro rata share of monopoly profits. But as more bidding rivals are bribed to join the cartel, the pro rata share of each falls. There comes a point at which the pro rata share is either very low or zero. At that point it will pay the next bidding rival who has not yet joined the cartel to refuse the offer and grab the entire market by bidding a price lower than the cartel's price.

may pay more for more transportation, service, or "container" per unit of a good purchased, as in the examples above. In this section, however, we shall see that a certain combination of market structure and monopoly might result in different prices being charged to different customers or to the same customer without these extras. Some examples would be hard-cover and soft-cover books, movies released to first-run theaters at a high price and later to neighborhood theaters at a low price, and a physician charging a higher fee to a rich patient than to a poor patient. An electric company might charge higher rates to households compared with industrial users and different rates to the same customer depending on the amount of electricity used.

11.4a Perfect Discrimination

If a monopoly makes a commodity that cannot be transferred from one consumer to another, it has an incentive to institute a policy of quantity discrimination. It will charge relatively high prices for the first units sold, and lower prices for the second and third units sold. Such price setting is possible only if the product cannot be resold, as with electricity and telephone services. The monopoly cannot successfully engage in this form of price discrimination if the product can be resold, because some consumers will inevitably buy large quantities and resell them at a personal profit in small quantities.

Let us now focus on Figure 11-7. Under normal conditions a monopoly would maximize its profit by seeking the point of intersection between marginal revenue (MR) and marginal cost (MC); this point of intersection is depicted by G, where output would be produced at a rate of X_0 units per unit of time and price would be set at P_0 dollars. You will recall from Section 7.4 that the area under the marginal cost curve amounts to total variable cost. This was explained by noting that total variable cost may be viewed as the additional cost of the first unit, plus the additional cost of the second unit, and so on up to the last unit. Applying the same procedure, we can obtain total revenue received by the monopolistic firm by adding the additional revenue from the first unit to the additional revenue of the second unit, and so on up to the last unit. This adds up to the area under the MR curve. In consequence, the producer's surplus of the monopoly would be the area bordered by the MR curve, the MC curve, and the price axis as indicated by LMG in Figure 11-7. Now, profit may be written as $\pi = R - \text{VC} - \text{FC}$ (π, R, VC, and FC stand for profit, total revenue, total variable cost, and total fixed cost as defined in Sections 7.2 and 6.2). Since by definition the producer's surplus is total revenue minus total variable cost we can write $\pi = (R - \text{VC}) - \text{FC}$; in words, profit is the difference between the producer's surplus and total fixed cost. Consequently, profit is positively related to the producer's surplus; in the long run the two are identical.

Now, suppose you are the manager of a company that produces electric power. You know that consumers cannot sell electricity to one another, either because it is illegal or because of the technical problems and cost involved. In Figure 11-7 curve D represents the market demand curve for

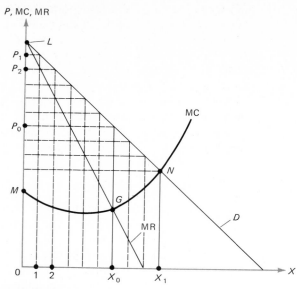

FIGURE 11-7   PERFECT DISCRIMINATION

If units of output cannot be sold from one consumer to another, then the monopoly, instead of selecting equilibrium where marginal cost curve MC cuts marginal revenue curve MR at point G, would follow a scheme of charging P_1 for the first unit, P_2 for the second unit, and so on. By following such a scheme, demand curve D would become the marginal revenue curve, and the monopolistic firm would consider point N as the equilibrium point. It would produce X_1 units and its producer's surplus would increase by the area LGN.

electric power; you can increase the producer's surplus of the company by charging a price of P_1 for the first unit, a price of P_2 for the second unit, and so on. Thus the net additional gain on the first unit is the price minus the MC, rather than MR minus the MC, and so on for the second and third, up to the last unit. Under such a scheme, which is known as *perfect discrimination*, it will benefit the company to increase the rate of production so long as the price (as indicated by the demand curve) is above the marginal cost (as indicated by the marginal cost curve). Your optimum level of output will be X_1. This level is determined by point N, where the MC curve crosses the demand curve. If you continue with this scheme beyond point N, your profit will begin to decline because the additional cost of producing an additional unit of electric power will exceed the price.

What have we learned from this exercise? The producer's surplus of a monopoly that institutes perfect discrimination is the area bordered by the demand curve, the MC curve, and the price axis as indicated by LMN in Figure 11-7. The monopolist has increased the producer's surplus, and hence the profit, by an area indicated by LGN. In reality, if there are a million consumers and if a price P_1 is set for the first unit, P_2 for the second unit, and so on, the monopolist will sell the first million units at a price of P_1 dollars, the second million units at a price of P_2 dollars, etc. If public opinion objects to such practices, the monopolist who happened to be, say, an electricity company, may set only two prices, one for households and one for industry. This variety of price discrimination will be discussed in the next section.

An interesting note: Although the entire consumer's surplus is "stolen" by the monopolistic firm, under perfect discrimination there is no welfare loss: There is no deadweight loss to society. The monopoly behaves as if it were a competitive firm: It produces where $P = $ MC. Accordingly, the consumer's surplus remains intact; it is transferred as a whole to the monopoly.

As indicated by Figure 11-7, perfect discrimination would require a declining rate for increasing quantities that would exactly trace out the demand curve. Since the precise shapes of demand curves are not known, electricity companies may change the rate by the block rather than unit by unit as displayed in Figure 11-8, where the first block B_1, sells for P_1 dollars, the second block, B_2, sells for a reduced rate of P_2 dollars, and the final block, B_3, sells for P_3 dollars. Such a quantity discrimination is less than perfect: Instead of the entire consumer surplus (the area of triangle LHN) the monopolist "grabs" only the shaded area from consumers. Accordingly, we may call this case *imperfect discrimination*.

11.4b Market Partitioning

Monopolies may be able to treat different parts of the market differently. If the domestic market is protected, a monopoly may dump its product abroad

FIGURE 11-8 IMPERFECT DISCRIMINATION

Only if the monopoly had perfect knowledge of the shape of demand curve D could its manager follow a scheme of perfect discrimination as in Figure 11-7. The alternative is to divide output into blocks, such as B_1, B_2, and B_3, and charge a price of P_1 (per unit) for the first block, P_2 for the second block, etc. Although this scheme does not enable the monopoly to transfer to itself the entire consumer's surplus, it transfers the shaded areas.

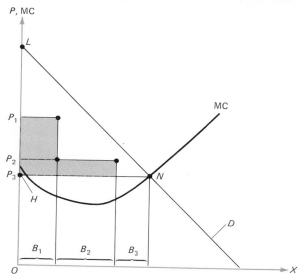

at a price that is lower than the domestic price. The partitioning of the *international market* into a *domestic* and a *foreign* market is accomplished by the protective act of a government. A movie may be released to a first-run theater and sold at a very high price; later it may be released to neighborhood theaters and sold at a relatively low price. In this example the partitioning of the market is accomplished by showing the movie first to the eager viewers and later to the less eager viewers. A more sophisticated technique is applied when a book is first published in hard cover for exorbitant prices and later published in soft cover at a much lower price. As in the case of perfect discrimination, the precondition for the feasibility of price discrimination between two (or more) parts of the market is the *impossibility of reselling*. In the above examples of dumping in foreign markets, separating the markets for movies between first-run and neighborhood theaters, and publishing books first in hard cover and later in soft cover, the partitioning satisfies the requirement of the impossibility of reselling.

We are now ready to prove the following theorem:

> *A monopolistic firm will charge a higher price in the segment of the market where the demand curve is relatively less elastic.*

The above theorem is proved in two stages: First, note that if a monopolist produces a fixed rate of output and is confronted with two separate parts of a market, what we shall call the *first* and the *second* market, the two marginal revenues have to be equated to maximize profit. If the two marginal revenues are denoted by MR_1 and MR_2, respectively, and if, for example, $MR_1 = \$7$ and $MR_2 = \$4$, it pays the monopolist to increase sales in the first market at the expense of the second market: The net gain from transferring the first unit from the second to the first market is $\$7 - \$4 = \$3$. However, since the marginal revenue curve has a negative slope, transferring output from the second to the first market will depress MR_1 and raise MR_2. It will pay the monopolist to continue transferring output from the second to the first market just until $MR_1 = MR_2$. Second, if MC is less than MR (which is either MR_1 or MR_2), it will pay the monopolist to expand. The gain per unit expanded will be $MR_1 - MC$ (which is the same as $MR_2 - MC$). The monopolist will expand just until the following holds:

$$MC = MR_1 = MR_2 \qquad (11\text{-}8)$$

If MC is in excess of MR, it will pay the monopolist to contract just until Equation 11-8 is satisfied. Geometrically, this optimal point of production is obtained by deriving the aggregate MR curve. This geometric procedure is carried out in Figure 11-9. We assume that the monopolist can partition the market into two markets: Market 1, whose demand curve D_1 is displayed in panel (*a*), and market 2, whose demand curve D_2 is displayed in panel (*b*). The associated marginal revenue curves are MR_1 and MR_2, respectively. We assume that demand curve D_2 is more elastic than D_1. This assumption should be qualified. As explained in Section 11.2b, price elasticity may be written as $\eta = (P/X)/(\text{slope})$. Since the slope of a linear demand curve is fixed, η, in absolute value, must be very small in the neighborhood of the quantity intercept and increase steadily as we climb up the linear demand curve toward the price intercept. As a matter of fact, as we move up from the quantity intercept to the price intercept, the absolute value of price elasticity of the linear demand curve varies from zero to infinity; at the midpoint on the demand curve it assumes a value of unity. Accordingly, when we say that demand curve D_2 is more elastic than D_1, we mean that it is more elastic in the respective neighborhoods of equilibrium. Next, MR_1 and MR_2 curves are aggregated horizontally. (The process of horizontal aggregation was explained in detail in Section 3.1a.) The result is the aggregate marginal revenue curve in panel (c), denoted by MR_t. The MC curve of the monopolist intersects with the aggregate marginal revenue curve MR_t at point W. Total output produced per unit of time is X_t^0 in panel (c). This amount is divided between the two markets as indicated by their respective marginal revenue curves. Geometrically, this is achieved by extending a horizontal (dashed) line at the $\overline{X_t^0 W}$ level back to panel (b) and panel (a). Thus the same marginal revenue which is equal to $\overline{X_t^0 W}$ prevails in each market. The quantity sold in market 1 is X_1^0 and in market 2 is X_2^0; and of course, by the construction of MR_t, $X_1^0 + X_2^0 = X_t^0$. Note that P_1 is higher than P_2. To achieve maximum profit, the monopolist must equate the two marginal revenues, but since the two demand curves have different elasticities, the price in the market with the less elastic demand curve is higher than the price in the market with the more elastic demand curve. To put it differently, P_1 is the only price in market 1 which would yield a marginal revenue of $\overline{X_t^0 W}$, and P_2 is the only price in market 2 which would yield the same marginal revenue of $\overline{X_t^0 W}$

FIGURE 11-9   PRICE DISCRIMINATION BETWEEN TWO MARKETS
The market is partitioned into two segments, one with the less elastic demand curve D_1 in panel (a) and one with the more elastic demand curve D_2 in panel (b). (Since the demand curves are linear, elasticities are compared only at small neighborhoods, not for the entire curves.) The associated marginal revenue curves are MR_1 and MR_2. These curves are aggregated into MR_t in panel (c); MR_t intersects with the marginal cost curve of the monopoly (MC) at point W. The solution is that monopoly produces X_t^0 units per unit of time, of which X_1^0 are sold in the first segment at a price of P_1 and X_2^0 units are sold in the second segment at a lower price of P_2.

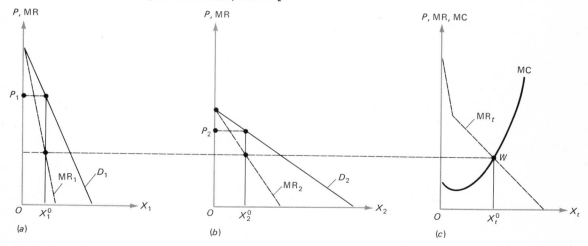

We now understand why at the turn of the century the Germans dumped their iron and steel abroad at half the price they charged at home: The demand outside Germany was by far more elastic than the domestic demand for steel and iron. Those willing to pay a very high price for a hard-cover novel or for a movie in a first-run theater are the eager readers and viewers; their demand curves are relatively less elastic than the demand curves of readers who patiently wait for the soft-cover book or of viewers who wait for the movie to reach neighborhood theaters.

What was demonstrated with the aid of Figure 11–9 can be done formally as follows: The marginal revenues in the two respective markets are

$$MR_1 = P_1 \left(1 + \frac{1}{\eta_1}\right) \qquad MR_2 = P_2 \left(1 + \frac{1}{\eta_2}\right)$$

Since profit maximization requires that $MR_1 = MR_2$, we obtain the equality

$$P_1 \left(1 + \frac{1}{\eta_1}\right) = P_2 \left(1 + \frac{1}{\eta_2}\right)$$

Since by assumption D_2 is a more elastic demand curve than D_1, we can write that $|\eta_2| > |\eta_1|$, and since both demand curves are respectively elastic, we obtain

$$\left(1 + \frac{1}{\eta_2}\right) > \left(1 + \frac{1}{\eta_1}\right)$$

but in order for the above inequalities to hold, we must have $P_1 > P_2$. *In summary, the monopolist will charge a higher price in the segment of the market where the demand curve is relatively less elastic.*

The theory and application of price discrimination among more than two parts of a market (that can be partitioned by a monopolist) is the same as the theory in the case of two parts only.

11.5 AN APPLICATION: THE MARKET FOR PHYSICIANS' SERVICES

The confusion and misunderstanding surrounding the issue of doctors' fees is amazing. The confusion starts with the role of the American Medical Association (AMA) in imposing barriers to entry into the profession. Some believe that in addition to limiting the supply of physicians, the AMA aids physicians in establishing local monopolies; others claim that the existence of local monopolies of physicians has nothing to do with AMA practices. The President's Council on Wages and Price Stability further confused the issue. A 1978 staff report stated that the increase in the supply of physicians gave rise to higher physicians' fees, because of *desired fixed income levels* for physicians. According to this doctrine, as the number of physicians rises, they raise their fees to maintain the fixed level of income.[8] The diffi-

---

[8]Zachary Y. Dyckman, "A Study of Physicians' Fees, *A Staff Report Prepared by the President's Council on Wages and Price Stability*, Government Printing Office, Washington, 1978.

As pointed out by Keith Leffler, the above report reached results that fly in the face of microeconomic theory by committing a common error in econometrics (statistics applied to

culty with the doctrine of desired fixed income levels is exposed by simple logic: At what level do physicians fix their desired income? If the level is $60,000 per annum, why not fix it at $100,000 per annum? After all, according to this doctrine, all that physicians have to do is to raise the fees they charge to a level that will yield an annual income of $100,000. Clearly, this issue is relevant for policy makers: If they believe in the *desired fixed income levels* doctrine, they should not subscribe to a policy aimed at increasing the supply of physicians in the United States; in fact, they should aid the AMA in further tightening the entry rules and regulations in order to decrease the supply of physicians. A physician who treats a larger number of patients will be able to charge a smaller fee to maintain the desired fixed level of income.

This section presents a microeconomic analysis of the market for physicians' services. Some studies are also cited that clearly test and confirm the implications of microeconomic theory versus the doctrine of desired fixed income levels.

11.5a Barriers to Entry

The American Medical Association (AMA) was founded in 1847. At the turn of the century the Carnegie Foundation issued the famous *Flexner Report*, which stressed the fact that too many medical schools provided low-level medical education. Armed with the *Flexner Report*, the AMA convinced all state legislatures to establish state medical examining boards, which were awarded the authority to license physicians. What is more important, only graduates of schools approved by the AMA were licensed by the state medical examining boards. The number of medical schools declined sharply from 162 in 1906 to 69 in 1944.

The issue of imposing barriers to entry into labor markets will be discussed in Chapter 15. For example, barbers in Illinois restricted supply by lobbying successfully for a state law requiring that licenses to cut hair be awarded only to those who studied a year in the barber school. Notice that barriers to entry into a profession do not necessarily lead to a monopolistic solution. Figure 11–10 illustrates the impact of the AMA on incomes of physicians under the assumption that competition prevails. The marginal cost curves of physicians are positively sloped, reflecting the rise in the marginal utility of leisure as leisure becomes scarce. In panel (*a*) the demand for physicians' services increases over time. If, in the face of this rise in demand, the AMA is able to block net entry into the profession, the aggregate MC curve ($\overset{m}{\Sigma}MC_i$) does not shift over time. As a result, physicians' fees rise sharply from P_0 to P_1. Had the number of physicians been allowed to grow freely, say from *m* to *n*, the aggregate MC curve would have shifted from

$$\overset{m}{\Sigma}MC_i \text{ to } \overset{n}{\Sigma}MC_i$$

and physicians' fees would have risen only to P'. In panel (*b*), originally the producer's surplus of a typical physician is the crosshatched area. Without the restriction imposed by the AMA, his or her producer's surplus would have increased over time by the shaded area. The fact that the AMA restricted the number of physicians to *m* enabled the typical physician to earn an extra producer's surplus, as indicated by the striped area. The reader is cautioned that the area with the diagonal stripes is not strictly a transfer of money from patients to physicians: Since the mechanism set by the AMA to inhibit an increase in supply over time boils down to limiting the number of medical schools and setting high standards to screen applicants, patients who are interested in high-quality medical services are saved the transaction costs of obtaining information about the credibility of physicians.

---

economics). The report used cross-sectional data from 124 metropolitan areas to estimate physicians' fees as a function of physicians' supply (physicians per 1000 population) and other factors. The report failed to recognize the fact that in metropolitan areas in which demand for physicians was relatively high, fees were relatively high, and these high fees attracted physicians from low-demand areas. Leffler comments that only if physicians dropped at random into the 124 metropolitan areas and were not allowed to relocate could one infer from the statistical results that increased supply leads to higher fees. (Keith B. Leffler, ''Explanations in Search of Facts: A Critique of a Study of Physicians' Fees,'' an Occasional Paper, Law and Economics Center, University of Miami School of Law, 1978.)

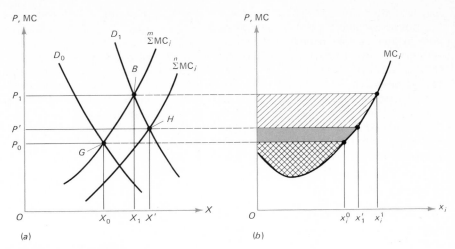

FIGURE 11-10 BARRIERS TO ENTRY

The marginal cost curve of a single physician (MC_i) is shown in panel (b). Assuming that perfect competition dominates and there are m physicians, $\overset{m}{\Sigma}MC_i$ in panel (a) is the supply curve of physicians' services. Initially, this supply curve cuts the demand curve D_0 at point G. The fee is P_0 and the producer's surplus is the crosshatched area in panel (b). Without barriers to entry, over time demand in panel (a) would shift from D_0 to D_1, the number of physicians would grow from m to n, leading to a supply increase from $\overset{m}{\Sigma}MC_i$ to $\overset{n}{\Sigma}MC_i$; the new point of intersection would be point H and the price would be P'. In panel (b) the producer's surplus of a single physician would increase by the shaded area. However, if barriers to entry would freeze the number of physicians at m, D_1 would intersect with $\overset{m}{\Sigma}MC_i$ at point B, with a fee of P_1. In panel (b) the producer's surplus of physicians would increase additionally by the striped area.

11.5b Local Monopolies

There are two basic hypotheses concerning the source of local monopolistic power of physicians. The first hypothesis by Reuben Kessel[9] is based on institutional arrangement as follows: Licensed physicians are organized in county medical societies. Most doctors must have excess to hospitals in order to practice. Certified hospitals are advised (Mundt Resolution) that their staff of physicians must be composed solely of members of the local county medical society. The "prize" for the hospitals is the allocation of positions to be filled by interns. Since wages of interns and residents are set by the AMA at a very low level, it benefits the certified hospitals to obey the rule

of restricting access to members of the county medical societies in order to qualify for the cheap source of labor. According to Kessel, the power of the county medical society lies in expulsion: A doctor expelled from the county medical society loses access to the hospital and thus cannot practice. The main evidence of monopolistic behavior is market partitioning between the poor and the rich. To illustrate, Kessel quotes from an unnamed physician who said: "I operated today upon two people for the same surgical condition—one a widow whom I charged $50, another a banker whom I charged $250. I let the widow set her own fee. I charged the banker an

---

[9]Reuben A. Kessel, "Price Discrimination in Medicine," *Journal of Law and Economics,* vol. 1, October 1958, pp. 20–53.

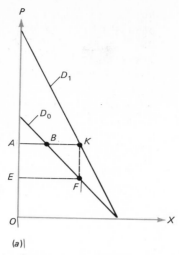

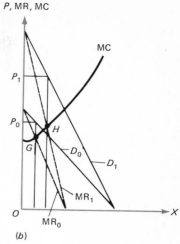

FIGURE 11-11 THE IMPACT OF INSURANCE PHYSICIANS' FEES

In panel (a), D_0 is the demand curve for services rendered by the physician. At a price of $\overline{OA}$ the quantity demand is $\overline{AB}$. After patient becomes insured, he or she pays out of pocket only $\overline{OE}$ dollars. As indicated by D_0, the quantity demanded is $\overline{EF}$; however, since the physician continues to receive a price of $\overline{OA}$ ($\overline{EA}$ dollars from the insurance company and $\overline{OE}$ from the patient), to the physician it looks as if the quantity demanded is $\overline{AK}$ at a price of $\overline{OA}$. This means that the physician perceives a demand shift from D_0 to D_1. Panel (b) shows that as the demand shifts from D_0 to D_1 the associated marginal revenue curve also shifts rightward. As a result, the intersection between the marginal revenue curve and the marginal cost curve shifts from G to H, and the physician's fee increases from P_0 to P_1.

amount which he probably carries around in his wallet to entertain his business friends."[10] In a more recent study Joseph Newhouse confirmed what Kessel had hypothesized, namely, that physicians charge higher fees to richer patients.[11] He found that doctors' fees are positively correlated with incomes of patients. Newhouse, however, developed a second alternative

hypothesis explaining the source of local monopolistic power of physicians: Since physicians are prohibited from advertising, information is imperfect and thus patients cannot very effectively compare prices; even if information were perfect, patients who trust a certain physician would not be lured to other physicians by small price cuts.

11.5c The Impact of Insurance on Physicians' Fees

Insurance increases the demand for physicians' services. A person who is insured by a plan that covers 80 percent of the physician's fees will find that a visit that previously cost $10 now costs only $2. Assuming a negatively sloping demand curve, this person will go down along the demand curve. To physicians, this

will appear as a shift to the right in the demand because they continue to charge $10 and the demand for their services is higher. In panel (a) of Figure 11-11 the demand curve of a certain patient for physicians' services is denoted by D_0. Prior to becoming insured, a patient pays $\overline{OA}$ dollars and the

---

[10]Ibid. Reprinted with permission from *Journal of Law and Economics.* Copyright 1958 by the University of Chicago Law School.

[11]Joseph P. Newhouse, "A Model of Physician Pricing," *Southern Economic Journal*, vol. 37, October 1970, pp. 174–183.

quantity demanded is $\overline{AB}$ units. Insurance reduces the out-of-pocket fee to $\overline{OE}$ dollars. The quantity demanded increases to $\overline{EF}$ units. But since physicians continue to charge $\overline{OA}$ dollars (albeit $\overline{EA}$ is now paid to them by the insurance company), it appears to them that the impact of insurance increased demand from $\overline{AB}$ units to $\overline{AK}$ units. Panel (b) shows that since

the demand curve as perceived by the physician shifts to the right as a result of medical insurance, the fee charged by the physician rises from P_0 to P_1. The theory here predicts that increasing the percentage of population which becomes covered by medical insurance will cause physicians' fees to rise.[12]

11.5d The Impact of the Supply of Physicians on Physicians' Fees

Former Secretary of Health, Education and Welfare, Joseph Califano, warned in 1978 that the United States was threatened by a severe oversupply of physicians in the future. The Secretary was probably echoing the views expressed by the Council on Wages and Price Stability. The argument is that physicians have in mind a *target income*: If the number of physicians per 1000 population increases, physicians would raise the fees to maintain the target income. Microeconomic theory predicts the opposite. It rejects the doctrine of *desired fixed income levels* by appealing to good empirical tests. In Figure 11–12 the demand curve confronting a physician prior to the increase in the supply of physicians is D_0. After the supply of physicians increases (relative to the population), the demand faced by the individual physician

decreases, leading to a leftward shift from D_0 to D_1. If we do not accept the assumption that the demand facing the physician must fall, we must believe that new doctors who arrive in town never succeed in luring patients from established physicians. Also, we should not forget that intercity migration gives rise to a never-ending flow of new patients. As indicated by Figure 11–12, increasing the stock of physicians leads to a decrease in the demand confronting the individual physician, a displacement of equilibrium from point G to point H, and hence a fall in the physician's fee from P_0 to P_1. Thus the assumption that physicians constitute local monopolies is consistent with a decline in physicians' fees resulting from an increase in the supply of physicians.[13]

11.5e The Empirical Evidence and the Conclusion

Keith Leffler was able to explain physicians' earnings over the period 1947–1975.[14] As predicted by the theory, he found out that the income of general practitioners was negatively correlated with the stock of physicians (relative to the population) and negatively

correlated with the proportion of patients' out-of-pocket expenditures on physicians' services. This is the same as being positively correlated with the proportion of expenditures on physicians' services paid by insurance companies.[15] Note that the results by Lef-

---

[12]This analysis ignores the impact of the payment of insurance fees on the demand for physicians' fees. Fees paid to insurance companies are similar to income taxes which reduce the disposable income of the patient. Since medical services are superior goods, the demand for physicians' services (D_0) will shift slightly to the left owing to insurance (Section 3.3b).

[13]If the demand curve confronting the monopolistic physician is $P = a + bX$, ($b < 0$) and the MC curve is given by MC $= g + hX$, the physician's equilibrium will be given by

$$P = a + \frac{g - a}{2 + h/|b|}$$

The clockwise rotation of the demand curve (from D_0 to D_1) means increasing $|b|$ and hence a fall in P.

[14]Keith B. Leffler, "Explanations in Search of Facts: A Critique of a Study of Physicians' Fees," an Occasional Paper, Law and Economics Center, University of Miami School of Law, 1978.

[15]The actual results of the regression run by Leffler were

log (EARN) $= 4.01 - 0.685$ STCK $+ 0.794$ log (INC) $+ 0.158$ POP $- 0.485$ log (DIR)

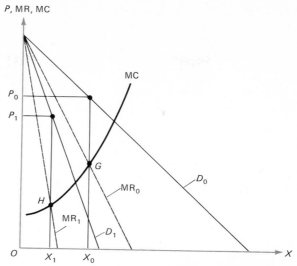

FIGURE 11-12 THE IMPACT OF A RISING SUPPLY OF PHYSICIANS ON PHYSICIANS' FEES
As the supply of physicians (relative to the population) increases, the demand curve confronted by a single physician rotates clockwise from D_0 to D_1. Simultaneously, the marginal revenue rotates from MR_0 to MR_1, leading equilibrium to change from point G to point H. Accordingly, the fee falls from P_0 to P_1.

fler would be in accord with either the assumption that physicians practice in a competitive market or, as we assume (following Kessel and Newhouse), that they are sheltered by local monopolies. The conclusion for policy making is unambiguous: If we want to lower physicians' fees, we should increase the supply of physicians relative to the size of the population. Increasing the supply would involve relaxing entry examinations administered to applicants. Thus a reduction in doctors' fees could be accompanied by a reduction in the quality of physicians' services.

11.6 PRICE LEADERSHIP

11.6a The Theory of Monopoly and Price Leadership

We now consider the case where an identical product is made by many small firms and one large firm. The large firm will be both a monopoly, in the sense that it will confront a negatively sloping demand curve, and a price leader. Aggregate demand in panel (a) of Figure 11–13 is D_0. Total supply of all the _small_ firms is S_0. If the price is, say, $\overline{OF}$, in panel (a), which is denoted by $\overline{OK}$ in panel (b), then small firms will supply $\overline{FG}$ units per unit of time;

where EARN, STCK, INC, POP, and DIR stand for median income of general practitioners, physicians stock, median family income, population, and the proportion of expenditures on physicians' services paid out-of-pocket by patients. (Keith B. Leffler, ''Explanations in Search of Facts: A Critique of a Study of Physicians' Fees,'' an Occasional Paper, Law and Economics Center, University of Miami School of Law, 1978.)

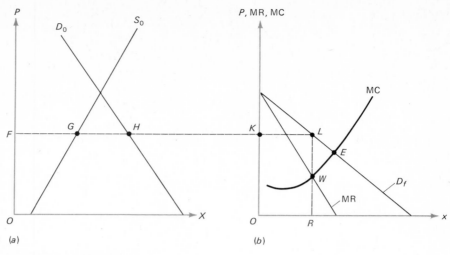

(a)   (b)

FIGURE 11-13 PRICE LEADERSHIP
There are n firms in the industry. In panel (a), S_0 is the supply of $n - 1$ firms; D_0 is the aggregate demand curve. If we subtract S_0 from D_0 horizontally, we get the curve D_f in panel (b). D_f is the (net) demand that is relevant for the price leader. The marginal revenue associated with D_f is denoted by MR. The marginal cost curve (MC) intersects with the MR curve at point W. Hence the leader produces $\overline{OR}$ units ($= \overline{KL} = \overline{GH}$) at a price of $\overline{RL}$, leaving to the many small firms $\overline{FG}$ units.

aggregate demand will amount to $\overline{FH}$ units; thus the excess demand will equal $\overline{GH}$ units ($= \overline{FH} - \overline{FG}$). This excess demand is the demand confronting the large firm: At a price of $\overline{OF}$ dollars the large firm could sell $\overline{GH}$ units in the market. In panel (b) we measure a price of $\overline{OK}$ ($= \overline{OF}$) along the price axis, and then we measure to the right a quantity $\overline{KL}$ which is equal to $\overline{GH}$. Thus L is one point on the demand curve confronting the large firm. Similarly, the entire demand curve D_f confronting the large firm is derived in panel (b) by subtracting, in panel (a), supply curve S_0 from demand curve D_0. The marginal revenue curve associated with the D_f curve in panel (b) intersects with the marginal cost curve of the large firm at point W. The large firm accordingly sells $\overline{OR}$ units at a price of $\overline{OK}$. This is the price which will be followed by the small firms. It is an equilibrium price, because as indicated before, the quantity demanded $\overline{FH}$ is equal to the combined quantity supplied at that price: The share of the small firms in production is $\overline{FG}$ and the share of the *leader* is $\overline{GH}$ ($= \overline{KL}$).

11.6b The Elasticity of the Leader's Demand Curve

Consider Figure 11–13, which illustrates how the demand curve confronted by a single large firm is derived. If the demand confronting the firm is denoted by D_f, the supply of all other firms by S, and the aggregate demand by D, we have $D_f = D - S$. Suppose that originally we have $D_{f0} = D_0 - S_0$ and after the price changes by ΔP we have $D_{f1} = D_1 - S_1$. Then of course,

$$\underbrace{D_{f1} - D_{f0}}_{\Delta D_f} = \underbrace{D_1 - D_0}_{\Delta D} - \underbrace{(S_1 - S_0)}_{\Delta S}$$

Multiplying through by $P/(D_f \cdot \Delta P)$, we obtain

$$\frac{P \cdot \Delta D_f}{D_f \cdot \Delta P} = \frac{P \cdot \Delta D}{D_f \cdot \Delta P} - \frac{P \cdot \Delta S}{D_f \cdot \Delta P}$$

or

$$\frac{P \cdot \Delta D_f}{D_f \cdot \Delta P} = \frac{D \cdot P \cdot \Delta D}{D_f \cdot D \cdot \Delta P} - \frac{S \cdot P \cdot \Delta S}{D_f \cdot S \cdot \Delta P}$$

which is

$$\eta_{Df} = \frac{D}{D_f} \cdot \eta - \frac{S}{D_f} \cdot \epsilon$$

where η_{Df} is the price elasticity of the demand curve facing the leader, η is the price elasticity of the aggregate demand curve, and ϵ is the price elasticity of the supply curve of all other (small) firms. It is obvious that η_{Df} will be larger, the larger D/D_f and S/D_f are. In other words, the smaller the share of the firm, the flatter its demand curve. When D/D_f and S/D_f are very large, η_{Df} is also very large, and for all practical purposes, we are justified in saying that the demand curve is horizontal.

For illustration consider two cases: Let $\eta = -1$ and $\epsilon = 2$. In the first case we assume that the share of the large firm is 50 percent of total output. The elasticity of the demand curve confronting the large firm is

$$\eta_{Df} = \frac{2}{1} \cdot (-1) - \frac{1}{1} \cdot 2 = -4$$

If, however, the share of this large firm is only a tenth of 1 percent (1/1000) of total production, the elasticity of the demand curve confronting this firm is

$$\eta_{Df} = \frac{1000}{1}(-1) - \frac{999}{1} \cdot 2 = -2998$$

In the first example an elasticity of -4 implies that the *price leader* is enjoying some monopolistic power: The gap between the MC and the price is 25 percent of the price. In the second example the firm is confronted with a demand curve with an elasticity of -2998 which, for all practical purposes, is negative infinity ($-\infty$). In other words, in the second example the single firm is competitive; it is a price taker, and we can say that it faces a horizontal demand curve.

11.7 TAXES AND MONOPOLIES (Optional)

Chapter 10 demonstrated how the imposition of an excise tax shifts the MC curve of the taxed good upward by the amount of the tax (Section 10.1b). If an excise tax is imposed on a product produced by a monopoly, the impact

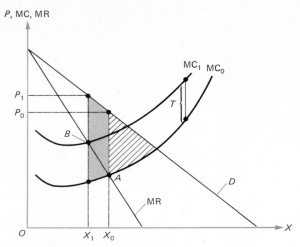

FIGURE 11-14 IMPOSING AN EXCISE TAX ON A MONOPOLY

Initially, D, MR, and MC_0 are the demand, marginal revenue, and marginal cost curves. Equilibrium occurs at point A, and the initial price and quantity are P_0 and X_0. After a unit tax of T dollars is imposed, the MC curves shifts upward by T dollars to MC_1. Equilibrium switches from point A to point B. New output and price are now X_1 and P_1. Welfare loss increases by the shaded area.

on the MC curve is the same: Its MC curve shifts upward by the amount of the tax. In Figure 11–14 a unit tax of T dollars is imposed by the government. As a result, the marginal cost curve shifts upward from MC_0 to MC_1. The vertical distance of MC_1 from MC_0 is T dollars. Originally, the point of intersection between the MC curve and the MR curve was depicted by A. The rate of production was X_0 and the price was P_0. After the tax is imposed, the intersection point between the new MC curve and the MR curve is B, the rate of production declines to X_1 and the price charged by the monopolistic firm rises to P_1. Notice that prior to the imposition of the unit tax the deadweight loss to society amounted to only the triangle with the diagonal stripes. After the tax is imposed, the deadweight loss to society increases by the shaded area. This should not surprise us: In Chapter 10 it was shown that an excise tax gives rise to a deadweight loss (Section 10.13). As a matter of logic, if the government wants to adopt a policy leading to a reduction of welfare losses due to monopolies, the government should offer monopolies excise subsidies. It is left as an exercise for the reader to show that the government can, in principle, by applying the proper combination of subsidy and tax, eliminate the welfare loss completely without any cost to the tax-payer.

11.8 DO MONOPOLIES SUPPRESS INVENTIONS?

There is a legend (popular among lay people) that monopolies suppress new inventions. It is said that American car manufacturers know how to produce cars with very long lives, but they produce cars with short lives to protect their own markets. Oil companies are also accused of not inventing substitutes for fossil fuels so as not to spoil the present market for gasoline. The issue of suppression of new inventions will now be analyzed by considering the following example: Assume that light bulbs are produced by a monopoly. It is rational to assume that consumers purchase light bulbs for their main *attribute*, namely, light, rather than as an ornament. The units of the main attribute can be measured by the durability of the light bulb, namely, months of light.[16] The dilemma of adopting an invention is illustrated in Figure 11–15. Along the X axis we measure months of light rather than light bulbs. Consider now panel (a); assume that before the new invention the monopolistic firm produces light bulbs that last 2 months. Two months' durability entails the lowest marginal cost curve. Thus, before the new invention, the marginal cost curve MC_0 corresponds to light bulbs with 2 months' durability. We recall (Section 11.4a) that the producer's surplus of the monopolistic firm is the area lying above the MC curve and below the MR curve, extending from the origin to the point of intersection between these two curves. We begin by considering the case in which the invention requires an additional fixed cost but no additional variable cost. [An invention which requires additional fixed and variable costs will be illustrated in panel (b).] Suppose an engineer invents a process to produce light bulbs with 4 months' durability. The invention is patented, and the inventor demonstrates that the production of the light bulbs with 4 months' durability is not more expensive than the production of light bulbs with 2 months' durability. Since MC_0 is the curve related to 2 months' durability, the new MC curve is likely to fall. The analysis is roughly the same as in the case of a downward shift of the MC curve due to a technological innovation (Section 8.4); if $\overline{OA}$ months of light are produced per unit of time ($\frac{1}{2} \cdot \overline{OA}$ light bulbs are produced per unit of time), the marginal cost is $\overline{AG}$. If the invention is adopted, the monopolistic firm could continue with the same rate of production of light bulbs. This rate, however, will double the production of months of light from $\overline{OA}$ to $\overline{OB}$ ($\overline{OB} = 2\overline{OA}$). Since the additional cost of producing one additional light bulb is the same, but the additional months of light per light bulb doubled, the marginal cost per month of light is cut by a half. The new marginal cost is then $\overline{BH}$, and $\overline{BH}$ is a half of $\overline{AG}$. We can proceed in this manner, step by step, to draw the new marginal cost curve MC_1. Before the invention was available, the MC_0 curve intersected with the MR curve at point K. The monopolistic firm produced $\overline{OE}$ months of light at a price of $\overline{EM}$ dollars. (The price per light bulb was $2 \cdot \overline{EM}$.) If the monopolistic firm decides to adopt the new invention, the new point of equilibrium will be L, where the new MC_1 curve intersects with the MR curve. Output of months of light will increase to $\overline{OF}$, and the price of 1 month of light will fall to $\overline{FN}$. (The price per light bulb will be $4 \cdot \overline{FN}$.) Let us ignore for a moment the royalties that will have to be paid to the inventor. Intuitively, it is clear that

---

[16] The example of light bulbs is adapted from Barzel, who used it to illustrate how specific taxes give rise to quality changes in commodities. See Section 10.1i.

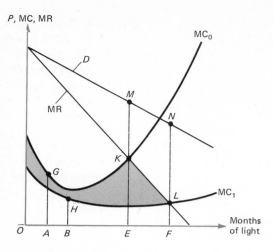

(a) Only fixed costs are involved

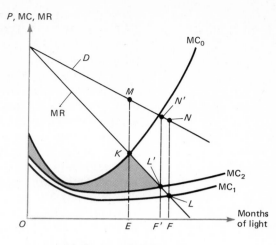

(b) Fixed and variable costs are involved

FIGURE 11-15   MONOPOLIES AND INVENTIONS

In both panels D denotes the demand curve for months of light, MR is the associated marginal revenue curve, MC_0 is the initial marginal cost curve, and MC_1 is the marginal cost curve under the assumption that illumination hours per light bulb double but variable cost is unchanged. In panel (a) we assume that variable cost of producing light bulbs is the same after durability doubles. Accordingly, after the invention is adopted, equilibrium shifts from point K to point L, and the shaded area is the additional producer's surplus. In panel (b) we assume that there is an additional variable cost involved in producing light bulbs that are twice as durable. Hence the marginal cost curve shifts upward from MC_1 to MC_2, and the remaining shaded area is the increment in the producer's surplus. In both panels, if the shaded area minus the increment in the fixed cost associated with the invention is positive, the monopoly will adopt the invention.

the monopolist is better off with the invention: Since normally $\overline{OF}$ is less than twice $\overline{OE}$, the monopolistic firm is producing a smaller amount of light bulbs in order to provide more months of light, implying a saving on costs. Also, under normal conditions the new price of a light bulb will be $4 \cdot \overline{FN}$, which is more than $2 \cdot \overline{EM}$. The increase in the producer's surplus is the shaded area. The monopolistic firm will purchase the invention from the inventor if the royalty (fixed cost) to be paid to the inventor will be less than the shaded area. (In the example the inventor will have to accept a royalty slightly less than the dotted area, because otherwise to whom would the invention be sold?) If the monopolistic firm has a research and development department, management will have to estimate the cost of such an invention and compare this estimate with the shaded area to decide whether to go ahead with development of the new idea.

Let us now shift our attention to panel (b). Suppose that in addition to the fixed cost incurred in inventing the 4-month light bulbs, the marginal cost of producing 4-month light bulbs exceeds the marginal cost of producing 2-month light bulbs, perhaps because of the need to use more expensive materials. As a result, the marginal cost curve must be adjusted by shifting it upward to a higher position depicted by MC_2; the new point of equilibrium is L' [instead of L in panel (a)]; the new quantity of months of light is $\overline{OF'}$ [smaller than $\overline{OF}$ in panel (a)], and the new price per month of light is $\overline{F'N'}$ [higher than $\overline{FN}$ in panel (a)]. The shaded area in panel (b) is the producer's surplus; it is smaller than the shaded area in panel (a). The test, however, is the same: If the shaded area in panel (b) exceeds the additional fixed cost associated with the invention, the monopolistic firm will go ahead and develop the new product with the higher quality (durability).

The conclusion we reach is that monopolies may or may not adopt new inventions, depending on whether or not the resulting increment in the producer's surplus is in excess of or short of the fixed cost associated with the invention.

11.9 CARTELS

11.9a The Theory of Cartels

Generally, *cartels* mean selling agencies. When economists refer to cartels, they mean a group of firms that organize for the purpose of decreasing the rate of production in order to increase profit. Thus if all or most firms in a competitive industry successfully collude and raise the price to a monopolistic level, a cartel has been formed. Since aggregate demand curves are negatively sloped, raising the price above the competitive level can be achieved only if the cartel can allot production quotas to member firms (or use similar techniques to be mentioned in the problem set). As will be explained, unless governments (as in OPEC) are involved as enforcers of contracts, cartels eventually break down because members have a tremendous incentive to cheat.

A cartel situation is pictured in Figure 11–16. In panel (a), MC_i is the marginal cost curve of a typical firm. In panel (b), ΣMC_i is the aggregate marginal cost curve, which is also the supply curve of the industry under competition (Section 8.1). The horizontal scales of the two panels are different: In panel (a), x, along the horizontal axis, measures the output of a single firm. In panel (b), X, along the horizontal axis, measures aggregate output of the entire industry. Competitive price P_0 is determined at the point of intersection between ΣMC_i and demand curve D. In the aggregate the industry produces X_0 units. In panel (a) each firm produces x_0 units, where price equals marginal cost. And of course, $X_0 = \Sigma x_0$. The crosshatched area plus the lightly shaded area are the producer's surplus of the competitive firm (Section 7.4). If MC_i is the long-run marginal cost curve, the producer's surplus is total revenue minus total variable cost, which boils down to the profit (rent) left for the entrepreneur. Now, let us return to panel (b). If all firms in the industry are in collusion, ΣMC_i is the MC curve of a monopoly facing the aggregate demand curve D. The aggregate profit of the industry will be maximized if the level of aggregate output is cut back to X_1, where ΣMC_i cuts the marginal revenue curve associated with the aggregate demand curve. Consider first the case where all firms are identical. Each firm will

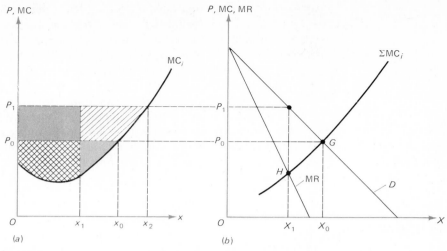

FIGURE 11-16   CARTEL

The marginal cost of the individual firm is depicted by MC_i in panel (a). The sum of all MC_i becomes the supply curve of the industry in panel (b). It is denoted by ΣMC_i. The market demand is denoted by D and its associated marginal revenue curve is denoted by MR. In perfect competition the ΣMC_i cuts D at point G, and the price is P_0. Total output is X_0 and the individual firm produces x_0, enjoying a producer's surplus depicted by the crosshatched area and the lightly shaded area. After the cartel is established, equilibrium shifts to point H, where ΣMC_i intersects with MR. Total output must be reduced to X_1 in order for the price to rise to the desired level of P_1. In other words, each individual firm must cut back on its production from x_0 to x_1. The individual firm loses the lightly shaded area, but it gains the heavily shaded area. The incentive of the individual firm to cheat is measured by the potential return to cheating, which is equal to the lightly shaded area plus the striped area.

have to agree to shrink its rate of production from x_0 to x_1. (x_1 must be related to x_0 as X_1 is related to X_0.) The producer's surplus of the firm will be the crosshatched area plus the heavily shaded region. The new producer's surplus must be greater than the precartel producer's surplus because the aggregate profit of the industry has increased and all firms are identical by assumption. If firms are not identical, the above analysis is only roughly correct; the management of the cartel might still require that each firm individually reduce its rate of production by the same fixed percentage of $[(X_0 - X_1) / X_0] \cdot 100$ but then redistribute profits to ensure that each cartel member earns at least a little more than before.

The incentive for individual cartel members to cheat is tremendous: The firm as depicted in panel (a) would like to expand all the way to a rate of production x_2, where the cartel price P_1 intersects with the MC_i curve. The additional profit (producer's surplus) to the firm would be the lightly shaded area plus the region with the diagonal stripes. Unless the cartel is strictly enforced by the government, cheating by members will sooner or later bring its downfall: The more sophisticated the methods of price fixing, the more sophisticated the cheating.

In the United States, conspiracy to fix prices is illegal. Hardly any serious cartels exist. Interestingly, the only significant cartel in agriculture is the famous tobacco cartel, which is based on an acreage allotment effectively enforced by the federal government. Cartels will now be illustrated by two examples.

11.9b An Example: A Cartel That Failed: The Electrical Conspiracy of the Early 1960s

In February 1961, General Electric, Westinghouse, Allis-Chalmers, and some other smaller companies pleaded guilty to charges of fixing prices of electrical equipment such as capacitors, insulators, circuit breakers, and transformers. Seven executives of these companies were sent to jail, and the companies were fined $2 million. The truth was that some of the top executives attempted to fix prices of electrical equipment (at a monopolistic level), but because of cheating, agreements to fix prices lasted for only short periods. According to testimony, some agreements did not last even a week. Cheating took place in the course of submitting sealed bids: A certain company was to receive a certain job; in a secret meeting all other companies agreed to submit higher bids. In their attempt to grab business from each other, however, the conspirators submitted lower bids than those agreed upon. In addition to this type of cheating, the unsuccessful cartel had to deal with outsiders whose appetite grew when prices were fixed at relatively high levels.[17]

The electrical equipment conspiracy had been in effect from 1956 to 1959. Yet a study by Armentano shows that the profitability of the major electrical companies declined during the period 1956–1959 compared with 1950–1955.[18] This evidence supports the testimony of the seven executives prosecuted, that the attempt to establish a cartel completely broke down.

11.9c An Example: A Cartel That Succeeded: OPEC

It is not surprising that the cartel created by OPEC (Organization of Petroleum Exporting Countries) succeeded: It involved governments and their power to enforce production quotas. Before the 1973 Yom Kippur War, the price per barrel of crude oil bought from Saudi Arabia was $2.10. The war was used as an excuse by OPEC members to raise the price in steps, until in October 1974 the price of a barrel increased fourfold. Table 11-2 presents some data concerning the price of oil produced by Saudi Arabia, a member of OPEC.

Although it seemed that the price set by OPEC continued to increase year in and year out, if we deflate the prices to obtain them in real terms, we notice that from 1974 to 1977 prices of crude oil in real terms fluctuated around $9 per barrel.[19]

The theory of OPEC can be explained by use of Figure 11-17 (which is almost a replica of Figure 11-13). For simplicity we can ignore the consumption of oil in OPEC countries which, relative to the consumption in the United States, Western Europe, and Japan, is negligible. Assume that the aggregate demand curve for oil in importing countries is depicted by D_0 in panel (a). The aggregate domestic supply of the importing countries is denoted by S_0. The net demand curve (obtained by subtracting S_0 from D_0) is D_f

---

[17]General Electric, Westinghouse, Allis-Chalmers, and Federal Pacific fixed prices of circuit breakers. I-T-E, an outsider at the time, bought a small firm and forced its way into the cartel: The agreement was that I-T-E's prices in southern California would be fixed at 15 percent off General Electric's book price, and elsewhere it would be 5 percent off. Even this agreement did not hold for a long time.

[18]D. T. Armentano, "Price Fixing in Theory and Practice," reprinted in *The Competitive Economy, Selected Readings*, Yale Brozen (ed.), General Learning Press, 1975, pp. 305–323.

[19]Part II of Chapter 16 shows that even if OPEC continues to operate as an uninterrupted cartel far into the future, since crude oil is an exhaustible resource, the price of oil will be expected to rise slowly over time. Interruptions such as the Iranian revolution in the late 1970s might cause sharp price changes followed by political repercussions.

TABLE 11-2   Prices of Crude Oil, 1973-1977

Date of change in price	Nominal price	Real price*
October 1973	$ 2.10	$2.10
October 1974	9.84	8.90
October 1975	11.28	9.30
1976†	11.28	8.80
Summer 1977	13.00	9.50

*Deflated by the Consumer Price Index, 1973 = 100.
†No change occurred.
Source: International Economic Report of the President, 1977, Government Printing Office.

in panel (*b*). The marginal cost curve, ΣMC in panel (*b*), could represent the sum of all marginal cost curves of OPEC countries. Before 1973, the price of $2.10 per barrel was determined by the intersection of ΣMC with d_f at point *E*. [The supply curve in panel (*b*) includes an element of paying royalties to the oil-exporting governments which we ignore here.] After the 1973 Yom Kippur War, the OPEC countries decided to move from point *E*, which was consistent with perfect competition, to point *L*, which is optimal from the cartel's viewpoint. As shown in Table 11-2, the price at point *L* is four times higher than the price at point *E*. It is interesting to note that during the life of the cartel there have been cases of countries producing more than their quotas. This cheating did not break down the cartel because Saudi Arabia was always willing to absorb these deviations by reducing its huge quota.

FIGURE 11-17   OPEC

In panel (*a*) the world demand for oil is depicted by D_0 and the supply of all non-OPEC members is depicted by S_0. If we subtract S_0 from D_0 horizontally, we get the demand curve confronting OPEC denoted by D_f. Before the 1973 Yom Kippur War, equilibrium was established at point *E*, where ΣMC, the marginal cost curve of OPEC (sum of all the MC curves of OPEC members), cut the D_f curve. The price per barrel was $2.10. After the Yom Kippur War, OPEC switched from point *E* to point *W*, where ΣMC and MR intersect. As a result, the price rose to $8.90.

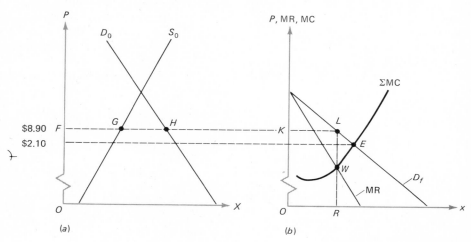

SUMMARY   We started out by seeing that the main difference between a monopoly and a firm in perfect competition is the negatively sloped demand curve faced by the monopoly. We saw again that the associated marginal revenue curve (MR) lies below the negatively sloping demand curve. Since profit is maximized at a rate of production where MR is equal to marginal cost (MC), monopolies produce less than an optimal level where the price P is equal to MC. It was stressed that the divergence between P and MC gives rise to a *welfare loss* (the "triangle"), which is a reduction in both consumer's surplus and producer's surplus that is not gained by any other entity in the economy. Economists who empirically estimated the welfare loss reached the conclusion that it is relatively minute. The reader was cautioned that this issue is not entirely settled. *Lerner's ratio* $(-1/\eta)$, which is applied to measure monopoly power, was derived; the caveat was that Lerner's ratio is not a perfect indicator of welfare loss resulting from monopolistic pricing.

Natural monopolies were defined as firms dominating whole markets as a result of two conditions: (1) large (internal) scale economies; and (2) the position of the market demand curve relative to the average cost curve (AC). Natural monopolies are mostly *utilities* producing services and goods such as garbage collection, water, and electricity at the municipal and the state level. Normally, such local utilities are regulated by public utilities commissions that require them to produce at a rate where AC equals P. Such a regulation results in a welfare loss. Demsetz challenged the practice of utilities regulation and suggested alternatives; experimentation by local governments would either refute or confirm Demsetz's challenge that alternatives superior to regulation do exist.

Discrimination by monopolies was then discussed. The precondition for discrimination is the impossibility of interconsumer sale of the good produced by the monopoly. *Perfect discrimination* was defined as pricing according to a declining schedule indicated by the demand curve of consumers; electric utilities could practice perfect discrimination if they were not regulated. *Discrimination by market partitioning* was defined as charging different prices in different segments of the market according to the rule that a higher price is charged in the market segment with the less elastic demand. An example of discrimination by market partitioning was selling hard-cover books at a relatively high price compared with prices of soft-cover books that appear later.

Microeconomic theory was then applied to the market for physicians' services. First, it was concluded that barriers to entry imposed by the American Medical Association (AMA) are consistent with the assumptions either that physicians constitute local monopolies or that they operate in an environment that comes close to perfect competition. One way or the other, barriers to entry increase rents claimed by physicians. Some evidence was then discussed that physicians do sell their services in sheltered markets and thus the local markets in which they operate can be approximated by monopolistic structures. Given this framework, it was concluded that physicians are likely to practice price discrimination by market partitioning and that they are expected to benefit from medical insurance. We saw why the doctrine of *desired fixed income* cannot stand any theoretical pressure, and how this doctrine was refuted by empirical tests; the tests showed that, in spite of local monopolies, increasing the number of physicians will result in lower physicians' fees.

The issue of *price leadership* was then considered. If, in the same industry, many small firms coexist with a large firm that contributes a large share of total output, the firm is a *price leader*. Equilibrium price is determined by deriving the *net demand curve* and then equating the MR associated with the net demand curve with the MC of the price leader.

Imposing an excise tax on a monopoly would result in an upward shift in the MC curve and thus a lower rate of production and a higher price. Additional welfare loss would also result.

The allegation that monopolies suppress inventions was discussed. By applying detailed geometric analysis, it was demonstrated that a monopolistic firm would adopt an invention if the expected resulting increment in its producer's surplus exceeded the expected increment in fixed costs (such as royalty to the inventor); otherwise the monopoly would simply not show interest in the invention.

At the end of the chapter *cartels* in theory and practice were discussed. Cartels were defined as groups of firms in an industry that organize for the purpose of decreasing the rate of production in order to raise the price to higher levels and achieve higher profits. The goal of the cartel is to restrict output to the rate where the MR curve intersects with the sum of all the MC curves of all the members. It was stressed that in practice, unless a strong agency (government or OPEC) backs it up, a cartel has very little chance to survive. Two illustrations were used: a cartel that failed and a cartel that survived.

GLOSSARY **Monopoly** A single firm that constitutes an entire industry. The monopoly faces the market demand curve; if there are good substitutes to the product produced by the monopoly, the demand it faces is very elastic and its monopoly power diminishes. If many substitutes exist, the industry is better classified as *monopolistic competition*.

Welfare loss due to monopolistic pricing A loss in consumer's surplus and producer's surplus not gained by any entity in the economy. If we pass a vertical line at the point of intersection between the MC and MR curves, the *area of the triangle* formed by this point of intersection, the point where this line cuts the demand curve and the point of intersection between the MC curve and the demand curve approximates the welfare loss due to monopolistic pricing.

Lerner's formula (ratio) The negative reciprocal of demand elasticity $(-1/\eta)$. This ratio measures market powers of monopolies; however, it is an imperfect measure because it is not a very good indicator of welfare loss.

Natural monopoly A monopoly arising as a result of the following two conditions: (1) large (internal) scale economies exist, and (2) the market demand curve occupies a unique position with respect to the AC curve. The above two conditions may lead either to a natural monopoly or to an *oligopoly*.

Public utility commision A commission charged with the responsibility to regulate the natural monopolies (utilities) at the local scene.

Price discrimination: perfect A scheme of charging a consumer a varying price which traces out his or her demand curve. According to this scheme the consumer pays a relatively high price for the first unit, a slightly lower price for the second unit, and so on. This scheme, in its perfect form, enables the monopoly to transfer the entire consumer's surplus from the consumer to the monopoly.

Price discrimination: market partitioning A scheme in which the monopoly partitions the market into segments and charges relatively high prices in segments with less elastic demand curves and relatively low prices in segments with more elastic demand curves.

Barriers to entry Devices aimed at artificially increasing the effort required to enter a profession. Certification, coupled with very difficult entrance examinations, is an example.

Desired fixed income levels doctrine A doctrine claiming that physicians have a goal of achieving a desired fixed income level, and owing to their power in local markets they can achieve this desired level of income, come what may. This doctrine is neither theoretically correct nor has it been confirmed by any serious empirical study.

Net demand curve Derived by horizontally subtracting the supply curve of $n - 1$ firms in an industry from the market demand curve. By assumption there are n firms in the industry.

Price leader (leadership) If a giant producer in an industry coexists with many small producers, the giant firm is known as the *price leader*. Price leaders set a monopolistic price except that they face the *net demand curve* rather than the market demand curve.

Cartels Selling agencies. In economic jargon a *cartel* means a group of firms that organizes for the purpose of decreasing the rate of production in order to increase price and their profit. A successful cartel would operate where the sum of the MC curves of its members intersects with the MR associated with the relevant demand curve.

PROBLEMS An asterisk indicates an advanced problem.

11-1. Must a monopoly know the shape of its MC curve in order to maximize its profit?

11-2. Does a monopolistic firm have a supply curve?

11-3. Consider a monopoly that is confronted with a linear demand curve. By using a diagram, indicate the rate of output that this monopoly would select if its MC is always zero.

11-4 Youths and students used to receive special air fares from airlines. Can you explain by applying economic theory?

11-5 Physicians sometimes argue that they charge the rich more than the poor in order to redistribute income more equally. What is your comment?

11-6 A monopoly considers setting a price in three separate segments of a market. Consider the following information:

Market	Price elasticity
1	−2
2	−5
3	−4

What prices should be set in these three segments, respectively, if MC is always $3?

11-7.* Consider Figure 11-6. If minimum point M of the AC curve of the utility happened to lie to the right of the demand curve, would regulation by equating the marginal cost with the price be desirable?

11-8. It is sometimes alleged that the MC curve of physicians' services (MC in Figures 11-11 and 11-12) bends backward (the higher their fees the less they work). Assuming such a backward-bending MC curve, answer the following:
(a) Would you expect physicians to work more or less as more patients become insured?
(b) Would you expect physicians to work more or less as the supply of physicians rises (relative to the population)?

11-9. A large firm produces 1/10 of the total production of an industry. The price elasticity of the market demand curve is −2, and the price elasticity of supply of all small firms is 1/3. What is the (relative) difference between the price and the MC of the price leader?

11-10. Cartels can be organized on the principle of "buying price" and "selling price": The cartel members agree to sell to the cartel all their output at the buying price that the management of the cartel decides to adopt. The management of the cartel then sells the output at a higher selling price, and the profit of the management (selling price minus buying price times output) is divided among the members of the cartel.
(a) By applying the correct geometric analysis, determine the "buying price" and "selling price."
(b) Would this cartel be effective if the profit of the management were to be divided among the members proportionately to their rate of production?

11-11.* Consider a cartel that operates by the formula indicated in problem

11-10. Suppose the government forces the cartel to raise its buying price and in response the cartel destroys a certain fraction of the output it purchased from its members. Explain.

11-12. A cartel of farmers has an agreement with the government according to which the government absorbs "surpluses" at a relatively low price. Suggest a profit-maximizing solution from the viewpoint of the cartel.

11-13.* Publishers pay authors royalties which are calculated by applying a certain percentage to the total value of sales. Should there be a conflict between author and publisher?

11-14. Is it possible (in principle) to force a monopoly to produce at a point where price is equal to MC by taxing and subsidizing the monopolist at the same time but without incurring any cost to the government?

11-15. If a fixed tax of $100,000 per annum is imposed on a monopoly, it will either close up or continue to produce the same amount. Do you agree with the above statement?

11-16. If a tax of 10 percent is imposed on its profits, the monopoly will cut down in production. Do you agree with the above statement?

11-17. Commodity X is produced by a monopoly. The monopoly is confronted with a negatively sloped demand curve at home and an infinitely elastic demand curve abroad. The government decides to impose a specific tax per unit of output sold by the monopoly at home. Analyze the domestic and foreign markets before and after the tax. A diagram will help. Assume that X can be shipped from the domestic market abroad but not vice versa.

11-18. The following is a demand schedule confronting a monopoly:

X	P
1	10
2	9
3	8
4	7
5	6
6	5
7	4

The marginal cost is always $6. (a) What is the price set by the monopolist and the quantity marketed if the monopoly is not regulated? (b) Can the government force the monopoly to "behave competitively" by taxing and subsidizing it at the same time without a loss to the government? Justify your answer numerically.

11-19. Multiple-plant monopoly: The demand schedule confronting a monopoly is like the one in problem 11-18. The monopolist operates two plants, A and B. The cost schedules of the two plants are:

Plant A		Plant B	
Quantity	Total cost	Quantity	Total cost
1	1	1	1
2	3	2	2
3	6	3	4
4	10	4	7
5	15	5	11

Determine the number of units that should be produced in each of the two plants in order to maximize profit. (Only whole units can be produced.)

MATHEMATICAL APPENDIX 11

M11·1 MARGINAL REVENUE AND ELASTICITY

Let total revenue be denoted by R. Differentiating R ($= P \cdot X$) with respect to X, we obtain

$$\frac{dR}{dX} = \frac{d\,(P \cdot X)}{dX} = P + X\frac{dP}{dX}$$

$$= P \cdot \left(1 + \frac{X \cdot dP}{P \cdot dX}\right) = P \cdot \left(1 + \frac{1}{\eta}\right) \tag{m11-1}$$

If the demand curve is given in a constant-elasticity form such as $X = kP^\eta$, total revenue is expressed as $R = KX^{1/\eta + 1}$, where $K = (1/k)^{1/\eta}$. Differentiating R with respect to X, we get

$$\mathrm{MR} = K\left(1 + \frac{1}{\eta}\right)X^{1/\eta}$$

Thus if $|\eta| < 1$, then $\left(1 + \dfrac{1}{\eta}\right)$ is negative and MR is negative.

Next, consider a linear demand curve in Figure 11-18 whose function is $X = aP + b$, where a is negative. This demand curve intersects with the quantity axis at $X = b$ and with the price axis at $P = -b/a$. Total revenue is

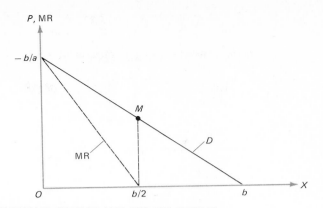

FIGURE 11-18 A LINEAR DEMAND CURVE AND ITS MR CURVE
Demand curve D has a linear equation $X = aP + b$. Its intercepts with the vertical and horizontal axes are $-(b/a)$ and b, respectively. The associated MR curve has intercepts of $-(b/a)$ and $b/2$, respectively.

found by multiplying the quantity demanded by the price, that is, $R = X \cdot P$ $= aP^2 + bP$. Rearranging we get $R = X^2/a - (b/a)X$. Differentiating with respect to X gives $MR = dR/dX = (2/a)X - b/a$; that is, MR is linear, too. For $X = 0$, $MR = -b/a$, and for $MR = 0$, $X = b/2$. In other words, the demand curve and the MR curve cut the vertical axis at the same point; the demand curve cuts the horizontal axis at $X = b$ and the MR curve cuts the horizontal axis at the midpoint between $X = b$ and $X = 0$. This is illustrated in Figure 11–18. The position of the MR curve in Figure 11-18 is consistent with a result obtained previously, namely, that the linear demand curve is inelastic along its lower half (between point M and the quantity intercept), elastic along its upper half (between point M and the price intercept), and of unitary elasticity at point M.

CHAPTER

MONOPOLISTIC COMPETITION
(optional)

As mentioned earlier, *monopolistic competition* is a market structure in which many firms, none of whom dominate the market, produce a good which is *slightly heterogeneous (differentiated)* and then sell it to a large number of consumers. Slightly differentiated means that the product made by any one firm in the industry is similar, but not identical, to the product made by any other firm in the same industry. The reason why goods are slightly heterogeneous has to do with both the nature of goods and the nature of consumers. First, most goods contain a variety of physical attributes that can be either brought out and enhanced or suppressed. Think of beer. Although all brands of beer are close substitutes for one another, no two manufacturers produce identical beer; rather, they stress different colors, flavors, weights, and other fine distinctions. Beer manufacturers may also suppress attributes, e.g., calories in light beer for slim consumers or those who aspire to be slim. Second, consumers have different tastes and preferences which encourage producers to differentiate their product.

If this line of logic is stretched a bit farther, we may think of all goods as a continuum of close substitutes. However, to render the theory useful, industry boundaries must be defined. This is achieved by dividing the continuum of substitute goods into groups of *close* substitutes. For example, the continuum of all drinks can be partitioned into the following groups: pop, juices, beer, milk, and so on.

Eggs are sold in *competitive markets*, and beer is sold in *monopolistically competitive markets*; producers of beer face demand curves with a negative slope, albeit very elastic curves. Producers of eggs face horizontal demand curves. Why are egg producers price takers? The reason is that chickens lay only homogeneous (round and white or round and brown) eggs. But suppose in the future the biological revolution enables farmers to raise chickens that can lay heterogeneous eggs, such as square and blue eggs or purple eggs with two yolks. Egg producers will then market their product in an environment of monopolistic competition; each of them will face a slightly negative-sloping demand curve. Eggs produced by farmer Peter would not be identical to eggs produced by farmer John. What is even more important, Peter and John and all other egg producers will find themselves engaged in *advertising*, an important aspect of monopolistic competition. Producers in monopolistic competition advertise in order to inform the customers about the special attribute of their differentiated good. Sometimes, when the good is homogeneous, firms differentiate the good through advertising. For example, firms can change the image of their product by package design and by ads on television and in magazines. An ad showing a smoker enjoying a cigarette in a fresh outdoor setting suggests to the consumer that the cigarette has a fresh taste. The product differentiation is psychological rather than "real."

To the individual firm it may seem that by advertising it could win customers over from other producers; however, since all firms are engaged in advertising, on average the net gain to the individual firm is nil. The value of advertisement lies in providing information about the various attributes of the good being sold, and in creating psychological attributes in the mind of consumers.

Product differentiation must not always give rise to monopolistic competition. Automobiles are heterogeneous goods; yet the automobile industry constitutes a typical *oligopoly*. In the United States only four companies produce cars; this is a result of the huge scale economies in automobile production. The following chapter will discuss the economic aspects of the automobile industry.

Examples of industries governed by monopolistic competition on the local scene are restaurants, grocery stores, and to a lesser extent gas stations. On the national scene, producers of furniture, soft drinks, and clothing fit the framework of monopolistic competition. Some industries are on the border between monopolistic competition and oligopoly; wine is a heterogeneous good: however, many small wine producers coexist with giants.

It is interesting to note that until 1930 economists had not developed a theory of monopolistic competition. They were aware that producers of slightly differentiated goods faced neither demand curves that were perfectly elastic as in perfect competition, nor market demand curves with low elasticity as in monopoly. They applied models of perfect competition to industries in which numerous firms sold a slightly differentiated good. In the early 1930s Joan Robinson and Edward Chamberlin developed theories of monopolistic competition. What follows will focus on the theory of monopolistic competition as developed by Chamberlin.[1] It should be understood that the model presented here is useful only for understanding the behavior of individual producers. When industry-wide problems, such as a rise in the demand for furniture in the United States in the wake of the baby boom, are considered we can gloss over the individuality of firms and apply a simple supply-demand apparatus, pretending that the furniture industry is perfectly competitive. In such an analysis the demand for furniture will increase, leading the demand curve to shift to the right and resulting in a higher price and a larger quantity marketed (Section 9.3b). Of course, the price of furniture is understood to be an average of all prices of all kinds of sofas, tables, and chairs. When to apply monopolistic competition models and when to apply perfect competition models is left for the individual researcher to decide.

12.1 THE THEORY OF PRICING UNDER MONOPOLISTIC COMPETITION

To understand how the price in monopolistic competition is determined, let us ignore for a moment the fact that a good sold by an industry governed by monopolistic competition is slightly differentiated. Imagine that there is a demand curve for the aggregated commodity such as the demand for furni-

---

[1]Edward H. Chamberlin, *The Theory of Monopolistic Competition*, Harvard University Press, Boston, Mass., 1958.

ture or for retail services provided by supermarkets. In Figure 12-1 this aggregate demand is depicted by ΣD. Next, assume that there are n producers of equal size in the industry. Had we divided the market among the n producers, each producer would have been confronted with a pro rata demand depicted by curve D in Figure 12-1. Now, let us assume, for the sake of theoretical argument, that the industry is dominated by a *multiple-plant monopoly*. Instead of n independent producers, there are n plants all belonging to a single corporation which is a monopolistic firm. In such a multiple-plant monopoly solution, each plant would be confronted with a pro rata demand curve D, to which corresponds a marginal revenue MR (D). This marginal revenue curve of the single plant cuts the marginal cost curve of the plant at point A. The management of the multiple-plant corporation will instruct each plant to produce at a rate of X_m, where the price is P_m (the subscript m stands for "multiple-plant monopoly"). Focusing on pro rata demand curve D is a geometric convenience. An alternative form of geometric presentation would be to aggregate all the MC curves of all the single plants. In Figure 12-1 this aggregate MC curve is denoted by ΣMC. The marginal revenue curve derived from the ΣD curve is denoted by MR(ΣD). The aggregate marginal cost curve, ΣMC, intersects with the MR(ΣD) at point B, where the total output produced per unit of time is ΣX_m. By geometric construction (since firms are of equal size), it must be true that $\Sigma X_m = nX_m$. For example, if there are 20 identical plants under the management of

FIGURE 12-1 MULTIPLE-PLANT MONOPOLY SOLUTION

The market demand curve is depicted by ΣD. The pro rata demand curve is depicted by D. The marginal cost curve (MC) intersects the marginal revenue curve associated with D [MR(D)] at point A. According to this monopolistic solution, the individual firm (which is treated as a plant owned by the monopolistic firm) produces X_m units per unit of time at a price of P_m. The solution for all the plants together obtains at point B, where the sum of all the MC curves (ΣMC) cuts the MR curve associated with D [denoted by MR(ΣD)]. The price is the same, P_m, and the quantity is ΣX_m. If there are n equal-sized firms, $\Sigma X_m = nX_m$.

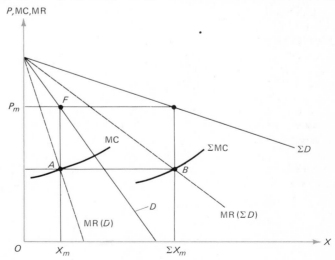

the multiple-plant corporation, then $\Sigma X_m = 20 X_m$. Notice that point B must be at the same height as point A and price P_m is the same price, regardless of the geometric technique selected.

Next we see why the multiple-plant monopoly solution could not apply to the case of monopolistic competition as defined above. Curve D would be valid if all firms were plants managed by some top management that allots each of them a pro rata share of the total market. But since under conditions of monopolistic competition each firm is legally and economically independent, the monopoly solution of Figure 12-1 cannot hold.

In order not to overcrowd Figure 12-1, we now shift to Figure 12-2, which focuses on the single firm rather than on the entire industry. Let us imagine that the single firm is currently at monopolistic point F, selling X_m units at price P_m. Would the single firm remain at point F for a long time? The answer is no. The independent firm will figure out that it can lure customers from other firms in the industry by lowering its price relative to the price charged by other firms. Thus the single independent firm has in mind demand curve d, which is more elastic than D. To this demand (depicted by curve d) there corresponds a marginal revenue curve denoted by MR(d), which cuts the MC curve at point E. The firm has temporarily moved from point F to point G, producing X at a price P_1. This happy situation cannot

FIGURE 12-2   THE SINGLE FIRM IN MONOPOLISTIC COMPETITION
The pro rata demand curve and its associated marginal revenue curve are denoted by D and MR(D). The marginal cost curve is MC, and the demand curve perceived by the firm and its associated marginal revenue curve are denoted by d and MR(d). If the firm is viewed as a plant owned and run by a monopoly, A is the equilibrium point, and price and quantity are X_m and P_m, as in Figure 12-1. If the firm is independent, it perceives demand curve d. The associated MR(d) intersects with MC at point E. The firm would attempt to produce X units at a price P_1. But if all firms do the same, the firm will have to retreat from G to H, that is, retreat to (point H on) the pro rata demand curve.

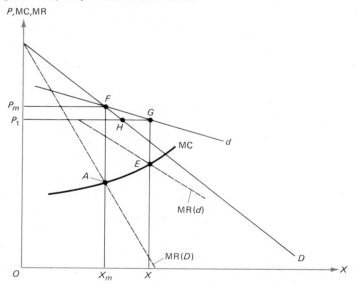

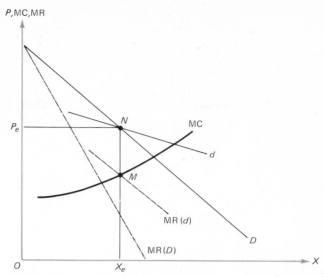

FIGURE 12-3 EQUILIBRIUM IN MONOPOLISTIC COMPETITION
The pro rata demand curve and its associated marginal revenue curve are depicted by curves D and MR(D); the marginal cost curve is denoted by MC; and the demand curve perceived by the individual firm and its associated marginal revenue curve are depicted by d and MR(d). Equilibrium occurs at point M, where MC cuts curve MR(d). Since the price P_e ($= \overline{X_eN}$) is consistent with both curve D and curve d, which cross one another at point N, this equilibrium satisfies both curves, and the industry is in equilibrium.

last long. Other firms will follow and reduce their price to P_1. At that price, the single firm cannot sell more than what is indicated by its pro rata demand curve D; it cannot sell more than $\overline{P_1H}$ units. The firm finds itself selling $\overline{HG}$ units less than it thought it would be able to sell. We can proceed with the analysis by passing another more elastic demand curve like d through point H. This process of passing a more elastic demand curve through points like F and then H on pro rata demand curve D continues until an equilibrium, as illustrated in Figure 12-3, is achieved.

The final equilibrium is displayed in Figure 12-3. Notice that in Figure 12-3, MR(d), which corresponds to some new demand curve d, cuts the MC curve at point M. The quantity sold is X_e and the price is P_e. But unlike the situations depicted in Figure 12-2, the combination of X_e and P_e satisfies both pro rata demand curve D and the more elastic demand curve d.

Before leaving this discussion, we should be aware of two aspects of monopolistic competition. First, consider Figure 12-4. If the average cost curve of the typical firm is like AC in panel (a), profit is above normal. In other words, the shaded area $[(P_e - \text{AC}) \cdot X_e]$ indicates that the entrepreneur enjoys economic rent (Section 9.10a). However, if we assume freedom of entry and an unlimited supply of entrepreneurial capacity, new firms will be attracted into the industry. The additional firms will lower pro rata curve D as well as the more elastic curve d, until the AC curve will be tangent to the more elastic demand curve d. This situation, known as the long-run solution, is presented in panel (b): The (lower) demand curve d' just touches the AC curve at point N. Accordingly, profit is zero, or put another way, there is no economic rent; the entrepreneur is earning an income which is equal to his or her potential return at the next-best job that he or she could get.

Second, to explain how monopolistic competition works the model was simplified and product differentiation was assumed to be so minute that prices were practially the same. But since differentiation in fact means that prices must differ from firm to firm, price P_e in Figure 12-4 cannot be the same for all firms. Nevertheless, the above analysis is valid. Pro rata demand curve D should represent a portion of the market assigned to each producer by some imaginary top management of a multiple-plant monopoly producing a variety of products which are differentiated in quality. The rest of the analysis follows.

12.2 AN EXAMPLE: PRICE DISPERSION AMONG SUPERMARKETS IN ALBUQUERQUE, NEW MEXICO

In any metropolitan area there are many retail grocery stores and supermarkets. The services they provide are slightly differentiated: Some supermarkets may be cleaner than others,, some may specialize in produce, and others may have delicatessen departments. Another aspect of their heterogeneity may be their distance from the customer. A consumer who lives next to supermarket A would be less sensitive to a price reduction in supermarket B than another consumer who lives in a neighborhood right between the two supermarkets. Accordingly, the demand curve confronting the single supermarket is negatively sloped but relatively elastic. There are many supermarkets and grocery stores serving the 400,000 people of Albuquerque. Since the services of these supermarkets are differentiated, prices are not expected to be identical. What is the typical price dispersion in such an industry? Data gathered by the New Mexico Public Interest Research Group for 1977 are presented to give the reader a feel for such a typical monopolistically competitive market. This group surveyed food prices in eight grocery stores throughout Albuquerque. The results (for four major supermarkets) are given in Table 12-1. The prices are averages for March, August, and December.

Chapter 9 showed that not all price dispersions are systematic in the sense that they reflect variations in quality. Unsystematic price dispersions may be present because obtaining information in the market is costly (Section 9.6). Households with high levels of income would be expected to spend less time seeking information about prices because the price of time is roughly equal to earnings per unit of time. On the benefit side, large families are expected to spend a great deal more time seeking information. The gross gain from information seeking for a family of six that spends large sums of money on food should exceed the gross gain for a family of three that spends relatively less on food. This issue will be discussed in depth in Section 12.4.

12.3 THE QUALITY DIMENSION

We have seen that, in the long run, free entry will guarantee that equilibrium will occur at a point like N in panel (b) of Figure 12-4, where average cost curve AC is tangent to special demand curve d'. Since monopolistic competition results from product differentiation, we might want to measure the quality dimension. Introducing a new variety of beer (light beer) or playing soft music in supermarkets are good examples of increasing the quality dimension of a good produced by firms in monopolistic competition. A more

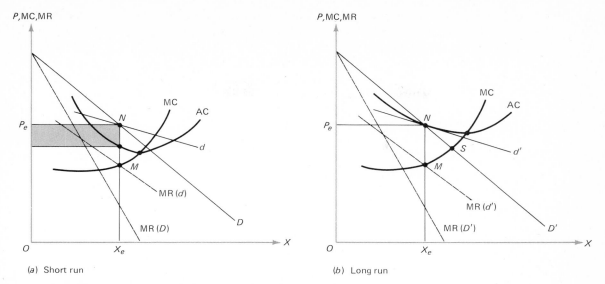

P,MC,MR

P_e

MC AC

N

d

M

MR (d)

MR (D)

D

O X_e X

(a) Short run

P,MC,MR

P_e

MC

AC

N

S

d'

M

MR (d')

MR (D')

D'

O X_e X

(b) Long run

FIGURE 12-4   EQUILIBRIUM IN MONOPOLISTIC COMPETITION

Both panels depict a firm in monopolistic competition after it has reached equilibrium. The letters D, MR(D), d, MR(d), MC, and AC denote the pro rata demand curve, its associated marginal revenue curve, the demand curve perceived by the individual firm, its associated marginal revenue curve, marginal cost, and average cost, respectively. The prime indicates long-run. In both panels equilibrium occurs at point M, where the MC curve intersects the MR(d) curve, leading to a price P_e and a rate of production X_e. In panel (a) the AC curve is lower than the demand curve (in the neighborhood of X_e); hence there is an economic rent measured by the shaded area. In panel (b) the AC curve is tangent to d' at point N, thus leaving no rent for the entrepreneur; this is an indication that long-run equilibrium has been achieved.

TABLE 12-1   **Price Dispersion in Four Supermarkets in Albuquerque, 1977**

Subtotal	Bag N' Save	Foodway	Piggly Wiggly	Safeway
Meat	$ 6.82	$ 6.83	$ 7.05	$ 6.60
Produce	3.12	4.18	3.95	3.47
Processed food	8.53	9.10	9.39	8.93
Baked goods, cereal staple	6.93	7.62	7.61	7.31
Nonfoods	3.36	3.73	3.98	3.73
Total	$28.76	$31.46	$31.98	$30.04
Percent higher than cheapest		9.38	11.2	4.45

Source: New Mexico Public Interest Research Group, 1977.

complete analysis could resort to a three-dimensional graph in which both quantity and quality are measured, respectively, along the two horizontal axes and dollars along the vertical axis.

Consider a firm in monopolistic competition that can vary both the rate of production and the quality of its product. (For simplicity of exposition assume that quality is continuous. In real life quality can be varied only in steps.) Figure 12-5 displays the axes of the three-dimensional diagram of a firm in monopolistic competition. Along one horizontal axis we measure the quantity denoted by x, and along the other horizontal axis we measure quality (some attribute) denoted by a, which is the degree of quality. The two-dimensional revenue surface is concave downward. The two-dimensional cost surface is convex downward. In the short run, the firm would seek the combination of x and a that would yield the maximum vertical distance between the revenue surface and the cost surface. This search is a two-dimensional extension of the process of searching for the maximum profit by the monopolistic firm as described in Section 11.1c and illustrated in panel (a) of Figure 11-2.

Assume that the greatest vertical distance between the two surfaces occurs at the combination of x_e units of x and a_e units of the variable attribute. (This combination is depicted by point E.) This distance is equal to $\overline{HK}$ dollars. First note that, parallel to the argument illustrated by Figure 11-2, when combination E (x_e, a_e) is produced by the firm, the marginal revenue of output is equal to the marginal cost of output, and the marginal revenue of the quality (attribute) is equal to the marginal cost of the quality. Marginal

FIGURE 12-5 TWO-DIMENSIONAL FIRM IN MONOPOLISTIC COMPETITION
We measure the *rate of production* x along one horizontal axis and the *quality* a along the other horizontal axis. Dollars are measured along the vertical axis. Instead of total revenue curve and total cost curve, *total cost surface* and *total revenue surface* are shown. Point E represents a pair of x_e units of x and a_e units of a. If we send a vertical line from E upwards, it will cut the cost surface at point H and the revenue surface at point K. Thus for that pair total cost is $\overline{EH}$, total revenue is $\overline{EK}$, and profit (economic rent) is $\overline{HK}$.

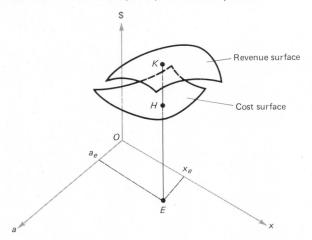

revenue and marginal cost of output are obtained by keeping quality constant (at a_e) and varying output by a small Δx. Marginal revenue and marginal cost of the quality are obtained by keeping output constant (at x_e) and varying the quality by a small Δa. In the long run, the positive (economic) rent of $\overline{HK}$ dollars will attract more firms into the industry. Accordingly, customers would be able to purchase from a wider selection of producers. Arithmetically, on average each individual firm will be selling to a smaller number of customers. The revenue surface would consequently begin to fall. In the end the two surfaces would be tangent to each other. (Point E may or may not remain the long-run equilibrium point.) This long-run solution is similar to the situation depicted by point N in panel (b) of Figure 12-4, where demand curve d' is tangent to AC. Figure 12-4 presented the geometry of attaining equilibrium by the individual firm under the assumption that quality had already been fixed at the optimal level.

12.4 WELFARE LOSS IN MONOPOLISTIC COMPETITION

In Figure 12-5, if $\overline{HK}$ shrinks to zero, it indicates that economic rent has been dissipated. In panel (b) of Figure 12-4 at point N the AC curve just touches demand curve d'; this also is a long-run equilibrium coupled with dissipation of economic rent. Rent dissipation should not be interpreted as a sign that there is no welfare loss. Since the rate of production is determined where MC cuts the MR(d') curve [point M in panel (b) of Figure 12-4] rather than where MC cuts demand curve D' [point S in panel (b) of Figure 12-4], welfare loss in monopolistic competition is present. However, since demand curve d' is more elastic than pro rata demand curve D', welfare loss is relatively small. Consider Figure 12-6. Competitive pricing would have implied that point S, where MC cuts pro rata demand curve D', is the point of equilibrium. There would be no welfare loss at point S. Monopolistic pricing would have been achieved if the firm selected point A as its equilibrium; at point A the MC curve intersects the MR(D') curve. Under such pricing, the welfare loss would have amounted to the area of triangle FAS, which is the area with the diagonal stripes plus the shaded area. However, the individual firm in monopolistic competition selects point M as its long-run equilibrium. At point M the MC curve intersects the MR(d') curve. The welfare loss is the striped area of triangle NMS, which is smaller by shaded area $FAMN$ than the welfare loss under monopoly. In the extreme case where d' is almost horizontal, monopolistic competition approaches perfect competition and welfare loss is next to nil. We can conclude that the larger the number of firms in the industry, and the higher the degree of substitutability among the differentiated goods, the more elastic curve d' will be and the smaller the welfare loss will be in monopolistic competition.

A solace for the concerned reader: In monopolistic competition, welfare loss (1) is very small relative to the loss in monopoly and (2) may be viewed as a price we all must pay for our unquenched thirst for variety.

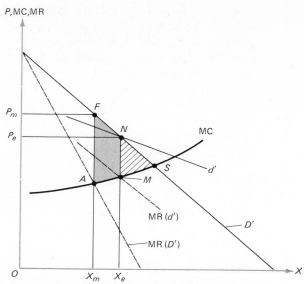

FIGURE 12-6 WELFARE LOSS IN MONOPOLISTIC COMPETITION
The pro rata demand and its associated marginal revenue are depicted by D' and MR(D');
the demand perceived by the individual firm and its associated marginal revenue are depicted
by d' and MR(d'). The marginal cost curve is denoted by MC. A monopolistic solution would
occur at point A, where MC cuts curve MR(D'). In that case welfare loss would be the area
of triangle *FAS* (shaded plus striped areas). The equilibrium under the assumption of
monopolistic competition occurs at point M, where MC cuts curve MR(d'). In that case the
welfare loss is only the striped area of triangle *NMS*. It is smaller by the shaded area than
the welfare loss under a (multiple-plant) monopoly.

12.5 PRICE DISPERSION

Price dispersion must not be taken as evidence that a market is dominated by
monopolistic competition. Price dispersion may result, partially or wholly,
from the fact that obtaining information is a costly process. The discussion in
Section 9.7 will be elaborated on because price dispersion may be used as
evidence that monopolistic competition (as contrasted with perfect competition) prevails. Accordingly, it becomes essential for economic researchers to
divide price dispersion into major components.

The consumer compares the cost to search for price information with the
benefit from the search. The amount of effort invested in search is determined by the point at which the marginal cost of search is equal to the
marginal revenue of search. Figure 12-7 measures the search effort of individuals along the horizontal axis and the marginal cost of effort and marginal
revenue of effort along the vertical axis. So long as the marginal revenue
from the search effort exceeds it marginal cost, individuals will expand their
effort in obtaining more information. They will expand the search effort up
to $\overline{OA}$ units, where marginal revenue equals marginal cost. The marginal
cost of effort is positively sloped because the time involved in the search is
the main input. Because the value of leisure is higher the scarcer it is, the

more time invested in the search effort, the higher is its alternative cost. We can predict that as income rises, the MC curve of effort in Figure 12-7 will shift upward and less effort will be devoted to search. The marginal revenue of effort is negatively sloped because, as illustrated in Section 9.7, marginal returns of canvassing salespeople diminish very rapidly. If the volume of the commodity purchased by individuals (and their families) is relatively high, the MR curve in Figure 12-7 will occupy a relatively high position: The gain is the reduction in price due to a search multiplied by the volume of the good purchased per unit of time. It is assumed that education makes the search more efficient. Thus the position of the MR curve of search effort should occupy a higher position, the more schooling the individual has had. A higher volume of purchases and a higher level of schooling per individual would lead to greater effort in the information search.

In summary, price dispersion is inversely related to the effort devoted by individuals to search. Price dispersion will diminish with rising levels of schooling and rising volumes of purchases per individual; price dispersion will increase with income.

As an example consider the retail market for gasoline in the United States. Some price dispersion in this market arises from product differentiation, such as courteous service performed by attendants. But lack of information about gasoline prices would also create price dispersion. The cost of search is mainly the time spent in searching. Since the cost per unit of time spent in

FIGURE 12-7 DETERMINING THE AMOUNT OF SEARCH EFFORT

We measure search effort along the horizontal axis and marginal cost and marginal revenue of search effort along the vertical axis. The marginal cost curve of search, MC, is positively sloping, reflecting the fact that the time that goes into search effort is more costly on the margin when leisure becomes scarcer. Since the main factor in search effort is time spent, its value is mainly determined by the income of the consumer conducting the search: The higher the income, the higher will be the position of the MC curve. The marginal revenue of search effort, MR, diminishes rapidly (Section 9.7). Its position will be higher, the more schooling the consumer has had and the larger the volume purchased.

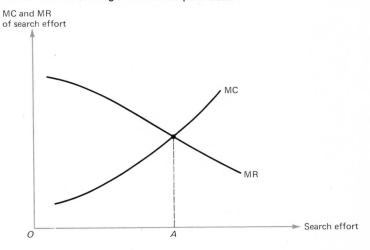

searching is roughly equal to the earnings of the consumer per unit of time, the theory developed previously predicts that the higher the income received by individuals, the less time they would devote to search. It might be repeated here that consumers with a higher level of schooling are expected to be more efficient in the process of search. The benefit from the search for information is simply the price reduction resulting from the search times the amount of gasoline purchased. Economic theory would accordingly predict that people who buy large amounts of gasoline would search more than those who purchase relatively small volumes. Howard Marvel has studied retail gasoline price dispersion.[2] He attempted to explain the price variability of gasoline prices by employing data provided by the Bureau of Labor Statistics. Monthly data were available for 10 standard metropolitan statistical areas and quarterly data for 13 other metropolitan areas. His empirical analysis confirmed what the theory predicts: Dispersion of gasoline prices was estimated statistically as a function of a variety of explanatory variables. The result was that price dispersion was negatively related to gallons consumed per car and to schooling, and positively related to family income. Gasoline is considered by many to be a typical case of monopolistic competition. But Marvel's study points out that monopolistic competition is not the sole factor contributing to gasoline price variability.

SUMMARY   *Monopolistic competition* arises in industries in which many small firms, none of whom dominates the market, produce a differentiated good. As a result, individual firms face demand curves that are very elastic but slightly negatively sloped. Also, firms in monopolistic competition engage in advertising. If all firms in an industry dominated by monopolistic competition were run as a high multiple-plant monopoly, each firm would have faced a pro rata demand curve which is a portion of the market demand curve. Under such (theoretical) conditions, a monopolistic solution could have been found. The analysis started from such a hypothetical solution and showed that if we relax the assumption of a multiple-plant monopoly, each individual firm would perceive a demand curve which is more elastic than the pro rata demand curve. This would trigger a process of adjustment in the industry until each individual firm would operate where its marginal cost curve intersects with the marginal revenue curve associated with the more elastic demand curve; an additional condition for equilibrium is that the price charged by the individual firm satisfies the point of intersection between the pro rata demand curve and the more elastic demand curve as perceived by the firm. In the long run, if the supply of entrepreneurial capacity is unlimited and there is freedom of entry into the industry, the average cost curve will be tangent to the more elastic demand curve where it cuts the pro rata demand curve.

---

[2]Howard P. Marvel, "The Economics of Information and Retail Gasoline Price Behavior: An Empirical Analysis," *Journal of Political Economy*, October 1976, vol. 84, pp. 1033–1066.

Our next step was to consider the quality dimension. We concluded that firms in monopolistic competition simultaneously vary quantity and quality and thus their cost and revenue graphs appear as three-dimensional surfaces rather than two-dimensional curves.

In the long run, if there is freedom of entry into the industry and an unlimited supply of entrepreneurial capacity, rent will completely dissipate. It has been noted that rent dissipation does not imply zero welfare loss. Since the demand curve perceived by the individual firm is slightly negatively sloped, there is a small welfare loss resulting from monopolistic competition. However, we may view the welfare loss due to monopolistic competition as the cost consumers incur to enjoy a variety of attributes.

Finally the issue of price dispersion was discussed. Price dispersion is sometimes taken as a sign that monopolistic competition (in contrast to perfect competition) prevails. Obtaining information in the marketplace has a cost, and the theory predicts that price dispersion would be directly related to income and inversely related to the consumer's level of education and volume of purchases. A study of gasoline price dispersion confirmed this theory; moreover, it indicated that the variability of prices of gasoline resulted to some extent from the fact that information in the market is costly to obtain. This finding verified the suspicion that only part of price variability resulted from monopolistic competition in the retail end of the gasoline distribution industry.

GLOSSARY   **Monopolistic competition** A market situation in which many firms, none of whom dominates the market, sell a differentiated product to many consumers. As a result, each individual firm faces a slightly negatively sloped demand curve.

Differentiated (heterogeneous) product Any pair of two close substitutes constitutes a differentiated product. Differentiation of a product may be achieved by bringing out and enhancing certain attributes and suppressing certain other attributes of the product.

Multiple-plant monopoly A monopolistic firm that operates many plants.

Pro rata demand curve The nth fraction of the market demand curve. For example, if $n = 3$, the pro rata demand curve is a third of the market demand curve. It is obtained by dividing the horizontal distance between the price axis and the market demand curve into three equal segments.

Price dispersion (Price variability). Let the mean of the prices in a certain market (industry) be denoted by μ. Then $\mu = (\Sigma P_i)/N$, if N prices were recorded. The variance is the arithmetic mean of the squares of the deviations from the mean, that is, $\sigma^2 = [\Sigma(P_i - \mu)^2]/N$. The standard deviation is the square root of the variance, namely, $\sigma = \sqrt{\sigma^2}$. The coefficient of variation is simply the standard deviation divided by the mean:

$$\text{Coefficient of variation} = \frac{\sigma}{\mu}$$

PROBLEMS An asterisk indicates an advanced problem.

12-1. In the long run rent in monopolistic competition is dissipated. Yet monopolistic competition gives rise to some welfare loss to society. Explain.

12-2. Do you think that all the supermarkets where you live could organize as a (clandestine) cartel and behave as if they were a multiple-plant monopoly? Why or why not?

12-3.* If an ad valorem tax (a tax imposed as a percentage of the price) were imposed on gasoline at the retail end, would you expect this to stimulate an increase in self-service pumps or vice versa?

12-4. "Farmers markets" (self-service markets for vegetables and fruit) are not air-conditioned. Moreover, services offered there do not come near to services one can get in supermarkets. Yet many consumers prefer "farmers markets" to clean supermarkets. Explain.

12-5. If in the long run rent is expected to dissipate, why should a brewery invent a new beer, say, the "light beer"?

12-6. Where would you expect to observe a higher degree of price dispersion, in neighborhood gas stations or in gas stations serving main arteries of traffic?

12-7.* Would you expect the quality of wine to increase as a result of an imposition of a unit tax (say a dollar per bottle) on wines?

12-8. Where do you expect lines for hamburger to be longer, in rich neighborhoods or in poor neighborhoods?

12-9. In some cities theaters sell cheaper movie tickets to students. Do you think they do it because they are fond of students?

12-10. Consider Figure 12-6. Assume that demand curve d' becomes perfectly elastic. Indicate the long-run equilibrium solution of the individual firm. What is the welfare loss of that firm?

C H A P T E R

OLIGOPOLY
(optional)

This chapter discusses a market situation known as *oligopoly*. Oligopoly was first defined in Chapter 7. There are two kinds of oligopolies: (1) The product is homogeneous, and a small number of firms dominate the market. An example is the steel industry. (2) The product is differentiated, and again, a small number of firms dominate the market. An example is the car industry. Note that we have not defined "a small number of firms." How small is small? There is no good definition of smallness that could be considered scientific. Economists use the *concentration ratio* as a measure to separate industries dominated by a large number of firms from industries dominated by a small number of firms. Thus the first topic to be covered in this chapter is concentration measures. The concentration ratio is the simplest and most popular measure of concentration. In the United States it is generally defined as *the share of the four largest firms in total output*. As we shall see later, other measures are used, too. It is used whenever an industry either is accused of having too much oligopolistic power or defends itself against such accusations. For instance, after the OPEC cartel raised the prices of oil in 1973 following the Yom Kippur War, the United States oil industry was accused of being an oligopoly of a few large vertically integrated companies. Exxon's response was a small booklet entitled *The Charge and the Facts*. As an example of the use of the concentration ratio, consider the following section in the Exxon booklet:

Charge:
The oil industry should be broken up because it is highly concentrated.

Facts:
Critics denounce the market share concentration of the top 20 oil companies but fail to note that few major industries have this many total competitors.

Market share concentration of typical industries (in %):

	Top 4	Top 8
Aluminum	96	100
Automobiles	91	97
Soap and detergents	70	79
Radio and TV sets	48	67
Average of all manufacturing	39	60
Petroleum production	31	49
refinng	32	55
sales	31	52
Total energy (oil, gas, coal, uranium)	21	34

Because concentration ratios are so widely used in real life, the concept will be discussed from both a theoretical and an empirical viewpoint right at the start. The theory of oligopoly, which consists of two major parts, *barriers to entry* and *price determination*, will then be examined.

The theory surrounding barriers to entry answers two important questions: (1) Why do we observe higher concentration ratios in manufacturing industries than in agriculture, retail trade, banking, and so on? (2) Why is the concentration ratio higher in some manufacturing industries, such as the automobile industry, than in other industries, such as the furniture industry?

There is no one theory to explain pricing under oligopoly, as there is under competition, monopoly, and monopolistic competition. The firm in competition has no appreciable influence over the price in the marketplace; hence it is a *price taker*. The monopoly faces the entire market demand and is therefore a *price maker*. The firm in monopolistic competition is a *limited price maker*: It faces a very elastic demand curve, so elastic that some would argue it should be viewed as a *price taker*. In oligopoly, however, there are a few dominant firms in the industry; we have neither the neat solution of *price taking* nor the neat solution of *price making*. The strategy adopted by one giant firm will affect the strategy of another giant firm, which in turn will affect the strategy of the first giant firm, and so on. If the oligopolists decide to enter into collusion, a theory of collusion may be sketched, similar to the theory of a multiple-plant monopoly (Section 12.1). However, if collusion cannot work, either because it is illegal or because the partners cheat one another, there is no single approach to resolving the conflict. Various theories of pricing exist under oligopolies. Most of these theories are stated mathematically and are only remotely related to real life; accordingly, they are covered in Mathematical Appendix 13. Some do relate to real life, as discussed in the course of the chapter. Real-life oligopoly is colorful and complex—a collection of many industries. The student of price theory is encouraged at least to look at how the profession analyzes these industries; to that end, three typical oligopolies—steel, airlines, and automobiles—will be examined.

13.1 CONCENTRATION RATIOS

13.1a Some Technical Aspects

It was mentioned earlier that in the United States the accepted measure of concentration is the share of the four largest firms in total output. Other countries have adopted different measures. For example, Canada counts the number of the largest firms that would be necessary to account for 80 percent of total output.

Another measure, more popular among economists than among laymen, is the Herfindahl (H) measure of concentration, which is defined as follows:[1]

$$H = s_1^2 + s_2^2 + \cdots + s_n^2 \qquad (13\text{-}1)$$

where s_1 is the share of the first firm, s_2 is the share of the second firm, and so on. For example, consider the shares of the car makers in the United States in 1950 as given in Table 13-1. The concentration ratio (the share of the four largest car makers) is 0.925 (92.5 percent). The Herfindahl measure is 0.3044. The Herfindahl measure has an advantage in that it will reflect changes in concentration not reflected by the share of the top four. Suppose that Studebaker-Packard and Willys were to merge. The concentration ratio

---

[1]Named after Orris C. Herfindahl.

TABLE 13-1   Shares of Car Makers in the United States, 1950

	Share expressed as a decimal	
	s_i	s_i^2
GM	0.459	0.2107
Ford	0.236	0.0557
Chrysler	0.180	0.0324
AMC	0.050	0.0025
Studebaker-Packard	0.051	0.0026
Willys Motors	0.023	0.0005
Crosley	0.001	*
Checker Cab	*	*
Total	1.000	0.3044

*Less than 0.1 percent.
Source: Calculated from manufacturers' unit production data reported in Motor Vehicle Manufacturers Association of the U.S., Inc., *Autombobile Facts and Figures*, 1961 edition.

would remain the same 92.5 percent. However, H would change as follows:

$$(s_5 + s_6)^2 = s_5^2 + s_6^2 + 2s_5 s_6$$

Thus, after the merger the new H is $2s_5 s_6$ higher than the original H.

In the illustration $2s_5 s_6 = 2 \cdot 0.051 \cdot 0.023 = 0.0023$, and the new H is 0.3067. Notice that if GM and Ford were to merge, the concentration ratio would rise from 0.925 to 0.975. H would rise from 0.3044 to 0.521, which is a relatively larger increase, reflecting the significance of the merger.

13.1b Some Theoretical Aspects

Can it be shown that the degree of competition declines as the concentration ratio rises? The answer is not simple. This section will try to shed light on this question by utilizing one of the many oligopolistic models.

Consider the *Cournot model*, which suggests that each oligopolist first records how much its rivals currently produce. Since it is very difficult to predict what those rivals are going to do next, it then assumes that they will not change their outputs. To illustrate this model, assume that there are three oligopolists (1, 2, 3) producing a homogeneous product. The amounts each produces are X_1, X_2, and X_3, respectively. Consider producer 1. When it makes a decision about how much to produce, it assumes that X_2 and X_3 are fixed. In other words, it varies X_1 until its profit is maximized and then waits for the reaction of the two rivals. Concurrently, the rivals are reacting to the first producer in the same way. Producer 2 assumes that X_1 and X_3 are fixed and varies X_2 until its profit is maximized. Producer 3 then assumes that X_1 and X_2 are fixed and varies X_3 until its profit is maximized. This interplay continues until equilibrium is reached: None of the rivals has an incentive to vary output further. Detailed theoretical discussion of the Cour-

TABLE 13-2 **The Relationship between the Concentration Measure *H* and the Extended Lerner Formula for Oligopoly: $\eta = -2$**

Number producers n	Concentration measure H	Markup (extended Lerner formula) $\dfrac{P - MC}{P} = \dfrac{-1}{n\eta}$
1	1	0.5
2	0.5	0.25
4	0.25	0.125
6	0.167	0.083
8	0.125	0.062
10	0.1	0.05

not model is postponed to Mathematical Appendix 13. Recall from Section 11.2b that with some qualifications, the distance between price and MC is a rough measure of monopoly power, sometimes known as the *Lerner formula*. George Stigler has extended the Lerner formula to the case of oligopoly governed by Cournot behavior with identical firms.[2] The extended Lerner formula for the Cournot case is

$$\frac{P - MC}{P} = \frac{-1}{n\eta} \qquad (13\text{-}2)$$

where n is the number of rival firms and η is the price elasticity of the market demand. The proof is given in Mathematical Appendix 13. If $n = 1$, we have the Lerner formula for monopoly. If $\eta = -2$, then, given monopoly, the distance between P and MC is half the price. The higher η, the smaller the distance and the closer we are to the case of competition in which $P = MC$. If we keep elasticity constant and increase the number of rivals, the distance between P and MC diminishes. Thus, for $n = 2$ ($\eta = -2$), the distance is a quarter of the price; and for $n = 3$, the distance falls to 1/6. Table 13-2 shows how, as the number of oligopolists increases, H decreases and the extended Lerner ratio also decreases.

As the number of oligopolists increases from 1 (monopoly) to 10, H decreases from 1 to 0.1 and the markup (extended Lerner formula) decreases from 0.5 to 0.05.

Two main empirical issues concern us with regard to the concentration ratios: First, there is the issue of concentration over time; does it rise or fall? Second, there is the issue of correlation between concentration ratios and the rate of return on equity (or other measures of capital). Most studies show that only for very high concentration ratios are profits significantly higher than normal. In Section 13.2 an example is cited in which the rate of return is related to the degree of barriers to entry. The following section presents an example of a study of concentration over time.

[2]George J. Stigler, *The Organization of Industry*, Richard D. Irwin, Inc., Homewood, Ill., 1968, chap. 4.

TABLE 13-3   Change in Concentration Ratios over Time

Change	By number of industries		By employment (*E*) or value of shipment (VS) in 1947 percentage	
			E	VS
	1947–1958	1947–1963	1947–1958	1947–1963
Increasing or constant	14	7	42.5	23.4
Decreasing	12	15	57.5	76.6
Total industries	26	22	100.0	100.0

Source: David R. Kamerschen, ''An Empirical Test of Oligopoly Theories, *Journal of Political Economy*, vol. 76, July/August 1968, pp. 615–634.

13.1c An Example: Concentration over Time

Do American manufacturing industries become more or less concentrated over time? David Kamerschen studied the trends in concentration ratios during the periods 1947–1958 and 1947–1963.[3] Oligopolies were defined as industries with concentration ratios equal to or above 75 percent. In 1947, twenty-six industries (including cereal preparation, cigarettes, synthetic fibers, tires and inner tubes, and typewriters) qualified as oligopolies. The results of this study are summarized in Table 13-3.

During 1947–1958, concentration decreased in about half of the 26 oligopolies. During 1947–1963, concentration decreased in about 15 out of the 22 industries with concentration ratios of 75 percent or over. That is, the concentration rate declined in about two-thirds of the industries. This is corroborated by statistics in which industries are weighted by employment (*E*) for the period 1947–1958, and by the value of shipments (of output) for the period 1947–1963. The conclusion reached by Kamerschen is that ''the odds are better than even that there has actually been some decline in concentration. It is a good bet that there has at least been no actual increase; and the odds do seem high against any substantial increase.''

We are now ready to investigate perhaps the most important issue of oligopolies; namely, why are some industries more concentrated than others? In particular, why are most manufacturing industries more concentrated than the rest of the industries?

13.2 BARRIERS TO ENTRY

13.2a The Theory

Section 6.5f explained that in the long run, up to a certain level of output, the production function obeys increasing returns to scale and consequently the long-run average cost curve (LRAC) is falling. From that certain level and beyond, the production function obeys decreasing returns to scale and LRAC is rising. The empirical phenomenon of increasing returns to scale is sometimes called *scale economies*; one of the examples in Chapter 6 demonstrated that firms generating electric power enjoy huge *economies of scale*:

---

[3]David R. Kamerschen, ''An Empirical Test of Oligopoly Theories,'' *Journal of Political Economy*, vol. 76, July/August 1968, pp. 615–634.

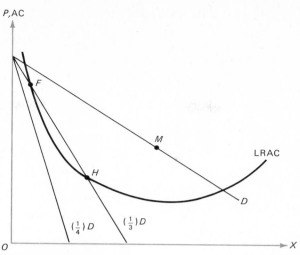

FIGURE 13-1   INTERNAL ECONOMIES OF SCALE
The market demand curve is denoted by D. Demand curves that cover one-third and one-fourth of the market demand are depicted by $(\frac{1}{3})D$ and $(\frac{1}{4})D$, respectively. These are known as pro rata demand curves. Between points F and H, $(\frac{1}{3})D$ lies above the long-run average cost curve (LRAC). Pro rata curve $(\frac{1}{4})D$ is entirely below LRAC. Thus there is room for only three firms in the industry.

in 1970, the minimum of the LRAC curve of a typical firm in the electricity generating sector was 20 billion kilowatthours (per annum). Section 11.3a noted that utilities at the local scene, such as electricity, water, and natural gas, are viewed by most people as being *natural monopolies*; natural monopolies result from economies of scale. A similar situation can arise in manufacturing industries. Because of scale economies, the long-run average cost curve in some manufacturing industries may be very high for relatively low levels of output and fall very rapidly over a wide range when the rate of production increases. This situation is illustrated in Figure 13-1. The market demand curve is D. The long-run average cost curve is denoted by LRAC. Let us assume that there are only three identical firms in the industry. If we take (horizontally) a third of the demand curve, we obtain a demand curve confronting each of the individual firms. Such a pro rata demand curve is denoted by $(\frac{1}{3})D$. Notice that there is room for only three firms in this particular market. If a fourth firm were to enter, the demand curve facing each firm would be $(\frac{1}{4})D$, and no firm would be able to make a profit. Geometrically, this is evident from observing that $(\frac{1}{3})D$ is above LRAC between points F and H; the attempt of a fourth producer to join the industry pushes $(\frac{1}{4})D$ to a position entirely below LRAC.

Clearly, the scale economies that cause the LRAC curve to fall very rapidly over a large range of production are a necessary condition for the existence of oligopoly. The position of the demand curve relative to the LRAC curve is the sufficient condition.

For an example of economies of scale, let us look at the glass industry.

According to H. Michael Mann,[4] the switch at the turn of the century from manpower to machine power necessitated large-scale plants to maximize efficiency. In 1960, Pittsburgh Plate operated four sheet-glass and four plate-glass plants; Libby-Owens-Ford operated one sheet-glass and three plate-glass plants and one that produced both sheet and plate. These plants accounted for 90 percent of plate-glass and 65 percent of all United States sheet-glass production. Thus Mann calculated that each of the plants accounted, on average, for slightly over 10 percent of total industry output; the minimum LRAC of these plants occurs at a very high level of output.

A second type of barrier to entry is *control of a scarce natural resource*. Mann also reports that in the 1960s, International Nickel and Falconbridge dominated 90 percent of the proven nickel ore reserves in the United States.[5] So long as no substitute is found for nickel in the production of stainless steel, control of nickel guarantees an oligopolistic position.

A third source of barriers to entry is patents. An example is the drug industry. Almost all drugs are protected by patents. A firm can enter the industry either by paying heavily for a license to use someone else's patent or by paying heavily for research and development of a new drug. Even if a new drug is successfully introduced into the market, the firm must pay for promotion.

A fourth source of barriers to entry is legal. In some states the number of licenses to sell liquor retail are fixed by the state government at arbitrary levels. A new entrant to the market must pay heavily to purchase a license.

Barriers to entry are not necessarily permanent. A change in technology may put an end to the economies of scale enjoyed by a certain industry. A discovery of a new ore may open the industry to new entrants. A technological innovation may introduce a substitute for a mineral hitherto sold at a very high price. The oligopoly may continue to exist formally, but its price must now decline to compete with the substitute mineral. Likewise, licensing could be abolished, restoring competition to the liquor business.

13.2b An Example: Rate of Return and Barriers to Entry

Mann also studied the relationship between barriers to entry and rates of return.[6] The motivation behind his study was the suspicion that concentration ratios may be misleading. If the barriers to entry are not severe, oligopolists may set a price that is not significantly above the competitive price and thus discourage potential entrants. To compare the profitability of various industries, a rate of return had to be calculated. Defining the rate of return as net income divided by the value of the stock would not have proved anything because the market value of the stock reflected the expected value of future net income (Section 9-10c). Accordingly, Mann defined the rate of return as the net income divided by the net worth of the corporation. First he divided 30 industries into two groups by concentration ratios: The first group included industries in which the top eight firms accounted for 70 percent or over of total industry pro-

---

[4]H. Michael Mann, "Seller Concentration, Barriers to Entry, and Rates of Return in Thirty Industries, 1950–1960," *The Review of Economics and Statistics*, vol. 48, August 1966, pp. 296–307.

[5]Ibid.

[6]Ibid.

TABLE 13-4   Average Rates of Return for Three Groups of Industry Classified by Degree of Barriers to Entry

Group	Average rate of return
Very high barriers	16.4
Substantial barriers	11.3
Moderate to low barriers	9.9

Source: H. M. Mann, "Seller Concentration, Barriers to Entry, and Rates of Return in Thirty Industries, 1950–1960," *The Review of Economics and Statistics*, vol. 48, August 1966, pp. 296–307.

duction. The second group included firms in which the top eight firms accounted for less than 70 percent of production. For the period 1950–1960 the average rate of return for the first group was 13.3 percent and for the second group, 9.0 percent.

Mann obtained a more revealing result when he divided the same industries into three groups: The first group (automobiles, chewing gum, cigarettes, ethical drugs, flat glass, liquor, nickel, and sulfur) had very high barriers to entry. The second group (aluminum products, biscuits, petroleum refining, steel, soap, farm machinery and tractors, copper, cement, and shoe machinery) had substantial barriers to entry. The third group (glass containers, tires and tubes, shoes, rayon, gypsum products, canned fruits and vegetables, meat packing, flour, metal containers, beer, backing, bituminous coal, textiles, and milk products) had moderate to lower barriers to entry. The results of Mann's study are summarized in Table 13-4.

In summary, we can say that barriers to entry may or may not lead to higher than normal rates of return. Only if the barriers to entry are very severe should the industry expect higher than normal rates of return. But as noted before, high barriers to entry need not be permanent.

13.3 THEORIES OF PRICE DETERMINATION

This section discusses some simple theories of price determination that might arise in oligopolies. The reader who is interested in more sophisticated oligopoly models of price determination should examine Mathematical Appendix 13.

13.3a The Case of Collusion and Homogeneous Product

In oligopoly the policy maker of a firm must contemplate possible retaliation from other firms. If the firm cuts its price, it may in the short run attract more customers. But other firms may cut their prices even further, thus winning over the customers to their product, and so on along the line. Eventually, the few firms in the industry will form a tacit merger or trust, and each firm will be allotted a certain fraction of total output. For example, an illegal merger of steel producers may decide to raise the price of steel by $6 per ton. Since it is illegal to conspire for the common prupose of limiting output, a secret meeting of the different producers may be called. Let us assume that steel producers will be convinced that the price elasticity is in the order of magnitude of -2. If the current price of steel is \$60, a \$6 increase is consistent with cutting down production 20 percent. So as not to arouse governmental suspicion, the producers will independently raise the price of steel a few weeks apart. This is a case in which antitrust laws may be ineffective because of the difficulty of proving that there has been collusion between producers. But even if it were possible to show collusion, it would be difficult to determine illegality, given the lack of data. For example, if raising the price of steel resulted from an upward shift in the rising marginal cost curve, then raising prices was justified.

In the absence of anticollusion laws, the few firms in the oligopolistic industry will tend to form a collusion and set a monopoly price. First, regardless of the price they set, oligopolistic firms will in the long run tend to divide output among themselves such that their respective marginal costs are the same. To illustrate this, consider a case of duopoly (an oligopoly of two producers). The outputs and marginal cost schedules of Firm A and Firm B are shown in Table 13-5. Let us assume that the entrepreneurs of the two firms made an agreement to peg the price at \$10, at which marginal revenue equals \$5. This is consistent with a price elasticity of -2. At that price, the market clears 10 units. Also, according to the agreement, Firm A and Firm B should share the market equally. Each of them will produce 5 units. This will not, however, be their final equilibrium.

The MC of Firm A is \$6 and the MC of Firm B is \$4. Firm B has an incentive to "bribe" Firm A to transfer one unit of output from its quota to the quota of B. By forgoing the production of one unit, Firm A will reduce its cost by \$6 and Firm B, by adding a unit, will increase its cost by \$5. Thus, between the two of them, A and B will increase their combined profit by \$1. How they will divide this extra profit will depend on their bargaining positions.

Saying that oligopolists tend to equate their respective marginal costs is equivalent to saying that they have a meaningful aggregate MC curve. Consider Figure 13-2. In panel (a), the marginal cost of Firm A is denoted by MC_a and that of Firm B by MC_b. In panel (b), the aggregate MC curve of the two firms is denoted by ΣMC. Curve ΣMC intersects curve MR at point L. Thus the optimum combination for the industry is quantity $\overline{KL}$ at a price $\overline{RS}$.

TABLE 13-5 MC Curves of a Duopoly

Firm A		Firm B	
Quantity	MC	Quantity	MC
1	2	1	½
2	3	2	1
3	4	3	2
4	5	4	3
5	6	5	4
6	7	6	5
7	8	7	6
8	9	8	7

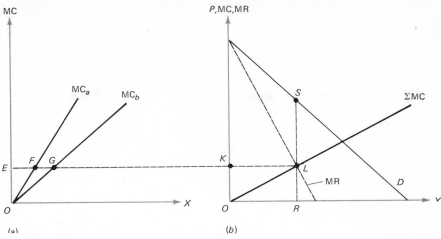

FIGURE 13-2 DUOPOLY COLLUSION

In panel (a), the marginal costs of duopolists A and B are depicted by curves MC_a and MC_b. In panel (b) the two MC curves are aggregated into the ΣMC curve. The market demand and its associated marginal revenue are depicted by curves D and MR. ΣMC intersects with curve MR at point L. Accordingly, the price set by the duopolists is $\overline{RS}$, the total rate of production is OR, of which A produces $\overline{EF}$, and B produces $\overline{EG}$ units.

$\overline{KL}$ in panel (b) equals $\overline{EF}$ plus $\overline{EG}$ in panel (a). Thus, after the long-run adjustment takes place, a quantity $\overline{EF}$ is produced by Firm A and a quantity $\overline{EG}$ is produced by Firm B, regardless of the original arrangement between them.

A market-sharing cartel is a market situation in which a few firms that dominate the production of a homogeneous product agree to share the market according to some regional, or any other, arrangement. The analysis above indicates that if the sharing agreement prohibits transferring output from one firm to another, the combined profit of the members of the cartel is less than the possible maximum. If the management of the cartel is wise, it should allow firms operating at a low marginal cost to "bribe" firms operating at a high marginal cost to yield some of their quotas.

Note that demand curve D in panel (b) is either the market demand curve or the net demand curve—the market demand curve minus the supply curve of all small firms as discussed in Section 11.6a.

Note also that even if collusion were legal, its success is not guaranteed. Collusions would collapse when the conspirators resort to secret price cutting. Secret price cutting would eventually lead to prices that roughly reflect competitive prices. (This topic was discussed in detail in Section 11.9.) Moreover, by secretly cutting prices, a firm could not lure customers from another firm's territory without detection. A possible solution to prevent secret price cutting is for legal collusions to fix market shares.

In summary, "chiseling" in the form of price cutting would be easier the larger the number of firms in collusion. The reason for this is that the impact of "chiseling" of a small firm on the rest of the producers is relatively small. Also, the smaller the number of customers, the easier it is to "chisel": The probability is less that one customer out of two will reveal a secret price-cutting transaction than it is that one out of ten customers (who benefit from price cutting) will reveal the transaction.

Collusion is unimportant if the demand curve confronting oligopolists is relatively elastic. A later section will discuss the steel industry. There it is noted that prices of steel rose rapidly when the domestic market was protected and rose hardly at all when true free trade prevailed between the United States and the rest of the world. In other words, when international trade was unrestricted, the demand curve for steel at home was relatively elastic and the oligopoly could raise the price only at the cost of losing a significant share of the market to foreign steel producers.

13.3b The Case of a Differentiated Product

If a differentiated product is made by a few firms, it is said to be produced by an oligopoly. Examples are the industries producing cars, tires, and cigarettes. Two market situations will be considered here: (1) Prices are flexible and rivalry results from altering prices; (2) there is nonprice rivalry, where the price is sluggish because, say, it is fixed and regulated by the government (as was the case in the airline industry from 1938 to 1978). In both market situations, advertising and changing the quality of the product are prevalent, as in the case of monopolistic competition (Chapter 12). First the case of flexible prices and then the case of nonprice rivalry will be discussed.

13.3c Flexible Prices

Pure competitive firms never advertise. After all, why should farmers waste money on advertising if for all practical purposes they sell the same kind of wheat? But when it comes to beer, for instance, each producer tries to convince consumers that the taste of its particular beer is the best. In terms of the formal individual equilibrium, there is no difference between a monopoly and an oligopoly producing a differentiated product. Like the monopoly, the oligopoly producing a differentiated product will operate where MC intersects MR. Thus, in both cases, the firm is able to charge a price higher than the marginal cost. But there is the following divergence: Normally, the oligopoly producing a differentiated product is confronted with a relatively more elastic demand curve. It is evident from the way curve MR is derived that the flatter the demand curve, the closer the marginal revenue curve is to it. Accordingly, the price charged by a firm producing a differentiated product cannot be set too high above the marginal cost. The demand curve confronting the rival producer of a differentiated product is not perfectly elastic; if the firm lowers the price of its product, it will win over many customers from other oligopolists, but not all of them. If the oligopolist raises its price, it will lose many customers to other oligopolists, but not all of them. For example, if Tareyton reduces the price of its cigarettes, it will attract a certain fraction of smokers of Kent and Pall Mall but not all cigarette smokers. Not all smokers will switch because there are differences in flavor, length, and filter that distinguish the various types of cigarettes from each other. Although these various types of cigarettes are heterogeneous, the element of substitution is quite strong. Thus the absolute value of the price elasticity of the demand curve for each brand of cigarettes is very high.

As in monopolistic competition, advertising creates a problem in oligopoly with a differentiated product. Because the products are differentiated, firms try to attract more customers by advertising. In economic terms, an oligopolistic firm attempts to change the tastes of consumers in favor of its product at the expense of substitutes made by the other oligopolists. Thus advertising entails the firm's spending money to shift the demand curve to the right. A rightward shift in the demand curve entails a rightward shift in the marginal revenue curve (MR). Recall that the producer's surplus is the area bordered by the MR curve, the marginal cost curve (MC), and the price axis (Section 11.4a). Assume first that advertising involves only a fixed cost to the firm. (This assumption will hold if advertising is carried out only in magazines and on TV.) Consider Figure 13-3. Advertising causes the demand curve to shift to the right. This shift is not shown in Figure 13-3. Following the shift in demand, the marginal revenue also shifts rightward from, say, MR_0 to MR_1. Originally, the producer's surplus was the area with the diagonal stripes. After the shift occurred, the producer's surplus increased by the shaded area. The net gain to the single

FIGURE 13-3 THE EFFECT OF ADVERTISING

Initially the marginal revenue and marginal cost curves of the oligopolist are depicted by MR_0 and MC. The producer's surplus is equal to the striped area. If advertising requires only fixed costs, it will result in a rightward shift in the marginal revenue curve from MR_0 to MR_1. The shaded area is the additional producer's surplus; if it exceeds the fixed cost associated with advertising, we conclude that advertising is profitable. If variable cost is also affected by advertising, the marginal cost curve will also shift upward from MC to MC'; the additional producer's surplus will decrease by striped area *GHLK* and increase by shaded area *EFKN*.

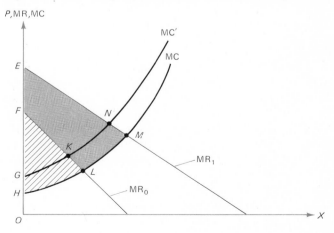

firm is the shaded area minus the additional (fixed) cost of advertising. Advertising may entail an upward shift in the MC curve. Suppose that the firm advertises by fancy packaging which costs an extra amount of, say, 10 cents a unit. In that case the marginal cost curve will shift from its original position MC to a new position MC' which is higher by 10 cents. The firm will lose the area marked by *GHLK* but gain the area marked by *EFKN*. The difference between the area lost and the area gained must be weighed against the additional fixed cost of advertising to determine whether advertising was profitable.

In the long run the gains from advertising may be dissipated because of retaliation by rivals. If a cigarette producer persuades the public to buy its cigarettes instead of a rival brand, other cigarette producers will retaliate by resorting to the same kind of advertising. This retaliation will cause the demand of the firm depicted by Figure 13-3 to decrease, leading the marginal revenue curve to shift back toward the intital MR_0 position. The conclusion is that the effects of advertising within the industry are roughly canceled out.

Since in the long run profits are dissipated, we must answer the following question: Is advertising a social waste? This issue was addressed in Chapter 12, where it was concluded that advertising is the cost consumers pay for information about product differentiation. In fact, there is evidence that variety is like a normal good: In Germany, after World War II, the relatively inexpensive Volkswagen dominated the car market for many years. However, in the 1960s when income per capita reached relatively high levels, Germans started to purchase other more expensive cars. It would seem, then, that the demand for variety is directly related to income.

Suppose that the few firms in an oligopolistic industry fixed their level of advertising. The following question remains to be answered: If a differentiated product is made by a small number of oligopolists, one oligopolist altering the price will affect the demand confronting the other firms. How do oligopolistic firms determine the price of their product? To answer this question, we shift our focus to Figure 13-4, depicting a case of duopoly. Panel (*a*) shows the demand curve confronting Firm A and its MC curve. Panel (*b*) shows the demand curve confronting Firm B and its MC curve. Originally, we assume that A is a monopolist and B exists only as a potential producer. The demand curve confronting A as a monopolist is $D(0)$. Given its associated MR curve, MR(0), A maximizes its profit by setting a price of P_{a0}. Next, we assume that B decides to enter the industry. Consider panel (*b*): Given a price of P_{a0} which is set by A, the demand curve confronting B is $D(P_{a0})$. By equating the associated marginal revenue, MR(P_{a0}), with B's marginal cost curve, Firm B will arrive at a maximum profit by setting a price of P_{b0}. Since some of the customers shifted from A to B, the demand curve confronting A shifts leftward from $D(0)$ to $D(P_{b0})$. As shown in panel (*a*), the associated marginal revenue curve, MR(P_{b0}), intersects MC_a at a lower point. This leads to a lower price of A, namely, P_{a1}. Since the price set by A has been reduced, A gained some customers away from B. Hence, as illustrated in panel (*b*), the demand curve confronting B shifts to the left from $D(P_{a0})$ to $D(P_{a1})$. The new marginal revenue curve of B, MR(P_{a1}), cuts the

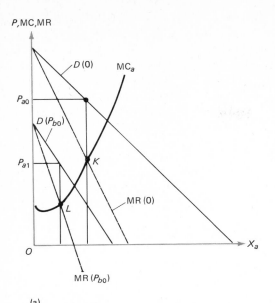

(a)

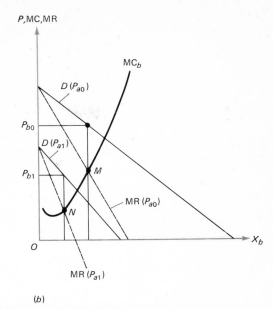

(b)

FIGURE 13-4   DUOPOLY: A CASE OF A DIFFERENTIATED PRODUCT

In panel (a) we start out assuming that Firm A is a monopoly facing an initial demand curve $D(0)$ and associated marginal revenue curve MR(0); the marginal cost curve MC_a cuts curve MR(0) at point K, leading to an equilibrium price P_{a0}. We shift to panel (b). Firm B now enters the industry. Given the price P_{a0} of the other producer, B faces a demand curve $D(P_{a0})$ with an associated marginal revenue curve MR(P_{a0}). Its marginal cost curve MC_b cuts MR(P_{a0}) at point M. B sets a price P_{b0}. Resulting from this, A loses some of its customers, and in panel (a) its demand curve shifts to $D(P_{b0})$; its associated MR(P_{b0}) cuts curve MC_a at point L, and consequently, A sets a new price P_{a1}. Since P_{a1} is less than P_{a0}, customers now shift from B to A. In panel (b) B's demand shifts leftward to a new position $D(P_{a1})$. Its associated MR(P_{a1}) cuts MC_b at point N. B sets a new price of P_{b1}, and so on.

marginal cost curve of B at a lower point. As a result, the new price set by B is P_{b1}, which is lower than P_{b0}. This process of adjustment continues until equilibrium is reached.

The process that determines the equilibrium in the industry is illustrated in Figure 13-5. The horizontal axis represents the price of A and the vertical axis the price of B. R_a is the *reaction curve* of A. It tells the price that A will set given the price of B. R_b is the *reaction curve* of B, telling what price B will set given the price of A. As shown in Figure 13-4, if A sets a price P_{a0}, then when B enters the market, it will set a price P_{b0}. To this A will react by setting a price of P_{a1}, triggering B to set a price of P_{b1}. This process, which is also shown in Figure 13-5, will continue until equilibrium is reached at point G (Figure 13-5). At point G neither of the duopolists has an incentive to change its price: Given P_a^*, B will set a price of P_b^*; given P_b^*, A will set a price of P_a^*.[7]

---

[7]It is easy to show that if R_a and R_b are interchanged, no stable equilibrium is attainable.

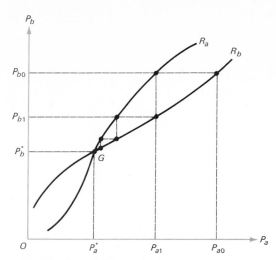

FIGURE 13-5 THE REACTION CURVES OF THE DUOPOLISTS

P_a is measured along the horizontal axis and P_b along the vertical axis. R_a is A's reaction curve. It tells what will be the price set by A given P_b. R_b is B's reaction curve. It tells what will be the price set by B given P_a. Thus, if we start with P_{a0}, as indicated by R_b, B will react by setting a price P_{b0}, but as indicated by R_a, A will react by setting P_{a1}, and as indicated by R_b, B will react by setting P_{b1}, and so on until they get to point G.

13.3d Nonprice Rivalry

As indicated before, the price of a differentiated product may be fixed in the marketplace either because of government regulation or because of other technical reasons. For example, vending machines selling a variety of brands of soft drinks would charge the same price per can of soft drink regardless of whether it is Coke, Pepsi, or Sprite. Had each producer of soft drinks attempted to sell its brand via its own vending machine at its own price, the maintenance cost would have been enormous. This type of transaction cost dictates a market structure based on nonprice rivalry among the oligopolists. Chapter 12 explained that when the product is differentiated, the individual firm can engage in product variation through advertising, packaging, and physical alterations. What follows will consider Chamberlin's model of nonprice rivalry.[8] Let us shift our attention to Figure 13-6. The price is fixed at level a $\overline{OE}$. To simplify the presentation of the theory, suppose that only two phases of the product are known to the producer, denoted X and Y. For example, X could represent no packaging (or simple packaging) and Y could represent fancy packaging; or X could represent advertising in magazines only, while Y could represent advertising both in magazines and on television. Since each phase entails a different cost of production, two distinct average cost curves are presented, one depicted by X and the other by curve

---

[8]Edward H. Chamberlin, *The Theory of Monopolistic Competition*, Harvard University Press, Boston, Mass., 1958.

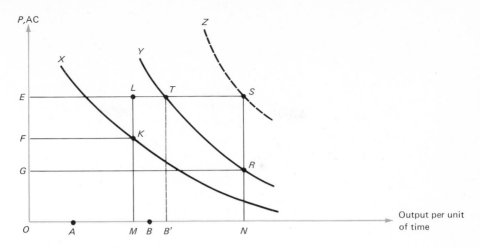

FIGURE 13-6   NONPRICE RIVALRY

$\overline{ES}$ is a price line, indicating the level of a rigid price prevailing in the market. *X, Y,* and *Z* represent average cost curves corresponding to three distinct strategies. Each strategy represents a certain advertising effort. If strategy *X* is selected, $\overline{OM}$ units are sold; the rent amounts to *EFKL*. If strategy *Y* is selected, $\overline{ON}$ units are sold and rent amounts to *EGRS.* If strategy *Z* is selected (as in the airlines example), rent is dissipated.

Y. Price line $\overline{ES}$ is not a demand curve with which the firm is confronted. How much will be demanded of each phase is determined by market conditions. Suppose we fix the market conditions and find out that if phase *X* is chosen, $\overline{OM}$ units are sold in the marketplace. The profit (economic rent) would be the quantity multiplied by the difference between the price and the average cost, namely, segment $\overline{OM}$ times segment $\overline{KL}$; this is equal to the area of rectangle *EFKL.* Suppose that if phase *Y* is chosen, $\overline{ON}$ units are produced; segment $\overline{RS}$ is the difference between the price and the average cost. Accordingly, the profit (economic rent) is the area of rectangle *EGRS.* Given the choice between the two phases, the firm should opt for phase *Y,* which yields the higher rent. If the profit depicted by area *EGRS* is sufficiently high, potential entrepreneurs may enter and establish firms in the industry. Entry of potential firms may mean a quantity smaller than $\overline{ON}$ for phase *Y* and a quantity smaller than $\overline{OM}$ for phase *X.* It is evident that if the firm can sell only $\overline{OA}$ units under phase *X* and only $\overline{OB}$ units under phase *Y,* the oligopolistic firm will discontinue production in the long run. It is very likely that in the long run the firm will end up producing $\overline{OB'}$ units as indicated by point *T,* where average cost curve *Y* intersects line $\overline{ES}$. In other words, the economic rent has completely dissipated.

13.4 THE MODEL OF A KINKED DEMAND CURVE

Before three examples of oligopoly in the United States are presented, two topics should be discussed:

1. The model of a *kinked demand curve*, which is very popular in textbooks. This topic will be covered in this section.

2. *Antitrust laws*, which make collusion among oligopolistic firms illegal. This topic will be covered in the next section.

Consider the oligopolist which believes that if it raises the price above the going market price, none of its rivals will imitate it, but if it lowers the price below the going market price, all the rivals will follow and reduce their prices. Accordingly, above the going price, the demand curve confronted by the individual oligopolist is very elastic. Below this price, it has a low elasticity. In Figure 13-7, the going market price is P_0, at which there is a kink. Above the kink, the demand curve is highly elastic. Below it, the elasticity of the demand curve is very low. The MR is smooth from point G to point L. Then, because of the kink, it falls to K and continues smoothly to H. This gives rise to price and quantity rigidities: The MC curve can shift up and down between K and L, leaving the quantity fixed at X_0 and the price at P_0. Thus this model attempts to rationalize price rigidities. There are two flaws in this model, however. First, the model implies that price rigidity coincides with quantity rigidity. In reality, this is not the case. Second, a good model of a kinked demand curve should be able to tell why the rigid price is set at one level and not another. There is nothing in the model of a kinked demand curve that explains why the kink was formed at a particular price. This model is included as part of the theory of oligopoly with the expectation that someday an economist will be able to explain why the kink occurs at a certain price P_0 rather than at any other price.

FIGURE 13-7   KINKED DEMAND CURVE

The oligopolist faces a demand curve D, which is more elastic above P_0 and less elastic below P_0. The kink occurs at output X_0 associated with P_0. As a result, at level X_0 marginal revenue curve MR falls vertically from point L to point K. Thus curve MC can shift up and down between L and K without any price fluctuation.

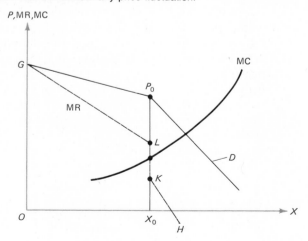

13.5 ANTITRUST LAWS

Antitrust laws are passed after the public becomes concerned that firms might either merge or organize in trusts for the common goal of restricting production to raise prices. For example, the *Sherman Antitrust Act*, passed in 1890, was designed to protect the American consumer from big mergers and trusts. Section 11.9b mentioned the case of the electrical conspiracy of the early 1960s. It was noted that the charge against electrical equipment companies was not that they constituted an oligopoly but that they fixed prices of electrical equipment. Thus it was concluded that collusion was *illegal* because of antitrust laws, and impractical because of the incentive to cheat. Given this background, the question arises: What mechanism of setting prices have American oligopolies adopted? The following sections will answer this question by discussing three oligopolies, i.e., steel, airlines, and automobiles. Attempt will also be made to answer another question: namely, why do oligopolies exist at all in some markets?

13.6 AN EXAMPLE: A HOMOGENEOUS PRODUCT—THE STEEL INDUSTRY

The oligopoly in steel production resulted from a special case of economies of scale. Stigler applied the survivor test to the steel ingots industry.[9] He found out that over the two decades from 1930 to 1951 very small firms, each with a share of less than ½ percent of the industry, declined rapidly. The one firm with more than 25 percent of the industry declined moderately. The intermediate-sized firms either grew or held their shares. The conclusion drawn from this study was that the optimum size of the firm producing steel extends over a large range of 2.5 to 25 percent of the industry capacity. This explains why moderate-sized firms coexist with giants in the steel industry. (Firms with size from ½ to 2.5 percent declined moderately. Thus it would be difficult to tell whether or not those smaller firms suffer from diseconomies of scale.)

How does a natural oligopoly like the steel industry, in which transportation costs are substantial, determine the price of its product? If collusive pricing were legal, the best procedure for the oligopoly would be to form a collusion consistent with the theory developed earlier and illustrated in Figure 13-2. Collusive pricing could be achieved by establishing a sales agency for the steel industry. The agency would establish a buying price and a selling price. The buying price would be a unique price applied to all firms, and it would be equal to $\overline{RL}$ in panel (b) of Figure 13-2. At each period, a firm would be willing to sell steel if its current marginal cost is less than or equal to the buying price. If the marginal cost of the firm is above the buying price, the firm will refuse to sell steel to the agency. This procedure would guarantee that marginal costs would tend to equalize, thus ensuring efficient allocation of resources among all producers. If the buying price is FOB mill,[10] the sales agency could refer the buyer to the firm whose distance from the buyer is the shortest. This would mean that the oligopoly as a whole satisfied the least-cost combination of factors of production, including the factors involved in transportation. Following the theory of collusion, the selling price should be fixed at a level $\overline{RS}$ in panel (b) of Figure 13-2. The agency would distribute the excessive profits at the end of a predetermined time period according to some agreed-upon key. If steel were produced by a duopoly, one firm would

---

[9]George J. Stigler, "The Economies of Scale," *Journal of Law and Economics*, vol. 1, October 1958, pp. 54–71.

[10]FOB: free on board. The term means price at the factory, not including transportation charges.

FIGURE 13-8   FOB MILL

The letters *A, B, C,* etc., represent different geographical locations. Firm I is located at *A* and firm II is located at *F*. The price that each firm must charge according to FOB mill is the mill price plus freight cost.

end up producing $\overline{EF}$ units and the other $\overline{EG}$ units [panel (*a*) of Figure 13-2]. The excessive profit to be divided among the duopolists would be $\overline{OR} \cdot \overline{LS}$.

Since collusion is illegal, the steel industry had to find more sophisticated solutions to pass the tests of antitrust legislation. Following is a discussion of these solutions:[11] Historically, the dilemma for the steel industry has been whether to adopt *FOB mill pricing* or *basing point pricing*. What is a basing point? For example, in 1920, Pittsburgh was one of a few cities that were fixed as a basing point on the map. The Pittsburgh price was fixed at $40 per ton. The price at any other point near Pittsburgh was determined by adding the freight charge to the basing point price. For example, the freight charge from Pittsburgh to Chicago was $7.60 per ton. Hence the Chicago price was fixed at $47.60. If a producer near Chicago shipped steel to Pittsburgh, that firm would have to accept a price of $40 at Pittsburgh and absorb $7.60 frieght charges; the mill revenue per ton would be $32.40. This is known as *absorbing freight cost*. On the other hand, a producer in Chicago shipping steel to a customer in Chicago had to charge $47.60. Although the actual freight charge was near zero, the official freight charge was $7.60. This is known as *phantom freight*. Following World War II, the steel industry temporarily adopted FOB mill price fixing, but during most of its history the industry has used basing point pricing. While we cannot be sure exactly how steel prices are determined in real life, a hypothesis can be presented that rationalizes why an oligopoly that produces a homogeneous product involving heavy transportation costs might prefer basing point pricing to other systems.

Consider two duopolists (I and II) and six markets (*A, B, C, D, E,* and *F*) spread evenly between geo-

graphic locations I and II. The duopolists agree to fix FOB mill at $60. The freight charge from I to *A* is $0 but then increases by $1 as we move from *A* to *B*, and so on. The freight charge from II to *F* is $0 and increases by $1 as we move from *F* to *E*, and so on. The geographic spread of the markets is illustrated in Figure 13-8. Look at Figure 13-8 and assume that the market is naturally divided between the two duopolists. I's territory covers *A, B,* and *C*; II's territory covers *F, E,* and *D*. Suppose that the demand is also equally divided between the two territories. If the duopolists do not cheat, that is, if they stick to their FOB mill of $60, their respective territories are indeed exclusive: Firm I will charge FOB mill plus freight prices of $60, $61, and $62 in markets *A, B,* and *C*. If Firm II does not cheat, it must charge prices of $65, $64, and $63 in these markets; customers will buy only from Firm I. The same argument in reverse applies to markets *F, E,* and *D*. If the demand for steel is geographically unstable, FOB mill price fixing may not work. Suppose that initially the demand was equally divided between the two territories. Later, demand shifted substantially from territory I (*A, B,* and *C*) to territory II (*F, E,* and *D*). In Stigler's words, Firm I is suffering a famine while Firm II is having a feast.[12] The incentive to cheat on the part of Firm I is substantial, and it will penetrate the territory of Firm II by freight absorption. For instance, in market *D* the price charged by Firm II is $62. To penetrate, Firm I will charge the same price of $62 per ton. It will have to subtract a freight charge of $3 from $62 and be left with an FOB mill net revenue per ton of $59. This is an absorption of $1. Similarly, if Firm I wants to penetrate market *E*, it must reduce its net FOB mill revenue per ton to $57. This freight absorption is in fact price discrimination played by Firm I in order to sur-

---

[11]George J. Stigler, "A Theory of Delivered Price Systems," *American Economic Review*, vol. 39, December 1949, pp. 1143–1159.

[12]Ibid.

vive. The reverse would occur if the demand shifted the other way from territory II to territory I. This geographic instability of the market demand causes the duopolists in a time of famine to cheat vis-à-vis freight absorption. Given this situation, the leaders of the industry need a pricing system that will fix delivered prices rather than FOB mill prices. This would allow the duopolists to penetrate faraway territories in times of famine without having to cheat. In fact, as Figure 13-9 will demonstrate, a basing point (delivered prices) system would impose a moderate penalty on territory penetration, making such penetration worthwhile only in times of famine. For simplicity of presentation, assume that A and F are the two selected basing points. The price from A to C rises linearly; the price from F to D also rises linearly. The formula used to fix the delivered prices is given by

Price at basing point + (distance between destination and basing point) · (unit shipping cost per mile) = delivered price

For simplicity of presentation, the delivered price between C and D is assumed to be $62. The solid curve in Figure 13-9 depicts the delivered prices at different points on the map. The net mill revenue of Firm I is the dashed curve. Note that in its own territory net mill revenue is $60. But penetrating to market D drives I's net mill revenue to $59, and so on. The dotted curve is the net FOB mill revenue of Firm II.

Suppose that a small number of producers are located at point A and point F, respectively. A and F then become two centers of production and basing point pricing solves the problem of territorial distribution between the centers. In each center the oligopolists might resort to nonprice rivalry that might stress such things as delivery on time and personal relationship.

How does the oligopoly set the price at the basing points? In the hypothetical example, how is the price of $60 per ton at basing points A and F determined? A likely procedure would be *price leadership*. The agreed-upon leader would set the price, and the other oligopolists would follow in lockstep.

Given the theory developed above, can we advo-

FIGURE 13-9 BASING POINT PRICING
A and F are the two basing points. Firm I is located at A and Firm II is located at F. As the solid curve shows, the delivered prices are $60, $61, $62, $62, $61, and $60 at points A, B, C, D, E, and F. The dashed curve is the net mill revenue of Firm I. The dotted curve is the net mill revenue of Firm II. The net mill revenue of Firm I declines beyond point C. The net mill revenue of Firm II declines beyond point D. The net mill revenue (per ton) is calculated by subtracting freight charges from delivered prices. We assume that the freight charge is $1 between any two adjacent points.

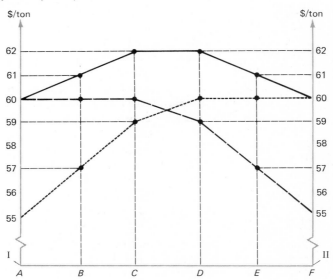

cate a policy? Toward the end of the 1950s steel prices were rising by more than 5 percent per annum. But between 1960 and 1968 steel prices hardly increased at all. This was due to import competition from Europe and Japan. Starting in 1969, after the State Department convinced the Europeans and the Japanese to accept voluntary quotas on their steel exports to the United States, imports of steel declined and prices of steel started to climb again. The lesson we learn from these observations: Free international trade will help tp keep the prices of steel down better than any form of regulation or policing.

13.7 AN EXAMPLE OF NONPRICE RIVALRY: THE AIRLINES— AN OLIGOPOLY CREATED BY THE FEDERAL GOVERNMENT

In 1938 the Civil Aeronautics Act created the Civil Aeronautics Board (CAB). The CAB, which consists of five members appointed by the President of the United States, is charged with the task of economic regulation of interstate flights. (The CAB does not regulate aviation safety, which is the responsibility of the Federal Aviation Administration.) Until 1978 the CAB's powers were mainly the following:

1. To determine whether or not an airline can serve a particular market (a pair of cities), thereby controlling entry into the industry.
2. To approve rate filings, thereby controlling rates.
3. To approve and confer antitrust immunity upon mergers and carriers agreements.
4. To administer the subsidy (Section 10.1h) program to local service airlines.

In 1938, the "big four" airlines—American, Eastern, TWA, and United—dominated the industry. Between 1938 and 1976, the services rendered by the industry increased 300-fold. Yet in 1976, the industry was dominated by the "big five" (Delta joined the industry). They provided roughly two-thirds of the domestic revenue passenger miles. Two points are worth stressing here: First, the existence of only the big four in 1938 was due to the uneven distribution of government subsidies for mail carriers before 1938. Second, there seem to be no economies of scale in the airline industries. Yet the structure of the market remained basically unchanged between 1938 and 1976, even though demand increased 300-fold: A small number of firms continued to dominate the industry, clearly showing that the airlines industry was a huge oligopoly facilitated by CAB regulation of market entry.

There is ample evidence that by exercising its entry authority the CAB preserved the industry for the airlines that existed in 1938 (except for Delta). The only competition allowed was by means of fringe groups, such as local service and supplemental carriers. This small amount of competition was allowed only after sustained congressional pressure, and it was confined to no more than 10 percent of the business. The mechanism adopted by the CAB to block the entry of new firms was extreme regulatory delay, which became de facto moratorium on competitive route applications.

In addition to controlling entry very tightly, the CAB opposed any fare competition during the period 1938–1978. Fares were established by the CAB, and various studies indicated that these fares were way above what would have been competitive fares.

There is a legend that the CAB is needed to provide transportation to small and remote towns. The legend is wrong: First, airlines that serve small cities could be subsidized under competition. Such subsidy would be no more distorting than any other subsidy (Section 10.1h). But the truth is that the CAB has generally allowed carriers to abandon unprofitable towns. Between 1948 and 1976, 294 points in the continental United States lost service by CAB-certificated carriers.

How do we know where the unregulated free market would have set prices? We can evaluate intrastate markets which were not regulated by the CAB. California and Texas furnish the data that can be used to compare regulated with unregulated fares. Pacific Southwest Airlines operates in California and Southwest Airlines operates in Texas. Table 13-6 shows the difference between the unregulated and regulated fares: It seems that competition cut prices by almost one-half. Regulatory high prices coupled with barriers to entry led the airlines to resort to nonprice competition. The airlines engaged in product differentiation and service competition. They embarked on advertising campaigns, attractively painted their aircraft, provided movies, better food, and free drinks. But most importantly, they provided more frequent flights and more convenient departure times. Indeed in Theodore Keeler's statistics relating to load

TABLE 13-6 **Comparison of One-Way Fares between Regulated Markets and Unregulated Markets in California and Texas**

Market*	Free market: Pacific Southwest Airlines†	Regulated market: CAB formula fare‡
Los Angeles–San Francisco	$25.20	$48.00
Fresno–Los Angeles	20.00	37.00
San Diego–San Francisco	31.75	60.00

Market*	Free market: Southwest Airlines§	Regulated market: certified carriers
Dallas–Houston	$15.00/25.00	$29.00
Dallas–San Antonio	15.00/25.00	41.00
Harlingen–Houston	15.00/25.00	45.00

*Only nonstop markets served by both certificated and intrastate carriers have been listed.
†*Official Airline Guide*, April 1, 1977.
‡Standard coach fare as prescribed by the CAB.
§Off-peak fare/peak fare.

factors (seats occupied divided by seats available), he has shown that for the period from 1951 to 1965 the load factor for regulated trunk airlines was 60.6 percent and for California intrastate airlines it was 71.5.[13] Keeler has also demonstrated that in the final analysis, airline regulation leads to a government-enforced cartel from which even the airlines do not benefit. The resources invested in nonprice rivalry led to a complete rent dissipation, and for the 30 years up to 1960 the airlines earned a rate of return on capital of 7.5 percent, which is roughly the same as the rate of return for the entire corporate sector (Section 5.1a). For the period 1960–1966 the rate of return for the entire corporate sector was 7.8 percent (11.7 per-

cent before taxes) and for the airlines 7.5 percent.[14]

That the airlines had a rate of return roughly equal to the average of the entire corporate sector illustrates a point that was made earlier when the theory of nonprice rivalry was discussed. When the oligopoly was established, the average cost curve of a typical airline could have been either X or Y in Figure 13-6. However, in spite of the fact that the CAB practically blocked entry to all interstate markets, the nonprice rivalry among the small number of protected airlines caused the cost of service to rise, leading to an upward shfit in the average cost curve until it reached level Z, which cut the price line at point S, thus leaving no profit (economic rent) to the airlines.

13.8 AN EXAMPLE OF A DIFFERENTIATED PRODUCT AND FLEXIBLE PRICES: THE CAR INDUSTRY

Today there are only four car makers in the United States, of which only three are major producers, and one of the three cannot survive without governmental support. Until the early 1970s, we could view the American market as independent of the European and Japanese markets. American producers specialized in relatively large cars, while the Europeans and the Japanese specialized in compact cars. Thus

---

[13]Theodore E. Keeler, "Airline Regulation and Market Performance," *The Bell Journal of Economics and Management Science*, vol. 3, autumn 1972, pp. 399–424.
[14]Ibid.

TABLE 13-7 **Survivor Test: The Car Industry, 1950–1974, Percentage of Total Domestic Production**

	1950	1960	1974
General Motors (GM)	45.9	47.7	48.9
Ford	23.6	28.2	30.1
Chrysler	18.0	15.2	16.1
American Motors Corp. (AMC)	5.0	7.2	4.8
Studebaker-Packard	5.1	1.6	
Willys Motors	2.3		
Crosley	0.1		
Checker Cab	*	0.1	0.1

*Less than 0.1 percent.

Source: Calculated from manufacturers' unit production data reported in Motor Vehicle Manufacturers Association of the U.S., Inc., *Automobiles Facts and Figures*, 1975 edition.

we were justified in viewing the American car oligopoly separately from the foreign car makers. After the early 1970s, particularly following the dramatic raising of oil prices by OPEC, the increasing interest of the American consumer in compact cars opened the American markets for European and Japanese car manufacturers. Consequently, today one can talk about the world oligopoly of car producers. What follows will focus on the American oligopoly up to 1974. We note, however, that presently the world oligopoly of cars has a similar structure: A relatively small number of car producers dominate the market; the commodity is differentiated and prices are flexible.

The car industry is a typical example of an oligopoly engaged in the production of a differentiated product. It appears that the reason for the presence of such a small number of producers is economies of scale. Stigler applied the survivor test to the car industry. In the period between 1936 and 1955, Stigler reports that the share of General Motors in the market for passenger automobiles increased from 42.9 to 50.2 percent. The share of Chrysler declined from 23.6 to 17.2 percent. The share of Ford increased from 22.6 to 28.2 percent. Other car makers such as Hudson, Nash, Kaiser, Willys-Overland, Packard, and Studebaker did not survive at all. Some had to merge with other firms, and others simply vanished.[15]

Investigating a more recent period, 1950–1974, we observe again that small firms could not survive for longer than a few years (Table 13-7).

Table 13-7 clearly shows that economies of scale are very significant. Studebaker-Packard, Willys Motors, and Crosley did not survive. It seems that because the fixed cost of machinery is huge, a new entrant must quickly grab a relatively huge share of the market if it is to succeed. The lesson we learn from examining the data of American Motors Corporation (AMC) is that the minimum scale needed for survival is 5 percent of the market. The survival of Checker Cab must be explained by the fact that cabs are significantly different from regular cars, and General Motors (GM), Ford, or Chrysler cannot easily stretch their equipment to produce cabs.

The survivor test is corroborated by a closer look at the process of production. John McGee investigated the engineering and economic aspects of automobile body manufacturing.[16] McGee reports that most automobile body parts are made by *stamping*, which means pressing a sheet of metal into a desired shape between two matted dies under heavy load. Steel and cast-iron body dies are expected to provide more than a million first-class parts. When the lifetime of a die is over, it is relatively less expensive to duplicate the old die rather than to design a new die. Moreover, by attaching *stretch inserts* to existing dies, different parts can be produced by using the same dies. In order to produce a new model, a car manufacturer does not need to invest in a new line of dies. First, the manufacturer can use many dies of the old model in production of the new

---

[15]Stigler, op. cit.

[16]John S. McGee, "Economies of Size in Auto Body Manufacture," *Journal of Law and Economics*, vol. 16, October 1973, pp. 239–274.

model. Second, it can use stretch inserts to produce a new variety of parts. Thus it would be much cheaper for an existing car manufacturer to introduce a new model based on an older one than for a new entrant to produce a new car based on a completely new design.

Let us elaborate further on the issue of scale economies in the production of cars. Consider the following hypothetical problem: In a certain country, given a certain price, consumers would buy a million cars per year. Suppose that stamping equipment for parts costs $100 million. The dies are good for a million parts. Take two extreme cases: First, 10 manufacturers could each produce 100,000 cars per year using the same equipment for 10 years. Second, one manufacturer could produce a million cars per year and retool at the end of each year. Assume that the cost of capital is the only fixed cost involved. We can see that the average fixed cost of producing a million cars a year is significantly less than the average fixed cost of producing 100,000 cars a year. Chapter 16 will derive a formula of calculating the cost of capital. For the time being we shall be satisfied with an intuitive explanation. Assume that the interest rate is 5 percent. A single firm that sells a million cars per year and retools at the end of each year spends $100 million on the equipment and forgoes $5 million on interest that could have been earned alternatively elsewhere in the economy. Its total fixed cost is $105 million. The average fixed cost is $105 as follows:

$$\$105 = \frac{\$105 \text{ million}}{1 \text{ million cars}}$$

If 10 firms are each producing 100,000 cars, the cost of capital is a bit more difficult to calculate: First, there is the interest forgone, which is the same $5 million per annum. But in addition, the firm must put aside a certain amount of money at the end of each year such that at the end of the economic lifetime of the equipment (10 years in the example) a sufficient amount of money will have accumulated to purchase the identical equipment. Such an amount of money should be equal to $7.95 million. Without understanding how this is calculated (see Chapter 16), you can check that if the first allocation of $7.95 million grows at 5 percent for 9 years, the second allocation of $7.95 million grows at 5 percent for 8 years, and so on up to the last allocation at the end of the tenth year. All these allocations aggregated will amount to $100 million. The average fixed cost is calculated as follows:

$$\$129.5 = \frac{\$7.95 \text{ million} + \$5 \text{ million}}{100,000 \text{ cars}}$$

Thus the advantage of a large-scale production of 1 million cars versus a small-scale production of 100,000 cars is $29.5 per $100.

The above hypothetical exercise illustrates another interesting fact. Consider a remote country with a limited market for only 100,000 cars per annum. Would it pay to establish a car factory in that country instead of importing from a car manufacturer abroad? The answer depends on the cost of shipping. In the example, if the cost of shipping a car is in excess of $24.5 (= $129.5 − $105), then a factory that produces 1 million cars over a period of 10 years could survive. This analysis would be correct under the assumption that consumers in the relatively small country do not care for a change of model every year. Volvo in Sweden exemplifies the survival of a car manufacturer producing a relatively small number of cars.

So far we have explained how economies of scale resulted in oligopoly in the car industry. How are prices of cars determined, given a differentiated commodity and price flexibility? Our best conjecture is that the car industry follows the model in Figure 13-5. Each oligopolist adopts a selling strategy and then determines its price by approaching point G in Figure 13-5 through a process of trial and error. The student is cautioned that setting prices is not the main concern of car producers: An error in setting the price of a certain model can be corrected with relative ease. However, an error in a (nonprice) strategy may be very costly. In the late 1970s, Chrysler failed to read some important messages transmitted by its hundreds of dealers all over the United States. Had the federal government not come to the rescue, Chrysler would have gone the way of Studebaker-Packard, Willys Motors, and Crosley.

Some laypeople and policy makers occasionally advocate breaking down giant car producers into many small firms to enhance competition. Professionally, this is known as *dissolution*. But dissolution may lead to results less attractive then the current situation. Consider Figure 13-10. Assume that GM faces a demand curve as depicted by D. The marginal revenue curve associated with D is denoted by MR. At point A the marginal cost curve of GM (MC) cuts the MR curve. Price is P_0 and quantity is X_0. Stockholders reap an economic rent as depicted by the shaded area. This shaded area is returns due to

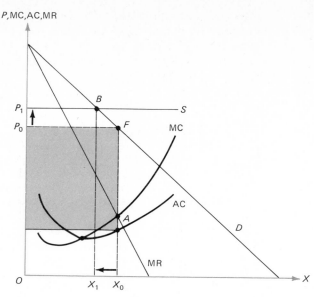

FIGURE 13-10   DISSOLUTION

The giant car manufacturer faces demand curve D. Its associated marginal revenue curve is MR. The average cost curve and marginal cost curve are AC and MC, respectively. MC intersects MR at point A; hence the car manufacturer sells X_0 cars per year at a price P_0. The rent of the stockholders is represented by the area of the shaded rectangle. Dissolution would lead to a situation of having many small firms, each with a much higher AC curve compared with the AC curve in the diagram. We assume that the supply curve of the many small firms is the horizontal line denoted by S. Its level is determined by the minimum of the AC curves of the small firms. It cuts the demand curve at B: As a result consumers pay a higher price P_1 and lose $P_1 P_0 FB$ of their initial consumer's surplus. Producers lose the entire shaded area.

the oligopolistic position of GM. Now, suppose that GM were forced to dissolve itself into many small firms. As illustrated in the hypothetical example, the new small firms will have to stretch fixed capital over a longer time period, causing average cost curves to shift upward. (In the example, dissolving one large firm into 10 small firms resulted in the average fixed cost rising by 29.5 percent.) In Figure 13-10 we assume that the many small firms will produce at their minimum average cost curve (AC). Thus we assume that the supply curve of the small firms is a horizontal line depicted by S (Section 10.4). The vertical distance of S from the horizontal axis measures the

minimum of the AC curve of a small car manufacturer. In the example the supply curve of the small firms cuts the demand curve at point B. Under such conditions consumers would pay a higher price of P_1 and purchase a smaller quantity of X_1. The rent to producers, the shaded area, would be completely dissipated. The consumer's surplus would decline by the area $P_1 P_0 FB$. Of course, theoretically, it is possible that horizontal line S will cut the demand curve at a point lower than F. But given the huge economies of scale in the car industry, the odds are against such a possibility.

SUMMARY   The chapter began by explaining the meaning of *concentration ratios* that are used to classify oligopolies and also to provide a boundary between oligopolies on one end and perfect and imperfect competition on the other end. The next step was to discuss *barriers to entry*. It was concluded that the most prevalent barrier to entering an industry is scale economies. Other barriers to entry could result from control of a natural resource by a few firms, ownership of a patent, or licensing requirements. A few studies were mentioned that indicate that highly concentrated industries do not necessarily benefit from significant economic rents (profits). The reasons for this could be either that barriers to entry are not too high and thus the incumbents charge prices that are nearly competitive to weaken the appetite of potential entrants, or that rent is completely dissipated in the process of nonprice rivalry.

Next, some theories of price determination under oligopoly were discussed. The theory of collusion might be tried if the good is homogeneous and collusion is legal. Theoretically, collusion would mean determining the total output of the industry at the point where the sum of all the MC curves of all the oligopolists intersects the marginal revenue curve associated with the market demand curve. There are two solutions for an oligopoly producing a differentiated product. In the first solution, prices are flexible and each individual firm maximizes its profit using the prices of other firms as parameters. This idea was translated into *reaction curves*. Equilibrium was achieved where the reaction curves intersected. In the second solution, price was somehow fixed and sharing the market was determined by *nonprice rivalry*. In both solutions, it was noted that since the good is assumed to be differentiated, firms resort to intensive advertising, as in monopolistic competition.

The model of a *kinked demand curve* was mentioned as an incomplete theory: No one has been able to show how to determine the price where the kink occurs. Why does the price become rigid at one level rather than another? The theory was accompanied by three major illustrations. First, we looked at the steel industry in which oligopoly resulted from increasing returns to scale and a wide range of constant returns to scale. It was conjectured that the steel industry has been following a model of setting prices sometimes according to *FOB mill* and at other times according to *basing points*. It was noted that industries producing a homogeneous product that is costly to ship tend to follow similar patterns of price setting. Second, we examined the airlines industry from 1938 to 1978. The airlines oligopoly was created and protected by the federal government. Its oligopolistic prices were determined by the Civil Aeronautics Board (CAB). However, rents in this oligopoly were dissipated because of heavy expenses involved in nonprice rivalry. Third, we looked at the car industry and noted that oligopoly resulted from huge economies of scale. It was conjectured that the car industry followed the model of flexible prices (reaction curves) in price setting. Finally, dissolution was analyzed as an option for the car industry. It was concluded that consumers might end up losing from dissolution of large corporations.

GLOSSARY **Oligopoly** A market situation in which production is dominated entirely, or almost entirely, by a small number of firms.

Concentration ratio The share of the four largest firms in total output.

Herfindahl measure of concentration The sum of the squares of the shares of the firms. Share is defined as the production of the firm divided by total output of the industry.

Cournot model A model of oligopoly based on the assumption that each oligopolist treats the amounts produced by rivals as parameters.

Extended Lerner's formula (Stigler's formula) $(P - MC)/P = -1/n\eta$, where n is the number of rivals (Cournot) and η is price elasticity of market demand.

Barriers to entry Factors such as scale economies, ownership of a patent, or legal requirements which make it difficult for more than a small number of firms to survive in a specific industry.

Collusion An agreement by the oligopolistic firms to fix a price at a level that would be consistent with monopolistic pricing. Technically, such a price should be associated with the aggregate level of output, where the sum of all MC curves intersects with curve MR associated with the market demand curve.

Reaction curve In case of duopolists A and B, the reaction curve of A tells what price A will charge, given a price of B. In other words, A perceives the price of B as a parameter, and B perceives the price of A as a parameter.

Nonprice rivalry Sometimes, when the price of a differentiated good is fixed by some mechanism, the oligopolists compete for market shares through intensive advertising. This is known as nonprice rivalry.

Kinked demand curve A demand curve that has a kink at a certain point. The segment of the demand curve above the kink is more elastic than the segment below the kink.

Antitrust laws Laws that make mergers, trusts, and collusion illegal.

FOB mill pricing Price at the factory, not including transportation charges.

Basing point pricing A certain center of production is determined as the *basing point*. Prices in the neighborhood of the basing point are determined by adding transportation cost per unit to the basing point price.

Absorbing freight cost Delivered price minus the freight cost. This term is used when a firm encourages sales in faraway territories by absorbing the cost of freight.

Phantom freight If a producer is located at some point other than the basing point and sells the product to a next-door neighbor, the official delivered price includes freight cost although freight is zero or near zero. This freight cost is known as phantom freight.

Price leader The firm in oligopoly assigned the role of determining the price for the entire industry. If collusion is illegal, the nonleaders will follow the leader in lockstep.

Dissolution Dissolving a large corporation into small-sized firms.

PROBLEMS An asterisk indicates an advanced problem.

13-1.   The concentration ratio may not reflect merger. The H measure always reflects merger. Explain why.

13-2. Consider a case of duopoly. Show that price leadership (one rival determines the price; the other is a price taker) is better for society than collusion (Section 11.6a).

13-3. If oligopoly arises because of economies of scale, dissolution is undesirable. Explain.

13-4. Explain why the degree of barriers to entry is better correlated with the rate of return than with the concentration ratio.

13-5. Some people say that legal protection for patent holders should be abolished. They say this will enhance competition in the drug industry, for example. Would you go along with this view? Why or why not?

13-6. How would the steel industry change if the federal government legalized collusion and eliminated all barriers to international trade (especially with Japan and Europe)?

13-7. Airlines did not benefit from deregulation, but consumers did. Comment.

13-8. Do you think the government could induce the car industry to emulate perfect competition by subsidizing and taxing it simultaneously?

13-9.* The market for a homogeneous product is entirely dominated by three oligopolists. The industry is described by the following table:

Market demand curve			Producer (1)		Producer (2)		Producer (3)	
X	P	MR	MC_1	TVC_1	MC_2	TVC_2	MC_3	TVC_3
1	20	20	1	1	3	3	5.5	5.5
2	19	18	3	4	5	8	5.5	11.0
3	18	16	5	9	7	15	5.5	16.5
4	17	14	7	16	9	24	5.5	22.0
5	16	12	9	25	11	35	5.5	27.5
6	15	10	11	36	13	48	5.5	33.0
7	14	8	13	49	15	63	5.5	38.5
8	13	6	15	64	17	80	5.5	44.0
9	12	4	17	81	19	99	5.5	49.5

Assume that only whole units can be produced. (a) How many units should each firm produce under collusion? Assume that none of the firms incurs fixed costs. (b) How many units should each firm produce if $FC_1 = \$10$, $FC_2 = \$10$, and $FC_3 = \$20$? Assume that the fixed costs (FC) are avoidable (Section 7.2h).

MATHEMATICAL APPENDIX 13

This mathematical appendix derives the extended Lerner formula (Stigler's formula) and then proceeds to the famous theoretical models of oligopoly based on different modes of behavior.

M13.1 THE EXTENDED LERNER FORMULA (Due to Stigler; see text)

We assume that there are n rivals each producing x_i units of output per unit of time. Since the rivals have identical production functions, we can write that

$$X = \sum_{i}^{n} x_i \text{ and } x_i = X/n, \text{ where } i = 1, 2, \ldots, n.$$

Since price is a funtion of total output, namely, $P = f(X)$, we can write

$$P = f(x_1 + x_2 + \cdots + x_n) \tag{m13-1}$$

Revenue of the ith producer is expressed as $R_i = P \cdot x_i$. Hence the marginal revenue of the ith firm (MR_i) is

$$MR_i = \frac{d(P \cdot x_i)}{dx_i} = P + x_i \frac{dP}{dX}$$

since $(dX/dx_i) = 1$.

The single firm must equate its MR_i with MC in order to maximize profit; this implies

$$P + x_i \frac{dP}{dX} = MC$$

If we multiply the above equation by (the number of firms) n, we get

$$nP + nx_i \frac{dP}{dX} = nMC$$

Since $nx_i = X$, we can, by substituting, rearranging, and dividing both sides by nP, obtain

$$\frac{P - MC}{P} = \frac{-1}{n\eta} \tag{m13-2}$$

M13.2 THEORETICAL MODELS OF OLIGOPOLY

In most textbooks the theoretical models are presented in the text. Only models that can shed light on real life were presented in the text here. Note, however, that two of the basic models to be discussed soon were presented geometrically in the text. For example, the model of *price leadership* was presented in Section 11.6. The model of *collusion* was presented in Section 13.3a. The *Cournot* model was mentioned in conjunction with the extended Lerner's formula (Stigler). This section will present the *Cournot*, *price leadership*, *collusion*, and *market sharing* models by examining numeric examples.

A. A Homogeneous Product

Unlike competition or monopolistic competition, in oligopoly each producer must take into account the acts of other producers. In oligopoly, various models based on various modes of behavior are possible. In the case of a homogeneous product, the following are the most important models:

1. *Cournot.* The Cournot model (named after the French economist Augustin Cournot) assumes that each producer treats as parameters the quantities produced by other producers. Accordingly, differentiating its own profit function with respect to its own output and setting the derivative equal to zero, each producer ends up with a *reaction function* in which the outputs of other producers are the independent variables and its own output is the dependent variable.

2. *Price leadership.* There are n oligopolists; $n - 1$ oligopolists agree to sell their output at whatever price is set by the nth firm. Here, $n - 1$ firms are the *price followers* and the nth firm is the *price leader*. It is clear that $n - 1$ followers behave like competitive firms. To maximize their profit, they equate their marginal costs with the price established by the leader. See Section 11.6a.

3. *Collusion.* The oligopolists agree to form a management whose goal is profit maximization for the industry as a whole. Since the collusion yields the highest possible aggregate profit, each producer can earn at least as much as it did prior to the establishment of the collusion. Formally, collusion is identical with the case of a multiple-plant monopoly. See Section 13.3a.

The mathematics is easy but very lengthy; what follows is an example of three cost functions of three oligopolists and a market demand function. The reader is asked to verify that the answers provided in the summary tables are correct. Recall that the commodity is homogeneous and the price is uniform.

The example is:

$$\text{Demand: } P = 200 - X$$

Producer	Cost function	
1	$C_1 = 0.5x_1^2$	
2	$C_2 = x_2^2$	
3	$C_3 = 10x_3$	(m13-3)

$$X = x_1 + x_2 + x_3$$

The results are summarized as follows:

Summary of Profits (Dollars)

Firm	Cournot	Price leadership	Collusion
		Mode of behavior	
1	2059.80	1012.50	
2	1220.68	506.25	
3	4110.73	3062.50*	
Total	7391.21	4581.25	9100

*Leader.

Summary of Quantities and Prices

	Cournot	Price leadership	Collusion
		Mode of behavior	
Price, $	74.11	45	105
Quantity	125.89	155	95

B. A Heterogeneous Product

In the case of a differentiated product, each oligopolist is confronted by a separate demand curve. The position of the demand curve confronting each producer is affected by the quantities sold by the other firms. The models discussed here are the Cournot and collusion models, plus a new model known as *market shares*. In the market shares model, all firms but one maintain a fixed share of total output regardless of the price they secure in the market. In the following example we assume that Firm 2 maintains a share of one-third of total output and Firm 3 maintains a share of one-fifth of total output. In other words, if X is total output, $x_2 = 1/3X$ and $x_3 = 1/5X$.

The example is:

Firm	Demand function	Cost function	
1	$P_1 = 100 - 2x_1 - x_2 - x_3$	$C_1 = 0.5x_1^2$	
2	$P_2 = 100 - x_1 - 2x_2 - x_3$	$C_2 = x_2^2$	(m13-4)
3	$P_3 = 100 - x_1 - x_2 - 2x_3$	$C_3 = 10x_3$	

The results, which the reader is asked to verify, are:

Summary of Profits (Dollars)

Firm	Cournot	Market shares	Collusion
		Mode of behavior	
1	524.61	686.27	579.00
2	402.87	499.80	434.09
3	510.72	321.75	556.65
Total	1438.20	1507.82	1569.74

Summary of Quantities and Prices

Firm	Cournot		Market shares		Collusion	
	x	P	x	P	x	P
1	14.49	$43.45	13.72	$56.88	11.58	$55.79
2	11.59	46.35	9.80	60.80	8.68	58.69
3	15.98	41.98	5.88	64.72	12.37	55.00
Total x	42.06		29.40		32.63	
Average P		$43.69		$59.75		$56.26

PART FIVE

DISTRIBUTION THEORY: PRICING OF FACTORS OF PRODUCTION

The following three chapters are concerned with the theory of the market for factors of production, which differs completely from the microtheory covered so far. Refer to Figure I-2. Note that in the market for finished goods (upper box) households are the demanders and firms are the suppliers. In the market for factors of production (lower box) the roles are switched: Households are the suppliers of the factors of production and firms are the demanders. Households supply labor as well as services rendered by capital, land, and other natural resources that they own. The role reversal between households and firms (or to use earlier terms, between consumers and producers) requires a new theory of demand, which is derived from the behavior of the firm.

Chapter 14 will discuss the theory of the demand for inputs, the supply of inputs, and some special problems related to input markets.

Chapter 15 will discuss labor. Labor is a unique factor of production, for two reasons: First, returns to labor account for more than half of the gross national product in the United States. Second, since the abolition of slavery, owners of labor and labor services have been united. The fact that the owner and the input owned are one entity raises special problems, as does the presence of labor unions and trade associations.

Previous chapters mentioned the importance of capital in human history (Section 5.1a). In the very early stages of human history, people used their own power (*labor*) and *natural resources* (water and land) in the process of production. Civilization started when people began to produce *capital*, say, in the form of bows and arrows. Even in its most primitive form, accumulating capital always meant sacrificing present consumption for the sake of future consumption; to make a bow and arrows, a person had to give up immediate tasks such as gathering and hunting in order to hunt more efficiently in the future. In modern economics, abstinence from present consumption for the sake of future consumption is known as *saving*. Producing factors of production that are nonhuman, such as machinery and structures, is known as *investment*. Savers are not necessarily investors. Savers may lend their money to investors who later pay them a *rate of interest* in return for agreeing to sacrifice present consumption for future consumption. These issues of saving, investment, and capital formation will be discussed in Chapter 16.

Natural resources are inputs of singular concern in a modern economy. Thus Chapter 14 will analyze *water rights* and the issue of *commonality*, e.g., fishing grounds. Chapter 16 will examine intertemporal pricing of exhaustible natural resources, e.g., crude oil. Fast-rising demands for water in the Southwest and escalating prices of crude oil in the 1970s have brought these issues to the frontier of economic analysis.

C H A P T E R

14

DEMAND AND SUPPLY OF INPUTS

447

The demand curve for a factor of production tells how many units of the factor will be employed by a firm or an industry given different prices of the factor in the marketplace. Intuitively we feel that, like the demand curve for goods, the demand curve for an input should be negatively sloped. Intuition, however, is insufficient for providing a useful theory of demand for inputs. We need a theory that will tell us under what conditions the demand for labor is going to be very elastic, in contrast to conditions under which the demand for labor will be very inelastic. We need a theory that will tell us how the demand for capital will change as a result of a rise in the price of energy in the production of shoes. We need a theory that will tell us whether or not farm labor will benefit from an agronomic innovation or from a subsidy on fertilizers.

The following steps will be taken to develop the theory of *demand and supply of factors*, known also as the *theory of distribution*. First, the theory of demand for an input by a single competitive firm will be developed; it will be extended later to an industry in perfect competition. Parallel to the theory of the consumer (Section 2.4g), the change in the quantity demanded for a factor of production will be divided into the *substitution effect* and the *expansion effect*. The supply of an input confronting an entire industry will then be discussed.

The previous three chapters discussed imperfect market structures. Although monopolies, oligopolies, and firms in monopolistic competition are normally price takers in input markets, their demand curves for inputs are slightly different from the demand of competitive firms. Accordingly, the theory of the demand for an input by monopolistic firms (firms facing negatively sloping demand curves for their output) will be adjusted to account for their power in the market, whether minute or significant.

By and large, firms purchase inputs in competitive markets. Put another way, firms are primarily price takers in the factor markets. Yet there are some insignificant cases in which a single firm may wield power in a local market for a factor of production. An example would be the only hospital in a small city that is the sole employer of nurses. A whole section will be devoted to this topic, known as *monopsony*.

Natural resources play a large role in modern economics. Accordingly, at the end of the chapter the example of water rights and the issue of commonality, e.g., fishing, will be presented.

14.1 THE DEMAND FOR AN INPUT BY A COMPETITIVE INDUSTRY

This section derives the demand curve for an input in perfect competition. First, a single firm isolated from the rest of the industry and employing only one variable input is considered. Second, the assumption that only one input is variable is relaxed and the demand curve is derived for an input where at least one other factor of production is variable. Third, the assumption that the firm is isolated from the rest of the industry is relaxed and the aggregate demand curve for an input is considered as a sum of all demand curves by all firms in the industry.

14.1a A Single Firm and a Single Variable Factor

Consider a competitive firm. For simplicity, its production function, as previously defined by Equation 5-1, is

$$X = f(A, B) \tag{14-1}$$

where B is assumed to be held constant, A is the variable factor of production, and X is output. Recall from Section 5.2d that the marginal physical product of an input is the change in total production over a small change in the variable input. Or, put differently, it is the extra output added by employing one extra unit of the variable input. Marginal physical product of factor A was denoted by MP_a (Section 5.2d) and written formally (Equation 5-3) as

$$MP_a = \frac{\Delta X}{\Delta A} \tag{14-2}$$

where ΔX is the small change in output and ΔA is the small changes in the variable input. Chapter 6 defined marginal cost as the additional (variable) cost divided by the additional output with which it is associated. Accordingly, we saw that if it takes ΔA additional units of input A to increase output by ΔX units of output X, the marginal cost is extra cost divided by extra output: $(P_a \cdot \Delta A)/(\Delta X)$. Note that because the firm is very small and has no influence on the price of A, we can assume that it is confronted with a horizontal supply curve of factor A, which can be drawn (Figure 14-1) at the level of P_a. (The introduction to this chapter mentioned that a firm may be the sole buyer of an input, for example, the only hospital in a small city hiring nurses. Such a firm would be known as a *monopsony* and would face a positively sloping supply of the variable input. The flatness of the supply curve of the input confronting the single firm, in fact, means that the firm has no *monopsonistic* power in the factor market: It is a price taker.) Formally, the marginal cost MC is written (Equation 6-10) as

$$MC = \frac{P_a}{MP_a} \tag{14-3}$$

Chapter 7 discussed the process of the profit maximization of the competitive firm. Two important conclusions were reached: First, since the competitive firm is a price taker, its marginal revenue curve is identical with the demand curve confronting it. Such a curve can be drawn at the level of the price of output, denoted by P_x [panel (*b*) of Figure 7-2]. Second, we have seen that maximum profit occurs where marginal revenue equals marginal cost (Section 7.2c). But because marginal revenue is identical with price of output in competition, using Equation 14-3, we obtain

$$\frac{P_a}{MP_a} = P_x \tag{14-4}$$

Equation 14-4, which specifies the condition for profit maximization in competition, can be rearranged (by multiplying both sides by MP_a) to yield

$$P_a = MP_a \cdot P_x \tag{14-5}$$

Notice that in Equation 14-5 the condition for profit maximization is the same as in Equation 14-4, except that the focus has switched from equating MC with P_x to equating P_a with a new term $MP_a \cdot P_x$. That term is, intuitively, the value of the additional output sold in the market, resulting from the fact that one additional unit of input A was added to the process of production. Formally, this new term is called the *value of the marginal physical product*. It is defined as follows:

The value of the marginal physical product is equal to the marginal physical product of the variable input (MP_a) times the price of output (P_x). It is denoted by VMP. In summary,

$$VMP_a = MP_a \cdot P_x \tag{14-6}$$

The competitive firm maximizes its profit when the price of final output is equal to its MC. If we focus on the variable input, we can say that maximization of profit occurs when the price of the variable input is equal to its VMP, as stated by Equation 14-5. In Chapter 7 profit attained its maximum level geometrically where price cut the MC curve. (For example, see Figure 7-4.) What follows will describe the geometry of profit maximization when the focus is on the variable input. Section 5.3b discussed the MP_a curve given the production function $X = f(A, B)$ and given that B is held constant. Figure 5-8 illustrates how MP_a rises from zero to a level of A_1 units of A and thereafter falls until it vanishes at a level of A_3 units of A. If the firm were to employ more than A_3, units of A per unit of time, marginal physical product of A would be negative, as in the case of a big tractor cultivating a too small field of wheat. The reader is reminded that only domain $\overline{A_2 A_3}$ (Figure 5-8) is of interest to the firm. As explained in Section 7.2h, producing a level of output associated with employing A in the domain extending from the origin to A_2 would be inferior to hiring zero units of A. MP_a as shown in panel (b) of Figure 5-8 is redrawn in Figure 14-1; the irrelevant portion is indicated by a dashed line. In the future the irrelevant portion of the MP and its associated VMP curves will be completely ignored. The VMP_a curve is drawn by vertically measuring $P_x \cdot MP_a$ rather than MP_a. For example, if P_x is $2, VMP_a occupies a position twice as high as MP_a. If the price of input A is currently P_{a0}, the firm will maximize its profit by employing A_0 units of A, where the price line denoted by S_0 cuts the VMP_a curve (point H). The intersection of price line S_0 with the VMP_a curve guarantees that Equation 14-5 (and also Equation 14-4) is satisfied. At levels of employment smaller than A_0, VMP_a exceeds P_{a0}. Thus it pays the firm to expand by employing more units of A per unit of time; the gain is $VMP_a - P_{a0}$ dollars per unit of A added to the process of production. At levels of employment greater than A_0, it pays the firm to contract by employing fewer units of A. The reasons are symmetrical. As mentioned before, S_0 is the supply curve of the factor with which the competitive firm is confronted.

We shall now see that the VMP curve is the demand curve of the competitive firm for a factor. In Section 8.3a it was concluded that the MC curve shifts in the same direction as the change in the price of the variable factor of production. Thus a decline in the price of A would lead to a downward shift

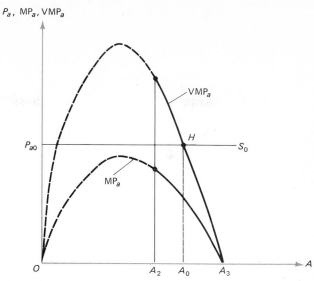

FIGURE 14-1 OPTIMAL FACTOR EMPLOYMENT

The marginal physical product curve is denoted by MP_a. If we assume that the price of output P_x is \$2, the value of the marginal physical product curve denoted by VMP_a is obtained by multiplying values of MP_a by 2. Assuming that the price of input A is P_{a0}, the supply of A confronting the competitive firm is S_0, which cuts the vertical axis at a level P_{a0}. S_0 cuts the VMP_a curve at point H, and hence A_0 units of A are employed per unit of time.

in MC and an expansion of output. Let us turn to the variable input. In Figure 14-2, as the price of A falls from P_{a0} to P_{a1}, the price line (supply) of A falls from S_0 to S_1. The intersection point falls from point H to point K. The firm increases the use of A from A_0 to A_1. We can generalize this finding with the following definition:

> *The VMP curve tells how many units of the variable input the firm will use at a given price of the variable input. The VMP curve is thus identical with the demand curve for the variable factor.*

In summary, we can say that the demand curve for a factor is negatively sloped because of the law of diminishing marginal physical product (Section 5.3b). A later section will show that when an entire industry is considered, the change in P_x also contributes to the negative slope of the demand for the factor.

Suppose you are the manager of a plant. You employ labor and capital denoted by A and B, respectively, in the production of whatnots, denoted by X. The engineer tells you that your production function is $X = \sqrt{A \cdot B}$, as in Equation 5-2. Suppose in the short run you are stuck with 10 units of capital. You now want to derive the VMP_a schedule under the assumption that whatnots sell in the marketplace for \$2 a unit. To simplify the process, assume that you can apply only whole units of A to the process of produc-

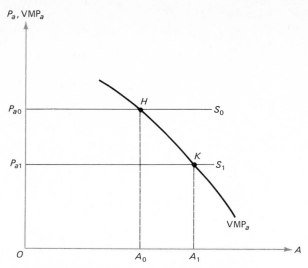

FIGURE 14-2 THE VMP CURVE IS THE DEMAND CURVE FOR INPUT A
The value of the marginal physical product of input A is depicted by the curve denoted by VMP_a. If the price of A in the marketplace is P_{a0}, the firm will face the horizontal supply curve S_0; this supply curve will cut the VMP_a curve at point H, and the firm will employ A_0 units of A. If the price of A drops to a lower level of P_{a1}, the firm will face a horizontal supply curve denoted by S_1; this supply curve will cut the VMP_a curve at point K and the firm will employ A_1 units of A per unit of time. This proves that points (like H and K) on the VMP_a curve constitute the demand curve for input A.

tion.[1] In Table 14-1 you vary the amount of A employed per unit of time from zero to 8 units of labor; in the second column you record the level of output by employing the above production function; in the third column you calculate the MP of labor (MP_a) by taking the first differences of column 2 ($1.31 = 4.47 - 3.16$) and recalling that $\Delta A = 1(1 = 2 - 1)$; in the fourth column you calculate the value of the marginal physical product of labor (VMP_a) by multiplying the MP_a in the third column by \$2. ($2.62 = 2 \cdot 1.31$.) Given Table 14-1, and given a price of labor of \$1.55, you would employ 4 units of labor. Since you can employ only whole units, it would not pay you to employ the fifth unit: It will yield an additional revenue of only \$1.50 and cost you \$1.55, a marginal loss of \$0.05.

14.1b A Single Firm and Two (or More) Variable Factors

The analysis will now be extended to the case in which there are at least two variable factors of production. To avoid the theorietical complexity arising

---

[1]If the assumption (in Table 14-1) that only whole units can be produced is relaxed, the results are slightly different. While the additional output from adding the fifth unit of labor is 0.75, when $A = 4$ and $B = 10$, the marginal physical product of labor (MP_a) is actually 0.79 for a very small ΔA: $X_0 = \sqrt{4 \cdot 10} = 6.3245$, $X_1 = \sqrt{4.1 \cdot 10} = 6.4031$. Hence,

$$MP_a = \frac{6.4031 - 6.3245}{4.1 - 4} = 0.79$$

TABLE 14-1   **Deriving VMP$_a$ for**
$X = \sqrt{A \cdot B}$, B = 10 units,
P_x = \$2

A	X	MP$_a$	VMP$_a$
1	3.16	3.16	6.32
2	4.47	1.31	2.62
3	5.48	1.01	2.02
4	6.32	0.84	1.68
5	7.07	0.75	1.50
6	7.75	0.68	1.36
7	8.37	0.62	1.24
8	8.94	0.57	1.14

from the case where all inputs are variable and the production function obeys constant returns to scale,[2] we assume that the production function is of the form

$$X = f(A, B, H) \tag{14-7}$$

where H is the fixed factor.

In Chapter 6 we saw that for two inputs to satisfy the least-cost combination criterion, the following must hold (Equation 6-15):

$$MC = \frac{P_a}{MP_a} = \frac{P_b}{MP_b} \tag{14-8}$$

Similar to deriving Equation 14-5 from 14-4, two conditions are derived that must be satisfied to achieve maximum profit. Since in perfect competition (prevailing in both input and output markets) the condition for profit maximization is $P_x = MC$, we can replace MC by P_x in Equation 14-8 to obtain

$$P_x = \frac{P_a}{MP_a} = \frac{P_b}{MP_b} \tag{14-9}$$

which can be written as two separate conditions, namely,

$$P_a = MP_a \cdot P_x \tag{14-10}$$

and

$$P_b = MP_b \cdot P_x \tag{14-11}$$

If there are n variable factors of production, n conditions like Equations 14-10 and 14-11 must be satisfied.

Intuitively, what is said in Equations 14-10 and 14-11 is very simple: In

---

[2]In Section 6.5d we saw that if the production function obeys constant returns to scale, and if all inputs, including the entrepreneurial capacity, are variable, then the long-run marginal cost curve is a horizontal line. Correspondingly, under such conditions the demand curve for a factor of production is also horizontal. The discussion of this unique case is postponed to Mathematical Appendix 14 (M14.1).

equilibrium the VMP of A must equal P_a and the VMP of B must equal P_b. Surely, if too little A is employed, the firm could increase its employment of A; the gain would be $\text{VMP}_a - P_a$ per unit of A added until Equation 14-10 is satisfied. If too little of B is employed, the firm could increase the employment of B and would gain $\text{VMP}_b - P_b$ until Equation 14-11 is satisfied. If too much of either A or B is employed, the argument is symmetrical.

Recall from Section 5.6 that two inputs may relate as MP-enhancing: When A is increased, MP_b increases; when B is increased, MP_a increases. This property, called *positive dependence*, is illustrated in panel (*a*) of Figure 5-13. Normally, positive relationship would dominate the process of production. The two inputs may (theoretically) relate to each other as MP-shrinking. This property, called *negative dependence*, is illustrated in panel (*b*) of Figure 5-13. Theoretically, it is also conceivable that two factors of production are *independent* of each other. Let us denote two inputs that satisfy positive dependence as *cooperative* and two inputs that satisfy negative dependence as *noncooperative*.[3]

Suppose, as is usually the case, that there are (at least) two variable factors of production, A and B, and a single fixed factor of production denoted by H. The two variable inputs are cooperative in the process of production. In Figure 14-3 equilibrium of the single firm is depicted by point K. The VMP_a is equal to the initial price of A, denoted by P_{a0}. But because B is also a variable factor of production, in equilibrium P_{b0} is equal to VMP_b. The initial situation at point K can be summarized as follows:

$$P_{a0} = \text{MP}_{a0} \cdot P_{x0}$$

$$P_{b0} = \text{MP}_{b0} \cdot P_{x0}$$

$$A = A_0 \quad B = B_0$$

We proceed in two stages: First, we allow the price of A to fall from P_{a0} to P_{a1} but keep the amount of B used at B_0. In that case the firm will consider the VMP_a for $B = B_0$ which is denoted by $\text{VMP}_a(B = B_0)$. As shown in Figure 14-3, the firm will move from point K to point L, increasing its use of A from A_0 to A_1 units per unit of time. But as the amount of A applied in the process of production increases, MP_b increases too. Since MP_b increases, $\text{MP}_b \cdot P_{x0}$ also increases and the firm hires more units of input B. Because the employment of B increases, the marginal physical product of curve A shifts upward [panel (*a*) of Figure 5-13]. In Figure 14-3 curve VMP_a shifts from the original position $\text{VMP}_a(B = B_0)$ to a higher position $\text{VMP}_a(B = B_1)$. After this occurs,

---

[3] Most texts denote inputs satisfying a positive relationship as *complements*. Note, however, that *complementarity* and *substitutability* are terms used to describe the relationship between any two consumer goods, with the constraint that utility is held constant, namely, that the consumer is restricted to his or her *n*-dimensional indifference surface (see Sections 2.4g and 3.3c). When we defined a positive relationship between inputs A and B, we did not require the firm to remain on the same isoquant. However, if the theory of the producer is to be formally similar to the theory of the consumer, complementarity ought to indicate a situation in which the firm is limited to moving only on its *n*-dimensional isoquant, and if A and B are complements, a fall in P_a results in increasing the employment of A as well as the employment of B.

at point L, VMP_a is in excess of P_{a1}. Thus the firm expands the amount of A it uses from A_1 to A_2.

In summary, the movement from point K to point L was temporary. After the assumption that B is held constant was relaxed, the firm moved to point M. The curve connecting points like K and M is the true demand curve for factor A when two factors are variable. This demand curve is denoted by D_a. We see that under the assumption that two factors are variable, the firm responded to a decline in the price of A by increasing its employment by $A_2 - A_0$—a change greater than the change of $A_1 - A_0$ associated with the assumption that B, the other factor, is held constant. The above analysis can be summarized as follows:

If the firm employs (at least) two variable inputs, the firm's demand curve for one input is more elastic if the other input is variable, as compared with a situation in which the other input is held constant.

The formal summary of the above analysis is as follows:

Point K	Point L ($B = B_0$)	Point M
$P_{a0} = \text{MP}_{a0} \cdot P_{x0}$	$P_{a1} = \text{MP}_{a1} \cdot P_{x0}$	$P_{a1} = \text{MP}_{a2} \cdot P_{x0}$
$P_{b0} = \text{MP}_{b0} \cdot P_{x0}$	$P_{b0} < \text{MP}_{b1} \cdot P_{x0}$	$P_{b0} = \text{MP}_{b2} \cdot P_{x0}$
	$\text{MP}_{a1} < \text{MP}_{a0}$	$\text{MP}_{a2} = \text{MP}_{a1}$
	$\text{MP}_{b1} > \text{MP}_{b0}$	$\text{MP}_{b2} = \text{MP}_{b0}$

If two inputs are noncooperative [negatively dependent upon each other as in panel (*b*) of Figure 5-13], the above results are preserved: D_a in Figure 14-3 will be more elastic than $\text{VMP}_a(B = B_0)$. This is left as an exercise for the student.

These results raise some immediate implications. Suppose A denotes energy and B denotes capital. The firm initially maximizes its profit at point M. Now, the price of energy rises from P_{a1} to P_{a0}. At first, capital is fixed at $B = B_1$ units. The firm moves from point M to point R. In the long run, as the amount of capital is reduced from B_1 to B_0, the firm adjusts by moving from point R to point K. The demand for energy in the long run is more elastic than in the short run.

If we were to apply the example $X = \sqrt{A \cdot B}$ (to illustrate Figure 14-3), the result would be an infinitely elastic demand curve for A (and for B), because the "square root" type of production function obeys constant returns to scale. We recall from Sections 6.5d and 7.2f that this case is inconsistent with perfect competition. Had we wanted to illustrate Figure 14-3 numerically, a production function that is mathematically more sophisticated would be required; at this level this is not a worthwhile price to pay.[4]

---

[4]An appropriate production function could be

$$X = K \cdot A^\alpha \cdot B^\beta \cdot H^\gamma$$

which is known as the *Cobb-Douglas production function*. Suppose we set $\alpha = 0.25$, $\beta = 0.5$, and $\gamma = 0.25$. To generate curves as in Figure 14-3, we could first hold B and H constant and vary only A, and then hold only H constant and vary A in response to a change in P_a, allowing B to adjust such that $P_b = \text{MP}_b \cdot P_x$.

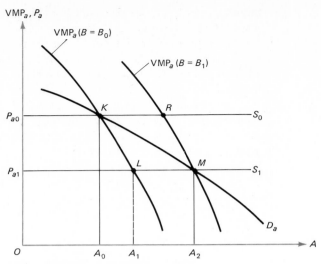

FIGURE 14-3   A SINGLE FIRM AND TWO VARIABLE INPUTS
First input B is held unchanged at $B = B_0$. The associated VMP curve is VMP_a $(B = B_0)$. As the price of A drops from P_{a0} to P_{a1}, the individual firm moves from point K to point L on this curve and increases its rate of employment of A from A_0 to A_1. But as more A is employed, the marginal physical product of B (MP_b) increases. (We assume that A and B are cooperative.) Hence the VMP_a curve shifts upward to a new position denoted by VMP_a $(B = B_1)$. The new (lower) supply curve cuts the new VMP_a curve at point M when new equilibrium is achieved. Employment of A increases to A_2 units. The revised demand curve for A is the curve depicted by D_a passing through points like K and M.

14.1c The Competitive Industry

To complete the analysis of the demand for a factor, we now shift our attention from the individual firm to the whole industry. Consider Figure 14-4. The industry demand for an input is derived in stages. First, the demand curves of all the single firms are added horizontally (as in Section 3.1a). The result of this aggregation is the curve denoted by $\Sigma D_a(P_x = P_{x0})$ in panel (a). Such a demand curve is obtained by adding horizontally all the demand curves of the type D_a in Figure 14-3. Recall that we assumed that the price of the product is unchanged at level P_{x0} along such a demand curve. But the price P_{x0} can hold only for a certain level of output, say, X_0. In panel (b), X_0 is produced by the industry where the demand curve for the product D_0 intersects with the supply S_0. But previously (Section 8.3b) we saw that if the price of a variable factor falls, the supply curve of the entire industry shifts downward. In panel (b), as the price of A falls from P_{a0} to P_{a1}, the supply of the product shifts downward from S_0 to S_1, and the price of the product falls from P_{x0} to P_{x1}. Since VMP_a is equal to $MP_a \cdot P_x$, the decline in the price of the product entails a downward shift in curve ΣD_a from ΣD_a $(P_x = P_{x0})$ to a new position depicted by $\Sigma D_a(P_x = P_{x1})$. Instead of employing ΣA_2, all firms in the industry together will employ $\Sigma A_2'$ units of the factor. In other words, instead of moving from point K to point M, all the firms in the industry will adjust for the fall in P_x and move from K to N. The demand curve going through points like K and N is denoted by D_A. Demand curve D_A is less elastic than $\Sigma D_a(P_x = P_{x0})$ because as we go down such a curve, MP_a declines owing to the law of diminishing marginal physical product and, additionally, P_x declines because more output is produced by the entire industry.

Let us return to the example in Table 14-1. Suppose the current price of labor is \$1.55, the price of whatnots is \$2, and 4 units of labor are employed per unit of time. Assume the whatnot industry is in equilibrium. Because of migration of cheap labor, however, the price of labor falls from \$1.55 to \$1.30. You decide to employ 6 units of labor. But, since all other whatnot producers also increase units of labor, the supply of whatnots increases and the price of whatnots falls to \$1.75. You adjust your VMP_a schedule as shown (partially) in Table 14-2. Given this new information about VMP_a, you revise your decision: Instead of increasing labor from 4 to 6 units, you

FIGURE 14-4 THE DEMAND FOR AN INPUT BY THE WHOLE INDUSTRY
In panel (a) the initial demand of the whole industry for input A is depicted by ΣD_a $(P_x = P_{x0})$. Along this demand curve P_x is held constant at P_{x0}. In panel (b) P_{x0} reflects equilibrium between initial supply (curve) S_0 and initial demand (curve) D_0. At point K in panel (a), the supply of input A, at a level P_{a0}, intersects the ΣD_a $(P_x = P_{x0})$ curve. The industry is in a complete equilibrium. The industry employs ΣA_0 units of A (as well as a certain amount of B which is not shown here) and produces X_0 units of output per unit of time. After the price of A drops from P_{a0} to P_{a1}, if we continue to hold the price of output unchanged at P_{x0}, the firms in the industry will move downward along the ΣD_a $(P_x = P_{x0})$ curve, and employment will increase to a level ΣA_2. But a fall in a price of a variable input will cause the supply curve in panel (b) to shift downward to a new position S_1 (Section 9.4), and hence the price of output will drop to a lower level of P_{x1}. Since VMP_a is the product of MP_a and P_x, the VMP_a of each firm will shift downward, leading to a shift in panel (a) from ΣD_a $(P_x = P_{x0})$ to ΣD_a $(P_x = P_{x1})$. The firms in the industry will revise their intentions concerning the employment of A: They will retreat from point M to point N, employing on the aggregate only $\Sigma A_2'$ units of A. Thus the curve denoted by D_A crossing through points like K and N is the true demand curve for input A by the entire industry. This demand curve takes into account the change in P_x.

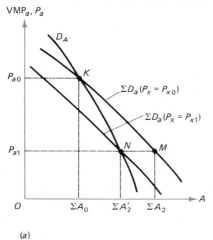

(a)

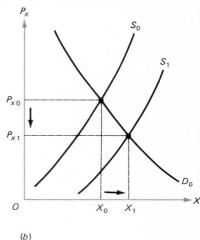

(b)

A	X	MP_a	VMP_a
4	6.32	0.84	1.47
5	7.07	0.75	1.31
6	7.75	0.68	1.19

increase it only to 5 units. This is the meaning of adjusting from point M to point N in panel (a). By implication, industry-wide changes would lessen the impact of a change in the price of an input as perceived initially by the individual entrepreneur.

14.1d A Shift in the Demand for the Product

It is intuitively clear that the demand for input A will shift in the same direction as the demand for the product X. Consider a point like K in panel (a) of Figure 14-4. Assume that the demand for product X increases, leading to a rightward shift of D in panel (b) of Figure 14-4, which is not shown there. If all the firms were to continue to employ the same combination of A and B as they did before such a change, production of output would continue at a rate X_0, and P_x would rise. With a higher price of X, the VMP of A (as well as of all other variable factors) would rise, thus shifting upward the demand curve for factor A. We can summarize this discussion as follows:

Ceteris paribus, the demand curves for the variable factors shift in the same direction as the demand curve for the final product.

14.1e A Technological Change

Section 8.4 discussed the case of a neutral technological innovation. It concluded that such a technological innovation would cause the marginal physical products of all inputs to rise. Consequently, the marginal cost curves of all the firms in the industry will fall, leading to a higher rate of production and a lower price of the product. This does not mean, however, that demand for variable inputs will increase. As a matter of fact, it is conceivable that following a technological innovation there will be more output by employing less of all variable inputs.

To illustrate technological innovation, the case of hybrid corn (Section 9.5b) is presented in Figure 14-5. Panel (a) displays the demand curve of an individual farm for some variable factor A. The horizontal line denoted by $\hat{S}_0$ is the supply curve of input A confronting the individual farm. In panel (b) the market for corn is displayed. Originally, the price of the variable input is P_{a0}, and A_0 units are employed by the farm. The price of corn is P_{x0}, and X_0 bushels of corn are produced and sold in the market. We now utilize some results from Section 8.4. For example, if the innovation of hybrid corn increases productivity by 10 percent, MP_a will increase by 10 percent: $\overline{MP}_a$ = 1.1 MP_a, where, as in Section 8.4, $\overline{MP}_a$ is the postinnovation marginal physical product of A. Since the demand for A is $MP_a \cdot P_x$, the technological innovation per se will lead to a (10 percent) upward shift in the demand for A, from position D_a to $\overline{D}_a$. Along $\overline{D}_a$ the following is satisfied: $VMP_a = \overline{MP}_a \cdot P_{x0}$. But recall from Figure 8-6 that this type of technological innovation will give rise to a downward shift of the farm's MC curve, from MC_0 to MC_1. Since the supply curve is the sum of all MC curves of all firms in the industry (Section 8.2a), the supply curve in panel (b) (of Figure 14-5) will shift downward from S_0 to S_1. As a result, the price will fall from P_{x0} to P_{x1}. The decline in the price of corn will tend to pull the demand curve for A downward because it would shrink the VMP of input A. Thus, we have two opposing effects: the increase in MP_a (from MP_a to $\overline{MP}_a$), which increases VMP_a and shifts the demand for A upward, and the fall in the price of the product (from P_{x0} to P_{x1}), which pulls the demand for A downward. Along the new demand curve D'_a the following is true: $VMP_a = \overline{MP}_a \cdot P_{x1}$. If the increase-in-the-MP_a effect is stronger than the fall-in-the-price effect, the new demand curve for the factor will occupy a position somewhere between $\overline{D}_a$ and D_a. (This case is not displayed in Figure 14-5.) If the reverse is the case, the new demand curve for A, D'_a will lie below D_a. In this illustration we assumed that the fall in the price of corn dominated. Thus, although more corn was produced, the

FIGURE 14-5   INPUT DEMAND AND TECHNOLOGICAL INNOVATION
In panel (a) D_a is the original demand curve for input A by a farm producing corn. Each point on D_a measures vertically $P_x \cdot MP_a$. A technological innovation (hybrid corn) results in an increase in MP_a (Section 8.4), and hence, to the first approximation, the demand for input A shifts upward to position $\overline{D}_a$. In panel (b) the technological innovations result in a downward shift in the supply curve from S_0 to S_1 (Section 9.5). As a result, the price of corn falls from P_{x0} to P_{x1}. The fall in P_x shrinks the VMP_a, and thus the demand curve for input A in panel (a) shifts back from $\overline{D}_a$ to a lower position D'_a. The net result is a decrease in the employment of A from A_0 to A_1. In this example we assumed that the fall in P_x dominated the rise in MP_a. Had we assumed the opposite, D'_a would have occupied a position between $\overline{D}_a$ and D_a.

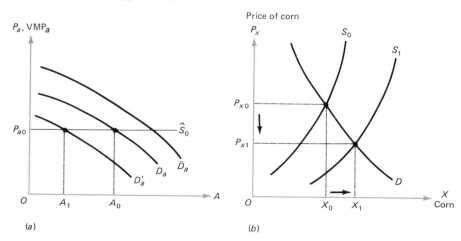

(a)

(b)

innovation of the hybrid corn led to a decline in the employment of A, from A_0 to A_1 units.

Indeed, if technological innovation leads the demand for an input to shift to the left [from D_a to D_a' in panel (a)], there are serious consequences. A certain amount of the inputs in the industry affected by technological change must seek employment elsewhere in the economy. Owners of fixed resources, such as land in corn production, suffer a loss.

14.2 THE SUBSTITUTION AND EXPANSION EFFECTS

The analysis so far is useful in solving problems such as demand-for-input shifts resulting from either a change in the demand for the final output or a technological innovation. It is not very efficient, however, when we consider the following two issues: First, what makes a demand curve for an input either elastic or inelastic (less elastic)? Second, where does the demand curve for an input shift after a change in the price of another input? The following analysis will provide the apparatus needed to solve these two issues.

14.2a A Geometrical Illustration

When the price of a factor falls, the industry will produce more output because the marginal cost curves of all the firms shift downward. Each firm will use more of the input whose price fell, for two reasons: First, since the price of the input declined relative to prices of other variable factors, the firm would substitute the input that became cheaper for other variable inputs. Second, the decline in the marginal cost would induce each firm to produce more. Consider Figure 14-6. Panel (a) displays an isoquant denoted by $X = X_0$. The original equilibrium is attained at point E_0, where tangency between this isoquant and an original isocost, C_0, occurs. Recall from Section 6.5b that at any least-cost-combination point the slope of the isoquant (RTS $= -\text{MP}_a/\text{MP}_b$) is equal to the slope of the isocost ($-P_a/P_b$). Panel (b) shows the MC and the demand curve confronting the competitive firm. Originally, the price of the product is P_{x0} and the marginal cost curve is MC_0. The intersection between these two curves leads to a level of output of X_0 units. After the price of A declines from P_{a0} to P_{a1}, the marginal cost curve shifts down to MC_1 (Section 8.3b), but as shown before (Figure 14-4), the price also declines from P_{x0} to P_{x1}. As a result, the rate of production increases from X_0 to X_1. (It is possible that one or a few firms will actually shrink their level of production. But for most firms in the industry, X_1 must be greater than X_0. Can you explain why?) We now shift our attention back to panel (a). We know that the rate of production increased to a level X_1. Since X_1 is greater than X_0, isoquant $X = X_1$ must lie to the right of $X = X_0$. We also know that there must be a new point of equilibrium on isoquant $X = X_1$. This point is E_1. Let us elaborate. At E_0, the original isocost line C_0 with a slope of $-P_{a0}/P_{b0}$ just touched isoquant $X = X_0$. After the price of A fell to a

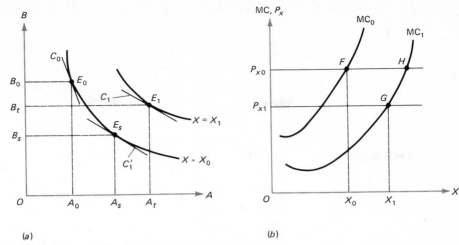

(a)

(b)

FIGURE 14-6 THE SUBSTITUTION AND EXPANSION EFFECTS

In panel (a) we measure the employment of A along the horizontal axis and the employment of B along the vertical axis. E_0 depicts the original point of equilibrium: The isocost C_0 is tangent to the isoquant $X = X_0$. In panel (b), point F is associated with E_0; initially, marginal cost curve MC_0 intersects with the demand for the firm's output at a level P_{x0}. Output is produced at a rate of X_0 units. After the price of A falls, the marginal cost curve falls to a lower level depicted by MC_1. Because of industrywide effects, the price of output falls from P_{x0} to P_{x1}. As a result, the firm moves from point F to point G and increases its rate of production from X_0 to X_1. Going back to panel (a), we note that point E_1 is associated with point G. At E_1 a new (and higher) isocost, C_1, is tangent to the new isoquant $X = X_1$. The total use of A increases from A_0 to A_t, and the total use of B decreases from B_0 to B_t. C_1' is an isocost which is parallel to C_1 and is tangent to $X = X_0$ at point E_s. The movement from E_0 to E_s along the initial isoquant ($X = X_0$) is the *substitution effect*. The movement from E_s to E_1 is the *expansion effect*. In the case of factor A, $A_s - A_0$ is the substitution effect; $A_t - A_s$ is the expansion effect. The two effects reinforce one another. In the case of factor B, $B_s - B_0$ is the substitution effect; $B_t - B_s$ is the expansion effect. The two effects offset one another.

level of P_{a1}, the slope of the new isocost denoted by C_1 became $-P_{a1}/P_{b0}$. Relative to C_0 the new isocost has rotated counterclockwise. The new isocost just touches the isoquant $X = X_1$ at point E_1. The total impact on the employment of input A is the movement from A_0 to A_t. Suppose, after the price of A declined, that the producer was forced to produce the original amount of X_0 units per unit of time. In that case the least-cost principle (Section 6.5b) would be satisfied at point E_s where the isocost C_1', which is parallel to C_1, is tangent to isoquant $X = X_0$. At that point A_s units of A are employed by the firm. Notice that if the firm moves along isoquant $X = X_0$ from E_0 to E_s, then $A_s - A_0$ units of input A are substituted for $B_s - B_0$ units of B, while the rate of production remains fixed. This is why the amount $A_s - A_0$ is termed the *substitution effect*. The remaining portion of the change in the employment of A, namely, $A_t - A_s$, is termed the *expansion effect*. The student should find it useful to compare this analysis with Section 2.4g in which we used a similar (but not identical) analysis to dissect the change in the quantity demanded for a good into the *substitution effect* and the *income effect*.

We are now ready to discuss the factors affecting the elasticity of the demand curve for an input.

14.2b The Elasticity of the Demand for an Input

Three rules goven the size of input-demand elasticity. These rules will, in general, apply to industry-wide changes. As before, elasticity is defined as the relative change in the quantity demanded for a factor over a small relative change in its price (Section 2.2). This elasticity is denoted by E_{AP_a}. The three rules are as follows:

1. *The larger the degree of substitutability between A and other inputs (B in the example), the more elastic the demand for A.* The geometrical interpretation for this is that if A and B are relatively good substitutes for each other, the change indicated by $A_s - A_0$ in panel (a) of Figure 14-6 will be relatively large.

2. *The more elastic the demand for output (X), the more elastic the demand for input A.* This can be illustrated by considering Figure 14-6: If the demand curve confronting the industry [D in panel (b) of Figure 14-5] were perfectly elastic, the price of X would have remained unchanged at P_{x0}. In that case, equilibrium in panel (b) of Figure 14-6, after the price of A falls, would have been achieved at point H rather than point G. Output would have been larger than X_1, and the new isoquant would have occupied a higher position than $X = X_1$ in panel (a) of Figure 14-6. The result must be that the expansion effect would exceed $A_t - A_s$. Generalizing, we can say that the more elastic the demand for the finished product, the smaller the fall in the price of the finished product, as a result of the fall in the price of the input, and the larger the expansion effect.

3. *The more elastic the supply curves of other inputs, the more elastic the demand for input A.* First, consider the substitution effect, going from E_0 to E_s along the original isoquant in panel (a) of Figure 14-6. If the supply of B confronting the industry were very inelastic, then as the amount of B diminished from B_0 toward B_s the price of B would decrease. This would mitigate the counterclockwise rotation of the isocost line, and the point of tangency on $X = X_0$ would occur somewhere between E_0 and E_s. (E_s is achieved under the assumption that P_b remained unchanged at a level P_{b0}, namely, that the industry is confronted with a perfectly elastic supply of input B.) Thus the more elastic the supply of B confronting the industry, the stronger would be the substitution effect. Second, consider the expansion effect: As the firms in the industry expand, they use more of input B. But if the supply of B facing the industry is very inelastic, the price of B will rise, thus mitigating the fall of curve MC in panel (b) in Figure 14-6. If the supply of B is perfectly elastic, the price of B remains unchanged at P_{b0} and thus there is no less of a downward shift of curve MC.[5]

---

[5]If the supply of B is perfectly elastic, or nearly so, and if the production function obeys

TABLE 14-3 Annual Percentage Changes of Production and Employment of Labor and Capital, Bituminous Coal Industry, 1929–1954

	Percentage change
Cost of labor	2.8
Labor employment	− 3.1
Coal production	− 1.3
Capital use	2.7

Source: Table 9-2.

Section 9.4b discussed the example of the bituminous coal industry. Some of the figures of Table 9-2 will now be transformed into annual percentage changes, as presented in Table 14-3. Although the data in Table 14-3 do not enable us to separate the expansion effect from the substitution effect, the fact that capital use rose 2.7 percent per annum shows a significant degree of substitution between labor and capital in the production of coal.

14.2c Demand Shifts due to Changes in Price of Other Factors

Table 14-3 demonstrates how the rise in the cost of labor induced owners of coal mines to substitute capital for labor. The use of capital increased 2.7 percent per year despite a 1.3 percent decline in the production of coal: The substitution effect exceeded the expansion effect. This section develops the relevant theory for analyzing the impact of a change in the price of one factor on the use of another factor.

How would the demand curve for factor B shift as a result of a decline in the price of factor A? Consider again panel (a) of Figure 14-6. As a result of a decline in the price of A, the firm decreased the amount of B used from B_0 to B_s, which we called the *substitution effect*, and then increased the amount of B used from B_s to B_t, which we termed the *expansion effect*. In the example, as displayed in panel (a) in Figure 14-6, the substitution effect happened to dominate. But it is clear from examining the diagram that if isoquant $X = X_1$ shifted far enough outward, the expansion effect would dominate. Let the

---

constant returns to scale, then the elasticity of the demand curve for A with respect to the price of A can be stated as

$$E_{AP_a} = -(K_b\sigma + K_a|\eta|)$$

where E_{AP_a} stands for the elasticity of the demand curve for factor A, K_a and K_b are the respective shares of factors A and B in the total cost, σ is the elasticity of substitution between the two factors (Section 5.4a), and η is the demand elasticity of the finished product. The Mathematical Appendix will show that $K_a + K_b = 1$. We can substitute $1 - K_a$ for K_b in the above formula and find out that K_a has an ambiguous effect on the elasticity. The reader can show that only if $\sigma < |\eta|$ would a higher K_a lead to a more elastic demand curve for A. Since E_{AP_a} is negative, it is clear that the higher the values of σ and $|\eta|$, the more elastic the demand for A. For proof of the above formula see R. G. D. Allen, *Mathematical Analysis for Economists*, Macmillan, London, 1956, chap. 19.

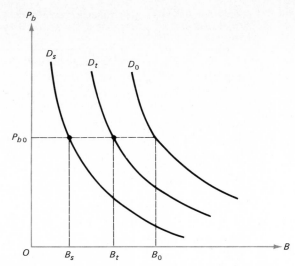

FIGURE 14-7 THE IMPACT OF A DECLINE IN P_a ON THE DEMAND FOR B

Initially, the demand for input B is depicted by D_0. It is assumed that A and B are competitive inputs. After the price of A falls, the demand curve for B shifts leftward to position D_s as a result of the substitution effect, and rightward from position D_s to the final position D_t as a result of the expansion effect. This example assumes that the substitution effect dominates the expansion effect. Had it been the other way around, D_t would lie to the right of D_0.

cross elasticity of the demand for B with respect to P_a be denoted by E_{BP_a}. We can summarize as follows:

Following a decline in the price of A, the demand curve for B will shift to the left because of the substitution effect, and it will shift to the right because of the expansion effect. It is impossible to determine a priori which of the two effects will dominate. If the substitution effect dominates, E_{BP_a} is positive. If the expansion effect dominates, E_{BP_a} is negative.[6]

Figure 14-7 illustrates the shift in the demand curve for B resulting from a fall in the price of A. (A rise in the price of A would reverse the direction of the substitution effect and expansion effect, respectively.) The change in employment from B_0 to B_s reflects the substitution effect. The backward movement from B_s to B_t is the expansion effect. Since this analysis can be applied to every possible price of B (not only to P_{b0}), we can say that the decline in the price of A shifted the demand for B leftward (from D_0 to D_s)

---

[6]Following Footnote 5, under the assumption that the industry is confronted with flat supply curves of variable inputs, and assuming constant returns to scale, the cross elasticity of B with respect to P_a can be written as

$$E_{BP_a} = K_a(\sigma - |\eta|)$$

Thus $K_a \cdot \sigma \cdot$ (percentage change in P_a) would amount to the substitution effect, and $-K_a \cdot |\eta| \cdot$ (percentage change in P_a) would amount to the expansion effect, as illustrated in Figure 14-7. For proof, see Allen, op. cit.

because of the substitution effect and rightward (from D_s to D_t) because of the expansion effect.

Two comments are relevant at this point:

First, if the demand for output is very elastic, it is likely that the expansion effect will dominate, and vice versa.

Second, it has been assumed that the two factors are related as *competitive* inputs ($\sigma > 0$). This is true if only two inputs are employed by the firm. If three or more inputs are employed by the firm, two inputs may be related as *complements* to each other.[7] In that case, following a decline in the price of A, the firm may use more of B because of the substitution ("complementarity") effect; in a three-dimensional diagram $B_s - B_0$ would be positive ($\sigma < 0$).

14.2d An Application: Who Is Not Afraid of the Energy Crisis?

Farmers drive tractors that run on diesel fuel; they apply fertilizers that take great amounts of energy to produce; and they use energy to generate heat needed for drying some crops. However, microeconomics tells us that, as unbelievable as it may sound, farmers should welcome the energy crisis.

Consider land, which is a fixed factor at the industry level. In Figure 14-8, services rendered by land per unit of time are measured along the horizontal axis. (For example, the use of 1 acre of land per annum is a service rendered by 1 acre per year; accordingly, it is a flow and not a stock.) Land rentals and the VMP of land are measured along the vertical axis. Land rentals should be distinguished from the price of land: It is the price one must pay for renting land for a period of time. Agricultural economists were able to show that the price elasticity of demand for farm output is very low—on the order of -0.2. A very inelastic demand for farm output implies a weak expansion effect. This is true because the less elastic the demand for farm output, the smaller the decrease in farm production following a rise in energy cost. Recall, a rise in the cost of energy would result in an upward shift in the supply of farm output (Sections 8.3 and 9.4). If the demand curve is perfectly inelastic, the expansion effect vanishes completely. On the other hand, there is sufficient evidence to convince us that the degree of substitutability between energy and land is relatively high. Also, assuming that the cost of energy rises relative to prices of all other inputs used on the farm, the demand for land services will shift from D_0 to D_s (Figure 14-8) as a result of the substitution effect. This movement will be mitigated by a leftward shift in the demand curve from D_s to D_t as a result of the expansion effect. D_t is the final position of the demand curve. This new demand curve will cut the vertical supply curve of land services at a higher point, and land rentals will rise from P_0 to P_t: Farmland owners will benefit from the energy crisis.

---

[7]The reader is reminded again that in some textbooks inputs A and B are called *complements* if there is a positive relationship between A and B, that is, if $(\partial^2 X)/(\partial A \cdot \partial B) > 0$. Following Allen (op. cit., chap. 19) and conforming to the definition of complementarity as in consumer's theory the following notations were adopted.

A and B are *cooperative* if A and B are related positively; mathematically, $(\partial^2 X)/(\partial A \cdot \partial B) > 0$.

A and B are *noncooperative* if A and B are related negatively; mathematically, $(\partial^2 X)/(\partial A \cdot \partial B) < 0$.

Following Allen (op. cit., chap. 19):

A and B are *competitive* (substitutes) if a decline in the price of A will lead to a reduction in the employment of B when the producer is restricted to moving along the (n-dimensional) isoquant; mathematically, $\sigma > 0$.

A and B are *complements* if a decline in the price of A will lead to an increase in the employment of B when the producer is restricted to moving along the (n-dimensional) isoquant; mathematically, $\sigma < 0$.

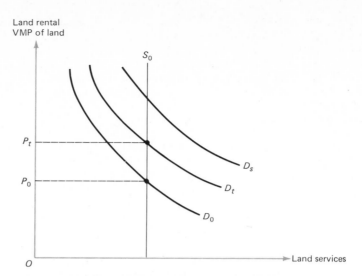

FIGURE 14-8 THE IMPACT OF RISING ENERGY PRICES ON LAND RENTALS
The initial demand for land is depicted by curve D_0. The supply of land facing the farm sector is depicted by vertical line S_0. Initial rental is equal to P_0. Land and energy are competitive (substitute) inputs. As the price of energy rises, resulting from the substitution effect, the demand for land shifts rightward to position D_s. Under the assumption that the expansion effect is weaker than the substitution effect, resulting from the (negative) expansion effect, the demand for land shifts back to the left to an intermediate position D_t. As a result, land rentals increase from P_0 to P_t.

14.2e An Example: The Energy Crisis and United States Manufacturing

Recall that if only two factors are employed by a firm, they must relate to each other as competitive inputs (Section 5.6). If the production process is expanded from two to n inputs, any two factors can become complementary. For example, if we consider a three-dimensional production function in which labor, capital, and energy are used, then equilibrium (least-cost combination of inputs) is achieved when the three-dimensional isocost plane is tangent to the three-dimensional isoquant (surface). Now, suppose that the price of energy rises and the firm moves to a new point of tangency where it hires more labor but decreases the use of both energy and capital. In that case energy and capital are related as complements to each other and energy and labor are competitive. In Section 5.4a the elasticity of substitution σ was defined (Equation 5-8 and Figure 5-9). Without going into complicated mathematics, we note that the elasticity of substitution is positive for a pair of competitive (substitute) inputs and negative for a pair of complementary inputs. From that viewpoint it is similar to the cross elasticity in consumption (Section 3.3d).

R. Ernst Berndt and D. O. Wood studied the degree of substitutability among energy, labor, and capital in the United States.[8] They reached the conclusion that substitution occurs among the three major factors in United States manufacturing, although to a limited extent. More specifically, they found that for the period 1947–1971 the elasticity of substitution between energy and labor was 0.65 and between energy and capital −3.2. (As shown by other studies, the elasticity of substitution between labor and capital is unity.) According to this study, energy and labor are competitive (substitute) inputs and energy and capital

---

[8]R. Ernst Berndt and D. O. Wood, "Technology, Prices, and the Derived Demand for Energy," *The Review of Economics and Statistics,* vol. 57, August 1975, pp. 259–268.

are complementary inputs. This study leads to the conclusion that the energy crisis should have an adverse effect on returns to capital: As the price of energy rises, the demand for capital services would decline because of both the expansion (contraction) effect and the complementarity effect. The demand for labor would increase because of the substitution effect and decrease because of the expansion (contraction) effect. In industries in which the substitution effect dominates, labor will benefit from the energy crisis. (*Note*: Labor will benefit relative to capital, not necessarily in absolute terms.) There is a policy implication: Accelerated depreciation allowances and investment tax credits would cheapen capital services and stimulate more investment; this would lead to a higher demand for energy and would be counterproductive to any energy conservation policy.

The student should be aware that during the period 1947–1971 real prices of energy were either stable or slightly declining. Accordingly, manufacturing industries had no inducement to search for energy-saving technologies. Thus, the results of Berndt and Wood's study have short-run policy implications. There is historical evidence that over a long period changes in relative factor prices induce new technologies which "stretch" the isoquants in the desirable direction. This stretching of the isoquant, discussed in the next section, makes economics a bit less of a dismal science.

14.2f What Came First, the Chicken or the Egg?

Do technological changes induce changes in factor use proportion, or do technological changes occur in response to changes in relative factor prices? The *induced innovation hypothesis* claims that isoquants shift and change over time in response to changes in relative prices of inputs. This hypothesis is an optimistic one. As we saw in the previous section, if technological innovations were not induced by a change in the price of energy, consumers might have to wait for a technological miracle to happen. If innovations are induced by factor price changes, the energy crisis will stretch the production isoquants to an extent unfamiliar to present researchers. Following Yujiro Hayami and Vernon Ruttan,[9] a diagram is presented that summarizes the idea of the induced innovation hypothesis. There are two quadrants. In the upper quadrant we measure energy along the vertical axis and "other factors" along the horizontal axis. In the lower quadrant we measure some technology index along the vertical axis going in the southerly direction. Isoquant x_0 represents a certain technology depicted by T_0 in the lower quadrant. This technology corresponds to a certain price of energy represented by isocost line P_0. (We assume that the cost of energy substitutes is held constant.) Originally, the proportion of energy to energy substitutes is B_0 to A_0. When the price of energy rises from P_0 to P_1, and the isoquant is x_0, producers reduce the amount of energy they use from B_0 to B_1 and increase the amount of substitutes they use from A_0 to A_1. Given the technology as represented by T_0, all that producers can do is to "scallop" isoquant x_0. But as more energy substitutes are used, there is an inducement to innovate, and a new technology denoted by T_2 becomes available. As a result, the isoquant shifts down to a new position x_0^*. The tangency between an isoquant reflecting the new price of energy, P_1, and x_0^* occurs at a much lower point. A much

[9]Yujiro Hayami and Vernon W. Ruttan, "Factor Prices and Technical Change in Agricultural Development: The United States and Japan, 1880–1960," *Journal of Political Economy*, vol. 78, September/October 1970, pp. 1115–1141.

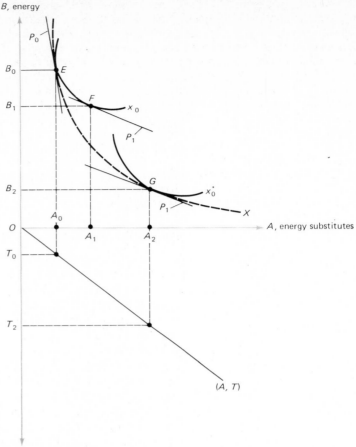

FIGURE 14-9   INDUCED INNOVATION
Along the horizontal axis we measure energy substitutes. Along the vertical axis pointing
north we measure energy, and along the vertical axis pointing south we measure technological innovation. In the lower quadrant, the (A, T) curve symbolizes the idea that as energy becomes more and more expensive, producers will adopt new technologies to produce the
same levels of output with many more energy substitutes and much less energy. In the upper
quadrant, initially the relative price of energy is P_0. An isocost associated with P_0 just touches
isoquant x_0 at point E. A_0 units of energy substitutes and B_0 units of energy are employed. As
the relative price of energy rises from P_0 to P_1, the firm moves to a new point of tangency
between an isocost associated with P_1 and isoquant x_0; this point of tangency is denoted by
F. The use of energy slightly decreases to B_1 and the use of energy substitutes slightly increases to A_1. Isoquant x_0 corresponds to a level of technology of T_0, as shown in the lower
quadrant. Given time for adjustment, the rise in the price of energy causes technology to
shift to T_2. As a result, the isoquant for x_0 units of output shifts southeasterly to a new position depicted by x_0^*. The isocost associated with P_1 now touches the new isoquant x_0^* at point
G. The employment of energy substitutes increases further to a level of A_2 units. The use of
energy declines further to a new low level of B_2. X is the envelope of x_0, x_0^*, and so on.

smaller amount of energy, B_2, and a much larger number of units of energy substitutes, A_2, respectively, are now used.

As for the chicken-and-the-egg issue, there is evidence that innovations tend to be induced by changes in factor prices. In the United States, land is abundant relative to Japan. United States farmers confronted a more elastic supply of land and a less elastic supply of labor. In Japan the reverse situation was the case. Thus, over a long period the price of labor relative to the price of land increased sharply in the United States. The opposite was observed in Japan. Hayami and Ruttan[10] studied the history of agricultural development in the two countries. Both countries experienced a spectacular rate of growth in farm production between 1880 and 1960. Laborsaving mechanical innovations (e.g., tractors) were introduced in the United States from 1880 to 1930. Only after the 1930s did United States farmers shift to biological innovations (e.g., crop varieties, hybrids) as a consequence of the significant decline in the price of chemical fertilizers. In contrast, Japanese farmers resorted to biological innovations as early as the 1880s: Their problem was to increase crops on limited lands. Note that with a fixed biological technology (e.g., fixed seed variety) the isoquant for land and fertilizers is represented by x_0 in Figure 14-9 (where A is fertilizers and B is land). But with an induced biological innovation, the isoquant shifts to x_0^*. It is as if the isoquant has been "stretched." We may consider X as some kind of a "super isoquant" that is the *envelope* of the isoquants like x_0 and x_0^*. It is interesting to note that in Japan an enormous rise in fertilizer input per acre was coupled with biological innovation, which was encouraged by the rising prices of land. In Japan the inducement toward laborsaving mechanisms appeared only at the end of World War II.

The hundreds of economic studies that have appeared regarding the energy crisis can be grouped into three general categories: (1) Studies that assume fixed proportions between energy and other factors. These doomsday studies are completely useless. They assume that isoquant x_0 is L-shaped [panel (*a*) of Figure 5-10], implying that $\sigma = 0$. (2) Studies that focus on the present degree of substitutability between energy and other inputs.[11] These studies serve a good purpose provided that we are aware that they are limited to isoquant x_0; they tell us very little about the stretched (or envelope) isoquant denoted by X in Figure 14-9. (3) Studies that tell us how innovations are induced by factor price changes.[12] Such studies provide real clues to solving the energy crisis.

14.3 THE SUPPLY OF AN INPUT FACING AN INDUSTRY

The individual firm is a price taker in the marketplace for factors of production. The only exception is the case of *monopsony*, which will be discussed

---

[10]Ibid.

[11]Berndt and Wood, op. cit.

[12]Hayami and Ruttan, op. cit.

in the next section. The fact that the firm is a price taker is translated geometrically into a horizontal supply curve of an input. For the individual firm to face a horizontal supply curve means that it can double its use of the factor or, alternatively, completely discontinue using the factor without having any impact on the factor price. For example, a single shoe manufacturer has no influence on the price of unskilled labor. But what about the entire shoe industry in the United States? Would this industry face a very elastic or a very inelastic supply curve of unskilled labor? Figure 14-10 helps to answer this question. Let A denote unskilled labor and X denote shoes. Let D in panel (a) denote the demand curve for unskilled labor by all the industries in the United States, except for industry X. Let the curve denoted by S in panel (a) depict the total supply of unskilled labor in the United States. We now subtract demand D from supply S in panel (a) to obtain supply curve S_I in panel (b) confronting industry X. Let us illustrate the process of deriving supply curve S_I. Suppose the price of A is $\overline{OF}$; in that case total quantity supplied in the entire economy is $\overline{FH}$ units of unskilled labor. As indicated by curve D, all other industries will employ $\overline{FG}$ units per unit of time, leaving a quantity of $\overline{GH}$ ($= \overline{FH} - \overline{FG}$) units of unskilled labor to be employed in industry X. Segment $\overline{GH}$ is plotted in panel (b) as a segment $\overline{KL}$. Thus we conclude that at a price of $\overline{OF}$ dollars $\overline{KL}$ units of input A will be supplied to industry X. These $\overline{KL}$ units are equal to $\overline{GH}$ units. Likewise, if the price of unskilled labor drops to $\overline{OR}$, total quantity supplied will amount to $\overline{RT}$; all other industries will demand only $\overline{RS}$ units, leaving for industry X a net quantity supplied of $\overline{ST}$. Segment $\overline{ST}$ is plotted as a segment $\overline{MN}$ in panel

FIGURE 14-10 THE SUPPLY OF AN INPUT FACING AN INDUSTRY

In panel (a) S denotes the total supply curve of input A; D is the demand curve for input A by $n - 1$ industries. (There are n industries in the economy.) In panel (b) S_I is obtained by subtracting curve D horizontally from curve S in panel (a). For example, $\overline{KL} = \overline{FH} - \overline{FG}$. As the demand for A by a single industry declines from D_{a0} to D_{a1}, equilibrium in the input market moves from point L to point N. Total quantity supplied of the input decreases from $\overline{FH}$ to $\overline{RT}$; total quantity demanded by the remaining $n - 1$ industries increases from $\overline{FG}$ to $\overline{RS}$ units.

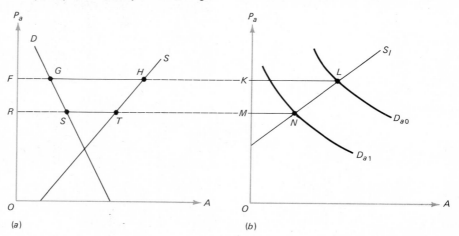

(a)

(b)

(b). Thus S_I in panel (b) is a curve connecting points like N and L. These points measure a horizontal distance from the price axis of panel (b), which is equal to the horizontal distance between curve S and curve D in panel (a).

Suppose the demand for unskilled labor in industry X is depicted by curve D_{a0} in panel (b). The intersection between D_{a0} and S_I occurs at point L. Industry X employs $\overline{KL}$ ($= \overline{GH}$) units of unskilled labor; all other industries employ $\overline{FG}$ units of labor. The market for input A is in equilibrium:

Demand for unskilled labor $=$ supply of unskilled labor

$$\underbrace{\overline{FG} + \overline{KL}} \qquad \underbrace{\overline{FH}}$$

Suppose the demand for unskilled labor in industry X shifts leftward from D_{a0} to D_{a1}. The new point of intersection between supply S_I and the new demand curve is N. Industry X now employs fewer units of input A. In fact, employment of A declined from $\overline{KL}$ units to $\overline{MN}$ units. Owners of factor A (in the example, unskilled workers) will start to cut prices of A. By so doing they will induce other industries to employ more of A. In fact, as indicated by curve D in panel (a), other industries will increase their quantity demanded for A from $\overline{FG}$ units to $\overline{RS}$ units. But since the price of A is declining, owners of input A will shrink the quantity supplied from $\overline{FH}$ units to $\overline{RT}$ units.

Note that if all other industries in the economy increase their demand for input A, demand curve D in panel (a) will shift rightward, but this in turn would mean that the supply of A facing industry X [S_I in panel (b)] will shift leftward and upward). Likewise, an upward shift in total supply S in panel (a) entails an upward shift in S_I in panel (b).

Let us now derive the formula for the elasticity of supply curve S_I in panel (b). The following notations relating to factor A are adopted:

$$\begin{array}{llll}
\overline{OF} = P_0 & \overline{FH} = S_0 & \overline{FG} = D_0 & \overline{KL} = S_{I0} \\
\overline{OR} = P_1 & \overline{RT} = S_1 & \overline{RS} = D_1 & \overline{MN} = S_{I1}
\end{array}$$
$$\Delta P = P_1 - P_0 \qquad \Delta S_I = S_{I1} - S_{I0} \qquad \Delta S = S_1 - S_0 \qquad \Delta D = D_1 - D_0$$

Then we have

$$S_{I0} = S_0 - D_0$$
$$S_{I1} = S_1 - D_1$$
$$S_{I1} - S_{I0} = S_1 - S_0 - (D_1 - D_0)$$
$$\Delta S_I = \Delta S - \Delta D$$

Multiplying through by $P/(S_1 \cdot \Delta P)$, we obtain

$$\frac{P \cdot \Delta S_I}{S_I \cdot \Delta P} = \frac{P \cdot \Delta S}{S_I \cdot \Delta P} - \frac{P \cdot \Delta D}{S_I \cdot \Delta P}$$

Rearranging, we obtain

$$\frac{P \cdot \Delta S_I}{S_I \cdot \Delta P} = \frac{S \cdot P \cdot \Delta S}{S_I \cdot S \cdot \Delta P} - \frac{D \cdot P \cdot \Delta D}{S_I \cdot D \cdot \Delta P}$$

or

$$\epsilon_I = \frac{S}{S_I}\,\epsilon - \frac{D}{S_I}\,\eta \qquad (14\text{-}12)$$

where ϵ_I is the elasticity of the supply curve facing industry $X[S_I$ in panel $(b)]$, ϵ is the elasticity of total supply of factor A in the economy $[S$ in panel $(a)]$, and η is the elasticity of the demand curve of all other industries for A $[D$ in panel $(a)]$.

To illustrate numerically, assume again that A is unskilled labor and the share of industry X in the labor market is one-tenth. Assume that $\epsilon = 1$ and $\eta = -2$. We can estimate the elasticity of supply of labor facing industry X as

$$\epsilon_I = \frac{10}{1}\cdot 1 - \frac{9}{1}\cdot(-2) = 10 + 18 = 28$$

It is a relatively elastic supply curve. To increase employment by 28 percent the wage rate will have to rise by only 1 percent. Accordingly, when you hear economists say that ''for all practical purposes'' the supply curve of a factor of production facing an industry can be assumed to be flat, they really mean that since the share of the industry in the total market of the input is rather small, for all practical purposes the elasticity of the supply curve confronting the industry is infinity. For example, if the share of the industry in the unskilled labor market is 1 percent, the elasticity of S_I rises to 298.

14.4 MONOPSONY

A *monopsony* in a factor market arises when an employer is confronted by a positively sloped supply of a factor of production. In the United States, monopsony is very rare. Perhaps a city with a single hospital may be the sole user of nurses' services. However, given the widespread ownership of cars and the extensive network of roads, it is difficult to conceive of a community so isolated that its workers are truly restricted to a single source of employment. The theory of monopsony will now be considered.

A firm in competition faces a horizontal supply curve of labor or of any other factor of production. This arises because the share of the individual firm in the market for resources is negligible. Thus the firm cannot affect the price of the resource it uses by deciding to use more or less of it. In contrast to the firm in competition, the sole buyer of an input faces the aggregate supply curve of the input. Since the supply curve is positively sloped under normal conditions, the firm has to pay higher prices per unit of the resource if it wants to use more of it.

An individual firm that purchases a certain input in a competitive market equates the VMP of the input with the market price. The firm is a price taker. However, in the case of a monopsony the firm is not a price taker: The more of the input the firm buys, the higher the price that must be paid for that input will be. Thus the monopsonistic firm must equate the VMP of the input

TABLE 14-4 An Illustration of Monopsony

Supply of labor				
Wage rate (1)	Quantity of labor offered (2)	Total cost of labor (1) × (2) (3)	Marginal factor cost (MFC) (4)	VMP of labor (5)
$1	1	$ 1	$ 1	$10
2	2	4	3	9
3	3	9	5	8
4	4	16	7	7
5	5	25	9	6
6	6	36	11	5
7	7	49	13	4
8	8	64	15	3
9	9	81	17	2

with the extra cost of one unit of the input, known as the *marginal factor cost* (MFC).

Table 14-4 shows a monopsony model in which the different functions are linear. For example, in column 4, the figure $3 is derived by taking $4 − $1, which is the firm's extra cost of labor, and dividing it by 2 − 1, which is extra labor used. Columns 5 and 2 show the hypothetical VMP curve of labor. In equilibrium, the firm will offer employment to 4 units of labor, because when 4 units are employed the marginal factor cost equals VMP, which is $7. For reasons previously discussed, it does not pay the firm to employ either less than or more than 4 units of labor. In equilibrium, the wage of $4 is lower by $3 than the marginal factor cost of labor. The case of monopsony furnishes the only example in which more employment will be created by enforcing a minimum wage rate above equilibrium. For example, if the minimum wage rate of $5 is enforced, 5 units of labor will be employed.

As noted before, the supply price of the input (column 1 in Table 14-4) is lower than its MFC (column 4). Accordingly, Figure 14-11 displays an MFC curve that lies above the supply curve of labor. The VMP curve of the firm cuts the MFC curve at point E. In monopsonistic equilibrium, $\overline{OA}$ units of labor will be employed at a wage rate of $\overline{OF}$ dollars. *Note*: In equilibrium, the wage rate is $\overline{OF}$ ($= \overline{AB}$) and the MFC is equal to $\overline{AE}$, which is higher than the wage rate by $\overline{BE}$ dollars. If a minimum wage rate of $\overline{OR}$ dollars was set and enforced by the government, the MFC curve would be the kinked $\overline{RGTU}$ curve intersecting the VMP curve at point M. Employment would rise to $\overline{OK}$ units of labor, and the wage rate would rise to $\overline{OR}$ dollars.

The next chapter will discuss the impact of the minimum wage rate in competitive markets.

In Section 3.2a a formula was proved that related MR to the demand price. In general, if A is a factor sold in a monopsonistic market, P_a is its price, and MFC is its marginal factor cost, then by applying the same procedure (replace X by A, P by P_a, R by C, MR by MFC, and η by ϵ), we obtain the following formula:

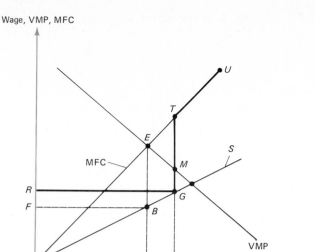

FIGURE 14-11 MONOPSONY IN THE LABOR MARKET
A single firm with a value of marginal product curve denoted by VMP faces a positively sloped supply curve of labor denoted by S; the corresponding marginal factor cost curve lies above the supply curve and is denoted by MFC. The VMP curve cuts the MFC curve at point E. Accordingly, $\overline{OA}$ units of labor are employed at a wage rate of $\overline{OF}$ dollars. If a minimum wage rate of $\overline{OR}$ dollars were imposed, the new MFC curve would be the one denoted by $RGTU$. This new curve would intersect with the VMP curve at point M, employment would increase to a new level of $\overline{OK}$ units, and the wage rate would rise to $\overline{OR}$ dollars.

$$\text{MFC} = P_a\left(1 + \frac{1}{\epsilon}\right) \tag{14-13}$$

where ϵ is the elasticity of the supply curve (S in Figure 14-11) confronting the monopsonistic firm. Since ϵ is positive, MFC must exceed the supply price. Accordingly, MFC lies above the supply curve.

It is left as an exercise for the student to show that if the government sets a minimum wage rate above $\overline{AE}$ dollars, employment will decline.

14.5 PRICING FACTORS OF PRODUCTION UNDER MONOPOLY

A monopoly is a price taker in the factor market. In that respect there is no difference between a monopoly and a competitive firm. But there is a difference between the demand curve of a monopoly and the demand curve of a competitive firm. As shown before, the demand curve of a competitive firm satisfies the equality $P_a = \text{MP}_a \cdot P_x$, where P_a is the price of the factor, P_x is the price of output, and MP_a is the marginal physical product of the factor. In other words, in equilbrium the price of an input equals its value of marginal physical product. So long as $\text{MP}_a \cdot P_x$ exceeds the price of the factor, it pays the firm to use more of the factor per unit of time because the amount by which the factor exceeds its market price is a net addition to the profit. Under monopoly, the extra contribution from adding one unit of input cannot be measured by the value of the marginal physical product. The price is not identical with marginal revenue. For example, suppose, by increasing employment by one worker, the monopoly increases production from 10 to 12 units of output, and this leads to a reduction in the market price from $105 to $100. Then marginal revenue equals $(1200 - 1050)/(12 - 10) = \$75$. The extra gross gain to the monopolistic firm is $MP_a \cdot MR = 2 \cdot \$75 = \$150$. Clearly, if the cost of one unit of labor is $60, it pays the monopoly to hire more labor, just until $MP_a \cdot MR$ equals $60. Note that this equality is obtained both by decreasing the MP_a because of the law of diminishing marginal physical product and by lowering the marginal revenue when more output is produced. In economic jargon $MP_a \cdot MR$ is called the *marginal revenue product* (MRP), as distinguished from the value of the marginal physical product, $MP_a \cdot P_x$, which was denoted by VMP.

Consider the demand for factor A. The following will hold at each point belonging to the demand curve: $P_a = MP_a \cdot MR_x$, where P_a is the price of the factor and MR is the marginal revenue. Since

$$MR = P_x\left(1 + \frac{1}{\eta}\right)$$

we obtain

$$P_a = MP_a \cdot P_x\left(1 + \frac{1}{\eta}\right)$$

The analysis is similar to that applied in cases of competition, except that VMP is multiplied by the coefficient $(1 + 1/\eta)$ to take into account the monopoly power over the market.

If the monopolist is confronted with a rising supply of the factor, then in equilibrium, $MFC = MP_a \cdot MR$, where MFC is the marginal factor cost. If supply elasticity of the factor is denoted by ϵ, then $MFC = P_a(1 + 1/\epsilon)$, and in equilibrium we have

$$\underbrace{MFC}_{P_a\left(1 + \dfrac{1}{\epsilon}\right)} = \underbrace{MP_a \cdot MR}_{MP_a \cdot P_x\left(1 + \dfrac{1}{\eta}\right)} \tag{14-14}$$

Consider a competitive industry whose demand curve for input A is denoted by VMP_a in Figure 14-12. Along such a demand curve the price of output X changes as indicated in Section 14.1c (D_A in Figure 14-4). If the industry were to become a cartel, marginal revenue product curve MRP would replace VMP. MRP is obtained by multiplying VMP by $(1 + 1/\eta)$. If the industry becomes monopolized, it will decrease the amount of the factor used from A_c to A_m. This confirms what was shown in Section 11.2a, namely, that a monopoly will produce less than if it were somehow induced to behave competitively. Figure 11-3 showed a monopoly that produced $\overline{AB}$ units less than the competitive solution would indicate.

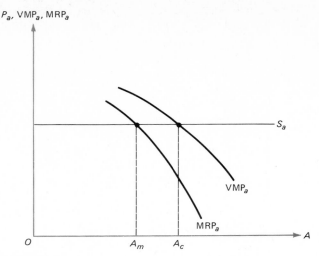

FIGURE 14-12   VMP VERSUS MRP

S_a is the supply curve of input A confronting a competitive industry. VMP_a represents the demand curve for A by this competitive industry. Under the assumption of competition, this industry employs A_c units of A per unit of time. $VMP_a = P_x \cdot MP_a$. If the industry organizes as a cartel, its demand curve for input A becomes *marginal revenue product* rather than *value marginal product*. Marginal revenue product (MRP) for input A is defined as $MR_x \cdot MP_a$, which can be written as $(1 + 1/\eta) \cdot P_x \cdot MP_a$. Since MR_x is lower than P_x, curve MRP_a occupies a lower position compared with VMP_a. Accordingly, employment of input A will fall to a new lower level of A_m units.

14.6   AN EXAMPLE: THE MARKET FOR WATER RIGHTS IN THE SOUTHWEST UNITED STATES

Where water is scarce, the issue of allocation predominates. This section will discuss the market for water rights in the Southwest United States, with emphasis on surface water.

In Eastern states the allocation of surface water is managed under the *riparian doctrine*. The riparian doctrine gives every landowner adjacent to a stream of surface water the right to use a "reasonable" amount of that water. Under this vague definition landowners can be deprived of water if their neighbors use too much. Nonetheless, the riparian doctrine survives in the East because surface water is available in such abundance that farmers normally get as much water as they require, except in times of drought.

In the Southwest, where water is scarce, the riparian doctrine could not survive. Instead, the *prior appropriation doctrine*, which clearly establishes

water rights, has been adopted. The principle is simple: So long as the flow of a stream or a river is not completely allocated, the right is established by being able to prove that water has been used by a person or a firm since a certain date. It is interesting to note that priority in time of appropriation gives the better right. As an illustration, if David appropriated his water rights prior to John, in the event of a severe drought John will have to give up his right to use water before David. David has senior rights and John has junior rights; in time of drought junior rights are called first. In some Southwestern states the *state engineer* oversees transactions in water rights. His or her main function is to ensure that the rights of third parties are not impaired and that the amount of water specified by a water rights agreement is correctly transferred from the seller to the buyer.[13]

For illustration consider Figure 14-13. Suppose

---

[13]This is technically complicated. The law refers to the right to the *consumptive use* of water,

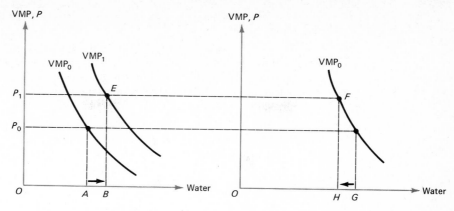

(a) David: a water user with a rising VMP curve   (b) John: a water user with a stable VMP curve

FIGURE 14-13   THE MARKET FOR WATER RIGHTS

David's VMP of water is displayed in panel (a). John's VMP of water is displayed in panel (b). Initially, David owns $\overline{OA}$ water rights and John owns $\overline{OG}$ water rights. The water market is in equilibrium: VMP of water is the same P_0 for both David and John. Owing to growth, David's VMP shifts upward to a new position depicted by VMP_1. If David continues to use only $\overline{OA}$ units of water, his VMP will exceed John's. Hence it behooves him to purchase $\overline{AB}$ water rights ($= \overline{HG}$) from John; David moves to point E on the new VMP_1 curve; John moves northwesterly along his old VMP_0 curve to point F. When new equilibrium is established, the value of the marginal physical product of water rises to P_1 dollars.

there are two users along the stream, David and John. David and John are in equilibrium in the sense that initially their VMPs are the same at P_0. Assume that David's VMP curve shifts from VMP_0 to VMP_1 [panel (a)]; thus, to the first approximation, the additional revenue that David derives from using the last unit of water exceeds the additional revenue that John derives from using the last unit of water. It behooves David to purchase $\overline{AB}$ units of water (rights) from John. John's water (rights) will then decrease by $\overline{HG}$ ($= \overline{AB}$). When the new equilibrium is attained, the VMP of both users rises from P_0 to P_1.

14.7 THE PROBLEM OF COMMON PROPERTY RESOURCE (Optional)

14.7a Exclusiveness

What is the main difference between farming and fishing? The answer is that a farmer owns his or her natural resource, the land. Ownership of the land enables the farmer to exclude others from appropriating his or her rent. Fishing grounds are not privately owned. Hence one fisherman cannot exclude others from sharing in the rent. This can be best illustrated by the case of demersal fish such as haddock which live on shallow continental

---

i.e., *water withdrawal* minus the *return flow*. Based on experience and involved calculations, the state engineer estimates the consumptive use of water in each economic category. If David, John, and Sam are three water users, David is located upstream, Sam is located downstream, and John is located midway between David and Sam, it is possible that when David buys water rights from Sam the flow of water will decrease at the point where John diverts it. If the decrement is substantial enough to reduce the amount of water John can divert, the state engineer will interfere on his behalf.

shelves. The feeding grounds of these fish are separated by deep water channels. Thus if the separate feeding grounds were privately owned, it would resemble farming; the owner of a fishing ground would legally be able to exclude others from fishing. In reality, however, fishing grounds are common properties and are not subject to any degree of exclusiveness.

Following the fishing tradition, management, labor, and capital (boats and fishing gear) are combined into one factor of production denoted by "fishing effort." We can assume that fishing firms can buy labor and capital services at competitive prices (without having any significant impact on the prices of these services). Hence the marginal factor cost curve of the fishing effort is assumed to be horizontal. As fishing efforts increase, the catch increases at a decreasing rate. Although as the effort expands, the fish population may shrink, for the time being we shall assume that the decline in the marginal physical product of effort results from diminishing returns to effort.

Let us illustrate the fishing operation with a numerical example. As in Table 14-1, assume that the fishing production function is given by $X = \sqrt{A \cdot B}$, where A is the variable fishing effort and B is the fishing ground, fixed at 10 units. Table 14-5 presents the values of X, MP_a, and AP_a for values of A extending from 1 to 10 units.

Suppose the price of fish P_x is \$1. Thus $MP_a = VMP_a$ and $AP_a = VAP_a$, where VAP_a is $P_x \cdot AP_a$. Assuming again that only whole units of effort can be applied and that the marginal factor cost of effort (MFC_a) is a flat \$1, a single fisherman who owned the fishing ground would apply 3 units of effort per unit of time. As before, the guiding principle is that so long as the value of the marginal physical product of effort exceeds its marginal factor cost, effort should be expanded. A fisherman who expanded effort to 4 units would receive additional revenue of only \$0.84, decreasing the profit by \$0.16 per unit of time.

Since $AP_a = X/A$, we can express total output as

$$X = A \cdot (AP_a) \tag{14-15}$$

Following an argument presented in Equation 11-5 and Section 11.1b, the following result is obtained for $\Delta A = 1$:

$$MP_a = A_0 \cdot [\Delta(AP_a)] + AP_a \tag{14-16}$$

As an illustration, consider the MP_a of the fourth level of effort.

$$MP_a = 3 \cdot (1.58 - 1.83) + 1.58$$

We can write it as an expression with two components as follows:

$$0.84 = -0.75 + 1.58$$

The first component may be viewed as a loss to the first three units already employed: the second component is the gain to the fourth unit of effort. Now, since the fishing ground is common property, a second fisherman may think: If I employ one unit of effort in this fishing ground, I will reduce the revenue of the other fellow by \$0.75 (\$1 · 0.75), but that is not my worry. My gain will be \$1.58, which still exceeds the MFC_a of \$1. If the first fisherman

TABLE 14-5   A Numerical Illustration for a Fishing Production Function $X = \sqrt{A \cdot B}$, $A =$ Fishing Effort, $B = 10$ Units of Fishing Ground

A	X	MP_a	AP_a
1	3.16	3.16	3.16
2	4.47	1.31	2.24
3	5.48	1.01	1.83
4	6.32	0.84	1.58
5	7.07	0.75	1.41
6	7.75	0.68	1.29
7	8.37	0.62	1.20
8	8.94	0.57	1.12
9	9.49	0.55	1.05
10	10.00	0.51	1.00

continues to employ 3 units of effort the MP_a of the second fisherman for the second unit of effort is calculated as follows:

$$MP_a = 1 \cdot (1.41 - 1.58) + 1.41 = -0.17 + 1.41 = 1.24$$

If we assume that the supply of fishing effort is infinitely elastic at \$1, so long as AP_a is in excess of MFC_a (which is \$1 in the example), more and more fishermen will be attracted to this fishing ground. As Table 14-5 shows, equilibrium will be reached when 9 units of effort are employed. Rent will be (almost) completely dissipated.

The geometrical analysis of common property is presented in Figure 14-14. Fishing effort is measured along the horizontal axis and VMP_a, VAP_a, and MFC_a are measured along the vertical axis. The VMP_a curve cuts the VAP_a curve at the maximum of the VAP_a curve. The MFC_a curve is horizontal, reflecting the assumption that relative to the size of the fishing industry the supply of fishing effort is infinitely elastic. One fisherman who owned a separate fishing ground would identify point F, where MFC_a intersects the VMP_a curve, as an optimal solution. The result would amount to employing $\overline{OA_1}$ units of effort per unit of time. But if other fishermen with identical MFC_a curves are not excluded from the fishing ground, the additional value of output resulting from an additional small fishing effort would appear to them to be segment $\overline{A_1G}$ rather than $\overline{A_1F}$. $\overline{A_1G}$ is the AP_a of the first fisherman, but as explained by the numerical example, it is MP_a as perceived by the second fisherman. (For convenience we continue to assume that $P_x =$ \$1.) If the first fisherman continues to employ $\overline{OA_1}$ units (3 units, in the numerical example), the second fisherman will expand along the dashed GN curve, which becomes the MP_a curve. This second fisherman would like to expand up to point F'. It is clear, however, that so long as VAP_a is higher than curve MFC_a, more fishermen will enter this fishing ground, and effort will be expanded to point H, where curve VAP intersects curve MFC_a. Equilibrium will occur when $\overline{OA'_1}$ units of effort are eventually employed. At

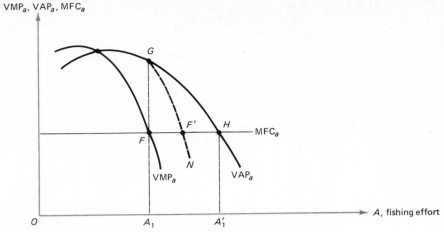

FIGURE 14-14 AN ILLUSTRATION OF A COMMON PROPERTY RESOURCE

The marginal factor cost of any fisherman is depicted by horizontal curve MFC_a. The fishing production function involves a fixed factor B, representing the fishing ground, and A, representing the fishing effort. A single fisherman who could exclude all other fishermen would select point F, where the MFC_a curve cuts the value marginal product of fishing denoted by VMP_a. The single fisherman would employ A_1 units of effort per unit of time. Since the fishing ground is common property, a new fisherman may enter and will perceive AP_a ($= \overline{A_1G}$) rather than MP_a ($= \overline{A_1F}$) as his relevant additional catch per additional unit of effort. Recall that in this example $P_x = \$1$, and hence $MP_a = VMP_a$ and $AP_a = VAP_a$. If the first fisherman continues to employ A_1 units of effort, the second fisherman's VMP_a curve will be the dashed GN curve. But even if the second fisherman were to stop at point F', a third fisherman will enter the fishing ground; this process will continue until total effort will amount to A_1' units, where VAP_a intersects MFC_a.

point H no rent will be left for fishermen. This is known as a point of complete rent dissipation.

If individual fishing firms owned their own fishing grounds, they would be able to exclude others from entering the grounds and thus they could produce at point F where VMP_a is equal to MFC_a. An alternative would be for the government to limit fishing efforts. Such a regulatory solution involves administrative and policing costs that must be taken into account.

14.7b A Renewable Natural Resource

We have seen that fishermen will reach an equilibrium, leaving them no rent. At that point of equilibrium, total cost of fishing will be equal to total value of fish landed (catch). The production function of fishing is related not only to effort but to the *fish population*, known as *biomass*. Corresponding to each level of biomass is an associated level of *natural growth*. At a particular natural growth the biomass remains constant. If the biomass is stable over time, it is said that the biological ecosystem has reached a *steady state*. The basic relationship between biomass and fishing is that up to a point the catch increases with steady-state biomass; beyond this point the catch falls as the steady-state biomass increases. Also, the smaller the biomass, the less productive the fishing effort. Thus the catch shows a steady-state curve which first rises and then falls as effort increases.

The relationship between biomass and fishing effort was described in Section 5.6, where we saw that if the two factors are cooperative, one factor enhances the marginal productivity of the other. In Figure 14-15 fishing effort, denoted by A, is measured along the horizontal axis and landing (the catch), denoted by X, is measured along the vertical axis. The three rays sent from the origin represent three different landing curves. Each ray represents a landing function as follows:

$$X = f(A, B) \qquad\qquad (14\text{-}17)$$

where biomass B is held constant along each ray. B_3 represents a higher level of biomass than B_2 and B_2 represents a higher level of biomass than B_1. The rays are linear for convenience of presentation. Consider an effort at a level A_0. If the biomass is B_1, landing will amount to $\overline{A_0E}$. If the biomass were to rise to B_2, landing would amount to $\overline{A_0F}$, and if the biomass were to rise to B_3, landing would be $\overline{A_0G}$. [$\overline{A_0E} = f(A_0, B_1)$, $\overline{A_0F} = f(A_0, B_2)$, and $\overline{A_0G} = f(A_0, B_3)$.] But as we noted before, for each level of biomass there is only one level of landing that will result in a steady state. Also, to each level of landing and population there is only one associated level of fishing effort. For example, for the ray denoted by B_3, point K represents the associated steady-state

FIGURE 14-15 THE STEADY-STATE LANDING FUNCTION

Fishing effort A is measured along the horizontal axis, and catch is measured along the vertical axis. B_3 is the total catch curve derived from the production function $X = f(A, B)$, where B, the fish population, is held constant at B_3. The linearity of such curves (rays) is assumed for simplicity of presentation. $B_3 > B_2 > B_1$, and so on. K is a steady state on ray B_3; L is a steady state on ray B_2, and M is a steady state on ray B_1. If we connect all the steady-state points like K, L, and M, we obtain the steady-state landing curve X.

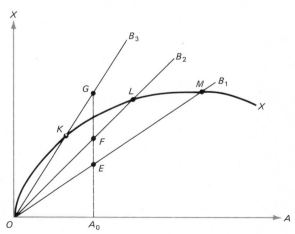

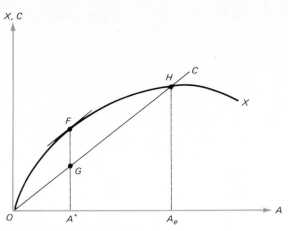

FIGURE 14-16 EQUILIBRIUM IN A FISHING GROUND
Fishing effort is measured along the horizontal axis. Catch (landing) and total cost of fishing
are measured along the vertical axis. If, as in reality, the fishing ground is common property, effort will amount to A_e where the total cost curve cuts the steady-state landing curve
($P_x = \$1$). If a single fisherman owned the fishing ground and could exclude other fishermen,
the effort would amount to A^* units, and there would be economic rent amounting to $\overline{GF}$ dollars per unit of time.

pair of A and X. If we connect steady-state points like K, L, and M, we
obtain the *steady-state landing curve* denoted by X. Curve X is concave
downward because landing increases with effort, and up to a point the
steady-state population declines as landing increases.

In the previous section we assumed that MFC_a is horizontal. Accordingly, the total cost function is the ray denoted by C in Figure 14-16. This
curve is derived from the MFC_a curve in Figure 14-14 in the same way that
the LRC curve in panel (*a*) of Figure 6-9 would be derived from the LRAC
(or LRMC) curve in panel (*b*) of Figure 6-9. (You may want to review
Chapter 6, in particular Section 6.5d.) Landing curve X is a replica of the
landing curve in Figure 14-15. To simplify the analysis, we assume that units
of fish are defined such that $P_x = \$1$. Accordingly, curve X is also the value
of landing curve or, simply, the revenue curve. Point H, where curve C
intersects curve X, is a point at which equilibrium will be established in the
long run. At that point the VAP is equal to MFC_a. Note, however, that the
amount of effort A_e in Figure 14-16 is not necessarily the same as the amount
A_1' in Figure 14-14. In Figure 14-14 the issue of biomass as related to landing
was completely ignored in favor of the commonality aspects of the fishing
ground. At point H rent is completely dissipated. The optimal solution would
have occurred at point F, where a tangent to curve X is parallel to curve C.
The tangent to curve X is its slope, namely, $\Delta X / \Delta A$, and the slope of curve C
is $\Delta C / \Delta A$, which is MFC_a. The amount of effort associated with this point is
A^*. This is not the same as A_1 in Figure 14-14 for similar reasons: A^* would

be the level of effort employed by a fisherman who would be able to exclude others from the fishing ground. In selecting A^* the fisherman will take into account the need to select the optimal biomass.[14]

The bottom line of all this is that if a natural resource cannot be privately owned such that all nonowners are excluded from using the resource, misallocation of the resource will occur: An amount of effort A_e will be employed. The optimal level of employment is A^*, which is smaller than A_e. Provided that transaction costs do not exceed the benefit, economists would advocate taking measures that would cut the level of fishing effort from A_e to A^*.

SUMMARY This chapter started by focusing on a demand for a factor of production by a single firm. The demand for a factor was defined as the *marginal physical product* of the factor (MP) times the price of the output (P_x). The product of MP and P_x was denoted VMP, namely the *value of the marginal physical product* of the factor. We saw that if the assumption that other factors of production are kept constant is relaxed, the demand curve for an input becomes more elastic. But if industry-wide changes are considered, then because of the change in the price of output, the demand curve for an input becomes less elastic.

It was demonstrated that the demand for a factor will shift in the same direction as the demand for output. The shift in the demand for a factor of production resulting from a neutral technological innovation is ambiguous: The rise in MP helps to shift it upward, and the fall in the price of output helps to shift it downward.

Next, the change in quantity demanded for a factor, as well as a shift in the demand for a factor due to a change in the price of another factor, were divided into the *substitution effect* and the *expansion effect*. The substitution effect was defined exactly as in the theory of the consumer. The expansion effect was defined as the total effect minus the substitution effect. It was concluded that the demand for an input will be more elastic the larger the degree of substitutability between it and other variable inputs, the more elastic the demand for output, and the more elastic the supply of other inputs. It was also demonstrated that if the price of one input falls, then if a second input is *competitive* with this input, the demand for the second input will shift to the left as a result of the substitution effect, and to the right as a result of the expansion effect. The importance of this approach to the theory of distribution was illustrated by a study related to the energy crisis. The *induced innovation hypothesis* was also discussed and evidence was introduced indicating that to a large extent innovation is induced by changes in relative prices.

The elasticity of the supply curve of a factor of production facing an entire

---

[14]We have ignored the rate of discount. Incorporating the discount rate into the fishery model would slightly change the optimal situation.

industry was analyzed, with the conclusion that in most cases this supply curve is extremely elastic. There are some exceptions to this rule, such as the supply of land confronting the farm sector.

The market situation known as *monopsony*, in which a single firm is the only employer in a certain factor market, was then analyzed. It was demonstrated how under such conditions it is possible to increase the level of employment by enforcing a minimum wage rate. It was stressed that monopsony is rare in a modern economy.

The slight difference in the monopoly's demand curve for a factor from the demand of a firm selling in a perfectly competitive market was demonstrated. Instead of VMP, the monopoly's demand curve was defined as the product of MP and marginal revenue (MR), known as the *marginal revenue product* (MRP).

The chapter ended with a discussion of the market of water rights as well as the problem of a *common property resource*, where a resource cannot be exclusively owned and used by a single firm. It was demonstrated how, in the absence of *exclusiveness*, resources are misallocated and economic rents are completely dissipated. This topic was illustrated by considering the case of demersal fishes which live on shallow continental shelves.

GLOSSARY

Factors of production Resources transformed into output in the process of production. Also known as inputs.

Firm An agency engaged in transforming *inputs* into *outputs*.

Production function Given a firm, to any feasible combination of inputs there corresponds a maximum output that can be produced from this specific combination; this is a *relation* between a combination of inputs and a level of output. The collection of all such possible relations is the production function. For the case of output X and two inputs, A and B, the production function is expressed as $X = f(A, B)$.

Marginal physical product The change in total output over a small change in one input ($\Delta X/\Delta A$), when all other factors of production are held unchanged. The marginal physical product of factor A is denoted by MP_a. Geometrically, the marginal physical product is the slope to the total output curve.

Average physical product Total output divided by the total amount of an input used per unit of time (X/A). Geometrically, it is the slope of a line connecting the origin and a point on the total output curve. The average physical product of factor A is denoted by AP_a.

Value of the marginal physical product The marginal physical product (MP) multiplied by the price of output. It is denoted by VMP. If the firm is competitive, the VMP curve is identical with the demand curve for an input. VMP is the additional revenue obtained by the competitive firm if it increases the use of the factor under consideration by one unit. Formally, $VMP_a = MP_a \cdot P_x$, when input A is involved in producing output X.

Cooperative factors If two factors A and B are positively related (when A

rises, MP_b rises, and when B rises, MP_a rises), they are known as cooperative factors. In some texts such a relationship is known as *complementarity*.

Noncooperative factors If two factors A and B are negatively related (when A rises, MP_b falls, and when B rises, MP_a falls), they are known as noncooperative factors.

Independent factors If two factors A and B are related to one another neither negatively nor positively (a change in A does not induce a change in MP_b, and a change in B does not induce a change in MP_a), they are known as independent factors.

Competitive factors Two inputs that are substitutes for one another. Substitutability is measured when production is restricted to an (n-dimensional) isoquant.

Complementary factors Two factors that are complementary to one another. Complementarity is measured when production is restricted to an (n-dimensional) isoquant. However, for complementarity to be feasible, there must be more than two factors in the process of production.

Substitution effect The effect of a change in the price of an input on its employment and the employment of other inputs, when the firm is restricted to movement along the (n-dimensional) isoquant.

Expansion effect The total effect of a change in the price of an input minus the substitution effect. The expansion effect arises because when the price of an input changes the marginal cost curve shifts, thus leading to a change in the rate of production.

The induced innovation hypothesis Isoquants shift and change over time in response to changes in relative prices of inputs.

Monopsony A market situation in which a single buyer is confronted with many sellers. In labor markets monopsony occurs when a single employer faces many workers in a certain labor market.

Marginal factor cost The extra cost that a firm must pay to increase the employment of a certain input by one unit per unit of time. Marginal factor cost (MFC) is related to the supply curve of the input facing the firm as marginal revenue is related to the demand curve; for factor A, $MFC_a = P_a(1 + 1/\epsilon)$.

Marginal revenue product In general, marginal revenue product (MRP) is the additional revenue obtained by the firm as a result of increasing the employment of a certain input by one unit per unit of time. In the case of monopoly MRP is the product of marginal physical product of the factor times marginal revenue. For factor A and output X it is $MRP_a = MP_a \cdot MR_x$. If the firm is competitive, $MR_x = P_x$, and the formula for marginal revenue product becomes $MRP_a = MP_a \cdot P_x$, which is VMP_a.

Riparian doctrine A doctrine of water allocation in Eastern states in the United States. This doctrine gives every landowner adjacent to a stream of surface water the right to use a reasonable amount of water.

Prior appropriation doctrine A doctrine of water allocation in Southwestern states in the United States. This doctrine gives rights to use water according to historical priority. It establishes water rights equivalent in many respects to ownership of water. Adoption of this doctrine has lead to active markets of water rights in many Western states.

Common property resource A resource which is owned by the entire community, usually a country or a state. Fishing grounds are an example.

Exclusiveness The ability to exclude others from using a resource. This ability obtains by private ownership.

Renewable natural resource A natural resource that can grow because of natural forces. One example would be the fish population (biomass) in fishing grounds. Another example would be underground water that feeds on rainfalls and melting snows.

Steady state of a renewable natural resource A state in which the rate of production equals the natural rate of growth of the resource.

PROBLEMS An asterisk indicates an advanced problem.

14-1. Will a rise in the price of farm machinery entail a rise in land rentals? Assume that (a) the supply curve of land is perfectly inelastic, (b) the substitution effect dominates the expansion effect, and (c) land and machinery are competitive inputs (substitutes).

14-2. Repeat problem 14-1, except assume that the expansion effect now dominates the substitution effect.

14-3. Can a monopolist get away with paying wages below the market wage rate?

14-4. Normally, the demand curve for a factor of production is negatively sloped because both the substitution and the expansion effects lead to a change in the same direction in the quantity demanded. Do you agree? Why or why not?

14-5. The union of workers in industry A raises wages above the equilibrium rate. As a result, will entrepreneurs in industry A demand more capital services? Assume that (a) the substitution affect dominates, (b) labor and capital are competitive inputs (substitutes), and (c) monopsony does not exist.

14-6. Repeat problem 14-5, except assume that the expansion effect now dominates.

14-7. Will farm landlords benefit from a subsidy on fertilizers? Assume that the substitution effect dominates and that land and fertilizers are competitive inputs.

14-8. Will wages in industry A rise in the short run if entrepreneurs invest in better equipment?

14-9. Repeat problem 14-8, but this time for the long run. Assume that labor mobility is perfect.

14-10. A single hospital in a small town is the sole buyer of nursing services. The supply curve of nurses is positively sloped. Nurses claim that enforcing a minimum wage rate would force the hospital to use more nurse hours. By drawing the right diagram, explain under what conditions this may be true.

14-11. Would the analysis displayed in Figure 14-3 be the same [D_a will be more elastic than $VMP_a(B = B_0)$] if negative dependence between A and B is assumed?

14-12. If industry A benefits from a technological innovation, in the short run workers in industry A may or may not benefit. In the long run they should not care. Explain by focusing on Figure 14-10.

14-13. Stimulating investment may worsen the energy crisis (given a fixed technology). Explain. (Use the results in Section 14.2e.)

14-14. If innovation is indeed induced by changes in relative prices of factors, what would be the most desirable policy for dealing with the energy crisis?

14-15.* The AP_a of effort in a fishing ground is given by the equation $AP_a = 100 - A$ and MFC = \$10, where A is the fishing effort and P_x = \$1.

(a) What would be the optimal solution under the assumption of private ownership (exclusiveness)?
(b) What would be the additional product for the outsider who is the first to enter the fishing ground after the fishing ground becomes common property?
(c) What is the equilibrium in the fishing ground after many fishermen enter it?

14-16. American Indians (sheepherders) tend to overgraze their land. Normally, grazing land is common property. Explain.

14-17. Show that if in Figure 14-11 the government sets a minimum wage rate higher than $\overline{AE}$, employment will decline.

14-18.* Those who oppose water markets (prior appropriation doctrine) claim that persons who own water rights downstream demonstrate the inefficiency of the water market: Had they released their water to upstream users, more water would be available because of less evaporation. How should the definition of water be formulated to eliminate this argument?

MATHEMATICAL APPENDIX 14

M14.1 THE DEMAND FOR AN INPUT WHEN ALL FACTORS ARE VARIABLE AND THE PRODUCTION FUNCTION IS HOMOGENEOUS OF DEGREE 1

Recall from Mathematical Appendix 5 (m5.1) that if the production function is homogeneous of degree 1, the MP function is homogeneous of degree zero (if $h = 1$, $h - 1 = 0$). When the firm expands along the expansion line in Figure 5-11, the ratio A/B is unchanged and MP_a and MP_b are also unchanged. Accordingly, a competitive firm that is a price taker has constant VMP_a and VMP_b curves as displayed (only for one factor) in Figure 14-17.

As we mentioned previously, the size of the firm is indeterminate under such conditions.

M14.2 THE PRODUCT IS EXHAUSTED: $h = 1$

Consider a production function $X = f(A, B)$ obeying constant returns to scale. This means that Equation m5-3 is satisfied and it can be written as ($h = 1$)

$$X = A \cdot f_a + B \cdot f_b \qquad \text{(m14-1)}$$

Multiplying Equation m14-1 by P_x, and assuming competition in the product market, we get

$$R = A \cdot VMP_a + B \cdot VMP_b$$

But since in competition (in the input market) $VMP_a = P_a$, etc. we have

$$R = A \cdot P_a + B \cdot P_b \qquad \text{(m14-2)}$$

That is, $R = C$. Dividing through by R (or C), we obtain

$$1 = K_a + K_b \qquad \text{(m14-3)}$$

which is a fact used in Footnote 5 in this chapter.

M14.3 THE MOST GENERAL CASE OF DEMAND FOR INPUTS

Let the production function of a monopoly be $X = f(A, B)$, where A is a factor bought in a monopsonistic market, that is, $P_a = F(A)$, and B is a factor bought in a competitive market. The assumption of a monopoly also implies that $P = \phi(X)$. The profit (rent) function is

$$\pi = P \cdot f(A, B) - P_a \cdot A - P_b \cdot B \qquad \text{(m14-4)}$$

The necessary conditions for profit maximization are

$$\frac{\partial \pi}{\partial A} = P \frac{\partial X}{\partial A} + X \cdot \frac{dP}{dX} \; \frac{\partial X}{\partial A} - P_a - A \cdot \frac{dP_a}{dA} = 0 \qquad \text{(m14-5)}$$

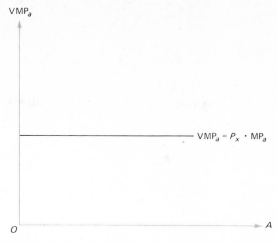

FIGURE 14-17
THE DEMAND FOR A VARIABLE INPUT, $h = 1$; ALL FACTORS ARE VARIABLE
If all factors of producton are variable and the production function obeys constant returns to scale, the MP_a (as well as MP_b, etc.) is constant. VMP_a is a horizontal curve at a level of $P_x \cdot MP_a$.

$$\frac{\partial \pi}{\partial B} = P \cdot \frac{\partial X}{\partial B} + X \cdot \frac{dP}{dX} \cdot \frac{\partial X}{\partial B} - P_b = 0$$

Rearranging Equation m14-5, we obtain

$$\left(P + X\frac{dP}{dX}\right)\frac{\partial X}{\partial A} = P_a + A \cdot \frac{dP_a}{dA}$$

$$\left(P + X\frac{dP}{dX}\right)\frac{\partial X}{\partial B} = P_b$$

(m14-6)

Factoring out prices and recognizing that

$$\eta = \frac{P \cdot dX}{X \cdot dP} \quad \text{and} \quad \epsilon = \frac{P_a \cdot dA}{A \cdot dP_a}$$

we obtain

$$P\left(1 + \frac{1}{\eta}\right) MP_a = P_a \left(1 + \frac{1}{\epsilon}\right)$$

$$P\left(1 + \frac{1}{\eta}\right) MP_b = P_b$$

(m14-7)

Since $P(1 + /\eta)$ is marginal revenue and $P_a(1 + 1/\epsilon)$ is marginal factor cost, Equation m14-7 can be written

$$MRP_a = MFC_a$$

$$MRP_b = P_b$$

(m14-8)

If the product is sold in a competitive market, $\eta \to -\infty$ and $P(1 + 1/\eta) = P$. Equation m14-8 becomes

$$VMP_a = MFC_a$$
$$VMP_b = P_b \qquad \text{(m14-9)}$$

M14.4 VMP FOR SPECIFIC PRODUCTION FUNCTIONS

Sections m5.5 and m5.6 derived the MP for specific production functions. The VMP in each case would be obtained by multiplying the MP by the price of the product (if competition prevails). In the case of the Cobb-Douglas funtion, where $\alpha + \beta = 1$, we can write (Section m5.5)

$$VMP_a = P_x \cdot MP_a = P_x \cdot \alpha\left(\frac{X}{A}\right) \qquad \text{(m14-10)}$$

Multiplying Equation m14-10 by A, we obtain ($VMP_a = P_a$ in competition)

$$A \cdot P_a = \alpha \cdot R \qquad \text{(m14-11)}$$

This means that if the process of production is governed by a Cobb-Douglas type of production function which is also homogeneous ($\alpha + \beta = 1$), the share of the factor is fixed. For example, if $\alpha = 0.4$, this means that revenue (equals total cost) will be distributed 40 percent to factor A and 60 percent to factor B. Recall that the Cobb-Douglas production function can be applied only if $\sigma = 1$.

CHAPTER

15

THE LABOR MARKET
(optional)

Wages and salaries account for about two-thirds of personal income and half of the gross national product in the United States. Over two-thirds of American families rely on wages and salaries as their main or only source of income. As mentioned in the previous chapter, the demand for labor is not different from the demand for any other factor of production: It is defined simply as the value of the marginal physical product of labor. (In the case of monopolistic firms, demand for labor is defined as the marginal revenue product of labor.)

The supply of labor, however, is different from the supply of other inputs. The change in the supply of labor over time is crucial for the welfare of workers. If the increase in demand for labor outstrips the increase in supply, real wages and salaries will increase over time. Demographic factors determine the change in labor supply in both developing countries and developed countries. For example, a massive development program leading to a 3 percent growth in the demand for labor would not benefit workers in an economy in which the labor force is growing at the same rate: Under such conditions the real wage rate would not change. The supply of labor is also affected by unions. Unions shrink the supply of labor in unionized industries while increasing the supply of labor in nonunion industries. We shall also see that the main impact of unions is not to inflict heavy losses on consumers, as is widely believed, but to redistribute income among the various groups of workers in the economy. The supply of labor is unique because the service and the person rendering it are inseparable. Where wage differences do exist, they can sometimes be explained by the mere fact that workers cannot leave their eyes, noses, ears, and emotions at home when they go on the job. We shall see in this chapter how some labor groups invented sophisticated means of limiting supply in order to increase returns to incumbent members of these specific groups. Interestingly, this type of supply manipulation was always achieved with government collaboration.

This chapter opens by considering the broad issue of wage determination over time.

15.1 WAGE CHANGES OVER TIME: MACROECONOMIC PERSPECTIVE

15.1a What Determines Wages

Approaching the economy from a macroeconomic perspective, we shall pretend there is one labor force represented by a single supply curve and confronted by a single demand curve for labor. The value of such an aggregative model is that it sheds light on the forces determining the change in the average wage rate over time without getting entangled in internal labor problems. Look at Figure 15-1. The initial aggregate demand for labor in the economy is depicted by the curve denoted by D_0. Such a demand curve is derived by assuming a fixed technology and a given amount of capital and other nonlabor resources (such as water, land, and minerals). This demand curve is defined as the marginal physical product of labor times the price of the finished product. It is akin to VMP_a curve displayed in Figure 14-2 for

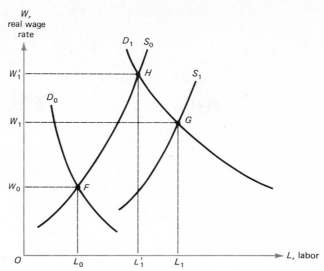

FIGURE 15-1 THE AGGREGATE LABOR MARKET
The initial supply and demand of labor are depicted by the curves S_0 and D_0. Equilibrium occurs at point F; L_0 units of labor are employed at an average wage rate of W_0. Had the demand curve shifted alone to position D_1, H would be the new equilibrium point and L_1' units of labor would have been employed at an average wage rate of W_1' dollars. However, if the demand shift is accompanied by a supply shift to position S_1, G is the new point of equilibrium and L_1 units of labor are employed at an intermediate wage rate of W_1 dollars.

two reasons: First, all factors are kept constant along the aggregate demand curve for labor. It is convenient to shift the demand for labor resulting from either technological innovations or capital accumulation rather than to incorporate these elements in one demand curve. Second, at this high level of aggregation, output is in terms of "units" of GNP (gross national product). Intuitively, a unit of GNP is the dollar value of a typical basket of goods and services consumed by the average consumer. More formally, GNP in real terms is obtained by deflating the nominal dollar values of aggregates of goods produced and sold in the economy by appropriate price indices (Section 4.1c). Since the price of a unit of GNP has no relative sense, we assume it is unity: $P_x = \$1$. The initial aggregate supply of labor is depicted by curve S_0. Such a curve is obtained by adding horizontally all the supply curves of labor of all the persons in the labor force. The intersection between initial demand curve D_0 and initial supply curve S_0 occurs at point F. As a result, initially L_0 units of labor are employed aggregately at an average wage rate of W_0 dollars.

We are now ready to consider long-run changes in factors that will displace either the aggregate demand for labor or the aggregate supply of labor, or both, thus giving rise to long-run changes in wages and aggregate employment. First, however, we must look at the process of aggregating the individual supply curves.

15.1b The Supply of Labor

Chapter 1 implicitly derived the individual's supply of labor when it considered the issue of leisure versus all other goods. Recall from Section 1.6 that work is equivalent to forgoing leisure. The amount of work performed by an individual is determined mainly by the wage rate, because the wage rate is in fact the price of leisure: When a laborer decides to perform one additional hour of work, it is equivalent to trading off one hour of leisure for all other goods. Figure 1-18 measured leisure along the horizontal axis and all other goods along the vertical axis. The point of tangency E between indifference curve U_0 and a budget line I_0 was the point of maximum utility. The amount of work performed was $L_1 - L_0$, where L_0 was the maximum leisure a worker can buy. As the wage rate rises, the budget line in Figure 1-18 rotates clockwise where point L_0 serves as the pivot. Recall that the slope of the budget line between leisure and all other goods is $\Delta Y/\Delta L = -W$, where Y is all other goods. Thus as W increases the additional amount of goods one can buy (ΔY) per one hour of leisure sacrificed (ΔL) also increases.

We now see that a supply curve of labor may bend backward. Consider Figure 15-2.

Panel (a) measures leisure along the horizontal axis and all other goods along the vertical axis. As before, L_0 on the leisure axis represents the maximum leisure a worker can buy (24 hours per day). As a result of a rise in the wage rate, the budget line rotates from I_1 to I_2, and so on to I_4. Connect-

FIGURE 15-2 THE BACKWARD-BENDING SUPPLY CURVE OF LABOR
Panel (a) presents the space of leisure (horizontal axis) and all other goods (vertical axis). Point L_0 represents the maximum leisure possible (24 hours per day). As the hourly wage rate rises, the budget line of the employee rotates clockwise from I_1 to I_2, and so on. The resulting PCC curve (Section 2.4b) first slopes negatively and then slopes positively. In panel (b) work performed along the horizontal axis and the wage rate along the vertical axis are measured. Corresponding to the negatively sloping portion of the PCC curve, the supply curve is positively sloped. Corresponding to the positively sloping portion of the PCC curve, the supply curve is negatively sloping (backward-bending).

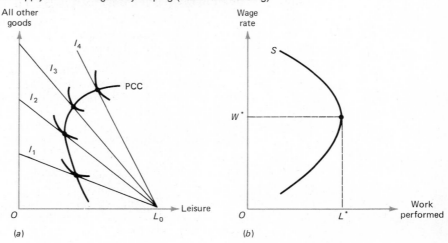

(a)

(b)

ing all points of tangency yields the PCC curves (Section 2.4b). We have drawn the lower portion of the PCC curve with a negative slope, implying that the *substitution effect* dominates. The upper part of the PCC curve slopes positively, implying that the *income effect* dominates. Panel (*b*) measures work performed (labor supplied) along the horizontal axis and the wage rate along the vertical axis. The lower part of the supply curve of labor slopes positively because less leisure is purchased owing to the substitution effect, as demonstrated in panel (*a*). Beyond a certain wage rate, say W^*, the PCC curve begins to slope positively and the supply of labor begins to slope negatively, reflecting the dominance of the income effect: With more income the worker desires more leisure.

Supply curve S_0 in Figure 15-1 is the sum of many individual supply curves. Although all individual supply curves may bend backward, their sum must not. This is so because when the wage rate rises, the size and the composition of the labor force change; secondary wage earners, such as teenagers, are attracted to the labor force, thus leading to a positive change in the quantity of labor supplied.

We now return to long-run shifts in the supply and demand for labor.

15.1c Long-Run Shifts in Demand and Supply of Labor

Let us focus again on Figure 15-1. Initially the labor market is in equilibrium at the point of intersection between supply S_0 and demand D_0. This point is denoted by F; initial employment is L_0 and the initial wage rate is W_0. Over time the demand for labor shifts from D_0 to D_1, and the supply of labor shifts from S_0 to S_1. Because the demand shift outstrips the supply shift, the wage rate rises from W_0 to W_1. The economic forces that underlie the demand-for-labor shift relate mainly to capital accumulation and technological change. The economic forces that underlie the supply-of-labor shift relate mainly to cost and utility of raising children. We turn first to the demand shift.

The main factor contributing to the demand-for-labor shift over time is technological change. We discussed the technological change in Section 14.1e. Since for the aggregate demand we assume that $P_x = \$1$, we should be interested only in the impact of technological change on the marginal physical product of labor. Robert Solow studied the technological change in the United States economy over the period 1909–1949.[1] He estimated that as a result of technological change the marginal physical product of nonfarm labor increased during that period at a rate of 1.5 percent per annum. The theory of the relationship between two inputs was discussed in Section 14.1b. If there is a positive relationship between two factors, the increase in the amount of one factor used will enhance the marginal physical product of the other. Figure 14-3 illustrated how the increase in the amount of B used led to an upward shift of VMP_a. Solow demonstrated that the capital ac-

---

[1] Robert M. Solow, "Technical Change and the Aggregate Production Function," *The Review of Economics and Statistics*, vol. 39, August 1957, pp. 312–320.

cumulation contributed only 10 percent to the total increase in the marginal physical product of labor over time.[2] What we learn from Solow's study is that technological progress and innovations are crucial for the increase in returns to labor over time. If a relatively high level of education is a precondition for technological progress, the Solow study also offers a lesson to developing countries: Do not neglect investment in schooling.

Now let us return to Figure 15-1. The Solow study shows that the demand for nonfarm labor in the United States would shift upward by 1.5 percent per year because of technological change and by another 0.15 percent because of capital accumulation. If the supply of labor were vertical and fixed at L_0, the real wage rate would rise by 1.65 percent per annum (not shown in the diagram). If the supply of labor were positively sloped but did not shift over time, the movement over time would be from point F to point H and the wage rate would rise to W_1'. This would slightly reduce the gain to labor from technological change. But if the supply of labor shifted from S_0 to S_1, the movement would be from point F to point G, increasing the wage rate to W_1, which is even lower than W_1'. This leads to the second aspect of the aggregate labor market, namely, supply shifts over the long run.

The importance of supply shifts over time cannot be exaggerated because the growth of labor supply can be so high as to completely dissipate any growth in real wages. In Figure 15-1 this would occur if the supply curve had shifted far enough to the right to intersect D_1 at the W_0 level. This situation is sometimes known in economic jargon as a *Malthusian nightmare*.

15.1d The Malthusian Theory of Population

Consider Figure 15-1 again. Suppose that in response to the demand shift from D_0 to D_1, the supply of labor were to shift far enough to the right that it intersected the demand at the previous W_0 level. There then would be no gain in real wages over time. This "nightmare" is redrawn in Figure 15-3. The two points of equilibrium in the labor market, F and K, are connected by a horizontal line called the long-run supply curve of labor. This long-run supply curve is denoted by S_m, where subscript m stands for Malthus: It is indeed the *Malthusian supply curve of labor*. Thomas Robert Malthus published his famous book on population in 1803. The crude Malthusian theory of population stated that labor is an input which is "produced" at a cost. The cost of labor is the minimum standard of living that is necessary to sustain the worker. In Figure 15-3 this standard of living is assumed to cost W_0 per unit of work performed. If the demand curve happens to increase from D_0 to D_1, the wage rate will temporarily rise above the level required to sustain the worker, say, to W_1, but then, according to this crude theory, marriages would occur earlier and more children would be born; with this and a fall in

---

[2]Actually Solow estimated the change in total output per unit of labor. But because he used a Cobb-Douglas production function it is legitimate to interpret it as a (relative) change in the marginal physical product of labor which is $\propto$(total output)/(labor). By switching from the Cobb-Douglas to the CES function (see Sections M5.5 and M5.6), economists were able to obtain slightly different results.

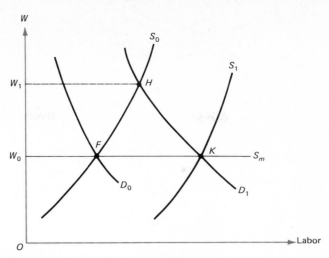

FIGURE 15-3   A MALTHUSIAN SUPPLY CURVE OF LABOR

W_0 is the Malthusian cost of a unit of labor. Initially, the short-run supply of labor S_0 intersects with the demand for labor D_0 at point F, at level W_0. Next, the demand curve for labor shifts rightward to a new position D_1. As a result, in the short run the labor market equilibrium settles at point H. Temporarily, the wage rate rises to W_1. As a result, marriages occur earlier and the death rate falls. This causes the population to increase relatively faster, thus shifting the short-run supply curve to position S_1, where it again intersects with demand curve D_1 at level W_0.

the death rate, the short-run supply of labor would shift to position S_1, where it again intersects with the demand for labor at W_0.

Although it would be difficult to find a developing country where the Malthusian model would be completely consistent with the population and GNP data, in some developing countries the Malthusian model explains time trends better than other models. For example, in Egypt between 1950 and 1970 population grew at a rate of 2.5 percent, while the real gross domestic product grew at a rate of 3.8 percent. During that period per capita income grew at a rate of 1.3 percent per year, not enough to get Egypt out of the vicious circle of poverty. Table 15-1 displays the rate of population growth of more developed and less developed countries from 1850 to 1975. It seems that during the period 1850–1900 population grew faster in the more developed countries of the world because technological change shifted the demand for labor relatively fast, and the population responded in a Malthusian fashion. During the period 1900–1950 the rate of population growth in more developed countries was declining, and the less developed countries caught up with the more developed countries. During the period 1950–1975 the growth rate of less developed countries significantly exceeded that of the more developed countries. These data are contrary to the crude Malthusian model of population growth, which would predict just the opposite. In countries like Japan and West Germany the rate of growth of real GNP was somewhere between 5 and 10 percent per annum in the post-World War II

TABLE 15-1 **Population Growth of More Developed and Less Developed Regions, 1850–1975**
(Percentage of annual increase since the preceding date)

	1850	1900	1950	1975
Total world	—	0.54	0.83	1.85
More developed regions	—	1.03	0.81	1.11
Less developed regions	—	0.32	0.85	2.18

Source: *World Population Trends and Policies, 1977 Monitoring Report*, vol. 1, Population Trends, United Nations, New York, 1977.

period, while their population growth rate declined gradually; West Germany reached a steady state in population. Faced with such data, economists abandoned the crude Malthusian doctrine of population and developed a more elaborate theory, which is capable of explaining the observed trends in both developed and developing countries.

15.1e The Modern Population Doctrine

The modern population doctrine views children as consumer durables (Sections 2.1 and 3.5). Services rendered by children are costly. The cost of raising children is compared with the costs of other goods consumed by the household. The demand for children can be analyzed in the framework of the demand theory for any good in the budget of the consumer. This theory focuses on the three major factors affecting the demand for children: (1) income effect; (2) substitution, or cost effect; and (3) schooling.

Income effect Children are assumed to be normal (superior) goods. Hence, *ceteris paribus*, the demand for children is predicted to increase as the income of parents grows.

Substitution, or cost effect In rural underdeveloped economies the cost of raising children had to be weighed against returns from children. Families were traditionally large because, as they grew older, children provided labor power on farms. When a family migrated from the farm to the city, however, it was soon clear that the cost of raising children increased steadily while returns from children vanished completely. The result was a decline in the size of urban families compared with rural families.

The cost of raising children is different in a modern city than it used to be in rural areas. Because the burden of raising children falls mainly on women, income forgone by mothers while raising a child constitutes a major cost item. The theory accordingly predicts that the substitution effect (cost effect) will carry more weight as a higher proportion of married women join the labor force, and as wages paid to women increase.[3]

---

[3]Wages paid to women and the rate of women participating in the labor force are positively correlated.

Schooling The level of schooling of parents affects their demand for children. We will examine (1) how schooling affects the demand for children when the cost of raising children is assumed fixed and (2) how schooling affects the cost of raising children.

Parents with a higher level of education may desire to give their children more education. Given a fixed, but relatively high cost of raising children, such parents may opt for having a smaller number of children to provide a higher level of schooling per child. Note, however, the contrary influences of education and income on the demand for children: With more schooling parents earn more income, leading to an increase in their demand for children.

Schooling also directly changes the cost of raising children. Parents with a higher level of education earn higher incomes, thus raising the cost of time parents devote to their children.

Finally, schooling may influence the actual demand for children. Parents with a relatively high level of schooling may be more efficient in obtaining information about birth control methods. This hypothesis is in accord with the general theory of information (Section 12.5). As an example, if two families decide to reduce their demand for children, the family with a higher level of schooling will have a better chance of actually succeeding in keeping the number of children at a lower level.

Do we have a strong theory of demand for children? The answer is no. We predict that with more income the demand for children will increase, but we also predict that with more income the cost of time, which is a major component in the cost of raising children, will rise. We suspect, however, that since the burden of raising children falls mainly on women, the cost of raising children will rise as wages earned by women increase and the rate of women's participation in the labor force rises.

The modern theory of population has been tested in various countries. The following section will discuss an empirical study that attempted to explore the modern theory of population in the United States.

15.1f An Example: The Demand for Children—An Empirical Study

Fertility rate is used as a proxy for the demand for children. The fertility rate is roughly defined as the number of births that a woman would have in her lifetime. We note that population may continue to grow for a few decades even if the fertility rate declines over time. The reason is that in the short run the distribution of women by age also determines the rate of population growth. In the United States a fertility rate of 2.11 represents the replacement level that would eventually leave the population at a steady state. Between 1970 and 1971, the United States fer-

tility rate fell from above the replacement rate to below it, yet the population continued to grow because of a time lag between the fall in the fertility rate and the impact on the population growth rate.

Table 15-2 displays some data on married women in the labor force and fertility. The data seem to indicate a negative correlation between the rates of participation by married women and fertility rates. Glen Cain and Martin Dooley attempted to estimate the statistical fertility function of married women in the United States for various age groups.[4] They statisti-

---

[4]Glen G. Cain and Martin D. Dooley, "Estimation of a Model of Labor Supply, Fertility, and Wages of Married Women," *Journal of Political Economy*, vol. 84, August 1976, pp. s179–s199.

TABLE 15-2   Fertility Rates and Married Women Participation Rates in the United States

Fertility		Married women in labor force	
Year	Rate	Year	Percentage
1940–1944	2.52		
1950–1954	3.34	1950	23.8
1960–1964	3.46	1960	30.5
1970	2.48	1970	40.8
1975	1.80	1975	44.4

Source: U.S. Bureau of the Census, *1978 Statistical Abstract of the United States*, p. 60, no. 80; p. 405, no. 657.

cally estimated fertility as a function of full-time earnings of wives, labor force participation rate of wives, husband's income, nonlabor income, wife's education, and several other variables. The fertility rate was defined as the number of children ever born per 1000 women ever married. The most important finding was the negative coefficient of the participation rate, for both black and white wives. The coefficient of the wife's earning was negative for blacks and mixed for whites. The coefficient of husband's income was mostly negative for whites and mostly positive for blacks, and the result was similar for nonlabor income. In the case of black families, the picture is clear: The income effect dominates when the earnings of the husband and nonlabor income are involved. For the black wife, the substitution effect dominates. In the case of white families, the negative coefficients of husband's and nonlabor income show that the substitution effect dominates. That the earnings of white wives did not have a negative coefficient

for two age groups (40 to 44 and 45 to 49) surprised the researchers. The results for the education variable were mixed. For reasons discussed above, this should not surprise us.

In summary, it may be concluded that developed countries are slowly approaching a stage of economic development in which the supply curve of labor will not shift at all, like S_0 in Figure 15-1. In contrast, as a result of never-ending technological innovations, the demand curve will continue to shift rightward, as illustrated by the shift from D_0 to D_1 in Figure 15-1. In consequence, returns to labor will increase more rapidly. Again, in Figure 15-1, returns to labor will rise over time from W_0 to W_1' rather than from W_0 to W_1. The long-run equilibrium will shift from point F to point H rather than to point G. This gain is mainly attributable to the fact that in the long run both returns to female laborers and the rate of women participation in the labor force will rise.

15.2 WAGE DIFFERENTIALS: MICROECONOMIC PERSPECTIVE

The theory of the demand for labor was spelled out in Chapter 14: In competitive markets the demand for labor is determined by the value of the marginal physical product of labor. In a slave society the theory of the supply of labor would be identical with the theory of the supply of nonhuman factors of production. A slave owner is interested neither in the leisure of the slave nor in the working conditions per se. A slave owner would force the slave to produce where the value of the marginal physical product of the slave is equal to the marginal factor cost. The cost of the slave is determined by such things as food, shelter, and health. It should be added that the leisure and working conditions of the slave enter the cost formula indirectly:

The less leisure provided and the worse the working conditions, the higher the cost of policing. In a free society, leisure and working conditions are important determinants in the labor-supply equation. The economic theory claims that a slave owner would manage slaves rationally. For example, the slave owner would feed them nutritional food to maintain their good health and would encourage them to consume more calories to maintain physical stamina.

15.2a An Example: Black Enslavement in the South

Slavery in the United States did not terminate voluntarily. Rather, it came to an abrupt end as a result of the violent Civil War. Owners of plantations and farms in the South considered their slaves good investments and fought for the continuation of the system. Fogel and Engerman, in studying the enslavement era, concluded that slave owners were perfectly rational.[5] The caloric content of slaves' diet exceeded that of free men by 10 percent. It consisted mainly of sweet potatoes and corn. The diet of free men consisted mainly of white potatoes and wheat. Slaves consumed on average 6 ounces of meat daily, 1 ounce less than free men. Again, as expected, the food of free men tasted better and consisted of more fresh beef; the slave ate more smoked pork. Fogel and Engerman also claim that, in general, slave owners tried to preserve the stability of the slave family simply because it reduced the cost of policing; slave owners who sexually exploited their slaves and broke up families arbitrarily were the exception to the rule. More importantly, as predicted by economic theory, southern slave farms were 28 percent more efficient than southern farms utilizing free labor.

In the following section we shall turn our attention to free labor markets.

15.2b Identical Wages for Identical Workers Working under Identical Conditions

We are now ready to see how the labor market equates the wage rate of identical workers who work under identical working conditions.

Assume that there are only two industries in the economy, X and Y. The two industries produce two different commodities, X and Y, by utilizing different methods of production. We assume, however, that working conditions in the two industries are equally pleasant with respect to the environment inside the plants as well as the convenience of the plants to the workers' residences. We also assume that the two industries recruit employees from a homogeneous labor force. In other words, *nonpecuniary* conditions are so similar in the two industries that workers do not care where they find employment so long as the wage rate is the same. Under such conditions there will always be economic forces that will equate the wage rate in industry X with the wage rate in industry Y.

Consider Figure 15-4. The labor market of industry X is displayed in panel (a) and the labor market of industry Y in panel (b). The demand curves for labor, D_x and D_y, reflect the value of the marginal physical product of labor in the two industries, respectively. The two supply curves are represented by S_x and S_y, respectively. The positive slopes of the supply curves indicate that either workers will buy less leisure as the wage rate rises or the labor

---

[5]R. W. Fogel and S. L. Engerman, *Time on the Cross*, Little, Brown, Boston, 1974.

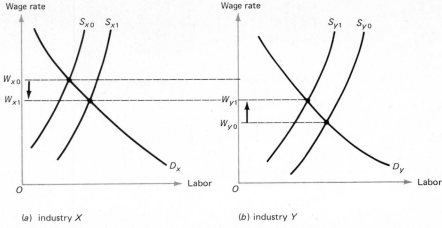

(a) industry X (b) industry Y

FIGURE 15-4   IDENTICAL WAGES FOR IDENTICAL WORKERS UNDER IDENTICAL CONDITIONS

Industries X and Y are depicted by panels (a) and (b), respectively. For the sake of argument, initially the supply of labor in industry X, denoted by S_{x0}, cuts the demand curve for labor in X, D_x, at a relatively high wage rate of W_{x0} dollars. Initially, the supply curve of labor in industry Y, S_{y0}, cuts the demand curve for labor in Y, D_y, at a lower wage rate, W_{y0}. The wage differential $W_{x0} - W_{y0}$ reflects equilibrium if either (1) nonpecuniary advantages are associated with employment in Y, or (2) employees in X and in Y are noncompeting groups, or (3) if employees in X imposed barriers to enter their trade. If none of the above is the case, employees in Y will relocate to X, the supply curve in Y will shift to the left to position S_{y1}, the supply curve in X will shift to the right to position S_{x1}, and an equilibrium wage rate of W_{x1} will prevail in both industries.

force participation rate will increase as a result of a rise in the wage rate, or both. (If the supply curves of individual workers are negatively sloped as illustrated in Figure 15-2, a positive slope of the aggregate supply curve is still possible if a higher wage rate induces a large influx of workers to enter the labor force.) Assume that originally S_{x0} intersects D_x at a wage rate of W_{x0}. Similarly, S_{y0} intersects with D_y at W_{y0}. For the sake of argument assume that W_{x0} is greater than W_{y0}. This is not an equilibrium solution because workers will move from the low-wage industry to the high-wage industry. As a result, the supply of labor in Y will shift to the left, and the supply of labor in X will shift to the right. This process of relocation will continue until the two wage rates are equal. The new supply curves will occupy positions S_{x1} and S_{y1}, respectively. The new wage rate in X will be W_{x1}, which is equal to W_{y1} in Y.

In the mid-1800s the farm labor force accounted for 50 percent of the American labor force. Today it accounts for 5 percent. The process of farm outmigration resulted from a continuous process of technological innovation coupled with an inelastic demand curve for output. As explained in Section 14.1e, the decline in the prices of farm goods dominated the rise in marginal physical product of farm labor, leading to a fall in the demand for farm labor. This in turn led to a differential between returns to farm and nonfarm labor.

In terms of Figure 15-4, in response to this wage differential, the supply curve of farm labor S_y constantly shifted to the left, and the supply curve of nonfarm labor constantly shifted to the right.

15.2c Equalizing Differences in Wages

Sometimes we observe that identical workers earn different wages even though labor mobility is practically perfect. Consider Figure 15-4 again. It is possible that the wage rates in the two industries are, respectively, W_{x0} and W_{y0} and that workers in industry Y are aware that W_{x0} is significantly higher than W_{y0}. Yet there is no migration from industry Y to industry X. This situation is explained by nonpecuniary advantages in Y relative to X. For example, graduates of business schools may earn more money than their professors. The reason we do not observe an exodus of business professors to the nonacademic labor markets is the convenience they associate with academic life. Let us rank all workers in industry Y according to their eagerness to move to industry X. If the most eager workers consider the wage differential $W_{x0} - W_{y0}$ as just a cut below the pecuniary compensation that will induce them to move to industry X, the labor market is in equilibrium and the wage differential is an *equalizing difference*.

It is evident from the above discussion that a major function of a free labor market is to create equalizing differences in wages in order to allocate labor properly among various industries associated with different nonpecuniary advantages. It is important to note that variations in nonpecuniary advantages may also arise from factors such as climate. Table 15-3 compares the adjusted average hourly earnings of production workers in New York State and in Hawaii. (The adjustment is carried out by taking into account that the cost of living in Honolulu is higher than in Buffalo.) We notice that the hourly earnings of production workers in Hawaii are 15 percent lower than in New York. This is an equalizing difference that compensates production workers in New York for the climatic disadvantage relative to Hawaii.

15.2d Differences Arising from Natural Noncompeting Groups

Human beings are distinguished by wisdom, brilliance, dexterity, imagination, and a host of other traits. These different traits give rise to *noncompeting* groups in the labor force: Acapulco divers and the rest of us, bank tellers and comptrollers, professors and clerks, engineers and skilled workers, pilots and bus drivers are just a few examples of pairs of noncompeting groups. Assume that in Figure 15-4, S_{y0} is the supply of tellers [panel (b)] and S_{x0} is the supply of comptrollers [panel (a)]. $W_{x0} - W_{y0}$ is the earning differential between the two groups. The two groups are noncompeting because bank tellers must receive a B.A. degree in accounting before they may train to become comptrollers. Thus the two labor markets, X and Y, are in equilibrium even though comptrollers earn more money than tellers. Table 15-4 displays differences in median weekly earnings arising from noncompeting groups. The noncompeting groups are defined in very broad terms. It

TABLE 15-3 Equalizing Differences in Wages (Data for 1977)

	Average hourly earnings, $	Cost of living per annum, $	Adjusted hourly earnings (New York = base), $	Percentage change
New York	5.67	18,298*	5.67	
Hawaii	5.51	20,883†	4.82	−15

*Urban intermediate budget for a family of four living in Buffalo,
†Urban intermediate budget for a family of four living in Honolulu.
Source: U.S. Bureau of the Census, *1978 Statistical Abstract of the United States,* p. 495, no. 798; p. 424, no. 687.

seems safe to speculate that *managers and administrators* and *private household workers* are noncompeting groups owing to a difference in both natural ability and level of schooling. The difference between *clerical workers* and *private household workers* is due more to a difference in the level of schooling than any other factor.

It is stressed that the differences arising from noncompeting groups are due to the position of the supply relative to the demand for the services rendered by each particular group. Thus professors of economics earn more money than professors of sociology because the supply of economists is scarcer relative to demand [S_{x0} in panel (*a*) of Figure 15-4] compared with the supply of sociologists relative to demand [S_{y0} in panel (*b*) of Figure 15-4]. It is correct to say that economists are scarce relative to sociologists because it is more difficult to do economics than sociology. As a result, in Figure 15-4, S_{x0} occupies a higher position relative to D_x, compared with the position S_{y0} occupies relative to D_y.

15.2e Differences Arising from Artificial Noncompeting Groups

Artificial noncompeting groups result from *occupational licensing,* that is, from the imposition of artificial barriers to entry into a certain trade. This section will discuss the economics of occupational licensing. Examples abound. In New Mexico a license to enter the liquor trade can cost more than $100,000. In New York City the cost of entering the taxi trade is the price of a medallion. Because medallions are in very short supply relative to the demand, the price is often extremely high. In many states barbers must be licensed to practice. License requirements include specified schooling. The cost of this schooling is tuition plus income forgone. The enforcement of licensing laws is usually vested in state and local government. The power behind such laws is normally in the hands of *boards of examiners.*

Licensing is prevalent in occupations where labor is self-employed, e.g., plumbers, electricians, barbers, physicians, and beauticians. The pretexts to pass licensing laws vary from occupation to occupation. Barbers, physicians, and pharmacists are allegedly licensed to protect the health of the

504 CHAPTER 15

TABLE 15-4 Differences Arising from Noncompeting Groups

Group	Median weekly earnings, $, 1977
Managers and administrators	302
Clerical workers	167
Farm workers	127
Private household workers	59

Source: U.S. Bureau of the Census, *1978 Statistical Abstract of the United States*, p. 423, no. 685.

public. Plumbers and electricians are licensed because services are not performed continuously for one buyer. Hence, allegedly, the buyer cannot have information about the quality of those who render the service. Liquor licenses are issued because some religious groups view drinking as immoral.

We are now ready to see that if licensure involves the imposition of barriers to entry such as schooling requirements, age limitations, or limited issuance of transferable permits, then only the incumbents benefit. The net returns to nonincumbents in the licensed trade should be the same as in the unlicensed trade.

Let us now focus on Figure 15-5. Let X and Y represent two free trades. Assume that returns to effort are the same in both trades; thus, originally in panel (a), the supply of professionals S_{x0} intersects demand D_x at level W_{x0}. In panel (b) the initial supply of professionals S_{y0} intersects demand D_y at level W_{y0}. Initially, returns to labor in X, W_{x0}, is the same as returns to labor in Y, W_{y0}. Also, initially L_{x0} units of labor are employed in X, and L_{y0} units of labor are employed in Y. Next, assume that the lobby of the employees in trade X bore fruit: Under pressure, the state legislature passed a law requiring a year of special schooling before a person can enter trade X. Thus a cost is now associated with entering trade X that is absent from trade Y. Assume that the equality between W_{x0} and W_{y0} will be temporarily preserved. As employees in trade X retire, job seekers will avoid trade X, for a while at least: Why should a person enter X if the return to effort in Y is the same and the cost of entry there is zero? Because new entrants will completely avoid trade X for a while, the supply of labor in X will fall from S_{x0} to S_{x1}. (Retired employees will not be replaced.) During this period the supply of labor in Y will increase from S_{y0} to S_{y1}. Employment in Y will rise from L_{y0} to L_{y1}, and employment in X will fall from L_{x0} to L_{x1}. An earning differential of $W_{x1} - W_{y1}$ will be created. This differential will be sufficient to compensate new entrants to X for the losses due to a year of special schooling. Thus we see that for those who entered trades X and Y after the licensure was introduced, returns to labor *adjusted* for the relative cost of entry are the same. For incumbents in X, a quasi-rent of $W_{x1} - W_{x0}$ accrues. Suppose a license to sell liquor is transferable, and it costs $100,000. Then at a going interest of 5 percent $W_{x1} - W_{y1}$ should amount roughly to $5000. In this example, X would be the retail end of the liquor business and Y could be any unlicensed retail business. Note that a new entrant into the liquor retail business earns

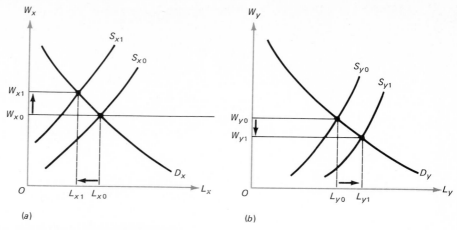

(a)   (b)

FIGURE 15-5   THE IMPACT OF LICENSURE
The labor markets in sectors X and Y are depicted by panels (a) and (b), respectively. Originally, the supply curve of labor in X, S_{x0}, cuts the demand curve for labor in X, D_x, at W_{x0};
also, the supply curve of labor in Y, S_{y0}, intersects with the demand for labor in Y, D_y, at W_{y0}.
The two wage rates are equal: $W_{x0} = W_{y0}$. After the incumbents in X impose barriers to enter
this trade (a specified amount of schooling, etc.), the supply of labor in X shifts leftward to
position S_{x1}, and the supply curve in Y shifts rightward to position S_{y1}. As a result, the wage
rate in X rises to W_{x1} and the wage rate in Y falls to W_{y1}. The differential $W_{x1} - W_{y1}$ is sufficient to compensate new entrants who opt for industry X. In equilibrium, new entrants should
be indifferent between entering X or entering Y.

$5000 more than could have been earned elsewhere, but the entrant also
borrowed $100,000 at 5 percent interest in order to purchase the license: In
the case of barbers, income forgone while attending the special school plus
tuition would be analogous to the purchase of a license to sell liquor, the only
difference being that an incumbent barber cannot sell the license to an outsider.

Consider again the case of liquor licensing. Let us change the previous
assumptions to the following: Licenses to sell liquor are *limited*, *nontransferable*, and *costless*. Then $W_{x1} - W_{x0}$ reflects quasi-rent. There is no
entry cost to X, and net returns to effort are at first not equal in X and Y.
What happens, however, when incumbents in X retire? Assuming a reasonable level of corruption, potential entrants will compete in bribing bureau-
crats, thus raising the cost of entry above zero. This process may lead to a
complete dissipation of quasi-rents for new owners. The American Medical
Association (AMA) limited the number of medical schools over the years
(Section 11.5a). Also, the period of training for a physician is longer than for
comparable professions. Thus the relatively high income of physicians reflects, in part, a higher return, which compensates for tuition and income
forgone while attending medical school. In part, however, it reflects quasi-
rent to limited licenses that are nontransferable.

A combination of a relatively high cost of entry and an arbitrary limitation
on the number of licenses is shown in Figure 15-6. If no extra schooling was

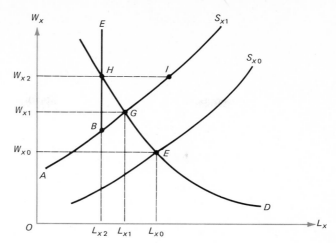

FIGURE 15-6 BARRIERS TO ENTRY

Services rendered by physicians are measured along the L_x axis. The price of services rendered by physicians is measured along the vertical axis. If no extra schooling were required to become a physician, the supply curve of services S_{x0} would cut the demand curve for physicians' services at point E. L_{x0} units of services would be sold to patients at a price W_{x0}. If extra medical schooling plus an internship were required (without other limitations), the supply would shift to the left to position S_{x1} and the new equilibrium would be depicted by G. L_{x1} units of services would be sold to patients at a price W_{x1}. Finally, if the AMA imposed barriers to entry, quantity supplied would be limited to L_{x2}, and the price per unit of service charged to patients would rise to W_{x2}. Unlike point G, point H does not reflect equilibrium in its normal sense.

required to become a physician, the supply curve would be S_{x0}. L_{x0} physicians would practice at an average income of W_{x0}. If medical schooling plus internship was required (over the schooling required for other academic professions) but the number of medical schools was not limited, the supply curve would be S_{x1}. L_{x1} physicians would practice at an income of W_{x1}. The differential between W_{x1} and W_{y1} [as in panel (b) of Figure 15-5, but not shown in Figure 15-6] would compensate for the fact that the cost of entry to the medical profession was higher than the cost of entry to other academic fields. (We assume that the talent required of Ph.D. holders is comparable with the talent required to become a physician.) If the number of licenses is limited by fixing the number of medical schools and other similar means (Section 11.5a), the number of certified physicians is artificially limited to L_{x2}. (The supply of services rendered by physicians becomes ABE.) The resulting differential $W_{x2} - W_{x1}$ is a quasi-rent accruing to the lucky ones who entered medical schools and were able to pass the examinations.

Note: In Figure 15-6, point G reflects equilibrium from two viewpoints: First, for persons endowed with equal talents, returns to effort in trade X, adjusted for the cost of entry, are the same as returns to effort in Y. Second, there are no waiting lines. Point H does not represent equilibrium: Quasi-rents accrue to incumbents; a waiting line amounting to $\overline{HI}$ exists.

15.2f An Example: Barbers in Illinois

Once the mechanism of some sort of licensure has been established, incumbents will continuously press for imposing additional barriers to entry to increase their quasi-rents. In particular, those who recently entered the trade can benefit from licensure only if additional barriers to entry are imposed. Simon Rottenberg studied the case of licensing barbers in Illinois.[6] The history of licensing barbers in Illinois started in 1909, and following Rottenberg, could be summarized as adding one barrier to entry on top of another:

1909: To be licensed, a person must either attend a special school or serve an apprenticeship and pass an examination.

1927: Only persons who had completed eight grades of school can quality for apprenticeship.

1929: The law is amended: *Both* six months of barber schooling and an apprenticeship are required for license.

1937: Minimum age requirements are added.

1939: Only citizens and aliens who had filed for naturalization can enter.

1947: The barber school term was lengthened from six to nine months.

1951: Completion of 10 years of schooling is required to enroll in the barber school.

The examination administered to candidates covers, among other things, "anatomy, physiology, skin diseases, hygiene and sanitation, bacteriology, barber history and law, pharmacology, electricity and light. . . ." As a result of licensing, from 1920 to 1950 the numbers of barbers per 1000 people declined as shown in Table 15-5.

Part of the reduction in the barber/population ratio might be explained by technological innovation. Rottenberg writes: "While the invention of the safety razor produced a good substitute for barber shaving services, there does not seem to be a good substitute for haircutting services"[7]

15.2g Differences Arising from Discrimination

Consider the data in Table 15-6 from the *Statistical Abstract of the United States*. Do such data reflect discrimination against women and blacks? Before we attempt to answer this sensitive question, let us develop a simple theory that explains discrimination.

As explained in Chapter 14, a firm will maximize its profit at the point where the value of the marginal physical products (VMP) is equal to the price of the factor of production. Similarly, an employer will pay an employee a wage rate that is equal to the VMP of the employee. Now, as an example, if male employers dislike associating with women at work, it means that the presence of women at work reduces their utility. What it implies is that male employers will not employ women unless their wages are

---

[6]Simon Rottenberg, "The Economics of Occupational Licensing," in *Aspects of Labor Economics*, NBER, Princeton University Press, Princeton, 1962.
[7]Ibid.

TABLE 15-5   **Barbers per 1000 People**

	Illinois Census count	
	1950	1920
Total population	1.4	2.0
Active population	3.2	4.9

sufficiently reduced to compensate for the welfare loss of the employers: Employers would pay women the going wage rate, minus an amount of money sufficient to offset the nonpecuniary loss due to their presence. This theory is very general and hence almost entirely nonoperational. For example, what if an average woman possesses a lower level of schooling and hence, on average, she performs less well than men? Or what about the legitimate argument that women are expected to quit their jobs more frequently then men because of childbearing? After all, replacing an employee is not costless. This type of argument led economists to embark on econometric studies where they attempted to test to what extent a presumption of economic discrimination against a certain minority group in the population can be empirically supported. Such econometric tests seek to disjoint earnings differentials that can be explained by differences in economic factors (such as schooling and age) from unexplained differentials. The unexplained differentials are assumed to result from discrimination.

15.2h An Example: Discrimination against Employees of Spanish Origin in the Southwest United States

This section presents an example that illustrates how economists study the impact of discrimination against employees of Spanish origin on earnings.

Richard Moss studied the earnings of Spanish-origin males relative to white (non-Spanish) males in the Southwest United States (Arizona, California, Colorado, New Mexico, and Texas).[8] He used data made available by the 1970 Census. Moss reports that in 1969 the median income of a white (non-Spanish) family in Texas was $9636. The median income of a family of Spanish origin in Texas for the same year was only $5897. The income differential is $3739, or 39 percent of the income of the white (non-Spanish)

family. Moss estimated an empirical earnings function by employing econometric methods. Earnings, the dependent variable, was explained by age, the level of schooling, family attributes, class of worker, occupation, mobility, and Spanish versus white (non-Spanish) origin. He found out that in Texas the earnings liability associated with being of Spanish origin was $1738. It is interesting to note that in California the income differential between a white (non-Spanish) and a family of Spanish origin was $2763. The earnings liability associated with being Spanish in California was estimated by Moss at $938, indicating lesser discriminatiion in California than in Texas.

15.3 THE ROLE OF UNIONS

15.3a The Theory of Unions

There is a strong temptation to define unions as labor-selling cartels (Section 11.9a). There are indeed some similarities: Under United States labor laws a union is elected democratically to represent all workers in a certain industry. Bargaining by other unions or by individuals is ruled out. Thus the power of the union to bargain is backed up by the government. We recall, however, that the goal of a cartel is to maximize profit, that is, to sell an amount of product at which the marginal revenue is equal to marginal cost. If we

---

[8]Richard L. Moss, "Earnings of Spanish-Origin and Non-Spanish-Origin Males in 1969, in Five Southwestern States." Ph.D. dissertation, Department of Economics, University of New Mexico, 1973.

attempted to define unions as cartels striving to maximize profit, we would run into two serious problems: The first problem would be to define the entity that claims the profit. If the entity is the collective of all workers who are currently employed by the industry, what about those who would later be laid off as a result of the rising wage rate? So long as demand curves for labor are negatively sloped, any increase in the wage rate by unions must lead to a reduction in employment. The second problem relates to the definition of profit. If the management of the union viewed the supply of labor confronting the industry as the marginal cost curve and attempted to fix the wage rate at a level of employment where this supply curve intersects with a marginal revenue curve derived from the demand-for-labor curve, it would not achieve any equilibrium so far as individual employees are concerned. Employees with a small probability of being laid off would be in favor of further raising the wage rate. Employees with a very high probability of being laid off would be opposed to it. Only if unions had the power to (1) limit the size of the labor force available for a certain industry and (2) ration the number of hours each employee could perform per week would they be able to function like cartels. We are thus led to the conclusion that unions' bargaining is subject to a very simple tradeoff: Given a demand function (curve) for labor, the higher the wage rate attained by bargaining, the greater will be the number of employees who will be laid off and forced to relocate. Thus the desire of unions to raise wages endlessly is limited by the welfare loss of employees who would be laid off as a result of the union's demand. In Figure 15-7 the labor market is displayed by considering two industries, U and N. During the preunion era the wage rates prevailing in the two industries are respectively equal to W_0. Assume that industry U now becomes unionized. The bargaining results in a higher wage rate W_u, and as indicated by the negatively sloped D_u, management lays off $L_u^0 - L_u'$ workers. These workers seek employment in the nonunion industry N, thus causing the supply of labor in N to increase, leading to a shift from S_{n0} to S_{n1}. As a result, employment in industry N increases from L_n^0 to L_n' and the wage rate is depressed from a level of W_0 to a lower level of W_n. The above analysis indicates that:

1. Unions give rise to labor relocation ($L_u^0 - L_u'$) and to wage differentials ($W_u - W_n$) that benefit the employees who remain in the union industry but adversely affect all other nonunion employees.

2. Unions can succeed only if there is a large nonunion sector (industry N in the model) that can absorb laid-off workers. Thus labor market equilibrium is unattainable in countries like England and Israel where there is almost no nonunion sector.

15.3b An Example: Unionism and Its Impact on Wages in Clothing Manufacturing

In 1914, the Amalgamated Clothing Workers of America (ACWA) was formed. By 1919, the union organized more than half of the workers in the men's clothing industry. Workers in cities like New York, Chicago, and Rochester were completely unionized. Cities like Buffalo, St. Louis, and Cleveland were not

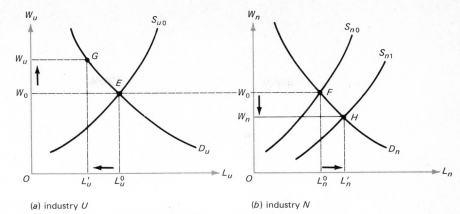

(a) industry U   (b) industry N

FIGURE 15-7   THE IMPACT OF THE UNION ON THE LABOR MARKET

Two labor markets in two industries, U and N, are depicted by panels (a) and (b), respectively. Initially, the supply curve of labor in U, S_{u0}, cuts the demand curve for labor in U, D_u, at point E. L_u^0 units of labor are employed at a wage rate of W_0. Initially, the supply curve of labor in industry N, S_{n0}, cuts the demand curve for labor in industry N, D_n, at point F. L_n^0 units of labor are employed at the same wage rate of W_0. Next, workers in industry U organize in a union. They bargain and succeed in raising their wage rate from W_0 to a higher level of W_u. As a result, employers cut back on employment from L_u^0 to L_u'. Workers who are laid off seek employment in industry N. Their relocation causes the supply curve to shift rightward from S_{n0} to S_{n1}. Thus, in the nonunion sector, N, the new point of equilibrium is H. This sector now employs L_n' units of labor at a lower wage rate of W_n. The wage differential due to unionism is measured by $W_u - W_n$.

unionized during the period 1919–1932. Table 15-7, which is based on H. Gregg Lewis,[9] shows how during the period 1911–1932, the ratio of union to nonunion earnings fluctuated between 1.20 and 1.39.

After 1932, most workers in the men's clothing industry joined the unions. Thus it became difficult to estimate the impact of the union on the wage differential. Table 15-7 illustrates that in real life the ratio $(W_u - W_n)/W_n$ (Figure 15-7) fluctuated between 0.20 and 0.39. As we shall see in the next section, this does not necessarily imply a great welfare loss.

15.3c An Example: Welfare Loss due to Unions

H. Gregg Lewis estimated that in the late 1950s labor unions were able to raise their wages 10 to 15 percent relative to wages of nonunion labor. Lewis also estimated that the displacement effect due to union bargaining amounted to roughly 10 to 15 percent.[10] These data can help us estimate the welfare loss due to unionism. First, note that the area under a demand for-labor curve is equal to the total value of output.

This is true because the demand-for-labor curve is defined as being equal to the VMP of labor. Since $VMP = MP_a \cdot P_x$ (Section 14.1), we can write it as $VMP = (\Delta X \cdot P_x)/\Delta A$. Thus $(\Delta A) \cdot (VMP_a) = \Delta X \cdot P_x$. A process of aggregation similar to the proof that the producer's surplus equals the area under curve MC (Figure 7-9) would show that the area under the demand for labor is equal to the dollar value of total

[9]H. Gregg Lewis, *Unionism and Relative Wages in the United States*, the University of Chicago Press, Chicago, 1963. Lewis reports a study by Elton Rayack, "The Effect of Unionism on Wages in Men's Clothing Industry, 1911–1955." Ph.D. dissertation, University of Chicago, Chicago, 1957.

[10]Ibid.

	Preunion 1911–1913	1914	1922	1924	1926	1928	1930	1932
Mean of union cities		51.7	79.8	85.7	87.6	87.4	80.7	58.4
Mean of nonunion cities	24.6	41.8	66.5	73.4	72.3	67.0	60.2	42.0
Ratio: union/nonunion		1.24	1.20	1.17	1.21	1.30	1.34	1.39

Source: H. Gregg Lewis, *Unionism and Relative Wages in the United States*, The University of Chicago Press, Chicago, 1963.

output. The latent assumption underlying this type of analysis is that capital is held constant along the demand curve for labor. This assumption is acceptable provided that labor displacements are not too large.[11]

In Figure 15-8 the aggregate demand for labor in the union sector is depicted by D_u in panel (a), and the demand for labor in the nonunion sector is depicted by D_n in panel (b). If unions did not exist, the same wage rate, W_0, would prevail in both sectors. The supply of labor would amount to $L_u^0 + L_n^0$. Following the method applied by Albert Rees, we now see how the loss in production due to unionism can be estimated.[12]

If by collective bargaining unions are able to raise the wage rate in the union sector [panel (a)] from W_0 to W_u, firms will respond by moving up along their demand-for-labor curve from point G to point H. Employment will reduce from L_u^0 to L_u'. These laid-off workers will seek employment in the nonunion sector. Employment in the nonunion sector will increase from L_n^0 to L_n' [panel (b)]. Assuming a vertical supply curve of labor implies that

$$\Delta L = L_u^0 - L_u' = L_n' - L_n^0$$

where ΔL is labor displaced due to union bargaining. The wage rate in the nonunion sector will be depressed to a lower level W_n, and the *wage differential*

is written as

$$\Delta W = W_u - W_n$$

The gain in production in the nonunion sector is the added area under D_n in (panel (b) which is covered by diagonal stripes. The loss in production in the union sector is the shaded area under D_u in panel (a). If we subtract the *gain* from the *loss*, we are left with the small loss depicted by the area of *EFGH* [panel (a)]. Simple geometry shows that

$$\text{Loss} = \tfrac{1}{2} \cdot \Delta W \cdot \Delta L$$

Rees estimated the loss for 1957 as follows:[13] In 1957, labor displacement ΔL amounted to 1.7 million workers. The wage differential was $700 per year. The loss then was

$$\text{Loss} = \tfrac{1}{2} \times 1,700,000 \times 700 = \$595,000,000$$

Since GNP in that year was $443 billion, the loss amounted to 0.14 percent GNP.

Note that in calculating the loss we ignore the issue of redistribution of income in favor of union members. If we assume that in 1957, $W_u - W_0 = \$350$, then the transfer from nonunion workers amounted to approximately $6 billion, more than 5 percent of GNP. The reasons why economists can say very little about this transfer were given in Section 11.2a.

---

[11] If we keep capital constant along the demand curve for labor, we follow a curve similar to VMP_a in Figure 14-2. If we allow capital to vary along the demand curve for labor, we follow a demand curve like D_a in Figure 14-3. Measuring the variation in output along D_a (Figure 14-3) is more difficult than measuring it along VMP_a (Figure 14-2).

[12] Albert Rees, "The Effect of Unions on Resource Allocation," *The Journal of Law and Economics*, vol. 6, October 1963, pp. 69–78.

[13] Ibid.

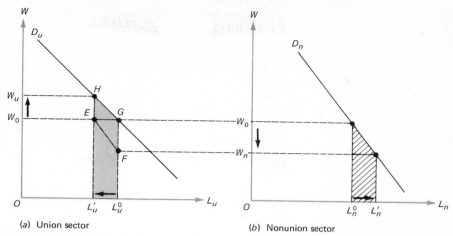

(a) Union sector (b) Nonunion sector

FIGURE 15-8 THE WELFARE LOSS DUE TO UNIONS

The labor markets in the union sector, U, and the nonunion sector, N, are depicted by panels (a) and (b), respectively. The demand for labor (VMP) in the two sectors is depicted by curves D_u and D_n, respectively. Prior to unionization in sector U, L_u^0 units of labor are employed in U and L_n^0 units of labor are employed in N. The same wage rate W_0 prevails in both sectors. For simplicity, the supply curves of labor are assumed to be vertical. After employees in U become unionized, they raise the wage rate to W_u. As a result, employers lay off $L_u^0 - L_u'$ units of labor. These units of labor relocate and find employment in N, increasing employment there to L_n' and depressing the nonunion wage rate to W_n. The area covered by diagonal stripes in panel (b) is production gain in the nonunion sector. The shaded area in panel (a) is the production loss in the union sector. The net loss is the area in panel (a), denoted by $HEFG$. This is equal to $\frac{1}{2} \cdot (\Delta L) \cdot (\Delta W)$.

15.4 MINIMUM WAGE LAWS

15.4a Minimum Wages—The Theory

Chapter 10 discussed the economics of regulation. Section 10.5 illustrated how legislating good things for the people leads to welfare losses because basically there is no such thing as a free lunch. In particular, the example of rent control (Section 10.5b) is relevant here: The idea that everyone should live in a decent apartment led to rent controls. In turn, rent controls resulted in shortages, waiting lines, and welfare dissipation through "key monies." The same idea of legislating good things for the people led to the notion that everyone should earn decent wages. Thus, in 1938, policy makers legislated a statutory minimum wage rate as part of the *Fair Labor Standards Act*. In what follows we shall see how the imposition of a minimum wage, which amounts to setting a floor on wages, increases the rate of unemployment. (We ignore the case of monopsony discussed in Section 14.4. Recall that if a labor market is governed by a monopsonistic market, a statutory minimum wage rate might raise the level of employment.) Consider Figure 15-9. Assume that all workers are of equal efficiency. Without minimum wage rates, the labor market will clear at a level of employment of L_0 and a wage rate of

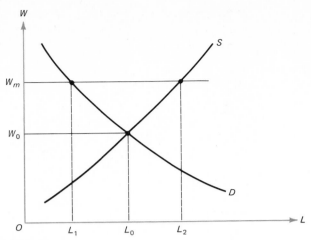

FIGURE 15-9   MINIMUM WAGES

Supply and demand of unskilled labor are depicted by curves S and D. Initially, L_0 units of unskilled labor are employed at a wage rate of W_0. After a minimum wage rate of W_m is enforced, employment of unskilled labor decreases to a new level of L_1 units. But at a high wage rate of W_m, L_2 units of unskilled labor offer to be employed. The result is unemployment amounting to $L_2 - L_1$ units of labor.

W_0. But after a floor of W_m is set legally, actual employment will fall to level L_1. Notice that the level of unemployment will amount to $L_2 - L_1$, where $L_0 - L_1$ arises because employers will substitute away from unskilled labor and $L_2 - L_0$ arises because at a higher wage rate more workers will be attracted to join the labor force. Note also, however, that although $L_2 - L_1$ is a measure of potential unemployment, unskilled workers who wait for a job at an attractive wage rate of W_m may be discouraged and drop out of the labor force altogether.

   The analysis in Figure 15-9 conceals some relevant aspects of the issue. For example, since fringe benefits are not covered by the minimum wage law, employers are expected to cut back on all kinds of fringe benefits offered to unskilled low-paid labor. By so doing, employers might succeed in keeping the *cost* of labor fixed in spite of the imposition of a minimum wage rate. A similar example would be a reduction or complete elmination of on-the-job training. Consider an employer who currently trains an unskilled worker. Assume that the degree of specificity of the skill acquired on the job is very low; the employer has no guarantee that investment in this type of on-the-job training will be recovered. If the VMP of the worker is currently $3 an hour but the employer estimates that on-the-job training costs $0.50 an hour, the employer will pay a (net) wage of $2.50 per hour. If, however, a minimum wage rate of $3 is imposed, the employer will discontinue the on-the-job program. Although the worker continues to work, his or her welfare diminishes because an option previously available no longer exists. We can summarize this as follows: (1) The potential $L_2 - L_1$ is unlikely to be reflected totally in unemployment statistics because of the *discouraged-worker effect*; (2) the impact of the minimum wage legislation is mitigated by narrowing of options, which in turn leads to (latent) welfare loss.[14]

15.4b Some Studies about the Impact of Minimum Wage Legislation

All empirical studies that tested the mechanism of minimum wage legislation verified that its main implication was a reduction in employment of the lowest-paid groups in the labor force. In particular, Jacob Mincer demonstrated that the imposition of minimum wage rates reduced the employment of all teenagers, the employment of males 20 to 24 years of age, the employment of white males 65 years and over, and the employment of females 20 years old and over.[15] Mincer also tested the hypothesis that the minimum wage laws discouraged many workers from remaining in the labor force. He verified the implication that the labor force participation rate, like the employment rate, was negatively correlated with the minimum wage rate.[16]

The statutory minimum wage rate is set at a certain date. Then inflation slowly erodes it until legislation again raises the minimum wage, and so on. An interesting puzzle (raised by Milton Friedman) is: If the minimum wage legislation mainly hurts the poor, why is it that legislators by and large support it? Keith Leffler was challenged by this puzzle, which is sharpened because the greater the proportion of low-wage constituents, the more likely the legislator is to support increasing the statutory minimum wage rate.[17] The attitude taken by Leffler was that politicians are utility maximizers. Hence they would not vote for measures that would adversely affect their constituents and thus erode their political base. Leffler argued that if those who lose their employment as a result of the imposition of minimum wages are left with zero income, the political puzzle is valid. However, if what happens is simply that those who lose their jobs relocate in the *nonmarket* where generous public welfare programs are available, legislators behave rationally: They increase the wages of the lucky ones who remain employed (L_1 in Figure 15-9) from W_0 to W_m. Those who lose their jobs become eligible for the generous welfare programs and may not be worse off. In summary, the Leffler argument is that the political perpetuation of relatively high statutory minimum wages does not stem from ignorance of legislators. Rather, it rests on a generous welfare system that provides a haven for minimum wage "victims."[18]

---

[14]For an excellent detailed analysis of the nonpecuniary impact of minimum wages see Finis Welch, *Minimum Wages Issues and Evidence*, American Enterprise Institute for Public Policy Research, Washington, D.C., 1978.

[15]Jacob Mincer, "Unemployment Effects of Minimum Wages," *Journal of Political Economy*, vol. 84, August 1976, pp. s87–s104.

[16]Ibid.

[17]Keith B. Leffler, "Minimum Wages, Welfare and Wealth Transfer to the Poor," *The Journal of Law and Economics,* vol. 21, October 1978, pp. 345–358.

[18]Ibid.

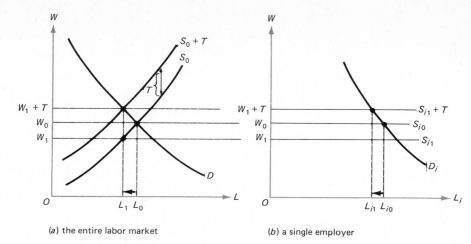

(a) the entire labor market   (b) a single employer

FIGURE 15-10   A PAYROLL TAX

The aggregate labor market is depicted by panel (a). The initial supply and demand curves of labor are S_0 and D_0, respectively. In equilibrium, L_0 units of labor are employed and the wage rate is W_0. Panel (b) depicts the demand for labor by a single employer. Its demand for labor is depicted by curve D_i. The single employer initially employs L_{i0} units of labor. Back in panel (a), after a payroll tax of T dollars is imposed, the supply of labor shifts upward by T dollars, employment shrinks to a new level L_1, the wage rate paid by employers to workers net of the tax is W_1, and with the tax, the cost per unit of labor is $W_1 + T$. In panel (b) the supply curve facing the single employer shifts from S_{i0} upward to $S_{i1} + T$. The cost of labor to employers rises by less than T dollars.

15.5 TAXES ON LABOR EARNINGS

Taxes on labor earnings or, as they are sometimes called, *payroll taxes* are analyzed like other excise taxes (Section 10.1). Employers are confronted with a supply curve of labor that tells them what is the wage rate that must be paid to lure a certain amount of labor. If a tax of T dollars per hour of labor is imposed by the government, then in addition to the wage rate, employers also have to pay T dollars to the government. Consider Figure 15-10. In panel (a) the entire labor market is displayed. Originally the aggregate demand for labor D cuts the supply of labor S_0 at a wage rate W_0 and an aggregate quantity of labor employed of L_0. Panel (b) presents an individual employer who is a price taker: This employer is confronted with a flat supply curve of labor S_{i0} at a wage level of W_0. This supply curve cuts the demand curve for labor at a point that induces the employer to employ L_{i0} units of labor per unit of time. After a payroll tax of T dollars is imposed, the supply curve in panel (a) shifts upward to $S_0 + T$ (Section 10.1). As a result, total employment shrinks to L_1, and the wage rate actually paid to employees is W_1. The amount of money paid per hour of labor is $W_1 + T$. Thus in panel (b) the new flat supply curve confronting the single employer is $S_{i1} + T$, inducing the employer to hire only L_{i1} units of labor. In conclusion, the payroll tax does not raise the cost of labor to employers by the amount of the tax per hour (T). Rather, because of the positive slope of the aggregate supply curve of labor, the cost of labor to the single employer rises by less than the full amount of the tax.

SUMMARY The chapter started by discussing the long-run macroeconomic perspective of the labor market. It was pointed out that in the long run the demand for labor increases mainly because of technological progress. In the United States the long-run trend during the twentieth century was estimated as a 1.5 percent per year increase in the marginal physical product of labor due to technological changes, and only a 0.15 percent annual increase due to capital accumulation. The long-run changes in supply of labor are determined by demographic factors. In this conjunction the *crude Malthusian theory* of population was mentioned, which held that labor is an input which is "produced" at a cost. According to this gloomy doctrine, the long-run supply of labor is horizontal, and regardless of technological progress and capital accumulation, the wage rate is doomed to remain at the level of the cost that it takes to "produce" labor. In contrast to the Malthusian theory of population, the modern population doctrine views children as consumer durables. The demand for children would increase with a rise in income, but it would decrease with the rise in the cost of raising children. It was mentioned that a major component in the cost of raising children is income forgone by the working wife. Thus in modern societies fertility rates are declining mainly as a result of the fact that a growing number of women are joining the labor force.

The second main topic was the microeconomic perspective of the labor market. The analysis began by proving that under identical conditions market forces will bring about equilibrium in which identical workers are paid identical wages. *Equalizing differences* in wages arise because working conditions vary from one industry (or geographical location) to the next. Wages and salaries will be relatively higher where nonpecuniary disadvantages exist relative to other industries (or geographical locations). Differences in returns to labor also arise because of *noncompeting groups,* such as bank tellers and comptrollers. Some noncompeting groups are created artificially by imposing barriers on entry to a trade. Most of these barriers are in the form of *occupational licensing.* Occupational licensing may take the form of limiting the number of medallions issued to taxi drivers in New York City or more sophisticated entry tests administered to medical school applicants. At the end of this section the differences in wages arising from *discrimination* against minority groups were discussed. Econometric studies are capable of separating differences in wages arising from discrimination from differences in wages arising from other factors such as education and age.

The third major topic was the role of unions in labor markets. The conclusion was that after a union raises the wage rate in the union sector, laid-off workers shift to the nonunion sector. As a result, the wage rate rises in the union sector and falls in the nonunion sector. It was concluded that unions benefit employees who remain in the union sector but adversely affect employees in the nonunion sector. One study was mentioned in which the welfare loss (to consumers) due to unionism was estimated as being only 0.14 of 1 percent of GNP, contrary to the belief that consumers bear the brunt of union demands.

The fourth major topic was minimum wage laws. We have seen that the theory predicts that minimum wage laws will give rise to a relatively higher rate of unemployment, especially among teenagers of minority groups. The theory was confirmed by various econometric studies. It was pointed out that minimum wage laws give rise to the abolition of on-the-job training programs, "free" lunches, and the like. Yet minimum wage laws are popular among politicians because those who lose their jobs relocated in the *non-market* where generous public welfare programs are available.

The chapter concluded by showing that payroll taxes are borne by both employees and employers. The burden of payroll taxes depends on the shapes of the supply and demand curves of labor.

GLOSSARY

Malthusian supply curve of labor This is a long-run horizontal supply curve of labor, at the level of the cost it takes to "produce" a unit of labor.

Modern population doctrine This doctrine views children as consumer durables. According to this doctrine, since children are superior goods, the demand for children increases with income but decreases with the cost of children.

Fertility rate The number of births that a woman would have in her lifetime.

Equalizing differences in wages Differences in wages arising in the labor market to compensate employees for nonpecuniary differences in working conditions.

Differences in wages arising from natural noncompeting groups Differences in wages arising from differences in natural ability of human beings.

Differences in wages arising from artificial noncompeting groups Artificial noncompeting groups result from *occupational licensing*. Occupational licensing limits the supply of a certain professional group, thus causing the returns to labor performed by this group to increase over what it would have been in a free market.

Union A labor organization whose main function is to bargain with management concerning the wages and working conditions of employees.

Minimum wage laws A law that sets a statutory minimum wage rate as a floor to wages. Such a law makes it illegal to pay less than the minimum wage rate.

Payroll taxes Taxes imposed on labor earnings.

PROBLEMS An asterisk indicates an advanced problem.

15-1. Where would you expect lines for hit movies to be longer, in rich neighborhoods or in poor neighborhoods? Why?

15-2. Would you expect the energy crisis to increase or decrease the rate of fertility in the United States? Why?

15-3. Will more schooling acquired by women in developing countries lead to a higher or lower fertility rate?

15-4. Do you think slave owners could entirely ignore the working conditions of their slaves?

15-5. Public school systems pay standard salaries to all teachers. Do you think that this is in accord with local government policy to send the best teachers to the slums? Why or why not?

15-6. In Figure 15-5 assume that X represents a city in which barbers must acquire 1 year of specified schooling before being licensed and Y is a city without such licensing requirements. Explain why the quasi-rent to incumbent barbers is $W_{x1} - W_{x0}$ rather than $W_{x1} - W_{y1}$.

15-7. If licensing to sell liquor is limited by the state, who loses and who gains?

15-8. Who would be more inclined to discriminate against a minority group, the majority stockholder or the chief executive of a large corporation? Explain your choice.

15-9. Describe the dilemma of the union in a country in which the entire labor force is unionized.

15-10. After the minimum wage was raised, the so-called "free lunch" was abolished. Is there a "free lunch"?

15-11. Under what conditions would farm labor benefit from the energy crisis?

15-12. Analyze the issue of a payroll tax under the assumption that the aggregate supply curve of labor [S_0 in panel (a) of Figure 15-10] is perfectly inelastic. Who bears the burden of the tax?

15-13. Would the results of Section 15.5 be changed if the tax of T dollars per hour were imposed on employees instead of employers?

15-14.* In a state in which *workmen's compensation laws* do not exist, wages are higher in industries in which the risk of on-the-job injuries is higher than in other industries. What would be the result of passing workmen's compensation laws that force employers to pay payroll taxes to the government, if the revenue from these taxes is earmarked to fully compensate workers who are injured on the job?

C H A P T E R

THE THEORY OF INTEREST, CAPITAL, AND EXHAUSTIBLE RESOURCES

(optional)

In Chapters 1 to 4 we saw how consumers allocated their budgets among the various goods available in the market. This chapter introduces time as another dimension to the theory of the consumer. Consumers can abstain from consuming part of their income at present in order to be able to consume more in the future. This is known as *saving*. Or consumers can consume in excess of their current income by borrowing money from savers. This is known as *dissaving*. Both saving and dissaving involve *intertemporal choices*. In a static economy saving is equal to dissaving; some people consume less than their income currently allows while others consume more than their income allows. In a growing economy producers borrow money in order to *invest*. *Investment* means the formation of capital in the form of machines, inventories of raw material, and structures. Saving is absorbed by both dissavers and investors. Chapter 5 to 8 discussed the theory of production, which emphasizes the least-cost combination of inputs and the optimal level of output. This chapter adds investment to the theory of production as a new dimension involving intertemporal choices. Part I of this chapter is devoted to the theory of saving, investment, and capital.

The 1974 energy crisis has turned attention to the issue of exhaustible natural resources. Lay people tend to have nightmares of running out of oil and other exhaustible minerals. If a certain mineral is finite and relatively scarce, the issue before producers is one of intertemporal choices: How should the rate of mining be distributed over time until the mineral is exhausted? As we shall see, today's nightmares have no foundation in reality: The price of a mineral must gradually rise over time, until at the time of exhaustion a substitute appears in the market. Some related but more complicated issues involving intertemporal choices concern natural resources that are both minable minerals and renewable resources. One example would be groundwater, which could be mined to the point where net pumping must equal the net natural recharge from rain and snow. Another example would be timber, which could be either mined or used at a rate equal to its natural rate of growth. Part II of this chapter will discuss these issues. You may skip Part I provided that you read Section 16.1, which discusses elementary concepts such as the *interest rate*, converting *present values* into *future values*, and alternately, converting future values into present values.

PART I THE THEORY OF CAPITAL

16.1 GENERAL CONCEPTS

16.1a Future Values and the Rate of Interest

Consider a consumer, Jerry, who purchases $100 worth of securities yielding 5 percent interest per year. This transaction means that he forgoes the consumption of $100 worth of goods in exchange for consuming $100 + 0.05 · ($100) one year hence. The fact that consumers will abstain from present consumption only if they are compensated indicates that they value a dollar's worth of present consumption more than a dollar's worth of future consumption, probably because the future holds less certainty than the present. The probability of death, sickness, etc., reduces the value of future consumption. In the example, Jerry is willing to part with a present consumption of $100 only if he is compensated by a rate of 5 percent, that is, only if he is given a premium of 5 percent of $100 one year hence. This allows us to define the rate of interest as a *premium paid to an individual for sacrificing present consumption*. Now, suppose that interest is compounded annually and Jerry purchases promissory notes from Lois that will mature two years hence; his compound value will be $100(1 + 0.05) \cdot (1 + 0.05) = $100(1 + 0.05)^2$. If consumption is postponed n years, the compound value of the promissory notes will be $100 \cdot (1 + 0.05)^n$. In general, if X denotes the present value of the flow and Y denotes the future value, the future (compound) value is related to the present value as

$$Y = X(1 + r)^n \tag{16-1}$$

where r is the going rate of interest expressed as a decimal or a percentage. Normally, interest rates are given as annual percentages, e.g., 5 percent, which should be written in calculations as a decimal, 0.05. Now, if the rate of interest is compounded quarterly instead of annually, the formula of the future value will be

$$Y = X(1 + r/4)^{4n} \tag{16-2}$$

and so on.

As an example, the (compound) future value of $100 two years hence at a rate of interest of 5 percent compounded annually is $100(1 + 0.05)^2 = 110.25. If in the above example the same rate of interest is compounded quarterly, the answer is $100(1 + 0.0125)^8 = 110.45. If the compounding is carried out monthly, the answer is $100(1 + 0.00417)^{24} = 110.49$. We notice that making the compounding period smaller and smaller does not increase the future value endlessly. It can be shown that the increase in the future is bounded.[1]

16.1b Present Values

The previous section examined future (compound) values. That is, intertemporal transactions were looked at from the viewpoint of the saver who is the lender. Jerry was willing to forgo $100 now in exchange for $105 one year hence. But Lois, who sold Jerry the promissory notes, would forgo the consumption of $105 in the future if she can receive $100 now. For her, the $100 is equal to a future stream of $105 *discounted* at 5 percent, namely, $100 = $105/(1 + 0.05)$. In general, solving for X (the present value) in Equation 16-1 gives

---

[1]The limit of the compound value is achieved when the rate of interest is compounded continuously. In that case it can be proved that $Y = X \cdot e^{rt}$. In the example, $100 \cdot e^{0.10} = 110.52$.

$$X = \frac{Y}{(1 + r)^n} \qquad (16\text{-}3)$$

We note that Equations 16-1 and 16-3 are in essence the same: The first gives the future value in terms of the present value; the second gives the present value in terms of the future value.

As an example, if Jerry offers Lois $1000 one year hence in exchange for X dollars now, what is the value of X if they agree to apply the current rate of interest of 7 percent? The answer is $X = \$1000/(1 + 0.07) = 934.58$.

16.2 LENDING AND BORROWING IN A STATIC ECONOMY

16.2a A Two-Period Model

We begin our investigation of intertemporal consumer behavior by considering the case in which the horizon of the consumer is limited to only two periods, say, this year and next year. Selecting the length of the period is arbitrary, a matter of convenience. Recall that we dealt with two goods, say, X and Y as in Chapter 1. Here we deal with *present consumption* and *future consumption*, which we shall denote by C_0 and C_1, respectively. In what follows, the subscripts 0 and 1 will denote "this year" and "next year," that is, the *present* and *future*. Chapter 1 assumed that the consumer was endowed each year with a certain budget and his or her problem was to allocate this budget optimally among the various goods available in the market. This chapter introduces another dimension to the analysis of the consumer's behavior: Given this year's income of Y_0 and next year's income of Y_1, how should the consumer allocate the combined flows of present and future income between present and future consumption? Figure 16-1 measures present consumption and income along the horizontal axis and future consumption and income along the vertical axis. The indifference curves in Figure 16-1 are convex and negatively sloped for reasons that were analyzed in Chapter 1. The intertemporal budget line, however, requires some elaboration. The consumer receives an income of Y_0 this year and expects to earn Y_1 next year. In the space of Y_0 and Y_1 his or her endowment is denoted by point A. But he or she must not be limited to consuming goods worth Y_0 this year and Y_1 next year. Consumers can either borrow money and enhance their present consumption at the expense of the future or lend money and enhance their future consumption at the expense of the present. We obtain the slope of the intertemporal budget line by recalling that abstaining from the consumption of ΔC_0 this year will yield $\Delta C_0(1 + r)$ to the consumer next year. Following Equation (1-6), we can write

$$-\Delta C_0(1 + r) = \Delta C_1 \qquad (16\text{-}4)$$

As in the previous examples, abstaining from consuming $100 now will enable consumers to enhance their consumption 1 year hence by $105 if $r = 0.05$.

From Equation 16-4 the slope of the intertemporal budget line is

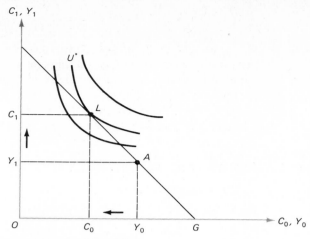

FIGURE 16-1 AN ILLUSTRATION OF A LENDER
The endowment of a person is denoted by point A: He or she is endowed with Y_0 dollars this year and an expectation to earn Y_1 dollars next year. He or she moves from point A to the point of tangency (between the intertemporal budget line and an intertemporal indifference curve) denoted by L. The person lends $Y_0 - C_0$ dollars this year, in exchange for $C_1 - Y_1$ dollars $[= (1 + r) \cdot (Y_0 - C_0)]$ next year.

$$\frac{\Delta C_1}{\Delta C_0} = -(1 + r) \tag{16-5}$$

If a market for funds is open to consumers, they can either borrow money, that is, follow their budget line from initial point A in a southeasterly direction, or lend money, that is, follow their budget line in a northwesterly direction. Since the tangency between an indifference curve U^* and the budget line occurs at L, the consumer moves from point A to point L along the budget line. He or she lends $Y_0 - C_0$ now, in exchange for $C_1 - Y_1$ one year hence. Since the intertemporal movement is restricted to the budget line, it must be true that $-(C_0 - Y_0)(1 + r) = (C_1 - Y_1)$.

Individual wealth is defined as the *present value of all the consumer's future income streams*. Geometrically, consumers can convert their claim against Y_1 next year into a present value of $Y_1/(1 + r)$. Technically, they can make this exchange by selling a note which promises to pay, say, Y_1 dollars 1 year hence in exchange for a present flow of $Y_1/(1 + r)$. Such an action, in Figure 16-1, is a movement along the budget line from point A to point G. Thus $\overline{OG}$ represents present income $\overline{OY_0}$, plus the present value of future income $\overline{Y_0G}$. We can write it as

$$\text{Wealth} = \overline{OG} = \overline{OY_0} + \overline{Y_0G}$$

$$= 1 \cdot Y_0 + \frac{1}{1 + r} \cdot Y_1 \tag{16-6}$$

Recall from Chapter 1 that the budget-line equation was written as $I = P_x \cdot X + P_y Y$. Wealth $\overline{OG}$ is comparable with budget I, and 1 and $1/(1 + r)$ are comparable with P_x and P_y, respectively. Although it is clear that unity is the price of present income flows in terms of present flows, the meaning of $1/(1 + r)$ needs some explanation: It is the price of future income streams converted to present values: If r is equal to 0.05, then \$1 next year is presently equal to $\$1/(1 + 0.05) = \$0.95$. The price of future streams expected 1 year hence is 0.95. It is clear that, *ceteris paribus*, if either Y_0 or Y_1 or both increase, the budget line will shift outward, parallel to its original position. The wealth of the individual will be greater: The intercept of the budget line on the horizontal axis will shift to the right. Such a shift in the intertemporal budget line is called a shift due to *the wealth effect*.

16.2b The Lender's Curve

How would consumers respond to a rise in the interest rate? More specifically, would lenders lend more as a result of a rise in the rate of interest? To answer this question, we focus on Figure 16-2. Let W' represent the original budget line for a rate of interest r_0. As the rate of interest rises from r_0 to r_1, the budget line rotates clockwise about the point of endowment A. The new budget line is W''. *Note*: All intertemporal budget lines must pass through point A. This is true because, borrowing or lending, the consumer always starts with an endowment of Y_0 and Y_1 dollars, respectively. Also, as indicated by Equation 16-5, as the rate of interest rises, the absolute value of ΔC_1 rises relative to the absolute value of ΔC_0, leading to a clockwise rotation. Before the change in the rate of interest took place, the consumer maximized her utility at point L. Her lending amounted to $Y_0 - C_0$ dollars. After the rise in interest occurred, she moved to point M. Let us follow Section 2.4g in order to distinguish the wealth (income) effect from the substitution effect. First, we temporarily confiscate a sufficient amount of wealth leading to an inward shift of the budget line from W'' to W^h. W^h is tangent to the original indifference curve U^* at point H. The movement from L to H is the *Hicksian substitution effect*. Since the indifference curve is convex and negatively sloped, the result is unambiguous: The pure substitution effect leads the consumer to lend more. Her lending increases by $C_0 - C_0^h$. When the confiscated wealth is returned, the consumer moves back to point M. If both C_0 and C_1 are normal goods, the HM path must point in the northeasterly direction (Section 2.3d). The movement from H to M is the wealth (income) effect. Since, a priori, it is impossible to tell which of the two effects will dominate, M can fall either to the left of L or to its right. Accordingly, the consumer may end up lending either more or less than $Y_0 - C_0$, resulting from a rise in the rate of interest. To reflect this uncertain response of the lender to a change in the rate of interest, the lender's curve denoted by L in Figure 16-4 is shown to be positively sloped in its lower part and negatively sloped in its upper part.

16.2c The Borrower's Curve

The response of the borrower to a rise in the rate of interest is analyzed by focusing on Figure 16-3. The original budget line of the consumer is W', and

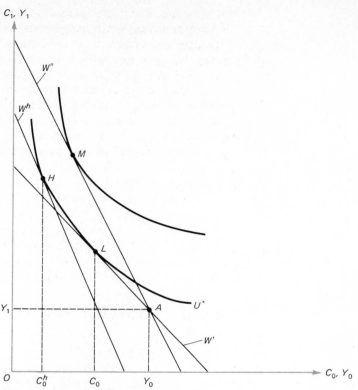

FIGURE 16-2 A LENDER'S RESPONSE TO A RISE IN r

A person who is endowed with point A (Y_0, Y_1) moves to optimal point L by lending $Y_0 - C_0$ dollars. As the rate of interest rises, the intertemporal budget line rotates about point A clockwise. The person now moves to point M. The new budget line W'' is shifted back—parallel to itself until it just touches original indifference curve U^* at point H. The movement from L to H (from C_0 to C_0^h) is the substitution effect. The movement from H to M is the wealth effect. The two effects work at cross purposes.

A represents the endowment. The consumer maximizes his utility at point B, indicating borrowing of $C_0 - Y_0$ at a rate of interest r_0. After the interest rate rises to r_1, the budget line rotates clockwise about point A. Notice that a clockwise rotation of the budget line, where A is the pivot, increases the opportunities open for the lender and diminishes the opportunitites open for the borrower: In Figure 16-2 the lender moved outside the area confined by W'; in Figure 16-3 the borrower moves deeper inside that area. The new budget line of the borrower in Figure 16-3 is W''. The new point of equilibrium is M. As before, to obtain the Hicksian substitution effect, wealth is temporarily added to the consumer such that his budget line shifts parallel to W'' to a new position W^h, where it just touches U^* at point H. The movement from B to H is the Hicksian substitution effect. Borrowing is unambiguously reduced by an amount $C_0 - C_0^h$. The movement from H back to M is the wealth (income) effect. Since both C_0 and C_1 are assumed normal, path HM

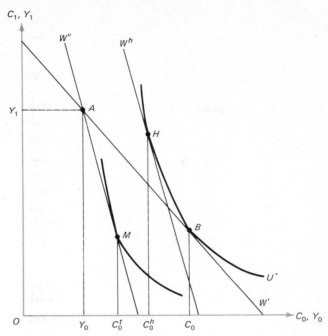

FIGURE 16-3 A BORROWER'S RESPONSE TO A RISE IN r

A person who is endowed with point A (Y_0, Y_1) moves to optimal point B by borrowing $C_0 - Y_0$ dollars. After the rate of interest rises, the intertemporal budget line rotates clockwise to a new position W'', and the person moves to point M. W'' is shifted parallel to itself until it just touches initial indifference curve U^* at point H. The movement from B to H (from C_0 to C_0^h) is the substitution effect. The movement from H to M is the wealth effect. The two effects coincide.

must point in the southwesterly direction, and the additional reduction of borrowing from C_0^h to C_0^t is unambiguous. Thus both the substitution effect and the wealth (income) effect lead the borrower to borrow less when responding to a rise in the rate of interest. That is why the borrower's curve denoted by B in Figure 16-4 slopes negatively throughout.

16.2d Equilibrium in a Static Economy

The previous two sections have shown that while lenders respond ambivalently to a rise in interest, the response of borrowers is clear: As the interest rate rises, they borrow less. This information is summarized in Figure 16-4. Equilibrium in the market for loanable funds is achieved at a rate of interest of r^* where $L^* = B^*$, that is, when a saving equal to the amount L^*, which savers lend, is equal to a dissaving equal to the amount B^*, which dissavers borrow. If the rate of interest were lower than r^*, borrowers would want to borrow more than lenders want to lend. This typical situation of excess demand over supply would bid up the rate of interest. Likewise, a rate of interest higher than r^* would generate market forces that would propel the

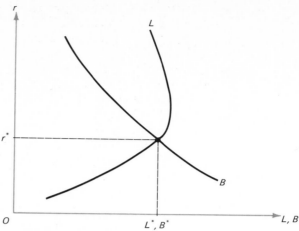

FIGURE 16-4   EQUILIBRIUM IN A STATIC ECONOMY
Lending and borrowing is measured along the horizontal axis. The interest rate is measured
along the vertical axis. Equilibrium is obtained at the point of intersection between lending
curve L and borrowing curve B. At the point of equilibrium the rate of interest is r^*, and
$L^* = B^*$.

rate of interest back to r^*. As was discussed in Section 9.2, as long as a rate
higher than r^* leads to an excess of lending over borrowing and a rate lower
than r^* leads to an excess of borrowing over lending, the market will be
stable.

16.3 A GROWING ECONOMY: INVESTMENT IN CAPITAL

16.3a Investment

Investment is the act of augmenting *capital*. In a primitive economy a farmer
may decide to devote less effort in cultivating a field in order to dig an
irrigation ditch. Income will fall this year, but the farmer expects that the
ditch will make it possible to cultivate a significantly greater acreage in the
future. In a modern economy a farmer may borrow money, or save, or both,
in order to pay a contractor to dig the irrigation ditch. It is clear that no
farmer would invest in a ditch who did not expect wealth to increase as a
result. Similarly, a carpenter may purchase a machine to increase productivity in the future. Or, a person may invest in schooling, by attending a
university for 8 years to become a physician. Such an investment would
amount to the cost of schooling and income forgone while attending the
university. This is an investment in human capital.

16.3b Investment Decisions

Now let us consider in Figure 16-1 an individual with an endowment represented by point A, and a rate of interest r that dictates a budget line W'

with a slope $-(1 + r)$ which passes through A. The entire wealth presently available to this individual is $\overline{OG}$. Look at it differently; he or she can borrow $\overline{Y_0G}$ in exchange for a promise to pay in the future $\overline{Y_0A}$ ($= Y_1$). The investment analysis begins by assuming that the individual has at present a maximum amount of cash amounting to $\overline{OG}$. If desired, he or she can climb along the budget line to a point like L. But suppose this individual happens to be an entrepreneur. He or she can produce a certain commodity and sell it in the market. This means that he or she can consider a variety of investments. If all the feasible investment projects were arranged by size, it is likely that their returns would increase with their size, but because of the fixity of entrepreneurial capacity, the investment curve would display diminishing marginal returns.

Now, in Figure 16-5 investment is measured along the horizontal axis going from point G to the left. Suppose a certain project was selected and thus a certain distance was traveled from G to some intermediate point between G and the origin. To find the expected return (in terms of Y_1) from that project, we have to trace a vertical line from that point up to the investment curve. Note also that the investment curve represents many alternative projects, not a continuous project. The concavity of the investment curve is due to the law of diminishing marginal returns. The goal of the individual is

FIGURE 16-5 INVESTMENT

We assume that an individual is endowed with point A (Y_0, Y_1). He or she can borrow $\overline{Y_0G}$ dollars and move to point G. The individual is an entrepreneur: He or she can invest in various projects as indicated by investment curve I. The entrepreneur selects point T where an intertemporal budget line W_i, which is parallel to the original budget line W', just touches investment curve I. Accordingly, the individual invests $\overline{FG}$ dollars expecting to be rewarded with $\overline{FT}$ dollars in the future. The indifference map of the individual does not determine the level of investment. It only determines point M; that is, it only determines how the individual will divide his or her consumption intertemporally.

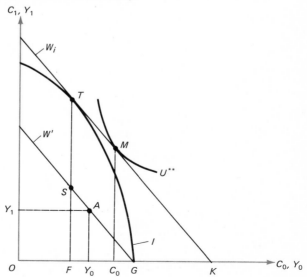

to maximize his or her wealth. Since, for each budget line, wealth (present income plus the present value of all future income streams) is represented by its intercept with the horizontal axis, the goal of the individual is to shift his or her intertemporal budget line as far outward as possible, and still have at least one point in common with investment curve I. Budget line W_i, which is parallel to W' and is tangent to the investment curve at point T, is the highest one which satisfies these requirements. The individual invests $\overline{FG}$ dollars (going from point G to point F). The expected return from this project is $\overline{FT}$ dollars, much better than sheer saving would yield. Wealth increases from $\overline{OG}$ to $\overline{OK}$.

The reader may get the wrong impression that an infinite blessing is hidden in Figure 16-5: The individual may sell the claim against the future stream of $\overline{FT}$ dollars, "slide" back on W_i to point K, and start a new investment project much bigger than the first one. The flaw in this procedure is easy to unveil: The expected return of $\overline{FT}$ involves the entrepreneurial capacity of the investor: Suppose a farmer invested a sum of $\overline{FG}$ dollars in a tractor. As a result expected return next year rises to $\overline{FT}$ dollars. Can the tractor be sold for the present value of $\overline{FT}$ dollars? No. A tractor can be bought from a factory for $\overline{FG}$ dollars this year, which is less than the present value of $\overline{FT}$ dollars. (The present value of $\overline{ST}$ dollars is the difference.) The answer to this "puzzle" is in combining the entrepreneurial capacity of the farmer with the services of the tractor in a specific process of production in order to yield $\overline{FT}$ dollars. In fact, the limitation of the entrepreneurial capacity was the factor that fixed the position of the investment curve to begin with.

16.3c The Arithmetics of Saving and Investment

Consider Figure 16-5 again. If the consumer chooses point T as his or her optimal point, the arithmetics of saving and investment will be the following:

$$\underbrace{\overline{FY_0}}_{} \qquad \underbrace{\overline{Y_0G}}_{} \qquad \underbrace{\overline{FG}}_{} \qquad (16\text{-}7)$$

$$\text{Self-saving} + \text{borrowing others' savings} = \text{investment}$$

The individual moved along W_i from T to M, his or her utility was maximized: At point M indifference curve U^{**} just touches new budget line W_i. In our accounting system we can state that the entrepreneur borrowed an additional amount of $\overline{FC_0}$ for the purpose of enhancing his or her consumption this year at the expense of consumption next year. As stated in Section 16.2c, $\overline{FC_0}$ is dissaving which must be provided by another person's saving. Combining the above results, we get the following summary:

$$\text{Total saving} = \text{total dissaving} + \text{investment}$$

$$\underbrace{\hphantom{\text{Total saving}}}_{\text{Lending}} \qquad \underbrace{\hphantom{\text{total dissaving} + \text{investment}}}_{\text{Borrowing}} \qquad (16\text{-}8)$$

Before we can come to a conclusion, we show that investment is nega-

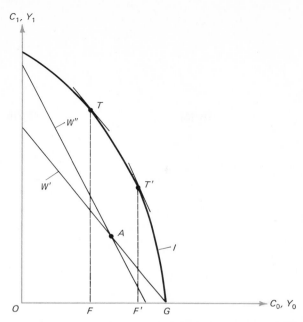

FIGURE 16-6 THE IMPACT OF A CHANGE IN THE RATE OF INTEREST ON INVESTMENT
Initially, the slope of the intertemporal budget line is represented by W'. A line which is parallel to W' is tangent to investment function I at point T. Investment amounts to $\overline{GF}$. As the rate of interest rises, the budget line rotates clockwise from W' to W''. A line parallel to W'' is tangent to the investment curve at point T'. Investment shrinks from $\overline{GF}$ to $\overline{GF'}$ dollars.

tively sloped with respect to the rate of interest. In Figure 16-6 the budget line is originally W', and the associated investment curve is I. Investment amounts to $\overline{FG}$ and expected returns are $\overline{FT}$. A rise in the rate of interest leads to a clockwise rotation of the budget line from W' to W''. Let us take a further step toward making our model closer to real life. Assume that the entrepreneur is endowed with a talent to combine factors of production and produce a commodity that can sell in the marketplace. We may summarize this by saying that he or she is endowed with investment curve I. Regardless of his or her current cash flow (Y_0), the entrepreneur can borrow any desirable amount of money not exceeding $\overline{OG}$ minus Y_0 dollars. He or she can invest this money in any single project, as indicated by investment curve I. Initially the entrepreneur invested $\overline{FG}$ dollars, expecting a return of $\overline{FT}$ dollars next year. After the rate of interest rises, the tangency point shifts from point T to point T'. Thus, to maximimize his or her wealth, the entrepreneur cuts back on the levels of investment from $\overline{FG}$ to $\overline{F'G}$ dollars. Point F' is associated with the new point of tangency T'. It is clear that as the rate of interest rises, the point of tangency between investment curve I and the relevant intertemporal budget line moves along the investment curve in the southeasterly direction. That is, a higher rate of interest results in a lower investment. Panel (a) of Figure 16-7 reproduces Figure 16-4. Since the L curve is also the gross saving curve and the B curve is the dissaving curve,

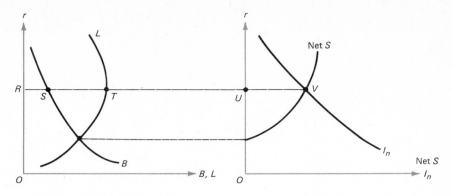

(a) consumer's lending and borrowing curves   (b) net lending (saving) and investment curves

FIGURE 16-7   GLOBAL EQUILIBRIUM IN THE SAVING-INVESTMENT MARKET
Panel (a) is a replica of Figure 16-4. L is the lender's curve and B is the borrower's curve. In panel (b) the net S (net saving) curve is drawn by subtracting the B curve horizontally from the L curve. Negatively sloped investment curve I_n intersects with the net S curve at point V. Net saving is equal to investment, and geometrically it is the segment $\overline{UV}$ ($=\overline{SS}$). Dissaving is equal to $\overline{RS}$. The interest is equal to $\overline{OR}$ ($=\overline{OU}$).

the horizontal subtracting of B from L yields the net saving curve (net S) in panel (b); the procedure is the same as in Section 14.3. The net S curve tells us the size of saved funds that remain available for investment after consumers have borrowed what they need for dissaving. The negative relationship between the rate of interest and the level of investment is depicted by curve I_n. In equilibrium curves I_n and net S intersect and the rate of interest is $\overline{OR}$; total saving is $\overline{RT}$, of which $\overline{RS}$ is absorbed by consumers and $\overline{ST}$ ($=\overline{UV}$) is invested.

16.4 CAPITAL BUDGETING

The previous sections were strictly theoretical. Rules will now be derived from the theory of capital which prove useful in daily applications. *Capital budgeting*, used in ranking investment projects, is an important field of applied economics. A bank deciding to rent computer services or buy a computer, the federal government deciding whether or not to invest in a big dam on a river, a manager of a manufacturing firm deciding between investing in a machine that cost more and lasts longer, or an alternative machine that costs less and has a shorter life expectancy—all these are decisions requiring the knowledge of capital budgeting.

What follows will argue that, logically, the only way to resolve such issues is the *present value rule*. In practice, however, other rules of ranking investment projects have been adopted by businessmen. These rules are acceptable so long as they coincide with the present value rule. When they do not coincide with the present value rule, they should not be applied. The most popular of the other rules is the *internal rate of return rule*. The next sections will show that under some circumstances the internal rate of return rule fails to guide the investor in making a logical choice.

16.4a The Present Value Rule

Let us reexamine Figure 16-5. The individual invests $\overline{FG}$ dollars at present and expects a return of $\overline{FT}$ dollars 1 year hence. This is a good investment because $\overline{FT}$ is greater than $\overline{FS}$, thus enabling the individual to move to a higher intertemporal budget line. Investment $\overline{FG}$ is a reduction from current income, and thus it is negative. From the construction of budget line W' we know that the present value of $\overline{FS}$ is $\overline{FG}$. Thus, if we were to add the present value of the postive $\overline{FS}$ to the negative value of $\overline{FG}$, the sum of the two would be zero. Hence, if $\overline{FT}$ is greater than $\overline{FS}$, the sum of the present value of $\overline{FT}$ plus the negative $\overline{FG}$ must be positive. Let us denote the investment which takes place now by I_0 and the return (net future income stream) next year by R_1 (I_0 = negative $\overline{FG}$, $R_1 = \overline{FT}$). Then the present value of the investment is

$$V = I_0 + \frac{R_1}{1 + r} \tag{16-9}$$

The basic practical rule of capital budgeting is as follows:

> A project should be considered for adoption only if its present value V is positive. If more than one investment project yields a positive V, the project with the highest value of V should be adopted.

The above rule is valid regardless of the shape of the indifference map of the individual. In Figure 16-5, a shift of the entire indifference map in the southeasterly direction or in the northwesterly direction will only change the point of tangency on the W_i line. But the position of the line is invariant to the indifference map. To put it differently, the goal of the individual is to maximize wealth. How to distribute the consumption of wealth over time is a matter of taste.

For example, suppose $\overline{FG}$ and $\overline{FT}$ in Figure 16-5 are \$10,000 and \$14,000, respectively. Calculate V for $r = 0.08$:

$$V = -10,000 + \frac{\$14,000}{1 + 0.08} = \$2963$$

If there are more than two periods within the horizon of the individual, the extension from $t = 2$ to $t = n$ is achieved by stretching Equation 16-9 as follows:

$$V = I_0 + \frac{R_1}{1 + r} + \frac{R_2}{(1 + r)^2} + \cdots + \frac{R_t}{(1 + r)^n} \tag{16-10}$$

Where I_0 is negative and $R_1, R_2, \ldots, R_n$ are positive. As an example, consider the investment project described in Table 16-1. (It could be a machine that initially costs \$10,000 and has an economic lifetime of 4 years. We assume that during the first year the entrepreneur expects to use the

TABLE 16-1   Benefit-Cost Analysis of an Investment Project

End of year	Investment (year O) and cost, $	Revenue, $	Net revenue, $	Present value coefficient $1/(1 + r)^n$ $r = 0.05$	Present value of net revenue, $
0	10,000		−10,000		−10,000
1	1,000	7,000	6,000	0.952	5,712
2	3,000	8,000	5,000	0.907	4,535
3	7,000	6,000	− 1,000	0.864	− 864
4	2,000	4,000	2,000	0.823	1,646
					1,029

machine to produce whatnots that will sell in the marketplace for $7000 and to incur current expenses of $1000, and so on.) An investment of $10,000 is made at the end of the present year: Following, at the end of each year in the future the project incurs a cost and yields a revenue. The present value of this project is $1029. The project shows a positive V and thus should be considered for investment. If better projects are not available for the individual, this project should be undertaken.

This section concludes by considering a project that yields a certain flow of returns in perpetuity. For such a project we can write $R = R_1 = R_2 = \cdots = R_n$. If n is very large, which is what perpetuity implies, it can be shown that

$$V = I_0 + \frac{R}{r} \qquad (16\text{-}11)$$

The proof of Equation 16-11 is straightforward.[2] Thus an investment of $1,000,000 in a project which is expected to yield an annual return of $100,000 in perpetuity has a present value of $1,000,000 at a going rate of interest of 5 percent:

$$V = -\$1,000,000 + \frac{\$100,000}{0.05} = \$1,000,000$$

16.4b Capital Recovery Factor

In Chapter 6 it was assumed that factors of production render services and that entrepreneurs pay a fee per unit of time for these services. Can the price

---

[2] Let $s = R/(1 + r) + R/(1 + r)^2 + \cdots + R/(1 + r)^n$. Denote $1/(1 + r)$ by g. S can be written as $R(g + g^2 + \cdots + g^n)$. From this we can get $g \cdot S = R(g^2 + g^3 + \cdots + g^{n+1})$. Upon subtraction we get $S - g \cdot S = R(g - g^{n+1})$. Hence

$$S = R \cdot \frac{g - g^{n+1}}{1 - g}$$

Since g is less than unity, for a very large n the expression g^{n+1} is very small and can be ignored. Substituting $1/(1 + r)$ for g in the expression $g/(1 - g)$ yields the result

$$S = R \cdot \frac{1}{r}$$

which is paid for an asset, such as a tractor, be converted into a cost per unit of service per unit of time? To illustrate how the price of an asset can be converted into a cost of a flow of a service per unit of time, consider the following example: A machine is purchased at a cost of $1000. The economic lifetime of the machine is 10 years. The going rate of interest is denoted by r. In order for the sum of $1000 to be an investment in permanent capital, the owner of the machine must accumulate a fund, which will amount to $1000 ten years hence. This is done by writing off an equal amount of X dollars at the end of each year, satisfying

$$X \cdot (1 + r)^9 + X(1 + r)^8 + \cdots + X(1 + r) + X = \$1000$$

Thus, by carrying out simple calculations,[3] we get

$$X \cdot \frac{(1 + r)^{10} - 1}{r} = \$1000$$

Solving for X, we obtain

$$X = \frac{\$1000 \cdot r}{(1 + r)^{10} - 1}$$

where X may be considered as annual capital replacement. If we add the interest payment forgone to this, we obtain

$$\text{Annual cost of capital} = \frac{\$1000 \cdot r}{(1 + r)^{10} - 1} + \$1000 \cdot r$$

In general, assuming an investment of $1, an economic lifetime of n years, and a rate of interest r, the cost of capital per annum is

$$\frac{r}{(1 + r)^n - 1} + r$$

which is known as the *capital recovery factor* (CRF). Suppose, for example,

---

[3] Let R replace $1 + r$. We can write

$$S = 1 + R + R^2 + \cdots + R^{n-1}$$
$$R \cdot S = R + R^2 + \cdots + R^{n-1} + R^n$$

Now $S - R \cdot S = 1 - R^n$. Accordingly, we obtain the result

$$S = \frac{1 - R^n}{1 - R}$$

and, upon substituting,

$$S = \frac{1 - (1 + r)^n}{1 - (1 + r)} = \frac{(1 + r)^n - 1}{r}$$

Since

$$X \cdot \frac{(1 + r)^n - 1}{r} = I_0$$

where I_0 is the initial investment, we can express X as a function of r, n, and I_0 as follows:

$$X = \frac{r}{(1 + r)^n - 1} \cdot I_0$$

TABLE 16-2
Capital Recovery Factor, $r = 0.05$

n	5	6	7	8	9	10	11	12	13	14	15
CFR	0.231	0.197	0.173	0.155	0.141	0.130	0.120	0.113	0.106	0.101	0.096
Rule of thumb	0.225	0.192	0.168	0.150	0.136	0.125	0.116	0.108	0.102	0.096	0.092

that a sum of $1000 is invested in a machine whose lifetime is 10 years. The rate of interest if 5 percent. Then the annual cost of capital is

$$\frac{r}{(1 + r)^n - 1} + r = \frac{0.05}{(1 + 0.05)^{10} - 1} + 0.05 = 0.130$$

$$0.130 \times \$1000 = \$130$$

and accordingly, the annual alternative cost of capital worth $1000 is $130.

The capital recovery factor, like the factors converting future dollars to present worth and vice versa, is found in tables calculated for different values of r and n. A sample table, for $r = 0.03$, 0.05, and 0.08 and $n = 1, 2, \ldots$, 10 years, is presented in Appendix 16.

If a table for CRF is not available, a rule of thumb can be used for approximation. According to this rule, we multiple I_0, the initial investment, by the expression $1/n + \frac{1}{2} \cdot r$. For example, consider in Table 16-2 a comparison of CRF with the rule of thumb for $r = 5$ percent and $n = 5, \ldots$, 15.

16.4c The Internal Rate of Return

The *internal rate of return test* is very popular among investors. Yet it may lead the investor to the wrong decision.

The internal rate of return is defined as that rate of return which would equate the present value of future returns (income streams) to the cost of the investment. For example, what is the internal rate of return i on an investment of, say $285.70 which takes place at the beginning of the year, if the only expected yields are $100 one year hence and $200 two years hence? Solve

$$285.7 = \frac{100}{1 + i} + \frac{200}{(1 + i)^2}$$

or in general solve

$$V' = \frac{R_1}{1 + i} + \frac{R_2}{(1 + i)^2}$$

where R_1 and R_2 are the expected yields. V' should not be confused with V in Equation 16-10; it is simply the investment. The value of i cannot be obtained as a simple solution for a linear equation. Let the right-hand member of this equation be denoted by H; then we go through a process of iteration as in Table 16-3.

TABLE 16-3   **Calculating** *i*

i	*H*	*H* relative to *V*'
0.04	281.1	Low; try a lower *i*
0.02	290.3	High; try a higher *i*
0.035	283.3	Low; try a lower *i*
0.025	287.9	High; try a higher *i*
0.03	285.6	Very close; stop iteration

In this example, the internal rate of return is roughly 3 percent.

Whenever the internal rate of return has to be determined for a project in which yield R_i varies from year to year, a process of iteration must be applied to obtain a solution. However, if the yield is R dollars in perpetuity, Equation 16-11 can be utilized to solve for the internal rate of return without applying a process of iteration. Now, to require that the present value of future returns be equal to the cost of the investment means to set $V = 0$, thus obtaining the result that $-I_0 = R/r$. Since in Equation 16-11, I_0 is negative, $-I_0$ is a positive number. In the internal rate of return formulation we termed it V'. Also, r now becomes the unknown, which we termed i. The problem is to find an internal rate of return i that will equate V' ($= -I_0$) with R/i.

Practical businessmen apply the following rule: Accept the project if the internal rate of return is higher than the rate of interest. Reject the project if the internal rate of return is lower than the rate of interest. In what follows we see that the internal rate of return rule is valid provided that V' and i are negatively related. Moreover, it is tempting to extend the internal rate of return rule to ranking two or more (exclusive) projects. We shall see that in many cases this type of ranking might lead to illogical results.

It is evident that if the yield is R dollars per annum in perpetuity, the curve relating V' to i is a *rectangular hyperbola*.[4] Curve VV relating V' to i for $R = \$10$ is depicted in Figure 16-8. Suppose the cost of the investment is $200. Then the internal rate of return is 5 percent. If the going interest rate is 3 percent, this project should be accepted according to the above test. The true test, however, as the theory indicates, is to compare the present value of future yields at the going 3 percent interest rate with the cost of the investment. In the example, the discounted present value of future yields is $333, and it exceeds the cost of investment of $200. Clearly, this is a worthwhile investment, because the present value is $V = -200 + 333 = \$133$.

From the construction of Figure 16-8 it is clear that if VV is negatively sloped, the internal rate of return test is in accord with the true present value test. As indicated by Figure 16-8, if the interest rate is lower than the internal

---

[4] $V' = R/i$. We can multiply both sides by i to obtain

$$i \cdot V' = R$$

which is the formula of a *rectangular hyperbola*. In this formulation, R is held constant and i and V' vary.

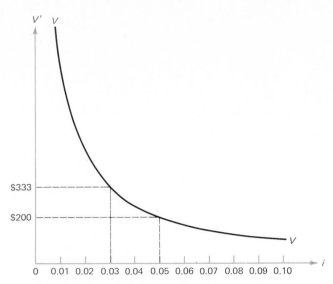

FIGURE 16-8 PRESENT VALUE VERSUS INTERNAL RATE OF RETURN
Along the horizontal axis we measure the internal rate of return i and the interest rate r.
Along the vertical axis we measure V' and $\hat{V}$. Curve VV is the locus of points generated by
$V' \cdot i = \$10$ or $\hat{V} \cdot r = \$10$. For example, if the initial investment is $200, then $\$200 \cdot i = \$10$
and $i = 0.05$. If the rate of interest is 0.03, then $\hat{V} \cdot 0.03 = \$10$ and $\hat{V} = \$10/0.03 =$
$333.33. Since VV is negatively sloped, the internal rate of return test $(i > r)$ is in accord with
the present value test: Present value of project $= -200 + 333.33 + \$133.3$. $\hat{V}$ is the present
value of all future yields.

rate of return, the discounted present value of future yields must exceed the
cost of the investment.

But consider a project in which the discounted present value of future
yields is positively related to the interest rate. For example, consider
a hypothetical project which yields $50 at the end of the first year and $-\$60$
at the end of the tenth year. Table 16-4 describes how the discounted present
value of this project rises with interest rate.

Suppose the cost of the investment is $18.50. Then, as indicated by Table
16-4, the internal rate of return is 8 percent. If the going rate of interest is 6
percent, the above test is misleading, because it tells us to accept the project.
But as indicated by Table 16-4, at a 6 percent interest rate, the discounted
present value of the project is $13.7, which is less than the cost of $18.50.
Thus investment in such a project would give rise to a wealth loss of $4.8.

Finally, consider two projects, say A and B, for which the cost of investment is the same, but curves VV are different. This case is depicted in Figure

TABLE 16-4 **A Failure of the Internal Rate of Return Test**

i	0.01	0.02	0.03	0.04	0.05	0.06	0.07	0.08	0.09	0.10
$V'(\$)$	-4.8	-0.2	4.0	7.5	10.8	13.7	16.4	18.5	20.5	22.3

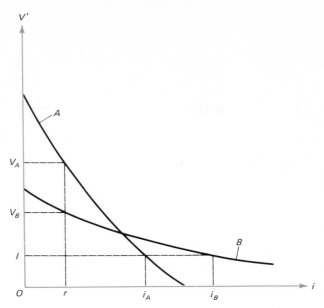

FIGURE 16-9   SELECTING THE BETTER PROJECT
Along the horizontal axis we measure the internal rate of return i and the rate of interest r. Along the vertical axis we measure $\hat{V}$ and V'. Curves A and B are VV-type curves as in Figure 16-8 ($V' \cdot i = R$ or $\hat{V} \cdot r = R$). Both projects require the same initial investment I. However, if we apply the internal rate of return test, since $i_B > i_A$, we rank project B over project A. But, given a rate of interest r, the present value of project A is higher than the present value of project B: $\hat{V}_A > \hat{V}_B$. The conclusion is that the internal rate of return test is misleading in this example.

16-9. It is left for the reader to show that the internal rate of return test for profitability fails if the problem at hand is to select only one of the two projects.

16.4d An Example: The Trans-Alaskan Pipeline

In the late 1950s a major oil field was discovered in the North Slope of Alaska. The oil companies involved in a huge investment in the Trans-Alaskan pipeline considered a few alternatives, one of which was an 800-mile-long pipeline from Prudhoe Bay to Valdez, and then from Valdez to California by tankers. Since it was to carry hot oil through seismically sensitive zones and across permanently frozen arctic tundra, environmentalists protested against the pipeline. Had it not been for an act of Congress in 1973, amending the Mineral Leasing Act of 1920 and authorizing the construction of the Trans-Alaskan pipeline, it might have been buried in complex legal

procedures and never seen the light. Two issues were debated before the construction of the pipeline: first, the straightforward economic issue of the present value of the benefit as related to the investment and second, the environmental issue. If the damage to the environment could be assigned a dollar value, it should have been subtracted from the future benefits of selling oil in the American market. This example abstains from the environmental issues because its goal is to focus on the procedure of comparing the present value of future benefits with the investment in the pipeline.

The example presented here is based on a study

TABLE 16-5 Present Value of Future Benefits

Interest rate, percent	Present value of benefits ($ billion)
8	7.25
10	5.68
12	4.52

by Charles Cicchetti,[5] completed in 1972, before the Yom Kippur War touched off the energy crisis (Table 11-2), making his data outdated. Nevertheless, given the information available prior to 1972, his study provides an excellent illustration of applying capital budgeting to real problems.

Investment in the pipeline was estimated in the range of $1.75 to $2.50 billion. The interest rate was assumed to range between 8 and 12 percent.

It was also assumed that Alaskan oil would replace Iranian light oil: After adjustments for weight and other considerations the Alaskan oil could command a price of $2.13 per barrel. The variable costs involved in getting a barrel of oil from the North Slope of Alaska to the West Coast were as follows:

Field costs	$0.245
Operating the pipe	0.13
Tankers	0.35
Total	$0.725

The net benefit per barrel was accordingly estimated at $2.13 − $0.725. Let us denote the expected throughput during the first year by F_1, during the second year by F_2, and so on, up to the last year's throughput of F_n. Then, the present value of all the future benefits is

$$\text{Present value of benefits} = \frac{(2.13 - 0.725) \cdot F_1}{1 + r}$$

$$+ \frac{(2.13 - 0.725) \cdot F_2}{(1 + r)^2} + \cdots + \frac{(2.13 - 0.725) \cdot F_n}{(1 + r)^n}$$

The results are given in Table 16-5. Subtracting the values of the investment, namely, the range $1.75 to $2.50 billion, we obtain a table of present values of the Trans-Alaskan pipeline as in Table 16-6 (Equation 16-10): Thus the present value (V) of the Trans-Alaskan pipeline was in the range $2.02 to $5.50 billions: A good project!

16.5 TAXES ON INCOME FROM CAPITAL

Corporate income taxes are in fact taxes imposed on income from capital. Because such taxes are imposed only on capital invested in the corporate sector, overinvestment of capital in the noncorporate sector results. The corporate sector in the United States covers industries such as mining, most manufacturing, energy products, contract construction, transportation, public utilities, and services. The noncorporate sector covers industries such as agriculture, crude oil and gas, real estate, and some services and manufacturing. In Figure 16-10, panel (a) represents the corporate sector and panel (b) represents the noncorporate sector. The VMP curve of capital in the corporate sector is denoted by D_0 and that of the noncorporate sector by D_0'. In the absence of any taxes on capital, owners of capital will allocate capital among the two sectors such that VMP is equal for the two sectors. This VMP is equal to $\overline{OK}$ in the diagram.

Originally, $\overline{OA}$ units of capital are employed in the corporate sector and

---

[5]Charles J. Cicchetti, *Alaskan Oil, Alternative Routes and Markets*, The Johns Hopkins Press, Baltimore, 1972.

TABLE 16-6

TABLE 16-6 **Values of V for the Trans-Alaskan Pipeline**

Rate of interest, percent	Initial investment ($ billion)	
	1.75	2.50
8	5.50	4.75
10	3.93	3.18
12	2.77	2.02

Source: C. Cicchetti, *Alaskan Oil, Alternative Routes and Markets*, The Johns Hopkins Press, Baltimore, 1972.

$\overline{OF}$ in the noncorporate sector. Upon the imposition of taxes on income from capital in the corporate sector, owners of capital are faced with a net VMP curve in panel (*a*) denoted by D_1. Curve D_1 is lower by the tax T than D_0. The reason for this is simple: If $\overline{OA}$ units of capital are currently employed in the corporate sector, VMP is $\overline{AR}$ dollars. $\overline{AR} = \overline{FI} = \overline{OK}$. But if owners of capital must pay T ($= \overline{SR}$) dollars per unit of capital per annum to the government, they are left with a net return of only $\overline{AS}$ dollars. Applying this

FIGURE 16-10 CORPORATE INCOME TAX

Initially, D_0 in panel (*a*) is the VMP curve of capital in the corporate sector, and D_0' in panel (*b*) is the VMP curve of capital in the noncorporate sector. $\overline{OA}$ units of capital are employed in the corporate sector and $\overline{OF}$ units of capital are employed in the noncorporate sector. VMP of capital is the same in both sectors: $\overline{AR} = \overline{FI}$. After corporate income tax is imposed, the VMP curve in panel (*a*) shifts downward by T dollars, the amount of the tax. To the first approximation, returns to corporate capital decrease by $\overline{SR}$ dollars. Capital relocates from the corporate to the noncorporate sector: $\overline{AB}$ units of capital move from the corporate to the noncorporate sector ($\overline{AB} = \overline{FG}$). The VMP of capital in the corporate sector is now $\overline{BZ}$ dollars, but net of the tax it is $\overline{BW}$ ($= \overline{BZ} - \overline{WZ}$). $\overline{BW}$ is equal to the new VMP in the noncorporate sector, which is equal to $\overline{GV}$.

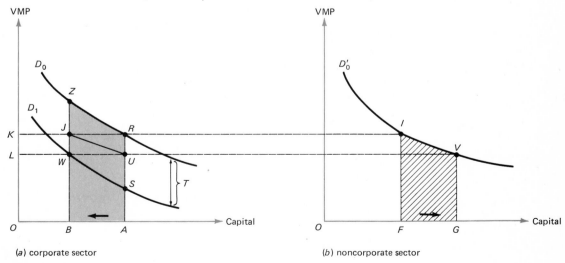

(*a*) corporate sector

(*b*) noncorporate sector

analysis along the D_0 curve yields net curve D_1, which is the VMP curve net of the tax. Since immediately after such a tax is imposed returns to capital in the corporate sector are lower than returns to capital in the noncorporate sector, capital will move from the corporate to the noncorporate sector. If the amount of capital is fixed, the capital leaving the corporate sector will be equal to the amount of capital being added to the noncorporate sector. In Figure 16-10, $\overline{AB}$ units of capital left the corporate sector, and the same amount, $\overline{FG}$ units, were absorbed in the noncorporate sector. In the new equilibrium, the (gross) VMP of the capital in the corporate sector is $\overline{BZ}$ dollars. Subtracting the tax ($\overline{WZ}$) from this value leaves owners of capital with a net return of $\overline{BW}$ dollars, which is equal to the return on noncorporate capital, namely $\overline{GV}$ dollars in panel (b).

Section 15.3c argued that for small variations in an input the area under its VMP curve equals the variation in output. Thus area IFGV with the diagonal stripes [in panel (b)] measures the value of the additional output in the noncorporate sector. Shaded area $ZBAR$ [in panel (a)] measures the value of the lost output in the corporate sector. We recall from Section 15.3c that such measurements are only roughly correct for small capital shifts, where the assumption that the other factor (labor) is unchanged does not introduce significant errors of measurements. The area lost minus the area gained yields a net loss indicated by area $ZJUR$ in panel (a). This loss in output is equal to half the tax times the relocated capital: $\frac{1}{2} \cdot T \cdot (\overline{AB})$.

Arnold Harberger estimated that for the period 1953–1959 the welfare loss to society due to corporate income taxes amounted to 0.5 to 1.0 percent of GNP.[6] Applying more sophisticated methods (general-equilibrium analysis), John Shoven confirmed this order of magnitude in welfare loss due to corporation income taxes.[7]

Recall from Section 11.2c that Harberger estimated the welfare loss due to monopolistic pricing in manufacturing industries at 0.1 percent of GNP.[8] Comparing the two estimates, we conclude that corporate income taxes give rise to a greater loss when compared with monopolistic pricing.

PART II EXHAUSTIBLE AND SEMIEXHAUSTIBLE NATURAL RESOURCES

Up to the time of the 1974 energy crisis, economists devoted relatively little effort to the topic of *exhaustible resources*. The energy crisis reminded everybody that some resources are subject to exhaustion. Many lay people were panic-stricken by the prospect that one morning all oil resources would

---

[6]Arnold C. Harberger, "Efficiency Effects of Taxes on Income from Capital," in Marian Krzyzaniak (ed.), *Effects of Corporation Income Tax*, Wayne State University Press, Detroit, 1966.

[7]John B. Shoven, "The Incidence and Efficiency Effects of Taxes on Income from Capital," *Journal of Political Economy*, vol. 84, December 1976, pp. 1261–1283.

[8]Arnold C. Harberger, "Monopoly and Resource Allocation," *American Economic Review*, vol. 44, May 1954, pp. 77–87.

be depleted and there would be no gasoline to run their cars. Fortunately, microeconomic theory shows that the nightmare of one day running out of energy has no logical basis. Part II of this chapter will show that even if all deposits of a certain natural resource (such as oil) are finite and known, and even if their quality is uniform (in the sense that the cost of exploring and pumping is the same for all oil fields), the price of this natural resource must rise over time such that at the time of exhaustion a new resource appears in the market. What is more important, at the time of switching, the new resource will be sold at the last price of the old resource. Semiexhaustible resources such as timber and water will also be considered here.

16.6 EXHAUSTIBLE NATURAL RESOURCES

16.6a A Numerical Illustration

We now consider a hypothetical example in which there is a market for a certain mineral denoted by X. The demand function for X is given by $X = 100 - P$. All mines of mineral X are owned by many small miners; competition prevails. The marginal cost of mining is $2 regardless of the scale of operation. The going rate of interest is 5 percent[9]; miners can save the proceeds from selling X at a rate of interest of 5 percent. Assume that the total deposit of X that remains in the ground amounts to exactly 125.73 units. All miners are aware of the aggregate amount of X still available in the ground. Also, all are aware of the form of the demand curve. To avoid the mathematical difficulty of having a price which changes continuously, let us assume that once the price is fixed at the beginning of the year it cannot be changed until the beginning of the next year. The demand function is given in units per annum, and the highest price that can be charged in the market is $99. An attempt to sell at a price higher than $99 will induce producers of a substitute to ship their product to the market. The principle that guides mine owners is that they must sell the mineral such that no one year in the future is more attractive than the other. Let us agree that the first year of production extends between now and 1 year hence, the second year extends between 1 year hence and 2 years hence, and so on. Let *royalty* be defined as the difference between the price and the marginal cost of mining. The principle mentioned above tells us that if the present value of the royalty in the ith year is higher than the present value of the royalty in the jth year, producers will shift production from the jth to the ith year. Such an intertemporal shift of output will depress the price in the ith year relative to the jth year until the present values of the two royalties are equal. This principle is summarized as follows:

$$\frac{P_1 - \mathrm{MC}}{1 + r} = \frac{P_2 - \mathrm{MC}}{(1 + r)^2} = \cdots = \frac{P_n - \mathrm{MC}}{(1 + r)^n} \qquad (16\text{-}12)$$

[9]This is the *real rate of interest*, which does not include the inflation-expectation component. For example, if the expected change in the general price level is 8 percent, the *nominal rate of interest* would be 13 percent (= 5 percent + 8 percent).

TABLE 16-7   A Hypothetical Example of an Exhaustible Resource

Year	Price, $ P	Royalty, $ P − MC	Quantity of the mineral, physical units, mined and sold in the marketplace X = 100 − P
8	99.00	97.00	1.00
7	94.38	92.38	5.62
6	89.98	87.98	10.02
5	85.79	83.79	14.21
4	81.80	79.80	18.20
3	78.00	76.00	22.00
2	74.38	72.38	25.62
1	70.94	68.94	29.06
		Total	125.73

Where P_1 is the price 1 year hence, P_2 is the price 2 years hence, and so on. r denotes the rate of interest and MC is the marginal cost of mining. If we divide the present value of the royalty of the second year by the present value of the royalty of the first year, the present value of the royalty of the third year by the present value of the royalty of the second year, and so on, we obtain

$$\frac{P_2 - MC}{P_1 - MC} = \frac{P_3 - MC}{P_2 - MC} = \cdots = \frac{P_n - MC}{P_{n-1} - MC} = 1 + r \qquad (16\text{-}13)$$

That is, from one year to the next, royalty grows at a rate r. The result for the example is given in Table 16-7. The table is calculated by first figuring out the royalty of the last year and then solving back until the mineral is exhausted.

Note: The price during the last year must be $99. As indicated by the demand curve, mining must be equal to 1 unit. Royalty is $97 (= $99 − 2). The royalty in the previous year must be $97/(1 + 0.05) = $92.38. The price that year must be $92.38 + $2 = $94.38, and as indicated by the demand function, quantity mined during that year must be 5.62 units.

If the stock of the mineral is relatively large, we can treat it as if it were infinite. To illustrate, assume that the stock of mineral X is estimated at 11,685.01. If we were to solve back, as we did in Table 16-7, the result would be as presented in Table 16-8.[10] In fact the result of Table 16-8 shows that for a very large stock the price is approximately equal to the marginal cost. In Table 16-8 the stock of 11,685 units would last for 140 years.

The results of the above analysis can be summarized as follows: It is assumed that a stock of a mineral (still remaining in the ground) is finite and its size is known to all miners who constitute a competitive industry. The demand function is also known to all miners. In particular, the intercept of the demand curve with the vertical axis which is defined as the *Choke-off*

---

[10]The numbers in Table 16-8 were derived with the aid of a computer.

TABLE 16-8　A Hypothetical Example of an Exhaustible Resource

Year	Price, $ P	Royalty, $ P − MC	Quantity of the mineral, physical units, mined and sold in the marketplace X = 100 − P
140	99.0000	97.0000	1.00
...	....	....	....
...	....	....	....
...	....	....	....
5	2.1337	0.1337	97.87
4	2.1274	0.1274	97.87
3	2.1213	0.1213	97.88
2	2.1155	0.1155	97.88
1	2.1100	0.1100	97.89
		Total	11,685.01

price is known. The quality of the deposits is uniform. Then (if P denotes the price and MC denotes the marginal cost of mining),

> 1. *The royalty $(P − MC)$ must rise over time at the rate of interest. As the royalty rises over time, price must be rising too. Thus the quantity mined per unit of time falls over time.*
> 2. *The period of exploitation ends when the price rises to the choke-off level and the deposits of the mineral are completely exhausted.*

16.6b　The Geometrical Analysis

The results of the previous discussion are summarized in Figure 16-11. In panel (a) time is measured along the horizontal axis, and price and marginal cost along the vertical axis. In panel (b) a regular demand curve for the mineral is drawn. Since in most cases minerals are inputs, this demand curve is the VMP curve for the particular mineral.

Initially, the price is $\overline{OF}$ and the royalty is $\overline{GF}$ ($= \overline{OF} − \overline{OG}$), which is the initial price minus the marginal cost. Over time, royalty grows at the rate of interest, and accordingly the price rises too. Finally, at the end of the period of exploitation $\overline{OT}$, the choke-off price $\overline{OH}$ is attained and the deposits are competely exhausted. The apparatus presented in Figure 16-11 is useful in analyzing markets for exhaustible natural resources. Only a few cases will be illustrated in what follows.[11]

Note that attaining the choke-off price must coincide with deposit exhaustion. First, if the mineral is exhausted before reaching the choke-off price, producers could have benefited from higher profits by charging higher prices over time. In panel (a) they could have started with an initial royalty greater than $\overline{GF}$. Second, if we suppose that the choke-off price of $\overline{OH}$

---

[11] For a detailed and exhaustive analysis of the most important cases, see Orris C. Herfindahl, "Depletion and Economic Theory," in Mason Gaffney, (ed.), *Extractive Resources and Taxation*, University of Wisconsin Press, 1967.

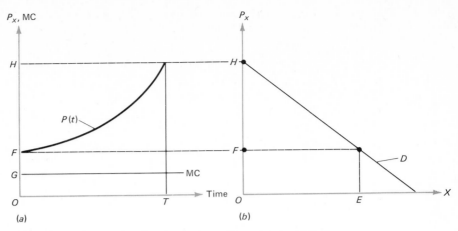

FIGURE 16-11 THE PRICE OF AN EXHAUSTIBLE RESOURCE OVER TIME
In panel (a) time is measured along the horizontal axis, and price and MC along the vertical axis. Panel (b) shows the demand curve for the mineral, denoted by D. $\overline{OG}$ is the marginal cost of mining. The marginal cost curve of mining is a flat line at the $\overline{OG}$ level. Initially, the price is $\overline{OF}$ and the royalty is $\overline{GF}$. Over time, the price rises such that in panel (a) the price, as indicated by $P(t)$, minus the marginal cost of mining, as indicated by MC, increases at the rate of interest from one year to the next. In panel (b), as the price rises, less and less is consumed of the exhaustible resource (mineral). Finally, at time $\overline{OT}$, the mineral is exhausted, the choke-off price is $\overline{OH}$, and demand for the resource is zero.

dollars has been reached and the mineral has not been exhausted, it leads to a contradiction: Miners with some deposits left in the ground will have to sell the leftovers at a price slightly lower than the choke-off price $\overline{OH}$; otherwise they will not be able to compete with the sellers of the mineral substitute which will become available at the choke-off price.

Case I: A rise in the cost of mining Consider Figure 16-12. Suppose the marginal cost rises from $\overline{OG}$ to $\overline{OG}'$. Then, for the sake of argument, suppose the initial price remains unchanged at a level $\overline{OF}$. Prices in the future must be lower than the prices indicated by solid curve FH because the initial royalty is smaller. Recall that the royalty (not the price) grows at the rate of interest over time. Such a lower set of prices will lead to a premature exhaustion of the deposits at time T_1, as indicated by the dashed curve. The only optimal solution to the problem would be to raise the initial price to $\overline{OF}'$. The early prices will be higher, but the later prices will be lower, as indicated by the new solid curve $F'H'$. The main result is that the exploitation time is extended from $\overline{OT_0}$ to $\overline{OT}'$. The same result will be obtained if instead of a rise in the marginal cost we consider a severance tax[12] at the level of $\overline{GG}'$ per unit of the mineral mined. Such a tax would lengthen the exploitation time. This result is intuitively clear: A severance tax or a rise in the cost of mining will

---

[12] A tax imposed on *severing* (depleting) an exhaustible natural resource. Such a tax may be imposed either as a unit tax or as an *ad valorem* tax.

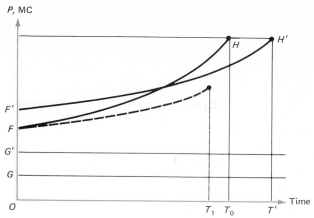

FIGURE 16-12 CASES I, II, AND V
Time is measured along the horizontal axis, and price and MC along the vertical axis. Initial intertemporal price curve FH is the same as curve $P(t)$ in panel (a) of Figure 16-11. Either a rise in the MC of mining or an imposition of a severance tax or a fall in the rate of interest, unless followed by an increase in the initial price, will result in the dashed intertemporal price curve, leading to premature exhaustion of the mineral at time T_1. Hence the solution must be to raise the initial price to a higher level $\overline{OF'}$, thus obtaining a new intertemporal price curve denoted by $F'H'$. The exploitation period is accordingly extended from T_0 to T'.

induce mine owners to postpone mining to the future to mitigate the impact of the additional cost at present.

Case II: A fall in the rate of interest We can also use Figure 16-12 to illustrate this case. The price is initially $\overline{OF}$, and the intertemporal price curve is FH. If the rate of interest falls but the initial price $\overline{OF}$ is retained, prices in the future will be lower, as indicated by the dashed curve. As in the previous case, premature exhaustion of the deposits will occur. The solution, as in the previous case is then to raise the initial price to $\overline{OF'}$, leading to intertemporal curve $F'H'$.

Case III: A discovery of new deposits This is left as a problem for the student.

Case IV: A change in demand Consider a case of an increase in the quantity demanded: At each price users of the mineral are willing to buy a certain percentage more. For example, originally the demand function is $X = 100 - P$. After a 10 percent shift occurs, the new demand curve is $X = 1.1(100 - P)$. In Figure 16-11 such an increase in demand would be reflected by a counterclockwise rotation of the demand curve, where point H in panel (b) is the pivot. Let us now shift to Figure 16-13. The intertemporal price curve FH is associated with the original demand curve. Had mine owners continued to follow this original curve after the demand increased, premature exhaustion would occur. The solution is to charge a higher price initially and also later. The result is a new higher intertemporal price curve indicated by $F'H'$; the exploitation time is shortened from $\overline{OT_0}$ to $\overline{OT'}$.

Case V: Monopoly Assume that at time $t = 0$ the entire industry is organized in an effective cartel (Section 11.9a). Since a cartel would operate like a monopoly, its royalty would be defined as marginal revenue minus marginal cost. The rule which the monopoly will adopt is that the present value of future royalties should be equated. Instead of Equation 16-12, the monopoly would adopt the following equation:

$$\frac{MR_1 - MC}{1 + r} = \frac{MR_2 - MC}{(1 + r)^2} = \cdots = \frac{MR_n - MC}{(1 + r)^n} \qquad (16\text{-}14)$$

Consider Table 16-7 again. Recall that the demand curve for the mineral was assumed to be $X = 100 - P$; hence the marginal revenue is $MR = 100 - 2X$. If at the beginning of the first year the competitive industry is organized as a cartel, it will not follow the price pattern of \$70.94, \$74.38, and so on. This pattern will be associated with marginal revenues of \$41.88, \$48.76, and so on. The royalties will be \$39.88, \$46.76, and so on. But these royalties will grow at a rate in excess of the interest rate of 5 percent. For example, \$46.76/\$39.88 = 1.17; that is a rate of growth of 17 percent instead of 5 percent. To achieve a rate of growth of 5 percent, the monopoly will have to shift output from the present to the future. This will lead to a rise in the initial price, but to lower prices later. We can use Figure 16-12 to illustrate the case of monopoly. The competitive intertemporal price curve is FH. If a cartel is organized at $t = 0$, the initial price rises to $\overline{OF'}$ and the monopolistic intertemporal price curve is $F'H'$. Curve FH satisfies Equation 16-12. Curve $F'H'$ satisfies Equation 16-14.

Those who believe that the period of oil exploitation should be extended should not complain about OPEC. As indicated by the analysis here, the mere creation of the oil cartel in 1973 should extend the exploitation period from $\overline{OT_0}$ to $\overline{OT'}$ in Figure 16-12. The choke-off price in the case of OPEC ($\overline{T'H'}$ in Figure 16-12) could be guessed by considering the best substitute, say, the price per equivalent barrel of synfuel,[13] or any other reasonable substitute for light oil.

16.6c An Example: Forecasting OPEC Prices in the Future

Economists attempted to forecast the prices of oil that will be set by OPEC. For example, Robert Pindyck, instead of assuming a choke-off price, assumed a rising cost of mining function. On this basis he derived a Herfindahl-type intertemporal function for prices of crude oil expressed as dollars per barrel. Based on this model, he theorized that in the years 1975, 2000, and 2010 real (1975) prices under competition should be \$4.62, \$15.65, and \$25.48, and under monopoly \$13.24, \$14.46, and \$20.29, respectively.[14] Note that these predictions are in agreement with intertemporal price curves FH and $F'H'$ as shown in Figure 16-12.

Jacques Cremer and Martin Weitzman predicted that in the periods 1975–1985, 1995–2005, and 2005–2015, real (1975) prices under monopoly will be \$9.8, \$14.7, and \$20.8. They assumed a choke-off price (in 1975 dollars) of \$35.[15]

---

[13] An example of synfuel would be liquid fuel produced from coal.

[14] Robert S. Pindyck, "Gains to Producers from the Cartelization of Exhaustible Resources," *Review of Economics and Statistics*, vol. 60, May 1978, pp. 238–251.

[15] Jacques Cremer and Martin L. Weitzman, "OPEC and the Monopoly Price of World Oil," *European Economic Review*, vol. 8, 1976, pp. 155–164.

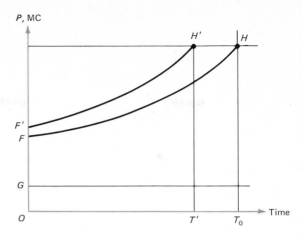

FIGURE 16-13   CASE IV

Time is measured along the horizontal axis. Price and MC are measured along the vertical axis. Initially, the intertemporal price curve is *FH*. After the demand for the mineral increases, the curve shifts upward, leading to a new curve denoted by *F'H'*, and as a result the exploitation period is shortened from T_0 to T'

16.6d Concluding Comments

The economic theory of exhaustible resources which we developed in this section provides a loose framework for organizing our thoughts, rather than a tight model that can be tested empirically. To begin with, most of the minerals in the earth are still available in such huge quantities that conventional economic theory suffices for analysis of their markets. Energy resources, except for oil, are relatively plentiful. Oil resources are limited, but the extent of their reserves cannot be determined with certainty. For example, at the time of this writing oil was discovered in Mexico. Also, the choke-off price can only be roughly estimated. For example, synfuel is produced in large quantities in South Africa. We can use South African synfuel data to arrive at an estimate of the choke-off price for crude oil. Shocks in the system such as discoveries of new oil fields or new technologies, or political unrest in oil-producing countries like Iran, leading to new choke-off prices, are always possible. The main value of the theory of exhaustible resources, in spite of all the caveats, is to assure that free markets will lead us gradually away from an exhaustible resource which will eventually be depleted to a new substitute through a slow intertemporal rise in the price of the mineral.

16.7 SEMIEXHAUSTIBLE RESOURCES

Examples of semiexhaustible natural resources are water, trees, and fish. These resources grow naturally over time. Their rate of growth is functionally related to the size of the existing stock. If production is equal to the flow provided by natural growth, the resource is *renewable*. If production is in excess of the flow provided by natural growth, mining of the natural resource occurs. In what follows two examples of semiexhaustible resources are discussed.

16.7a Water

In semiarid regions such as the Southwestern United States and Israel, water is a scarce resource. It appears in nature in two basic forms: *surface water* and *groundwater*. Surface water is a renewable resource. Its scarcity in the Southwest led to the establishment of property rights (Section 14.6). Its *scarcity*, however, should not be confused with *exhaustibility*: Its price over time may rise or fall depending on whether the demand for surface water increases or decreases. Groundwater, on the other hand, may be entirely exhaustible as in West Texas, or semiexhaustible as in most of the aquifers in the Southwestern United States.

A typical groundwater aquifer would be a natural underground water storage which is naturally recharged by water flows from melting snows and rainfalls. A typical farm situation would be one in which farmers irrigate the land overlying the aquifer. The fact that only farmers who own land overlying the aquifer can pump groundwater limits the acreage that can be irrigated by a specific aquifer. If irrigation farmers use more water than the natural recharge plus the return flow from irrigation, the aquifer is said to be mined. As the stock of water in the aquifer is being mined, the water table falls and the cost of pumping consequently increases. If each farmer owned a separate aquifer, each would take into consideration the going rate of interest and distribute pumping intertemporally as would any mineral mine owner. But since the aquifer is commonly pumped, it does not make sense for the individual farmer to allow such a scheme for water use. As a matter of fact, although the stock of water is fixed in the aggregate, each individual farmer treats it as if it were an unlimited source of water available at the cost of pumping. Accordingly, the individual farmer would pump water up to the point where the marginal cost of pumping intersects with the VMP of water.[16]

Figure 16-14 presents a model of one individual farmer. It starts at $t = 0$. The marginal cost of pumping is MC($t = 0$). This curve cuts the VMP of the water curve at E. The individual farmer uses A_0 units of water for irrigation. But since other farmers also pump, and aggregately they mine water, the water table falls, and during the next period the water table is deeper and the marginal cost of pumping rises to MC($t = 1$). The farmer contracts along the VMP curve from E to F and now uses only A_1 units of water for irrigation. So long as water is being mined the water table must fall, leading the farmer to climb higher and higher along the VMP curve. Let us assume that

---

[16]Section 14.7a argued that nonexclusiveness, as in the case of fishing grounds, will lead producers to operate where the marginal cost of effort is equal to the VAP rather than to the VMP (Figure 14-14). Irrigation of groundwater is different in the sense that farmers who do not own land overlying the aquifer are excluded.

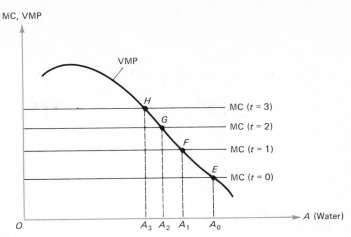

FIGURE 16-14 GROUNDWATER MODEL
Water pumped by a single farmer is measured along the horizontal axis. Marginal cost of pumping (MC) and VMP of water are measured along the vertical axis. Initially, the marginal cost of pumping is MC ($t = 0$). The farmer pumps A_0 units of water, where VMP is equal to MC (point E). But since water is being mined by all farmers together, next year the water table is lower and the MC of pumping, as perceived by the farmer, rises to a higher level of MC ($t = 1$). The new point of equilibrium is F, and the farmer decreases use of water to A_1 units. This process continues: Each year the cost of pumping rises, thus inducing all farmers to use less and less water. Finally, as the MC of pumping rises to MC ($t = 3$), the aggregate amount of water pumped by all farmers is equal to the natural replenishment of water (natural recharge plus return flow, assuming zero natural discharge). Steady state has been achieved. The MC of pumping does not shift any more.

when MC rises to MC($t = 3$) the amount of water pumped, ΣA_3, equals the natural replenishment of water (natural recharge plus return flow from irrigation). In that case the water consumed by farmers is equal to the renewable supply, and a *steady-state equilibrium* has been achieved: Unless the system will be disturbed by a change in the real cost of pumping or a shift in the VMP curve, farmers will continue to pump ΣA_3 units of water per unit of time forever.[17]

As a short example (Section 9.6c), in 1926 the elevation of the water table of the main aquifer in the Pecos Basin, New Mexico, was 3451 feet above sea level. It receded to 3403 feet in 1969. This amounted to an increase of 48 feet of lift over a period of 43 years. At a cost of 3 cents per foot of lift, this meant that the marginal cost of pumping shifted upward by $1.44 per acre foot.

16.7b Trees

Suppose a lumber company purchases a tract and plants it with trees. In the future the company intends to cut the trees for sale as timber. Consider

---

[17] If the aquifer has a *bottom*, a steady-state solution may not be reached. In that case farmers must be assigned water pumping rights which aggregately amount to the natural recharge plus return flow from irrigation.

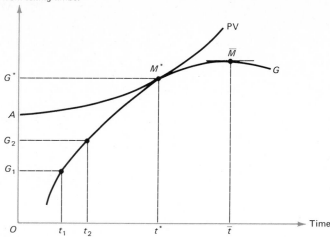

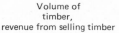

FIGURE 16-15 CUTTING TREES

We measure time along the horizontal axis. We measure the volume of timber times its price along the vertical axis. The price is assumed to be $1, for convenience. G is the growth curve of timber. It shows the value of timber at each point of time. Maximum growth occurs at time $\bar{t}$. But maximum wealth is attained if the trees are cut at time T^*, when the rate of growth of the trees is equal to the rate of interest. PV is but one of many present value curves. It is tangent to curve G at point M^*. Tracing back on the PV curve leads us to point A: The (maximum) present value of the trees is $\overline{OA}$. $\overline{AA}$ should exceed the initial investment in the tract to justify the project.

Figure 16-15. Time is measured along the horizontal axis (the origin is planting time), and the volume of timber is measured along the vertical axis. For simplicity, the unit of timber is defined such that its price is $1. That way the volume of timber sold is equal to revenue from selling the timber. The growth is represented by the G curve, indicating the volume of timber that could be obtained from cutting the trees at each point in time. The shape of the growth curve indicates that trees are growing at a declining rate. At time $\bar{t}$ the volume of timber is maximized. Beyond this point there is no growth; in fact, the volume of timber may even slightly decline.

Let us now illustrate what is meant by a *rate of growth*. At time t_1 the volume of the trees amounts to G_1. At time t_2 the volume of the trees has grown to G_2. We can accordingly write

$$\text{Growth rate} = \frac{(G_2 - G_1)/(t_2 - t_1)}{G_1} = \frac{\Delta G/\Delta t}{G_1} \qquad (16\text{-}15)$$

If Δt is 1 year, we have in mind an *annual growth rate* that can be compared with the rate of interest.

The rule of determining the optimal cutting time is as follows: So long as the rate of growth of the trees exceeds the rate of interest, the trees should continue to grow. The reason for this can be figured out as follows: If this rule is not followed, cutting the trees is equivalent to shifting one's money from a "bank" that pays a relatively high rate of interest to a bank that pays a relatively low rate of interest. For example, suppose that at the end of the ninth year the value of the trees is $1000 and during the tenth year they are expected to grow 12 percent. Then, while the rate of interest is only 7 percent, by cutting at the end of the ninth year rather than waiting for the end of the tenth year, the owner of the tract would lose $50. Since the growth curve is concave, eventually a time will be reached when the growth rate of the trees is equal to the rate of interest. At that time the trees should be cut. In Figure 16-15 the equality between the rate of interest and the growth rate occurs at $t = t^*$.

Curve PV has a special meaning in the theory of cutting trees. Moving forward with time, this curve generates future values. Accordingly, moving backward with time, this curve generates present values. For example, at the time of planting ($t = 0$) we start with a value of $\overline{OA}$. After the first year passes, the curve would yield a (vertical) value of $\overline{OA} \cdot (1 + r)$, after 2 years $\overline{OA} \cdot (1 + r)^2$, and after n years $\overline{OA} \cdot (1 + r)^n$, where n can be a very large number.[18] Clearly, if t^*M^* is equal to $\overline{OA} \cdot (1 + r)^{t^*}$, $\overline{OA}$ is equal to $t^*M^*/(1 + r)^{t^*}$; that is, $\overline{OA}$ is the present value of any point on curve PV. We can conceive of a map of PV curves constructed by applying the going rate of interest to a series of initial values. The highest such curve that has at least one point in common with the growth curve is tangent to the growth curve. At the point of tangency the rate of interest is equal to the rate of growth of the trees. In Figure 16-15, M^* is the point of tangency. The optimal growing time is thus t^*. In the future, the optimal volume of timber will be $\overline{OG^*}$. But as shown by the PV curve, the present value of $\overline{OG^*}$ is $\overline{OA}$. If the initial investment is the tract and planting trees is less than $\overline{OA}$, the investment is good: It augments the wealth of the investor. The following additional points result from the above analysis:

1. The concavity of the growth curve implies that the lower the rate of interest, the longer the growth period will be.
2. At time $\bar{t}$ the trees achieve their maximum growth. However, point $\overline{M}$ is optimal only under the unlikely event that the rate of interest is zero.

The conclusion we reach is that the optimal time of cutting trees is simultaneously determined by physical factors such as natural growth rate, as well as economic factors such as the rate of interest.

SUMMARY   Part I

First, it was explained how consumers can forgo consumption in the present by saving or consume in excess of their present income by dissaving. The intertemporal budget line of the consumer has a slope of $-(1 + r)$, where r is the rate of interest. This means that forgoing the consumption of $1 today

---

[18] In fact, the curve is drawn under the assumption of continuous compounding, namely, $PV = \overline{OA} \cdot e^{rt}$.

will yield the consumer $(1 + r)$ times the dollar 1 year hence. The intertemporal point of equilibrium of the consumer occurs where an intertemporal indifference curve is tangent to the intertemporal budget line.

In a static economy the rate of interest is determined by achieving an equilibrium between savers and dissavers: Saving must be equal to dissaving or, put in other words, where the lender's curve intersects with the borrower's curve. The function of investment in a dynamic economy was introduced. We have seen that investment is undertaken by entrepreneurs whenever they expect the act of investment to augment their wealth. We have also seen that the decision of the individual investor is invariant to his or her intertemporal tastes. Finally, we demonstrated that the investment function is negatively related to the rate of interest. In a dynamic economy the rate of interest is determined at the point where investment is equal to net saving; net saving is equal to saving minus dissaving.

The theory of capital gave rise to one of the most useful fields in economics, capital budgeting. First the *present value rule* was derived from the theory of capital. This is the only rule that never fails. The rule says that an investment should be undertaken only if the present value of the project under consideration is positive. Ranking among a few (exclusive) projects is carried out by selecting the project with the highest present value. The *internal rate of return* rule was mentioned with the conclusion that it can be used in capital budgeting only if it is in agreement with the present value rule.

The issue of *corporate income taxes* was then considered. We have seen why such taxes on income from corporate capital lead to a shift of capital from the corporate to the noncorporate sector. Some empirical studies concluded that the welfare loss due to corporate income taxes is in the order of magnitude of 0.5 to 1.0 percent of GNP.

Part II

This part analyzed the market for exhaustible resources. We saw that in competitive markets, if the size of the deposit, the demand function, and the *choke-off price* are known, *royalty*, which is price minus the marginal cost of mining, must grow over time at the rate of interest. This means that the price of a finite resource must rise over time until at the time of exhaustion it is equal to the choke-off price. We showed that either (1) a rise in the cost of mining, (2) an imposition of a severance tax, or (3) a fall in the rate of interest will induce mine owners to postpone mining to the future and will also lengthen the exploitation period. An increase in demand for the deposit will increase intertemporal prices and reduce the exploitation period. The most striking result of the theory is that formation of a cartel would postpone mining to the future. Accordingly, compared with a competitive market, prices will be higher at the present and in the near future, but lower in the far future. This leads to the conclusion that OPEC helps to conserve crude oil for the future.

The economic theory of semiexhaustible resources such as groundwater and trees (timber) was also discussed. We saw that in the case of groundwater it would sometimes be possible to reach equilibrium where the water used by farmers is equal to natural replenishment. In the case of trees, it was proved that the wealth of a tract owner is maximized if he or she cuts the trees when the rate of growth of the trees is equal to the rate of interest.

GLOSSARY　**Interest rate**　A premium paid to an individual for sacrificing present consumption.

Compound value　If r is the interest rate, the compound value of X n years hence is $Y = X(1 + r)^n$.

Future value　The same as compound value.

Present value　If $Y = X(1 + r)^n$, then X is the present value of Y. We write it as $X = Y/(1 + r)^n$.

Intertemporal budget line　If present income is measured along the horizontal axis and future income along the vertical axis, a line that passes through the endowment of the individual consumer (Y_0, Y_1) and has a slope of $-(1 + r)$ is the *intertemporal budget line*.

Intertemporal indifference curve　If present consumption is measured along the horizontal axis and future consumption along the vertical axis, an intertemporal indifference curve in that space is the locus of points that are equally desirable by the consumer.

Wealth　The present value of all expected income streams (of an individual).

Lender's curve　A curve relating the amount of lending per unit of time to the interest rate. Lending is identical with (gross) saving. The lender's curve can be either positively sloped or negatively sloped.

Borrower's curve　A curve relating the amount of borrowing per unit of time to the rate of interest. The borrower's curve is negatively sloped. Borrowing is identical with dissaving.

Net saving　Saving minus dissaving.

Investment　The act of augmenting capital. Capital is augmented by producing more machines, constructing more structures, increasing inventories, and so on.

Investment curve　A curve relating investment to the rate of interest. This curve is negatively sloped.

Capital budgeting　The theory of ranking investment projects.

The present value rule　An investment project has future returns that are expected to be positive but could be negative, and a cost of investment which is a negative flow. If the present value of all these flows is positive, the project should be undertaken. If the present value of all these flows is negative, the project should be rejected. If a few (exclusive) projects are considered, the one with the highest present value should be undertaken, provided it is positive.

Capital recovery factor　A factor that converts the initial cost of investment in capital into a cost per unit of time. If r and n denote the interest rate and the expected lifetime of the asset (in years), the capital recovery factor (CRF) is CRF $= r/[(1 + r)^n - 1] + r$.

Internal rate of return rule The internal rate of return is that rate which equates the present value of all future returns with the initial cost of the investment. The rule is to undertake the project if the internal rate of return is higher than the rate of interest, and to reject it if the internal rate of return is lower than the rate of interest.

Corporate income taxes Taxes imposed on corporate profit. Such taxes are in fact imposed on income from capital invested in corporations. Capital invested either in partnerships or in single proprietorships is exempted.

Exhaustible natural resources Resources in nature that are in finite supply. Example: crude oil.

Royalty Has many meanings. In the theory of exhaustible natural resources royalty is marginal revenue minus the marginal cost of mining.

Choke-off price The price of a resource at which its deposit is completely exhausted and a substitute appears in the market and sells for the same price. The choke-off price must coincide with the intercept of the demand curve for the resource with the vertical axis.

Exploitation period The period between the present and the time of exhaustion.

Severance tax A tax imposed on severing (depleting) exhaustible resources.

Semiexhaustible natural resource Natural resources that grow naturally over time. Their rate of growth is normally a function of their stock. Such resources are mined if production is in excess of their natural rate of growth.

Steady-state equilibrium If the production of a semiexhaustible natural resource is equal to the amount provided by its natural growth, a steady state has been achieved. The resource may be viewed as a renewable resource.

PROBLEMS An asterisk indicates an advanced problem.

16-1. How many years would it take an investment of $100 to grow to $147 at a compounded 8 percent interest rate?

16-2. The lifetime of a well-built structure is 10 years. Its cost is $10,000. The lifetime of an inferior structure is 5 years. Its cost is $7000. If the rate of interest is 5 percent, would you prefer to invest once in a superior structure or twice in an inferior structure?

16-3. Consider buying a machine which will last 4 years. After 4 years the machine disintegrates and has no scrap value. Given the table at the top of the next page, which shows the expected revenues and operation and maintenance costs, does it pay to invest $22,000 in the machine, knowing that the going interest rate is 8 percent?

16-4.* Prove that the CRF $\{r/[(1 + r)^n - 1] + r\}$ can be expressed as

$$\frac{r(1 + r)^n}{(1 + r)^n - 1}$$

Table for problem 16-3

Time (1)	Expected total revenues, $ (2)	Expected current costs, excluding interest and depreciation, $ (3)
End of year 1	10,000	5,000
End of year 2	8,000	3,000
End of year 3	12,000	2,000
End of year 4	7,000	4,000

16.5. An asset whose lifetime is 10 years costs $10,000. The going rate of interest is 8 percent. (a) What is the sum that must be written off at the end of each year to obtain $10,000 10 years hence? (b) What is the CRF and the annual cost of this asset?

16-6. Project A is expected to sell 100,000 whatnots annually at $1 apiece. The annual current cost of labor, electricity, maintenance, etc., is expected to amount to $60,000. The investment includes one asset at the cost of $100,000 and a lifetime of 10 years, and another asset at a cost of $80,000 and a lifetime of 5 years. The going interest rate is 5 percent. Is this a good project?

16-7. After the rate of interest rose, the wealth of a certain wage earner fell. In spite of this, the person welcomed the rise in the rate of interest. Explain.

16-8. Would the discovery of a new technology enabling energy companies to produce relatively cheap liquid fuel from solar energy cause the rate of interest to rise or to fall?

16-9. Explain under what circumstances the internal rate of return test should not be applied in capital budgeting problems.

16-10. Currently (January 1) you hold two bonds, A and B. Both pay a dividend of $100 at the end of each calendar year. Both have a redemption value of $1000. A will mature in 5 years and B will mature in 10 years. Would the market value of the bonds increase or decrease as a result of a decline in the going interest rate? Which of the market prices of the two bonds will change more drastically? Why?

16-11. In Figure 16-12 curve $F'H'$ must cross curve FH. Why?

16-12. Assume that new desposits of a certain exhaustible resource are discovered. Will this cause a change in the exploitation period? Would prices over time increase or decrease?

16-13.* A certain mineral appears in nature in two grades, one of which is more costly to mine than the other (offshore oil). Which of the two grades would you expect to be mined earlier?

16-14. "Doomsday" studies apply the current rate of oil consumption to calculate the date of running out of oil. What is wrong with "doomsday" studies?

16-15. Farmers who pump groundwater to irrigate their fields reached a steady state in the sense that the water table of the aquifer has been stable for many years. Assume that suddenly the cost of pumping increases sharply. How would farmers behave in the future? In particular, refer to the level and cost of pumping over time.

16-16. A tract of trees grows at a rate of 10 percent during the first year, 9 percent during the second year, and so on. Maximum growth is achieved at the end of the tenth year. Because of increasing demand for timber, the real price rises at a rate of 3 percent per annum. When should the trees be cut if the going interest rate is 4.9 percent?

APPENDIX 16

A Table of Capital Coefficients

Interest year	Future value coefficient $(1 + r)^n$			Present value coefficient (discount rate) $1/(1 + r)^n$			Capital recovery factor $r/[(1 + r)^n - 1] + r$		
	3%	5%	8%	3%	5%	8%	3%	5%	8%
1	1.030	1.050	1.080	0.971	0.952	0.926	1.030	1.050	1.080
2	1.061	1.103	1.166	0.943	0.907	0.857	0.523	0.538	0.561
3	1.093	1.158	1.260	0.915	0.864	0.794	0.354	0.367	0.388
4	1.126	1.216	1.360	0.889	0.823	0.735	0.269	0.282	0.302
5	1.159	1.276	1.469	0.863	0.784	0.681	0.218	0.231	0.250
6	1.194	1.340	1.587	0.838	0.746	0.630	0.185	0.197	0.216
7	1.230	1.407	1.714	0.813	0.711	0.584	0.161	0.173	0.192
8	1.267	1.477	1.851	0.789	0.677	0.540	0.142	0.155	0.174
9	1.305	1.551	1.999	0.766	0.645	0.500	0.128	0.141	0.160
10	1.344	1.629	2.159	0.744	0.614	0.463	0.117	0.130	0.149

MATHEMATICAL APPENDIX 16

M16.1 CONTINUOUS COMPOUNDING

Footnote 1 noted that if the rate of interest is compounded continuously the future value formula is

$$Y = X \cdot e^{rt} \tag{m16-1}$$

Accordingly, the present value for the continuous case is

$$X = Y \cdot e^{-rt} \tag{m16-2}$$

M16.2 CUTTING TREES

Assume that K dollars is currently invested in a tract of newly planted trees. The growth function of the trees is $G(t)$. The present value of the venture is

$$V = [G(t)] \cdot e^{-rt} - K \qquad \text{(m16-3)}$$

Let dG/dt be denoted by G'. Then the first-order condition for present value maximization is

$$\frac{\partial V}{\partial t} = G(t) \cdot (-r) \cdot e^{-rt} + e^{-rt} G' = 0 \qquad \text{(m16-4)}$$

Upon dividing by e^{-rt} and rearranging, we obtain

$$r = \frac{G'}{G(t)} \qquad \text{(m16-5)}$$

where $G'/G(t)$ is the rate of growth of the trees at time t. Equation m16-5 is the necessary condition for present value maximization. As mentioned in the text, in order for the investment to increase wealth, after we solve for time in Equation m16-5, we ought to plug this value of t into Equation m16-3 and invest in the tract only if the resulting value of V is positive.

PART SIX

SPECIAL ISSUES AND APPLICATIONS

Chapters 17 and 18 are related to the previous 16 chapters in a variety of ways.

Chapter 17 covers the broad topic of welfare economics. Chapter 1 discussed the welfare losses resulting from such programs as food stamps (versus cash subsidies), and Chapter 4 considered welfare measurements vis-à-vis quantity index numbers. Chapter 10 analyzed the welfare loss resulting from unit taxes, and Chapter 11 devoted a lot of space to welfare losses due to monopolies. The topic of social versus private costs was briefly discussed in Chapter 6. The issue of monopsony was analyzed in Chapter 14. The previous chapters applied *partial-equilibrium analysis* to welfare issues. In Chapter 17, for the first time, *general-equilibrium analysis* is applied to shed further light on the issues of welfare economics. In particular, the chapter expands on the topic of social versus private costs known as *externalities*, which, given the practical problems of water and air pollution, has become one of the most important issues in modern microeconomics. In addition to this, the problems of *income inequality* and *public goods* are discussed.

Chapter 18 covers the quantitative tools applied by economists. In almost all the previous chapters the theory was illustrated by statistical studies. Time and again it was repeated that economics is a science because economic theories can be either confirmed or refuted by econometric tests. Recall the demand for electricity in the United States (Chapter 3), empirical cost functions (Chapter 6), or testing for price discrimination among physicians (Chapter 11). These empirical tests were based on *econometrics*, which is a branch of applied mathematics and statistics, essential for confirming or refuting economic theories. The meanings of econometrics will be discussed in the first part of Chapter 18.

Economists apply optimization procedures, known as *operations research*, to the solutions of numerous practical problems. The second part of Chapter 18 will discuss in a nonmathematical fashion the meaning of operations research in the field of applied economics.

C H A P T E R

WELFARE
ECONOMICS
(optional)

Welfare economics deals with two major issues, *economic efficiency* and *economic equity*. It so happens that microeconomic theory can say a lot about efficiency and little about equity. Practically all questions arising from governmental economic policies, however, involve evaluation of both *efficiency* and *equity*. As an example consider two taxes: a progressive income tax and a per capita lump-sum tax. The first is an inefficient tax; the second is an efficient tax. Which is more equitable? Most people would say that the first is more equitable than the second. But unfortunately economists have failed to provide a useful theory to determine equity.

Sometimes the question arises regarding the need to initiate an economic policy. For example, should the government do something about monopolies? Welfare economics demonstrates that monopolies are inefficient (Section 11.2). But consider a monopolistic firm which is owned by a single individual. Owing to the monopolistic position, the person earns a higher level of income relative to other individuals, who must suffer the "slings and arrows" of competition. Should income be redistributed from the monopoly owner to the others? This is an equity issue about which welfare economics is able to say very little. Governmental policies which do redistribute incomes through progressive income taxes rest on *value judgments* rather than on economic theory.

This chapter will first discuss *general equilibrium*, an important component in the apparatus of *welfare economics*. Next it will consider economic efficiency known as *Pareto optimum*. It will show that if laissez-faire and competition prevail, economic efficiency is achieved, as if by Adam Smith's *invisible hand*. Then the notorious situations leading to efficiency loss, e.g., monopolies and taxes, will be presented. Inefficiency resulting from externalities such as water and air pollution will be analyzed, and remedies discussed for cases of externalities. The end of the chapter will briefly review the issues of *equity* and *public goods*.

17.1 GENERAL EQUILIBRIUM

Preceding chapters focused on markets for certain goods, paying little or no attention to the economy as a whole. In the discussion of competitive markets (Chapters 9 and 10) some attention was paid to closely related markets (e.g., imposing a unit tax on margarine and the subsequent impact on the market for butter) but none to remotely related markets (e.g., imposing a unit tax on margarine and the subsequent impact on the market for pianos). The type of analysis applied up to this point is termed *partial-equilibrium analysis*. When a duty is eliminated, a tax is levied, or a monopoly is created, partial-equilibrium analysis focuses on the market that is immediately involved as well as on closely related markets. It ignores the interrelationships among the many less related markets in the economy.

Section 11.2c mentioned that, based on partial-equilibrium analysis, Arnold Harberger reached a conclusion that welfare loss due to monopolistic pricing was in the order of magnitude of 0.1 percent of GNP.[1] Harberger touched off a controversy which still lives. Part of the controversy stems from economists' uneasiness with partial-equilibrium analysis, particularly when economic welfare issues are involved. In contrast to *partial-equilibrium analysis*, *general-equilibrium analysis* leaves much less to the realm of *ceteris paribus*. If a tax is imposed on margarine, general-equilibrium analysis does not leave the market for pianos for the domain of *ceteris paribus*. Rather, it formally treats such remote markets in exactly the same fashion as it does closely related markets. Note, however, the famous law relating to economic theories:

> There is a tradeoff between the domain of ceteris paribus and economic theory: The larger the first, the more efficient the second.

We might note, at this point, that in general-equilibrium analysis *ceteris paribus* does not vanish: Technology, tastes, and government and other institutional frameworks are held constant.

In light of the above law of economic theories, why did economists become involved in general-equilibrium analysis? The answer lies mainly in their curiosity. They wanted to solve the following puzzle: In an economy where many producers, by using a multitude of inputs, produce and sell a great variety of goods to a large number of consumers via a system of interrelated markets, is there a set of prices that would bring all markets into a simultaneous equilibrium? Mathematical economic analysis, which started with the pioneering work of Leon Walras, provided an affirmative answer to the puzzle.[2] But economists took a further step. They applied general-equilibrium apparatus to test the precision of welfare loss estimates based on partial-equilibrium analysis. As an example, in the previous chapter we mentioned that Harberger applied partial-equilibrium analysis and estimated the welfare loss due to corporation income taxes between 0.5 and 1 percent of GNP.[3] John Shoven applied general-equilibrium apparatus and verified Harberger's results (Section 16.5).[4]

The analysis that follows will present a limited general-equilibrium model in which two consumers trade in two goods. The goods are produced by two sectors, each using only two factors. The *ceteris paribus* domain in this model does not entirely vanish: Tastes (indifference maps), technology (production indifference maps), and the intitial endowment of factors are held constant.

---

[1] Arnold C. Harberger, "Monopoly and Resource Allocation," *American Economic Review*, vol. 44, May 1954, pp. 77–87.

[2] Leon Walras, *Elements of Pure Economics*, published in French in 1874.

[3] Arnold C. Harberger, "Efficiency Effects of Taxes on Income from Capital," in M. Krzyzaniak, (ed.), *Effects of Corporation Income Tax*, Wayne State University Press, Detroit, 1966.

[4] John B. Shoven, "The Incidence and Efficiency Effects of Taxes on Income from Capital," *Journal of Political Economy*, vol. 84, December 1976, pp. 1261–1283.

17.2 ECONOMIC EFFICIENCY

An economic change is efficient if it leads to an improvement in economic welfare. Economic welfare is improved when either some individuals in society are better off and none are worse off, or all are better off. If such an efficient economic change leads the economy from situation E to situation F, then F is said to be *Pareto preferred* to E.[5]

What follows will first assume that money and prices do not exist. Pareto optimum conditions between any two consumers, between any two productive sectors, and between consumers and producers will be derived. The *law of the invisible hand*, which states that perfect competition (assuming no externalities) leads inevitably to the satisfaction of Pareto optimum conditions, will then be proved.

17.2a Exchange

Consider two consumers, 1 and 2, who have only two commodities in their budgets, X and Y. Consumer 1 is initially endowed with X_1^0 units of X and Y_1^0 units of Y. Consumer 2 is initially endowed with X_2^0 units of X and Y_2^0 units of Y. If the graph of consumer 2 is rotated 180° clockwise about its origin and the graph of 2 is brought together with the graph of 1, an *Edgeworth box diagram* is obtained. This diagram is shown in Figure 17-1. Point K represents the original endowments of the two consumers. U_1 and U_2 are indifference curves of 1 and 2, respectively, passing through point K. Let us denote the marginal rate of commodity substitution by RCS. Recall from Chapter 1 that RCS measures the marginal rate of substitution of one good for another along the indifference curve (Section 1.3d). From Figure 17-1 it is evident that (ignoring the negative sign) $\Delta Y_1/\Delta X_1$ exceeds $\Delta Y_2/\Delta X_2$. Consumer 1 can forgo ΔY_1 and add to his or her consumption ΔX_1, thus moving along his or her indifference curve from point K to point L. At point L consumer 1 is as well off as he or she was at point K. Consumer 2 can forgo the consumption of ΔX_2 and add to his or her consumption of ΔY_2, thereby moving from point K to point M. At point M consumer 2 is as well off as he or she was at point K. If 1 moves from K to L and 2 moves from K to M, both consumers are left with "free" $\overline{LM}$ units of X. They can move to any intermediate point such as N. At point N both consumers are better off. Each has moved to a higher indifference curve. Accordingly, the inequality of the marginal rates of substitution led consumer 1 to trade Y to consumer 2 in exchange for X. As long as the RCS of one consumer differs from the RCS of the other, it is worthwhile to continue trading and thereby climbing the utility hill.

Suppose now that 1 and 2 finally reach a point, such as S, where their indifference curves are tangent to each other. At point S the RCS of 1 and 2 is the same. Moving away from point S must lead to a welfare deterioration of at least one of the consumers. Curve CC, known as the *contract curve*, is

---

[5] Vilfredo Pareto, an Italian economist, the pioneer of welfare economics, 1848–1923.

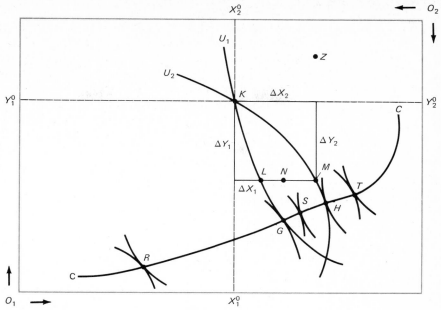

FIGURE 17-1　THE CONTRACT CURVE, TWO CONSUMERS

O_1 is the origin of consumer 1 and O_2 is the origin of consumer 2. At point K, which is the initial endowment of the two consumers, respectively, the indifference curve of consumer 1, U_1, intersects with the indifference curve of consumer 2, U_2. If consumer 1 decreases his or her consumption of Y by ΔY_1 and increases his or her consumption of X by ΔX_1, and if consumer 2 increases his or her consumption of Y by ΔY_2 and decreases his or her consumption of X by ΔX_2, both will remain with the same amount of utility, but they will be able to climb to a higher level of utilities by seeking a point between L and M. Contract curve CC is the locus of tangency points (between the indifference curves of consumer 1 and the indifference curves of consumer 2). Illustrations are points R, G, S, H, and T.

the locus of all tangency points such as R, G, S, H, and T. If 1 and 2 are at any point, such as K, which does not belong to the contract curve, it pays both of them to move through exchange to the contract curve. Note, however, that not every point on the contract curve is preferred to a point such as K. Only points that lie on the contract curve between G and H are preferred to point K. But the point has been made: If the marginal rates of commodity substitution of Y for X are not the same for the consumers, both consumers will upgrade their utility by exchanging commodities just until the marginal rates of commodity substitution are the same. Where on the contract curve between G and H the two consumers will settle depends on their bargaining positions. In summary, equilibrium of exchange between any two consumers trading in any two commodities occurs when

$$\text{RCS}_1 = \text{RCS}_2 \qquad (17\text{-}1)$$

We are now ready to consider equilibrium in production.

17.2b Production

Assume that there are only two sectors in the economy; one produces X and the other produces Y. The intital endowment of inputs A and B of the two sectors is indicated by point G in an Edgeworth box, in Figure 17-2. Thus initially A_x^0 units of A and B_x^0 units of B are tied up in the production of X, and A_y^0 units of A and B_y^0 units of B are tied up in the production of Y. I_x and I_y are the isoquants of X and Y passing through point G. Recall from Section 5.4a that RTS measures the marginal rate of substitution of one input for another, along the isoquant. Thus we can write

$$\text{RTS}_x = \frac{\Delta B_x}{\Delta A_x} = -\frac{\text{MP}_{ax}}{\text{MP}_{bx}} \quad \text{and} \quad \text{TRS}_y = \frac{\Delta B_y}{\Delta A_y} = -\frac{\text{MP}_{ay}}{\text{MP}_{by}}$$

It is clear from Figure 17-2 that (ignoring the negative sign)

$$\text{RTS}_x = \frac{\Delta B_x}{\Delta A_x} > \frac{\Delta B_y}{\Delta A_y} = \text{RTS}_y$$

Accordingly, ignoring the negative sign,

$$\frac{\text{MP}_{ax}}{\text{MP}_{bx}} > \frac{\text{MP}_{ay}}{\text{MP}_{by}}$$

Intuitively, this inequality indicates that on the margin, input A is relatively more productive in the production of X, and input B is relatively more productive in the production of Y. Hence more A and less B should be used in the production of X, and conversely, more B and less A should be used in the production of Y. One can see the benefit of factor substitution from observing that while $\Delta B_x = \Delta B_y$, ΔA_y exceeds ΔA_x. For example, suppose $\Delta B_x = \Delta B_y = 3$, $\Delta A_y = 4$, and $\Delta A_x = 1$. By moving from point G to point R, the producer of X releases 3 units of B and absorbs 1 additional unit of A. By moving from point G to point S, the producer of Y releases 4 units of A and absorbs 3 additional units of B. At points R and S, the production of X and Y, respectively, remains at the previous level, but $\overline{RS}$ (= 3) units of A are unused. The 3 units of A may be added to the production of both X and Y. This is achieved by moving to an intermediate point such as T. As in the case of consumption, if the marginal rate of technical substitution (RTS) in producing X is not equal to the marginal rate of technical substitution in producing Y, the production of both X and Y can increase through factor substitution. The equilibrium of production is achieved when the two marginal rates of technical substitution are equal. The RTS of X and the RTS of Y are equal when the isoquants of X and Y are tangent to each other. In Figure 17-2, H, L, W, M, and N are such points of tangency. The contract curve is the locus of all tangency points. Any point on the contract curve between L and M is preferred to G. W is an example. The requirement that the marginal rates of technical substitution in the production of any two goods in equilibrium should be equal can be formally stated:

$$\text{RTS}_x = \text{RTS}_y \tag{17-2}$$

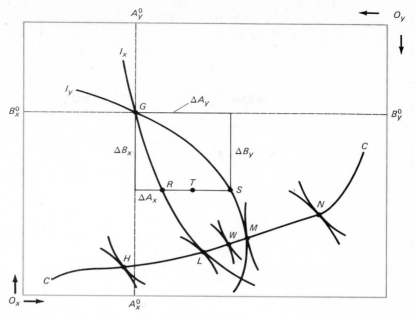

FIGURE 17-2 THE CONTRACT CURVE, TWO PRODUCERS

O_x is the origin of a producer in industry X, and O_y is the origin of a producer in industry Y. Point G denotes their initial endowment of inputs A and B, respectively. At point G isoquant I_x intersects with isoquant I_y. The first producer can increase the use of A by ΔA_x and decrease the use of B by ΔB_x. The second producer can decrease the use of A by ΔA_y and increase the use of B by ΔB_y. Both producers will remain on the same isoquants, and thus will continue to produce the same amounts as they did initially. But they can increase output by climbing to higher isoquants between points R and S.

The (production) contract curve CC is drawn by locating all tangency points (between isoquants of the first producer and isoquants of the second producer).

Another condition should be added to Equation 17-2: The equality between RTS_x and RTS_y implies that

$$\frac{\text{MP}_{ax}}{\text{MP}_{bx}} = \frac{\text{MP}_{ay}}{\text{MP}_{by}}$$

The above equality is a necessary condition for efficiency in production. The sufficient condition is that the marginal physical products of a certain factor used in a certain sector are the same for all firms:

$$\text{MP}_{ax}^\alpha = \text{MP}_{ax}^\beta \qquad (17\text{-}3)$$

where α and β represent any pair of firms in the sector producing X. The subscript ax can be replaced by bx or ay, etc. Clearly, if Equation 17-3 is not satisfied, say, $\text{MP}_{ax}^\alpha > \text{MP}_{ax}^\beta$, total output of X could be increased by shifting some units of A from firm β to firm α.

17.2c The Transformation Curve (Production-Possibility Curve)

We now develop a new concept known as the *transformation curve*. The transformation curve is derived by mapping contract curve CC from Figure 17-2 into a new space in which goods X and Y are measured along the axes. Such a space is shown in Figure 17-3. Recall from Section 2.3c that mapping simply means to utilize information from Figure 17-2 to draw a related curve in a different space. As an illustration, consider Figure 17-2. Suppose isoquant I_y represents a level of output of 50 units of Y; if the isoquant which is tangent to I_y at point M represents a level of output of 100 units of X, then point M is associated with pair of outputs (per unit of time) $X = 100$ and $Y = 50$. Point M is transformed from Figure 17-2 to Figure 17-3 by measuring 100 units along the X axis and 50 units along the Y axis. Thus, in principle, the transformation curve is drawn by mapping the contract curve from the Edgeworth box in Figure 17-2 into Figure 17-3, in which the axes are the outputs X and Y, respectively. Transformation curve T_r is concave from below. This may be true either because there are specific factors of production which are tied up in the production of X and Y or because one final good is capital-intensive and the other is labor-intensive. Points to the right of the transformation curve are unattainable. Points to the left of the transformation curve are inefficient since, given the inputs, less than the maximum output is produced.

The slope of the transformation curve is known as the *marginal rate of product transformation*. It is denoted by RPT. Thus

$$RPT = \frac{\Delta Y}{\Delta X} \qquad (17\text{-}4)$$

FIGURE 17-3 THE TRANSFORMATION CURVE

Transformation curve T_r is the locus of efficient rates of production of X and Y, drawn in the X, Y space for a given endowment of A and B. The transformation curve is obtained by mapping the production contract curve in Figure 17-2 into the X, Y space.

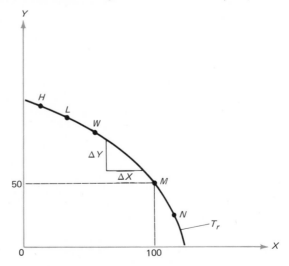

A firm in the Y sector can decrease the production of Y by ΔY, by reducing employment of factor A by ΔA. A firm in sector X will increase its use of A by the released ΔA and produce an additional ΔX units of X. This is summarized as

$$\Delta Y = \mathrm{MP}_{ay} \cdot \Delta A$$

$$\Delta X = \mathrm{MP}_{ax} \cdot \Delta A$$

If we divide the second into the first equality above (and add a minus sign to reflect the fact that ΔA is shifting from sector to sector), we can express RPT as $-\mathrm{MP}_{ay}/\mathrm{MP}_{ax}$. Similarly, a shift of ΔB from sector Y to sector X would yield two equalities:

$$\Delta Y = \mathrm{MP}_{by} \cdot \Delta B$$

$$\Delta X = \mathrm{MP}_{bx} \cdot \Delta B$$

In this case the RPT is expressed as $-\mathrm{MP}_{by}/\mathrm{MP}_{bx}$. In summary, we can write

$$\mathrm{RPT} = \frac{\Delta Y}{\Delta X} = -\frac{\mathrm{MP}_{ay}}{\mathrm{MP}_{ax}} = -\frac{\mathrm{MP}_{by}}{\mathrm{MP}_{bx}} \qquad (17\text{-}5)$$

17.2d Consumers and Producers

We have established that any two consumers must be on contract curve CC in Figure 17-1 in order to be in Pareto equilibrium. Any two sectors must be on contract curve CC in Figure 17-2 in order to be in equilibrium. This section discusses the simultaneous equilibrium conditions for the two groups.

There are many combinations of X and Y that the economy could produce. For any given endowment of inputs A and B there corresponds a transformation curve as illustrated in Figure 17-3. On each transformation curve there are an infinitely large number of points like H, L, W, M, and N. Each represents an efficient pair of X and Y from the producers' viewpoint. Let us now shift our focus to Figure 17-4. T_r is the transformation curve associated with a certain endowment of A and B. Let us assume that initially the economy produces X_0 units of X and Y_0 units of Y, as indicated by point R. Rectangle OX_0RY_0 is an Edgeworth box as in Figure 17-1 (O is O_1 and R is O_2). Assume that point S lies on the contract curve of this particular box (in order not to overcrowd the diagram the contract curve is not drawn); tangency between indifference curves U_1 and U_2 occurs at S. Line kk reflects the slope of U_1 and U_2 at S:

$$\text{Slope of } kk = \mathrm{RCS}_1 = \mathrm{RCS}_2$$

To put it differently, the two consumers initially select S as their temporary equilibrium. The slope of the transformation curve at R is represented by tangent line tt; hence,

$$\text{Slope of } tt = \mathrm{RPT}$$

Let us shift tt inward in a parallel manner until it crosses kk at point S; let

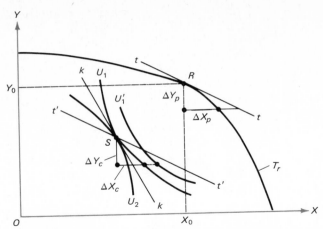

FIGURE 17-4 SEEKING A PARETO POINT FOR CONSUMERS AND PRODUCERS

The transformation curve is denoted by T_r. We should imagine a contract curve connecting point O and point R. Thus OX_0RY_0 is an Edgeworth box for two consumers. Point S is one point on such a contract curve. Indifference curve U_1 is tangent to indifference curve U_2 at point S. Line kk reflects the slope of the two indifference curves ($RCS_1 = RCS_2$). At point R line tt reflects the slope (RPT) of curve T_r. Line tt is shifted parallel to itself until it crosses point S. It is called $t't'$. Since the slope of $t't'$ is less (absolute value) than the slope of kk, we conclude that if consumer 1 forgoes the consumption of ΔY_c ($= \Delta Y_p$), and if production also shrinks by ΔY_c, which is equal to ΔY_p, resources can be released that can enhance the production of X by ΔX_p. But since $\Delta X_p > \Delta X_c$, consumer 1 can climb to higher indifference curve (U_1'), while consumer 2 is as well off as he or she was initially. Thus if RCS is not equal to RPT, a Pareto change is possible. The conclusion is that in order for Pareto optimum to be reached, RCS must be equal to RPT.

this new line be denoted by $t't'$. Since $t't'$ crosses kk from below going from left to right, RCS is greater than RPT (absolute value; ignore the negative value). What this means is that if consumer 1 will forgo the consumption of ΔY_c, he or she will have to add ΔX_c to remain on initial indifference curve U_1. But assume that simultaneously producers reduce the production of Y by ΔY_p, where $\Delta Y_p = \Delta Y_c$. As indicated by the slope of T_r at R (recall that this slope tt is parallel to $t't'$), resources that would be released by sector Y could be applied to increase production of X by ΔX_p. Since ΔX_p exceeds ΔX_c, consumer 1 can gain the difference of $\Delta X_p - \Delta X_c$, while consumer 2 could remain with his or her initial consumption of X and Y associated with point S.[6] To summarize, we have demonstrated that if RCS is not equal to RPT, at least one consumer could improve his or her lot through substitution in the production sector without adversely affecting other consumers. Consumer 1 will continue to substitute X for Y via the production sector, leading producers to move down along T_r in the southeasterly direction. This would constitute a *Pareto change*, since consumer 1 will be able to climb to a higher

---

[6] ΔX_p as measured by T_r is smaller than ΔX_p as measured by tt. This is due to the concavity of T_r. ΔX_c as measured by U_1 is greater than ΔX_c as measured by kk. This is due to convexity of U_1. When changes (Δ) are relatively small, these differences can be ignored.

indifference curve, such as U_1', while consumer 2, even if he or she stays with his or her initial basket, will be as well off as before. Notice, by the way, that this movement along the T_r curve requires a continuous drawing of new Edgeworth boxes with new CC curves. The two consumers will continue to trade with each other so long as producers are moving southeasterly along their T_r curve. This search will go on just until a point in the X and Y space is found where the marginal rate of product transformation will be equal to the marginal rate of commodity substitution for all consumers:

$$RCS_1 = RCS_2 = RPT \qquad (17\text{-}6)$$

After such a point is attained, Pareto changes would be impossible. Geometrically, Equation 17-6 implies that the slope of the transformation curve is the same as the slope of all indifference curves of all consumers.

The analysis focusing on Figure 17-4 is geometrically cumbersome. A considerable geometric simplification is achieved if we are willing to assume that all customers have identical tastes and identical initial endowments. Under such assumptions we can focus on one *representative consumer* whose indifference map is the same as the indifference maps of all other consumers. Assume that there are n consumers in this type of simplified economy. If the one consumer consumes a pair of X_0/n units of X and Y_0/n units of Y, the community will consume X_0 units of X and Y_0 units of Y. Moreover, for this (or any other) level of consumption, the indifference curve of the representative consumer and of the community have the same slope. Figure 17-5 shows the *community indifference map*, which in principle is obtained by drawing the indifference map of the representative consumer and then changing the scale of the axes such that each previous unit now becomes n units. The tangency between a community indifference curve and the transformation curve occurs at point R^*. There the community consumes a basket of X_0 and Y_0, and the representative consumer consumes X_0/n and Y_0/n units of X and Y, respectively. Equation 17-6 is satisfied at point R^*. Community indifference maps will be used in what follows for the sake of geometrical simplicity, keeping in mind that the results would not have changed if analysis as in Figure 17-4 had been used.

17.2e Pareto Optimum: A Summary

As mentioned earlier, an economic situation is defined as being a *Pareto optimum* if no individual can increase his or her welfare without adversely affecting the welfare of another individual. Four conditions must be satisfied to achieve Pareto optimum:

1. The marginal rates of commodity substitution between any two goods for any two consumers are equal:

$$RCS_1 = RCS_2 \qquad (17\text{-}1)$$

2. The marginal rates of technical substitution between any two inputs in the production of any two goods are equal:

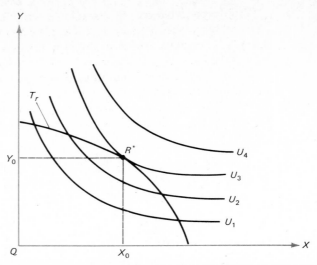

FIGURE 17-5   TRANSFORMATION CURVE AND COMMUNITY INDIFFERENCE CURVES
If we are willing to assume that consumers have identical tastes, we can draw the community indifference map, depicted by U_1, U_2, U_3, and U_4. Community indifference curve U_3 is tangent to transformation curve T_r at point R^*. Thus R^* is an efficient point: RCS = RPT.

$$RTS_x = RTS_y \qquad (17\text{-}2)$$

3. The marginal physical product of a factor of production engaged in the production of a certain good must be the same for all firms producing the good:

$$MP^\alpha_{ax} = MP^\beta_{ax} \qquad (17\text{-}3)$$

where α and β represent any pair of two firms. Also, the subscript ax can be replaced by bx, ay, and by.

4. The marginal rate of commodity substitution and the marginal rate of product transformation must be equal:

$$RCS_1 = RCS_2 = RPT \qquad (17\text{-}6)$$

17.2f The Law of the Invisible Hand

The above Pareto optimum conditions were derived without mentioning either prices or markets. In fact, the data consisted of consumers with fixed tastes, producers with a given technology, and a certain endowment of inputs. We are now ready to prove the famous *law of the invisible hand*. Adam Smith was the father of the dictum claiming that in a free market economy, each individual, by pursuing his or her own selfish economic goals, is led, as if by an *invisible hand*, to attain bliss for society as a whole.

Let us be more specific and qualify the law of the invisible hand. *Laissez-faire* is the necessary condition. The sufficient conditions are first that competition prevails and second that externalities are absent. What we are about to prove is that given laissez-faire, competition, and the absence of externalities, Pareto optimum (rather than maximum aggregate social welfare) is achieved. Pareto optimum implies efficiency but not necessarily maximum aggregate social welfare. We are not concerned in this section with the issue of income redistribution and whether or not such redistribution might render a higher level of utility to society as a whole.

The law of the invisible hand is proved as follows:

1. To maximize utility, the consumer allocates his or her budget among various goods and services such that the marginal rate of commodity substitution equals the price ratio of any pair of goods (Section 1.4b). That is,

$$\text{RCS} = -\frac{P_x}{P_y} \tag{17-7}$$

Goods X and Y represent any possible pair of commodities. Price uniformity in competition guarantees the equality of all the marginal rates of commodity substitution.

2. Consider the marginal rate of technical substitution between any two inputs A and B in the production of any output, say, X. The RTS has been defined to be $\Delta B_x / \Delta A_x$, which is equal to $-\text{MP}_{ax}/\text{MP}_{bx}$ (Section 5.4a). We can take advantage of the fact that in competition VMP_{ax} ($\text{MP}_{ax} \cdot P_x$) is equal to the price of A (Section 14.1a) to derive the following result:

$$\text{RTS}_x = \frac{\Delta B_x}{\Delta A_x} = -\frac{\text{MP}_{ax}}{\text{MP}_{bx}} = -\frac{\text{MP}_{ax} \cdot P_x}{\text{MP}_{bx} \cdot P_x} = -\frac{P_a}{P_b}$$

That is, in competition, RTS_x is equal to the ratio of P_a to P_b. (This relationship is also satisfied at each point on the expansion line, as explained in Section 6.5c.) The same relation for commodity Y can be derived. Then

$$\text{RTS}_x = -\frac{P_a}{P_b}$$
$$\text{RTS}_y = -\frac{P_a}{P_b} \tag{17-8}$$

The uniformity of prices of inputs in competition guarantees the equality of RTS_x with RTS_y.

3. As in 2, since in competition VMP_{ax} is equal to P_a (Section 14.1a), we can express MP_{ax}^α and MP_{ax}^β as follows:

$$\text{MP}_{ax}^\alpha = \frac{P_a}{P_x}$$
$$\text{MP}_{ax}^\beta = \frac{P_a}{P_x} \tag{17-9}$$

The uniformity of prices of inputs and outputs in competition guarantees the equality of MP_{ax}^α with MP_{ax}^β.

4. Competitive firms produce where the price is equal to the marginal cost (Section 7.2c); that is,

$$P_x = \mathrm{MC}_x = \frac{P_a}{\mathrm{MP}_{ax}} = \frac{P_b}{\mathrm{MP}_{bx}}$$

$$P_y = \mathrm{MP}_y = \frac{P_a}{\mathrm{MP}_{ay}} = \frac{P_b}{\mathrm{MP}_{by}}$$

Dividing the above equations gives

$$\frac{P_x}{P_y} = \frac{\mathrm{MP}_{ay}}{\mathrm{MP}_{ax}} = \frac{\mathrm{MP}_{by}}{\mathrm{MP}_{bx}}$$

This result together with Equation 17-5 gives

$$\mathrm{RPT} = -\frac{P_x}{P_y} \tag{17-10}$$

Price uniformity in competition coupled with Equation 17-7 gives

$$\mathrm{RPT} = \mathrm{RCS} = -\frac{P_x}{P_y} \tag{17-11}$$

We conclude that in a world in which perfect competition prevails and externalities are absent, Pareto efficiency is achieved. A major section will be devoted to the issue of externalities, which is perhaps the most important topic in modern welfare economics. First, however, we shall consider deviation from Pareto efficiency resulting from taxation and imperfect competition.

17.3 INEFFICIENCIES RESULTING FROM TAXATION AND IMPERFECT COMPETITION

In this section we shall see that, in general, taxation and imperfect competition lead to welfare losses. It will be stressed, however, that the initial condition of the economy is relevant for this type of efficiency analysis.

17.3a Indirect Taxes

Governments levy taxes to obtain revenues needed for providing the public with goods such as defense and education. Since we are interested in the welfare loss due to taxes per se, it will be assumed that after the tax is levied the proceeds are returned as a lump-sum subsidy to all citizens. This procedure makes it possible to leave the transformation curve and the indifference map unaltered. The problems of indirect taxes was discussed in Section 10.1.

Let us assume that there are only two goods in the economy, X and Y. Each of these commodities is produced competitively. Using the technique of Figure 17-5, we draw the aggregate transformation curve and an indifference curve U_2 in Figure 17-6. Indifference curve U_2 is tangent to the transformation curve at point R^*. At this point of tangency, the slope (of

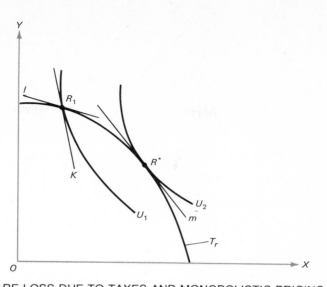

FIGURE 17-6 THE WELFARE LOSS DUE TO TAXES AND MONOPOLISTIC PRICING
At point R^*, community indifference curve U_2 just touches transformation curve T_r. Line m reflects the slope of both the T_r curve (RPT) and the U_2 curve (RCS). Hence RCS = RPT. If either a unit tax is imposed on X or producers of X organize in a cartel and price X monopolistically, there is a divergence between RCS and RPT: RCS > RPT, and a new non-Pareto equilibrium is found at point R_1, where RCS is represented by line k and RPT is represented by line l. U_1 represents less utility than U_2.

both curves), which is represented by line m, is (ignoring the negative sign)

$$\text{RPT} = \text{RCS} = \frac{P_x}{P_y}$$

Assume that the government imposes a tax of T dollars per unit of output X. Let us continue to denote the price net of the tax by P_x. This is the price received by producers of X and is therefore relevant for them. The price paid by consumers is $P_x + T$. The marginal rate of product transformation in production is no longer equal to the marginal rate of commodity substitution in consumption (ignoring the negative signs):

$$\text{RCS} = \frac{P_x + T}{P_y} > \text{RPT} = \frac{P_x}{P_y} \tag{17-12}$$

To find a new point of equilibrium after the tax is imposed, we start moving leftward along the transformation curve. We finally reach point R_1 at which line l is tangent to the transformation curve. Line l represents slope RPT = P_x/P_y. Line k, which is tangent to indifference curve U_1 at point R_1, represents slope RCS = $(P_x + T)/P_y$. Thus the diversion of RCS from RPT forced consumers to shift from a high level of utility U_2 to a lower level of utility U_1. The gap between RCS and RPT was caused by the indirect tax, which led the price ratio confronting consumers to divert from the price ratio confronting producers. The fact that the slope of l differs from the slope of

m shows that the price of X (relative to the price of Y) facing the producer has declined. Accordingly, the price paid by consumers has increased, but not by the full amount of the tax.

Section 10.1e applied partial-equilibrium analysis to show that indirect taxes give rise to welfare losses. In this section a simple general-equilibrium model was applied to confirm that result. In more advanced studies economists apply general-equilibrium analysis to investigate the order of magnitude of the welfare loss resulting from indirect taxation.

17.3b Income Taxes

Income taxes are not neutral taxes. The mere fact that a person who opts to spend 24 hours a day in leisure avoids paying income taxes completely indicates that such taxes are in effect imposed on all goods but leisure. Section 1.6 discussed the indifference map in the space where all other goods are aggregated into one good and leisure is the other good. In this section another concept is added to Section 1.6, that is, the transformation curve between leisure and all other goods. To conform to Figure 17-6, the vertical axis is assigned to leisure and the horizontal axis to all other goods. This reverses the axis assignments in Section 1.6.

Let X represent all the goods in the economy except leisure. Let Y represent leisure. We can imagine a tranformation curve in the space of all-other-goods and leisure. Moving along such a transformation curve in the southeasterly direction implies that leisure is being transformed into all-other-goods. The imposition of an income tax is equivalent to imposing a tax on all goods but leisure. As an example, if 1 hour of labor is worth \$10, and income tax is 10 percent, working 1 hour more is equivalent to selling an additional hour of leisure. The worker, however, cannot use the entire sum of \$10 to purchase X. He or she must pay \$1 to the government and can actually spend only \$9. Thus, if the worker forgoes 1 hour of leisure, as a consumer in the marketplace, he or she can purchase only ΔX worth \$9. But because the employer pays him or her \$10 an hour, his or her hour on the margin can be transformed into goods worth \$10. Hence the ΔX associated with the movement along the transformation curve is larger than the ΔX worth only \$9. This situation is geometrically depicted by point R_1 in Figure 17-6. We can formulate this situation as follows:

The employer pays the employee (who is also the consumer) his or her value of the marginal physical product of labor:

$$\text{MP}_{yx} \cdot P_x = P_y$$

MP_{yx} is $\Delta X/\Delta Y$, and the above equation can be written

$$\frac{\Delta Y}{\Delta X} = \frac{P_x}{P_y}$$

where the negative sign would appear if *labor* were replaced by *leisure*. In consumption we have

$$\Delta Y(P_y - T) + \Delta X \cdot P_x = 0$$

Thus (ignoring the negative sign), the subjective rate of substitution in consumption is

$$\frac{\Delta Y}{\Delta X} = \frac{P_x}{P_y - T} \qquad (17\text{-}13)$$

The marginal rate of substitution along the transformation curve (P_x/P_y) is represented by line l. The subjective marginal rate of substitution [$P_x/(P_y - T)$] is represented by line k. Without an income tax the two rates would be equated and the consumer would move to point R^*. The utility loss as a result of the tax is the difference between U_2 and U_1. We have confirmed that a tax on income from work gives rise to a welfare loss.

17.3c Monopolistic Pricing

Section 11.2 applied partial-equilibrium analysis to show that monopolistic pricing results in welfare loss to society. We now confirm these results by applying general-equilibrium analysis.

Suppose that commodity X is produced by monopoly and commodity Y is produced competitively. The reader can easily show that a monopolist combines factors of production efficiently in the process of production. In other words, rule 2 of Pareto optimality is not violated under monopolistic pricing. Consider any of the inputs used in the production of X and Y, say, input A. Firms producing Y equate the value of marginal product of A with the price of A while the monopoly equates the marginal revenue product of A with the price of A. This may be written as follows:

In competition $\qquad\qquad$ $\text{MP}_{ay} \cdot P_y = P_a$ $\qquad$ (Section 14.1a)

Under monopoly $\qquad\qquad$ $\text{MP}_{ax} \cdot \text{MR}_x = P_a$ $\qquad$ (Section 14.5)

Thus, since P_a is uniform for all firms,

$$\text{MP}_{ay} \cdot P_y = \text{MP}_{ax} \cdot \text{MR}_x$$

But since $\text{MR}_x < P_x$,

$$\text{MP}_{ay} \cdot P_y < \text{MP}_{ax} \cdot P_x$$

and rearranging the last inequality, we get

$$\frac{\text{MP}_{ay}}{\text{MP}_{ax}} < \frac{P_x}{P_y}$$

But utilizing Equation 17-5 and recalling that, for consumers, the marginal rate of commodity substitution equals the price ratio (Equation 17-7), we get (ignoring the negative sign)

$$\text{RPT} = \frac{\text{MP}_{ay}}{\text{MP}_{ax}} < \frac{P_x}{P_y} = \text{RCS}$$

To put it more rigorously,

$$\text{RPT} = \frac{\text{MR}_x}{P_y} = \frac{P_x\left(1 + \frac{1}{n}\right)}{P_y} < \frac{P_x}{P_y} = \text{RCS} \qquad (17\text{-}14)$$

We can use Figure 17-6 to demonstrate the position of the monopoly. RPT is a slope represented by l. RCS is a slope represented by line k. RPT, the marginal rate of product transformation at point R_1, is smaller than RCS, the marginal rate of commodity substitution at the same point. (Again, ignore the negative value of RPT and RCS.) It is left for the reader to show that the government can increase the welfare of consumers by subsidizing the monopolized commodity. In summary, monopolies reduce the economic welfare of society by creating a gap between RPT and RCS.

17.3d Monopsonistic Pricing

Section 14.4 discussed the case of monopsony in the labor market. Although it was stressed that monopsonies are hard to find in real life, for the sake of completing the theory the case of welfare loss due to monopsony will be discussed.

Consider a case in which a firm producing X uses two factors of production A and B. The firm faces a positively sloped supply curve of input A; i.e., the firm enjoys a monopsonistic position in the market for input A. In the market for A the supply elasticity is $\epsilon > 0$. The firm has no influence over the price of factor B or the price of output. Recall (Section 14.4) that the firm would employ inputs A and B such that the marginal factor cost of A equals the value of the marginal product of A, and the price of B equals the value of the marginal product of B. This can be written as

$$P_x \cdot \text{MP}_{ax} = P_a\left(1 + \frac{1}{\epsilon}\right)$$

$$P_x \cdot \text{MP}_{bx} = P_b$$

Dividing (recalling Section 5.4a and ignoring the minus signs) gives

$$\text{RTS}_x = \frac{\text{MP}_{ax}}{\text{MP}_{bx}} = \frac{P_a\left(1 + \frac{1}{\epsilon}\right)}{P_b}$$

Consider a firm in industry Y which sells its output and buys its inputs in competitive markets. There

$$P_y \cdot \text{MP}_{ay} = P_a$$

$$P_y \cdot \text{MP}_{by} = P_b$$

Dividing gives

$$\text{RTS}_y = \frac{\text{MP}_{ay}}{\text{MP}_{by}} = \frac{P_a}{P_b}$$

And combining the results for the two firms,

$$\text{RTS}_y = \frac{P_a}{P_b} < \frac{P_a\left(1 + \frac{1}{\epsilon}\right)}{P_b} = \text{RTS}_x \tag{17-15}$$

The student can easily show that the inequality of the marginal rates of technical substitution induces the two firms to be at a point like G in Figure 17-2 rather than at a point like W on the contract curve. This is a deviation from rule 2 of Pareto optimality.

17.3e A Caveat: The Initial Condition Is Relevant

In the preceding sections the intital position of the economy was assumed to be depicted by point R^* in Figure 17-6, where competition prevails and no taxes are imposed by the government. At such an initial equilibrium position the same price ratio P_x/P_y was seen by consumers and producers. A unit tax T imposed on good X led to a price ratio divergence and hence to a movement to a position associated with a lower level of utility denoted by R_1. The conclusion that a unit tax must result in a deviation from a Pareto optimum position is correct provided that R^* is the initial position. Given a noncompetitive initial position, the imposition of a unit tax may give rise to a higher level of utility. As an example, suppose the initial position of the economy is represented by point R_1 in Figure 17-6, because X is produced by a monopoly. A unit tax on Y, if imposed in the right size, may restore the optimal position R^* by simply eliminating the divergence caused by monopolistic pricing. In fact, the size of tax T should be such that

$$\text{RPT} = \frac{P_x\left(1 + \frac{1}{\eta}\right)}{P_y} = \frac{P_x}{P_y + T} = \text{RCS} \tag{17-16}$$

The following section will argue that a tax may be called for to remedy welfare losses resulting from externalities.

17.4 EXTERNALITIES

17.4a Externalities Defined

Externalities arise in production when *social costs* diverge from *private costs* (Section 6.1b). The most notorious examples of externalities are water and air pollution. A paper mill disposes of its production residuals into the river; downstream a fisherman and a swimmer suffer a loss which is not reflected in the cost function of the paper mill. A power station generates electricity by burning coal. In the process, sulfur dioxide is emitted. Sulfur dioxide is one of the worst forms of air pollution: It leads to health and property deterioration. Thus the social cost is the total cost to society, including the damage to health and property. The private cost to the power stations excludes the damages to health and property. A gang of motorcyclists ride through a quiet street in a suburb. A resident who enjoys listening to classical music is disturbed. In this case the private cost of consumption to the motorcyclists falls short of the social cost.

Externalities are not always adverse. They can sometimes be favorable. As an example, effluents which are spilled by cities into streams contain nitrogen. If not excessive, nitrogen may be useful to farmers who irrigate downstream.

The following section will formulate the theory of externalities in production. Next will be a discussion of *Coase's theorem*, which goes to the roots of externalities: Why do they arise to begin with?

At the end of this section it is noted that our analysis is limited to physical externalities. Pecuniary externalities, which were discussed in Section 9.5, are ignored in this chapter because they do not lead to Pareto inefficiencies.

17.4b Why Externalities Give Rise to Inefficiencies

Assume again an economy in which goods X and Y are produced and sold in the market. For simplicity, assume that only factor A is used in the production of X and Y and that its quantity is given. Assume that the production of X generates a by-product Z for which there is no market but which is either beneficial or detrimental in the production of Y. If X is apple farming and Y is beekeeping, then if apple farmers apply more effort to growing apples, there will be more apples to sell in the market but there will also be more nectar in apple blossoms for the bees. The nectar is factor Z, which, supposedly, farmers cannot sell in a market.[7] In another example, X could be a paper mill and Y a fisherman downstream. The paper mill does not pay for the water use. But the pollution resulting from the paper mill operations is harmful to fishing: It reduces the catch.

Assume that X is the paper industry, Y the fishing industry (downstream), and Z the water pollution. Two new terms of *marginal physical products* are introduced as follows: MP_{az} is $\Delta Z/\Delta A$; it is the additional pollution per additional unit of effort going into paper production. MP_{zy} is $\Delta Y/\Delta Z$; it is the reduction in fish catch per additional unit of pollution discharged into the stream by the paper mill. To find out the slope of the transformation curve, the following accounting is carried out:

A small amount of effort ΔA is diverted from X, the paper mill, into Y, the fishing industry.
The reduction in paper production: $\Delta X = \Delta A \cdot MP_{ax}$
The increase in fish catch: $\Delta Y = \Delta A \cdot MP_{ay} - \Delta A \cdot MP_{az} \cdot MP_{zy}$

Under these circumstances, if ΔY is divided by ΔX, the slope of the transformation curve is obtained as follows (ignoring the negative sign):

---

[7] The assumption that there is no market for the nectar was proved to be erroneous. See Section 17.4d.

$$\frac{\Delta Y}{\Delta X} = \frac{\mathrm{MP}_{ay} - \mathrm{MP}_{az} \cdot \mathrm{MP}_{zy}}{\mathrm{MP}_{ax}} = \mathrm{RPT} \qquad (17\text{-}17)$$

But the firms in both industries consider only private costs; they equate their marginal costs with the prices of paper and fish, respectively (Section 7.2c).

We can write

$$P_x = \mathrm{MC}_x = \frac{P_a}{\mathrm{MP}_{ax}}$$

$$P_y = \mathrm{MC}_y = \frac{P_a}{\mathrm{MP}_{ay}}$$

Dividing the above equations and making use of Equation 17-7, we get (ignoring the negative sign)

$$\mathrm{RCS} = \frac{P_x}{P_y} = \frac{\mathrm{MC}_x}{\mathrm{MC}_y} = \frac{\mathrm{MP}_{ay}}{\mathrm{MP}_{ax}} \qquad (17\text{-}18)$$

Equations 17-17 and 17-18 tell us that externalities lead to an inefficient position

$$\mathrm{RCS} = \frac{P_x}{P_y} = \frac{\mathrm{MP}_{ay}}{\mathrm{MP}_{ax}} < \frac{\mathrm{MP}_{ay} - \mathrm{MP}_{az}\mathrm{MP}_{zy}}{\mathrm{MP}_{ax}} = \mathrm{RPT} \qquad (17\text{-}19)$$

As an illustration, assume that a unit of A is shifted from the paper industry to the fishing industry ($A = 1$). As a result, the following happens on the margin: The production of paper falls by, say, 3 units ($\mathrm{MP}_{ax} = 3$). The direct fish catch increases by 6 units ($\mathrm{MP}_{ay} = 6$). Pollution decreases by 1.5 units ($\mathrm{MP}_{az} = 1.5$), but since each additional unit of pollution causes the catch to decline by 2 units ($\mathrm{MP}_{zy} = -2$), the total external gain to the fishing industry is 3 units. Thus, while RCS is 2 (6/3), RPT is 3 (9/3). In Figure 17-7 equilibrium is achieved at point R_1. RPT, which is represented by tangent line l, is greater than RCS, which is represented by line k (negative values are ignored). The efficient position of the economy is attained at point R^*, where RCS is equal to RPT. To reach R^* the production of paper would be cut back from X_1 to X^*. The released resources should be employed in the enhancing of the catch of fish by $Y^* - Y_1$. The welfare loss is indicated by the difference between U_2 and U_1.

Why do fishermen not bribe the paper mill to decrease its production from X_1 to X^*? This question takes us to the heart of the issue, that is, to *Coase's theorem*.

17.4c Coase's Theorem

If property rights for resources such as land, water, and air were properly defined, or if property rights for these resources were completely absent, and if the operation of the pricing system imposed no cost, then physical externalities as described in the previous section would not lead the *invisible hand* astray. This is the thrust of *Coase's theorem*.

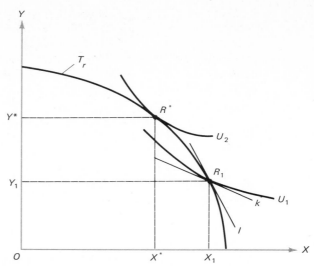

FIGURE 17-7 EXTERNALITIES

Without externalities R^* would be the equilibrium point consistent with Pareto optimum: At point R^* community indifference curve U_2 is tangent to transformation curve T_r. But if we assume that the production of X (paper) releases an effluent Z which affects adversely the production of Y, then there is a divergence between RCS and RPT: In fact RCS < RPT. This new situation is depicted by point R_1 where line l represents the slope of T_r and line k represents the slope of U_1. U_1 represents less utility than U_2. R_1 is non-Pareto optimal.

The following example, which is based on Ronald Coase's article,[8] will illustrate Coase's theorem. A factory which emits smoke is built in a small town. Assume that the damage to the community from the air pollution is estimated at $100 per year. The factory can install scrubbers that will completely eliminate the air pollution at a cost of $90 a year. The members of the community can move to another smoke-free location at an annual cost of $40. There are bargains that might be concluded here if *transaction costs* are zero.[9] First, assume that the members of the community have property rights to the air and that the factory is liable for $100 worth of damage. If the factory paid $90 for scrubbing, it could save $10. But there is a better bargain: If the factory bribed the members of the community to the tune of $40 to move to a smoke-free location, they would be as well off. But the community members can bargain with the factory to pay them a sum which is higher than $40 but lower than $90. If, for example, they agree on $60, the members of the community will be $20 (= $60 − $40) better off, and the factory will be $30 (= $90 − $60) better off. Second, suppose that either nobody has property rights to the air or the factory has the rights to the air. In that case the factory is not liable for damage. The strong point made by Coase was that

---

[8] Ronald H. Coase, "The Problem of Social Cost," *Journal of Law and Economics*, vol. 3, October 1960, pp. 1–44.

[9] Transaction costs are usually legal, administrative, and other similar costs involved in bargaining and signing contracts.

from the viewpoint of efficiency the result would be the same: Rather than suffering a damage of $100, the community would move to another location at an annual cost of $40. From the viewpoint of equity, the two solutions are different. But as pointed out earlier, equity is an ethical rather than an economic issue. The upshot of all this is that in the absence of transaction costs, externalities would not lead the economy to an inefficient point like R_1 in Figure 17-7. Rather, it would, through bargaining, lead the parties involved to point R^*: Either the paper mill will be liable for damage to the fishermen and reduce its level of output to save some of the damage fees or the fishermen will bribe the paper mill to reduce its production.

Note that if transaction costs are nil, a tax properly imposed will lead to the same optimal result: A tax of $100 imposed on the factory will result in the same deal as in the case of damage liability. The factory will pay the members of the community more than $40 but less than $90 to move elsewhere.

Now, assume that transaction costs are extremely high. For example, transaction costs may be nil for the community but so high for the factory that under a system of damage liability it decides to install a scrubber for a cost of $90. Since the factory cannot negotiate with the members of the community, the alternative optimal solution is not reached. A system of no liability, on the other hand, would induce the members of the community to move away for $40, which is the optimal solution. This should not lead us to the conclusion that no liability is preferred to a system of damage liability: If the cost of moving rises from $40 to $95 and transaction cost for the community is high, the result is reversed.

If transaction costs are extremely high, externalities can be *internalized* by a merger between the two parties involved. Thus, if the entire stock of the smoke-emitting factory is owned by the residents of the adjacent town, the optimal solution will be reached without any bargaining. Or if the paper mill is owned by the fishermen downstream, the Pareto optimal solution will be reached in a natural way. In reality, where numerous parties may be involved, internalization of externalities may involve heavy transaction costs and may thus be impractical.

Lest the reader begin to think that transaction costs are always so high as to prevent Pareto equilibrium from ever being reached in face of externalities, a classic example follows in which externalities exist and bargains lead to optimal solutions.

17.4d An Example: The Fable of the Bees

For decades economists argued that market failures occurred because of externalities. Unfortunately for those economists, they invented the example of the bees and the apple trees (Section 17.4b): Apple orchards provided free nectar to owners of beehives, and the bees provided free pollinating services to orchard owners. Then Steven Cheung explored the beekeeping and orchard industries and published his results.[10] He found that beekeepers either reached verbal contracts or signed written contracts with

[10]Steven N. S. Cheung, "The Fable of the Bees: An Economic Investigation," *The Journal of Law of Economics*, vol. 16, April 1973, pp. 11–33.

farmers. Where nectar was available in relative abundance, beekeepers signed apiary lease contracts specifying the rent beekeepers must pay farmers for the right to locate their hives in a specific orchard. The apiary rent was paid mostly in honey based either on the current honey yield or the yield of the preceding year. Where nectar was scarce, farmers had to lure beekeepers by offering them attractive pollination contracts. Such contracts specified the rental fee per hive, the strategic location of the hives, and even such things as protection of bees from chemical spraying. What went on in the orchards of Washington indicated that not only did farmers and beekeepers sign contracts, they also minimized the transaction costs of contracting in a variety of ingenious ways. For example, farmers may take a free ride; they may not rent beehives and yet will benefit from the spillover from neighbors who have entered pollinating contracts. To prevent free rides, farmers adhere to the *custom of the orchards*, whereby during the pollination period farmers either keep their own beehives or hire as many hives per acre as are hired by the other neighbors. A farmer who fails to comply would be rated as a *bad neighbor*, which according to Cheung, would result in a number of inconveniences.

In addition to verifying Coase's theorem,' Cheung may have warned economists that "failing to investigate the real world situation and [in] arriving at policy implications out of sheer imagination" may give them the rate of "bad neighbors."

17.4e Water and Air Pollution

Section 17.4b discussed the case where the production of good X generates Z, which inhibits (or enhances) the production of Y. It mentioned water pollution (production of paper and fishing) and air pollution (emission of sulfur dioxide by power stations). It is convenient to organize our thinking by focusing on Z, the water or air pollution, rather than by using a diagram as in Figure 17-7. This is achieved by focusing on Figure 17-8. Along the horizontal axis we measure the pollution, which is denoted by Z. Along the vertical axis we measure the costs and gains, in dollars. Curve $\Delta Y/\Delta Z$ (previously MP_{zy}) could be the marginal loss of fish due to water pollution. In that sense fish lost is a factor in the production of paper. The curve denoted by Δ(gain to X)/ΔZ tells about the cost the polluter avoids on the margin by being able to discharge waste into the stream (or into the atmosphere). For the paper mill (X) in the previous example the gain is due to the fact that the next best alternative to discharging waste into the stream is more expensive.

If transaction costs are zero, there could be two market solutions: First, if producers of X are liable for the damage which they inflict upon producers of Y, they will discharge waste amounting to Z^*. Since under this system $\Delta Y/\Delta Z$ becomes the marginal damage curve, pollution beyond Z^* would mean paying marginal damages in excess of marginal gains. Next, if a system of no damage liability prevails, producers of Y will bribe producers of X to cut back on waste discharged from Z_1 to Z^*. You can show that so long as the waste discharge is in excess of Z^*, say, $\overline{OK}$, the bribe for agreeing to discharge one unit less is somewhere between $\overline{KL}$ and $\overline{KM}$.

Second, if transaction costs are extremely high, producers of X will discharge Z_1 units of waste. However, a tax which is equal to the damages will make it unprofitable for the producers of X to discharge in excess of Z^*. Although taxes on waste could lead to point Z^*, which is Pareto optimal (associated with R^* in Figure 17-7), in the United States, by and large, the government has resorted to administrative regulation of pollution.

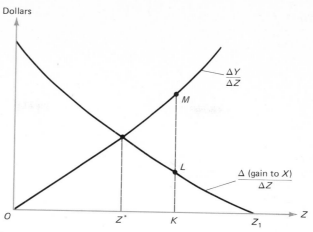

FIGURE 17-8 POLLUTION

Pollution Z is measured along the horizontal axis and dollars along the vertical axis. The downward-sloping curve is the marginal gain from disposing of the effluent into the environment. The gain is due to the fact that the next-best alternative is more expensive. The upward-sloping curve depicts the marginal damage to another industry, say, fishing. The optimal amount of effluent that should be discharged per unit of time is Z^*, where the two curves cross each other. If the amount of effluent currently discharged is $\overline{OK}$, even if property rights to water (or air) do not exist, if transaction costs are nil, the suffering industry (Y) will bribe the polluting industry by an amount of money that is equal to a segment somewhere between $\overline{KL}$ and $\overline{KM}$ in order to induce it to reduce pollution by one unit. This process will continue until the optimal pollution of Z^* per unit of time is achieved.

17.4f An Example: The Proposed Proxmire Tax on Sulfur Dioxide

Property rights cannot be assigned to air. Even if proper property rights could be assigned to air, the fact that numerous small entities (households) suffer from air pollution would render transaction costs extremely high. It is a known technological fact that when coal is burned by industries and power stations, sulfur dioxide is emitted into the air. Sulfur dioxide is harmful to health and property. Currently being motivated more by politics than by good economic analysis, the federal government forces all sizable coal burners to install scrubbers. This, of course, is not an efficient rule in face of the fact that Western coal (relative to that in the East) is low in sulfur content. Senator Proxmire suggested a tax at a rate of 5 cents or more per pound of emitted sulfur. Such a tax would be more efficient than the current regulation in that it would induce the coal burners to select the best alternative available. For example, if a power station

in the East calculated that shipping clean coal from the West is cheaper than scrubbing Eastern coal, it would so do.

Alan Schlottman and Lawrence Abrams applied linear programming techniques (Chapter 18) to estimate the impact of such a tax on the American economy.[11] Among other things, they found that at a tax rate of 15 cents per pound of emitted sulfur the use of high-sulfur coal would be reduced by 50 percent. Some of the results of this study are shown in Table 17-1. Notice that while coal extraction in the Middle West would decline from 150 to 78 million tons as the tax rises from 0 to 20 cents per pound emitted, Western extraction of relatively clean coal would rise from 49 to 90 million tons. In addition, as the tax rises, total extraction of coal in the United States falls from 507 to 427 million tons because of both a reduction in the demand for electricity and fuel substitution.

---

[11] Alan Schlottman and Lawrence W. Abrams, "Sulfur Emission, Taxes and Coal Resources," *Review of Economics and Statistics*, vol. 59, February 1977, pp. 50–55.

TABLE 17-1 **The Regional Impact of a Tax on Coal Extraction**
(Millions of Tons)

Coal-producing region	Sulfur emissions tax, $/lb.				
	0	0.05	0.10	0.15	0.20
Northern Appalachia	167.5	151.3	142.9	128.8	113.2
Central Appalachia	122.1	129.6	129.3	128.4	126.5
Southern Appalachia	20.1	20.1	19.7	19.4	19.3
Total, Appalachia	307.9	301.0	291.9	276.6	259.0
Middle West	150.0	135.1	93.3	88.8	77.7
West	48.9	55.7	73.8	83.5	89.8
United States	506.8	491.8	459.6	448.9	426.5

Source: Alan Schlottman and Lawrence Abrams, "Sulfur Emission, Taxes and Coal Resources," The *Review of Economics and Statistics*, vol. 59, February 1977, pp. 50–55.

Table 17-2 presents the attempt of Schlottman and Abrams to calculate the marginal benefits of pollution abatement and its marginal cost. *Note*: They obtained the damage function to the environment by multiplying the sulfur emission by $756 per ton of sulfur, a figure provided by the Environmental Protection Agency. Although the author does not believe that such a figure can be estimated, it is nevertheless presented for the sake of illustration. Roughly, a tax of 15 cents is optimal: First, the marginal benefit of abatement of $0.76 billion is still in excess of the marginal cost of abatement of $0.33 billion. Second, total increase in benefits of $1.18 + $0.76 billion is in excess of the added cost due to abatement of $1.25 + $0.33 billion.

17.5 INCOME DISTRIBUTION AND THE SOCIAL WELFARE FUNCTION

The attainment of *Pareto optimum* is a *necessary*, but not a *sufficient condition* for reaching maximum *social welfare*. We have already seen that given input endowment and income distribution a Pareto optimum position can be found (Section 17.2d). For example, in Figure 17-4 point S represented an initial endowment which summarizes a certain income distribution for a given endowment of inputs. Recall that since S was not Pareto optimal, consumers traded with each other and also triggered production changes until they had reached a point where $RCS_1 = RCS_2 = RPT$. There are many other initial endowment points reflecting a multitude of schemes of income distribution. Even if we do not know which of these many combinations of X and Y coupled with a certain income distribution will lead to the point of maximum social welfare, we are certain that that point of maximum social welfare must be Pareto optimal; otherwise the welfare of some or all members of society could increase by moving away from such a point.

To summarize, in Sections 17.5a to 17.5c we shall see that there are an infinitely large number of Pareto optimal equilibrium positions, only one of which, however, is *the* position of *maximum social welfare*. It should be stressed that although discussing the nature of the maximum social welfare position is an interesting intellectual exercise, it leads to no policy implications: Because of our inability to make interpersonal utility comparisons, it

TABLE 17-2 **Costs and Benefits of the Sulfur Emission Tax**
(Benefits and costs are in billions of dollars)

	Sulfur emission tax, $/lb				
	0.00	0.05	0.10	0.15	0.20
Total emission, million tons	11.41	10.02	8.45	7.45	6.65
Total damage	8.62	7.57	6.39	5.63	5.03
Marginal benefits of abatement		1.05	1.18	0.76	0.60
Increased oil use		0.63	2.01	2.43	3.40
Total coal costs	5.11	5.04	4.91	4.82	4.70
Total cost of energy	5.11	5.67	6.92	7.25	8.10
Marginal cost of abatement		0.56	1.25	0.33	0.85

Source: Alan Schlottman and Lawrence Abrams, "Sulfur Emission, Taxes and Coal Resources," *The Review of Economics and Statistics*, vol. 59, February 1977, pp. 50–55.

is impossible to tell which of the many Pareto equilibrium points is that precious one which yields the maximum social welfare.

17.5a The Utility Possibility Frontier

Consider again the transformation curve as presented in Figure 17-3. For each point on the curve, say, M, there corresponds an Edgeworth box as in Figure 17-1. Inside such a box we can draw the contract curve. Let us draw such a contract curve for consumers 1 and 2 in panel (*a*) of Figure 17-9. The origin of the indifference map of consumer 1 is point *0* and that of consumer 2 is point M. Recall that (if M is fixed) the contract curve is efficient from the consumers' viewpoint. In panel (*b*) we measure the utility of consumer 1, denoted by U_1, along the horizontal axis, and the utility of consumer 2, denoted by U_2, along the vertical axis. The contract curve is mapped from the X, Y space into a $V_m V_m'$ curve in the $U_1 U_2$ space, as shown in panel (*b*). Mechanically, this mapping procedure is similar to that of mapping the production contract curve in Figure 17-2 into a transformation curve in Figure 17-3. The $V_m V_m'$ curve is known as the *utility possibility curve*. The movement from origin *0* to point M in panel (*a*) involves a rise in U_1 from zero to some positive level and a fall in U_2 from some positive level to zero. Put differently, as we move from *0* to M, U_1 increases at the expense of U_2. The utility possibility curve slopes downward to reflect the tradeoff between U_1 and U_2 as we move along the contract curve in panel (*a*). However, the ordinal nature of utility measurement does not permit us to assume either convexity or concavity. Thus the $V_m V_m'$ curve is drawn as a wavy line.

At M', which lies on the contract curve in panel (*a*), the indifference curves of the two consumers are tangent to each other. Assume that at that point their slopes are respectively equal to the slope of the transformation

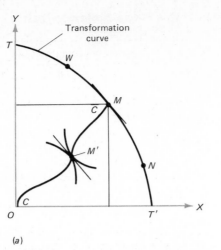

(a)

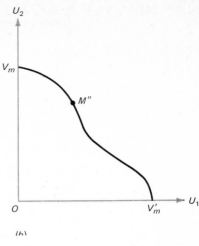

(b)

FIGURE 17-9 DERIVING THE UTILITY POSSIBILITY CURVE
In panel (a) we measure X and Y along the two axes, respectively. We select any point M on transformation curve TT'. The selection of M creates an Edgeworth box for two consumers. Consumer 1 has an origin at O and consumer 2 has an origin at M. The contract curve (as in Figure 17-1) is denoted by CC. At point M' on curve CC the slopes of the two indifference curves are equal to one another and to the slope of the transformation curve at point M; $RCS_1 = RCS_2 = RPT$. In panel (b) we measure the utility of consumer 1 (U_1) along the horizontal axis and the utility of consumer 2 (U_2) along the vertical axis. We map curve CC into the U_1, U_2 space and obtain the V_mV_m' curve, which is known as the utility possibility curve. This curve is wavy to reflect the ordinal nature of utility. Going from V_m to V_m' along the curve in panel (b) is equivalent to going from O to M along curve CC in panel (a). Point M' in panel (a) was mapped into point M'' in panel (b).

curve at M. In other words, $RCS_1 = RCS_2 = RPT$. Point M' in the X, Y space is mapped as point M'' into the U_1, U_2 space. M'' in panel (b) is the only point on the utility possibility curve which is Pareto optimal.

Now imagine a movement along the transformation curve in panel (a) from T' to T. As we move along the curve, for each point such as N, M, and W we can fit an Edgeworth box and draw an associated contract curve. For example, the contract curve corresponding to N [not shown in panel (a)] could be mapped into V_nV_n' in Figure 17-10. Also, if N' on such a curve represents equality among RCS_1, RCS_2, and RPT at N, this unique point could be mapped into N'' on this utility possibility curve (V_nV_n') in the U_1, U_2 space. There are an infinitely large number of utility possibility curves. In Figure 17-10 only three of the multitude of such curves are drawn—the dashed, wavy lines V_mV_m', V_nV_n', and V_wV_w'. If we connect all points like M'' and N'' of all the utility possibility curves, we obtain the *envelope curve* of all the utility possibility curves denoted by VV'. This curve is termed the *utility possibility frontier*. Each and every point on the utility possibility frontier is Pareto optimal. Moreover, all the possible Pareto optimal points lie on the utility possibility frontier.

Consider the Edgeworth box corresponding to point W in panel (a) of

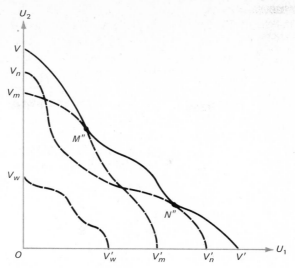

FIGURE 17-10   THE UTILITY POSSIBILITY FRONTIER
We measure the utility of consumer 1 (U_1) along the horizontal axis, and the utility of consumer 2 along the vertical axis. To each point on the transformation curve in panel (a) of Figure 17-9 there corresponds a CC curve that can be transformed into a $V_m V_m'$ type of curve in panel (b) of Figure 17-9. Had we drawn all such curves of the $V_m V_m'$ type in the U_1, U_2 space, the envelope of these curves would be the *utility possibility frontier*. Only three such utility possibility curves ($V_m V_m'$, $V_n V_n'$, and $V_w V_w'$) are shown. The envelope of these curves (and the many others that are not shown) is curve VV'. *Note*: The points of tangency between the VV' and the utility possibility curves are M'' and N'', which are Pareto optimal (efficient) in the sense that $RCS_1 = RCS_2 = RPT$ at each and every tangent point. Curve VV' is the utility possibility frontier.

Figure 17-9 (not shown). Suppose we could find not even one point on the associated contract curve at which the slopes of two indifference curves and the slope of the transformation curve (at W) are the same. In that case the entire associated utility possibility curve would lie below the utility possibility frontier.

17.5b Social Welfare Functions

So far the term *social welfare* has been used rather loosely. Social welfare may be defined as being the *aggregate utility of all consumers in the economy*. The utility function of consumer 1 in a two-good economy can be written as

$$U_1 = f_1(X_1, Y_1) \tag{17-20}$$

And that of consumer 2 is written as

$$U_2 = f_2(X_2, Y_2) \tag{17-21}$$

It is important to remember than U_1 and U_2 are *ordinal numbers*.

Let us ignore the impossibility of interpersonal comparison of utility. We can then arrive at an aggregate utility function as follows:

$$W = W(U_1, U_2) \tag{17-22}$$

where W is the *social welfare*. Equation 17-22 tells us that the utility of the entire society is dependent upon the utilities of all individuals who make up the society.

Given a utility function of the type $U = f(X, Y)$, an indifference map for an individual consumer can be derived (Chapter 1). In exactly the same manner an indifference map can be derived from the social welfare function as specified by Equation 17-22, the only difference being that since U_1 and U_2 are measured ordinally, social welfare indifference curves do not have to be convex; rather they are drawn wavy to indicate that they must only be negatively sloped.

If society were ruled by a dictator, it would have been up to him or her to construct the social indifference map. No doubt such a map would reflect his or her tastes rather than society's preferences. In a free society, where the construction of the social welfare function must be done by voting, this task becomes an impossibility.[12] On a more intuitive basis, the construction of social welfare functions requires a comparison of losses of utility of some individuals with gains of utility of other individuals. Since there is no measuring rod for comparing the utilities of two individuals, the social welfare function cannot be constructed.

In the following section we will pretend that social welfare functions can be constructed and will try to see what lessons can be learned from such a theoretical undertaking.

17.5c The Maximum Social Welfare

Consider Figure 17-10: Points inside the utility possibility frontier are attainable but non-Pareto. Points outside the frontier are unattainable. So we must search for the best point along the utility possibility frontier itself. Formally, our problem is stated as follows:

Maximize:

$$W = W(U_1, U_2)$$

Subject to the constraint of the utility possibility frontier VV'

Geometrically, the point of maximum social welfare is found by imposing the social indifference map on the U_1, U_2 space. This social indifference map is represented by only four social indifference curves (out of an infinite number), W_1, W_2, W_3, and W_4 in Figure 17-11. The highest level of social welfare is achieved at point G, where social welfare indifference curve W_3 is

---

[12] Arrow provided a rigorous proof known as the *theorem of impossibility*: Kenneth J. Arrow, *Social Choices and Individual Values*, John Wiley & Sons, New York, 1951.

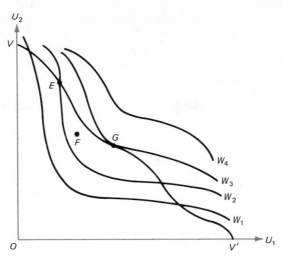

FIGURE 17-11 ATTAINING SOCIAL WELFARE MAXIMUM
The utility of consumer 1 (U_1) is measured along the horizontal axis, and the utility of consumer 2 (U_2) is measured along the vertical axis. The utility possibility frontier is depicted by curve VV'. The social indifference map is depicted by indifference curves W_1, W_2, W_3, and W_4. Social welfare is maximized at point G, where social indifference curve W_3 is tangent to utility possibility frontier VV'.

tangent to the utility possibility frontier. Thus W_3 is the highest level of social welfare attainable.

But if social indifference curves like W_1, W_2, etc., cannot be constructed, what have we gained from the above analysis? Perhaps the best answer is: Consider point E in Figure 17-11. It is Pareto optimal, and therefore it is an efficient point but not necessarily the point of maximum social welfare. Only if by sheer chance E happened to coincide with G would we be allowed to say that the economic policy leading to E is optimal. Moreover, compare the Pareto optimal E with the non-Pareto optimal F (which may arise owing to a monopoly). In Figure 17-11, F reflects a higher level of social welfare than E. This is what we mean by stating that Pareto optimum is a *necessary* but not a *sufficient condition* for maximum social welfare.

The upshot of all this is that if the four Pareto optimum conditions are satisfied, it is not a sign that maximum social welfare has been achieved. Moreover, even if somehow it is evident that maximum social welfare has not been achieved, there is no rule to guide us to that desirable precious point hidden somewhere on the utility possibility frontier.

17.5d Some Practical Considerations of Income Distribution

The fact that the impossibility of interpersonal comparison of utility renders the social welfare function nonoperational does not imply that economists shied away from the practical aspects of inequalities. Economists invented technical measures of income inequality. The best-known measure of income inequality is the *Lorenz curve*, which is associated with the *Gini coefficient*, to be discussed shortly.

In all Western countries progressive income taxes and other taxes are imposed. Such taxes, if they are imposed in a competitive environment, will lead to deviations from Pareto optimum. If such taxes are imposed in a noncompetitive economy, they may lead the economy either closer to Pareto optimum or farther away from it. If, in addition to giving governments revenues to purchase public goods (such as defense), the purpose of taxes is to modify the income distribution in favor of the poor, an apparatus is needed to compare the income distribution before and after the tax. Such a comparison can be performed with the aid of the *Lorenz curve*.

Suppose we lined up all families according to the size of their income, beginning with the lowest level of income and ending with the highest level of income. We could then measure the share of a certain percentile of the population in total income. For example, the share of total money income in the United States (before the deduction of income and social security taxes) is given in Table 17-3. From Table 17-3 we learn that in 1977 the lowest fifth (20 percent) of the population claimed only 5.2 percent of total income (before income taxes), the lowest 40 percent shared only 16.8 percent, and so on. This information can be mapped into a curve on a graph in which the lowest population percentage is measured along the horizontal axis and the share of the group in total income is measured along the vertical axis. Such a curve is known as the *Lorenz curve*, and Table 17-3 furnishes six points for the construction of such a curve (0,0 . . . 20,5.2 . . . 40,16.8 . . . 60,34.2 . . . 80,58.4 . . . 100,100). In principle, given continuous data on income sharing, a smooth Lorenz curve can be constructed, as illustrated in Figure 17-12, where $\overline{OG}$ measures 100 percent population and $\overline{OK}$ measures 100 percent income. If income were equally distributed, the cross diagonal $\overline{OH}$ would represent the Lorenz curve. On the other hand, if the entire national income were received by a single family, the Lorenz curve would boil down to OGH. Assume that the true Lorenz curve is marked by $OBEH$. From the above argument we deduce that the more it bulges toward the corner de-

TABLE 17-3 **Money Income of United States Families, Percent of Aggregate of Income Received by Each Fifth, 1977**

	Share	Accumulative share
Lowest fifth	5.2	5.2
Second fifth	11.6	16.8
Middle fifth	17.4	34.2
Fourth fifth	24.2	58.4
Highest fifth	41.6	100.0

Source: Statistical Abstract of the United States, 1978, p. 455, no. 734, Bureau of the Census, Washington, D.C., 1978.

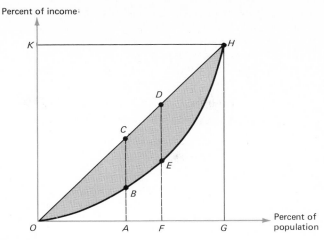

FIGURE 17-12 THE LORENZ CURVE

Cumulative percent population is measured along the horizontal axis. Cumulative percent share of income is measured along the vertical axis. The curve which depicts an actual income distribution is *OBEH*. The shaded area divided by the area of triangle *OGH* is the Gini coefficient.

noted by point G, the higher the degree of inequality in the economy is. Put in other words, the degree of inequality is represented by the ratio of shaded area to the area of triangle OGH. If instead of percents we used decimals (such that 10 percent is 0.1), the shaded area could be calculated by dividing $\overline{OG}$ into many small segments such as $\overline{AF}$. Shaded area $BEDC$ is obtained by taking the difference

$$BEDC = AFDC - AFEB = AFDC - \left(\overline{AF} \cdot \frac{\overline{AB} + \overline{FE}}{2}\right)$$

If we sum, we get

$$\Sigma BEDC = \Sigma AFDC - \Sigma\left(\overline{AF} \cdot \frac{\overline{AB} + \overline{FE}}{2}\right) = \frac{1}{2} - \Sigma\left(AF \cdot \frac{\overline{AB} + \overline{FE}}{2}\right)$$

The *Gini coefficient* is defined as the shaded area divided by the area of OGH, which is equal to 1/2 (under the decimal notations $\overline{OG}$ is unity). Thus we have a formula for the Gini coefficient as follows:

$$\text{Gini coefficient} = 1 - \Sigma[\overline{AF} \cdot (\overline{AB} + \overline{FE})] \tag{17-23}$$

It is left as an exercise for the student to calculate the Gini coefficient for data in Table 17-3.

17.5e An Example: Farms under Stress in Arid Environments

During droughts farmers who use surface water for irrigation must devise a procedure for allocating scarce water among the many users. Conventional wisdom holds that the allocation procedures that rank high in efficiency will rank low in equity and vice versa. Arthur Maass and Raymond Anderson studied water allocation procedures in arid environments in the United States and Spain.[13] They simulated allocation of water by following nine different procedures, only one of which was *market*. The other eight procedures were *nonmarket*. Contrary to the conventional wisdom, they discovered that the Gini coefficient which resulted from the market simulation was the lowest. For example in the United States the Gini coefficient for 75 percent water availability ranged from market 0.0254 to farm priorities 0.7942. In Spain the range was from market 0.1365 to farm priorities 0.5861.

17.5f Developed versus Developing Countries

Let us agree to classify income distribution by degree of inequality as follows: high inequality, $G > 0.50$; moderate inequality, $0.40 < G < 0.50$; low inequality, $G < 0.40$. Michael Todara finds that most Western countries fall into the *low inequality* category. (France and Germany are exceptions.) Most developing countries fall into the *high* and *moderate* inequality categories. (Taiwan and South Korea are exceptions.)[14] Thus we confirm that economic development fosters income equality.

17.6 PUBLIC GOODS

17.6a The Theory of Public Goods (Samuelson Conditions)

This chapter concludes with a discussion of public goods.

If no one's satisfaction from the consumption of a good is diminished from the satisfaction gained by others who consume the same good, the good is said to be a *public good*. Broadcasting is an example of a public good. Assuming that all consumers are equipped with radios, the fact that Robert listens to a broadcast does not reduce the satisfaction derived by Gail. In fact, the quantity and the quality of the broadcasting enjoyed by Robert is the same regardless of whether he listens to a certain program alone or with a million other listeners.

Notice that public goods are sometimes owned privately, e.g., TV and radio stations in the United States. "Private" goods such as schooling are owned both publicly and privately. At the municipal level, such "private" goods as water and garbage collection are often publicly owned.

The Pareto optimality conditions for a public good will now be derived. These are also known as *Samuelson conditions*.[15]

In Figure 17-13, Z is the public good and X is the private good. The public good is represented by the horizontal axis. The indifference curves in panels

---

[13] Arthur Maass and Raymond L. Anderson, *. . . and the Desert Shall Rejoice: Conflict, Growth, and Justice in Arid Environments*, The MIT Press, Cambridge, Mass., 1978. The areas studied were Valencia, Murcia-Orihuela and Alicante in Spain, and South Platte and Kings River in the United States. Procedures of allocation could be *fixed shares*, under which each farmer receives water according to priorities based on the time of settlement, etc.

[14] Michael P. Todaro, *Economic Development in the Third World*, Longmans, London, 1978, p. 106.

[15] Paul A. Samuelson, "Diagramatic Exposition of a Theory of Public Expenditure," *Review of Economics and Statistics*, vol. 37, November 1955, pp. 350–356.

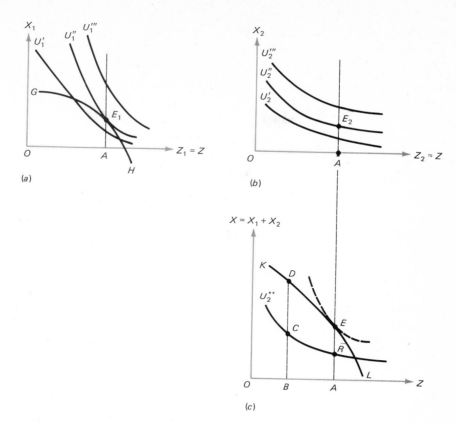

FIGURE 17-13 PARETO OPTIMALITY CONDITIONS FOR A PUBLIC GOOD

Z is the public good and X is the private good. The indifference maps of consumers 1 and 2 are shown in panels (a) and (b), respectively. U_2^{**} in panel (c) is identical with U_2'' in panel (b). The transformation between Z and X is depicted by curve LK in panel (c). The vertical distance between curve LK and U_2^{**} is drawn as curve HG in panel (a). The indifference curve of consumer 1, U_1'', is tangent to curve HG at point E_1. At point E_1, the utility of consumer 1 is maximized subject to the constraint that the utility of consumer 2 is held constant at a level of U_2'' ($= U_2^{**}$). Thus $\overline{OA}$ units of public good Z are produced. Consumer 1 consumes $\overline{AE_1}$ units of X [$= \overline{RE}$ units of X in panel (c)]. An amount of $\overline{AR}$ units of X is left for consumer 2.

(a) and (b) display the preferences of consumers 1 and 2 between the public good and the private good, respectively. The transformation curve in panel (c), denoted by KL, relates the production of the public good to the total production of the private good. Because of the definition of public goods, namely, $Z_1 = Z$ and $Z_2 = Z$, the three panels are lined up with exactly the same horizontal scale. Put differently, since the production of a public good simultaneously enhances the utility of every consumer, we must be at the same horizontal distance from the origin in all three panels.

The next step is to maximize the utility of one consumer subject to given utility levels of all other consumers. In this case, "all other consumers" are represented by consumer 2 in panel (b). Let us assume that we arbitrarily decide to maximize the utility of consumer 1 subject to a level of utility of U_2'' of consumer 2. Given the assumption that consumer 2 is restricted to U_2'', what would be the best combination of Z and X_1 for consumer 1? To get an answer, we first reconstruct indifference curve U_2'' in panel (c) and denote it by U_2^{**}. The vertical distance between the transformation curve and U_2^{**} tells how much of the private good is left for consumer 1, given a certain point on the fixed indifference curve of consumer 2. For example, if consumer 2 is at point C on U_2^{**}, both consumers (each separately) enjoy $\overline{OB}$ units of the public good, and $\overline{CD}$ units of the private good are left for consumer 1.

The next step is to move from left to right in panel (c), subtract U_2^{**} vertically from the transformation curve, and plot the result in panel (a). This process yields curve GH in panel (a). Again, GH tells what combinations of Z and X are available to consumer 1 as consumer 2 moves along the U_2'' indifference curve. While consumer 2 is indifferent among different points on U_2'', consumer 1, moving along GH, can locate point E_1, where the maximum level of utility is achieved: At E_1, GH is just tangent to U_1''. This determines the point of equilibrium, at which an amount of $\overline{OA}$ units of Z is produced. This same amount is simultaneously consumed by both consumers. Examining panel (a), we find that consumer 1 consumes $\overline{AE_1}$ units of X. This amount is (by the geometrical construction) equal to $\overline{RE}$ in panel (c). Thus an amount of $\overline{AR}$ is left for consumer 2. Note that $\overline{AR}$ in panel (c) is equal to $\overline{AE_2}$ in panel (b).

In what follows we see the algebraic meaning of the point of tangency E_1 in panel (a). The subscript will indicate from what curve the slope is derived.

First, the tangency between U_1'' and GH in panel (a) is written as

$$\left(\frac{\Delta X_1}{\Delta Z} \right)_{U_1''} = \left(\frac{\Delta X_1}{\Delta Z} \right)_{GH}$$

But

$$\left(\frac{\Delta X_1}{\Delta Z} \right)_{GH} = \left(\frac{\Delta X}{\Delta Z} \right)_{KL} - \left(\frac{\Delta X_2}{\Delta Z} \right)_{U_2^{**}}$$

Upon substituting and rearranging, we get

$$\left(\frac{\Delta X_1}{\Delta Z} \right)_{U_1''} + \left(\frac{\Delta X_2}{\Delta Z} \right)_{U_2^{**}} = \left(\frac{\Delta X}{\Delta Z} \right)_{KL}$$

or

$$\text{RCS}_1^{(x,z)} + \text{RCS}_2^{(x,z)} = \text{RPT}^{(x,z)} \tag{17-24}$$

where (x, z) indicates a slope $\Delta X / \Delta Z$. Let the private good X be the numeraire. Accordingly, we can set P_x to be equal to unity. As indicated by Equation 1-8, RCS_1 is the price consumer 1 is willing to pay for Z. Now, from Equation 17-5 we recall that $\text{RPT} = \text{MP}_{ax}/\text{MP}_{az}$. Since $P_x = 1$ and $\text{MP}_{ax} \cdot P_x = P_a$ in equilibrium (P_a is the price paid for factor A; see Equation 14-5), we obtain the result that RPT is the marginal cost of producing the public good (Equation 6-10). Thus Equation 17-24 can be written as

$$P_{z1} + P_{z2} = MC_z \qquad (17\text{-}25)$$

In other words, in order for the Pareto optimum to be achieved, the price as indicated by the demand curve of consumer 1 plus the price as indicated by the demand curve of consumer 2 must be equal to the marginal cost of producing the public good. In Figure 17-14, to obtain this result the demand curves of the two consumers are aggregated *vertically* to obtain the vertical sum of the two demand curves denoted by ΣD. MC_z intersects ΣD at point A. The Pareto level of output is Z' and the marginal cost at that level is $\overline{Z'A}$. Clearly (by geometrical construction) $\overline{Z'A}$ equals $P_{z1} + P_{z2}$.

If the producer of the public good was a monopolist, would he or she apply Equation 17-25 and charge two different prices to the two consumers? The answer is ambivalent. Even if consumers who are reluctant to pay for the public good could be excluded, a monopolist would apply a price discrimination scheme (Section 11.4b) which involves horizontal aggregation of the two marginal revenue curves rather than a vertical aggregation of the two demand curves. If the goods were produced competitively, the price would be uniform, again a violation of Pareto optimum as stated in Equation 17-25. We conclude that there is no market mechanism that will bring about a Pareto solution. This, by the way, does not mean that the government could do better than the market: There is no practical way by which the government would ever be able to estimate the *true* RCS of each and every consumer in the economy. Moreover, even if it were possible to estimate the price each consumer is willing to pay for every conceivable quantity of the

FIGURE 17-14   PARETO PRICING OF A PUBLIC GOOD

Public good Z is measured along the horizontal axis and marginal cost of Z (MC_z) and the price of Z (P_z) along the vertical axis. The demands (for Z) of two individuals are depicted by curves D_1 and D_2. D_1 and D_2 are aggregated vertically into curve ΣD. Curve ΣD intersects with curve MC_z at point A. Accordingly, Z' units of the public goods are produced per unit of time. Samuelson conditions are satisifed: $P_{z1} + P_{z2} = MC_z$.

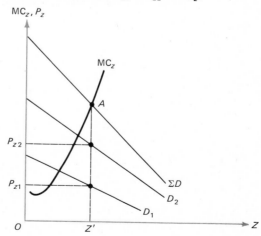

public good, the cost of collecting such information would be enormous. This is one of those economic problems for which there is no neat solution.

17.6b Public Goods in Practice

The army, in providing defense services, furnishes an example of a public good. Defense services are paid for by general taxes. Radio and TV stations, which are privately owned, also produce public goods in the form of programs and "viewpoints." Since a scheme to charge for programs and viewpoints would be administratively complex and costly, the stations in fact produce programs and viewpoints to attract viewers. They sell the time and attention of the viewers to manufacturers who advertise to inform the viewers about their product. Thus, in reality, the manufacturers are the customers, the TV and radio stations are the producers, and the good delivered is defined as total time of viewers devoted to watching TV (or listening to the radio). The public good becomes the "raw material" in the process of production.

Newspapers and radio and TV stations are regulated by the Federal Communications Commission (FCC). To own a TV station requires a license from the FCC. Allen Parkman was able to demonstrate that licensing leads to flows of cash from the public to the pockets of some individuals who know how to play a game.[16] In allocating limited licenses among numerous applications, the FCC stressed qualitites such as broadcasting experience, diversification of media ownership, and local ownership. As an example, McClatchy Broadcasting Company wanted to obtain a license for a TV station in Sacramento, California. McClatchy was found superior in all aspects except diversity. Hence the license for the channel (10) was awarded to Sacramento Telecasters. Sacramento Telecasters in 1954 estimated that the cost of constructing the station would be $715,000. In 1958, they sold Channel 10 for the huge sum of $4.5 million. This clearly shows that had the FCC auctioned the channel, a sum in the neighborhood of $4 million would have flown to the public rather than to the pocket of Sacramento Telecasters. The epilogue is that in 1964 McClatchy bought another channel (13) for $7.8 million. Thus McClatchy achieved what it wanted initially, while the public lost some $4 million.

SUMMARY   *General equilibrium* versus *partial equilibrium* was discussed first. It was explained that general-equilibrium analysis takes into consideration the entire economy for the analysis of a particular market. In contrast, partial equilibrium takes into consideration only one market, and at most, it also considers one or two closely related markets. In many situations, when welfare economic issues are discussed, general-equilibrium analysis follows partial-equilibrium analysis for the purpose of confirming the results of partial-equilibrium analysis.

---

[16]Allen M. Parkman, "An Economic Analysis of the FCC's Multiple Ownership Rules," *Administrative Law Review*, vol. 31, no. 2, Spring 1979.

The next topic was economic efficiency. It was stated that economic welfare is improved when either some individuals in society are better off and none are worse off, or all are better off. An economic change leading to such results is termed a *Pareto change*. An economic state is Pareto optimal if the Pareto change from that state is impossible. The four *Pareto optimum conditions* ($\mathrm{RCS}_1 = \mathrm{RCS}_2$, $\mathrm{RTS}_x = \mathrm{RTS}_y$, $\mathrm{MP}_{ax}^\alpha = \mathrm{MP}_{ax}^\beta$, and $\mathrm{RCS}_1 = \mathrm{RCS}_2 = \mathrm{RPT}$) were then derived, and the *law of the invisible hand* was proved; it states that under conditions of laissez-faire, perfect competition, and absence of externalities, Pareto optimum conditions are satisfied.

We saw that indirect taxes and income taxes lead to deviations from the fourth rule of the Pareto optimum. Likewise, either monopoly or monopsony leads to deviations from the fourth and second rules, respectively. The reader's attention was called to an important caveat: The intitial condition of the economy is relevant. For example, if a certain good is produced by a monopoly, then imposing a unit tax on the other good (or goods) might lead the economy back to a Pareto optimum.

We then considered *externalities*. Externalities arise when *social costs* diverge from *private costs*. In the modern era externalities are important because of the problems arising in conjunction with air and water pollution. *Coase's theorem* was then discussed; it proves that if the operation of the pricing system were costless, that is, if *transaction costs* were nil, externalities would not arise. But if transaction costs are significant, externalities do arise. Externalities in production were defined as a situation in which the production of one good X indirectly affects the physical environment of the production of another good Y and thus either enhances the level of the production of the other good or diminishes it. If the production of X has a negative indirect impact on the production of Y, then, relative to Pareto optimum, too much of X and too little of Y is produced per unit of time. The end of the section concluded that in some examples in the economy the producers of goods that allegedly create externalities bargain in the marketplace, and thus Pareto optimum is achieved (bees and orchards). In some other situations a tax is called for (burning coal to generate electricity and the Proxmire tax).

Next the issue of income distribution and the social welfare function was discussed. It was determined that social welfare functions are impossible to construct, but a very important conclusion was reached: Pareto optimum is a *necessary* but not a *sufficient condition* for attaining maximum social welfare. Since it is impossible to construct social welfare functions, we do not know how to achieve social welfare maximum. On the practical side of income distribution it was explained how inequality in income distribution is measured either by the famous *Lorenz curve* or by the associated *Gini coefficient*. Gini coefficients are used to compare income inequality among different countries or to compare two situations in the same country, such as before and after taxes.

Last, the theory of public goods (Samuelson conditions) was presented. It was proved geometrically that to attain Pareto optimum, the demand curves of all consumers should be added vertically, and the point of equilibrium should be determined where the marginal cost of the public good intersects with the vertically aggregated demand curve. It was indicated that neither a monopoly nor a competitive market will lead to the satisfaction of these conditions. Moreover, even if a public good is produced by the government, it would be very difficult if not entirely impossible for the government to price the public good such that Samuelson's conditions are satisfied.

GLOSSARY

Welfare economics A branch in economics that deals with economic efficiency and economic equity.

General-equilibrium analysis An economic analysis that focuses on the economy in its entirety. The *ceteris paribus* is reduced to technology (state of the art), input endowment and the initial distribution of wealth.

Partial-equilibrium analysis An economic analysis that focuses on a single market and one or two closely related markets. The rest of the markets in the economy are in the realm of the *ceteris paribus*.

Pareto change If, resulting from an economic change, some individuals are better off and none are worse off, or all are better off, this is a *Pareto change*. It is also known as an *efficient economic change*.

Pareto preference If a *Pareto (efficient) change* leads the economy from point E to point F, then point F is said to be *Pareto preferred* to E.

Edgeworth box diagram A box whose edges serve as the two goods axes, or the two inputs axes. The southwesterly corner of the box serves as the origin for one consumer (or producer) and the northeasterly corner of the box serves as the origin for the other consumer (or producer).

Contract curve In an Edgeworth box, the locus of all tangency points between the indifference curves (isoquants) of one consumer (producer) and the indifference curves (isoquants) of the other consumer (producer).

Transformation curve (also known as the *production-possibility curve*) Given an endowment of inputs (A and B), the transformation curve is the locus of all efficient combinations of production rates of X and Y in the X, Y space. It is obtained by mapping the production contract curve into the X, Y space.

Marginal rate of product transformation (RPT) The slope of the transformation curve: $\Delta Y/\Delta X$. It tells by how much the production of one good will increase if the production of the other good decreases by a relatively small amount, thus releasing small amounts of the variable factors of production.

Community indifference map Obtained by assuming that all consumers are identical, then drawing the indifference map of one consumer and changing the scale of the axes to reflect the size of the community.

Pareto optimum Implies that four conditions are satisfied: $RCS_1 = RCS_2$, $RTS_x = RTS_y$, $MP^\alpha_{ax} = MP^\beta_{ax}$, and $RCS_1 = RCS_2 = RPT$.

The law of the invisible hand Under laissez-faire, perfect competition, and absence of externalities, *Pareto optimum* obtains. This means that under such conditions the economy reached a point of *efficiency* at which a *Pareto change* is impossible.

Externality A situation in which the production of good X has an indirect physical impact on the production of good Y. This impact can be positive or negative, and it leads to divergence of the social cost from the private cost of producing X and Y, respectively. A divergence of social cost from private cost results in a deviation from *Pareto optimum*. Externalities in consumption are similar to externalities in production.

Coase's theorem A theorem that states that if *transaction costs* are nil, that is, if the operation of the pricing system is costless, externalities will not result in any deviation from Pareto optimum.

The utility possibility frontier Given that the utility function of two individuals are denoted by U_1 and U_2, respectively, then the locus of all points in the U_1, U_2 space satisfying the fourth Pareto optimum condition is the *utility possibility frontier (curve)*.

Social welfare function The aggregate of all utilities of all individuals in the community. Given that the utility functions of two individuals consuming two goods are $U_1 = f_1(X_1, Y_1)$ and $U_2 = f_2(X_2, Y_2)$, then social welfare W is $W = W(U_1, U_2)$. The social welfare function is a theoretical concept. In real life social welfare functions cannot be constructed.

Lorenz curve If we line up all families in an economy according to size of their income, beginning with the lowest income and ending with the highest income, and calculate the cumulative share of cumulative population percentiles, and if we measure the cumulative population percentiles along the horizontal axis and the cumulative income percentiles along the vertical axis and then plot the pairs of cumulative population percentiles and cumulative income percentiles, we obtain the Lorenz curve.

Gini coefficient Let the area under a Lorenz curve drawn for an egalitarian society (the cross diagonal) be denoted by S. Let the area below this curve but above the actual Lorenz curve be denoted by T. The Gini coefficient is then T/S.

Public good If no one's satisfaction from the consumption of a good is diminished from the satisfaction gained by others who consume the same good, then the good is said to be a public good.

Samuelson conditions Pareto optimum in the consumption of a public good is obtained at the point of intersection between the *vertical* aggregated demand curve for the good and its marginal cost curve.

PROBLEMS An asterisk indicates an advanced problem.

17-1.* Show that if the transformation curve in Figure 17-6 is linear, the price received by producers does not change as a result of the tax.

17-2. Show that, roughly speaking, a subsidy of S dollars per unit of X would lead to the same utility loss as a tax of T dollars per unit of X. Assume that $T = S$.

17-3.* Show that a monopoly combines factors of production efficiently. That is, if X is output and A and B are any two imputs, then for the monopoly (as for other competitive firms) $\text{RTS}_x = -P_a/P_b$.

17-4. Show that if initially unit taxes are absent, X is produced by a monopolist and Y is produced competitively, then either a tax on Y or a subsidy per unit on X could restore Pareto optimum.

17-5. Show that price discrimination between two markets by a monopolist leads to a deviation from Pareto optimum. Assume that commodity X is made by the monopolist while commodity Y is produced competitively; consumers are divided into two groups, 1 and 2. The monopolist charges a higher price to group 1.

17-6. Show that a lump-sum tax does not lead to a deviation from the Pareto optimum.

17-7. Explain why, if the pricing system were costless, physical externalities would not lead the invisible hand astray (Coase).

17-8. Explain why, in Figure 17-8, in the absence of damage liability laws but assuming that the pricing system is costless, fishermen would be willing to pay the paper mill a sum of less than $\overline{KM}$ but higher than $\overline{KL}$ if the paper mill would in return agree to reduce waste discharge from $\overline{OK}$ to $\overline{OK} - 1$.

17-9. Explain why the proposed Proxmire tax on sulfur dioxide emission is more efficient than mandating that each coal burner must install a scrubber.

17-10. Pareto optimum is a *necessary* but not a *sufficient condition* for social welfare maximum. Does this mean that we should not fight monopolies?

17-11. Draw a diagram in which *my income* ("my" refers to the reader) is measured along the horizontal axis. and *your income* is measured along the vertical axis. Draw the indifference map in this space. What should be the slope of my budget line? What determines its position? Where would you expect a point of equilibrium? Draw a cross diagonal starting at the origin. Can equilibrium occur above the cross diagonal?

17-12. Calculate the Gini coefficient for Table 17-3.

17-13. Suppose the government attempts to price defense services according to Samuelson conditions (Equation 17-25). Indicate the kind of practical difficulties the government should expect to encounter.

CHAPTER

QUANTITATIVE TOOLS
(optional)

Economists apply a variety of quantitative tools in their daily work. The most important of these tools are *econometrics* and optimization methods known as *operations research*.

Econometrics is a branch of mathematical statistics that is used in empirical testing and estimation. Econometrics is essential to confirm (or refute) theories as well as to improve the ability of economists to predict.

Operations research is a branch of applied mathematics which aids economists in practical problems involving optimization. Examples are solving problems of profit maximization and the more limited goals of cost minimization.

The purpose of this chapter is to introduce the major quantitative tools that are used by economists. First econometrics and then operations research will be discussed.

PART I ECONOMETRICS

18.1 ECONOMIC THEORIES

Any economic theory is developed through a process consisting of three essential steps:

1. Stating the *postulates*.
2. Making refutable assumptions (which is the main body of the theory).
3. Testing the assumptions empirically, and either confirming the theory or refuting it.

This three-step process will be illustrated by two examples.

First, Chapter 1 asserted the postulate that consumers maximize their utility. Chapter 2 developed assumptions derived from that basic postulate. The collection of these assumptions was called the *theory of consumer behavior*. Perhaps the most important part of the theory of consumer behavior is the assumption that the demand curve is negatively sloped. That is, *ceteris paribus*, consumers are expected to consume less when the price of a good rises, and vice versa. The assumption that the demand curve is negatively sloped is refutable because demand curves could be either negatively or positively sloped. If instead the assumption was made that a demand curve is either negatively or positively sloped, it would be a nonrefutable assumption: Clearly, what is predicted will logically occur. Finally, to illustrate how economists test refutable assumptions, recall the pioneer work of Henry Schultz. He confirmed that the demand for sugar was negatively sloped.[1] Note that *confirming* that the demand curve is negatively sloped is not a *proof* that the theory is correct. Theories cannot be proved. They can only be confirmed. And the more times they are confirmed, the better. By confirming the negative slope of the demand curve, Henry Schultz (as well as other pioneers) helped to upgrade economics from a branch of logic to a

---

[1]Henry Schultz, *The Theory and Measurement of Demand*, University of Chicago Press, Chicago, 1938. For a discussion see Section 2.5.

science. Since Schultz studied the demand for sugar, many other studies have confirmed the theory that the demand curve is negatively sloped. With each additional study confirming it, economists feel more confident that they can trust the negatively sloping demand curves when they predict the behavior of consumers in a world of changing prices.

Second, Chapter 7 asserted the postulate that firms maximize their profits. In Chapter 8, based on that postulate, the theory of supply under competition was developed. A basic assumption was that the supply curve is positively sloped. The theory clearly predicted that firms will respond to positive changes in prices by increasing the quantity of output supplied. Marc Nerlove did pioneer work in confirming the positive slope of the supply curve of cotton, wheat, and corn.[2]

Like Henry Schultz and Marc Nerlove, hundreds of other economists who followed in their footsteps have applied econometric methods in order to confirm (or refute) economic theories.

18.2 PREDICTION AS AN AID IN POLICY

It is not always the case that a postulate will lead to a strong theory which is then tested empirically in order to either confirm it or refute it. Sometimes there is no theory as such. But there is a question about economic relationships. Econometrics can be employed to investigate such questions. For example, the economic profession wanted to know whether energy and capital and energy and labor are, respectively, pairs of competitive inputs (substitutes) or pairs of complements. Recall that the study by Ernst Berndt and D. O. Wood was mentioned in Chapter 14. By employing econometrics, they reached the conclusion that energy and labor are substitutes and energy and capital are complements.[3] Thus the theory and its confirmation were born simultaneously. Of course, more confirmations would be needed before economists would feel at ease with this theory. If further confirmed, its value to policy makers could not be ignored: A subsidy to capital would increase the demand for energy.

A study of the demand for electricity in the United States was mentioned in Chapter 3. Recall that in that study Robert Halvorsen confirmed again the negative sign of the price elasticity, and the positive sign of the cross elasticity between electricity and natural gas. He obtained a positive sign for income elasticity, which confirmed a weak theory that electricity is a normal good.[4] We say "weak" theory because there is nothing in the theory to

---

[2]Marc Nerlove, "Estimates of the Elasticities of Supply of Selected Agricultural Commodities," *Journal of Farm Economics*, vol. 33, May 1956, pp. 496–509. For a discussion see Section 8.2e.

[3]R. Ernst Berndt and D. O. Wood, "Technology, Prices, and the Derived Demand for Energy," *Review of Economics and Statistics,* vol. 57, August 1975, pp. 259–268. For a discussion see Section 14.2e.

[4]Robert Halvorsen, "Demand for Electric Energy in the United States," *Southern Economic Journal*, vol. 42, April 1976, pp. 610–625. For a discussion see Section 3.4a.

suggest strongly that a good should be superior rather than inferior or vice versa. The contribution of Halvorsen's econometric study is twofold: First, it confirms one more time theories that had been confirmed before. Second, it places in the hands of the electric utilities and policy makers a tool that might aid them in predicting the future demand for electric power.

In summary, economists empirically estimated demand functions for a variety of goods, production functions, cost functions, and supply functions. By and large, economists have been able to confirm the theories presented in the previous 17 chapters. But we must note before passing that confirmation was not always easy. At times it was rather vague. A first example is the theory that local markets for physician's services are monopolized. Circumstantial evidence exists that led to the formulation of the theory. But a strong confirmation based on econometric studies has not been presented so far. Chapter 11 mentioned the study by Joseph Newhouse, who, by applying econometric methods, found that doctors' fees are positively correlated with incomes of patients.[5] Since it was theorized that the demand curve of rich patients is relatively less elastic than the demand curve of poor patients, this finding might confirm a practice of price discrimination. But because the service rendered by physicians is far from homogeneous, Newhouse's study might simply indicate that the rich pay more in order to get higher-quality service. The conclusion is that more studies confirming (or refuting) the theory of local monopolies are needed.

Sometimes very simple techniques are required in order to confirm a theory. For example, H. Michael Mann theorized that oligopolies will benefit from significantly higher than average rates of return when barriers to entry are severe, rather than when concentration ratios are relatively high. The logic of the theory was that if barriers to entry were mild, oligopolists with high concentration ratios would charge competitive prices in order not to raise the appetite of potential rivals. The empirical test Mann applied was simple: First, he partitioned a group of 30 industries into subgroups according to the severity of barriers to entry. He then recalculated the average rate of return for each subgroup. He was able to confirm that barriers to entry explain oligopolistic rates of return better than concentration ratios.[6]

18.3 TECHNICAL ASPECTS OF ECONOMETRICS

18.3a Economic Functions

Economic theories boil down to economic functions or, in relatively complicated cases, to sets of economic functions. An economic function is a relationship between economic variables. Most of Chapter 2 was devoted to

---

[5]Joseph P. Newhouse, "A Model of Physician Pricing," *Southern Economic Journal*, vol. 37, October 1970, pp. 174–183. For a discussion see Section 11.5b.

[6]H. Michael Mann, "Seller Concentration, Barriers to Entry, and Rate of Return in Thirty Industries, 1950–1960," *Review of Economics and Statistics*, vol. 48, August 1966, pp. 296–307. For a discussion see Section 13.2b.

developing the theory of the demand function of the individual consumer. It was hypothesized that the quantity demanded for a good is negatively related to the price and, if the good is normal, positively related to the income of the individual. In Chapter 3 the price of a related good was added as a fourth variable to the demand relation. This demand relation can be expressed as follows:

$$X = f(P_x, I, P_y) \tag{18-1}$$

where X is the quantity demanded of good X, P_x is its price, I is the income of the individual consumer, and P_y is the price of a closely related good. If X is normal and X and Y are a pair of substitute goods, we have a theory that X and P_x are negatively related to one another, X and I are positively related to one another, and X and P_y are also positively related to one another. But Equation 18-1 is general and thus cannot be estimated empirically. We must specify the form of the general relation as given by Equation 18-1. The simplest form is a linear one as follows:

$$X = a + bP_x + cI + dP_y \tag{18-2}$$

where a, b, c, and d are unknown parameters that can be estimated empirically. Note that a is the intercept of the demand curve, while b, c, and d are slopes measuring $\Delta X/\Delta P_x$, $\Delta X/\Delta I$, and $\Delta X/\Delta P_y$.[7]

Chapter 8 discussed the supply curve. It was hypothesized that the quantity of a good supplied by a firm in perfect competition is positively related to the price of the good produced and negatively related to the price of any variable input it uses in the process of production. The supply relation can be expressed as follows:

$$X = F(P_x, P_j) \tag{18-3}$$

where X is the quantity supplied, P_x is the price of X in the marketplace, and P_j is the price of a variable input.

The linear form of Equation 18-3 is

$$X = g + hP_x + iP_j \tag{18-4}$$

where g, h, and i are unknown parameters that can be estimated empirically. Note that g is the intercept of the supply function, while h and i are slopes measuring $\Delta X/\Delta P_x$ and $\Delta X/\Delta P_j$.

Equation 18-1 (and Equation 18-2) is the demand function as perceived by an individual consumer. In some circumstances such a function can be estimated separately from the supply relation. Likewise, in some circumstances the supply function as given by Equation 18-3 (Equation 18-4), which is perceived by a single producer, can be estimated separately from the demand relation. Section 9.3a explained that for the individual consumer and the individual producer the price P_x is exogenous. But when we consider the competitive market, the price is no longer an exogenous variable. Rather it

---

[7] If X, P_x, I, and P_y are given in logarithms, then parameters b, c, and d are price elasticity, income elasticity, and cross elasticity, respectively.

becomes an endogenous variable. How can we describe a competitive market as a system of equations? Let us simplify our notations and assume that quantity demanded is related only to the price of the good and to income per capita of consumers. Let the superscript d indicate the aggregate quantity demanded. Likewise, we can assign the superscript s to the aggregate quantity supplied. The competitive market, expressed in a linear form, is then

Demand: $$X^d = a + bP_x^d + cI$$

Supply: $$X^s = g + hP_x^s + iP_j$$

$$(18\text{-}5)$$

In Equations 18-5, X^d, X^s, P_x^d, and P_x^s are endogenous variables. Income per capital I and the price of a variable input P_j are the exogenous variables. In fact we have only two endogenous variables, because in equilibrium the price that is paid by consumers is received by producers, that is,

$$P_x^d = P_x^s \qquad (18\text{-}6)$$

Also, the quantity brought to the marketplace by producers is taken by consumers, that is,

$$X^d = X^s \qquad (18\text{-}7)$$

A system of functions as described by Equations 18-5 is more difficult to estimate empirically than a single equation as described by either Equation 18-2 or Equation 18-4. It should be intuitively clear that since the price and the quantity are determined simultaneously in the marketplace, parameters a, b, c, g, h, and i in Equations 18-5 cannot be estimated empirically separately for each equation; they must be estimated simultaneously.

We now turn our attention to some data problems that economists must always face.

18.3b Data Problems

To make it possible to apply econometric methods to economic data, exogenous variables must vary. Consider first the case of a single function. Electric utilities are regulated monopolies not subject to short-run market forces. For all practical purposes the price of electricity can be considered an exogenous variable. If the price of electricity does not vary, all we observe is a single point on a demand curve and we cannot estimate a demand function. A variation of the price would generate different responses by consumers, which would make it possible to estimate a demand function empirically.

Next, consider the case of a system of equations, like the market supply and demand functions represented by Equations 18-5. Figure 18-1 illustrates how the changes in the exogenous variables give rise to demand and supply shifts, leading to the generation of data that are essential for econometric estimation. Initially income per capita is at I_0 and the price of the variable input, say, energy, is at P_{j0}. The associated demand and supply are $D(I_0)$ and $S(P_{j0})$. The initial equilibrium occurs at point K. If I and P_j were to remain at the levels of I_0 and P_{j0}, respectively, economists would not be able to esti-

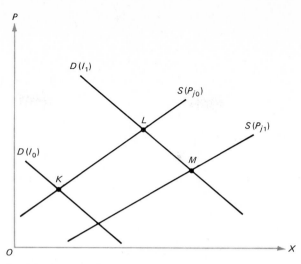

FIGURE 18-1 SUPPLY AND DEMAND SHIFTS
Initially the demand is depicted by curve $D(I_0)$ and the supply is depicted by curve $S(P_{j0})$. Initial equilibrium occurs at point K. As income (per capita) increases from I_0 to I_1, the demand curve shifts from $D(I_0)$ to $D(I_1)$, and it intersects with $S(P_{j0})$ at point L. Point L represents a new observation in the set of data. Another observation is generated when the price of an input falls from P_{j0} to P_{j1}, leading the supply curve to shift downward to a new position $S(P_{j1})$, where it cuts $D(I_1)$ at point M.

mate supply and demand empirically: only point K would be observed. Economists must count on variations in I and P_j in order to generate many observations. For example, when I increases from I_0 to I_1, and assuming that X is a normal good, the demand for X increases from $D(I_0)$ to $D(I_1)$, and we obtain a new point denoted by L. As the price of energy falls from P_{j0} to P_{j1} the supply curve shifts downward from $S(P_{j0})$ to $S(P_{j1})$ and still another observation, namely, point M, is obtained. Thus, each time a change in either I or P_j occurs, a new observation is generated. The nature of econometrics is such that, *ceteris paribus*, the more observations we have the better is the chance to obtain reliable empirical estimates.

Basically two types of data are used in econometric studies: *time-series data* and *cross-sectional data*. Henry Schultz used time-series data when he estimated the demand for sugar in the United States.[8] Hendrik Houthakker used cross-sectional data when estimating income elasticities for groups of goods in selected countries.[9] In time-series data the variation in the exogenous variable occurs as time progresses. Intertemporal variations in the price of electricity may result from the varying costs of fossil fuels. It is interesting

[8]Schultz, op. cit.
[9]Hendrik S. Houthakker, "An International Comparison of Household Expenditure Patterns, Commemorating the Century of Engel's Law," *Econometrica*, vol. 25, October 1957, pp. 532–551. For a discussion see Section 2.3h.

TABLE 18-1 Hypothetical Data of a Consumer

Price, $	Quantity consumed per unit of time
15.12	72
21.70	55
5.00	93
30.00	41
18.30	60
10.12	79
27.21	47
29.10	43
6.90	87
7.14	85
22.23	53
16.20	69
19.60	62
25.99	49
12.40	78
6.30	88
15.75	72
24.10	54
20.11	61
25.20	50

to note, however, that until the 1974 energy crisis, prices of energy resources were relatively stable over time. Thus time-series data could not be used to estimate demand curves for electricity. While time-series data are obtained by recording the response of one group (such as a nation) to the intertemporal variations of the exogenous variables, cross-sectional data are obtained by recording the response of different cross sections of the population (such as states or counties) to the exogenous variable which varies from one section to another section at a point in time. For example, the price of electricity varied from region to region in the United States even before the 1974 energy crisis, mainly because in different regions different resources (hydropower, oil, natural gas, and coal) were used to generate electricity.

We now see how a statistical demand curve can be estimated from hypothetical data.

18.3c An Illustration of a Statistical Demand Curve

Consider the hypothetical data in Table 18-1. The first column shows prices of a certain good. The second column shows the response of a consumer in terms of quantity of the good consumed per unit to time. In order to estimate a demand function empirically, we specify a linear relation, namely,

$$X = a + bP_x \tag{18-8}$$

By applying a method known as *regression analysis* (which is too mathematical to be discussed here) the following result is obtained:

$$X = 101.09 - 2.02P_x \qquad (18\text{-}9)$$

Note: The most important finding is the negative sign of parameter b. It confirms the theory that demand curves are negatively sloped. But the value of b, that is, -2.02, tells us that $\Delta X / \Delta P_x$ has the same value: If the price of X rises from \$10 to \$15, we can predict that consumption of X will decrease by 10.1 units per unit of time. The pairs of prices and quantities, known as observations, as well as estimated Equation 18-9 are depicted by dots and a negatively sloping line in Figure 18-2.

PART II OPERATIONS RESEARCH

Operations research is a branch of applied mathematics dealing with optimization problems. In most cases operations research is useful when issues of profit maximization or cost minimization at the firm level are involved. For example, a farmer who raises chickens buys feed grains for his chickens. Since the prices of grains in the market change frequently, the farmer wants to adjust the grain mix quickly so as to guarantee the least-cost combination of grains at all times (Section 6.5b). A similar problem would be one in which

FIGURE 18-2 EMPIRICAL DEMAND CURVE
The dots represent the observations as given in Table 18–1. Line $X = 101.09 - 2.02P$ was empirically estimated from the data in Table 18-1 by running a *regression*.

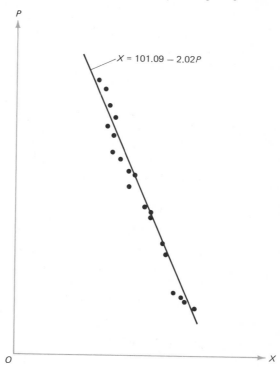

a manufacturer wants to blend various alloys each containing a certain percentage of metals such as copper, tin, and zinc. Assume that the contents of the alloys are specified and that 10 different alloys are available in the market at different prices. Operations research would be the natural apparatus that the economist could employ in order to find the least-cost blend of the alloys. A transportation problem arises when a moving firm has trucks spread all over the country and has to assign these trucks "jobs," where each job consists of a point of loading, a point of unloading, and selection of a route between the two points. More sophisticated practical problems that could be solved with the aid of operations research might involve complicated water systems. For example, given a complex of rivers, dams, and lakes that are interconnected, the problem is to maximize the aggregate benefit from irrigation, electricity, and recreation by releasing the proper flows of water from the various dams in the system. Another example would be a river polluted by factories and municipalities. Clearly, here is a case of externalities that cannot be solved optimally vis-à-vis bargaining because of heavy transaction costs (Section 17-4). Imposing a tax on polluters that could be proportional to the waste discharged into the river could not be expected to lead to a Pareto optimal solution because the impact from the waste disposal upstream exceeds the impact from the waste disposal downstream. Assume that all the communities along the river reach consensus concerning the degree of water cleanliness to be reached throughout the river. In that case, operations research can be used to formulate the least-cost program of pollution abatement leading to the desirable goal of water cleanliness.

While econometrics is essential for testing refutable theories, operations research is neither used in testing refutable theories nor is it a part of the economic theory. It is a useful apparatus that may be used in applied practical daily economic activities.

What follows will discuss some of the major areas of operations research without becoming involved in the mathematical complexities of this apparatus. Suffice it to say that the field of operations research is so rich that some universities offer it as an independent graduate program.

18.4 LINEAR PROGRAMMING

18.4a Introduction[10]

Linear programming is an optimization apparatus that can be applied only in cases in which all functions are linear. Linearity arises in competitive situa-

---

[10] A mathematical solution to the linear programming problem was not available until World War II. (The Russian economist L. V. Kantorovich started to work on linear programming in 1939.) During World War II, a group headed by Marshall K. Wood was involved in analyzing the problem of resource allocation for the United States Air Force. In 1947, George B. Dantzig, a member of that group, formulated the linear programming problem and developed a mathematical technique known as the *simplex method* for maximizing or minimizing the objective function.

TABLE 18-2
Two
Processes of
Production

tions in which the firm is a price taker. Thus linear programming can be applied in the case of the chicken farmer mentioned earlier because the behavior of a single chicken farm can have no influence either on the price of grains or on the price of eggs (Section 7.2a). On the other hand, a utility that generates electric power could not employ *linear programming* in order to solve some of its economic problems (involving revenue). This is true because it is confronted with a negatively sloped demand curve and its revenue function is not linear (Section 11.1c). It is interesting to note, however, that if, as normally is the case, the monopoly purchases its inputs in a competitive market, linear programming might be applied to discover the least-cost combination of inputs associated with each plausible level of output. What follows will present the concept of linear programming by considering a few simple numerical examples.

18.4b Formulating the Problem

A girl scout group raises money to fly to Walt Disney World. A bakery donated to the group 14 pounds of flour, 8 pounds of sugar, and 24 ounces of butter. The group can bake two kinds of cookies, Crunchies and Munchies. The profit from selling a box of Crunchies is $15, and from selling a box of Munchies it is $20. It takes 1 pound of flour, 1 pound of sugar, and 4 ounces of butter to bake one box of Crunchies. It takes 2 pounds of flour, 1 pound of sugar, and 1 ounce of butter to produce one box of Munchies. Given that the group of girl scouts is stuck with the above supplies of flour, sugar, and butter, the problem is: What is the combination of Crunchies and Munchies that will yield the greatest profit for them?

Let Crunchies and Munchies be denoted by X and Y, and flour, sugar, and butter be denoted by A, B, and C.

The production information is summarized in Table 18-2, which is sometimes called the *input-output table*.

Table 18-2 shows two *processes of production*. Sometimes a process of production is called an *activity*. Each of the two columns in Table 18-2 represents a process of production. The phrase "process of production" tells us what combination of inputs it takes to produce a certain level of output.

When discussing processes of production, the following should be noted:

1. Processes X and Y can be two separate activities employed in the production of the same commodity.[11]

Earlier, in 1945, George J. Stigler used another technique to solve the least-cost balanced diet, which can be formulated as a linear programming problem.

Dantzig's technique and the postwar development of electronic computers rendered linear programming a very important tool in business and economics. Today, linear programming is widely used in solving problems of resource allocation, blending, animal feeding, transportation, and timing inloads and outloads in warehouses.

[11]As an example, let a firm in competition be engaged in the production of whatnots. Let A stand for labor, B for land, and C for capital. If process X is used, it takes 1 unit of labor, 1 unit of land, and 4 units of capital to make one whatnot. If process Y is employed, it takes 2 units of labor, 1 unit of land, and 1 unit of capital to produce one whatnot.

**TABLE 18-3
An Illustration
of Divisibility**

X	Y	
2.5	6.4	A
2.5	3.2	B
10.0	3.2	C

2. Each process of production is governed by *fixed proportions* and constant returns to scale. Fixed proportions means that if, say, Crunchies are produced, then the proportion of flour to sugar is 1 and the proportion of butter to sugar is 4. These proportions cannot change. For example, if 2 pounds of flour are used, 2 pounds of sugar and 8 ounces of butter must be used in the process of production. Constant returns to scale (Section 5.4c) imply that if 2 pounds of flour, 2 pounds of sugar, and 8 ounces of butter are used, 2 boxes of Crunchies will be produced, etc.

3. The production processes are independent of one another. Changing the level of X neither requires a change in the level of Y, nor does it give rise to such a change, and vice versa.

Divisibility is taken for granted here, but let us illustrate what it means. If the firm decides to produce 2.5 units of Crunchies and 3.2 units of Munchies, the activities will be as illustrated by Table 18-3. The assumption of divisibility may be relaxed in the solution of specific problems.

Let us denote profit (net revenue) by π. Then the profit function becomes

$$\pi = 15X + 20Y$$

This function is called the *objective function*. Here linearity is made possible by the assumption of perfect competition: The group of girl scouts has no influence on prices of cookies.

Finally recall that not more than 14 pounds of flour (A), 8 pounds of sugar (B), and 24 ounces of butter (C) are available to the group of girl scouts. Then, if X boxes of Crunchies and Y boxes of Munchies are baked, the following are the constraints by which the group must abide:

$$1 \cdot X + 2 \cdot Y \leq 14$$
$$1 \cdot X + 1 \cdot Y \leq 8$$
$$4 \cdot X + 1 \cdot Y \leq 24$$

The problem is to maximize profit subject to the above constraints. Formally this is a linear programming problem that can be stated as
Maximize:

$$\pi = 15 \cdot X + 20 \cdot Y$$

Subject to:

$$1 \cdot X + 2 \cdot Y \leq 14$$
$$1 \cdot X + 1 \cdot Y \leq 8$$
$$4 \cdot X + 1 \cdot Y \leq 24$$
$$X \geq 0$$
$$Y \geq 0$$

where the last two constraints ensure that activities are used only at positive levels.

18.4c Linear Programming Applied to Allocation of Limited Resources

The example in the previous section is a typical problem of allocating limited resources among several processes of production. The allocation of limited resources should be optimal. That is, it should lead to profit maximization. Limited resources are normally not flour, sugar, and butter. Rather, in real life limited resources may be machine time, plant size, space availability in warehouses, water, and land. But regardless of the technical nature of the limitation, if competition plus the other "linear" assumptions can be made, the solution to the problem can be accomplished by applying linear programming.

We are now ready to develop the geometrical solution of the problem. Figure 18-3 measures units generated by process Y along the horizontal axis and units generated by process X along the vertical axis. Consider first the constraint $X + 2Y \leq 14$. Line AA represents the equality $X + 2Y = 14$. The region to the left of (or below) AA represents the (strict) inequality $X + 2Y < 14$. This region plus line AA represents the inequality $X + 2Y \leq 14$. Thus, if A were the only limitation, the region to the left of AA plus AA would form the *feasible region* of production. Attempting to produce combinations of X and Y represented by points in the region to the right of AA would not be feasible because production would take more input A than is available. If we add the limitation of input B, the feasible region becomes the region to the left of and including LGH. Finally, if the limitation of input C is added, the feasible region becomes the region to the left of and including $EFGH$. Since we limited ourselves to positive levels of production, the feasible region becomes the shaded region bordered by $OEFGH$, including the boundaries.

It is evident from the graph that the point of maximum profit must lie on the frontier of the feasible region. Recall that both X and Y are profitable. Then, logically, we can find points on the frontier which yield more profit than any point inside the region, such as point R. This is true because moving away from point R, either rightward or upward or generally in the northeasterly direction, implies an increased production of either X or Y or both. Recall also that the assumptions of constant returns to scale and competition eliminate the presence of either diminishing or increasing returns to scale, diminishing prices or output, or rising prices of variable inputs. Accordingly, such a movement away from R and in the northeasterly direction toward the frontier must lead to increasing profits.

What linear programming does, essentially, is locate the optimal point on the frontier, indicated here by $EFGH$. With that in mind, let us describe the geometrical solution. The profit function in the example is $\pi = 15X + 20Y$. One can imagine an infinitely large number of *isoprofit lines* corresponding to the profit function. Only three such isoprofit lines[12] are illustrated in Figure 18-4. These are $\pi_1 = \$80$, $\pi_2 = \$150$, and $\pi_3 = \$300$.

Suppose we start to move rightward from π_1 to higher isoprofit lines. We

---

[12]Isoprofit line means a line along which profit remains unchanged.

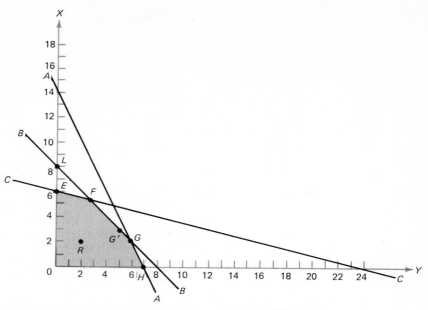

FIGURE 18-3 A GEOMETRICAL ILLUSTRATION OF LINEAR CONSTRAINTS
Lines *AA*, *BB*, and *CC* are boundaries representing constraints in a profit-maximization linear programming problem. Points to the left of each line satisfy a particular inequality. For example, points to the left of *AA* and points on *AA* satisfy the inequality $1 \cdot X + 2 \cdot Y \leq 14$. Shaded area *OEFGH* satisfies all three inequalities (plus $X \geq 0$ and $Y \geq 0$) simultaneously. It is known as the feasible region of production. The producer will seek a point on frontier *EFGH* in the process of profit maximization. The reason for this is that moving either upward or rightward (or generally in a northeasterly direction) away from an interior point like *R* leads to a rise in profit.

seek the highest isoprofit line which contains at least one feasible point. The feasible point is the corner denoted by G. This is known as *a corner solution*: Point G yields the maximum profit.

The solution may not be a corner. For example, suppose the isoprofit lines happen to be parallel to segment $\overline{FG}$. In that case, the points which lie on this segment, including corners F and G, are optimal. This implies that each of the points belonging to the optimal segment must yield the same profit.

The reader can imagine a situation in which the profit of X increases following a rise in the price of Crunchies. This would lead to a counterclockwise rotation of the isoprofit lines. If the increase in the profit of X is substantial, F will eventually become the corner solution, leading to a decline in the production of Y and a rise in the production of X. This in turn will lead to increasing the demand for input C and reducing the demand for input A.

It is left for the reader to show that at point G the group produces 2 units of X (2 boxes of Crunchies) and 6 units of Y (6 boxes of Munchies). Accordingly the maximum profit amounts to $\$150 = 2 \cdot \$15 + 6 \cdot \$20$.

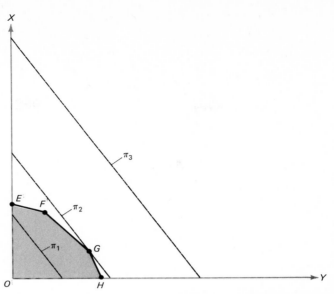

FIGURE 18-4 A GEOMETRICAL ILLUSTRATION OF A LINEAR PROGRAMMING SOLUTION
The shaded area is the feasible region: it satisfies the three constraints (inequalities) simultaneously. The lines denoted by π_1, π_2, and π_3 are isoprofit lines ($\pi = 15X + 20Y$) for profit levels of $80, $150, and $300. Profit line π_2 just touches frontier *EFGH* at one point, that is, corner *G*. Point *G* represents the optimal solution. Maximum profit is $150.

Notice finally that input *C* (butter) is not exhausted in the process of production. You should find it instructive to show that only 14 units of input *C* are used up in the process of production. Accordingly, input *C* is a "free" input.

18.4d Linear Programming and Shadow Prices

Shadow prices are akin to marginal revenue products (Sections 14.1a and 14.5). The *shadow price* is defined as the change in profit per unit change in one of the constraining factors. The shadow price of an input is determined by first reaching the optimal solution yielding the maximum profit. The second step is to vary by one unit the use of the constraining input whose shadow price we want to measure. Let us calculate the shadow price of flour, denoted by *A*: If we reduce *A* by one unit, the first constraint becomes $X + 2Y \leq 13$. The line represented by $X + 2Y = 13$ would be parallel to *AA* and would cut *BB* at *G′* in Figure 18-3. At *G′* the firm would produce 3 units of *X* and 5 units of *Y*, and the new profit would be $145 = 3 \cdot \$15 + 5 \cdot \$20$. Thus the shadow price of *A* would be

$$\text{Shadow price of } A = \frac{\$145 - 150}{13 - 14} = \$5$$

That is, in the example, if the group received 1 pound less of flour, its profit would decrease by $5. Shadow prices may be relevant in furnishing the management of the firm with data needed to reach long-run decisions. For example, assume that A is land and opportunity arises to rent land at $4 per unit; this would be a profitable proposition.

18.4e Linear Programming and Supply Curves

We now abandon the girl scouts and instead assume that there is a competitive firm which is stuck with 14 units of factor A, 8 units of factor B, and 24 units of factor C. We ask the following question: If this competitive firm is managed by applying linear programming, would its supply curve be the same as in the theories developed in Chapters 5, 6, 7, and 8? The answer is affirmative, except that the supply curve is *step-shaped* rather than smooth. This section illustrates how a positively sloped, step-shaped supply curve is derived for such a firm. We assume that X and Y are two different goods. The response of the firm to a continuous rise in the price of X will be investigated. We assume, as before, that the profit per unit of Y is unchanged at a level of $20. In other words, the price of Y and prices of variable inputs are unchanged in the market. Suppose that it takes $15 to pay for the variable inputs required for the production of one additional unit of X, and the price of X may vary in the marketplace.

If the price of X is between $0 and $15, the profit per unit of X is negative. Accordingly the firm would produce 7 units of Y as indicated by point H in Figure 18-3. Output of X would be zero.

Moving from H to G along the AA line, the firm gives up 1 unit of Y for 2 units of X. Thus, if the profit per unit of X were $10, the firm would forgo $20 by giving up 1 unit of Y, but it would regain the same amount because two additional units of X would yield $20 = 2 \cdot $10. Since the average variable cost of X is $15, the entrepreneur would be indifferent between point H and G only if the price of X is $25.

Moving from G to F along line BB, the firm gives up 1 unit of Y for 1 unit of X. Thus, in order for the entrepreneur to be indifferent between G and F, the profit per unit of X must be equal to the profit per unit of Y. Accordingly, the profit per unit of X must be $20. This implies that the price per unit of X must be $35.

TABLE 18-4 **Deriving a Step-Shaped Supply Curve**

Segment	Corner	Y	X	Profit per unit of Y, $	Profit per unit of X, $	Price of X, $
	H	7	0			
$\overline{HG}$				20	10	25
	G	6	2			
$\overline{GF}$				20	20	35
	F	2 2/3	5 1/3			
$\overline{FE}$				20	80	95
	E	0	6			

Moving from F to E along line CC, the firm gives up 1 unit of Y for ¼ unit of X. In order for the entrepreneur to be indifferent between points F and E, the profit per unit of X must be $80. Thus, the gain of $20 = 0.25 \cdot 80 is equal to the loss of $20 per 1 unit of Y diverted from the process of production. The price of X must be $95. The price of X may continue to rise, but the firm will continue to make 6 units of X. This is summarized in Table 18-4. The resulting supply curve of X is presented in Figure 18-5, which is a positively sloped step-shaped supply curve. However, if all supply curves of all firms in the industry were step-shaped, the aggregate supply curve of the industry, which is obtained by horizontally adding all the individual supply curves, will be smooth for all practical purposes (Section 8.2a).

18.4f Least-Cost Combination of Inputs and Linear Programming

There are cases in which the process of profit maximization can be broken into two parts: (1) determining the expansion path of the firm and (2) locating

FIGURE 18-5 A STEP-SHAPED SUPPLY CURVE DERIVED FROM FIGURE 18-3

This supply curve is a geometric representation of the data in Table 18-4. It was derived by assuming that a producer has the same feasible region as in Figure 18-3 (or 18-4), that the profit per unit of Y is $20, and that it takes $15 to pay for the variable inputs required for the production of one additional unit of X. The procedure is to vary the price of X from $0 to a very high price. The vertical segments of this supply curve reflect the property that once the producer is at a corner, there is a price range within which the producer will continue to produce the same amount. For example, if the price of X is between $25 and $35, the producer will remain at point (corner) G. The horizontal segments of this supply curve reflect situations in which the isoprofit line is parallel to a segment on the frontier. For example, when the price of X is $35, the profit per unit of X is $20 and also the profit per unit of Y is $20. The slope of constraint BB (Figure 18-2) is -1.

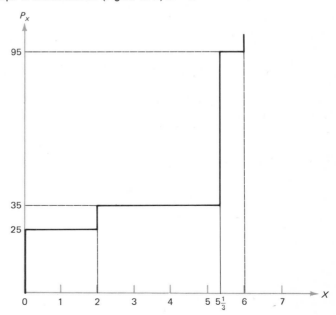

TABLE 18-5
Nutrient
Content in
Grains, an
Example

Nutrient	Grain X	Y
A	1	3
B	1	1
C	8	2

the optimal point on the expansion path. The chicken farmer is confronted with the problem of finding the least-cost combination of grains that will yield at least the minimum amount of each of many nutrients that must be fed to a single chicken. A bushel of barley is known to contain a certain amount of each of the variety of nutrients that must be fed to chickens. The same is true with respect to corn and all the other grains available in the feed market. The problem, then, is to find the least-cost combination of barley, corn, and so on that will satisfy the nutrient constraints.

Consider the following hypothetical problem: A farmer has to find the least-cost combination of two grains X and Y. The nutrient content of the grains are shown in Table 18-5. Assume that one chicken must be fed each day at least 9, 5, and 16 units of nutrients A, B, and C, respectively. Accordingly the constraints are

$$1 \cdot X + 3 \cdot Y \geq 9$$

$$1 \cdot X + 1 \cdot Y \geq 5$$

$$8 \cdot X + 2 \cdot Y \geq 16$$

In Figure 18-6 the first, second, and third inequalities are denoted by AA, BB, and CC, respectively. The difference between Figure 18-6 and Figure 18-3 is that in Figure 18-3 the feasible region lies to the left of the frontier, while in Figure 18-6 the feasible region lies to the right of the frontier.

Suppose the farmer is confronted with a market in which the price of X is $4 and the price of Y is $6. Then the problem is

Minimize:

$$C = 4 \cdot X + 6 \cdot Y$$

Subject to:

$$1 \cdot X + 3 \cdot Y \geq 9$$

$$1 \cdot X + 1 \cdot Y \geq 5$$

$$8 \cdot X + 2 \cdot Y \geq 16$$

$$X \geq 0$$

$$Y \geq 0$$

where $C = 4 \cdot X + 6 \cdot Y$ is the objective function and the last two inequalities ensure that X and Y are nonnegative.

The problem is solved by selecting the lowest isocost line which contains at least one feasible point. In Figure 18-7 only three isocost lines are shown. These are $C_1 = \$36$, $C_2 = \$24$, and $C_3 = \$12$. C_2 is the lowest isocost line containing at least one feasible point. This point, which is denoted by L, is a corner solution. If the price of Y would decrease relative to the price of X, such that the isocost lines would rotate counterclockwise until they are parallel to segment $\overline{LM}$, then the least-cost combination would be any point on segment $\overline{LM}$, including points L and M. A further reduction in the relative

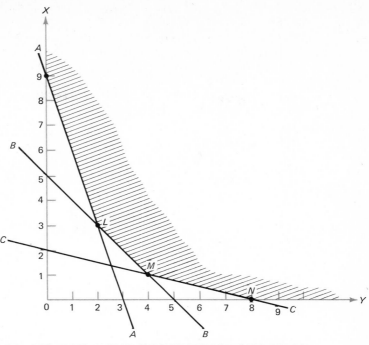

FIGURE 18-6 LINEAR CONSTRAINTS IN THE CHICKEN FEEDING PROBLEM
Lines *AA*, *BB*, and *CC* are boundaries. Points to the right of each line satisfy the constraints of the chicken feeding problem. For example, points to the right of *AA*, and the line *AA* itself, together satisfy the inequality $1 \cdot X + 3 \cdot Y \geq 9$. The area covered by diagonal stripes satisfies all three constraints simultaneously. It is known as the feasible region of production. The cost-minimization problem is to find the minimum cost of feeding on the frontier *KLMN*.

price of Y would lead to switching the point of tangency from L to M. As indicated by Figure 18-7, the farmer would substitute grain Y for grain X.

At corner L, $X = 3$ and $Y = 2$. Accordingly the cost is $24 = $4 \cdot 3 + $6 \cdot 2$. A single chicken is fed 9 units of nutrient A, 5 units of nutrient B, and 28 units of nutrient C. The first two inequalities are just satisfied; the third is oversatisfied.

Shadow prices in cost-minimization problems provide additional information about the constraints. The shadow price of a constraint, such as nutrient A, is determined by first reaching the optimal (minimum-cost) solution. Then the constraint is changed by 1 unit. Lowering the minimal use of nutrient A from 9 to 8 would lead to a new optimal point where $X = 3.5$ units and $Y = 1.5$ units. The new cost would be $23 (= $4 \cdot 3.5 + $6 \cdot 1.5)$. Accordingly,

$$\text{Shadow price of nutrient } A = \frac{23 - 24}{8 - 9} = \$1$$

From the above analysis it is clear that passing a ray from the origin of Figure 18-7 through point L provides the short-run expansion path of the

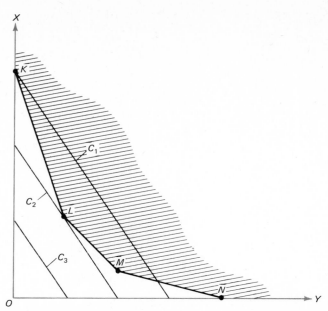

FIGURE 18-7   APPLYING LINEAR PROGRAMMING TO A LEAST-COST COMBINATION OF INPUTS PROBLEM
The frontier is denoted by *KLMN*. The area covered by diagonal stripes represents the feasible production region. Three isocosts ($C = 4X + 6Y$), C_1($24), and C_3($12), are shown. Isocost C_2 just touches the frontier at point L, which is the least-cost point. The minimum cost is accordingly $24.

chicken farm (Section 6.5c). Such a ray tells us what the least-cost combination of inputs (grains) X and Y should be in the process of producing eggs.

18.5 NONLINEAR PROGRAMMING

Nonlinear programming problems arise when a firm is confronted with a noncompetitive market for its product. Alternatively nonlinear programming problems may arise when a firm purchases its inputs in noncompetitive markets. The latter case is very unlikely to occur. A nonlinear programming problem will be illustrated by assuming that a firm is bound by the constraints as presented in Figure 18-3, but that the firm enjoys a monopolistic position in the markets for X and Y, respectively. Thus the firm is assumed to be confronted with two negatively sloped demand curves as follows:

$$P_x = 8 - 0.5X$$

$$P_y = 12 - Y$$

If for simplicity we assume that variable cost of production is zero, the profit function of the firm becomes

$$\pi = 8X - 0.5X^2 + 12Y - Y^2$$

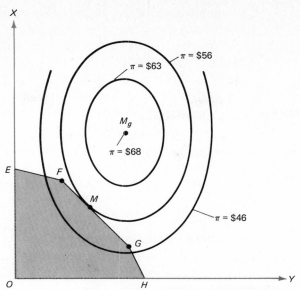

FIGURE 18-8   A GEOMETRICAL ILLUSTRATION OF A NONLINEAR PROGRAMMING
PROBLEM

The shaded area represents the feasible region of production. It is identical to the shaded
area in Figure 18-3. Since by assumption the firm enjoys monopolistic power in the markets
of X and Y, the isoprofit curves are nonlinear. M_g represents global maximum ($68). If the
firm were not constrained by $EFGH$, it could produce a combination of 8 units of X and 6
units of Y and could earn $68 per unit of time. But since the firm is constrained, it will select
point M, at which an isoprofit curve is tangent to the frontier. The highest attainable level of
profit subject to the constraints is accordingly $56.

The resulting isoprofit curves are nonlinear. Three such nonlinear isoprofit
curves are shown in Figure 18-8: $\pi = \$46$, $\pi = \$56$, and $\pi = \$63$. The highest
isoprofit curve that is still feasible is for $\pi = \$56$. This curve is tangent to the
frontier at point M on constraint BB. This tangency occurs where $Y = 4$ and
$X = 4$. Note that if the firm were not confined by any constraint it would
have produced the combination M_g where $Y = 6$ and $X = 8$. M_g is known as
the *global maximum*. The example can be stated as follows:

Maximize:

$$\pi = 8X - 0.5X^2 + 12Y - Y^2$$

Subject to:

$$1 \cdot X + 2 \cdot Y \leq 14$$

$$1 \cdot X + 1 \cdot Y \leq 8$$

$$4 \cdot X + 1 \cdot Y \leq 24$$

$$X \geq 0$$

$$Y \geq 0$$

The mathematics of nonlinear programming are complex. There are several known procedures that may be applied in solving nonlinear programming problems. None, however, can solve *all* the nonlinear programming problems that might arise.

18.6 DYNAMIC PROGRAMMING

Another useful branch of operations research is *dynamic programming*. *Dynamic programming* is a logical apparatus which can be applied to either cost-minimization problems or profit-maximization problems, where a system of interrelated economic activities is involved. Dynamic programming will be illustrated by two cases.

18.6a Water Pollution along a River

Consider a river which is polluted by factories and municipalities located along the river from its head source all the way down to its sink. The problem of maintaining a certain degree of cleanliness along the river at a minimum cost may be formulated as a dynamic programming problem. In particular, assume that the waste discharged into the river is of the biological oxygen demand type, known as BOD. It is known that BOD wastes, if discharged in excessive amounts, are harmful to fishing and recreation. Because anaerobic organisms predominate, fish die off and a stench rises. The level of cleanliness in the river may be approximated by the amount of *dissolved oxygen* in the river, denoted by DO. Figure 18-9 measures time along the horizontal axis and DO along the vertical axis. Note that if the velocity of the water flowing in the river is stable, the horizontal axis also indicates the distance from the head source as we move downstream. The curve presented in Figure 18-9 is known as the *dissolved oxygen sag*. This curve shows the amount of dissolved oxygen in water. Let the origin mark the head source of the river. The first waste discharger is located at point A. Between point A and A_m, DO falls because the utilization of oxygen in the process of biochemical oxidation exceeds the natural process of photosynthesis[13] and absorption of oxygen from the atmosphere. Beyond A_m the reverse occurs; photosynthesis and atmospheric absorption of oxygen exceed the process of biochemical oxidation, and the DO rises. The second waste discharger is located at B, and so on. The waste discharger farthest downstream is located at point D. In the absence of waste discharging, the level of DO would have been $\overline{OL}$ (parts per million). Let us assume that the communities located near the river decide that they cannot tolerate the present state of the DO in the river and that they want to enforce a minimum DO level of $\overline{OK}$ (parts per million) along the entire river. The issue for them is to solve the following problem:

---

[13]The hydrogen of the water is used to convert carbon dioxide into carbon hydrate. The oxygen of the water is freed and thus increases the DO.

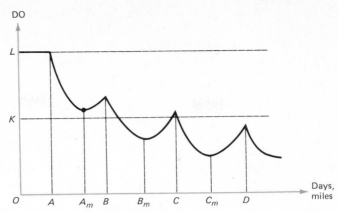

DO

L

K

O   A A_m B B_m C C_m D

Days, miles

FIGURE 18-9   THE DISSOLVED OXYGEN SAG CURVE

Along the horizontal axis we measure days (or miles) from the head source of a river. Along the vertical axis we measure dissolved oxygen (DO). A, B, C, and D denote the locations of producers who discharge effluent into the river. DO is at its natural level at point A; then it falls because of effluent discharge, until at point A_m it reaches its minimum and thereafter, because of photosynthesis and atmosphere absorption, it begins to rise again, and so on. Suppose the community wants to enforce a floor of $\overline{OK}$ parts per million of DO. The problem is how to minimize the cost of abating pollution subject to this constraint (of $\overline{OK}$ parts per million). This is a typical dynamic programming problem.

Minimize the total cost of waste treatment of polluters A, B, C, and D.

Subject to the constraint that the DO level must be at least $\overline{OK}$ (parts per million) everywhere.

This cost-minimization problem can be formulated as a dynamic programming problem because there is a sequence of waste dischargers along the river, each affecting the position and shape of the *dissolved oxygen sag curves* of all waste dischargers located downstream.

Although the dynamic programming involved in solving the above problem is simple, the physics and mathematics involved in calculating the dissolved oxygen sag curves are beyond our level. Accordingly, in order to give the student the flavor of dynamic programming, the solution to a simpler problem will be illustrated.

18.6b The Problem of Finding the Minimum-Cost Route

Consider Figure 18-10. Letters a, b, c, and so on, up to i depict towns. Lora, a sales representative, has to fly from a to i. As Figure 18-10 indicates, there is no direct flight from a to i. Lora has to select four legs in order to reach destination i. For example, she can fly from a either to b or to c. Suppose she decided to fly from a to b, she can now fly to d, e, or f, and so on. The question is how to select the legs from origin a to destination i so as to minimize the cost of flying. Note that one possible solution would be to enumerate all possible routes (each route includes four legs) and to select the lowest-cost route. Such a solution, however, might prove to be very costly in terms of

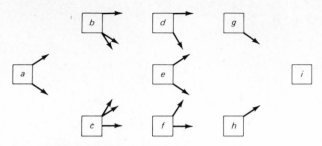

FIGURE 18-10 FLYING ROUTES CONSIDERED BY LORA

Letters *a, b, c,* and so on up to *i* denote towns. *a* denotes the origin and *i* denotes the destination. Lora can fly from *a* to *i* by selecting legs, such as *a→b*, then *b→e*, then *e→g*, and finally *g→i*. The problem is, given ticket prices (Table 18-6), how to find the least-cost combination of legs. This is a typical dynamic programming problem.

computer time. Thus, in what follows a logical procedure that will lead Lora to the minimum-cost route will be presented. This procedure requires a minimal amount of computer time. Table 18-6 presents the ticket cost from airport to airport. (For example, a ticket from *c* to *e* costs $30.)

TABLE 18-6 **Flying Costs ($) from Airport to Airport**

	b	c			d	e	f			g	h			i
a	20	10		b	60	40	60		d	20	50		g	20
				c	50	30	40		e	40	30		h	10
									f	20	20			

For reasons that will be intuitively clear at the end of the process, the optimization process in dynamic programming problems starts from the end (town *i*). We begin to solve the problem of minimizing the cost of flying from *a* to *i* by considering, in Table 18-7, the last leg, which could be either *g→i* or *h→i*. This is a trivial stage.

TABLE 18-7 **Optimal Solution for the Last Leg**

	Minimum cost from g or h to i	Destination
g	20	i
h	10	i

Next, if she has only two legs left, Lora's optimal solution is illustrated in Table 18-8, where, for example, $40 from *d* to *i* via *g* is $20 plus $20. Also $60 from *d* to *i* via *h* is $50 plus $10, and so on. The minimum cost is simply ob-

tained by taking the lowest of $40 and $60, $60 and $40, and $40 and $30, respectively.

TABLE 18-8 **Optimal Solution When Two Legs Are Left**

	Cost from d, e, f to i via		Optimal solution	
	g	h	Minimum cost	Destination
d	40	60	40	g
e	60	40	40	h
f	40	30	30	h

The next stage in this sequence is to select the optimal route from either b or c all the way to i. The solution to this stage is presented in Table 18-9.

TABLE 18-9 **Optimal Solution When Three Legs Are Left**

	Cost from b, c, to i via			Optimal solution	
	d	e	f	Minimum cost	Destination
b	100	80	90	80	e
c	90	70	70	70	e or f

Notice, for example, that in Table 18-9 the cost of $100 from b to i via d is calculated by adding to the $60, the cost from b to d, the minimum cost from d to i, which amounts to $40 and which uses the route $d \rightarrow g \rightarrow i$.

The final optimal solution is obtained when we select the cheaper of the two routes, namely, $a \rightarrow b$ or $a \rightarrow c$. This is carried out in Table 18-10.

TABLE 18-10 **The Optimal Solution**

	Cost from a to i via		Optimal solution	
	b	c	Minimum cost	Destination
a	100	80	80	c

We now trace the optimal solution from Table 18-10 back to Table 18-7 and conclude that the two (equally) optimal routes for Lora are

$$a \rightarrow c \underset{\searrow f \rightarrow h \rightarrow i}{\overset{\nearrow e \rightarrow h \rightarrow i}{}}$$

at a cost of $80.

18.7 PROBABILISTIC MODELS

Probabilistic models, as their name indicates, involve optimization procedures in which the theory of probability plays a major role (Section 4.2a). This section will be restricted to some of the most important branches of probabilistic optimization models. Detailed description of these techniques are avoided for two main reasons: First, unlike linear programming, non-linear programming, and dynamic programming, probabilistic models do not easily yield to geometric or simple tabular presentation. Second, they are applied in specialized cases of optimization rather than in the more general cases of optimal resource allocation.

18.7a Queuing Theory

Queuing is the study of waiting lines. An example would be a barber shop serving its customers on a first come, first served basis. Occasionally waiting lines (queues) form in the barber shop. These lines are at times very long and at other times very short. Sometimes the waiting lines completely vanish, and some barbers are idle until there is a new influx of customers. The arrival of customers is a random process. This means that the time gap between one arrival and the next is a random number. Also, the time it takes to cut the hair of a single customer is a random process. Owners of barber shops face a dilemma: On the one hand, they can increase the number of barbers in the shop to the point where it would be very rare indeed to find even one customer waiting in line for service. Such a strategy will increase the cost of service but will bring the waiting time to a minimum. On the other hand, they can leave only a single barber to serve all the customers. Such a strategy will drive the cost of service to a minimum but will give rise to long queues, resulting eventually in a loss of customers. The above discussion can be summarized as follows: When the number of barbers is very small, say, only one barber, the cost of waiting is extremely high and the cost of service is relatively low. As the number of barbers increases, the cost of waiting in line falls but the cost of service rises; at first the decline in the cost of waiting dominates, and hence the sum of the two costs falls. At a certain point the rise in the cost of service begins to dominate, and accordingly the sum of the two costs begins to rise. Figure 18-11 illustrates the dilemma of the barber shop: The larger the number of barbers employed, the smaller the cost of waiting per unit of time and the higher the cost of barbers (wages) per unit of time. The sum of the two costs declines up to point M and rises thereafter. Calculating the cost of waiting function involves the theory of probability because, as mentioned earlier, arrival of customers and cutting hair are, respectively, random numbers.

Queuing theory is applied in solving optimization problems whenever waiting for a service is involved. In chemical industries the issue may be how many reactors to keep in order to process batches of various chemical mixes. In a supermarket the issue may be to find the optimal number of cash

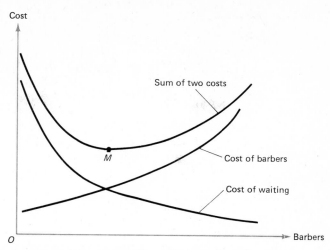

FIGURE 18-11 THE QUEUING DILEMMA: OPTIMAL NUMBER OF BARBERS
The number of barbers (servers) is measured along the horizontal axis. The cost of the operation (cutting hair) is measured along the vertical axis. The cost-of-barbers curve is rising because the more barbers the shop employs, the greater is the salary that must be paid to them. The cost of waiting is interpreted as the loss of customers because of waiting time: As the number of barbers increases, the *expected* waiting time of customers decreases, and thus the loss of customers declines. The sum of the two curves is U-shaped. The construction of the cost-of-waiting curve involves probability theory. The barber's dilemma is a classic example of queuing.

registers needed in order to accommodate outgoing customers. In a tool crib the problem may be to determine the optimal number of clerks required to serve the mechanics in the shop.

18.7b Theories of Inventories

Inventories are held by producers, wholesalers, and retailers. Chapter 9 mentioned that inventories are at the heart of the market adjustment mechanism. If the price is above the equilibrium level, excess supply over demand will cause a temporary accumulation of unwanted inventories, leading store owners and producers to reduce prices in order to get rid of these inventories. On the other hand, if the price in the market is lower than the equilibrium level, inventories will shrink, leading to a rise in the price. From the discussion in Chapter 9 it was evident that producers, wholesalers, and managers of retail operations have some idea of an optimal level of inventories to which they try to adhere. While the "Five and Ten" stores may apply some rules of thumb based on experience in order to formulate their inventory policies, giant stores and supermarkets may be able to save considerable amounts of money by applying probabilistic models in order to arrive at optimal ordering procedures. The main costs of inventories arise from *storage per se, interest forgone, ordering,* and the *penalty from run-*

ning out of inventories (loss of customers). The problem may be defined as determining the frequency of ordering inventories that will minimize all the above costs.

To illustrate a simple inventory problem which does not involve probablistic procedures, consider a food store. Let food be ordered at equal time intervals. An order of inventories would amount to X units. Let the rate of inventory depletion be r units per unit of time. The total cost per order is $A + bX$, where A denotes a fixed cost incurred each time an order is made and b denotes the cost per unit ordered. Let m be the cost of storage per unit of the commodity per unit of time. Since the commodity is being depleted at a rate of r units per unit of time, inventories on shelves as a function of time has the following form:

$$X(t) = X - r \cdot t \qquad (18\text{-}10)$$

where t denotes time. If the store does not wish ever to be left without inventories, an order must arrive exactly when the X units are depleted. Geometrically this situation is described in Figure 18-12. The problem is, what should be the size of the order of inventories to minimize the cost of inventories? Calculus must be applied in order to solve for the minimum cost order. The solution is $X^* = \sqrt{2A \cdot r/m}$. The optimal time interval between one order and the next (t^*) is derived by dividing X^* by the rate of depletion as follows: $t^* = X^*/r = \sqrt{2A/(m \cdot r)}$.

If rate of depletion r is a random number, the theory of probability must be used in order to arrive at an optimal solution of ordering inventories. In spite of the mathematical difficulties, solutions for the case of a random rate of depletion were found by researchers in the field of operations research.

18.7c Simulation

To *simulate* means to pretend. In operations research *simulation* means pretending that a system can be created on a computer which is sufficiently similar to a real system. For example, the solution to the barber shop queuing problem can be obtained by evaluating the random behavior of customer arrivals and hair cutting and assigning to the computer the role of both arrivals and barbers. The barber shop situation can be simulated on the computer for equivalent long periods such as years. Simulating a barber shop for an equivalent period of a year may take only minutes on the computer. To determine the best policy, first a barber shop with one barber is simulated, then a barber shop with two barbers is simulated, and so on. The simulation that yields the highest profit is selected as the optimal one. Simulation analysis is applied in order to determine the optimal policy for complex systems such as combinations of river dams and lakes. Probability theory enters into such issues because the flow of water in river and streams follows a random pattern. Decisions must be made concerning releasing water from dams. The benefit to be maximized is usually threefold: irrigation of farmland, generation of electricity, and recreation. Given more than one river and more than one dam, it is almost hopeless to attempt to derive an optimal

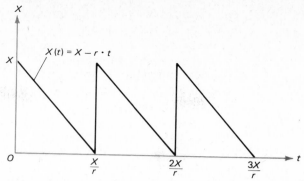

FIGURE 18-12 A MODEL OF ORDERING INVENTORIES AT EQUAL TIME INTERVALS
Time is measured along the horizontal axis and X, the inventories, along the vertical axis.
The rate of depletion is denoted by r. If an amount of X is ordered at time O, then X, as a
function of time, is given by $X(t) = X - r \cdot t$. Inventories vanish at $t = X/r$, $t = 2X/r$, . . . , and
so on.

water release policy by applying analytical methods. However, simulation
can lead to the optimal policy.

SUMMARY Part I

Economic theories are developed through a process consisting of three
steps: stating the *postulates*, making *refutable assumptions*, and testing the
assumptions empirically. *Econometrics* is applied in the third step. Added to
this, however, is the fact that econometrics is also applied in formulating
theories when assumptions are weak, standing on logical grounds alone.
Finally the fact was stressed that econometrics is an extremely useful tool in
the hands of policy makers when economic predictions are made. It was
noted that economic relations are estimated empirically either as single
equations or as systems of simultaneous equations. One way or the other,
variations in exogenous variables must be present in order for good data,
suitable for empirical estimation, to be available. Economists mainly use
time-series and cross-sectional data in empirical studies.

Part II

Operations research is a branch of applied mathematics dealing with optimization problems such as profit maximization and cost minimization. In most
cases operations research is applied to practical problems in real-life situations.

Of all the fields in operations research, *linear programming* is the most
popular among economists. It deals with the issues of optimization when
perfect competition prevails and when the process of production is governed
by constant returns to scale and production activities are separable. Linear
programming is applied in problems of profit maximization when firms are

stuck with fixed amounts of inputs, in problems of least-cost combinations of inputs in a variety of problems such as mixing feeds or chemicals subject to some constraining specifications, and in various other problems involving transportation and storage.

When imperfect competition prevails, optimization problems normally become *nonlinear*. The nature of nonlinear programming was illustrated geometrically, and it was stressed that mathematical procedures are much more complicated for solving nonlinear programming problems than for linear programming problems.

Dynamic programming is a logical (rather than mathematical) apparatus applied to problems of profit maximization or cost minimization, where systems of interrelated economic activities are involved. An example is dynamic programming as a tool applied to find the least cost of pollution abating along a river in which the waste discharged by producers upstream affects the welfare of water users downstream.

Probabilistic models involve optimization procedures in which the theory of probability plays a major role. They include *queuing theory*, which analyzes waiting lines and optimal number of servers (barbers); *inventory theory*, which deals with optimal inventory size given the cost of stocking and holding inventories, and the rate of depletion; and *simulation*, which helps economists to solve complicated queuing and inventory problems when analytical solutions are impossible.

GLOSSARY

Econometrics A branch in mathematical statistics used in empirical testing of economic theories and empirical estimation of economic functions.

Postulates Propositions concerning the behavior of economic entities. Example: Consumers maximize their utility.

Theory A set of assumptions based on the postulate(s). Such assumptions must lead to refutable implications.

Exogenous variables Variables that originate from external causes. For example, if a demand function of an individual consumer is considered, the price is exogenous and the quantity demanded is endogenous. Income per capita is exogenous.

Endogenous variables Variables that originate from internal causes. For example, in demand-supply analysis, price and quantity are endogenous variables. Income per capita and prices of variable inputs are exogenous variables.

Time-series data Data obtained by recording the response of one group (such as a nation) to the intertemporal variations of the exogenous variables.

Cross-sectional data Data obtained by recording the response of different cross sections of the population (such as states or counties) to the exogenous variables which vary from one section to another section at a point in time.

Regression analysis A mathematical technique used in empirical estimation of functions.

Operations research A branch in applied mathematics dealing with optimization problems.

Linear programming An optimization technique that can be applied only when all functions involved are linear.

Input-output table A table that shows the amount of each input required to produce one unit of each output.

A process of production Also known as an *activity*. A column (vector) showing the amount of each input required to produce one unit of a certain output. The collection of all activities is the *input-output table*.

Objective function A function in which the dependent variable is either profit or cost and the dependent variables are the levels of the activities and either the profits or the costs associated with the respective activities. In operations research the goal is to either maximize (profit) or minimize (cost) the value of the objective functions, subject to a variety of constraints.

A constraint A function of the activities levels as well as technical and economic parameters. The value of such a function must either exceed (or be equal to) a certain value or be less than (or equal to) a certain value. In most operations research problems the goal is to maximize the value of the objective function subject to a set of constraints.

Feasible region of production In linear (and nonlinear) programming problems, it is the collection of all combinations of activity levels (outputs) that do not violate the constraints.

Isoprofit curve In the X, Y space, it is the locus of points yielding a fixed level of profit (or cost for isocost curves). In linear programming problems, isoprofit curves are linear.

Shadow price A change in the value of the objective function per unit change in one of the constraints.

Nonlinear programming An optimization problem in which either the objective function or one or more of the constraints are nonlinear.

Dynamic programming A logical apparatus which can be applied to problems of optimization when a system of interrelated economic activities is involved.

Probabilistic models Optimization procedures in which the theory of probability plays a major role.

Queuing The study of waiting lines. Belongs to the field of probabilistic models. In most cases the goal of queuing theory is to determine the optimal number of servers.

Inventory theory A study of the optimal time interval between inventory orders. Belongs to the field of probabilistic models.

Simulation Pretending that a system can be created on a computer. Simulation is applied when analytical solutions to complicated economic systems are impossible.

PROBLEMS An asterisk indicates an advanced problem.

18-1. "The supply is positively sloped." Is this a *theory*, a *postulate*, or just a *refutable* implication?

18-2. Theories cannot be proved, only confirmed. Do you agree?

18-3. How can the theory stating that indifference curves are convex be confirmed?

18-4.* The *Barzel law* claims that specific taxes on cigarettes would lead to quality improvements (Section 10.1j). To confirm this law, Barzel had to show statistically that a 1-cent increase in taxes would give rise to more than a 1-cent increase in the retail price of cigarettes. Explain.

18-5. When we watch ships approaching the coast from a far distance, they gradually become visible from top to bottom. Is this sufficient confirmation that the earth is round?

18-6. Over the years the supply of whatnots shifted all over the place. The demand for whatnots hardly shifted at all. Can econometrics be applied in order to estimate supply and demand simultaneously?

18-7.* How many units (of X and Y, respectively) does the group produce at point G in Figure 18-3?

18-8. Show that at point G in Figure 18-4 only 14 units of input C are employed.

18-9. Calculate the shadow price of B and C in Figure 18-4.

18-10. Draw the supply curve of X under the assumption that prices of variable inputs fall, thus leading to a reduction of the average variable cost of X from \$15 to \$5.

18-11. Calculate the shadow prices of B and C in Figure 18-7.

18-12.* A homogeneous product is produced in $i = 1, 2, 3$ origins. The respective quantities produced are x_1, x_2, x_3. There are $j = 1, 2, 3, 4$ shipping destinations. The respective quantities demanded in these destinations are d_1, d_2, d_3, d_4. The amount which is shipped from location i to destination j is denoted by x_{ij}. Supply equals demand; that is, $\Sigma x_i = \Sigma d_j$. Finally, the cost of shipping one unit from location i to destination j is C_{ij}. Formulate (write the objective function and the constraints) the linear programming problem for this problem (known as the *transportation problem*).

18-13. A farm is restricted to 200 units of labor and 100 units of land. Let labor be denoted by A and land by B. Wheat can only be produced according to the following three processes:

	Processes		
	I	II	III
Wheat	1	1	1
Labor (A)	1	2	4
Land (B)	3	2	1

It is given that the price of wheat is $24 per unit. Formulate the problem as a linear programming problem. How would you determine if it is worthwhile for the farm to buy more labor if all of a sudden labor becomes available at a cost of $3 per unit of labor?

18-14. Enumerate all the possible solutions in the dynamic programming problem as depicted by Figure 18-10. Could we count on enumeration as a procedure to solve dynamic programming problems?

HINTS AND NUMERICAL ANSWERS

CHAPTER 1

1-1. (a) 2 utils. (b) Recall the law of diminishing MU.

1-2. If marginal utility is constant, the gain from transferring money from Y to X will not diminish.

1-3. (a) MU is the same, regardless of the supermarket where the bread is purchased. (b) If a person has a pair of shoes, adding a right (left) shoe would not add anything to his or her utility.

1-4. The budget line must cross through A (10, 30). Recall that a point and a slope are sufficient to determine a straight line.

1-5. The budget line must cross through the point of in-kind endowment (7, 8).

1-6. Select a point on the vertical axis. First draw a very steep budget line. Then, starting at the same point, draw a negatively sloped and convex indifference curve that lies above the budget line.

1-7. The present shifts John's budget line by three units to the right. Going from right to left, this budget line comes to its end 3 units short of the vertical (Y) axis.

1-8. Start at L = 24 hours/day. Each time you sell an hour of leisure, you receive a net amount of $4 instead of $5: Note: $4= $5 − 0.2 · $5.

1-9. Let the tax collected be $T = t(Y - Y_0)$. Let the rate of the tax $\hat{t}$ be $\hat{t} = T/Y$.

1-10. Work is a source of disutility.

1-11.* Consider panels (*a*) and (*b*) of Figure 1-19. Merge the two into a single panel. The new equilibrium should occur at the point of intersection of I_1 associated with a lump-sum tax with I_1 associated with a proportional tax.

CHAPTER 2

2-2. If two ICC intersected, then at the point of intersection two indifference curves would have to intersect.

2-3. Income elasticity = $(\Delta X/\Delta I)/(X/I)$.

2-4. The baskets for which the slopes of the associated budget lines are identical.

2-5. − 0.25.

2-6. − 2 percent.

2-7. $X \cdot P_x + Y \cdot P_y = I$.

2-8. Assume that initially $20 is spent on food and that the initial budget is I_0 = $100.

2-9. 3.

2-10. See comment to problem 2-2.

2-11. − 12.6 percent.

2-12. (a) 0 percent. (b) 37.8 percent.

2-13. − 10 units.

2-14. The strength of the income effect.

2-15.* Draw a diagram in which you show both effects. Be consistent.

2-16.* Price elasticity is $(\Delta X/\Delta P) \cdot [P/(aP+ b)]$ or $(\Delta X/\Delta P) \cdot [(X-b)/aX]$, where $X= aP+ b$.

2-17.* $25.

CHAPTER 3

3-1. Focus on the MR.

3-2. 1 percent.

3-3. Separate the effect of a rising income from the effect of a higher price.

3-4. Figure 3-8.

3-5. 4.13 percent.

3-6. The demand for farm output is price-inelastic.

3-7. $X \cdot P_x + Y \cdot P_y = I. \; Y = (I - X \cdot P_x)/P_y$.

3-8.* First, express quantity as a function of price. Then solve.

3-9.* $P = 8 - 0.2 X_t \cdot P$ is given in $.

3-10.* What is the necessary condition? What is the sufficient condition?

CHAPTER 4

4-1. Properties of indifference curves.

4-2. Table 4-2.

4-3. Base year is 1974.

4-4. (a) Calculate his quantity index numbers. (b) 35 percent. (c) In Figure 4-9, point A reflects equilibrium in the United States and point A' reflects equilibrium in Brazil.

4-5. Assume that initially the first, second, and third consumers purchased 20, 30, and 50 units of X and 80, 70, and 50 units of Y, respectively. Assume that initially $P_x = \$1$ and $P_y = \$1$.

4-6. Draw a diagram in which X is natural gas and Y is all other goods. The analysis should follow the procedures in Figure 4-9.

4-7. 2.5 utils.

4-8. Where, on a utility curve (Figure 4-12) should the person be?

4-9.* If we assume that professor was just barely induced to join the faculty club when the annual membership fee was set at \$20, his demand function is $X = -250P + 350$.

CHAPTER 5

5-2. For a check: AP = 0.96 when 120 pounds of nitrogen are applied. $MP_a = 0.27$ when the application of nitrogen rises from 120 to 160 pounds.

5-3. Figure 5-8, panel (b).

5-4. $E_a = (\Delta X / X)/(\Delta A / A)$. Rearrange until you obtain E_a in terms of AP_a and MP_a.

5-5. Let $K > 1$. Instead of A and B, let us employ KA and KB.

5-6.* Up to the point where $B = B_0$, the production function obeys constant returns to scale, and both A and B are variable.

5-7. Entrepreneurial capacity.

5-8. -3.65.

5-9. Along the isoquant $-\Delta A \cdot MP_a = \Delta B \cdot MP_a$.

5-10. For a check: When A grows from 3 to 4 units, for $B_0 = 2$, $MP_a = 0.38$ and for $B_1 = 3$, $MP_a = 0.46$.

CHAPTER 6

6-1. Alternative earnings.

6-2. (a) Damage liabilities. (b) What will the fishermen do?

6-3. It has to do with the shape of the MC curve in that neighborhood.

6-4. Let the producer move a small distance by withdrawing ΔB from the process of production. Show that the ΔA that will return the producer to the isoquant is smaller than the ΔA that the producer can purchase with $-\Delta B \cdot P_b$.

6-5. Imagine that in Figure 6-8, at point J, $A_0 = 8$, $B_0 = 2$, and $X_0 = \sqrt{A_0 \cdot B_0} = 4$. The producer wants to move to point K, and $X_1 = 5$. Consider also Figure 6-9.

6-6. For $\Delta A = \Delta B = 0.1$, respectively, calculate MP_a, MP_b, and check if RTS is equal to the slope of the new isocost.

6-7. What is the value of ΔX in the shortest run?

6-8. What is the amount of B used when $X = 0$?

6-9. Distinguish between a shift in a curve and going along a curve.

6-10.* Focus on LRAC.

6-12. The tax may be viewed as a cost.

6-13. Figure 6-11 should give you the clue.

6-14. Start by considering Figure 6-9.

CHAPTER 7

7-2. The minimum fixed profit should be treated like fixed costs.

7-3. Start by assuming that the price is higher than the LRMC of the least efficient firm.

7-4. Assume that the cost functions of Mr. Matson are depicted by Figure 7-6.

7-5. Did the government create some false expectations among farmers regarding the long-run prices of farm products?

7-6. Figure 6-3 should provide the clue. You might want to review Section 7-2h.

7-7.* Recall $MC = P_a/MP_a$. Thus, for Plant 1, MC when 80 megawatthours are produced is $2.5 \cdot 15 = \$37.5$ (3.75 cents per kilowatthour). You should calculate the MC schedules of Plant 1 and Plant 2, respectively. Then apply the principle as shown in Figure 7-8. Allocation should be 100 megawatthours to Plant 1 and 50 megawatthours to Plant 2. (b) Allocate production only to Plant 1.

7-8. Assume no scrap value to machinery. Also assume that life of machinery is 10 years and depreciation is $16,000. The cost of machinery is unavoidable.

7-9. 2.

7-10. (a) $10. (b) $12.

7-12.* Focus on the producer's surplus.

CHAPTER 8

8-1. 30 percent.

8-2. 2.

8-3. About 2 cents.

8-4. Additional producer's surplus is roughly $110. The additional total variable cost is roughly $210.

8-5.* The issue of positive relationship was discussed in Section 5-6. Focus on panels (b) and (c) of Figure 8-5.

8-6. In the long run, labor and electricity are competitive (substitutes) inputs.

8-7. How would the MC of the individual producer shift?

8-9. Supply elasticity is $(\Delta X/X)/(\Delta P/P)$. Rearrange the formula such that elasticity will be an expression of $\Delta X/\Delta P$ and X/P.

8-10. Section 8-3a should provide the clue.

CHAPTER 9

9-1. Focus on the MC of the individual firm.

9-2. Demand shifts.

9-3. Coffee and tea are substitutes. You may ignore the income effect.

9-4. Assume a neutral shift in the production function.

9-5. Bus services and cab services are substitutes.

9-6.* The supply of oil is obtained by aggregating the domestic supplies with the import component. If you are interested in an elaborate model, read Section 10.2a.

9-7. See Section 9.3d.

9-8. Cars and gasoline are complementary goods.

9-9. Assume that the firm in Figure 9-9, panel (*a*), is typical.

9-10.* The aggregate consumer's and producer's surplus is the area extending from the origin to the point of intersection between the supply curve and the demand curve, bounded by the vertical axis, the demand curve, and the supply curve.

9-11. 2700 million bushels are produced after the hybrid corn is adopted. Gain to consumers is $340 million. Net gain is $247 million.

9-12. Suppose you are an individual producer in the microelectronics industry.

9-13. Are there any limitations on how far down ΣMC_1 can shift?

9-14. The demand for farm output is price-inelastic.

CHAPTER 10

10-2. Find the point at which the two after-tax supply curves intersect.

10-3. Assume that $|\eta| = \epsilon$.

10-4. As the tax increases, the quantity marketed decreases.

10-5. The length of cigarettes prior to the imposition of the tax was optimal.

10-6. Compare the rate of a 10 percent sales tax calculated for two persons: The first saves 10 percent, the second saves 20 percent.

10-7. The price of gasoline covers the cost of attendants.

10-8. The segment $\overline{FE}$ in Figure 10-8 covers the unit cost of shipping, duties, etc.

10-9.* In Figure 10-9, draw a less elastic (than D_d) demand curve and let it go through point H.

10-10. Remember, you pay taxes to your government.

10-11. Shift the S_m curve in Figure 10-10 upward by the unit tax. Show that at the new point of equilibrium $P_w + P_m - T = MC_s$.

10-13. Compare C with P.

10-14. The fraudulent activities of timber companies were not costless.

10-15. A geometric analysis will help.

10-17. Where would you shift the net demand curve of speculators, and the net supply curve of hedgers?

CHAPTER 11

11-1. If you were a manager of a monopolistic firm, would you be able to find the level of output yielding maximum profit, even if you did not know the shape of your demand curve and cost curves?

11-2. What is the definition of a supply curve (Section 7.2d)?

11-3. The rule of profit maximization.

11-4. Section 11.4b.

11-6. $6, $3.75, and $4.

11-7.* Taxes give rise to welfare losses.

11-8. The MC curve should cross the MR curve from below, going from left to right.

11-9. $(P - MC)/P = 0.043$.

11-10. (a) The supply curve becomes the MC curve of the cartel.

11-11.* Consider the case where raising the buying price leads to a situation in which, if the entire aggregate output were dumped in the marketplace, MR would be negative. A diagram will help.

11-12. Section 11.4b. The cartel will view the government as a separate market.

11-13.* Formulate the royalties paid to authors as $k \cdot R$. The profit of publishers is $(1 - k) \cdot R - C$, where C is a regular cost function, covering both fixed and variable costs.

11-14. The subsidy and the tax are imposed differently. Start by extending a subsidy that will induce the monopolistic firm to behave competitively $(MC = P)$.

11-15. Focus on the AC curve. Does the MC curve shift at all?

11-16. Draw the net profit curve as a function of production before and after the tax.

11-17. Section 11.4b; you cannot shift the MC curve. Hence, shift the domestic demand curve.

11-18. Assume whole units are produced. (a) Produce either 2 units or 3 units. (b) The subsidy should induce the monopoly to produce 5 units.

11-19. One solution: A produces 2 units, B produces 3 units.

CHAPTER 12

12-2. What could supermarkets invent in order to lure customers from one another?

12-3.* The cost of attendants is covered by the price one pays for gasoline at the gas station.

12-4. Time spent in "Farmers Markets" is relatively less pleasant as compared with time spent in modern supermarkets. On the margin, the value of time is not the same for different customers.

12-5. Consider the short run.

12-6. Apply Section 12.5. Make your own assumptions.

12-7.* Section 10.1i.

12-8. See the hint to problem 12-4. Where is time on the margin more precious?

12-9. Section 11.4b.

12-10. We are now back in the world of perfect competition.

CHAPTER 13

13-1. Compare $s_5^2 + s_6^2$ with $(s_5 + s_6)^2$.

13-2. Section 11.6a.

13-3. Dissolution is likely to cause the MC of each small firm to shift upward.

13-4. At what level would the oligopolists set the price of the good they produce if barriers to entry are low?

13-6. Focus on the elasticity of demand which steel producers in the United States face.

13-8. Go back to Chapter 11. Consider again Problem 11-14.

13-9.* (a) 3, 2, 3. (b) 4, 3, 0.

CHAPTER 14

14-1. Draw a vertical supply curve of land. Then shift the demand for land, once due to the substitution effect and once due to the expansion effect.

14-3. The monopolist (producing output X) is not a monopsonist.

14-4. Figure 14-6 should provide the clue.

14-5. Shift the demand curve for capital, once due to the substitution effect and once due to the expansion effect.

14-7. Draw a vertical supply curve of land. Shift the demand for land, once due to the substitution effect and once due to the expansion effect.

14-8. Section 14.1e and Figure 14-5 should give you the clue.

14-9. What is the shape of the long-run supply of labor facing industry A?

14-10. Figure 14-11. Start with point E as the initial equilibrium ($\overline{AB}$ is the initial wage rate).

14-11. As the firm moves from K to L, MP_b will decrease, VMP_b will decrease, too. Q.E.D.

14-12. In the short run, the demand for labor may shift either way. In the long run, you should focus on the elasticity of supply of labor facing the industry.

14-13. Energy and capital are complementary inputs.

14-15.* (a) $A = 45$. (b) For his first unit, 54. (c) $A = 90$.

14-16. Assume that grazing effort is given by $AP_a = 100 - A$.

14-17. What will be the shape of the new MFC curve?

14-18.* The consumptive use of the down-stream user should include an evaporation component.

CHAPTER 15

15-1. The value of time on the margin is different for different people.

15-2. How would the cost of energy affect (a) the cost of raising children and (b) income of parents.

15-3. Consider the impact of schooling on women's labor force participation rate and earnings.

15-4. No. The cost of policing is related.

15-5. Is VMP of teachers equal to their pay?

15-6. Compare W_{x1} with what W_x would have been without licensing.

15-7. Focus on sellers and consumers.

15-8. Section 7.1b.

15-9. In Figure 15-7, industry N [panel (b)] does not exist.

15-10. There is no such thing as a free lunch.

15-11. Labor and energy are competitive (substitute) inputs. Assume that as a result of a rise in the price of energy we observed a substitution effect and an expansion effect. Which of the two should dominate?

15-12. Section 10.1d. You may want to shift the demand curve.

15-13. The result is the same regardless of which is shifted, the supply upward by the tax or the demand downward by the tax.

15-14.* Focus on the supply of labor in a risky industry versus a risk-free industry.

CHAPTER 16

16-1. 5 years.

16-2. Once.

16-3. Substract the expected current costs from the expected total revenue. Then calculate V as in Equation 16-10. $V = -\$2,940$.

16-5. (a) \$690. (b) 0.149, \$1490.

16-6. Yes. Profit per year = \$8,520.

16-7. Figure 16-2.

16-8. Figure 16-7.

16-9. First, the shape of the VV curve in Figure 16-8 is relevant. Second, if two VV curves representing two projects cross one another, we may run into a problem.

16-10. Calculate the present values of the two bonds. Let r fall from 8% to 5%.

16-11. If it does not, the choke-off price will be reached prior to exhaustion of the mineral.

16-12. If FH is not revised, at time T_0 some deposits will be left in the ground.

16-13.* The best grade should be mined first. Trying to mine the low-grade first will lead to a contradiction.

16-14. Answer this question while focusing on Figure 16-11.

16-15. MC $(t=3)$ will shift upwards. The typical farmer will pump less than A_3 (in Figure 16-14).

16-16. After (approximately) 9 years.

CHAPTER 17

17-1.* The slope of T_r is the same at R^* and R_1.

17-2. Assume that T_r is roughly symmetrical in the neighborhood of R^*.

17-3.* A monopoly is not a monopsony.

17-4. Equation 17-16.

17-5. Use Figure 17-1.

17-6. A lump-sum tax does not destroy any of the price ratios mentioned in Section 17.2f.

17-7. The example in Section 17.4c.

17-8. Show that both parties will benefit.

17-9. Scrubbing Western coal, etc.

17-10. No.

17-11. The slope of my budget line is -1.

17-12. 0.34.

17-13. For example, to determine $RCS_i^{(x, z)}$, where i goes from 1 to many millions, is practically impossible.

CHAPTER 18

18-1. A theory.

18-3. Section 1.4c.

18-4.* Recall that if the supply curve is horizontal, without qualitative changes, the price to consumers rises by the unit tax.

18-5. This could confirm different theories regarding the shape of light rays.

18-6. Draw a diagram. Assume that only the supply curve shifts.

18-7.* 2 units of X and 6 units of Y.

18-8. Use the information given by the last row in Table 18-2.

18-9. \$10 and \$0.

18-10. Use the same procedure as in Section 18.4e.

18-11. \$3 and \$0.

NAME INDEX

Mann, H. Michael, 418, 419, 608
Markowitz, Harry, 141
Marshall, Alfred, 16, 144
Marvel, Howard P., 408
Matson, Randall, 244, 252
Mercado, Abraham, 300
Mill, John S., 219
Mincer, Jacob, 515
Moss, Richard L., 509

Neiderhoffer, Victor, 306
Nerlove, Marc, 266, 267, 607
Newhouse, Joseph P., 377, 379, 608
Newton, Sir Isaac, 3
Noyce, Robert N., 295

Olson, Edgar O., 339

Pareto, Vilfredo, 566
Parkman, Allen M., 600

Pindyck, Robert S., 548
Proxmire, William, 587

Rayack, Elton, 511*n*.
Rees, Albert, 512
Regan, Patrick J., 306
Robinson, Joan, 398
Rottenberg, Simon, 508
Russel, Louise B., 110
Ruttan, Vernon W., 467, 469

Samuelson, Paul A., 596
Savage, Leonard J., 136, 137*n*.
Schlottman, Alan, 587–589
Schultz, Henry, 79*n*., 606, 607, 611
Shoven, John B., 542, 565
Siegfrid, John J., 364, 365
Slutsky, Eugene, 75
Smith, Adam, 7, 154, 574
Solow, Robert M., 495, 496*n*.
Stigler, George J., 74, 213*n*., 219,

Stigler:
   220, 301, 364, 365*n*., 415, 429,
   430, 434, 438, 440, 441, 615*n*.

Tieman, Thomas K., 364, 365
Todaro, Michael P., 596*n*.

Walras, Leon, 16, 565
Weitzman, Martin L., 548
Welch, Finis, 515*n*.
Wildhorn, Sorrel, 290*n*.
Wold, Herman, 61
Wood, D. O., 466, 469, 607
Wood, Marshall K., 614*n*.
Worcester, Dean A., Jr., 365

Yeh, Chung J., 308

Zapp, A. D., 305, 306

SUBJECT INDEX